MHT CET

Engineering Entrance Exam

Latest Edition Practice Kit

20 Tests
20 Mock Test

Based On Real Exam Pattern

✓ Thoroughly Revised and Updated
✓ Detailed Analysis of all MCQs

Title	: MHT CET Engineering Entrance Exam
Author Name	: Mr. Rohit Manglik
Published By	: EduGorilla Community Pvt. Ltd.
Publishers Address	: 12/651, First Floor Opp. Arvindo Park, Near Jama Masjid, Indira Nagar, Lucknow, Uttar Pradesh-226016, India

Copyright EduGorilla

ISBN : 978-93-90257-81-2

First Edition

No part of this book may be reproduced, distributed, or transmitted in any form by any means, without the prior written permission of the publisher.

All Right Reserved

© by EduGorilla Community Pvt. Ltd

Disclaimer EduGorilla

Although the author and publisher have made every effort to ensure the accuracy of information in this book, we do not assume any responsibility to errors and hereby disclaim any liability to any party for any loss, damage, or disruption caused by errors or omissions, whether such errors or omissions result from negligence, accident, or any other cause.

Compiled and created by EduGorilla Community Pvt. Ltd

Printed By EduGorilla Community Pvt. Ltd.

ROHIT MANGLIK
CEO, EduGorilla

Dear Applicants,

People say *"Success comes to those who work hard."* But I've seen people working hard for their exams day in and day out for marginal success. While others succeed in their examinations by putting in just half the work. So are they God Gifted? No! I believe that it's because they work *smart* and not just *hard*. Similarly, for your exams, you should strategize your preparation so as to increase the likelihood of success. Well with EduGorilla get ready to increase your *chances of selection* in your exam by *16x*.

EduGorilla helps you in not only working *hard* but also working in a *smart and strategic* manner. With EduGorilla's preparation package, you get a chance to make your exam preparation easy, and a fun learning path towards selection. Finding the right path to your preparations can be difficult if you don't know in which direction to head. Don't worry, we have you covered! EduGorilla will be your guide to success in your journey. With our Preparation Package, you can prepare strategically and beat the exam in just one attempt.

EduGorilla's Preparation Package includes-
- Test Series
- Books

Our preparation package is handcrafted as per the latest changes, expert opinions, and students' discretion. Thus, enabling you to get through each stage of the selection process for your exam.

Our Books are designed by the teachers and experts of the respective exam with a combined 150+ years of experience; to provide you with easy, efficient, and effective learning. Our books are smart, in the sense that not only do they give you the answers to the questions but also provide similar questions for practice.

EduGorilla's competent Test Series gives you real-time experience and confidence through which you can clear your offline or online exam in just one attempt. We currently host 83,000+ mock tests for 1,440+ competitive and academic exams.

Thus, EduGorilla misses no chance to assist you in your preparation and covers all stages of the exam, so that you don't have to look anywhere else.

We provide complete preparation packages for defense, banking, teaching, and other National & State-Level exams. Hence, it doesn't matter which exam you aspire to because you will reach your success.

ALL THE BEST !
Let EduGorilla be your Guide to Success.

Rohit Manglik,
Founder and CEO, EduGorilla

INTRODUCTION

EduGorilla focuses on guiding students to succeed in their examinations. With that in mind, our book, titled "MHT CET : Engineering Entrance Exam", has been drafted through the collective efforts of our distinguished experts with 150+ years of combined experience. This book consists of questions that are created following the latest changes in the syllabus and exam pattern. We compiled the book on the basis of questions that are most likely to appear in the MHT CET. Through EduGorilla's "MHT CET : Engineering Entrance Exam" your chances of success will increase 16x.

EduGorilla does this through our Complete Preparation Package. This package consists of well-conceptualized and structured content in the form of questions that are tailor-made according to your needs and will help you practice for exams in a smart way by pinpointing all the necessary information. It also provides hints and solutions, along with a smart answer sheet for your self-evaluation. You can assess your shortcomings and work accordingly on areas that may require more of your attention.

EduGorilla promises to help you succeed in your examination and accomplish your dream goals. We believe in our aspirants and see them at the top of the merit list. And the first step towards the top is to start preparing with us. EduGorilla's "MHT CET : Engineering Entrance Exam" includes the following attributes.

➤ Well-Researched Content

➤ Top-Notch Quality

➤ Detailed Answers and Analysis

➤ Smart Answer Sheet

➤ Exam Relevant Questions

Therefore, EduGorilla fortifies your preparation and makes it durable enough to help you stand tall and beat the examination.

MHT CET
Scan QR code for Eligibility, Exam Pattern, Syllabus and more.

Book ID: 0236

TABLE OF CONTENTS

Mathematics : Mock Test — 1-172

Mathematics : Mock Test - 1	1-17
Mathematics : Mock Test - 2	18-34
Mathematics : Mock Test - 3	35-50
Mathematics : Mock Test - 4	51-66
Mathematics : Mock Test - 5	67-84
Mathematics : Mock Test - 6	85-102
Mathematics : Mock Test - 7	103-119
Mathematics : Mock Test - 8	120-137
Mathematics : Mock Test - 9	138-155
Mathematics : Mock Test - 10	156-172

Physics & Chemistry : Mock Test — 173-420

Physics & Chemistry : Mock Test - 1	173-196
Physics & Chemistry : Mock Test - 2	197-220

Physics & Chemistry : Mock Test - 3	221-244
Physics & Chemistry : Mock Test - 4	245-269
Physics & Chemistry : Mock Test - 5	270-293
Physics & Chemistry : Mock Test - 6	294-320
Physics & Chemistry : Mock Test - 7	321-344
Physics & Chemistry : Mock Test - 8	345-369
Physics & Chemistry : Mock Test - 9	370-394
Physics & Chemistry : Mock Test - 10	395-420

Mathematics : Mock Test 01

Q.1 How many different words can be formed by using all the letters of the word, ALLAHABAD if both L's do not come together?
A. 1680   B. 7500   C. 5880   D. 7560

Q.2 Find $2X - Y$ matrix such as $X + Y = \begin{bmatrix} 7 & 5 \\ 3 & 4 \end{bmatrix}$ and $X - Y = \begin{bmatrix} 1 & -3 \\ 3 & 0 \end{bmatrix}$.

A. $\begin{bmatrix} 3 & 4 \\ 0 & -2 \end{bmatrix}$ B. $\begin{bmatrix} 5 & -2 \\ 6 & 2 \end{bmatrix}$
C. $\begin{bmatrix} 5 & 4 \\ 3 & -2 \end{bmatrix}$ D. $\begin{bmatrix} -3 & 4 \\ 0 & -2 \end{bmatrix}$

Q.3 If $A = \begin{bmatrix} 0 & -i \\ i & 0 \end{bmatrix}$ and $B = \begin{bmatrix} 1 & 0 \\ 0 & -1 \end{bmatrix}$ are matrices, then $AB + BA$ is:
A. A diagonal matrix   B. An invertible matrix
C. A unit matrix   D. A null matrix

Q.4 What is the order of $\begin{bmatrix} 4 & 4 & 1 \end{bmatrix} \begin{bmatrix} 3 & 2 & 5 \\ 9 & 7 & 4 \\ 6 & 4 & 1 \end{bmatrix}$?
A. 1×1 B. 1×3 C. 3×3 D. 3×1

Q.5 In the given figure, lines PQ and ST intersect each other at O. If ∠ROQ = 90° and a : b = 4 : 5. What is the value of angle c?

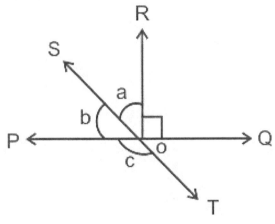

A. 120°   B. 100°   C. 130°   D. 145°

Q.6 Find the general solution of given differential equation $\frac{xdy}{dx} + 3y = 4x^3$?
A. $x^3 \cdot y = \frac{2}{3} \cdot x^5 + c$ B. $x^3 \cdot y = 3x^6 + c$
C. $x^3 \cdot y = \frac{2}{3} \cdot x^6 + c$ D. None of these

Q.7 The general solution of $\frac{dy}{dx} + y\tan x = 2\sin x$ is:
A. $\frac{\log\sec^2 x + C}{\sec x}$ B. $\sec^2 x$
C. $\log\sec^2 x + C$ D. $2\log\sec^2 x + C$

Q.8 The degree of the differential equation:
$\frac{d^2y}{dx^2} + 3\left(\frac{dy}{dx}\right)^2 = x^2 \log\left(\frac{d^2y}{dx^2}\right)$
A. 1   B. 2   C. 3   D. Not defined

Q.9 What are the two main types of measures of dispersion?
A. Real measure of dispersion and Relative measure of dispersion
B. Nominal measure of dispersion and Real measure of dispersion
C. Absolute measure of dispersion and Relative measure of dispersion
D. Nominal measure of dispersion and Relative measure of dispersion

Q.10 Find the value of $\lim_{x \to 5} \frac{x^2 - 25}{x^2 - 2x - 10}$
A. ∞   B. −1   C. 0   D. 1

Q.11 Find the area bounded by the curve $y = \sin x$ between $x = 0$ and $x = 2\pi$.
A. 16 sq. units   B. 4 sq. units
C. 8 sq. units   D. 2 sq. units

Q.12 Find the area between the curve $y = \sin x$ and lines $x = -\frac{\pi}{3}$ to $x = \frac{\pi}{3}$.
A. $\frac{1}{2}$ B. 1   C. $\frac{3}{2}$ D. 2

Q.13 Find the area under the curve $y = \cos x$ in the interval $0 < x < \frac{\pi}{2}$.
A. 0.5   B. 1   C. 0.7   D. 1.2

Q.14 Find the value of i^{1325} where $i = \sqrt{-1}$.
A. i B. $-i$ C. 1   D. −1

Q.15 Consider the following L.P.P. Maximize $Z = 3x + 2y$ Subject to the constraints:
$x + 2y \leq 10$
$3x + y \leq 15$
$x, y \geq 0$
Find the maximum value of Z.
A. 18   B. 20   C. 32   D. 16

Q.16 Maximise, $Z = x + y$, subject to $x - y \leq -1, -x + y \leq 0$, and $x, y \leq 0$.
A. one maximum value
B. no maximum value
C. two maximum value
D. zero maximum value

Q.17 Find graphically, the maximum value of $z = 2x + 5y$, subject to constraints given below:
$2x + 4y \leq 8$
$3x + y \leq 6$
$x + y \leq 4$
$x \geq 0, y \geq 0$

A. 11 B. 12 C. 10 D. 13

Q.18 If the distances of $P(x,y)$ from $A(4,1)$ and $B(-1,4)$ are equal, then which of the following is true?

A. $3x = 2y$ B. $5x = 3y$ C. $x = 2y$ D. $x = y$

Q.19 Find distance between the parallel lines $p(x+y) + q = 0$ and $p(x+y) - r = 0$?

A. $\frac{|q-r|}{\sqrt{2}p}$ B. $\frac{|q+r|}{\sqrt{2}p}$ C. $\frac{|q+r|}{2\sqrt{2}p}$ D. $\frac{|q-r|}{2\sqrt{2}p}$

Q.20 What is the product of the perpendiculars drawn from the points $(\pm\sqrt{a^2-b^2}, 0)$ upon the line $bx\cos\alpha + ay\sin\alpha = ab$?

A. a^2 B. b^2 C. $a^2 + b^2$ D. $a + b$

Q.21 A box contains 4 tennis balls, 6 season balls and 8 dues balls. 3 balls are randomly drawn from the box. What is the probability that the balls are different?

A. $\frac{1}{17}$ B. $\frac{2}{17}$ C. $\frac{4}{17}$ D. $\frac{3}{17}$

Q.22 For a distribution of student's height, the quartiles are $60.125, 61.345, 62.688$. The absolute measure of skewness is:

A. 0.321 B. 0.312 C. 0.231 D. 0.130

Q.23 If $\sin^{-1}x + \sin^{-1}y = \frac{5\pi}{6}$, then what is the value of $\cos^{-1}x + \cos^{-1}y$?

A. $\frac{\pi}{2}$ B. $\frac{\pi}{4}$ C. $\frac{\pi}{6}$ D. $\frac{\pi}{8}$

Q.24 The value of cosine of the angle between the x-axis and the vector $2\hat{i} + 2\hat{j} + \hat{k}$ is:
[UPSESSB TGT Mathematics, 2013]

A. $\frac{2}{3}$ B. $\frac{1}{3}$ C. $\frac{1}{2}$ D. $\frac{1}{\sqrt{2}}$

Q.25 If the position vectors of A and B are $\vec{a}$ and $\vec{b}$ respectively, then the position vector of mid-point of AB is:
[UPSESSB TGT Mathematics, 2013]

A. $\vec{a} + \vec{b}$ B. $\vec{a} - \vec{b}$ C. $\frac{1}{2}(\vec{a}+\vec{b})$ D. $\frac{1}{2}(\vec{a}-\vec{b})$

Q.26 If $\sec^2\theta + \tan^2\theta = 7$ then, find the value of $\sec\theta$:

A. 4 B. 2 C. 1 D. 0

Q.27 If $\sin x + \sin^2 x = 1$, then $\cos^4 x + \cos^2 x$ is equal to:

A. 0 B. 1 C. -1 D. 2

Q.28 Evaluate: $\frac{\cos x - \sin x + 1}{\cos x + \sin x - 1}$

A. $\cot x + \csc x$ B. $\cot x - \csc x$
C. $\tan x + \sec x$ D. $\tan x - \sec x$

Q.29 What is the degree of the differential equation
$\left(\frac{d^3y}{dx^3}\right)^{\frac{3}{2}} = \left(\frac{d^2y}{dx^2}\right)^2$?

A. 1 B. 2 C. 3 D. 4

Q.30 If $\lim_{x \to a} \frac{a^x - x^a}{x^x - a^a} = -1$, then what is the value of a?
[UPSC NDA, 2021]

A. -1 B. 0 C. 1 D. 2

Q.31 In a simultaneous throw of a pair of dice, the probability of getting a total more than 7 is:

A. $\frac{7}{12}$ B. $\frac{5}{36}$ C. $\frac{5}{12}$ D. $\frac{7}{36}$

Q.32 Evaluate $\int \frac{1-\cos 2x}{1-\sin^2 x}dx$.

A. $\tan x - 2x + c$ B. $2\tan x - x + c$
C. $2\tan x - 2x + c$ D. $2\tan x + 2x + c$

Q.33 Find the value of $\int \frac{dx}{1+e^{-x}}$, where c is the constant of integration.

A. $1 + e^x + c$ B. $\ln(1 + e^{-x}) + c$
C. $\ln(1 + e^x) + c$ D. $2\ln(1 + e^{-x}) + c$

Q.34 If $f(x)$ is a quadratic polynomial with vertex $V(1, \alpha)$, then the integral $I = \int_0^2 \frac{e^{f(x)}}{e^{f(x)} + e^{f(2-x)}} dx$ is equal to:

A. 1 B. 2 C. 3 D. 4

Q.35 The value of the integral $I = \int_{\frac{1}{\sqrt{3}}}^{\sqrt{3}} \frac{dx}{1+x^2+x^3+x^5}$ is equal to:

A. $\frac{\pi}{2}$ B. $\frac{\pi}{3}$ C. $\frac{\pi}{12}$ D. $\frac{\pi}{6}$

Q.36 The radius of a circle is changing at the rate of $\frac{dr}{dt} = 0.01$ m/sec. The rate of change of its area $\frac{dA}{dt}$, when the radius of the circle is 4 m, is:

A. 16π m²/sec B. 0.16π m²/sec
C. 0.08π m²/sec D. 0.04π m²/sec

Q.37 For the given curve: $y = 2x - x^2$, when x increases at the rate of 3 units/sec, then how the slope of curve changes?

A. Increasing, at 6 units/second
B. Decreasing, at 6 units/second
C. Increasing, at 3 units/second
D. Decreasing, at 3 units/second

Q.38 If at any instant t, for a sphere, r denotes the radius, S denotes the surface area and V denotes the volume, then what is $\frac{dV}{dt}$ equal to?

Mathematics : Mock Test - 1

A. $\frac{1}{2}S\frac{dr}{dt}$ **B.** $\frac{1}{2}r\frac{dS}{dt}$ **C.** $r\frac{dS}{dt}$ **D.** $\frac{1}{2}r^2\frac{dS}{dt}$

Q.39 The equation of the plane passing through the line of intersection of the planes $x + y + z = 1$, $2x + 3y + 4z = 7$, and perpendicular to the plane $x - 5y + 3z = 5$ is given by:

A. $x + 2y + 3z - 6 = 0$
B. $x + 2y + 3z + 6 = 0$
C. $x + 2y + 3z + 6 = 0$
D. $3x + 4y + 5z + 8 = 0$

Q.40 If $x = 2 + 3\cos\theta$ and $y = 1 - 3\sin\theta$ represent a circle then the centre and radius is:

A. $(-2, -1), 3$
B. $(1, 2), \frac{1}{3}$
C. $(2, 1), 3$
D. $(2, 1), 9$

Q.41 Let $f: R \to R$ be defined by $f(x) = 2x + 6$ which is a bijective mapping then $f^{-1}(x)$ is given by:

A. $6x + 2$ B. $x - 3$ C. $2x + 6$ D. $\frac{x}{2} - 3$

Q.42 The mean and standard deviation of a binomial distribution are 12 and 2 respectively. What is the number of trails?

A. 2   B. 12   C. 18   D. 24

Q.43 Consider a random variable X which follows Binomial distribution with parameters $n = 10$ and $p = \frac{1}{5}$. Then $Y = 10 - X$ follows Binomial distribution with parameters n and p respectively given by:

A. $5, \frac{1}{5}$ B. $5, \frac{2}{5}$ C. $10, \frac{3}{5}$ D. $10, \frac{4}{5}$

Q.44 What is $\int \frac{dx}{\sec^2(\tan^{-1}x)}$ equal to?

A. $\sin^{-1}x + C$
B. $\tan^{-1}x + C$
C. $\sec^{-1}x + C$
D. $\cos^{-1}x + C$

Q.45 The differential coefficient of $\log_{10}x$ with respect to $\log_x 10$ is:

A. $\frac{x^2}{100}$
B. $(\log_x 10)^2$
C. $-(\log_{10}x)^2$
D. 1

Q.46 If $\int_0^a \frac{1}{1+x^2}dx = \frac{\pi}{4}$ then, find the value of a ?

A. 1   B. 2   C. 3   D. 4

Q.47 Suppose a random variable X follows a Binomial distribution with parameters $n = 6$ and p. If $9P(X = 4) = P(X = 2)$, then the value of p is:

A. $\frac{1}{3}$ B. $\frac{1}{2}$ C. 1   D. $\frac{1}{4}$

Q.48 The equation of the locus of a point equidistant from the point $A(2, 3)$ and $B(-1, 2)$ is:

A. $2x + 6y = 8$
B. $6x + 2y = 8$
C. $x + y = 8$
D. $6x - 2y = 8$

Q.49 The statement $(\neg p) \Rightarrow (\neg q)$ is logically equivalent to which of the statements below?

I. $p \Rightarrow q$
II. $q \Rightarrow p$
III. $(\neg q) \vee p$
IV. $(\neg p) \vee q$

A. I only
B. II and IV only
C. II only
D. II and III only

Q.50 Let p, q, r denotes the statements "It is raining", "It is cold", and "It is pleasant", respectively. Then the statement "It is not raining, and it is pleasant, and it is not pleasant only if it is raining and it is cold" it represented by:

A. $(\neg p \wedge r) \wedge (\neg r \to (p \wedge q))$
B. $(\neg p \wedge r) \wedge ((p \wedge q) \to \neg r)$
C. $(\neg p \wedge r) \vee ((p \wedge q) \to \neg r)$
D. $(\neg p \wedge r) \vee (r \to (p \wedge q))$

Mathematics : Mock Test - 1

// Smart Answer Sheet //

Correct — Indicates percentage of students who answered questions correctly.

Skipped — Indicates percentage of students who skipped questions.

Q.	Ans.	Correct / Skipped	Q.	Ans.	Correct / Skipped	Q.	Ans.	Correct / Skipped	Q.	Ans.	Correct / Skipped	Q.	Ans.	Correct / Skipped
1	C	25.78 % / 16.21 %	11	B	33.19 % / 9.84 %	21	C	25.52 % / 13.5 %	31	C	27.26 % / 16.82 %	41	D	18.64 % / 14.29 %
2	B	36.15 % / 14.9 %	12	B	32.67 % / 16.46 %	22	D	11.85 % / 17.68 %	32	C	32.23 % / 17.16 %	42	C	28.4 % / 15.68 %
3	D	24.91 % / 16.03 %	13	B	38.33 % / 15.5 %	23	C	37.2 % / 12.63 %	33	C	30.49 % / 17.85 %	43	D	12.28 % / 16.81 %
4	B	38.59 % / 15.68 %	14	A	22.47 % / 15.68 %	24	A	22.47 % / 14.55 %	34	A	21.34 % / 15.86 %	44	B	34.32 % / 14.11 %
5	C	26.83 % / 18.55 %	15	A	25.87 % / 17.07 %	25	C	40.85 % / 14.99 %	35	C	21.95 % / 15.51 %	45	C	21.69 % / 16.64 %
6	C	27.7 % / 8.36 %	16	B	27.53 % / 12.37 %	26	B	32.67 % / 17.07 %	36	C	31.62 % / 13.94 %	46	A	27.35 % / 16.55 %
7	A	17.07 % / 16.21 %	17	C	25.7 % / 13.59 %	27	B	33.19 % / 15.94 %	37	B	29.44 % / 16.29 %	47	D	16.64 % / 12.37 %
8	D	23.08 % / 16.12 %	18	B	37.54 % / 10.98 %	28	A	14.37 % / 12.11 %	38	B	35.89 % / 14.2 %	48	B	33.97 % / 14.72 %
9	C	36.67 % / 14.03 %	19	B	31.36 % / 16.98 %	29	C	33.01 % / 15.77 %	39	A	18.55 % / 16.64 %	49	D	22.91 % / 12.98 %
10	C	32.84 % / 16.2 %	20	B	23.43 % / 7.75 %	30	C	30.75 % / 13.68 %	40	C	36.67 % / 10.89 %	50	A	30.4 % / 16.38 %

Performance Analysis	
Avg. Score (%)	29.0%
Toppers Score (%)	100.0%
Your Score	

//Hints and Solutions//

1. The word ALLAHABAD contains 9 letters, in which A occur 4 times, L occurs twice and the rest of the letters occur only once.

We know that:

Number of Permutations of 'n' things taken 'r' at a time:

$$p(n, r) = \frac{n!}{(n-r)!}$$

Number of Permutations of 'n' objects where there are n_1 repeated items, n_2 repeated items, n_k repeated items taken 'r' at a time:

$$p(n, r) = \frac{n!}{n_1! n_2! n_3! \ldots n_k!}$$

Therefore,

Number of different words formed by the word ALLAHABAD using all the letters.

$$= \frac{9!}{4! \times 2!}$$

$$= \frac{9 \times 8 \times 7 \times 6 \times 5 \times 4!}{4! \times 2}$$

$$= \frac{72 \times 7 \times 30}{2}$$

$$= 7560$$

Now, let us take both L together and consider (LL) as 1 letter.

Then, we will have to arrange 8 letters, in which A occurs 4 times and the rest of the letters occur only once.

So, the number of words having both L together will be:

$$= \frac{8!}{4!}$$

$$= \frac{8 \times 7 \times 6 \times 5 \times 4!}{4!}$$

$$= 1680$$

Therefore, the number of words with both L not occurring together will be:

$$= 7560 - 1680$$

$$= 5880$$

Hence, the correct option is (C).

2. Given,

$$X + Y = \begin{bmatrix} 7 & 5 \\ 3 & 4 \end{bmatrix} \ldots(i)$$

$$X - Y = \begin{bmatrix} 1 & -3 \\ 3 & 0 \end{bmatrix} \ldots(ii)$$

Adding the equations (i) and (ii), we get

$$2X = \begin{bmatrix} 8 & 2 \\ 6 & 4 \end{bmatrix}$$

$$\Rightarrow X = \begin{bmatrix} 4 & 1 \\ 3 & 2 \end{bmatrix}$$

Substracting (ii) from (i), we get

$$2Y = \begin{bmatrix} 6 & 8 \\ 0 & 4 \end{bmatrix}$$

$$\Rightarrow Y = \begin{bmatrix} 3 & 4 \\ 0 & 2 \end{bmatrix}$$

Let $A = 2X - Y$

$$A = 2 \times \begin{bmatrix} 4 & 1 \\ 3 & 2 \end{bmatrix} - \begin{bmatrix} 3 & 4 \\ 0 & 2 \end{bmatrix}$$

$$\Rightarrow A = \begin{bmatrix} 8 & 2 \\ 6 & 4 \end{bmatrix} - \begin{bmatrix} 3 & 4 \\ 0 & 2 \end{bmatrix}$$

$$\Rightarrow A = \begin{bmatrix} 5 & -2 \\ 6 & 2 \end{bmatrix}$$

$$\therefore 2X - Y = \begin{bmatrix} 5 & -2 \\ 6 & 2 \end{bmatrix}$$

Hence, the correct option is (B).

3. Given,

$$A = \begin{bmatrix} 0 & -i \\ i & 0 \end{bmatrix}$$

$$B = \begin{bmatrix} 1 & 0 \\ 0 & -1 \end{bmatrix}$$

$$\therefore AB = \begin{bmatrix} 0 & -i \\ i & 0 \end{bmatrix} \times \begin{bmatrix} 1 & 0 \\ 0 & -1 \end{bmatrix}$$

$$= \begin{bmatrix} 0+0 & 0+i \\ i+0 & 0+0 \end{bmatrix}$$

$$= \begin{bmatrix} 0 & i \\ i & 0 \end{bmatrix}$$

And $BA = \begin{bmatrix} 1 & 0 \\ 0 & -1 \end{bmatrix} \times \begin{bmatrix} 0 & -i \\ i & 0 \end{bmatrix}$

$$= \begin{bmatrix} 0+0 & -i+0 \\ 0-i & 0+0 \end{bmatrix}$$

$$= \begin{bmatrix} 0 & -i \\ -i & 0 \end{bmatrix}$$

$$\therefore AB + BA = \begin{bmatrix} 0 & i \\ i & 0 \end{bmatrix} + \begin{bmatrix} 0 & -i \\ -i & 0 \end{bmatrix}$$

$$= \begin{bmatrix} 0+0 & i-i \\ i-i & 0+0 \end{bmatrix}$$

$$= \begin{bmatrix} 0 & 0 \\ 0 & 0 \end{bmatrix}$$

So, $AB + BA$ is a null matrix.

Hence, the correct option is (D).

4. Let $\begin{bmatrix} 4 & 4 & 1 \end{bmatrix} \begin{bmatrix} 3 & 2 & 5 \\ 9 & 7 & 4 \\ 6 & 4 & 1 \end{bmatrix} - AB$

Order of matrix A is (1×3).

Order of matrix B is (3×3).

As we know,

To multiply an $m \times n$ matrix by $n \times p$ matrix, the n must be the same and the result is an $m \times p$ matrix.

So, Order of $A_{(1 \times 3)} B_{(3 \times 3)}$ is (1×3).

∴ Order of $\begin{bmatrix} 4 & 4 & 1 \end{bmatrix} \begin{bmatrix} 3 & 2 & 5 \\ 9 & 7 & 4 \\ 6 & 4 & 1 \end{bmatrix}$ is (1×3).

Hence, the correct option is (B).

5. Given:

∠ROQ = 90°

a : b = 4 : 5

Calculations:

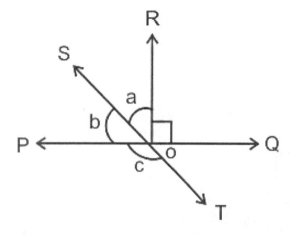

Let ∠a and ∠b be 4x and 5x

According to the question, we have,

∠a + ∠b = 90° (The angle subtended at a straight line is 180° and ∠ROQ = 90°)

⇒ 4x + 5x = 90°

⇒ 9x = 90°

⇒ x = 10°

∠b = 5x = 5 × 10° = 50°

Now,

∠b + ∠c = 180°

⇒ 50° + ∠c = 180°

⇒ ∠c = 130°

∴ The value of ∠c is 130°.

Hence, the correct option is (C).

6. Given,

$\dfrac{xdy}{dx} + 3y = 4x^3$

Now,

$\dfrac{dy}{dx} + \dfrac{3y}{x} = 4x^2$

By comparing with $\dfrac{dy}{dx} + Py = Q$

We get,

$P = \dfrac{3}{x}$ and $Q = 4x^2$

$\Rightarrow I.F. = e^{\int P dx} = e^{\int \frac{3}{x} dx}$

$\Rightarrow I.F. = e^{3\ln x}$

$\Rightarrow I.F. = e^{\ln x^3}$

$\Rightarrow I.F. = x^3 (\because e^{\ln x} = x)$

Now general solution will be,

$y \cdot (I \cdot F \cdot) = \int (Q\, I.F) dx + c$

$\Rightarrow y \cdot x^3 = \int (4x^2 \cdot (x^3)) dx + c$

$\Rightarrow x^3 \cdot y = \int 4x^5\, dx + c$

$\Rightarrow x^3 \cdot y = 4 \dfrac{x^6}{6} + c$

$\Rightarrow x^3 \cdot y = \dfrac{2}{3} \cdot x^6 + c$

Hence, the correct option is (C).

7. Given,

$\dfrac{dy}{dx} + y\tan x = 2\sin x$

By comparing with $\dfrac{dy}{dx} + Py = Q$

We get,

$P = \tan x$ and $Q = 2\sin x$

Integrating factor (I.F) of the equation is given by

$I.F = e^{\int P dx}$

$I.F = e^{\int \tan x dx}$

$= e^{\log \sec x}$

$= \sec x$

By solving,

$y \times (I.F) = \int [Q \times (I.F)] dx + C$

$\Rightarrow y \sec x = \int [2\sin x \times \sec x] dx + C$

$\Rightarrow y = \int \left[2\sin x \times \dfrac{1}{\cos x} \right] dx + C$

$\Rightarrow y = \int [2\tan x] dx + C = 2\log \sec x + C$

$\Rightarrow y = \dfrac{2\log \sec x + C}{\sec x}$

$\Rightarrow y = \dfrac{\log \sec^2 x + C}{\sec x}$

Hence, the correct option is (A).

8. Given,

$$\frac{d^2y}{dx^2} + 3\left(\frac{dy}{dx}\right)^2 = x^2 \log\left(\frac{d^2y}{dx^2}\right)$$

For the given differential equation the highest order derivative is 2.

The given differential equation is not a polynomial equation because it involved a logarithmic term in its derivatives so, its degree is not defined.

Hence, the correct option is (D).

9. Absolute measure of dispersion and Relative measure of dispersion are the two main types of measures of dispersion.

Absolute measure of dispersion indicates the amount of variation in a set of values in terms of units of observations. Relative measures of dispersion are free from the units of measurements of the observations. They are pure numbers. They are used to compare the variation in two or more sets, which are having different units of measurements of observations.

Hence, the correct option is (C).

10. Given,

$$\lim_{x \to 5} \frac{x^2 - 25}{x^2 - 2x - 10}$$

Putting the value $x \to 5$ in above equation, we get:

$$= \frac{5^2 - 25}{5^2 - 2 \times 5 - 10}$$

$$= \frac{0}{5}$$

$$= 0$$

Hence, the correct option is (C).

11. Given curve:

$$y = \sin x$$

The graph of $y = \sin x$ can be drawn as shown in the diagram:

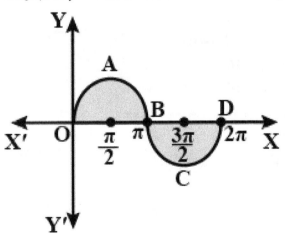

∴ Required area = Area $OABO$ + Area $BCDB$

$$= \int_0^\pi \sin x\, dx + \left|\int_\pi^{2\pi} \sin x\, dx\right|$$

$$= [-\cos x]_0^\pi + |[-\cos x]_\pi^{2\pi}|$$

$$= [-\cos\pi + \cos 0] + |-\cos 2\pi + \cos\pi|$$

$$= 1 + 1 + |(-1 - 1)|$$

$$= 2 + |-2|$$

$$= 2 + 2$$

$$= 4 \text{ sq. units}$$

Hence, the correct option is (B).

12. Given:

Curve 1: $y = \sin x = f(x)$ (say)

Curve 2: Lines $x = -\frac{\pi}{3}$ and $x = \frac{\pi}{3}$

It can be drawn as follows:

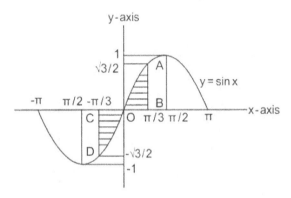

According to the figure the sum of area curve OAB and curve OCD.

Here, OAB and OCD are equal and limit 0 to $\frac{\pi}{3}$.

So,

Area $= 2 \times$ area of OAB.

The area between the curves $y_1 = f(x)$ and $y_2 = g(x)$ is given by:

Area enclosed $= \left|\int_{x_1}^{x_2} (y_1 - y_2)\, dx\right|$

Where, x_1 and x_2 are the intersections of curves y_1 and y_2

Now, the required area (A) is,

Area of $OAB = \left|\int_{x_1}^{x_2} f(x)\, dx\right|$

$$= \left|\int_0^{\frac{\pi}{3}} \sin x\, dx\right|$$

$$= \left|[-\cos x]_0^{\frac{\pi}{3}}\right|$$

$= \left|-\cos\frac{\pi}{3} + \cos 0°\right|$

$= \left|1 - \frac{1}{2}\right|$

$= \frac{1}{2}$

∴ Shaded Area $= 2 \times \frac{1}{2} = 1$

Hence, the correct option is (B).

13. Let us first draw the graph of $y = \cos x$ in the interval $0 < x < \frac{\pi}{2}$.

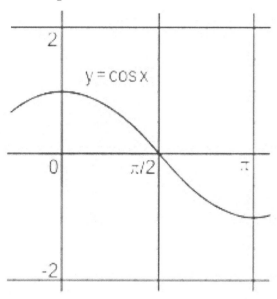

Let the required area of the positive enclosed region be A.

Using the formula of the area under the curve as,

$A = \left|\int_a^b f(x) - g(x)dx\right|$,

$\Rightarrow A = \left|\int_0^{\frac{\pi}{2}} \cos x \, dx\right|$

$= \left|[\sin x]_0^{\frac{\pi}{2}}\right|$

Using the value of $\sin 0 = 0$ and $\sin\frac{\pi}{2} = 1$

$\Rightarrow A = \left|\sin\frac{\pi}{2} - \sin 0\right|$

$= |1 - 0|$

$= 1$

Hence, the correct option is (B).

14. As we know,

$i = \sqrt{-1}$

$i^2 = -1$

$i^{4n} = 1$

Given,

i^{1325}

$= i^{(1324+1)}$

$= (i^4)^{331} \times i$

$= 1 \times i \quad [\because i^{4n} = 1]$

$= i$

∴ $i^{1325} = i$

Hence, the correct option is (A).

15.

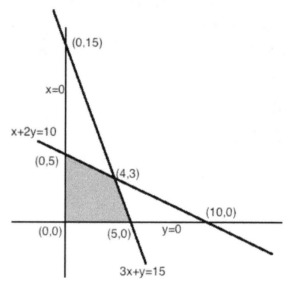

Given:

$Z = 3x + 2y$

subject to the constraints

$x + 2y \leq 10$

$3x + y \leq 15$

Convert these inequalities into equations

$x + 2y = 10$ .....(i)

$3x + y = 15$ .... (ii)

From (i), we get

$x = 0$ when $y = 5$ and $y = 0$ when $x = 10$

So, the points $(0,5)$ and $(10,0)$ lie on the line given in (i).

From (ii), we get the points

$(0,15)$ and $(5,0)$

Let's plot these point and we get the graph in which, shaded part shows the feasible region.

Lines (i) and (ii) intersect at $(4,3)$ and other corner points of the region are $(0,5), (5,0)$ and $(0,0)$.

To find the maximum value of Z, we need to find the value of Z at the corner points.

Corner points	$Z = 3x + 2y$
(0,0)	0
(5,0)	15
(0,5)	10
(4,3)	18

Thus, Z is maximum at $(4,3)$ and its maximum value is 18.

Hence, the correct option is (A).

16.

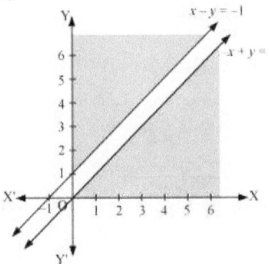

Maximize

$Z = (x + y)$

$\Rightarrow x - y \leq -1, y - x \leq 0, x, y \leq 0$

put $x = 0$ in $x - y = -1$............. (i)

$y = 1$

put $x = 1$ in equation (i)

$y = 2$

put $x = -1$

$-1 - y = -1$

$y = 0$

$y - x = 0$.......(ii)

put $x = 0$ in equation (ii)

$y = 0$

put $x = 1$

$y = 1$

put $x = 2$

$y = 2$

put $x = -1$

$y = -1$

No feasible region, hence, no maximum value.

Hence, the correct option is (B).

17. Given:

$z = 2x + 5y$

$2x + 4y \leq 8$

$\Rightarrow x + 2y \leq 4$

$3x + y \leq 6, x + y \leq 4, x \geq 0, y \geq 0$

Draw the lines $x + 2y = 4$ (passes through $(4,0\ ), (0,2)$)

$3x + y = 6$ (passes through $(2,0), (0,6)$ and

$x + y = 4$ (passes through $(4,0), (0,4)$

Shade the region satisfied by the given inequations;

The shaded region in the figure gives the feasible region determined by the given inequations.

Solving $3x + y = 6$ and $x + 2y = 4$ simultaneously, we get

$x = \frac{8}{5}$ and $y = \frac{6}{5}$

We observe that the feasible region $OABC$ is a convex polygon and bounded and has corner points.

$O(0,0), A(2,0), B\left(\frac{8}{5}, \frac{6}{5}\right), C(0,2)$

The optimal solution occurs at one of the corner points.

At $O(0,0), z = 2 \times 0 + 5 \times 0 = 0$

At $A(2,0),\ z = 2 \times 2 + 5 \times 0 = 4$

At B $\left(\frac{8}{5},\frac{6}{5}\right), z = 2 \times \frac{8}{5} + 5 \times \frac{6}{5} = \frac{46}{5}$

At $C(0,2),\ z = 2 \times 0 + 5 \times 2 = 10$

Therefore, z maximum value at C and maximum value $= 10$

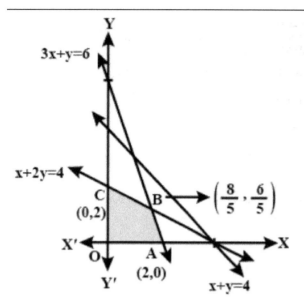

Hence, the correct option is (C).

18. Given,

The distances of $P(x, y)$ from $A(4,1)$ and $B(-1,4)$ are equal.

The distance 'd' between two points (x_1, y_1) and (x_2, y_2) is obtained by using the Pythagoras' Theorem: $d^2 = (x_1 - x_2)^2 + (y_1 - y_2)^2$.

Using the formula for the distance between two points:

$AP^2 = (x - 4)^2 + (y - 1)^2$

$BP^2 = (x + 1)^2 + (y - 4)^2$

Since the distances are equal, we have:

$AP^2 = BP^2$

$\Rightarrow (x - 4)^2 + (y - 1)^2 = (x + 1)^2 + (y - 4)^2$

$\Rightarrow x^2 - 8x + 16 + y^2 - 2y + 1 = x^2 + 2x + 1 + y^2 - 8y + 16$

$\Rightarrow 10x = 6y$

$\Rightarrow 5x = 3y$

Hence, the correct option is (B).

19. Given,

Two parallel line $p(x + y) + q = 0$ and $p(x + y) - r = 0$

The distance between the parallel lines $ax + by + c_1 = 0$ and $ax + by + c_2 = 0$ is given by:

$d = \left|\dfrac{c_1 - c_2}{\sqrt{a^2 + b^2}}\right|$

Here, we have to find the distance between the parallel lines $p(x + y) + q = 0$ and $p(x + y) - r = 0$

The given equations of line can be re-written as: $px + py + q = 0$ and $px + py - r = 0$

By comparing the equations of the given line with $ax + by + c_1 = 0$ and $ax + by + c_2 = 0$ we get,

$a = p, b = p, c_1 = q$ and $c_2 = -r$

As we know that, the distance between the parallel lines is given by:

$d = \left|\dfrac{c_1 - c_2}{\sqrt{a^2 + b^2}}\right|$

$d = \left|\dfrac{q + r}{\sqrt{p^2 + p^2}}\right|$

$= \dfrac{|q + r|}{\sqrt{2}p}$

Distance between the parallel lines $p(x + y) + q = 0$ and $p(x + y) - r = 0$ is $\dfrac{|q + r|}{\sqrt{2}p}$.

Hence, the correct option is (B).

20. $\dfrac{x}{a}\cos\theta + \dfrac{y}{b}\sin\theta = 1$

Or, $bx\cos\theta + ay\sin\theta - ab - 0$ ....(1)

Length of the perpendicular from point $\left(\sqrt{a^2 - b^2}; 0\right)$ to line (1) is

$P_1 = \dfrac{|b\cos\theta(\sqrt{a^2-b^2}) + a\sin\theta(0) - ab|}{\sqrt{b^2\cos^2\theta + a^2\sin^2\theta}} = \dfrac{|b\cos\theta\sqrt{a^2-b^2} - ab|}{\sqrt{b^2\cos^2\theta + a^2\sin^2\theta}}$ ....(2)

Length of the perpendicular from point $\left(-\sqrt{a^2 - b^2}, 0\right)$ to line (2) is

$P_2 = \dfrac{|b\cos\theta(-\sqrt{a^2-b^2}) + a\sin\theta(0) - ab|}{\sqrt{b^2\cos^2\theta + a^2\sin^2\theta}} = \dfrac{|b\cos\theta(-\sqrt{a^2-b^2}) - ab|}{\sqrt{b^2\cos^2\theta + a^2\sin^2\theta}}$

$P_2 = \dfrac{|b\cos\theta(-\sqrt{a^2-b^2}) + a\sin\theta(0) - ab|}{\sqrt{b^2\cos^2\theta + a^2\sin^2\theta}} = \dfrac{|b\cos\theta\sqrt{a^2-b^2} + ab|}{\sqrt{b^2\cos^2\theta + a^2\sin^2\theta}}$ ....(3)

On multiplying equations (2) and (3) we get,

$P_1 P_2 = \dfrac{|(b\cos\theta\sqrt{a^2-b^2} - ab)(b\cos\theta\sqrt{a^2-b^2} + ab)|}{\left(\sqrt{b^2\cos^2\theta + a^2\sin^2\theta}\right)^2}$

$= \dfrac{|(b\cos\theta\sqrt{a^2-b^2} - ab)(b\cos\theta\sqrt{a^2-b^2} + ab)|}{(b^2\cos^2\theta + a^2\sin^2\theta)}$

$= \dfrac{\left|(b\cos\theta\sqrt{a^2-b^2})^2 - (ab)^2\right|}{(b^2\cos^2\theta + a^2\sin^2\theta)}$ ($\because (a+b)(a-b) = a^2 - b^2$)

$= \frac{|b^2\cos^2\theta(a^2-b^2)-a^2b^2|}{(b^2\cos^2\theta+a^2\sin^2\theta)}$

$= \frac{|a^2b^2\cos^2\theta-b^4\cos^2\theta-a^2b^2|}{b^2\cos^2\theta+a^2\sin^2\theta}$

$= \frac{b^2|a^2\cos^2\theta-b^2\cos^2\theta-a^2|}{b^2\cos^2\theta+a^2\sin^2\theta}$

$= \frac{b^2|a^2\cos^2\theta-b^2\cos^2\theta-a^2\sin^2\theta-a^2\cos^2\theta|}{b^2\cos^2\theta+a^2\sin^2\theta}$ ∵

$[\sin^2\theta+\cos^2\theta=1]$

$= \frac{b^2|-(b^2\cos^2\theta+a^2\sin^2\theta)|}{b^2\cos^2\theta+a^2\sin^2\theta}$

$= \frac{b^2(b^2\cos^2\theta+a^2\sin^2\theta)}{(b^2\cos^2\theta+a^2\sin^2\theta)}$

$= b^2$

Hence, the correct option is (B).

21. Given,

A box contains 4 tennis balls, 6 season balls and 8 dues balls

We know that,

$\text{Probability} = \frac{\text{Favourable outcomes}}{\text{Total outcomes}}$

Let us assume that all balls are unique.

There are a total of 18 balls.

Number of all combinations of n things, taken r at a time, is given by $^nC_r = \frac{n!}{(r)!(n-r)!}$

Total ways $= 3$ balls can be chosen in $^{18}C_3$ ways

$= \frac{18!}{3! \times 15!}$

$= \frac{18 \times 17 \times 16}{3 \times 2 \times 1}$

$= 816$

There are 4 tennis balls, 6 season balls and 8 dues balls, 1 tennis ball, 1 season ball and 1 dues Ball drawn.

Therefore, favorable ways $= 4 \times 6 \times 8$

$= 192$

$\text{Probability} = \frac{192}{816}$

$= \frac{4}{17}$

Hence, the correct option is (C).

22. Given:

$\mu_1 = 60.125$

$\mu_2 = 61.345$

$\mu_3 = 62.688$

Skewness coefficient is denoted by β_1

$\beta_1 = \frac{(\mu_3)^2}{(\mu_2)^3}$

$= \frac{(62.688)^2}{(61.345)^3}$

$\Rightarrow \beta_1 = 0.0170$

Absolute skewness measurement $= \gamma_1$

$\Rightarrow \gamma_1 = \sqrt{(\beta_1)}$

$= \sqrt{0.0170}$

$= 0.130$

∴ Absolute skewness measurement is 0.130.

Hence, the correct option is (D).

23. Given,

$\sin^{-1}x + \sin^{-1}y = \frac{5\pi}{6}$ .... (1)

Let, $\cos^{-1}x + \cos^{-1}y = a$ .... (2)

Adding the two equation we get,

$(\sin^{-1}x + \cos^{-1}x) + (\sin^{-1}y + \cos^{-1}y) = \frac{5\pi}{6} + a$

$\Rightarrow \frac{\pi}{2} + \frac{\pi}{2} = \frac{5\pi}{6} + a$ [∵ $\sin^{-1}x + \cos^{-1}x = \frac{\pi}{2}$]

$\Rightarrow \pi - \frac{5\pi}{6} = a$

$\Rightarrow a = \frac{\pi}{6}$

So, $\cos^{-1}x + \cos^{-1}y = \frac{\pi}{6}$

Hence, the correct option is (C).

24. Unit vector along x-axis $= \hat{i} + 0\hat{j} + 0\hat{k} = \hat{i}$ .... (1)

Unit vector along y-axis $= \hat{j}$

Unit vector along z-axis $= \hat{k}$

And angle between two vectors $\vec{a}$ and $\vec{b}$.

$\cos\theta = \frac{\vec{a}.\vec{b}}{|\vec{a}|.|\vec{b}|}$

Where

$|\vec{a}| = \sqrt{a_1^2 + b_1^2 + c_1^2}$

$|\vec{b}| = \sqrt{a_2^2 + b_2^2 + c_2^2}$

Given,

Vector, $\vec{a} = 2\hat{i} + 2\hat{j} + \hat{k}$

By equation (1), unit vector along x -axis, $\vec{b} = \hat{i} + 0\hat{j} + 0\hat{k}$

Then, value of cosine,

$\cos\theta = \dfrac{(2\hat{i}+2\hat{j}+\hat{k})\cdot(\hat{i}+0\hat{j}+0\hat{k})}{\sqrt{2^2+2^2+1^2}\sqrt{1^2+0+0}}$

$\Rightarrow \cos\theta = \dfrac{2}{\sqrt{9}\cdot\sqrt{1}}$

$\Rightarrow \cos\theta = \dfrac{2}{3}$

Hence, the correct option is (A).

25. Section formula is given by $\dfrac{mA+nB}{m+n}$.

Given: Position vector of A and B are $\vec{a}$ and $\vec{b}$ respectively.

Let M be the mid-point of AB, such that $AM = MB$, it means that M divides AB in the ratio $1:1$, so by section formula, we get,

$\dfrac{(1)\vec{a}+(1)\vec{b}}{1+1} = \dfrac{1}{2}\left(\vec{a}+\vec{b}\right)$

Thus, we conclude that If the position vectors of A and B are $\vec{a}$ and $\vec{b}$ respectively, then the position vector of mid-point of AB is $\dfrac{1}{2}\left(\vec{a}+\vec{b}\right)$.

Hence, the correct option is (C).

26. Given,

$\sec^2\theta + \tan^2\theta = 7$ ......(i)

Adding 1 both sides in eqaution (i) we get,

$\sec^2\theta + \tan^2\theta + 1 = 7 + 1$

$\Rightarrow \sec^2\theta + \sec^2\theta = 8$ $(\because 1 + \tan^2\theta = \sec^2\theta)$

$\Rightarrow 2\sec^2\theta = 8$

$\Rightarrow \sec^2\theta = 4$

$\Rightarrow \sec\theta = 2$

$\therefore \sec\theta = 2$

Hence, the correct option is (B).

27. Given,

$\sin x + \sin^2 x = 1$

$\Rightarrow \sin x = 1 - \sin^2 x$ $(\because 1 - \sin^2\theta = \cos^2\theta)$

$\Rightarrow \sin x = \cos^2 x$ ......(i)

Sqauring both in equation (i) we get,

$\sin^2 x = \cos^4 x$

$\Rightarrow 1 - \cos^2 x = \cos^4 x$ $(\because \sin^2\theta = 1 - \cos^2\theta)$

$\Rightarrow \cos^4 x + \cos^2 x = 1$

Hence, the correct option is (B).

28. Given,

$\dfrac{\cos x - \sin x + 1}{\cos x + \sin x - 1}$

Assuming this as equation (i)

$\dfrac{\cos x - \sin x + 1}{\cos x + \sin x - 1}$ ......(i)

Now rationalizing eqution (i)

$\dfrac{\cos x - (\sin x - 1)}{\cos x + (\sin x - 1)} \times \dfrac{\cos x - (\sin x - 1)}{\cos x - (\sin x - 1)}$

$= \dfrac{[\cos x - (\sin x - 1)]^2}{\cos^2 x - (\sin x - 1)^2}$

Now using identity $(a-b)^2 = (a^2 - 2ab - b^2)$ we get,

$= \dfrac{\cos^2 x + (\sin x - 1)^2 - 2\cos x(\sin x - 1)}{-(\sin^2 x - 2\sin x + 1)}$

$= \dfrac{\cos^2 x + \sin^2 x - 2\sin x + 1 - 2\cos x(\sin x - 1)}{1 - \sin^2 x - (\sin^2 x - 2\sin x + 1)}$

$(\because \cos^2 x + \sin^2 x = 1$ and $\cos^2 x = 1 - \sin^2 x)$

$= \dfrac{1 - 2\sin x + 1 - 2\cos x(\sin x - 1)}{1 - \sin^2 x - (\sin^2 x - 2\sin x + 1)}$

$= \dfrac{2 - 2\sin x - 2\cos x(\sin x - 1)}{1 - \sin^2 x - \sin^2 x + 2\sin x - 1}$

$= \dfrac{2(1-\sin x) + 2\cos x(1-\sin x)}{2\sin x - 2\sin^2 x}$

$= \dfrac{(1-\sin x)(1+\cos x)}{\sin x(1-\sin x)}$

$= \dfrac{1+\cos x}{\sin x}$

$= \dfrac{1}{\sin x} + \dfrac{\cos x}{\sin x}$ $\left(\because \operatorname{cosec} x = \dfrac{1}{\sin x}, \cot x = \dfrac{\cos x}{\sin x}\right)$

$= \operatorname{cosec} x + \cot x$

Hence, the correct option is (A).

29. We have, $\left(\dfrac{d^a y}{dx^2}\right)^{\frac{3}{2}} = \left(\dfrac{d^2 y}{dx^2}\right)^2$

Squaring both the sides, we get,

$\left(\dfrac{d^3 y}{dx^3}\right)^3 = \left(\dfrac{d^2 y}{dx^2}\right)^4$

Here highest derivative is $\left(\dfrac{d^3 y}{dx^3}\right)^3$.

∴ Degree = power of $\left(\frac{d^3y}{dx^3}\right)^3 = 3$

Hence, the correct option is (C).

30. Given,

$\lim_{x \to a} \frac{a^x - x^a}{x^x - a^a}$

$= \frac{a^a - a^a}{a^a - a^a}$

$= \frac{0}{0}$, an indeterminate form.

Applying L'Hospital's rule,

$\lim_{x \to c} \frac{f(x)}{g(x)} = \lim_{x \to c} \frac{f'(x)}{g'(x)}$

After applying L'Hospital's rule we get,

$\lim_{x \to a} \frac{a^x - x^a}{x^x - a^a}$

$= \lim_{x \to a} \frac{a^x \log a - a x^{a-1}}{x^x (\log x + 1)} = \frac{a^a \log a - a \cdot a^{a-1}}{a^a (\log a + 1)}$

$= \frac{\log a - 1}{\log a + 1}$

According to the question,

$\frac{\log a - 1}{\log a + 1} = -1$

$\Rightarrow \log a - 1 = -\log a - 1$

$\Rightarrow 2 \log a = 0$

$\Rightarrow a = 1$

Hence, the correct option is (C).

31. Let S be sample space.

The probability of an event is $P(E)$.

$\Rightarrow P(E) = \frac{n(E)}{n(S)}$

Given, $S =$ a simultaneous throw of a pair of dice

$\{(1,1), (1,2), (1,3), (1,4), (1,5), (1,6), (2,1), (2,2), (2,3), (2,4), (2,5), (2,6)$

$(3,1), (3,2), (3,3), (3,4), (3,5), (3,6), (4,1), (4,2), (4,3), (4,4), (4,5), (4,6)$

$(5,1), (5,2), (5,3), (5,4), (5,5), (5,6), (6,1), (6,2), (6,3), (6,4), (6,5), (6,6)\}$

$\Rightarrow n(S) = 36$

$E =$ event of getting a total more than 7.

$E = \{(2,6), (3,5), (3,6), (4,4), (4,5), (4,6), (5,3), (5,4), (5,5), (5,6), (6,2), (6,3), (6,4), (6,5), (6,6)\}$

$\Rightarrow n(E) = 15$

The probability of getting a total more than 7 is $P(E)$.

$\Rightarrow P(E) = \frac{n(E)}{n(S)}$

$\Rightarrow P(E) = \frac{15}{36}$

$\Rightarrow P(E) = \frac{5}{12}$

Hence, the correct option is (C).

32. Let $I = \int \frac{1 - \cos 2x}{1 - \sin^2 x} dx$

$= \int \frac{2 \sin^2 x}{\cos^2 x} dx$

$= 2 \int \tan^2 x \, dx$

$= 2 \int (\sec^2 x - 1) dx$

$= 2[\tan x - x] + c$

$= 2 \tan x - 2x + c$

Hence, the correct option is (C).

33. Let, $I = \int \frac{dx}{1 + e^{-x}}$

$= \int \frac{dx}{1 + \frac{1}{e^x}}$

$= \int \frac{e^x dx}{e^x + 1}$

Now put $1 + e^x = t$

$e^x dx = dt$

$\therefore I = \int \frac{dt}{t}$

$\Rightarrow \ln t + c$

$\Rightarrow \ln(1 + e^x) + c \quad (\because t = 1 + e^x)$

Hence, the correct option is (C).

34. As vertex is $V(1, \alpha)$, thus the quadratic is symmetric about $x = 1$

$\Rightarrow f(1 + x) = f(1 - x)$

Replacing (x) by $(x - 1)$, we get,

$f(x) = f(2 - x)$

Applying $(a + b - x)$ in I and adding, we get,

$2I = \int_0^2 \frac{e^{f(x)} + e^{f(2-x)}}{e^{f(x)} + e^{f(2-x)}} dx$

$\Rightarrow 2I = \int_0^2 1 \, dx = [x]_0^2$

$\Rightarrow 2I = 2 - 0$

$\Rightarrow I = 1$

Hence, the correct option is (A).

35. Given integral is,

$I = \int_{\frac{1}{\sqrt{3}}}^{\sqrt{3}} \frac{dx}{(1 + x^2)(1 + x^3)}$

Let $\tan^{-1} x = \theta$

$\Rightarrow dx = \sec^2\theta d\theta$

$\therefore I = \int_{\frac{\pi}{6}}^{\frac{\pi}{3}} \frac{d\theta}{1+\tan^3\theta}$

$= \int_{\frac{\pi}{6}}^{\frac{\pi}{3}} \frac{\cos^3\theta}{\sin^3\theta+\cos^3\theta} d\theta$

Applying $(a+b-x)$ property and adding, we get,

$2I = \int_{\frac{\pi}{6}}^{\frac{\pi}{3}} \frac{\cos^3\theta+\sin^3\theta}{\sin^3\theta+\cos^3\theta} d\theta$

$2I = [\theta]_{\frac{\pi}{6}}^{\frac{\pi}{3}}$

$\Rightarrow 2I = \frac{\pi}{6}$

$\Rightarrow I = \frac{\pi}{12}$

Hence, the correct option is (C).

36. We know that the area of a circle of radius units is given by $A = \pi r^2$ sq.units.

$\therefore \frac{dA}{dt} = \frac{d}{dt}(\pi r^2) = 2\pi r \left(\frac{dr}{dt}\right)$

Now, $\left[\frac{dA}{dt}\right]_{r=4} = 8\pi(0.01)$ m^2/sec $= 0.08$ mm^2/sec

Hence, the correct option is (C).

37. Rate of change of 'x' is given by $\frac{dx}{dt}$

Given that, $y = 2x - x^2$ and $\frac{dx}{dt} = 3$ units /sec

Then, the slope of the curve, $\frac{dy}{dx} = 2 - 2x = m$

$\frac{dm}{dt} = 0 - 2 \times \frac{dx}{dt}$

$= -2(3)$

$= -6$ units per second

Thus, the slope of the curve is decreasing at the rate of 6 units per second when x is increasing at the rate of 3 units per second.

Hence, the correct option is (B).

38. Given, at any instant t, for a sphere, r denotes the radius, S denotes the surface area. Surface area $S = 4\pi r^2$

Differentiating w.r.to t, we get:

$\frac{dS}{dt} = 4\pi \cdot 2r \frac{dr}{dt}$

$\Rightarrow \frac{dS}{dt} = 8\pi r \frac{dr}{dt}$

$\Rightarrow \frac{dr}{dt} = \frac{1}{8\pi r} \frac{dS}{dt}$ ……(1)

Volume of sphere $V = \frac{4}{3}\pi r^3$

Differentiating w.r.to t, we get:

$\frac{dV}{dt} = \frac{4}{3}\pi \cdot 3r^2 \frac{dr}{dt}$

$\Rightarrow \frac{dV}{dt} = 4\pi r^2 \frac{dr}{dt}$

From equation (1), we have

$\frac{dV}{dt} = 4\pi r^2 \frac{1}{8\pi r} \frac{dS}{dt}$

$\Rightarrow \frac{dV}{dt} = \frac{r}{2} \frac{dS}{dt}$

Thus, if at any instant t, for a sphere, r denotes the radius, S denotes the surface area and V denotes the volume, then

$\frac{dV}{dt} = \frac{1}{2} r \frac{dS}{dt}$

Hence, the correct option is (B).

39. Let $P_1: x + y + z - 1 = 0$

$P_2: 2x + 3y + 4z - 7 = 0$

Then, equation of plane passing through the line of intersection of P_1 and P_2 is:

$x + y + z - 1 + \lambda(2x + 3y + 4z - 7) = 0$ ....(1)

$\Rightarrow x(1 + 2\lambda) + y(1 + 3\lambda) + z(1 + 4\lambda) - 1 - 7\lambda = 0$

It is perpendicular to the plane $x - 5y + 3z = 5$

$\therefore [x(1 + 2\lambda) + y(1 + 3\lambda) + z(1 + 4\lambda) - 1 - 7\lambda] \cdot [x - 5y + 3z - 5] = 0$

$\Rightarrow 1(1 + 2\lambda) - 5(1 + 3\lambda) + 3(1 + 4\lambda) = 0$

$\Rightarrow 1 + 2\lambda - 5 - 15\lambda + 3 + 12\lambda = 0$

$\Rightarrow -\lambda - 1 = 0$

$\Rightarrow \lambda = -1$

Putting $\lambda = -1$ in (1), we get the equation of required plane,

$x + y + z - 1 + (-1)(2x + 3y + 4z - 7) = 0$

$\Rightarrow x - 2x + y - 3y + z - 4z - 1 + 7 = 0$

$\Rightarrow -x - 2y - 3z + 6 = 0$

$\Rightarrow x + 2y + 3z - 6 = 0$

Hence, the correct option is (A).

40. The equation of a circle is:

$(x - h)^2 + (y - k)^2 = r^2$

Where (h, k) is the center of the circle and r is the radius

$x = 2 + 3\cos\theta$

$\cos\theta = \frac{x-2}{3}$

Also $y = 1 - 3\sin\theta$

$\sin\theta = \frac{1-y}{3}$

$\because \sin^2\theta + \cos^2\theta = 1$

$(y-1)^2 + (x-2)^2 = 9$

$\therefore h = 2, k = 1, r = 3$, i.e.,

Centre $= (h, k) = (2,1)$ and radius $= 3$

Hence, the correct option is (C).

41. Let $f(x) = y$

$\therefore f^{-1}(y) = x$

Now, $y = 2x + 6$

$2x = y - 6$

$x = \frac{y-6}{2}$

$\therefore f^{-1}(y) = \frac{y}{2} - 3$

$f^{-1}(x) = \frac{x}{2} - 3$

Hence, the correct option is (D).

42. We know that,

Mean $= \mu = np$

Standard deviation $= \sigma = \sqrt{npq}$

Where $n =$ number of trials; $p =$ probability of success; $q = (1-p) =$ probability of failure

Given: Mean $= \mu = np = 12$

Standard deviation $= \sigma = \sqrt{npq} = 2$

$\therefore$ Variance $= \sigma^2 = npq = 4$

$\Rightarrow 4 = np(1-p) = 12(1-p)$

$\Rightarrow \frac{4}{12} = (1-p)$

$\Rightarrow (1-p) = \frac{1}{3}$

$\Rightarrow p = 1 - \frac{1}{3}$

$\therefore p = \frac{2}{3}$

Again; $\mu = np = 12$

$\therefore n = \frac{12}{p} = 12 \times \frac{3}{2} = 18$

Hence, the correct option is (C).

43. Given: $n = 10$ and $p = \frac{1}{5}$

Therefore, $q = 1 - p$

$q = \frac{4}{5}$

Thus, the binomial distribution is given by:

$P(X = r) = {}^nC_r p^r q^{n-r}$

$P(X = r) = {}^{10}C_r \left(\frac{1}{5}\right)^r \left(\frac{4}{5}\right)^{10-r}$

If we put $Y = 10 - X$ that means we are writing $X = 10 - Y$.

Thus the corresponding binomial distribution is given as follows:

$P(X = 10 - Y) = {}^{10}C_{10-Y}(p)^{10-Y}(1-p)^{10-10+Y}$

$P(X = 10 - Y) = {}^{10}C_Y \left(\frac{1}{5}\right)^{10-Y}\left(\frac{4}{5}\right)^Y$

$(\because {}^nC_r = {}^nC_{n-r})$

Now, Compare with the standard equation

Therefore, $n, p = 10, \frac{4}{5}$

Hence, the correct option is (D).

44. Formula Used:

$\sec^2 x - \tan^2 x = 1$

$\frac{d}{dx}\tan(x) = \sec^2(x)$

$\int \frac{dx}{1+x^2} = \tan^{-1}x + C$

Where C is a constant

Let $I = \int \frac{dx}{\sec^2(\tan^{-1}x)}$

As we know that,

$\sec^2 x - \tan^2 x = 1$

$\Rightarrow I = \int \frac{dx}{1+\tan^2(\tan^{-1}x)}$

$\Rightarrow I = \int \frac{dx}{1+[\tan(\tan^{-1}x)]^2}$

$\Rightarrow I = \int \frac{dx}{1+x^2}$

As we know,

$\int \frac{dx}{1+x^2} = \tan^{-1}x + C$ where C is constant.

$\Rightarrow I = \int \frac{dx}{\sec^2(\tan^{-1}x)} = \tan^{-1}x + C$

Hence, the correct option is (B).

45. Let $y = \log_{10} x$ and $z = \log_x 10$

Now, $yz = (\log_{10} x) \times (\log_x 10)$

$\Rightarrow yz = 1$

Differentiating with respect to z, we get

$y\left(\frac{dz}{dz}\right) + z\left(\frac{dy}{dz}\right) = 0$

$y + z\left(\frac{dy}{dz}\right) = 0$

$\frac{dy}{dz} = -\frac{y}{z}$

$= -\frac{\log_{10} x}{\log_x 10}$

$= -\frac{\log_{10} x}{\frac{1}{\log_{10} x}}$

$= -(\log_{10} x)^2$

Hence, the correct option is (C).

46. Given:

$\Rightarrow \int_0^a \frac{1}{1+x^2} dx = \frac{\pi}{4}$

We know that,

$\int \frac{dx}{1+x^2} = \tan^{-1} x + C$

$\Rightarrow \int_0^a \frac{1}{1+x^2} dx = \frac{\pi}{4}$

$\Rightarrow [\tan^{-1} x]_0^a = \frac{\pi}{4}$

$\Rightarrow \tan^{-1}(a) - \tan^{-1}(0) = \frac{\pi}{4}$

$\Rightarrow \tan^{-1}(a) - 0 = \frac{\pi}{4}$

$\Rightarrow a = \tan\left(\frac{\pi}{4}\right)$

$\Rightarrow a = 1$

The value of a is 1.

Hence, the correct option is (A).

47. Given: $n = 6$ and $9P(X = 4) = P(X = 2)$

Using the definition $P(X = k) = {}^nC_k p^k (1-p)^{n-k}$

$9P(X = 4) = P(X = 2)$

$\Rightarrow 9 \times {}^6C_4 \times p^4 \times (1-p)^{6-4} = {}^6C_2 \times p^2 \times (1-p)^{6-2}$

$\Rightarrow 9 \times p^2 \times (1-p)^2 = (1-p)^4 \quad \ldots ({}^6C_4 = {}^6C_2)$

$\Rightarrow (1-p)^2 - 9p^2 = 0$

$\Rightarrow 1 - 2p + p^2 - 9p^2 = 0$

$\Rightarrow 8p^2 + 2p - 1 = 0$

$\Rightarrow p = \frac{-2 \pm \sqrt{2^2 - 4 \times 8 \times (-1)}}{2 \times 8} = \frac{-2 \pm \sqrt{4+32}}{16} = \frac{-2 \pm 6}{16}$

$\Rightarrow p = \frac{1}{4}$ or $\frac{-1}{2}$

Since p is positive, $p = \frac{1}{4}$ is the answer.

Hence, the correct option is (D).

48. Let $P(h, k)$ be any point on the locus. Then

Given: $PA = PB$

$\Rightarrow PA^2 = PB^2$

$\Rightarrow (h-2)^2 + (k-3)^2 = (h+1)^2 + (k-2)^2$

$\Rightarrow h^2 - 4h + 4 + k^2 - 6k + 9 = h^2 + 2h + 1 + k^2 - 4k + 4$

$\Rightarrow -4h - 6k + 9 = 2h - 4k + 1$

$\Rightarrow 6h + 2k = 8$

The equation of the locus of a point equidistant from the point $A(2,3)$ and $B(-1,2)$ is $6x + 2y = 8$

Hence, the correct option is (B).

49. Formula:

p ⇒ q ≡ ¬ p ∨ q

Derivation:

(¬ p) ⇒ (¬ q)

≡ ¬ (¬ p) ∨ (¬ q)

≡ p ∨ (¬ q)

Statement I,

p ⇒ q

≡ (¬ p) ∨ q,

Statement II,

q ⇒ p

≡ (¬ q) ∨ p

≡ p ∨ (¬ q)

Statement III,

(¬ q) ∨ p

≡ p ∨ (¬ q)

Statement IV,

(¬ p) ∨ q

Only II and III option matches with the given implication.

Hence, the correct option is (D).

50. Concept:

And operator - ∧

Only if meaning: q only if means that p is a necessary condition for q , denoted as : q → p

p = it is raining

q = it is cold

r = it is pleasant

¬ p = it is not raining

Now, "' It is not raining, and it is pleasant" = ¬ p ∧ r

"it is not pleasant only if it is raining and it is cold" denoted as = ¬ r → (p ∧ q)

So, the overall expression for "It is not raining and it is pleasant, and it is not pleasant only if it is raining and it is cold" will be:

(¬ p ∧ r) ∧ (¬ r → (p ∧ q))

Option (A) is true.

Hence, the correct option is (A).

Mathematics : Mock Test 02

Q.1 The number of ways in which 5 boys and 4 girls to sit around a table, so that, all the boys sit together is:
A. 9!
B. 5!5!
C. 4!5!
D. None of these

Q.2 If $x + 2y = \begin{bmatrix} 2 & -3 \\ 1 & 5 \end{bmatrix}$ and $2x + 5y = \begin{bmatrix} 7 & 5 \\ 2 & 3 \end{bmatrix}$, then y is equal to:
A. $\begin{bmatrix} 3 & 11 \\ 0 & 7 \end{bmatrix}$
B. $\begin{bmatrix} 3 & 5 \\ 0 & -7 \end{bmatrix}$
C. $\begin{bmatrix} 3 & 11 \\ 0 & -7 \end{bmatrix}$
D. $\begin{bmatrix} 3 & 5 \\ 0 & 7 \end{bmatrix}$

Q.3 Find the value of X and Y if $X + Y = \begin{bmatrix} 10 & 2 \\ 0 & 9 \end{bmatrix}, X - Y = \begin{bmatrix} 6 & 12 \\ 0 & -5 \end{bmatrix}$.
A. $X = \begin{bmatrix} 8 & 7 \\ 0 & -5 \end{bmatrix}, Y = \begin{bmatrix} 2 & 5 \\ 7 & -5 \end{bmatrix}$
B. $X = \begin{bmatrix} 8 & 7 \\ 0 & 2 \end{bmatrix}, Y = \begin{bmatrix} 2 & -5 \\ 0 & 7 \end{bmatrix}$
C. $X = \begin{bmatrix} 8 & 7 \\ 0 & 2 \end{bmatrix}, Y = \begin{bmatrix} 2 & 5 \\ 0 & 7 \end{bmatrix}$
D. $X = \begin{bmatrix} 8 & -7 \\ 0 & 7 \end{bmatrix}, Y = \begin{bmatrix} 2 & -5 \\ 0 & 7 \end{bmatrix}$

Q.4 If AB^T is defined as a square matrix then what is the order of the matrix B, where matrix A has order 2×3?
A. 3×3
B. 2×3
C. 4×2
D. 3×2

Q.5 In the given figure, BC || RS, ∠RAQ = ∠BAC, ∠SAD = 52°, then the value of x is:

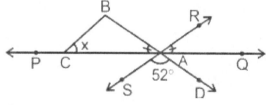

A. 64°
B. 26°
C. 38°
D. 52°

Q.6 Find the degree and order of differential equation:
$y''' - \sin(y') + y = 0$
A. Degree 3 and order 1
B. Degree 1 and order 3
C. Degree 1 and order 1
D. Cannot be determined

Q.7 Find the general solution of the differential equation:
$\frac{y^2}{x^2} = \frac{dy}{dx}$
A. $\frac{1}{y} = \frac{1}{x} + C$
B. $y = x + C$
C. $\frac{y^2}{2} = \frac{x^2}{2} + C$
D. $y^2 = x^2 + C$

Q.8 General solution of differential equation $\frac{dy}{dx} + y = 1, (y \neq 1)$, is:
A. $\log\left|\frac{1}{1-y}\right| = x + C$
B. $\log|1 - y| = x + C$
C. $\log|1 + y| = x + C$
D. $\log\left|\frac{1}{1-y}\right| = -x + C$

Q.9 If P_n denotes the product of all the coefficients in the expansion of $(1 + x)^n$, then $\frac{P_{n+1}}{P_n}$ is equal to:
A. $\frac{(n+2)^n}{n!}$
B. $\frac{(n+1)^{n+1}}{n+1!}$
C. $\frac{(n+1)^{n+1}}{n!}$
D. $\frac{(n+1)^n}{n+1!}$

Q.10 The means of two samples of sizes 50 and 100 respectively are 54.1 and 50.3 and the standard deviations are 8 and 7. Find the mean and the standard deviation of the sample of size 150 obtained by combining the two samples.
A. 7.71
B. 7.56
C. 2.89
D. 9.65

Q.11 What is $\int_0^1 \frac{e^{\tan^{-1}} dx}{1+x^2}$ equal to?
A. $e^{\frac{\pi}{4}} - 1$
B. $e^{\frac{\pi}{4}} + 1$
C. $e - 1$
D. e

Q.12 $\int \frac{e^x}{x}(1 + x \cdot \ln x) dx$
A. $e^x \ln x - c$
B. $e^x \ln x + c$
C. $e^x x - c$
D. $e^x x + c$

Q.13 What is the area bounded by $y = \tan x, y = 0$ and $x = \frac{\pi}{4}$?
A. ln 2 square units
B. $\frac{\ln 2}{2}$ square units
C. 2 (ln 2) square units
D. None of the above

Q.14 The area bounded by $y = \log x$, x-axis and ordinates $x = 1, x = 2$ is:
A. $\frac{1}{2}(\log 2)^2$ sq. unit
B. $\log\left(\frac{2}{e}\right)$ sq. unit
C. $\log\left(\frac{4}{e}\right)$ sq. unit
D. $\log 4$ sq. unit

Q.15 What is the area bounded by the curves $|y| = 1 - x^2$?
A. $\frac{4}{3}$ square units
B. $\frac{8}{3}$ square units
C. 4 square units
D. $\frac{16}{3}$ square units

Q.16 If $f: R \to R$ and $g: R \to R$ are two mappings defined as $f(x) = 2x$ and $g(x) = x^2 + 2$, then the value of $(f + g)(2)$ is:

[UPSESSB TGT Mathematics, 2013]

A. 8
B. 10
C. 12
D. 24

Q.17 For any positive integer n, $(-1\sqrt{-1})^{4n+5}$ is:
A. 1   B. -1 C. $-i$ D. i

Q.18 The problem of maximizing $z = x_1 - x_2$ subject to constraints $x_1 + x_2 \leq 10, x_1 \geq 0, x_2 \geq 0$ and $x_2 \leq 5$ has:
A. no solution
B. one solution
C. two solutions
D. more than two solutions

Q.19 If $x = (7 + 4\sqrt{3})^{2n} = [x] + f$, then $x(1-f)$ is equal to:
A. 1   B. 2   C. 3   D. 4

Q.20 Solve the following LPP by:
Minimize $z = 8x + 10y$
Subject to $2x + y \geq 7, 2x + 3y \geq 15, y \geq 2, x \geq 0, y \geq 0$
A. 52   B. 54   C. 36   D. 98

Q.21 The slope of the line perpendicular to the line passing through the points $(3,2)$ and $(1,-1)$ is:
A. $\frac{-2}{3}$ B. $\frac{2}{3}$ C. $\frac{3}{2}$ D. $\frac{-3}{2}$

Q.22 Find the value of k for which the distance of point $(k+2, 2k+3)$ is $\frac{4}{\sqrt{10}}$ from the line $x + 3y = 7$?
A. 9   B. -3   C. 2   D. 0

Q.23 The point whose abscissa is equal to its ordinate and which is equidistant from $A(-1,0)$ and $B(0,5)$ is:
A. $(1,1)$ B. $(2,2)$
C. $(-2,-2)$ D. $(3,3)$

Q.24 What is the equation of the straight line which joins the intersection of the line $x - y + 4 = 0$ and $y - 2x - 5 = 0$ and the point $(3,2)$?
A. $x + y - 11 = 0$ B. $x - 2y - 11 = 0$
C. $x + 3y - 11 = 0$ D. $x + 4y - 11 = 0$

Q.25 A continuous random variable X has the distribution function $F(x) = 0$ if $x < 1 = k(x-1)^4$ if $1 < x < 3 = 1$ if $x > 3$ The value of k is:
A. $\frac{1}{16}$ B. $\frac{1}{4}$ C. $\frac{1}{8}$ D. $\frac{1}{2}$

Q.26 A discrete random variable x has the probability functions as:

x	0	1	2	3	4	5	6	7	8
f(x)	k	2k	3k	5k	5k	4k	3k	2k	k

The value of $xf(x)$ is:
A. $\frac{97}{26}$ B. $\frac{107}{26}$ C. $\frac{93}{26}$ D. $\frac{103}{26}$

Q.27 If $\sin^4 x + 2\cos^4 x = \frac{2}{3}$, then what is the value of $\sec^2 x$?
A. 2   B. 3   C. 1   D. 4

Q.28 If $\vec{a} = 4\hat{\imath} + 6\hat{\jmath}$ and $\vec{b} = 3\hat{\jmath} + 4\hat{k}$, then the vector form of the component of $\vec{a}$ along $\vec{b}$ is:
A. $\frac{18(3\hat{\jmath}+4\hat{k})}{10\sqrt{3}}$ B. $\frac{18(3\hat{\jmath}+4\hat{k})}{25}$
C. $\frac{18(3\hat{\jmath}+4\hat{k})}{\sqrt{13}}$ D. $\frac{(3\hat{\jmath}+4\hat{k})}{25}$

Q.29 Let the unit vectors a and b be perpendicular to each other and the unit vector c be inclined at an angle θ to both a and b. If $c = xa + yb + z(a \times b)$, then:
A. $-\sin 2\theta$ B. $\sin 2\theta$ C. $\cos 2\theta$ D. $-\cos 2\theta$

Q.30 $\sin\theta + \sin 3\theta + \sin 5\theta + \sin 7\theta$ is equal to:
A. $\cos\theta\cos 2\theta\sin 4\theta$ B. $2\cos\theta\cos 2\theta\sin 4\theta$
C. $4\cos\theta\cos 2\theta\sin 4\theta$ D. None of the above

Q.31 The value of $\sin 25°\cos 65° + \cos 25°\sin 65°$ is:
A. 1   B. 2   C. $\frac{1}{2}$ D. 0

Q.32 The expression $\frac{\cot x + \csc x - 1}{\cot x - \csc x + 1}$ is equal to:
A. $\frac{\sin x}{1-\cos x}$ B. $\frac{1-\cos x}{\sin x}$ C. $\frac{1+\cos x}{\sin x}$ D. $\frac{\sin x}{1+\cos x}$

Q.33 What is $\lim_{x \to 2} \frac{x^3 + x^2}{x^2 + 3x + 2}$ equal to?

[UPSC NDA, 2021]

A. 0   B. 1   C. 2   D. 3

Q.34 There are 3 bags each containing 5 white balls and 3 black balls. Also, there are 2 bags each containing 2 white balls and 4 black balls. A white ball is drawn at random. The probability that this white ball is from a bag of the first group.
A. $\frac{45}{16}$ B. $\frac{15}{40}$
C. $\frac{45}{61}$ D. None of these

Q.35 If the third term in the binomial expansion of $(1+x)^m$ is $\left(\frac{-1}{8}\right)x^2$ then the rational value of m is:
A. 2   B. $\frac{1}{2}$
C. 3   D. None of these

Q.36 Evaluate $\int \frac{x}{3x^2+4} dx$.
A. $\frac{1}{3}\log(3x^2+4) + c$
B. $\frac{1}{6}\log(3x^2+4) + c$
C. $\frac{1}{6}\log(3x^2+4) + \tan^{-1}x + c$
D. None of the above

Q.37 The coefficient of the middle term in the expansion of $(1+x)^{10}$ is
A. $\frac{10!}{5!6!}$ B. $\frac{10!}{(5!)^2}$
C. $\frac{10!}{5!7!}$ D. None of these

Q.38 Find the value of $\lim_{x \to \infty} \frac{x^4+3x^2+5}{x^4+x^2-6}$

A. 1   B. -1   C. 0   D. 0.5

Q.39 Find the rate of change of area of the square at the edge length of 12 cm, if the rate of change of edge length of the square is 2 cm/s.

A. 32 cm²/s   B. 40 cm²/s
C. 45 cm²/s   D. 48 cm²/s

Q.40 The interval in which the function $f(x) = 2x^3 - 15x^2 + 36x + 12$ is increasing in:

A. $(-\infty, 2] \cup (3, \infty)$ B. $(-\infty, 2) \cup (3, \infty)$
C. $(-\infty, 2] \cup [3, \infty)$ D. $(-\infty, 2) \cup [3, \infty)$

Q.41 If $f(x)$ is an increasing function and $g(x)$ is a decreasing function such that $gof(x)$ is defined, then gof (x) will be:

A. $gof(x)$ is an increasing function
B. $gof(x)$ is decreasing function
C. $gof(x)$ is constant function
D. None of the above

Q.42 Find the equation of plane passing through the intersection of the planes $x + 3y - 2z + 5 = 0$ and $2x + 5y - 3z + 2 = 0$ and the point $(2,1,1)$?

A. $x + 2y + z + 3 = 0$
B. $x + 2y - z - 3 = 0$
C. $x + 2y + z - 3 = 0$
D. $x - 2y + z + 3 = 0$

Q.43 Find the range of the function $f(x) = \sqrt{20 - x^2}$.

A. $[0, 2\sqrt{5}]$ B. $(0, 2\sqrt{5})$
C. $(-2\sqrt{5}, 2\sqrt{5})$ D. $(0, 2\sqrt{5}]$

Q.44 If the equation of a circle is $ax^2 + (2a-3)y^2 - 4x - 1 = 0$, then its centre is:

A. $(1,1)$ B. $(2,0)$ C. $\left(\frac{2}{3}, 0\right)$ D. $\left(-\frac{2}{3}, 0\right)$

Q.45 In a Binomial distribution, the mean is three times its variance. What is the probability of exactly 3 successes out of 5 trials?

A. $\frac{80}{243}$ B. $\frac{40}{243}$ C. $\frac{20}{243}$ D. $\frac{10}{243}$

Q.46 Find out differentiation coefficient $\tan^{-1}\frac{2x}{1-x^2}$ with respect to $\sin^{-1}\frac{2x}{1+x^2}$.

A. 1   B. $1 + x^2$ C. $\frac{1}{1+x^2}$ D. -1

Q.47 If $x = a(\theta + \sin\theta)$ and $y = a(3 - \cos\theta)$ find $\frac{dy}{dx}$ at $\theta = \frac{\pi}{2}$.

A. 0   B. 1   C. 2   D. -1

Q.48 What is $\int_0^{2\pi} \sqrt{1 + \cos\frac{x}{2}}\, dx$ equal to?

A. $8\sqrt{2}$ B. $2\sqrt{2}$ C. 6   D. $4\sqrt{2}$

Q.49 If $\sec(5\theta - 50°) = cosec(\theta + 32°)$, then the value of θ is: $(0° < \theta < 90°)$

A. 108°   B. 18°   C. 36°   D. 54°

Q.50 Consider the following expressions:

(i) false
(ii) Q
(iii) true
(iv) P ∨ Q
(v) ¬ Q ∨ P

The number of expressions given above that are logically implied by P ∧ (P ⇒ Q) is _____

A. 2   B. 1   C. 3   D. 4

 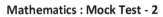

// Smart Answer Sheet //

Correct — Indicates percentage of students who answered questions correctly.

Skipped — Indicates percentage of students who skipped questions.

Q.	Ans.	Correct / Skipped
1	C	43.59 % / 2.56 %
2	C	64.1 % / 10.26 %
3	B	87.18 % / 7.69 %
4	B	46.15 % / 7.7 %
5	A	48.72 % / 7.69 %
6	D	41.03 % / 7.69 %
7	A	61.54 % / 7.69 %
8	A	41.03 % / 7.69 %
9	D	15.38 % / 7.7 %
10	B	53.85 % / 7.69 %
11	A	48.72 % / 7.69 %
12	B	76.92 % / 7.7 %
13	B	53.85 % / 10.25 %
14	C	25.64 % / 7.69 %
15	B	38.46 % / 7.69 %
16	B	71.79 % / 7.7 %
17	C	48.72 % / 10.25 %
18	B	64.1 % / 7.69 %
19	A	30.77 % / 7.69 %
20	A	61.54 % / 7.69 %
21	A	64.1 % / 7.69 %
22	D	43.59 % / 10.26 %
23	B	69.23 % / 7.69 %
24	D	58.97 % / 7.7 %
25	A	33.33 % / 7.7 %
26	D	33.33 % / 7.7 %
27	B	53.85 % / 10.25 %
28	B	64.1 % / 7.69 %
29	D	23.08 % / 10.25 %
30	C	53.85 % / 7.69 %
31	A	76.92 % / 10.26 %
32	C	38.46 % / 7.69 %
33	B	76.92 % / 10.26 %
34	C	30.77 % / 7.69 %
35	B	46.15 % / 7.7 %
36	B	71.79 % / 7.7 %
37	B	64.1 % / 7.69 %
38	A	58.97 % / 7.7 %
39	D	76.92 % / 7.7 %
40	C	30.77 % / 7.69 %
41	B	61.54 % / 7.69 %
42	B	66.67 % / 7.69 %
43	A	30.77 % / 7.69 %
44	C	30.77 % / 7.69 %
45	A	53.85 % / 7.69 %
46	A	61.54 % / 7.69 %
47	B	71.79 % / 7.7 %
48	D	46.15 % / 10.26 %
49	B	61.54 % / 7.69 %
50	D	20.51 % / 7.7 %

Performance Analysis

Avg. Score (%)	49.0%
Toppers Score (%)	94.0%
Your Score	

//Hints and Solutions//

1. Given that:

All boys are to sit together.

So, all boys can be considered as a single group.

∴ Total no. of students = 4 Girls + 1 Group = 5

Since, this is a cyclic permutation.

We know that, for cyclic permutation:

$${}^nP_r = (n-1)!$$

Therefore,

The number of ways of arranging 5 students in a round table is $(5-1)! = 4!$

Now, no. of the ways of arranging 5 boys is $5!$.

Therefore, the total number of ways $= 4!\,5!$

Hence, the correct option is (C).

2. Given,

$$x + 2y = \begin{bmatrix} 2 & -3 \\ 1 & 5 \end{bmatrix} \ldots(1)$$

$$2x + 5y = \begin{bmatrix} 7 & 5 \\ 2 & 3 \end{bmatrix} \ldots(2)$$

Multiplying by 2 in the equation (1), we get

$$2x + 4y = \begin{bmatrix} 4 & -6 \\ 2 & 10 \end{bmatrix} \ldots(3)$$

Subtracting equation (3) from equation (2), we get

$$(2x+5y)-(2x+4y) = \begin{bmatrix} 7 & 5 \\ 2 & 3 \end{bmatrix} - \begin{bmatrix} 4 & -6 \\ 2 & 10 \end{bmatrix}$$

$$\therefore y = \begin{bmatrix} 3 & 11 \\ 0 & -7 \end{bmatrix}$$

Hence, the correct option is (C).

3. Given,

$$X + Y = \begin{bmatrix} 10 & 2 \\ 0 & 9 \end{bmatrix} \ldots(1)$$

$$X - Y = \begin{bmatrix} 6 & 12 \\ 0 & -5 \end{bmatrix} \ldots(2)$$

Adding equation (1) and (2), we get

$$2X = \begin{bmatrix} 10 & 2 \\ 0 & 9 \end{bmatrix} + \begin{bmatrix} 6 & 12 \\ 0 & -5 \end{bmatrix} = \begin{bmatrix} 16 & 14 \\ 0 & 4 \end{bmatrix}$$

$$\therefore X = \begin{bmatrix} 8 & 7 \\ 0 & 2 \end{bmatrix}$$

Now, subtracting equation (2) from (1), we get

$$2Y = \begin{bmatrix} 10 & 2 \\ 0 & 9 \end{bmatrix} - \begin{bmatrix} 6 & 12 \\ 0 & -5 \end{bmatrix} = \begin{bmatrix} 4 & -10 \\ 0 & 14 \end{bmatrix}$$

$$\therefore Y = \begin{bmatrix} 2 & -5 \\ 0 & 7 \end{bmatrix}$$

So, the value of $X = \begin{bmatrix} 8 & 7 \\ 0 & 2 \end{bmatrix}$ and $Y = \begin{bmatrix} 2 & -5 \\ 0 & 7 \end{bmatrix}$

Hence, the correct option is (B).

4. Let the matrix B has an order $p \times q$, i.e, p rows and q columns.

Transpose of B is B' will have order $q \times p$.

For matrix, $AB^T = [A_{(2\times 3)} \times B^T_{(q \times p)}]$ is defined.

∴ $q = 3$

Given,

AB^T is a square matrix.

$$AB^T = [A_{(2\times 3)} \times B^T_{(3\times p)}]$$

∴ $p = 2$

So, the order of $B = p \times q = 2 \times 3$

Hence, the correct option is (B).

5. Given:

BC || RS, ∠RAQ = ∠BAC, ∠SAD = 52°

Calculation:

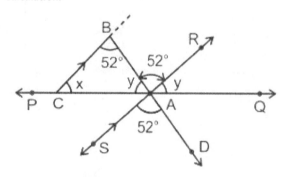

∠BAR = ∠SAD = 52° (Vertically opposite angle)

Let ∠ RAQ = ∠ BAC = y

52° + 2y = 180° (A straight line makes 180°)

⇒ 2y = 180° - 52°

⇒ y = 64°

In Δ ABC,

x + y + 52° = 180°

⇒ x + 64° + 52° = 180°

∴ x = 64°

Hence, the correct option is (A).

6. Given,

$$y''' - \sin(y') + y = 0$$

In the given equation the polynomial equation cannot be formed in y', so order and degree cannot be defined.

Hence, the correct option is (D).

7. Given,

$$\frac{y^2}{x^2} = \frac{dy}{dx}$$

Separate the variables,

$\frac{dx}{x^2} = \frac{dy}{y^2}$

On integrating both side,

We get,

$\int \frac{dx}{x^2} = \int \frac{dy}{y^2}$ $\left(\because \int \frac{1}{x^2} dx = \frac{-1}{x}\right)$

$\Rightarrow -\frac{1}{x} + C = -\frac{1}{y}$

$\Rightarrow \frac{1}{y} = \frac{1}{x} + C$

Hence, the correct option is (A).

8. Given,

$\frac{dy}{dx} + y = 1$

On seprating the variables

We get,

$\frac{dy}{1-y} = dx$

On integrating,

We get,

$\int \frac{dy}{1-y} = \int dx$

$\Rightarrow -\log(1-y) = x + C$

$\Rightarrow \log(1-y)^{-1} = x + C$ $[m\log n = \log n^m]$

$\Rightarrow \log\left|\frac{1}{1-y}\right| = x + C$

Hence, the correct option is (A).

9. Given:

$P_n = {}^nC_0 {}^nC_1 \cdot {}^nC_2 \ldots {}^nC_n$

Now,

$\frac{P_{n+1}}{P_n} = \frac{{}^{n+1}C_0 \cdot {}^{n+1}C_1 \cdot {}^{n+1}C_2 \ldots {}^{n+1}C_{n+1}}{{}^nC_0 \cdot {}^nC_1 \cdot {}^nC_2 \ldots {}^nC_n}$

$\Rightarrow \frac{P_{n+1}}{P_n} = {}^{n+1}C_0 \cdot \left(\frac{{}^{n+1}C_1}{{}^nC_0}\right) \cdot \left(\frac{{}^{n+1}C_2}{{}^nC_1}\right) \ldots \left(\frac{{}^{n+1}C_n}{{}^nC_n}\right) \cdot {}^{n+1}C_{n+1}$

Since ${}^{n+1}C_{r+1} = \frac{n+1}{r+1} \cdot {}^nC_r$

$\Rightarrow \frac{P_{n+1}}{P_n} = 1\left(\frac{n+1}{1}\right)\left(\frac{n+2}{2}\right)\ldots\left(\frac{n+1}{n}\right)1$

$\therefore \frac{P_{n+1}}{P_n} = \frac{(n+1)^n}{n!}$

Hence, the correct option is (D).

10. Combined standard deviation,

$\sigma_{12} = \sqrt{\frac{N_1\sigma_1^2 + N_2\sigma_2^2 + N_1 d_1^2 + N_2 d_2^2}{N_1 + N_2}}$

Where,

$N_1 = 50$,

$N_2 = 100$,

$\sigma_1 = 8$,

$\sigma_2 = 7$,

$\overline{X}_1 = 54.1$,

$\overline{X}_2 = 50.3$

Now,

To calculate combined standard deviation, we need to find the combined mean of the observations.

Thus, Combined mean is:

$\overline{X}_{12} = \frac{N_1\overline{X}_1 + N_2\overline{X}_2}{N_1 + N_2}$

$= \frac{50 \times 54.1 + 100 \times 50.3}{150}$

$= \frac{2705 + 5030}{150}$

$= \frac{7735}{150}$

$= 51.57$

Now,

$d_1^2 = \left(\overline{X}_1 - \overline{X}_{12}\right)^2 = (54.1 - 51.57)^2 = (2.53)^2 = 6.40$

$d_2^2 = \left(X_2 - \overline{X}_{1,2}\right)^2 = (50.3 - 51.57)^2 = (-1.27)^2 = 1.61$

Thus, Combined standard deviation will be:

$\sigma_{12} = \sqrt{\frac{50(8)^2 + 100(7)^2 + 50(6.4) + 100(1.61)}{150}}$

$\Rightarrow \sigma_{12} = \sqrt{\frac{3200 + 4900 + 320 + 161}{150}}$

$\Rightarrow \sigma_{12} = \sqrt{\frac{8581}{150}}$

$\Rightarrow \sigma_{12} = \sqrt{57.20}$

$\Rightarrow \sigma_{12} = 7.56$

So, the combined standard deviation is 7.56

Hence, the correct option is (B).

11. $I = \int_0^1 \frac{e^{\tan^{-1}x} dx}{1+x^2}$

Let $\tan^{-1} x = t$

$\frac{1}{1+x^2} dx = dt$

Lower limit $\rightarrow t = \tan^{-1} 0 = 0$

Upper limit $\to t = \tan^{-1} 1 = \frac{\pi}{4}$

$\therefore \int_0^{\frac{\pi}{4}} e^t \, dt = [e^t]_0^{\frac{\pi}{4}}$

$e^{\frac{\pi}{4}} - e^0 = e^{\frac{\pi}{4}} - 1$

Hence, the correct option is (A).

12. $\int \frac{e^x}{x}(1 + x\ln x) dx$

$= \int \frac{e^x}{x} dx + \int \frac{e^x}{x} x \ln x \, dx$

$= \int \frac{e^x}{x} dx + \int e^x \ln x \, dx$

Consider $\int \frac{e^x}{x} dx$

Integrating by parts,

Let $u = e^x \Rightarrow du = e^x dx$

$dv = \frac{1}{x} dx \Rightarrow v = \ln x$

$= e^x \ln x - \int \ln x \, e^x dx$

$\therefore \int \frac{e^x}{x} dx = e^x \ln x - \int \ln x \, e^x dx + c$

$\therefore \int \frac{e^x}{x} dx + \int e^x \ln x \, dx$

$= e^x \ln x - \int \ln x \, e^x dx + \int \ln x \, e^x dx + c$

$= e^x \ln x + c$ where c is the constant of integration.

Hence, the correct option is (B).

13. Given here,

$y = \tan x, y = 0$ and $x = \frac{\pi}{4}$

Let us first draw the graph for above, we get:

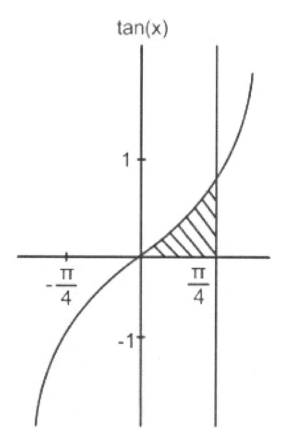

$\therefore$ Area $= \int_0^{\frac{\pi}{4}} y \, dx$

$= \int_0^{\frac{\pi}{4}} \tan x \, dx$

$= [\ln|\sec x|]_0^{\frac{\pi}{4}}$

$= \ln\left(\sec \frac{\pi}{4}\right) - \ln(\sec 0)$

$= \ln(\sqrt{2}) - \ln 1$

$= \ln(2)^{\left(\frac{1}{2}\right)}$

$= \frac{\ln(2)}{2}$

Hence, the correct option is (B).

14. We know that:

Area bounded by function f(x) and g(x) is given as,

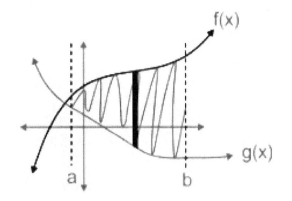

Area $= \int_a^b [f(x) - g(x)]dx = \int_a^b [\text{Top} - \text{bottom}]dx$

Given:

$y = \log x$

Then,

Area $= \int_1^2 \log x \, dx$

Applying by parts rule, we get:

$= [\log x \cdot x]_1^2 - \int_1^2 \frac{1}{x} \times x \, dx$

$= [x \log x]_1^2 - [x]_1^2$

$= [2\log 2 - \log 1] - [2 - 1]$

$= 2\log 2 - 1$

$= \log 2^2 - \log e$

$= \log 4 - \log e$

$= \log \left(\frac{4}{e}\right)$ sq. unit

Hence, the correct option is (C).

15. $|y| = \begin{cases} -y, & y < 0 \\ y, & y \geq 0 \end{cases}$

For $y \geq 0$

$y = 1 - x^2$

For $y < 0$

$-y = 1 - x^2$

$\Rightarrow y = x^2 - 1$

This can be drawn as:

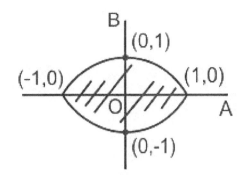

So, area under the curve $= 4 \times$ Area under the region OABO (symmetry)

$= 4 \times \int_0^1 (1 - x^2) \, dx$

$= 4 \times \left[x - \frac{x^3}{3}\right]_0^1$

$= 4 \times \left(1 - \frac{1}{3}\right)$

$= \frac{8}{3}$ square units

Hence, the correct option is (B).

16. Given, $f(x) = 2x, g(x) = x^2 + 2$

then, $(f + g)(2) = f(2) + g(2)$

$= (2 \times 2) + (2^2 + 2)$

$= 4 + 6$

$= 10$

Hence, the correct option is (B).

17. As we know,

$i = \sqrt{-1}$

$i^2 = -1$

$i^3 = -i$

$i^4 = 1$

$i^{4n} = 1$

Given,

$(-1\sqrt{-1})^{4n+5}$ (where n is a positive integer)

$= (-1 \times i)^{4n+5}$

$= (-i)^{4n+5}$

$= (-i)^{4n} \times (-i)^5$

$= (-i)^{4n} \times (-i)^4 \times (-i)^1$

$= 1 \times 1 \times (-i)$

$= -i$

Hence, the correct option is (C).

18.

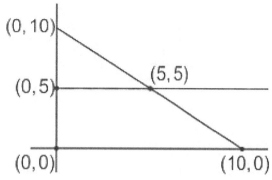

Maximizing $z = x_1 - x_2$

Constraints $x_1 + x_2 \leq 10$

$x_1 \geq 0$

$x_2 \geq 0$

$x_2 \leq 5$

Corner points are: $(0,0)(5,0), (5,5), (0,10)$.

$Z(0,0) = 0 - 0 = 0$

$Z(0,5) = 0 - 5 = -5$

$Z(5,5) = 5 - 5 = 0$

$Z(10,0) = 10 - 0 = 10$

Maximum $Z = Z(10,0) = 10$

Thus, problem has one optimum solution.

Hence, the correct option is (B).

19. Given:

$x = (7 + 4\sqrt{3})^{2n}$

$x = 3 + f$

f is fractional part of x:

$0 < f < 1$

Let $f' = (7 - 4\sqrt{3})^{2n}$

$0 < 7 - 4\sqrt{3} < 1$

$0 < (7 - 4\sqrt{3})^n < 1$

$0 < f' < 1$

$I + f + f' = 2[^{2n}C_0 (7)^{2n} + {}^{2n}C_2 (7)^{2n-2} + \cdots]$

= even

$0 + f + f' < 2$ is integer

$'I'$ is integer and $f + f'$ is also integer.

$\Rightarrow f + f' = 1$

$f' = 1 - f$

$x(1 - f) = xf' = (7 + 4\sqrt{3})^{2n}(7 - 4\sqrt{3})^{2n}$

$= 1$

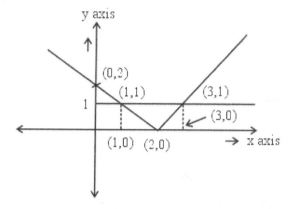

Hence, the correct option is (A).

20. First we draw the lines AB,CD and EF whose equations are $2x + y = 7, 2x + 3y = 15$ and $x + y = 5$ respectively.

Line	Equation	Point on the X-axis	Point on the Y-axis	Sign	Region
AB	$2x + y = 7$	A(3,5,0)	B(0,7)	$\geq$	non-origin side of line AB
CD	$2x = 3y = 15$	C(7,5,0)	D(0,5)	$\geq$	non-origin side of line CD
EF	$y = 2$	-	F(0,2)	$\geq$	non-origin side of line EF

The feasible region is EPQBY which is shaded in the graph.

The vertices of the feasible region are P, Q and B (0,7), P.

Substituting $y = 2$ in $2x + 3y = 15$, we get

$2x + 3y = 15$

$\therefore 2x = 9$

$\therefore x = (4.5)$

$\therefore P = (4.5, 2)$

Q is the point of intersection of the lines

$2x + 3y = 15$ ....(1)

and $2x + y = 7$ ....(2)

On subtracting, we get

$2y = 8$

$\therefore y = 4$

$\therefore$ from (2), $2x + 4 = 7$

$\therefore 2x = 3$

$\therefore x = 1.5$

$\therefore Q = (1.5, 4)$

The values of the object function $z = 8x + 10y$ at these vertices are

$z(P) = 8(4.5) + 10(2) = 36 + 20 = 56$

$z(Q) = 8(1.5) + 10(4) = 12 + 40 = 52$

$z(B) = 8(0) + 10(7) = 70$

z has minimum value 52, when $x = 1.5$ and $y = 4$.

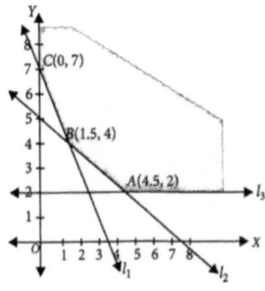

Hence, the correct option is (A).

21. Given,

The line passing through the points $(3, 2)$ and $(1, -1)$

Equation of a line passing through (x_1, y_1) and (x_2, y_2) is:

$\frac{y - y_1}{x - x_1} = \frac{y_2 - y_1}{x_2 - x_1}$

Therefore,

$\frac{y - 2}{x - 3} = \frac{-1 - 2}{1 - 3}$ $\left(\because \frac{y - 2}{x - 3} = \frac{-1 - 2}{1 - 3} \right)$

$3x - 2y - 5 = 0$

$y = \frac{3}{2}x - \frac{5}{2}$

$\Rightarrow$ Slope $(m_1) = \frac{3}{2}$ and $c_1 = \frac{-5}{2}$

Now for the slope of the perpendicular line (m_2)

$m_1 \times m_2 = -1$

$\Rightarrow \frac{3}{2} \times m_2 = -1$

$\Rightarrow m_2 = \frac{-2}{3}$

Hence, the correct option is (A).

22. Given,

The distance of the point $(k + 2, 2k + 3)$ from the line $x + 3y = 7$ is $\frac{4}{\sqrt{10}}$.

Let $P = (k + 2, 2k + 3)$

$\Rightarrow x_1 = k + 2$ and $y_1 = 2k + 3$

Here, $a = 1$ and $b = 3$

Now substitute $x_1 = k + 2$ and $y_1 = 2k + 3$ in the equation $x + 3y - 7 = 0$ we get,

$\Rightarrow |x_1 + 3 \cdot y_1 - 7| = |7k + 4|$

$\Rightarrow \sqrt{a^2 + b^2}$

$= \sqrt{1^2 + 3^2}$

$= \sqrt{10}$

As we know that, the perpendicular distance d from $P(x_1, y_1)$ to the line $ax + by + c = 0$ is given by:

$d = \left| \frac{ax_1 + by_1 + c}{\sqrt{a^2 + b^2}} \right|$

$d = \left| \frac{7k + 4}{\sqrt{1^2 + 3^2}} \right|$

$= \frac{4}{\sqrt{10}}$

$\Rightarrow |7k + 4|$

$= 4$

$\Rightarrow k = 0$ or $\frac{-8}{7}$

Hence, the correct option is (D).

23. Given,

Points are $A(-1, 0)$ and $B(0, 5)$.

The distance between tow points $A(x_1, y_1)$ and $B(x_2, y_2)$ is given by:

$AB = \sqrt{(x_1 - x_2)^2 + (y_1 - y_2)^2}$

Let the point which is equidistant from the points A and B be $C(x, x)$.

As the point is equidistant we have $AC = BC$.

Therefore, equating the right hand and left hand side using distance formula.

$AC = BC$

$\sqrt{(-1-x)^2 + (0-x)^2} = \sqrt{(0-x)^2 + (5-x)^2}$

$\Rightarrow (-1-x)^2 + (0-x)^2 = (0-x)^2 + (5-x)^2$

$\Rightarrow 1 + 2x + x^2 + x^2 = x^2 + 25 - 10x + x^2$

$\Rightarrow 1 + 2x = 25 - 10x$

$\Rightarrow 12x = 24$

$\Rightarrow x = 2$

Thus, the point which is equidistant from both points is $(2,2)$.

Hence, the correct option is (B).

24. Given,

Lines $x - y + 4 = 0$ ...(i)

$y - 2x - 5 = 0$ ...(ii)

The equation of the line with points (x_1, y_1) and (x_2, y_2)

$\frac{y-y_1}{x-x_1} = \frac{y_2-y_1}{x_2-x_1}$

Adding the 2 equation (i) and (ii)

$-x - 1 = 0$

$x = -1$

Putting it in equation (i) we get,

$-1 - y + 4 = 0$

$y = 3$

Intersection of the lines $(-1, 3)$

Now the equation of the line to be find out is

$\frac{y-3}{x-(-1)} = \frac{2-3}{3-(-1)}$

$4(y-3) = -1(x+1)$

$4y + x - 11 = 0$

Hence, the correct option is (D).

25. Concept:

For a continuous random variable, $f(x)$ is called probability density function if it satisfies-

$\int_{-\infty}^{\infty} f(x)dx = 1$

Relation between Probability density function $f(x)$ and Probability distribution function is:

$f(x) = \frac{d}{dx}\{F(x)\}$

Calculation:

Here Probability distribution function $F(x)$ is given

$\because \int_{-\infty}^{\infty} f(x)dx = 1$

$\Rightarrow \int_{-\infty}^{1} f(x)dx + \int_{1}^{3} f(x)dx + \int_{3}^{\infty} f(x)dx = 1$

$\Rightarrow \int_{-\infty}^{1} \frac{d}{dx}\{F(x)\}dx + \int_{1}^{3} \frac{d}{dx}\{F(x)\}dx + \int_{3}^{\infty} \frac{d}{dx}\{F(x)\}dx = 1$

$\Rightarrow \int_{-\infty}^{1} \frac{d}{dx}\{0\}dx + \int_{1}^{3} \frac{d}{dx}\{k(x-1)^4\}dx + \int_{3}^{\infty} \frac{d}{dx}\{1\}dx = 1$

$\Rightarrow \int_{1}^{3} 4k(x-1)^3 dx = 1$

$\Rightarrow 4\frac{k}{4}[(x-1)^4]_{1}^{3} = 1$

$\Rightarrow k[(3-1)^4] = 1$

$\Rightarrow k = \frac{1}{16}$

Hence, the correct option is (A).

26.

x	$f(x)$	$xf(x)$
0	k	0
1	$2k$	$2k$
2	$3k$	$6k$
3	$5k$	$15k$
4	$5k$	$20k$
5	$4k$	$20k$
6	$3k$	$18k$
7	$2k$	$14k$
8	k	$8k$
Total	$26k$	$103k$

We know that for random variable x sum of Probaboility $= 1$

$\Rightarrow \Sigma P_i = 1$

$\Rightarrow k + 2k + 3k + 5k + 5k + 4k + 3k + 2k + k = 1$

$\Rightarrow 26k = 1$

$\Rightarrow k = \frac{1}{26}$

$\therefore xf(x) = 103k$

$= 103 \times \frac{1}{26}$

$= \frac{103}{26}$

∴ The value of $xf(x)$ is $\frac{103}{26}$.

Hence, the correct option is (D).

27. Given:

$\sin^4 x + 2\cos^4 x = \frac{2}{3}$

$\Rightarrow \sin^4 x + \cos^4 x + \cos^4 x = \frac{2}{3}$

$\Rightarrow 1 - 2\sin^2 x \cos^2 x + \cos^4 x = \frac{2}{3}$

$\Rightarrow 1 - 2(1 - \cos^2 x)\cos^2 x + \cos^4 x = \frac{2}{3}$

$\Rightarrow 1 - 2\cos^2 x + 2\cos^4 x + \cos^4 x = \frac{2}{3}$

$\Rightarrow 9\cos^4 x - 6\cos^2 x + 1 = 0$

$\Rightarrow (3\cos^2 x - 1)^2 = 0$

$\Rightarrow \cos^2 x = \frac{1}{3}$

$\Rightarrow \sec^2 x = 3$

Hence, the correct option is (B).

28. Given:

$\vec{a} = 4\hat{\imath} + 6\hat{\jmath} + 0\hat{k}, \quad b = 0\hat{\imath} + 3\hat{\jmath} + 4\hat{k}$

$|\vec{b}| = \sqrt{(3j)^2 + (4k)^2}$

$= \sqrt{9 + 16} \quad [\because i^2 = 1, j^2 = 1, k^2 = 1]$

$= \sqrt{25}$

$= 5$

$\vec{a} \cdot \vec{b} = (4\hat{\imath} + 6\hat{\jmath} + 0\hat{k}) \cdot (b = 0\hat{\imath} + 3\hat{\jmath} + 4\hat{k})$

$= 4 \times 0 + 6 \times 3 + 0 \times 4$

$= 18$

Component of $\vec{a}$ along $\vec{b} = \frac{\vec{a} \cdot \vec{b}}{|\vec{b}|} = \frac{18}{5}$

Component of $\vec{a}$ along $\vec{b} = \frac{18}{5}\hat{b}$

$= \frac{18}{5}\left(\frac{\vec{b}}{|\vec{b}|}\right) \quad [\because \hat{b} = \left(\frac{\vec{b}}{|\vec{b}|}\right)]$

$= \frac{18}{5}\left(\frac{3\hat{\jmath}+4\hat{k}}{5}\right)$

$= \frac{18(3\hat{\jmath}+4\hat{k})}{25}$

Hence, the correct option is (B).

29. Given:

$c = xa + yb + z(a \times b)$

Let $c \cdot a = x$, $c \cdot b = y$, $x = y = \cos\theta$

Now, $c \cdot c = |c|^2$

So,

$[xa + yb + z(a \times b)] \cdot [xa + yb + z(a \times b)] = |c|^2$

$\Rightarrow 2x^2 + z^2|a \times b|^2 = 1 \quad [\because c \text{ is a unit vector}]$

$\Rightarrow 2x^2 + z^2[|a|^2|b|^2 - (a \cdot b)^2] = 1$

$\Rightarrow 2x^2 + z^2[1 - 0] = 1 \quad [\because a \perp b \therefore a \cdot b = 0]$

$\Rightarrow 2x^2 + z^2 = 1$

$\Rightarrow z^2 = 1 - 2x^2$

$= 1 - 2\cos^2\theta$

$= -\cos 2\theta$

Hence, the correct option is (D).

30. Given,

$\sin\theta + \sin 3\theta + \sin 5\theta + \sin 7\theta$

$= (\sin 3\theta + \sin\theta) + (\sin 7\theta + \sin 5\theta)$

$= 2\sin\left(\frac{3\theta+\theta}{2}\right)\cos\left(\frac{3\theta-\theta}{2}\right) + 2\sin\left(\frac{7\theta+5\theta}{2}\right)\cos\left(\frac{7\theta-5\theta}{2}\right) \quad \left(\because \sin x + \sin y = 2\sin\left(\frac{x+y}{2}\right)\cos\left(\frac{x-y}{2}\right)\right)$

$= (2\sin 2\theta \cos\theta) + (2\sin 6\theta \cos\theta)$

$= 2\cos\theta(\sin 2\theta + \sin 6\theta)$

$= 2\cos\theta(\sin 6\theta + \sin 2\theta)$

$= 2\cos\theta \times 2\sin\left(\frac{6\theta+2\theta}{2}\right)\cos\left(\frac{6\theta-2\theta}{2}\right)$

$\left(\because \sin x + \sin y = 2\sin\left(\frac{x+y}{2}\right)\cos\left(\frac{x-y}{2}\right)\right)$

$= 2\cos\theta \times 2\sin 4\theta \cos 2\theta$

$= 4\cos\theta \cos 2\theta \sin 4\theta$

$\therefore \sin\theta + \sin 3\theta + \sin 5\theta + \sin 7\theta = 4\cos\theta \cos 2\theta \sin 4\theta$

Hence, the correct option is (C).

31. Given,

$\sin 25° \cos 65° + \cos 25° \sin 65°$ ...(i)

We know that,

$\sin(A+B) = (\sin A \times \cos B + \cos A \times \sin B)$....(ii)

Comparing equation (i) with euation (ii) we get,

$A = 25°$

$B = 65°$

$\sin(25° + 65°)$

$\Rightarrow \sin 90° = 1$

Hence, the correct option is (A).

32. Given,

$\frac{cotx + cosecx - 1}{cotx - cosecx + 1}$

We know that,

$cosec^2 x = 1 + cot^2 x$

Therefore,

$\frac{cotx+cosecx-1}{cotx-cosecx+1} = \frac{cotx+cosecx-cosec^2x-cot^2x}{cotx-cosecx+cosec^2x-cot^2x}$

$\Rightarrow \frac{cotx+cosecx-1}{cotx-cosecx+1} = \frac{cotx+cosecx-cosec^2x-cot^2x}{cotx-cosecx+1}$

$\Rightarrow \frac{cotx+cosecx-1}{cotx-cosecx+1} = \frac{cotx+cosecx-(cosecx-cotx)(cosecx+cotx)}{cotx-cosecx+1}$

$\Rightarrow \frac{cotx+cosecx-1}{cotx-cosecx+1} = \frac{(cotx+cosecx)(cotx-cosecx+1)}{(cotx-cosecx+1)}$

$\Rightarrow \frac{cotx+cosecx-1}{cotx-cosecx+1} = (cotx + cosecx)$

$\Rightarrow \frac{cotx+cosecx-1}{cotx-cosecx+1} = \frac{cosx+1}{sinx}$

Hence, the correct option is (C).

33. Given,

$\lim\limits_{x \to 2} \frac{x^3 + x^2}{x^2 + 3x + 2}$

$= \lim\limits_{x \to 2} \frac{x^2(x+1)}{(x+1)(x+2)}$

$= \lim\limits_{x \to 2} \frac{x^2}{x+2}$

$= \frac{2^2}{2+2}$

$= \frac{4}{4}$

$= 1$

Hence, the correct option is (B).

34. Let E_1, E_2, A be the events.

E_1 be the selecting a bag from the first group.

E_2 be the selecting a bag from the second group.

And A be the ball drawn is white.

Since there are 5 bags out of which 3 bags belong to the first group and 2 bags to the second group.

$P(E_1) = \frac{3}{5}, P(E_2) = \frac{2}{5}$

E_1 has already occurred, then a bag containing from the first group is chosen. The bag chosen contains 5 white balls and 3 black balls.

Therefore the probability of drawing white balls from it is:

$P\left(\frac{A}{E_1}\right) = \frac{5}{8}$

Similarly $P\left(\frac{A}{E_2}\right) = \frac{2}{6} = \frac{1}{3}$

We have to find $P\left(\frac{E_1}{A}\right)$ i.e., given that the ball is drawn is white, the probability that it is drawn from a bag of the first group.

By Bayes rule,

$P\left(\frac{E_1}{A}\right) = \frac{P(E_1)P\left(\frac{A}{E_1}\right)}{P(E_1)P\left(\frac{A}{E_1}\right) + P(E_2)P\left(\frac{A}{E_2}\right)}$

$= \frac{\frac{3}{5} \times \frac{5}{8}}{\frac{3}{5} \times \frac{5}{8} + \frac{2}{5} \times \frac{1}{3}}$

$= \frac{\frac{8}{8}}{\frac{3}{8} + \frac{2}{15}}$

$= \frac{\frac{3}{8}}{\frac{45+16}{120}}$

$= \frac{\frac{3}{8}}{\frac{61}{120}}$

$= \frac{3}{8} \times \frac{120}{61}$

$= \frac{45}{61}$

Hence, the correct option is (C).

35. Given,

The third term in the binomial expansion of $(1+x)^m$ is $\left(\frac{-1}{8}\right)x^2$.

$(1+x)^m = 1 + mx + \frac{m(m-1)}{2!}x^2 + \frac{m(m-1)(m-2)}{3!}x^3 + ...$

So, the third term in the binomial expansion of $(1+x)^m$ is $\frac{m(m-1)}{2!}x^2$.

$\frac{m(m-1)}{2!}x^2 = \left(\frac{-1}{8}\right)x^2$

$\Rightarrow \frac{m(m-1)}{2} = \frac{-1}{8}$

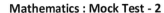

$\Rightarrow 4m^2 - 4m + 1 = 0$
$\Rightarrow (2m - 1)^2 = 0$
$\Rightarrow 2m - 1 = 0$
$\therefore m = \frac{1}{2}$

Hence, the correct option is (B).

36. $I = \int \frac{x}{3x^2+4} dx$

Let $3x^2 + 4 = t$

Differentiating with respect to x, we get

$6x\,dx = dt$

$\Rightarrow x\,dx = \frac{dt}{6}$

Now,

$I = \frac{1}{6}\int \frac{1}{t} dt$

$= \frac{1}{6}\log t + c \quad \left(\because \int \frac{1}{x}dx = \log x + c\right)$

$= \frac{1}{6}\log(3x^2 + 4) + c$

Hence, the correct option is (B).

37. The expansion of $(1 + n)^{10}$ will contain 11 terms,

$\therefore$ The middle term will be $\frac{11+1}{2} = 6^{\text{th}}$ term.

$T_{r+1} =\ ^nC_r a^{n-r} b^r$

$T_{r+1} =\ ^{10}C_{5(10)}{}^{10-5}n^5$

Coefficient $=\ ^{10}C_5$

$= \frac{10!}{5!5!}$

$= \frac{10!}{(5!)^2}$

Hence, the correct option is (B).

38. Given that:

$\lim_{x\to\infty} \frac{x^4+3x^2+5}{x^4+x^2-6}$

On putting the limits in above equation, we get:

$\lim_{x\to\infty} \frac{x^4+3x^2+5}{x^4+x^2-6} = \frac{\infty}{\infty}$

We know that:

L-Hospital Rule :

$\lim_{x\to c}\frac{f(x)}{g(x)} = \lim_{x\to c}\frac{f'(x)}{g'(x)}$

Applying L-Hospital Rule

$L(\text{say}) = \lim_{x\to\infty} \frac{\frac{d}{dx}(x^4+3x^2+5)}{\frac{d}{dx}(x^4+x^2-6)} \quad \left(\because \frac{d}{dx}(x^n) = nx^{n-1}\right)$

and differentiation of constant term is $0.$)

$= \lim_{x\to\infty} \frac{4x^3+6x}{4x^3+2x}$

$= \lim_{x\to\infty} \frac{4x^2+6}{4x^2+2} \quad ....(1)$

$= \frac{\infty}{\infty}$

Again applying L-Hospital Rule on equation (1), we get:

$L = \lim_{x\to\infty} \frac{\frac{d}{dx}(4x^2+6)}{\frac{d}{dx}(4x^2+2)}$

$L = \lim_{x\to\infty} \frac{8x}{8x}$

$L = \lim_{x\to\infty} 1$

$L = 1$

Hence, the correct option is (A).

39. Given that the edge length (L) of the square changes at the rate $= \frac{dL}{dt} = 2$ cm/s

Area of the square $A = L^2$

Rate of change of area $A = \frac{dA}{dt} = \frac{dA}{dL} \times \frac{dL}{dt}$

$\frac{dA}{dt} = \frac{d}{dL}[L^2] \times \frac{dL}{dt}$

$\frac{dA}{dt} = 2L \times 2 = 4L$

As, $L = 12$ cm

$\frac{dA}{dt} = 4 \times 12$

$\frac{dA}{dt} = 48$ cm^2/s

Hence, the correct option is (D).

40. If $f'(x) \geq 0$ at each point in an interval, then the function is said to be increasing.

Given, $f(x) = 2x^3 - 15x^2 + 36x + 12$

Differentiating, we get:

$f'(x) = 6x^2 - 30x + 36$

$f'(x)$ is increasing function:

$f'(x) \geq 0$

$= 6x^2 - 30x + 36 \geq 0$

$= x^2 - 5x + 6 \geq 0$

$= (x - 2)(x - 3) \geq 0$

Thus, $x \in (-\infty, 2] \cup [3, \infty)$

The interval in which the function $f(x) = 2x^3 - 15x^2 + 36x + 10$ is increasing in $(-\infty, 2] \cup [3, \infty)$

Hence, the correct option is (C).

41. Given: $f(x)$ is an increasing function and $g(x)$ is a decreasing function

If $f'(x) > 0$ then the function is said to be increasing.

If $f'(x) < 0$ then the function is said to be decreasing.

$\therefore f'(x) > 0$ and $g'(x) < 0$

Let, $h(x) = gof(x) = g(f(x))$

Differentiating with respect to x, we get

$h'(x) = g'(f(x)) \times f'(x)$

We know, $f'(x) > 0$ and $g'(x) < 0$

Therefore, $h'(x) = $ (Negative) $\times$ (Positive) $=$ Negative

$\therefore h'(x) < 0$

So, $gof(x)$ is decreasing function.

Hence, the correct option is (B).

42. Given:

$x + 3y - 2z + 5 = 0$ and $2x + 5y - 3z + 2 = 0$ are two planes

So, the cartesian equation of plane passing through the intersection of two planes is given by: $(x + 3y - 2z + 5) + \lambda(2x + 5y - 3z + 2) = 0$

$\Rightarrow (1 + 2\lambda)x + (3 + 5\lambda)y - (2 + 3\lambda)z + 5 + 2\lambda = 0$......(1)

Now, the plane represented by (1) passes through the points $(2,1,1)$. So, this point will satisfy the equation of plane represented by (1).

So, substitute $x = 2, y = 1$ and $z = 1$ in equation (1).

$\Rightarrow (1 + 2\lambda)2 + (3 + 5\lambda)1 - (2 + 3\lambda)1 + 5 + 2\lambda = 0$

$\Rightarrow 2 + 4\lambda + 3 + 5\lambda - 2 - 3\lambda + 5 + 2\lambda = 0$

$\Rightarrow 8\lambda + 8 = 0 \Rightarrow \lambda = -1$

So, substitute $\lambda = -1$ in equation (1)

$\Rightarrow (-1)x + (-2)y - (-1)z + 3 = 0$

$\Rightarrow x + 2y - z - 3 = 0$

Hence, the correct option is (B).

43. Given:

$f(x) = \sqrt{20 - x^2}$

It is defined only when $20 - x^2 \geq 0$

so, $y \geq 0$....(1)

Let, $y = f(x)$

$\Rightarrow y = \sqrt{20 - x^2}$

Squaring both sides, we get

$y^2 = 20 - x^2$

$\Rightarrow x^2 = 20 - y^2$

$\Rightarrow x = \sqrt{20 - y^2}$

It is defined only when $20 - y^2 \geq 0$

$\Rightarrow y^2 \leq 20$

$\Rightarrow y^2 - 20 \leq 0$

$\Rightarrow (y - 2\sqrt{5})(y + 2\sqrt{5}) \leq 0$

$\Rightarrow y \in [-2\sqrt{5}, 2\sqrt{5}]$....(2)

From eq (1) and eq (2), we get

$= y \in [0, 2\sqrt{5}]$

Hence, the correct option is (A).

44. Given equation of circle is $ax^2 + (2a - 3)y^2 - 4x - 1 = 0$......(1)

from circle $a = 2a - 3 \Rightarrow a = 3$

put in equation (1) we get

$\Rightarrow 3x^2 + 3y^2 - 4x - 1 = 0$

$\Rightarrow x^2 + y^2 - \left(\frac{4}{3}\right)x - \frac{1}{3} = 0$

on comparing with equation (1) we get,

$\Rightarrow 2g = -\left(\frac{4}{3}\right) \Rightarrow g = -\left(\frac{2}{3}\right)$

and $2f = 0 \Rightarrow f = 0$

Thus centre $(-g, -f) = \left(\frac{2}{3}, 0\right)$

Hence, the correct option is (C).

45. Given: Mean $(\mu_x) = 3 \times$ variance (σ_x^2)

$n \times p = 3 \times n \times p \times (1 - p)$

$\Rightarrow 1 - p = \frac{1}{3}$

$\Rightarrow p = \frac{2}{3}$

Probability of exactly 3 successes $= P(X = 3)$

$= {}^5C_3 p^3 (1-p)^{(5-3)}$

$$= \frac{5 \times 4 \times 3!}{2!3!} \times \left(\frac{2}{3}\right)^3 \times \left(\frac{1}{3}\right)^2$$

$$= 10 \times 8 \times \left(\frac{1}{3}\right)^5$$

$$= \frac{80}{243}$$

Hence, the correct option is (A).

46. If $f(x)$ and $g(x)$ are the functions in x, then

$$\frac{df(x)}{dg(x)} = \frac{\frac{df(x)}{dx}}{\frac{dg(x)}{dx}}$$

Let $f = \tan^{-1}\frac{2x}{1-x^2}$ and $g = \sin^{-1}\frac{2x}{1+x^2}$

Put $x = \tan\theta$

$$\frac{2x}{1-x^2} = \frac{2\tan\theta}{1-\tan^2\theta} = \tan 2\theta$$

$$\frac{2x}{1+x^2} = \frac{2\tan\theta}{1+\tan^2\theta} = \sin 2\theta$$

Now,

$f = \tan^{-1}\frac{2x}{1-x^2} = \tan^{-1}\tan 2\theta = 2\theta$
($\because \tan^{-1}\tan x = x$)

$g = \sin^{-1}\frac{2x}{1+x^2} = \sin^{-1}\sin 2\theta = 2\theta$
($\because \sin^{-1}\sin x = x$)

If $x = \tan\theta$ then $\theta = \tan^{-1}x$

Now, $f = 2\theta = 2\tan^{-1}x$

Differentiating with respect to x, we get

$$\frac{df}{dx} = \frac{2}{1+x^2}$$

$g = 2\theta = 2\tan^{-1}x$

Differentiating with respect to x, we get

$$\frac{dg}{dx} = \frac{2}{1+x^2}$$

$$D = \frac{f'}{g'} = \frac{\frac{2}{1+x^2}}{\frac{2}{1+x^2}}$$

$D = 1$

Hence, the correct option is (A).

47. Differentiate the x and y with respect to θ

$$\Rightarrow \frac{dy}{dx} = \frac{\frac{dy}{d\theta}}{\frac{dx}{d\theta}}$$

Given: $x = a(\theta + \sin\theta)$

Differentiation with respect to θ

$$\Rightarrow \frac{dx}{d\theta} = a(1 + \cos\theta)$$

Now, $y = a(3 - \cos\theta)$

Differentiation with respect to θ

$$\Rightarrow \frac{dy}{d\theta} = a(\sin\theta)$$

$$\Rightarrow \frac{dy}{dx} = \frac{\frac{dy}{d\theta}}{\frac{dx}{d\theta}}$$

$$\Rightarrow \frac{dy}{dx} = \frac{\sin\theta}{1+\cos\theta}$$

Putting the value of $\theta = \frac{\pi}{2}$ we get

$$\Rightarrow \frac{dy}{dx} = \frac{\sin\frac{\pi}{2}}{1+\cos\frac{\pi}{2}}$$

$$\Rightarrow \frac{dy}{dx}\theta = \frac{\pi}{2} = 1$$

Hence, the correct option is (B).

48. We know that,

$\sin^2 x + \cos^2 x = 1$

$\cos 2x = \cos^2 x - \sin^2 x$

Let, $I = \int_0^{2\pi}\sqrt{1+\cos\frac{x}{2}}\,dx$

$$\Rightarrow I = \int_0^{2\pi}\sqrt{\left(2\cos^2\left(\frac{x}{4}\right)\right)}$$

$$\Rightarrow I = \sqrt{2}\int_0^{2\pi}\cos\left(\frac{x}{4}\right)$$

$$\Rightarrow I = 4\sqrt{2}\left[\sin\left(\frac{x}{4}\right)\right]_0^{2\pi}$$

$$\Rightarrow I = 4\sqrt{2}\left[\sin\left(\frac{2\pi}{4}\right) - \sin 0°\right]$$

$$\Rightarrow I = 4\sqrt{2}\left(\sin\frac{\pi}{2}\right)$$

$$\Rightarrow I = 4\sqrt{2}$$

Hence, the correct option is (D).

49. Given:

$\sec(5\theta - 50°) = cosec(\theta + 32°)$

Formula used:

If $SecA = CosecB$ then, $A + B = 90°$

$Sec(5\theta - 50°) = Cosec(\theta + 32°)$

As we know

If $SecA = CosecB$

Then, $A + B = 90°$

$\Rightarrow (5\theta - 50°) + (\theta + 32°) = 90°$

$\Rightarrow 6\theta = 108°$

$\Rightarrow \theta = 18°$

$\therefore$ The value of θ is $18°$.

Hence, the correct option is (B).

50. $P \Rightarrow Q$ means $\bar{P} \vee Q$

$P \wedge (P \Rightarrow Q) = P \wedge (\bar{P} \vee Q) = P \wedge Q$

Let us consider P.Q as A.

We have to find which of the given expression is implied by A, that is, (A =>)

Construct the truth table for each option separately

Let $A \equiv P \wedge (P \Rightarrow Q)$

P	Q	P ⇒ Q	A
True	True	True	True
True	False	False	False
False	True	True	False
False	False	True	False

Consider all options one by one:

(i) False

P	Q	A	A ⇒ False
True	True	True	False
True	False	False	True
False	True	False	True
False	False	False	True

Here, all are not true. So, this option is incorrect.

(ii) Q

P	Q	A	A ⇒ Q
True	True	True	True
True	False	False	True
False	True	False	True
False	False	False	True

This option is implied by $P \wedge (P \Rightarrow Q)$.

iii) True

P	Q	A	A ⇒ True
True	True	True	True
True	False	False	True
False	True	False	True
False	False	False	True

iv) P ∨ Q

P	Q	A	A ⇒ P ∨ Q
True	True	True	True
True	False	False	True
False	True	False	True
False	False	False	True

This is a tautology. So, option is correct.

v) –Q ∨ P

P	Q	A ≡ P ∧ (P ⇒ Q)	A ⇒ –Q ∨ P
True	True	True	True
True	False	False	True
False	True	False	True
False	False	False	True

This is also a tautology.

Hence, the correct option is (D).

Mathematics : Mock Test 03

Q.1 The number of ways in which 4 boys and 4 girls can be arranged in a row so, that no two girls and no two boys are together is:
A. $(4!)^2$
B. $2(4!)^2$
C. $8!$
D. None of these

Q.2 Construct a 3×2 matrix whose elements are given by $a_{ij} = \frac{1}{3}|2i + j|$.

A. $\begin{bmatrix} 1 & \frac{5}{3} \\ \frac{4}{3} & 2 \\ \frac{7}{3} & \frac{8}{3} \end{bmatrix}$
B. $\begin{bmatrix} 1 & \frac{4}{3} \\ \frac{7}{3} & 2 \\ \frac{5}{3} & \frac{8}{3} \end{bmatrix}$
C. $\begin{bmatrix} 1 & \frac{4}{3} \\ \frac{5}{3} & 2 \\ \frac{8}{3} & \frac{7}{3} \end{bmatrix}$
D. $\begin{bmatrix} 1 & \frac{4}{3} \\ \frac{5}{3} & 2 \\ \frac{7}{3} & \frac{8}{3} \end{bmatrix}$

Q.3 If $2\begin{bmatrix} 1 & 3 \\ 0 & x \end{bmatrix} + \begin{bmatrix} y & 0 \\ 1 & 2 \end{bmatrix} = \begin{bmatrix} 5 & 6 \\ 1 & 8 \end{bmatrix}$ then find the value of $x + y$.
A. 6
B. 0
C. -6
D. -7

Q.4 If $A = \begin{bmatrix} \sin\alpha & -\cos\alpha \\ \cos\alpha & \sin\alpha \end{bmatrix}$, then for what value of α, A is an identity matrix?
A. 0°
B. 45°
C. 90°
D. 60°

Q.5 The solution of the differential equation $\frac{dy}{dx} = 2^{x-1}$ is:
A. $y = \frac{1}{\log 2} 2^x + c$
B. $y^2 = \frac{1}{\log 2} 2^x + c$
C. $2y = \frac{1}{\log 2} 2^x + c$
D. $2y^2 = \frac{1}{\log 2} 2^x + c$

Q.6 The differential equation of all parabolas whose axis is y-axis is:
A. $x\frac{d^2y}{dx^2} - \frac{dy}{dx} = 0$
B. $x\frac{d^2y}{dx^2} + \frac{dy}{dx} = 0$
C. $\frac{d^2y}{dx^2} - y = 0$
D. $\frac{d^2y}{dx^2} - \frac{dy}{dx} = 0$

Q.7 While calculating the standard deviation, the deviations are only taken from _____.
A. The mode value of a series
B. The median value of a series
C. The quartile value of a series
D. The mean value of a series

Q.8 Find the value of $\lim_{x \to 3} \frac{x^4 - 81}{x^3 - 27}$
A. 3
B. 4
C. 5
D. 9

Q.9 Find the area bounded by the curve between $y = \sin x + \cos x$ in the interval $0 < x < \frac{\pi}{2}$.
A. 1
B. 2
C. 3
D. 4

Q.10 Find the area of the region (in sq. units) bounded by the curve $y = e^{-2x}$ and x-axis for $x \in (-1,1)$.
A. $\frac{e^{2x}}{2}$
B. $\frac{e^2 + e^{-2}}{2}$
C. $\frac{e^{2x} + e^{-2x}}{2}$
D. $\frac{e^2 - e^{-2}}{2}$

Q.11 The volume generated by revolving the arc $y = \sqrt{1 + x^2}$ lying between $x = 0$ and $x = 4$ about x-axis is:
[UPSESSB TGT Mathematics, 2016]
A. $\frac{8\pi}{3}$
B. $\frac{49\pi}{3}$
C. $\frac{65\pi}{3}$
D. $\frac{76\pi}{3}$

Q.12 Find the real and imaginary part of the complex number $z = \frac{1-i}{1+i}$.
A. 1, 1
B. -1, 1
C. 0, 1
D. 0, -1

Q.13 Solve $3x + 2y \leq 12, x + 2y \leq 16, x + y \leq 10, x \geq 0, y \geq 0$.
A. $A(0,4), 0(0,0)$ and $B(6,0)$
B. $A(0,-4), 0(0,0)$ and $B(-6,0)$
C. $A(0,-3), 0(0,0)$ and $B(-5,0)$
D. $A(0,-3), 0(0,3)$ and $B(-8,0)$

Q.14 For the following LPP:
Max. $Z = -0.1x_1 + 0.5x_2$
$2x_1 + 5x_2 \leq 80$
$x_1 + x_2 \leq 20$
$x_1, x_2 \geq 0$
to get the optimum solution, the values of x_1, x_2 are:
A. $(20,0)$
B. $\left(\frac{20}{3}, \frac{40}{3}\right)$
C. $(0,16)$
D. $(3,16)$

Q.15 Solve the linear programming problem by graphical method.
Minimize $Z = 20x_1 + 40x_2$ subject to the constraints $36x_1 + 6x_2 \geq 108; 3x_1 + 12x_2 \geq 36$ $20x_1 + 10x_2 \geq 100$ and $x_1, x_2 \geq 0$.
A. 126
B. 160
C. 150
D. 123

Q.16 Find the equation of the line through the point $(-1,5)$ and making an intercept of -2 on the y-axis?
A. $7x - y - 2 = 0$
B. $7x + y + 2 = 0$
C. $7x + y - 2 = 0$
D. None of these

Q.17 What is the equation to the straight line passing through $(5, -2)$ and $(-4, 7)$?
A. $5x - 2y = 4$
B. $-4x + 7y = 9$
C. $x + y = 3$
D. $x - y = -1$

Mathematics : Mock Test - 3

Q.18 If a line is perpendicular to the line $5x - y = 0$ and forms a triangle of area 5 square units with co-ordinate axes, then its equation is:

A. $x + 5y \pm 5\sqrt{2} = 0$
B. $x - 5y \pm 5\sqrt{2} = 0$
C. $5x + y \pm 5\sqrt{2} = 0$
D. $5x - y \pm 5\sqrt{2} = 0$

Q.19 Find the equation of a line having a slope of -2 and passes through the intersection if $2x - y = 1$ and $x + 2y = 3$.

A. $y - 2x + 1 = 0$
B. $y + 2x - 3 = 0$
C. $2y - x - 3 = 0$
D. $2y + x + 1 = 0$

Q.20 A basket contains 6 blue, 2 red, 4 green and 3 yellow balls. If 5 balls are picked up at random, what is the probability that at least one is blue?

A. $\frac{137}{143}$
B. $\frac{37}{143}$
C. $\frac{113}{143}$
D. $\frac{117}{143}$

Q.21 The odds against an event A are $5:3$ and odds in favor of another independent event B are $6:5$. The chances that neither A nor B occurs is:

[IBPS PO, 2020]

A. $\frac{21}{88}$
B. $\frac{23}{88}$
C. $\frac{27}{88}$
D. $\frac{25}{88}$

Q.22 If $\cos^4\theta - \sin^4\theta = \frac{1}{3}$, then the value of $\tan^2\theta$ is:

A. $\frac{1}{2}$
B. $\frac{1}{3}$
C. $\frac{4}{3}$
D. $\frac{1}{5}$

Q.23 The vector moment about the point $\hat{\imath} + 2\hat{\jmath} + 3\hat{k}$ of the resultant of the forces $\hat{\imath} - 2\hat{\jmath} + 5\hat{k}$ and $3\hat{\jmath} - 4\hat{k}$ acting at the point $-2\hat{\imath} + 3\hat{\jmath} - \hat{k}$ is:

[UPSESSB TGT Mathematics, 2013]

A. $5\hat{\imath} + \hat{\jmath} - 4\hat{k}$
B. $5\hat{\imath} - \hat{\jmath} - 4\hat{k}$
C. $3\hat{\imath} + \hat{\jmath} - 3\hat{k}$
D. $3\hat{\imath} + \hat{\jmath} - 4\hat{k}$

Q.24 Evaluate the following expression: $\sin x + \sin(x - \pi) + \sin(x + \pi)$

A. $-\sin x$
B. $\sin x$
C. $\sec x$
D. $\cos x$

Q.25 If $2\sin^2 A + 3\cos^2 A = 2$, find the value of $(\tan A - \cot A)^2$ where, $\sin A > 0$

A. ∞
B. $\sqrt{3}$
C. 0
D. 1

Q.26 The value of $\lim\limits_{x \to a} \frac{x^2 - (1+a)x + a}{x^2 + (1-a)x - a}$

A. 1
B. a
C. $\frac{(a+1)}{(a-1)}$
D. $\frac{(a-1)}{(a+1)}$

Q.27 Differentiate $x^{\sin x}, x > 0$ w.r.t. x

A. $\left[\frac{\sin x}{x}\right]$
B. $x^{\sin x}\left[\frac{\sin x}{x} + \cos x\right]$
C. $\left[\frac{\sin x}{x} + \cos x \log x\right]$
D. $x^{\sin x}\left[\frac{\sin x}{x} + \cos x \cdot \log x\right]$

Q.28 Find out the differentiation of the function $x^5 + 2x^{-3}$.

A. $6x^4 - 5x^{-4}$
B. $6x^4 + 5x^{-4}$
C. $5x^4 - 6x^{-4}$
D. $5x^4 + 6x^{-4}$

Q.29 A balloon, which always remains spherical, has a variable diameter $\frac{3}{2}(4x + 3)$. Find the rate of change of its volume with respect to x.

A. $12\pi R^2$
B. $4\pi R^2$
C. $3\pi R^2$
D. $6\pi R^2$

Q.30 If $f(x) = X^5 - 20X^3 + 240X$ then $f'(x)$ is:

A. Monotonically decreasing everywhere
B. Monotonically decreasing on $(0, \infty)$
C. Monotonically increasing only in $(-\infty, 0)$
D. Monotonically increasing everywhere

Q.31 Which one of the following statements is correct?

A. e^x is an increasing function
B. e^x is a decreasing function
C. e^x is neither increasing nor decreasing function
D. e^x is a constant function

Q.32 Evaluate $\int \frac{\sin x}{(\cos x)^3} dx$.

A. $\tan x - \sin x + c$
B. $\frac{\tan^2 x}{2} + C$
C. $\frac{\sin^2 x}{2} + C$
D. $\log(\cos^2 x) + c$

Q.33 What is the coefficient of the middle term in the binomial expansion of $(2 + 3x)^4$?

A. 6
B. 12
C. 108
D. 216

Q.34 The 6th coefficient in the expansion of $\left(2x^2 - \frac{1}{3x^2}\right)^{10}$

A. $\frac{4580}{17}$
B. $-\frac{896}{27}$
C. $\frac{5580}{17}$
D. None of these

Q.35 Find the area of the region bounded by the curve $y^2 = x$ and the lines $x=1$, $x=4$ and the x-axis.

A. $\frac{8}{3}$
B. $\frac{14}{3}$
C. $\frac{7}{3}$
D. $\frac{1}{3}$

Q.36 From $x = 0$ to $x = \pi$, the area enclosed between $y = 6\sin x$ and $y + 8\sin^3 x = 0$ is (In square unit):

A. 10π
B. $\frac{34\pi}{3}$
C. 8
D. $\frac{68}{3}$

Q.37 If the integral is $I_n = \int_0^{\frac{\pi}{2}} \frac{\sin(2n-1)x}{\sin x} dx$, then the value of $[I_{20}]^3 - [I_{19}]^3$:

A. 400
B. 200
C. 361
D. 0

Q.38 Find equation of circle concentric with the circle $x^2 + y^2 - 2x - 4y - 5 = 0$ and area is double:

A. $x^2 + y^2 - 3x - 4y - 10 = 0$
B. $x^2 + y^2 - 2x - 4y - 15 = 0$
C. $x^2 + y^2 - 2x - 4y - 10 = 0$
D. $x^2 + y^2 - 3x - 4y - 15 = 0$

Q.39 What is the differential equation corresponding to $y^2 - 2ay + x^2 = a^2$ by eliminating a?

Mathematics : Mock Test - 3

Where $p = \dfrac{dy}{dx}$

A. $(x^2 - 2y^2)p^2 - 4pxy - x^2 = 0$
B. $(x^2 - 2y^2)p^2 + 4pxy - x^2 = 0$
C. $(x^2 + 2y^2)p^2 - 4pxy - x^2 = 0$
D. $(x^2 + 2y^2)p^2 - 4pxy + x^2 = 0$

Q.40 A card is drawn from a pack of 52 cards. The probability of getting a queen of club or king of heart is:

A. $\dfrac{1}{23}$ B. $\dfrac{2}{13}$ C. $\dfrac{1}{26}$ D. $\dfrac{1}{52}$

Q.41 Find the angle between the line $\dfrac{x}{6} = \dfrac{y+32}{2} = \dfrac{z-2}{3}$ and the plane $3x + 4y - 12z - 7 = 0$.

A. $\sin^{-1}\left(\dfrac{5}{91}\right)$ B. $\sin^{-1}\left(\dfrac{10}{91}\right)$
C. $\sin^{-1}\left(\dfrac{9}{91}\right)$ D. None of these

Q.42 What is the range of the function $f(x) = \dfrac{|x|}{x}, x \neq 0$?

A. Set of all real numbers
B. Set of all integers
C. $(1, -1)$
D. $(-1, 0, 1)$

Q.43 The proposition $(P \Rightarrow Q) \wedge (Q \Rightarrow P)$ is a:
A. tautology   B. contradiction
C. contingency   D. absurdity

Q.44 Let p, q, r, s represents the following propositions.
p: x ∈ {8, 9, 10, 11, 12}
q: x is a composite number
r: x is a perfect square
s: x is a prime number
The integer x ≥ 2 which satisfies ¬ p ⇒ q) ∧ (¬ r ∨ ¬ s is _____

A. 11   B. 13   C. 13   D. 15

Q.45 Consider an unbiased cubic dice with opposite faces coloured identically and each face coloured red, blue or green such that each colour appears only two times on the dice. If the dice is thrown thrice, the probability of obtaining red colour on top face of the dice at least twice is _____.

A. 0.259   B. 1.359   C. 2.529   D. 3.295

Q.46 In a binomial distribution, the mean is 4 and variance is 3. Then its mode is:
A. 5   B. 6
C. 4   D. None of these

Q.47 For the vectors $\vec{a} = -4\hat{i} + 2\hat{j}, \vec{b} = 2\hat{i} + \hat{j}$ and $\vec{c} = 2\hat{i} + 3\hat{j}$, if $\vec{c} = m\vec{a} + n\vec{b}$, then the value of $m + n$ is:

A. $\dfrac{1}{2}$ B. $\dfrac{3}{2}$ C. $\dfrac{5}{2}$ D. $\dfrac{7}{2}$

Q.48 If $\sin^{-1}x + \sin^{-1}y = \dfrac{3\pi}{4}$, then $\cos^{-1}x + \cos^{-1}y = ?$

A. $-\dfrac{3\pi}{4}$ B. $\dfrac{\pi}{4}$ C. $\dfrac{\pi}{4}$ D. $\dfrac{3\pi}{2}$

Q.49 If the two planes $3x - 2y + 4z + 1 = 0$ and $-6x + qy + rz + 8 = 0$ are parallel then q and r respectively.

A. 4,8   B. $-4, -8$ C. $-4, 8$ D. $4, -8$

Q.50 Given that $(1 + \cos^2 A) = 3\sin A \cdot \cos A$, then find the value of $\cot A$

A. -1 or $\dfrac{1}{2}$ B. 1 or $\dfrac{1}{2}$
C. 1 or $\dfrac{-1}{2}$ D. -1 or $\dfrac{-1}{2}$

// Smart Answer Sheet //

Correct — Indicates percentage of students who answered questions correctly.

Skipped — Indicates percentage of students who skipped questions.

Q.	Ans.	Correct / Skipped	Q.	Ans.	Correct / Skipped	Q.	Ans.	Correct / Skipped	Q.	Ans.	Correct / Skipped	Q.	Ans.	Correct / Skipped
1	B	34.29 % / 5.71 %	11	D	17.14 % / 20.0 %	21	D	28.57 % / 20.0 %	31	A	54.29 % / 22.85 %	41	B	42.86 % / 20.0 %
2	D	45.71 % / 22.86 %	12	D	57.14 % / 22.86 %	22	A	40.0 % / 25.71 %	32	B	42.86 % / 20.0 %	42	C	40.0 % / 20.0 %
3	A	65.71 % / 22.86 %	13	A	37.14 % / 22.86 %	23	B	22.86 % / 22.85 %	33	D	34.29 % / 22.85 %	43	C	45.71 % / 20.0 %
4	C	65.71 % / 20.0 %	14	C	40.0 % / 22.86 %	24	A	54.29 % / 20.0 %	34	B	31.43 % / 20.0 %	44	A	31.43 % / 22.86 %
5	C	57.14 % / 20.0 %	15	B	40.0 % / 22.86 %	25	A	37.14 % / 22.86 %	35	B	57.14 % / 20.0 %	45	A	42.86 % / 25.71 %
6	A	45.71 % / 20.0 %	16	B	57.14 % / 17.15 %	26	D	40.0 % / 22.86 %	36	D	31.43 % / 20.0 %	46	C	28.57 % / 20.0 %
7	D	60.0 % / 20.0 %	17	C	68.57 % / 20.0 %	27	D	48.57 % / 22.86 %	37	D	17.14 % / 20.0 %	47	C	40.0 % / 20.0 %
8	B	60.0 % / 20.0 %	18	A	40.0 % / 20.0 %	28	C	65.71 % / 25.72 %	38	B	42.86 % / 22.85 %	48	B	40.0 % / 22.86 %
9	B	51.43 % / 22.86 %	19	B	62.86 % / 22.85 %	29	A	34.29 % / 22.85 %	39	A	28.57 % / 20.0 %	49	D	48.57 % / 20.0 %
10	D	42.86 % / 22.85 %	20	A	25.71 % / 17.15 %	30	D	42.86 % / 20.0 %	40	C	60.0 % / 22.86 %	50	B	40.0 % / 20.0 %

Performance Analysis	
Avg. Score (%)	40.0%
Toppers Score (%)	86.0%
Your Score	

Mathematics : Mock Test - 3

//Hints and Solutions//

1. Given that:

4 boys and 4 girls can be arranged in a row so that no two girls and no two boys are together.

It means they can sit alternately.

Case-I: 1st person in the row is a boy.

$B_1 G_1\ B_2 G_2\ B_3 G_3\ B_4 G_4$

The no. of ways in which the boys can be rearranged among themselves is $4!$.

Similarly, the no. of ways in which the girls can be rearranged among themselves is $4!$

So, the total number of ways in this case $= 4! \times 4! = (4!)^2$

Case-II: 1st person in the row is a girl.

$G_1\ B_1 G_2\ B_2 G_3\ B_3 G_4\ B_4$

The no. of ways in which the girls can be rearranged among themselves is $4!$.

Similarly, the no. of ways in which the boys can be rearranged among themselves is $4!$

So, the total number of ways in this case $= 4! \times 4! = (4!)^2$

Therefore, Total Number of ways $= (4!)^2 + (4!)^2 = 2(4!)^2$

Hence, the correct option is (B).

2. As we know,

In general, a 3×2 matrix is given by,

$A = \begin{bmatrix} a_{11} & a_{12} \\ a_{21} & a_{22} \\ a_{31} & a_{32} \end{bmatrix}$

Given,

$a_{ij} = \frac{1}{3}|2i+j|$

Here $i = 1,2,3$ and $j = 1,2$

$a_{11} = \frac{1}{3}|2+1| = 1,\ a_{12} = \frac{1}{3}|2+2| = \frac{4}{3}$

$a_{21} = \frac{1}{3}|4+1| = \frac{5}{3},\ a_{22} = \frac{1}{3}|4+2| = \frac{6}{3} = 2$

$a_{31} = \frac{1}{3}|6+1| = \frac{7}{3},\ a_{32} = \frac{1}{3}|6+2| = \frac{8}{3}$

So, the required matrix is $\begin{bmatrix} 1 & \frac{4}{3} \\ \frac{5}{3} & 2 \\ \frac{7}{3} & \frac{8}{3} \end{bmatrix}$.

Hence, the correct option is (D).

3. Given,

$2\begin{bmatrix} 1 & 3 \\ 0 & x \end{bmatrix} + \begin{bmatrix} y & 0 \\ 1 & 2 \end{bmatrix} = \begin{bmatrix} 5 & 6 \\ 1 & 8 \end{bmatrix}$

$\Rightarrow \begin{bmatrix} 2 & 6 \\ 0 & 2x \end{bmatrix} + \begin{bmatrix} y & 0 \\ 1 & 2 \end{bmatrix} = \begin{bmatrix} 5 & 6 \\ 1 & 8 \end{bmatrix}$

$\Rightarrow \begin{bmatrix} 2+y & 6 \\ 1 & 2x+2 \end{bmatrix} = \begin{bmatrix} 5 & 6 \\ 1 & 8 \end{bmatrix}$

As we know,

If two matrices A and B are said to be equal, then

Order of matrix A = Order of matrix B

Corresponding element of matrix A = Corresponding element of B

So, equating the corresponding elements:

$\therefore 2 + y = 5$
$\Rightarrow y = 5 - 2$
$\Rightarrow y = 3$

And $2x + 2 = 8$
$\Rightarrow 2x = 8 - 2$
$\Rightarrow 2x = 6$
$\Rightarrow x = 3$

Now, $x + y = 3 + 3 = 6$

So, the value of $x + y$ is 6.

Hence, the correct option is (A).

4. Given,

$A = \begin{bmatrix} \sin\alpha & -\cos\alpha \\ \cos\alpha & \sin\alpha \end{bmatrix}$

As we know,

Any square matrix in which all the elements are zero except those in the principal diagonal is called a diagonal matrix. A diagonal matrix in which all the principal diagonal elements are equal to 1 is called an identity matrix. It is also known as a unit matrix whereas an identity matrix of order n is denoted by I.

Value of α such that A is an identity matrix.

i.e., $A = I$

$\begin{bmatrix} \sin\alpha & -\cos\alpha \\ \cos\alpha & \sin\alpha \end{bmatrix} = \begin{bmatrix} 1 & 0 \\ 0 & 1 \end{bmatrix}$

$\therefore \sin\alpha = 1$
$\Rightarrow \sin\alpha = \sin 90°$
$\Rightarrow \alpha = 90°$

And $\cos\alpha = 0$
$\Rightarrow \cos\alpha = \cos 90°$
$\Rightarrow \alpha = 90°$

$\therefore$ The required value of α is $90°$.

Hence, the correct option is (C).

5. Given,

$\frac{dy}{dx} = 2^{x-1}$

$\Rightarrow \frac{dy}{dx} = \frac{2^x}{2}$

$\Rightarrow 2dy = 2^x dx$

Now, variables are separated.

Integrating both sides,

We get

$2\int dy = \int 2^x dx \quad \left(\because \int a^x dx = \frac{a^x}{\log a}\right)$

$\Rightarrow 2y = \frac{1}{\log 2} 2^x + c$

Hence, the correct option is (C).

6. We know that,

Standard formula of y −axis parabola is:

$x^2 = 4ay$

Let,

Vertex of parabola be $(0, k)$

Then,

$(x - 0)^2 = 4a(y - k)$

$\Rightarrow x^2 = 4ay - 4ak$

Taking derivative on both side,

We get,

$\frac{d}{dx}(x^2) = \frac{d}{dx}(4ay - 4ak)$

$\Rightarrow 2x = 4a \frac{dy}{dx}$

$\Rightarrow \frac{1}{x}\frac{dy}{dx} = \frac{1}{2a}$

Again taking derivative on both side,

We get,

$\frac{d}{dx}\left(\frac{1}{x}\frac{dy}{dx}\right) = \frac{d}{dx}\left(\frac{1}{2z}\right)$

$\Rightarrow \frac{1}{x}\frac{d^2y}{dx^2} + \frac{dy}{dx}\left(\frac{-1}{x^2}\right) = 0$

$\Rightarrow x \times \frac{d^2y}{dx^2} - \frac{dy}{dx} = 0$

Hence, the correct option is (A).

7. While calculating the standard deviation, the deviations are only taken from the mean value of a series.

A standard deviation is a measure of how dispersed the data is in relation to the mean. Low standard deviation means data are clustered around the mean, and high standard deviation indicates data are more spread out.

Hence, the correct option is (D).

8. Given:

$\lim_{x \to 3} \frac{x^4 - 81}{x^3 - 27}$

On checking the limit by putting $x = 3$ in above equation, we get $\left(\frac{0}{0}\right)$ form.

We know that:

L-Hospital Rule as:

$\lim_{x \to c} \frac{f(x)}{g(x)} = \lim_{x \to c} \frac{f'(x)}{g'(x)}$

∴ By using the L-Hospital rule, we get,

$\lim_{x \to 3} \frac{x^4 - 81}{x^3 - 27} = \lim_{x \to 3} \frac{\frac{d}{dx}(x^4 - 81)}{\frac{d}{dx}(x^3 - 27)}$

$= \lim_{x \to 3} \frac{4x^3}{3x^2} \quad \left(\because \frac{d}{dx}(x^n) = nx^{n-1}\right.$ and differentiation of constant term is $\left. 0.\right)$

$= \lim_{x \to 3} \frac{4x}{3}$

Putting the value of $x \to 3$ in above equation, we get

$= \frac{4(3)}{3}$

$= 4$

Hence, the correct option is (B).

9. Given:

$y = \sin x + \cos x$ in the interval $0 < x < \frac{\pi}{2}$

Let the required area be A.

Using the formula of the area under the curve as:

$A = \left|\int_a^b f(x) + g(x) dx\right|$

$= \left|\int_a^b f(x) dx\right| + \left|\int_a^b g(x) dx\right|$

$\Rightarrow A = \left|\int_0^{\frac{\pi}{2}} (\sin x + \cos x) dx\right|$

$= \left|\int_0^{\frac{\pi}{2}} (\sin x) dx\right| + \left|\int_0^{\frac{\pi}{2}} (\cos x) dx\right|$

$= \left|[-\cos x]_0^{\frac{\pi}{2}}\right| + \left|[\sin x]_0^{\frac{\pi}{2}}\right|$

Using the value of $\cos 0 = 1, \sin 0 = 0, \cos \frac{\pi}{2} = 0$ and $\sin \frac{\pi}{2} = 1$

$\Rightarrow A = \left|-\cos \frac{\pi}{2} + \cos 0\right| + \left|\sin \frac{\pi}{2} + \sin 0\right|$

$= |0 + 1| + |1 - 0|$

$= 1 + 1$

$= 2$

Hence, the correct option is (B).

10. Given:

$f(x) = e^{-2x}$

and, $g(x) = 0$

$x_1 = -1$ and $x_2 = 1$

Let us plot a rough graph of given curves and shade the bounded area to be calculated as:

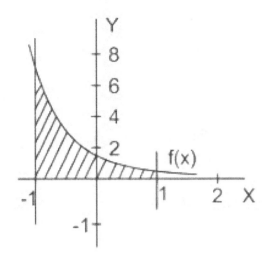

So, area under the curve $= \left| \int_{x_1}^{x_2} \{f(x) - g(x)\} dx \right|$

$= \left| \int_{-1}^{1} \{e^{-2x} - 0\} dx \right|$

$= \left| -\frac{e^{-2x}}{2} \right|_{-1}^{1}$

$= \frac{-e^{-2} - (-e^2)}{2}$

$= \frac{e^2 - e^{-2}}{2}$

Hence, the correct option is (D).

11. Given function:

$y = f(x) = \sqrt{1 + x^2}$ and $x = 0 = a$, $x = 4 = b$

We know that:

$V = \pi \int_a^b [f(y)]^2 dy$

Therefore,

Volume, $(V) = \pi \int_0^4 \left(\sqrt{1+x^2}\right)^2 dx$

$= \pi \int_0^4 (1 + x^2) dx$

$= \pi \left[x + \frac{x^3}{3}\right]_0^4$

$= \pi \left[(4 - 0) + \left(\frac{64}{3} - \frac{0}{3}\right)\right]$

$= \pi \left[\frac{12 + 64}{3}\right]$

$= \frac{76\pi}{3}$

Hence, the correct option is (D).

12. Given,

Complex number $z = \frac{1-i}{1+i}$

Multiplying by $(1-i)$ in the numerator and denominator, we get

$z = \frac{1-i}{1+i} \times \frac{1-i}{1-i}$

$\Rightarrow z = \frac{(1-i)(1-i)}{1-i^2}$

$\Rightarrow z = \frac{1+i^2-2i}{1+1}$ $[\because i^2 = -1]$

$\Rightarrow z = \frac{1-1-2i}{2}$

$\Rightarrow z = \frac{0-2i}{2}$

$\Rightarrow z = 0 - 1i$

The real and imaginary part of the complex number $z = 0, -1$

Hence, the correct option is (D).

13. Solving the question graphically

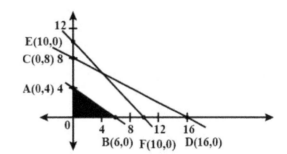

Given:

$3x + 2y \leq 12$

$x + 2y \leq 16$

$x \geq 0$

$y \geq 0$

Solution (i) $3x + 2y = 12$

x	0	6
y	4	0
Points	A(0,4)	B(6,0)

(ii) $x + 2y = 16$

x	0	16
y	8	0
Points	C(0,8)	D(16,0)

(iii) $x + y = 10$

x	0	0
y	10	0
Points	E(0,10)	F(10,0)

The feasible region is AOB since it is common to the three equation graphically with the points.

A(0,4), O(0,0) and B (6,0).

Hence, the correct option is (A).

14. Given:

$$\text{Max. } Z = -0.1x_1 + 0.5x_2$$

$$2x_1 + 5x_2 \leq 80$$

$$x_1 + x_2 \leq 20$$

$$x_1, x_2 \geq 0$$

Convert the inequality constraints into equations, we have

$$2x_1 + 5x_2 = 80$$

$$x_1 + x_2 = 20$$

$2x_1 + 5x_2 = 80$ passes through the point $(0,16)$ and $(40,0)$.

$x_1 + x_2 = 20$ passes through the point $(0,20)$ and $(20,0)$.

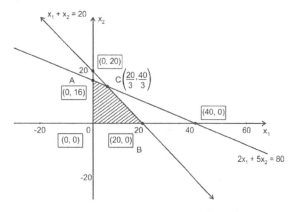

Now, the co ordinates of the point $A = (0,16), B = (20,0)$ and $C = \left(\frac{20}{3}, \frac{40}{3}\right)$

Corner Point	Coordinate of point & value of Z	
A	(0, 16)	8
B	(20, 0)	−2
C	$\left(\frac{20}{3}, \frac{40}{3}\right)$	6.06

Here, maximum value occurs at $(0,16)$

For given

$$\text{Max. } Z = -0.1x_1 + 0.5x_2$$

$$2x_1 + 5x_2 \leq 80$$

$$x_1 + x_2 \leq 20$$

$$x_1, x_2 \geq 0$$

to get the optimum solution, the values of x_1, x_2 are $(0,16)$.

Hence, the correct option is (C).

15. Given:

$36x_1 + 6x_2 \geq 108$

Let $36x_1 + 6x_2 = 108$

$6x_1 + x_2 = 18$

x_1	0	3	2
x_2	18	0	6

Also given that $3x_1 + 12x_2 \geq 36$

Let $3x_1 + 12x_2 = 36$

$x_1 + 4x_2 = 12$

x_1	0	12	4
x_2	3	0	2

Also given that $20x_1 + 10x_2 \geq 100$

Let $20x_1 + 10x_2 = 100$

$2x_1 + x_2 = 10$

x_1	0	5	4
x_2	10	0	2

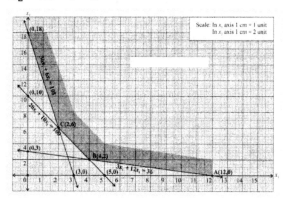

The feasible region satisfying all the conditions is $ABCD$.

The co-ordinates of the corner points are $A(12,0), B(4,2), C(2,6)$ and $D(0,18)$.

Corner points	$Z = 20x_1 + 40x_2$
$A(12,0)$	240
$B(4,2)$	$80 + 80 = 160$
$C(2,6)$	$40 + 240 = 280$
$D(0,18)$	720

The minimum value of Z occurs at $B(4,2)$

∴ The optimal solution is $x_1 = 4, x_2 = 2$ and $Z_{\min} = 160$

Hence, the correct option is (B).

16. As we know that, the equation of a line whose slope is m and which makes an intercept c on the y axis is given by:

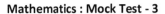

$y = mx + c$

Let the slope of the required line be m.

Here, we have $c = -2$

So, the equation the required line is $y = mx - 2$.....(i)

The required line passes through the point $(-1, 5)$

Therefore,

Substitute $x = -1$ and $y = 5$ will satisfy the equation (i).

$5 = -m - 2$

$\Rightarrow m = -7$

∴The equation of the required line is $7x + y + 2 = 0$.

Hence, the correct option is (B).

17. Given,

Straight-line passing through $(5, -2)$ and $(-4, 7)$

The slope of a line passing through the distinct points (x_1, y_1) and (x_2, y_2) is given by,

$m = \frac{y_2 - y_1}{x_2 - x_1}$

Where, $x_1 = 5$, $y_1 = -2$, $x_2 = -4$, and $y_2 = 7$

Slope of a line $= m = \frac{7-(-2)}{-4-5}$

$= \frac{9}{-9}$

$= -1$

Now, equation of line is:

$(y - y_1) = m(x - x_1)$

$y - (-2) = -1 \times (x - 5)$

$\Rightarrow y + 2 = -x + 5$

$\Rightarrow x + y = 3$

Hence, the correct option is (C).

18. Given,

The area of a triangle is 5 square units

Equation of line is $5x - y = 0$

The equation of a line perpendicular to a given line is

$x + 5y = \lambda$....(i)

$\Rightarrow \frac{x}{\lambda} + \frac{5y}{\lambda} = 1$

$\Rightarrow \frac{x}{\lambda} + \frac{y}{\left(\frac{\lambda}{5}\right)} = 1$

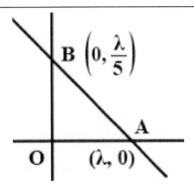

Area of triangle $= 5$ square units

Area of triangle $= \frac{1}{2} \times b \times h$

$\frac{1}{2} \times \lambda \times \frac{\lambda}{5} = 5$

$\Rightarrow \lambda^2 = 50$

$\Rightarrow \lambda = \pm 5\sqrt{2}$

Put the value of λ in equation (i) we get,

$x + 5y = \pm 5\sqrt{2}$

$\Rightarrow x + 5y \pm 5\sqrt{2} = 0$

Hence, the correct option is (A).

19. Given,

Slope of line = -2

Lines are:

$2x - y = 1$....(i)

$x + 2y = 3$...(ii)

On multiplying equation (i) by 2 we get,

$4x - 2y = 2$....(iii)

Adding equation (ii) and (iii) we get,

$5x = 5$

$\Rightarrow x = 1$

On putting value of x in equation (i),

$2(1) - y = 1$

$\Rightarrow y = 1$

Therefore,

The intersection point is $(1,1)$

So line has the slope m = -2 and passes through $(1,1)$

Therefore,

Equation of the perpendicular line is:

$(y - y_1) = m(x - x_1)$

$\Rightarrow y - 1 = -2(x - 1)$

$\Rightarrow y + 2x - 3 = 0$

Hence, the correct option is (B).

20. Given,

Total number of balls $= (6 + 2 + 4 + 3) = 15$

Number of all combinations of n things, taken r at a time, is given by $^nC_r = \dfrac{n!}{(r)!(n-r)!}$

Let E be the event of drawing 5 balls out of 9 non-blue balls.

$\therefore n(E) = {}^9C_5$

$= {}^9C_{(9-5)}$

$= {}^9C_4$

$= \dfrac{9!}{(4)!(5)!}$

$= \dfrac{9 \times 8 \times 7 \times 6}{4 \times 3 \times 2 \times 1}$

$= 126$

And, types of selecting 5 balls from 15 balls

$n(S) = {}^{15}C_5$

$= \dfrac{15!}{(5)!(10)!}$

$= \dfrac{15 \times 14 \times 13 \times 12 \times 11}{5 \times 4 \times 3 \times 2 \times 1}$

$= 3003$

$\therefore P(E) = \dfrac{n(E)}{n(S)}$

$= \dfrac{126}{3003}$

$= \dfrac{6}{143}$

$\therefore$ Required Probability $= \left(1 - \dfrac{6}{143}\right)$

$= \dfrac{137}{143}$

Hence, the correct option is (A).

21. Given,

The odds against an event A are $5:3$

Probability of not occurring the individual event $A = \dfrac{5}{8}$

Probability of occurring the individual event $A = \dfrac{3}{8}$

Again,

Odds in favor of another independent event B and $6:5$

Probability of occurring the individual event $B = \dfrac{6}{(6+5)}$

$= \dfrac{6}{11}$

Probability of not occurring the individual event $B = \dfrac{5}{(6+5)} = \dfrac{5}{11}$

The chances that neither A nor B occurs is $=$ Probability of not occurring event $A \times$ probability of not occurring event B
[As the two events are independent therefore multiplication will occur]

$= \dfrac{5}{8} \times \dfrac{5}{11}$

$= \dfrac{25}{88}$

Hence, the correct option is (D).

22. Given:

$\cos^4\theta - \sin^4\theta = \dfrac{1}{3}$

$a^2 - b^2 = (a - b)(a + b)$

$\Rightarrow (\cos^2\theta - \sin^2\theta)(\cos^2\theta + \sin^2\theta) = \dfrac{1}{3}$

$\Rightarrow (\cos^2\theta - \sin^2\theta) = \dfrac{1}{3}$ $(\because \cos^2\theta + \sin^2\theta = 1)$

$\Rightarrow \cos 2\theta = \dfrac{1}{3}$ $(\because \cos^2\theta - \sin^2\theta = \cos 2\theta)$

and $\cos 2\theta = \dfrac{1 - \tan^2\theta}{1 + \tan^2\theta}$

$\dfrac{1}{3} = \dfrac{1 - \tan^2\theta}{1 + \tan^2\theta}$

By cross multiplication,

$1 + \tan^2\theta = 3(1 - \tan^2\theta)$

$\Rightarrow 1 + \tan^2\theta = 3 - 3\tan^2\theta$

$\Rightarrow 4\tan^2\theta = 3 - 1$

$\Rightarrow 4\tan^2\theta = 2$

$\therefore \tan^2\theta = \dfrac{1}{2}$

Hence, the correct option is (A).

23. Moment of a force $= \vec{r} \times \vec{F}$ where $\vec{r}$ is vector joining point action of force $\vec{F}$ and the point about which it is calculated.

Given: $\vec{r} = (-2\hat{i} + 3\hat{j} - \hat{k}) - (\hat{i} + 2\hat{j} + 3\hat{k})$

$= -3\hat{i} + \hat{j} - 4\hat{k}$

Resultant $\vec{F} = (\hat{\imath} - 2\hat{\jmath} + 5\hat{k}) + (3\hat{\jmath} - 4\hat{k}) = \hat{\imath} + \hat{\jmath} + \hat{k}$

$\vec{r} \times \vec{F} = \begin{vmatrix} \hat{\imath} & \hat{\jmath} & \hat{k} \\ -3 & 1 & 4 \\ 1 & 1 & 1 \end{vmatrix}$

$= \hat{\imath}(1 - (-4)) - \hat{\jmath}(-3 + 4) + \hat{k}(-3 - 1)$

$= \hat{\imath}(1 + 4) - \hat{\jmath}(-3 + 4) + \hat{k}(-4)$

$= 5\hat{\imath} - \hat{\jmath} - 4\hat{k}$

Hence, the correct option is (B).

24. Given,

$\sin x + \sin(x - \pi) + \sin(x + \pi)$

We know that,

$\sin(\pi - x) = \sin x$

$\sin(\pi + x) = -\sin x$

$\sin(-x) = -\sin x$

Therefore,

$= \sin x - \sin(\pi - x) - \sin(\pi + x)$

$= \sin x - \sin(\pi - x) - \sin x$

$= -\sin(\pi - x)$

$= -\sin x$

Hence, the correct option is (A).

25. Given,

$2\sin^2 A + 3\cos^2 A = 2$

$\Rightarrow 2\sin^2 A + 3(1 - \sin^2 A) = 2$ ($\because \cos^2 A = 1 - \sin^2 A$)

$\Rightarrow 2\sin^2 A + 3 - 3\sin^2 A = 2$

$\Rightarrow -\sin^2 A = -1$

$\Rightarrow \sin^2 A = 1$

$\Rightarrow \sin A = 1$

$\Rightarrow \sin A = \sin 90°$

$\Rightarrow A = 90°$

Now, we will find

$(\tan A - \cot A)^2 = (\tan 90° - \cot 90°)^2$

$\Rightarrow (\tan A - \cot A)^2 = (\infty - 0)^2$

$\Rightarrow (\tan A - \cot A)^2 = \infty$

Hence, the correct option is (A).

26. $\lim_{x \to a} \frac{x^2 - (1+a)x + a}{x^2 + (1-a)x - a}$, This is $\frac{0}{0}$ form.

Here we use factorization method.

$\lim_{x \to a} \frac{(x-a)(x-1)}{(x-a)(x+1)}$

$\lim_{x \to a} \frac{(x-1)}{(x+1)} = \frac{(a-1)}{(a+1)}$

Hence, the correct option is (D).

27. Let $y = x^{\sin x}$

Apply logarithms on both sides $\log y = \sin x \cdot \log x$

Diff w.r.t x

$\frac{1}{y}\frac{dy}{dx} = \sin x \cdot \frac{d}{dx}(\log x) + \log x \cdot \frac{d}{dx}(\sin x)$

$\frac{1}{y}\frac{dy}{dx} = \sin x \cdot \frac{1}{x} + \log x \cdot \cos x$

$\frac{dy}{dx} = y\left[\frac{\sin x}{x} + \log x \cdot \cos x\right]$

$\therefore \frac{dy}{dx} = x^{\sin x}\left[\frac{\sin x}{x} + \log x \cdot \cos x\right]$

Hence, the correct option is (D).

28. We apply the formula,

$\frac{d}{dx}(x^n) = nx^{n-1}$

First, $n = 5$ so

First term, $5x^4$

Then $n = -3$, so

$= -3x^{-4}$

Second term, $-6x^{-4}$

Thus, complete value of differentiation $= 5x^4 - 6x^{-4}$.

Hence, the correct option is (C).

29. Given diameter of spherical balloon $D = \frac{3}{2}(4x + 3)$

Radius $R = \frac{D}{2} = \frac{3}{4}(4x + 3)$

Rate of change of radius R wrt $x = \frac{dR}{dx} = \frac{d}{dx}\left[\frac{3}{4}(4x + 3)\right]$

$\frac{dR}{dx} = \frac{3}{4} \times \frac{d}{dx}(4x + 3)$

$\frac{dR}{dx} = \frac{3}{4} \times 4 = 3$

Volume of the spherical balloon $V = \frac{4\pi}{3} \times R^3$

Rate of change of radius V wrt $x = \frac{dV}{dx} = \frac{dV}{dR} \times \frac{dR}{dx}$

Mathematics : Mock Test - 3

$\frac{dV}{dx} = \frac{d}{dR}\left[\frac{4\pi}{3} \times R^3\right] \times \frac{dR}{dx}$

$\frac{dV}{dx} = \frac{4\pi}{3} \times 3R^2 \times 3 = 12\pi R^2$

Hence, the correct option is (A).

30. Given:

$f(x) = X^5 - 20X^3 + 240X$

Differentiate w.r.t x,

$f'(x) = 5X^4 - 60X^2 + 240 = X^4 - 12X^2 + 48$

For checking whether the function is Monotonically increasing or decreasing put $X_1 = -1$

$f'(X_1) = (-1)^4 - 12(-1)^2 + 48 = 1 - 12 + 48 = 37$

Now, put $X_2 = 0$

$f'(X_2) = 0 - 0 + 48 = 48$

Therefore, $f'(X_1) \leq f'(X_2)$

From the above condition we can assume that given function is Monotonically increasing everywhere.

Hence, the correct option is (D).

31. If $f'(x) > 0$ at each point in an interval then the function is said to be increasing.

If $f'(x) < 0$ at each point in an interval I, then the function is said to be decreasing.

Here, derivative of e^x is e^x.

and it is greater than zero at any interval

$\therefore e^x$ is an increasing function.

Hence, the correct option is (A).

32. Let $I = \int \frac{\sin x}{(\cos x)^3} dx$

$= \int \tan x \sec^2 x\, dx$

Put $\tan x = t$

Thus, $\sec^2 x\, dx = dt$

Therefore, the integral becomes $= \int t\, dt$

$= \frac{t^2}{2} + C$

Re-substituting $t = \tan x$, we get

$= \frac{\tan^2 x}{2} + C$

Hence, the correct option is (B).

33. General term in the expansion of $(x+y)^n$ is given by

$T_{(r+1)} = {}^nC_r \times x^{n-r} \times y^r$

The middle terms is the expansion of $(x+y)^n$ depends upon the value of n.

If n is even, then total number of terms in the expansion of $(x+y)^n$ is $n+1$.

So there is only one middle term i.e. $\left(\frac{n}{2}+1\right)$ th term is the middle term,

$T_{\left(\frac{n}{2}+1\right)} = {}^nC_{\frac{n}{2}} \times x^{\frac{n}{2}} \times y^{\frac{n}{2}}$

If n is odd, then total number of terms in the expansion of $(x+y)^n$ is $n+1$.

So there are two middle terms i.e. $\left(\frac{n+1}{2}\right)^{th}$ and $\left(\frac{n+3}{2}\right)^{th}$ are two middle terms.

Here, we have to find the coefficient of the middle term in the binomial expansion of $(2+3x)^4$

Here $n = 4$ (n is even number)

$\therefore$ Middle term $= \left(\frac{n}{2}+1\right) = \left(\frac{4}{2}+1\right) = 3rd$ term

$\Rightarrow T_3 = T_{(2+1)} = {}^4C_2 \times (2)^{(4-2)} \times (3x)^2$

$\Rightarrow T_3 = 6 \times 4 \times 9x^2 = 216x^2$

$\therefore$ Coefficient of the middle term $= 216$

Hence, the correct option is (D).

34. As we know the general term in $(a+b)^n$,

$T_{r+1} = {}^nC_r a^{n-r} b^r$

Given,

$\left(2x^2 - \frac{1}{3x^2}\right)^{10}$

Here, $a = 2x^2, b = \frac{-1}{3x^2}$ and $r = 5$

6th coefficient $\rightarrow 5^{th}$ term

$T_6 = {}^{10}C_5 (2x^2)^5 \left(\frac{-1}{3x^2}\right)^5$

$= {}^{10}C_5 \times 2^5 \times \frac{-1}{3^5}$

$= -\frac{252 \times 32}{243}$

$= -\frac{896}{27}$

Hence, the correct option is (B).

35. Required area = Area of $ABCD = \int_1^4 y\, dx$

$= \int_1^4 \sqrt{x}\, dx$

$= \frac{2}{3}\left[(4)^{\frac{3}{2}} - (1)^{\frac{3}{2}}\right]$

$= \frac{2}{3}(8-1)$

$= \frac{14}{3}$ units

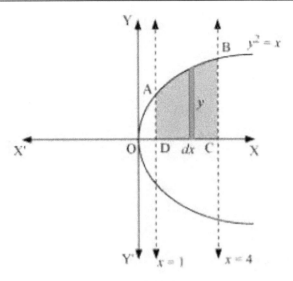

Hence, the correct option is (B).

36. Since, $6\sin x \geq 0$ and $-8\sin^3 x \leq 0$ is the intended area for all $x \in [0, \pi]$,

$A = \int_0^\pi 6\sin x - (-8\sin^3 x)dx$

$A = 2[\int_0^\pi 3\sin x + (3\sin x - \sin 3x)dx]$

$\Rightarrow 2[\int_0^\pi 6\sin x - \sin(3x)dx]$

$\Rightarrow 2\left[-6\cos x + \frac{\cos(3x)}{3}\right]_0^\pi$

$\Rightarrow 2[(6 - \frac{1}{3}) - (-6 + \frac{1}{3})]$

$\Rightarrow 2[12 - \frac{2}{3}] = \frac{68}{3}$ square unit

Hence, the correct option is (D).

37. $I_{20} = \int_0^{\frac{\pi}{2}} \frac{\sin 39x}{\sin x} dx$ ...(i)

$I_{19} = \int_0^{\frac{\pi}{2}} \frac{\sin 37x}{\sin x} dx$ ...(ii)

From equation (i) and (ii)

$I_{20} - I_{19} = \int_0^{\frac{\pi}{2}} \frac{\sin(39x) - \sin(37x)}{\sin x} dx$

$\Rightarrow I_{20} - I_{19} = \int_0^{\frac{\pi}{2}} \frac{2\sin x \cos(38x)}{\sin x} dx$

$\Rightarrow I_{20} - I_{19} = \int_0^{\frac{\pi}{2}} 2\cos(38x)dx$

$= \left[\frac{\sin(38x)}{19}\right]_0^{\frac{\pi}{2}}$

$= \frac{\sin\left(\frac{38\pi}{2}\right)}{19}$

$= 0$

$\therefore I_{20} = I_{19}$

So, $[I_{20}]^3 - [I_{19}]^3 = 0$

Hence, the correct option is (D).

38. The given equation of the circle is $x^2 + y^2 - 2x - 4y - 5 = 0$.

Comparing it with the general equation of the circle we get:

$g = -1, f = -2, c = -5$

Using the relation $r^2 = g^2 + f^2 - c$, we get:

$\Rightarrow r^2 = (-1)^2 + (-2)^2 - (-5)$

$\Rightarrow r = \sqrt{10}$

For doubling the area, the radius must become $\sqrt{2}$ times.

$\therefore$ Required radius $= \sqrt{20}$

Center is $(-g, -f) = (1, 2)$.

Equation of the circle is: $(x - 1)^2 + (y - 2)^2 = (\sqrt{20})^2$

$\Rightarrow x^2 + y^2 - 2x - 4y - 15 = 0$

Hence, the correct option is (B).

39. Given: $y^2 - 2ay + x^2 = a^2$ ....(1)

Differentiating both sides w.r.t x

$\Rightarrow \frac{2y dy}{dx} - 2a\frac{dy}{dx} + 2x = 0$

$\Rightarrow 2py - 2ap + 2x = 0$

$\Rightarrow py + x = ap$

$\Rightarrow \frac{py + x}{p} = a$

Put $a = \frac{py+x}{p}$ in equation (1)

$y^2 - 2y\left(\frac{py+x}{p}\right) + x^2 = \left(\frac{py+x}{p}\right)^2$

$\Rightarrow p^2 y^2 - 2py(py + x) + p^2 x^2 = (p^2 y^2 + x^2 + 2pxy)$

$\Rightarrow -2p^2 y^2 - 2pxy + p^2 x^2 - x^2 - 2pxy$

$\Rightarrow (x^2 - 2y^2)p^2 - 4pxy - x^2 = 0$

Hence, the correct option is (A).

40. Pobability of an outcome is defined as:

$P = \frac{n}{N}$

n = Number of favourable outcomes

Mathematics : Mock Test - 3

N = Total Possible Outcomes

N = Total number of possible outcomes = 52

In a pack of 52 cards, there are only 1 'queen of club' and 1 'king of heart'.

The required outcome is getting a queen of club or king of heart, i.e. the number of favourable outcomes ' n ' is 2.

So, $n = 2$ and $N = 52$

The probability (P) of getting a queen of club or king of heart will be:

$P = \dfrac{n}{N} = \dfrac{2}{52}$

$P = \dfrac{1}{26}$

Hence, the correct option is (C).

41. Given the equation of a line is:

$\dfrac{x}{6} = \dfrac{y+32}{2} = \dfrac{z-2}{3}$

$\Rightarrow a_1 = 6, b_1 = 2, c_1 = 3$

Equation of plane is:

$3x + 4y - 12z - 7 = 0$

$\Rightarrow a_2 = 3, b_2 = 4$ and $c_2 = -12$

$\Rightarrow \sqrt{a_1^2 + b_1^2 + c_1^2} = \sqrt{6^2 + 2^2 + 3^2} = 7$

$\Rightarrow \sqrt{a_2^2 + b_2^2 + c_2^2} = \sqrt{3^2 + 4^2 + (-12)^2} = 13$

We know that the angle between the line is given by:

$\sin\theta = \dfrac{|a_1 a_2 + b_1 b_2 + c_1 c_2|}{\left(\sqrt{a_1^2 + b_1^2 + c_1^2}\right)\left(\sqrt{a_2^2 + b_2^2 + c_2^2}\right)}$

$\Rightarrow \sin\theta = \dfrac{10}{7 \times 13} = \dfrac{10}{91}$

$\Rightarrow \theta = \sin^{-1}\left(\dfrac{10}{91}\right)$

Hence, the correct option is (B).

42. The range of $f(x)$ is all the y-values where there is a number x with $y = f(x)$.

To find the range of the function $f(x) = \dfrac{|x|}{x}, x \neq 0$, first split the function.

$f(x) = \dfrac{x}{x}, x > 0$

$f(x) = \dfrac{-x}{x}, x < 0$

We know that, the range of $f(x)$ is all the y-values where there is a number x with $y = f(x)$.

Now to find the range, take the limit of the function.

$\lim\limits_{x \to \infty} \dfrac{x}{x} = \lim\limits_{x \to \infty} 1 = 1$

Now,

$\lim\limits_{x \to \infty} \dfrac{-x}{x} = \lim\limits_{x \to \infty} -1 = -1$

The range of the function $f(x) = \dfrac{|x|}{x}, x \neq 0$ is $(1, -1)$.

Hence, the correct option is (C).

43. A compound proposition that is always false is called a contradiction.

Formula:

$a \Rightarrow b = \neg a \vee b$

$(P \Rightarrow Q) \wedge (Q \Rightarrow P)$

$(\neg P \vee Q) \wedge (\neg Q \vee P)$

replace ¬ with NOT ($\overline{}$), ∨ with OR (+) and ∧ with AND (.)

$(\overline{P} + Q).(\overline{Q} + P)$

$\overline{P}.\overline{Q} + \overline{P}.P + Q.\overline{Q} + QP$

$\overline{P}.\overline{Q} + QP$

$P \odot Q$

Truth Table:

Input P	Input Q	Output $Y = P \odot Q$
0	0	1
0	1	0
1	0	0
1	1	1

The proposition $(P \Rightarrow Q) \wedge (Q \Rightarrow P)$ is a contingency.

Hence, the correct option is (C).

44. Data:

p: x ∈ {8, 9, 10, 11, 12}

q: x is a composite number

r: x is a perfect square

s: x is a prime number

$p \Rightarrow q$ means $\overline{p} + q$

As, q is composite number So, $p \Rightarrow$ results in {8, 9, 10, 12}

As, r: x is a perfect square, ¬ r results in all the numbers which are not perfect square

So, ¬ r: {8, 10, 11, 12}

¬ s: {8, 9, 10, 12}

¬ r ∨ ¬ s = {8, 9, 10, 11, 12}

Now, $(p \Rightarrow q) \wedge (\neg r \vee \neg s)$ = {8, 9, 10, 12}

¬ $p \Rightarrow q) \wedge (\neg r \vee \neg s$ results in a number which is not present in $p \Rightarrow q) \wedge (\neg r \vee \neg s$

$\neg p \Rightarrow q) \wedge (\neg r \vee \neg s$ will give {11}

Hence, the correct option is (A).

45. Binomial distribution:

$$P(x = k) = n_{C_k} p^k q^{n-k}$$

Where,

p = Probability of success in one trial

q = Probability of failure in one trial $= 1 - p$

n = Total number of independent trials

k = Discrete random variable

$n = 3$

$P(\text{each colour}) = \frac{2}{6} = \frac{1}{3}$

$q = 1 - p = 1 - \frac{1}{3} = \frac{2}{3}$

Using binomial distribution

Probability of getting red on the top face at least twice is:

$P(x \geq 2) = P(x = 2) + P(x = 3)$

$P(x \geq 2) = n_{C_2} p^2 q^{n-2} + n_{C_3} p^3 q^{n-3}$

$P(x \geq 2) = 3_{C_2} \left(\frac{1}{3}\right)^2 \left(\frac{2}{3}\right)^1 + 3_{C_3} \left(\frac{1}{3}\right)^3 \left(\frac{2}{3}\right)^0$

$= \frac{6}{27} + \frac{1}{27} = \frac{7}{27} = 0.259$

Hence, the correct option is (A).

46. In Binomial distribution,

Mean = np, Variance = npq and the mode is r if for $x = r$, the probability function $p(x)$ is maximum.

Given: $np = 4$ and $npq = 3$

$\therefore q = \frac{3}{4}$ and $p = 1 - q = 1 - \frac{3}{4} = \frac{1}{4}$

Also, $n = \frac{4}{p} = \frac{4}{\frac{1}{4}} = 16$

Now, $(n+1)p = (16+1)\frac{1}{4}$

$= \frac{17}{4} = 4 + \frac{1}{4}$

Hence, the correct option is (C).

47. If two vectors $\vec{a} = a_1 i + a_2 j + a_3 k$ and $\vec{b} = b_1 i + b_2 j + b_3 k$ are equal, then $a_1 = b_1, a_2 = b_2$ and $c_1 = c_2$.

We have $\vec{c} = m\vec{a} + n\vec{b}$

$\Rightarrow 2\hat{\imath} + 3\hat{\jmath} = m(-4\hat{\imath} + 2\hat{\jmath}) + n(2\hat{\imath} + \hat{\jmath})$

$\Rightarrow 2\hat{\imath} + 3\hat{\jmath} = (-4m + 2n)\hat{\imath} + (2m + n)\hat{\jmath}$

Equating the scalar coefficients, we get:

$-4m + 2n = 2$ ....(1)

$2m + n = 3$ ....(2)

Multiplying equation (2) by 2 and adding to equation (1), we get:

$4n = 8$

$\Rightarrow n = 2$

Using either of the equations above, we also get:

$m = \frac{1}{2}$

$\therefore m + n = 2 + \frac{1}{2} = \frac{5}{2}$

Hence, the correct option is (C).

48. We know that,

$\sin^{-1}x + \cos^{-1}x = \frac{\pi}{2}$

$\sin^{-1}x + \sin^{-1}y = \frac{3\pi}{4}$

$\Rightarrow \left(\frac{\pi}{2} - \cos^{-1}x\right) + \left(\frac{\pi}{2} - \cos^{-1}y\right) = \frac{3\pi}{4}$

$\Rightarrow \pi - (\cos^{-1}x + \cos^{-1}y) = \frac{3\pi}{4}$

$\Rightarrow \cos^{-1}x + \cos^{-1}y = \frac{\pi}{4}$

Hence, the correct option is (B).

49. If plane $a_1 x + b_1 y + c_1 z + d_1 = 0$ and $a_2 x + b_2 y + c_2 z + d_2 = 0$ are a parallel i.e.

$\frac{a_1}{a_2} = \frac{b_1}{b_2} = \frac{c_1}{c_2} \neq \frac{d_1}{d_2}$

Given two planes are $3x - 2y + 4z + 1 = 0$ and $-6x + qy + rz + 8 = 0$

For the parallel planes;

$\frac{3}{-6} = \frac{-2}{q} = \frac{4}{r}$

Taking the first two ratios,

$\frac{3}{-6} = \frac{-2}{q}$

$\Rightarrow q = 4$

Taking first and last ratios,

$\frac{3}{-6} = \frac{4}{r}$

$-r = -8$

Hence, the correct option is (D).

50. Given,

$(1 + \cos^2 A) = 3\sin A \cdot \cos A$

Dividing by $\cos^2 A$;

$\Rightarrow (1 + \sec^2 A) = 3\tan A$

We know that: $\sec^2 A = (1 + \tan^2 A)$

$\Rightarrow 2 + \tan^2 A = 3\tan A$

$\Rightarrow \tan^2 A - 3\tan A + 2 = 0$

$\Rightarrow (\tan A - 1)(\tan A - 2) = 0$

$\Rightarrow \tan A = 1$ or 2

$\therefore \cot A = 1$ or $\dfrac{1}{2}$

Hence, the correct option is (B).

Mathematics : Mock Test 04

Q.1 Find the number of arrangements of letters in the word ASHUTOSH?
A. 10080 B. 11080 C. 21080 D. 20080

Q.2 The order of the given matrix is:
$$A = \begin{bmatrix} 2 & 4 \\ -1 & 0 \\ 6 & 5 \end{bmatrix}$$
A. 3×3 B. 3×2 C. 2×3 D. 2×2

Q.3 Find the value of x and y such that $\begin{bmatrix} x-y \\ x+y \end{bmatrix} = \begin{bmatrix} 2 \\ 16 \end{bmatrix}$.
A. $x = 7$ and $y = 9$
B. $x = 9$ and $y = 7$
C. $x = 8$ and $y = 5$
D. $x = 13$ and $y = 3$

Q.4 If $A = \begin{bmatrix} 1 & -5 \\ -3 & 7 \end{bmatrix}$ and $B = \begin{bmatrix} 8 & 4 \\ 1 & 3 \end{bmatrix}$ then the value of $(AB)^T$ is:
A. $\begin{bmatrix} 3 & -11 \\ -17 & 9 \end{bmatrix}$
B. $\begin{bmatrix} 3 & -17 \\ -11 & 9 \end{bmatrix}$
C. $\begin{bmatrix} -3 & 17 \\ 11 & -9 \end{bmatrix}$
D. $\begin{bmatrix} -6 & 17 \\ 22 & -9 \end{bmatrix}$

Q.5 Find the equation of line passing through the points $A(2,-3,1)$ and $B(3,-4,-5)$?
A. $\frac{x-2}{1} = \frac{y+3}{-1} = \frac{z-1}{-6}$
B. $\frac{x-2}{1} = \frac{y+3}{1} = \frac{z-1}{-6}$
C. $\frac{x-2}{1} = \frac{y+3}{1} = \frac{z-1}{6}$
D. $\frac{x-2}{1} = \frac{y+3}{-1} = \frac{z-1}{6}$

Q.6 Form the differential equation for the family of circle with center $(0,0)$ and radius r, where r is any constant:
A. $\frac{dy}{dx} = \frac{x}{y}$
B. $\frac{dy}{dx} = -xy$
C. $\frac{dy}{dx} = -\frac{x}{y}$
D. $\frac{dy}{dx} = xy$

Q.7 Find the general solution of $\frac{dy}{dx} = e^{x-y}$
A. $e^{-y} = e^x + c$
B. $e^y = e^{-x} + c$
C. $e^y = e^x + c$
D. None of these

Q.8 The differential form of the equation $(y - b) = a\sin x$:
A. $y'' + y' = 0$
B. $y'' + y'\tan x = 0$
C. $y'' + y'\sin x = 0$
D. $y'' + y'\cos x = 0$

Q.9 For a group of 100 males, mean and standard deviation of their daily wages are Rs. 36 and Rs. 9 respectively. For a group of 50 females, it is Rs. 45 and Rs. 6. Find the standard deviation for the whole group.
A. Rs. 9.16 B. Rs. 6.19 C. Rs. 9.6 D. Rs. 6.9

Q.10 Find the area of the region (in sq. units) bounded by the curve $y^2 = 2y - x$ and y-axis.
A. $\frac{8}{3}$ B. $\frac{4}{3}$ C. $\frac{5}{3}$ D. $\frac{2}{3}$

Q.11 The area bounded by curve $y = x|x|$, x axes and ordinates $x = 1, x = -1$ is given by:
A. 0 B. $\frac{2}{3}$
C. $\frac{1}{3}$ D. None of these

Q.12 The area of the region bounded by the curve $y = \sqrt{16 - x^2}$ and x-axis is:
A. 8π sq. units B. 20π sq. units
C. 16π sq. units D. None of these

Q.13 The function $f(x) = \sqrt{\cos(\sin x)} + \sin^{-1}\left(\frac{1+x^2}{2x}\right)$ is defined for:

[UPSESSB TGT Mathematics, 2016]

A. $x \in \{-1,1\}$ B. $x \in [-1,1]$
C. $x \in R$ D. $x \in (-1,1)$

Q.14 Find the value of θ for which $z = \frac{3-2i\sin\theta}{2-i\sin\theta}$ is purely real.
A. $\theta = n\pi$, where n belongs to an integer
B. No value of θ exists
C. 0
D. π

Q.15 Solve the following Linear Programming Problems graphically:
Minimise $Z = -3x + 4y$, subject to $x + 2y \le 8, 3x + 2y \le 12, x \ge 0, y \ge 0$
A. -13 B. +13 C. -12 D. +12

Q.16 In order that linear programming techniques provide valid results:
A. Relations between factors must be linear (Positive)
B. Relations between factors must be linear (Negative)
C. (A) or (B)
D. none of the above

Q.17 Consider the following Linear Programming Problem (LPP).
Maximise $Z = x_1 + 2x_2$
Subject to:
$x_1 \le 2$
$x_2 \le 2$
$x_1 + x_2 \le 2$
$x_1, x_2 \ge 0$ (i.e., +ve decision variables)
A. 2, 2 B. 0, 2 C. 2, 0 D. 0, 0

Q.18 The equation of a line which is parallel to the line $2y + 5x - 2 = 0$ and passing through $(-1,3)$ is:

Mathematics : Mock Test - 4

A. $2y - 5x - 11 = 0$
B. $2y + 5x - 1 = 0$
C. $2y + 5x - 4 = 0$
D. $5y + 2x - 13 = 0$

Q.19 The angle between the lines x − 2y = y and y − 2x = 5 is:

A. $\tan^{-1}\left(\frac{1}{4}\right)$
B. $\tan^{-1}\left(\frac{3}{5}\right)$
C. $\tan^{-1}\left(\frac{5}{4}\right)$
D. $\tan^{-1}\left(\frac{2}{3}\right)$

Q.20 The length of the perpendicular from the origin to a line is 7 and the line makes an angle of 150 degrees with the positive direction of the y-axis then, the equation of a line is:

A. $x + y = 14$
B. $\sqrt{3}y + x = 14$
C. $\sqrt{3}x + y = 14$
D. None of these

Q.21 $\cos\frac{\pi}{5} \cos\frac{2\pi}{5} \cos\frac{4\pi}{5} \cos\frac{8\pi}{5} = ?$

A. $\frac{1}{16}$
B. 0
C. $\frac{-1}{8}$
D. $\frac{-1}{16}$

Q.22 What is the value of λ for which the vectors $3\hat{\imath} + 4\hat{\jmath} - \hat{k}$ and $-2\hat{\imath} + \lambda\hat{\jmath} + 10\hat{k}$ are perpendicular?

[UPSC NDA, 2019]

A. 2
B. 3
C. 4
D. 1

Q.23 If vector b is vector whose initial point divides the join of $5i$ and $5j$ in the ratio $k:1$ and terminal point is origin and |vector b |$\leq \sqrt{37}$, then the set of exhaustive values of k is:

A. $\left[6, -\frac{1}{6}\right]$
B. $(-\infty, -6) \cup \left[-\frac{1}{6}, \infty\right)$
C. $[0,6]$
D. $\left[-\frac{1}{6}, \infty\right)$

Q.24 Evaluate the expression: $\sqrt{\frac{1+\cos\theta}{1-\cos\theta}} = ?$

A. $cosec\theta - \cot\theta$
B. $cosec\theta + \cot\theta$
C. $\tan\theta - \cot\theta$
D. None of these

Q.25 Which of the following equals $1 + \cot^2\theta$?

A. $\sec^2\theta$
B. $\cos^2\theta$
C. $cosec^2\theta$
D. $\cot^2\theta$

Q.26 If $xdy = ydx + y^2dy, y > 0$ and $y(1) = 1$, then what is $y(-3)$ equal to?

A. 3 only
B. -1 only
C. Both -1 and 3
D. Neither -1 nor 3

Q.27 If c is an arbitrary constant then solution of differential equation $x^2dy - y^2dx - xy^2(x - y)dy = 0$ can be:

A. $\ln\left|\frac{x-y}{xy}\right| = \frac{y^2}{2} - c$
B. $\ln\left|\frac{xy}{x-y}\right| = \frac{x^2}{2} + c$
C. $\ln\left|\frac{x-y}{xy}\right| = \frac{x^2}{2} + c$
D. $\ln\left|\frac{x-y}{xy}\right| = x + c$

Q.28 If a differentiable function $f(x)$ satisfies

$f(x) \lim_{x \to -1} \frac{f(x)+1}{x^2-1} = -\frac{3}{2}$ then what is $\lim_{x \to -1} f(x)$ equal to?

[UPSC NDA, 2021]

A. $-\frac{3}{2}$
B. -1
C. 0
D. 1

Q.29 In a trunk there are 3 types of ice cream of flavors vanilla, chocolate and blueberry. The probability of selecting one vanilla ice-cream is $\frac{1}{2}$ and probability of selecting one blueberry ice-cream is $\frac{2}{7}$. The total number of chocolate icecream is 6. Find the number of ice creams in the trunk.

A. 25
B. 30
C. 28
D. 32

Q.30 Find the minimum value of $3x^4 - 8x^3 + 12x^2 - 48x + 1$ on the interval $[1,4]$ and $x \in R$?

A. -25
B. -39
C. -75
D. -63

Q.31 Which of the following is true regarding the function $f(x) = \log(\sin x)$?

A. $f(x)$ is strictly increasing function on $\left(0, \frac{\pi}{2}\right)$
B. $f(x)$ is strictly decreasing function on $\left(\frac{\pi}{2}, \pi\right)$
C. $f(x)$ is neither strictly increasing nor strictly decreasing function on $\left(0, \frac{\pi}{2}\right)$
D. Both (A) and (B)

Q.32 Find slope of the tangent to the curve $2x^3 + 3y = 2y^3 + 3x$ at $p(x, y)$.

A. $\frac{6x^2-3}{6y^2+3}$
B. $\frac{6x^2-3}{6y^2-3}$
C. $\frac{6y^2-3}{6x^2-3}$
D. $\frac{6y^2+3}{6x^2-3}$

Q.33 The circumference of a circle is 66 cm. Find its radius (in cm).

A. 21
B. 10.5
C. 4.5
D. 9

Q.34 The value of $I = \int_0^{\frac{\pi}{2}} \frac{(\sin x + \cos x)^2}{\sqrt{1+\sin 2x}} dx$ is:

A. 3
B. 1
C. 2
D. 0

Q.35 $\int \frac{dx}{e^x + e^{-x}}$ equals:

A. $\log(e^x + e^{-x}) + c$
B. $\log(e^x - e^{-x}) + c$
C. $\tan^{-1}(e^x) + c$
D. $\tan^{-1}(e^{-x}) + c$

Q.36 $\int \frac{1}{x^2}(2x+1)^3 dx = ?$

A. $4x^2 + 12x + 6\log x - \frac{1}{x} + c$
B. $4x^2 + 12x - 6\log x - \frac{2}{x} + c$
C. $2x^2 + 8x + 3\log x - \frac{2}{x} + c$
D. $8x^2 + 6x + 6\log x + \frac{2}{x} + c$

Q.37 Consider a binomial random variable X. If $X_1, X_2, \ldots X_n$ are independent and identically distributed samples from the distribution of X with sum $Y = \sum_{i=1}^{n} X_i$ then the distribution of Y as $n \to \infty$ can be approximated as.

[GATE Mechanical Engineering ME, 2021]

A. Exponential
B. Bernoulli
C. Binomial
D. Normal

Q.38 Which among the following is the standard deviation of Binomial distribution?

Mathematics : Mock Test - 4

A. $\sqrt{npq}$ B. npq C. np^2q D. np

Q.39 What is the coefficient of the middle term in the expansion of $(1 + 4x + 4x^2)^5$?

[UPSC NDA, 2021]

A. 8064 B. 4032 C. 2016 D. 1008

Q.40 If the angle θ between the line $\frac{x+1}{1} = \frac{y-1}{2} = \frac{z-2}{2}$ and the plane $2x - y + \sqrt{\lambda}z + 4 = 0$ is such that $\sin\theta = \frac{1}{3}$. The value of λ is-

A. $-\frac{4}{3}$ B. $\frac{3}{4}$ C. $-\frac{3}{4}$ D. $\frac{5}{3}$

Q.41 If $f(x) = \begin{cases} \frac{\sin 3x}{e^{2x}-1}, & x \neq 0 \\ k-2, & x = 0 \end{cases}$ is continuous at $x = 0$, then $k = ?$

A. $\frac{3}{2}$ B. $\frac{9}{5}$ C. $\frac{1}{2}$ D. $\frac{7}{2}$

Q.42 Let x be a continuous variable defined over the interval $(-\infty, \infty)$ and $f(x) = e^{-x-e^{-x}}$. The integral $g(x) = \int f(x)dx$ is equal to

A. $e^{e^{-x}}$ B. $e^{-e^{-z}}$ C. e^{-e^x} D. e^{-x}

Q.43 Evaluate $\int e^{\sin^{-1}x} \frac{1}{\sqrt{1-x^2}} dx$:

A. $e^{\sin x} + c$ B. $2e^{\sin^{-1}x} + c$
C. $e^{\sin^{-1}x} + c$ D. $e^{\sin^{-1}x} + 2c$

Q.44 The value of $\int_0^1 |5x - 3| \, dx$ is:

A. $-\frac{1}{2}$ B. $\frac{13}{10}$ C. $\frac{1}{2}$ D. $\frac{28}{10}$

Q.45 If the slope of one of the lines represented by $ax^2 + 2hxy + by^2 = 0$ (be the square of the other, then):

A. $a^2b + ab^2 - 6abh + 8h^3 = 0$
B. $a^2b + ab^2 + 6abh + 8h^3 = 0$
C. $a^2b + ab^2 - 3abh + 8h^3 = 0$
D. $a^2b + ab^2 - 6abh - 8h^3 = 0$

Q.46 If $f(x) = \frac{\sin(e^{x-2}-1)}{\log(x-1)}, x \neq 2$ and $f(x) = k$. Then, the value of k for which f will be continuous at $x = 2$ is:

A. -2 B. -1 C. 0 D. 1

Q.47 Which one of the following well - formed formulae is a tautology?

A. $\forall x \exists y(x,) \mapsto \exists y \forall x R(x,y,$
B. $(\forall x [\exists y(x,) \to S(x,y)]) \to \forall x \exists y S(x,y,$
C. $[\forall x \exists y(P(x,y) \to R(x,y)] \leftrightarrow [\forall x \exists y(\neg P(x,y) \vee R(x,y)]$
D. $\forall x \forall y(x_1) \to \forall x \forall y P(y,x)$

Q.48 Consider the following two statements.

S1: If a candidate is known to be corrupt, then he will not be elected

S2: If a candidate is kind, he will be elected

Which one of the following statements follows from S1 and S2 as per sound inference rules of logic?

A. If a person is known to be corrupt, he is kind
B. If a person is not known to be corrupt, he is not kind
C. If a person is kind, he is not known to be corrupt
D. If a person is not kind, he is not known to be corrupt

Q.49 For any discrete random variable X, with probability mass function $P(X = j) = p_j, p_j \geq 0, j \in \{0, ..., N\}$, and $\sum_{j=0}^{N} p_j = 1$, define the polynomial function $g_X(z) = \sum_{j=0}^{N} p_j z^j$. For a certain discrete random variable Y, there exists a scalar $\beta \in [0,1]$ such that $g_Y(z) = (1 - \beta + \beta z)^N$. The expectation of Y is:

A. $N\beta(1-\beta)$
B. $N\beta$
C. $N(1-\beta)$
D. Not expressible in terms of N and β alone

Q.50 For the discrete random variable x having probability mass function $(1-p)^{k-1}p; k = 1,2,3,...; 0 < p \leq 1$, the mode of x is:

A. 1 B. 0 C. p D. 1-p

Mathematics : Mock Test - 4

// Smart Answer Sheet //

Correct Indicates percentage of students who answered questions correctly.

Skipped Indicates percentage of students who skipped questions.

Q.	Ans.	Correct / Skipped	Q.	Ans.	Correct / Skipped	Q.	Ans.	Correct / Skipped	Q.	Ans.	Correct / Skipped	Q.	Ans.	Correct / Skipped
1	A	69.23 % / 3.85 %	11	B	50.0 % / 3.85 %	21	D	53.85 % / 7.69 %	31	D	46.15 % / 7.7 %	41	D	34.62 % / 3.84 %
2	B	84.62 % / 3.84 %	12	A	50.0 % / 3.85 %	22	C	80.77 % / 3.85 %	32	B	76.92 % / 7.7 %	42	B	38.46 % / 7.69 %
3	B	92.31 % / 3.84 %	13	A	19.23 % / 7.69 %	23	B	57.69 % / 3.85 %	33	B	88.46 % / 3.85 %	43	C	73.08 % / 3.84 %
4	B	73.08 % / 7.69 %	14	A	73.08 % / 3.84 %	24	B	69.23 % / 3.85 %	34	C	61.54 % / 7.69 %	44	B	26.92 % / 3.85 %
5	A	73.08 % / 7.69 %	15	C	76.92 % / 3.85 %	25	C	88.46 % / 3.85 %	35	C	46.15 % / 3.85 %	45	A	42.31 % / 7.69 %
6	C	61.54 % / 3.84 %	16	C	65.38 % / 3.85 %	26	A	26.92 % / 7.7 %	36	A	57.69 % / 7.69 %	46	D	34.62 % / 7.69 %
7	C	76.92 % / 7.7 %	17	B	46.15 % / 0.0 %	27	A	26.92 % / 3.85 %	37	D	11.54 % / 7.69 %	47	C	46.15 % / 3.85 %
8	B	61.54 % / 3.84 %	18	B	69.23 % / 7.69 %	28	B	53.85 % / 3.84 %	38	A	76.92 % / 7.7 %	48	C	88.46 % / 3.85 %
9	A	23.08 % / 3.84 %	19	C	42.31 % / 7.69 %	29	C	61.54 % / 7.69 %	39	A	50.0 % / 3.85 %	49	B	23.08 % / 3.84 %
10	B	57.69 % / 3.85 %	20	C	34.62 % / 7.69 %	30	D	38.46 % / 3.85 %	40	D	42.31 % / 3.84 %	50	A	23.08 % / 7.69 %

Performance Analysis	
Avg. Score (%)	48.0%
Toppers Score (%)	98.0%
Your Score	

//Hints and Solutions//

1. Given word is : ASHUTOSH

Total 8 letters are there, in which letter S and H are repeated twice.

We know that:

Number of Permutations of 'n' things taken 'r' at a time:

$$p(n,r) = \frac{n!}{(n-r)!}$$

Number of Permutations of 'n' objects where there are n_1 repeated items, n_2 repeated items, n_k repeated items taken 'r' at a time:

$$p(n,r) = \frac{n!}{n_1! n_2! n_3! ... n_k!}$$

Therefore,

The number of arrangements will be:

$$p(8,2) = \frac{8 \times 7 \times 6 \times 5 \times 4 \times 3 \times 2!}{(2 \times 1)2!}$$

$$= 10080$$

Therefore, the number of arrangements of letters in the word ASHUTOSH will be 10080.

Hence, the correct option is (A).

2. As we know,
A matrix having m rows and n columns is called a matrix of order $m \times n$ or simply $m \times n$ matrix.
Given,

$$A = \begin{bmatrix} 2 & 4 \\ -1 & 0 \\ 6 & 5 \end{bmatrix}$$

As we can see that the given matrix A has 3 rows and 2 columns.

$\therefore$ The order of the given matrix A is 3×2.

Hence, the correct option is (B).

3. Given,

$$\begin{bmatrix} x - y \\ x + y \end{bmatrix} = \begin{bmatrix} 2 \\ 16 \end{bmatrix}$$

As we know,
If two matrices and are said to be equal, then
Order of matrix $A = $ Order of matrix B
Corresponding element of matrix $A = $ Corresponding element of B
So,
$x - y = 2$...(1)
$x + y = 16$...(2)
On adding equation (1) and (2) we get,
$2x = 18$
$\Rightarrow x = 9$

Substituting $x = 9$ in equation (2) we get
$9 + y = 16$
$\Rightarrow y = 16 - 9$
$\Rightarrow y = 7$
So, the value of $x = 9$ and $y = 7$
Hence, the correct option is (B).

4. Given,

$$A = \begin{bmatrix} 1 & -5 \\ -3 & 7 \end{bmatrix} \text{ and } B = \begin{bmatrix} 8 & 4 \\ 1 & 3 \end{bmatrix}$$

$$AB = \begin{bmatrix} 1 & -5 \\ -3 & 7 \end{bmatrix}\begin{bmatrix} 8 & 4 \\ 1 & 3 \end{bmatrix}$$

$$= \begin{bmatrix} (1 \times 8) + (-5 \times 1) & (1 \times 4) + (-5 \times 3) \\ (-3 \times 8) + (7 \times 1) & (-3 \times 4) + (7 \times 3) \end{bmatrix}$$

$$= \begin{bmatrix} 3 & -11 \\ -17 & 9 \end{bmatrix}$$

Now, we can get transpose of AB by switching its rows with its columns.

$$\therefore (AB)^T = \begin{bmatrix} 3 & -17 \\ -11 & 9 \end{bmatrix}$$

Hence, the correct option is (B).

5. Concept:

The cartesian equation of a line passing through $A(x_1, y_1, z_1)$ and $B(x_2, y_2, z_2)$ is given by: $\frac{x-x_1}{x_2-x_1} = \frac{y-y_1}{y_2-y_1} = \frac{z-z_1}{z_2-z_1}$

Given: $A(2, -3, 1)$ and $B(3, -4, -5)$ are two points

Let $x_1 = 2, y_1 = -3, z_1 = 1, x_2 = 3, y_2 = -4$ and $z_2 = -5$.

As we know that, equation of a line passing through $A(x_1, y_1, z_1)$ and $B(x_2, y_2, z_2)$ is given by: $\frac{x-x_1}{x_2-x_1} = \frac{y-y_1}{y_2-y_1} = \frac{z-z_1}{z_2-z_1}$

So, the required equation of line is: $\frac{x-2}{1} = \frac{y+3}{-1} = \frac{z-1}{6}$.

Hence, the correct option is (A).

6. The family of circle having centre $(0,0)$ and radius r is:
$x^2 + y^2 = r^2$

There is only one constant r.

Differentiating w.r.t. x

We get,

$$\frac{d}{dx}(x^2 + y^2) = \frac{d}{dx}r^2$$

$$\Rightarrow 2x + 2y\frac{dy}{dx} = 0$$

$$\Rightarrow \frac{dy}{dx} = -\frac{x}{y}$$

Hence, the correct option is (C).

7. Given,

$\frac{dy}{dx} = e^{x-y}$

$\Rightarrow \frac{dy}{dx} = \frac{e^x}{e^y}$

$\Rightarrow e^y dy = e^x dx$

Now,

Integrating both sides, we get

$\int e^y dy = \int e^x dx$

$\Rightarrow e^y = e^x + c$

Hence, the correct option is (C).

8. Given,

$y - b = a\sin x$

There are two constants a and b so differentiate two times

Differentiating w.r.t x

We get,

$y' = a\cos x \ldots (i)$

Again differentiating w.r.t x

$y'' = -a\sin x$

From equation (i),

$a = \frac{y'}{\cos x}$

$y'' = -\frac{y'}{\cos x} \times \sin x \quad y'' + y'\tan x = 0$

Hence, the correct option is (B).

9. Calculating combined standard deviation,

$\sigma_{12} = \sqrt{\frac{N_1\sigma_1^2 + N_2\sigma_2^2 + N_1 d_1^2 + N_2 d_2^2}{N_1 + N_2}}$

Where,

$N_1 = 100,$

$N_2 = 50,$

$\overline{X}_1 = 36,$

$\overline{X}_2 = 45,$

$\sigma_1 = 9,$

$\sigma_2 = 6$

Now,

To calculate combined standard deviation, we need to find the combined mean of the observations.

Thus, Combined mean is:

$\overline{X}_{12} = \frac{N_1\overline{X}_1 + N_2\overline{X}_2}{N_1 + N_2}$

$= \frac{100(36) + 50(45)}{150}$

$= \frac{3600 + 2250}{150}$

$= $ Rs. 39

Now,

$d_1^2 = (\overline{X}_1 - \overline{X}_{12})^2 = (36-39)^2 = (-3)^2 = 9$

$d_2^2 = (\overline{X}_2 - \overline{X}_{12})^2 = (45-39)^2 = (6)^2 = 36$

Thus, Combined standard deviation will be:

$\sigma_{12} = \sqrt{\frac{N_1\sigma_1^2 + N_2\sigma_2^2 + N_1 d_1^2 + N_2 d_2^2}{N_1 + N_2}}$

$\Rightarrow \sigma_{12} = \sqrt{\frac{100(9)^2 + 50(6)^2 + 100(9) + 50(36)}{150}}$

$\Rightarrow \sigma_{12} = \sqrt{\frac{8100 + 1800 + 900 + 1800}{150}}$

$\Rightarrow \sigma_{12} = \sqrt{\frac{12600}{150}}$

$\Rightarrow \sigma_{12} = \sqrt{84}$

$\Rightarrow \sigma_{12} = 9.16$

So, the combined standard deviation is Rs. 9.16

Hence, the correct option is (A).

10. Given:

$y^2 = 2y - x$

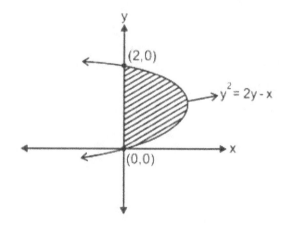

Here,

$y^2 = 2y - x$

$y^2 - 2y + 1 = -(x - 1)$

$(y - 1)^2 = -(x - 1)$

$x = 1 - (y - 1)^2$

Area under the curve is,

$= \int_{y=0}^{y=2} x \, dy$

$= \int_0^2 (1 - (y - 1)^2) \, dy$

$= \left[y - \frac{(y-1)^3}{3} \right]_0^2$

$= \left[2 - \frac{1}{3} \right] - \left[0 + \frac{1}{3} \right]$

$= \frac{4}{3}$

Hence, the correct option is (B).

11. Given curve and lines:

$y = x|x|$, x axes and ordinates $x = 1, x = -1$

Therefore,

Area under the curve $= \left| \int_{-1}^{1} x|x| dx \right|$

$= \left| \int_{-1}^{0} x|x| dx \right| + \left| \int_{0}^{1} x|x| dx \right|$

$= \left| \int_{-1}^{0} x(-x) dx \right| + \left| \int_{0}^{1} x \cdot x dx \right|$

$= \left| \int_{-1}^{0} -x^2 dx \right| + \left| \int_{0}^{1} x^2 dx \right|$

$= \left[\frac{-x^3}{3} \right]_{-1}^{0} + \left[\frac{x^3}{3} \right]_{0}^{1}$

$= \frac{2}{3}$

Hence, the correct option is (B).

12. Given:

$y = \sqrt{16 - x^2}$ and x-axis

At x-axis, y will be zero

$y = \sqrt{16 - x^2}$

$\Rightarrow 0 = \sqrt{16 - x^2}$

$\Rightarrow 16 - x^2 = 0$

$\Rightarrow x^2 = 16$

$\therefore x = \pm 4$

So, the intersection points are (4, 0) and (-4, 0)

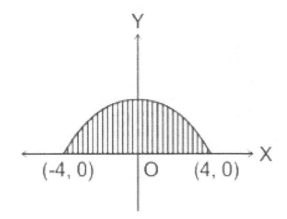

Area of the curve, $A = \int_{-4}^{4} \sqrt{16 - x^2} \, dx$ \qaud $\because$

$\int (\sqrt{a^2 - x^2}) = \frac{x}{2}\sqrt{a^2 - x^2} + \frac{a^2}{2} \sin^{-1} \frac{x}{a}$

$= \left[\frac{x}{2} \sqrt{4^2 - x^2} + \frac{4^2}{2} \sin^{-1} \frac{x}{4} \right]_{-4}^{4}$

$= \left[\frac{4}{2} \sqrt{4^2 - 4^2} + \frac{4^2}{2} \sin^{-1} \frac{4}{4} \right] - \left[\frac{-4}{2} \sqrt{4^2 - (-4)^2} + \frac{4^2}{2} \sin^{-1} \frac{-4}{4} \right]$

$= 8 \frac{\pi}{2} + 8 \frac{\pi}{2}$

$= 8\pi$ sq. units

Hence, the correct option is (A).

13. Given: function is $\sqrt{\cos(\sin x)} + \sin^{-1} \leq ft \left(\frac{1+x^2}{2x} \right)$

Range of $\sin x$ is $[-1, 1]$. so, $\cos(-ve)$ also positive value.

$\Rightarrow$ Defined for all real number .....(1)

$\sin^{-1}(x)$ is defined for $-1 \leq x \leq 1$

$-1 \leq \frac{1+x^2}{2x} \leq 1$

Case (1) $x^2 + 1 \geq -2x$

$(x + 1)^2 \geq 0$

Always positive and this is equal to zero when $x = -1$

Case (2) $1 + x^2 \leq 2x$

$(x - 1)^2 \leq 0$

This is equal to zero when $x = 1$

The function domain will be inter section of case (1) and (2) function

For function (2) $x \in \{-1, 1\}$

The final answer for this is $x \in \{-1, 1\}$

Hence, the correct option is (A).

14. Given,

$z = \dfrac{3-2i\sin\theta}{2-i\sin\theta}$

Multiplying the numerator and denominator by $(2+i\sin\theta)$, we get

$z = \dfrac{3-2i\sin\theta}{2-i\sin\theta} \times \dfrac{2+i\sin\theta}{2+i\sin\theta}$

$\Rightarrow z = \dfrac{6+3i\sin\theta-4i\sin\theta-2i^2\sin^2\theta}{(2)^2-(i\sin\theta)^2}$

$\Rightarrow z = \dfrac{6-i\sin\theta+2i^2\sin^2\theta}{4-i^2\sin^2\theta}$

$\Rightarrow z = \dfrac{6-i\sin\theta+2\times(-1)\sin^2\theta}{4-(-1)\sin^2\theta}$ $\quad [\because i^2 = -1]$

$\Rightarrow z = \dfrac{6-i\sin\theta+2\times(-1)\sin^2\theta}{4-(-1)\sin^2\theta}$

$\Rightarrow z = \dfrac{6-2\sin^2\theta}{4+\sin^2\theta} + i\left(\dfrac{-\sin\theta}{4+\sin^2\theta}\right)$

Imaginary part of z,

$Im(z) = \dfrac{-\sin\theta}{4+\sin^2\theta}$

As we know,

For z to be purely real, $Im(z) = 0$

$\therefore \dfrac{-\sin\theta}{4+\sin^2\theta} = 0$

$\Rightarrow \sin\theta = 0$

$\Rightarrow \theta = n\pi$, where n belongs to an integer

Hence, the correct option is (A).

15.

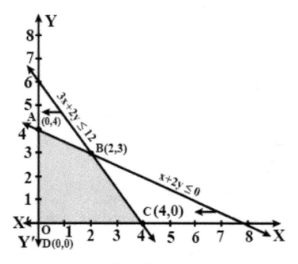

Objective function : $Z = -3x + 4y$

We have to minimize Z on constraints

$x + 2y \leq 8$

$3x + 2y \leq 12$

$x \geq 0, y \geq 0$

After plotting inequalities, we got feasible region as shown in the image.

Now, there are 3 corner points $(0,4), (2,3)$ and $(4,0)$.

At $(0,4)$, value of $Z = -3 \times 0 + 4 \times 4 = 16$

At $(2,3)$, value of $Z = -3 \times 2 + 4 \times 3 = 6$

At $(4,0)$, value of $Z = -3 \times 4 + 4 \times 0 = -12$

So, minimum value of $Z = -12$.

Hence, the correct option is (C).

16. Linear Programming: Linear programming is an important optimization (maximization or minimization) technique used in decision making in business and every - day life for obtaining the maximum or minimum values as required of linear expression, subjected to satisfy a certain number of given linear restrictions.

Linear programming problem (LPP): The linear programming problem is general calls for optimizing (maximizing/minimizing) a linear function of variables called the objective function subject to a set of linear equations and/or linear inequations called the constraints or restrictions.

The function which is to be optimized (maximized or minimized) is called the objective function.

The system of linear inequations (or equations) under which the objective function is to be optimized are called the constraints.

A primary requirement of an LPP is that both the objective function and all the constraints must be expressed in terms of linear equations and inequalities.

Hence, the correct option is (C).

17. Given:

Objective function,

Maximize, $Z = x_1 + 2x_2$

Constraints:

$x_1 \leq 2$

$x_2 \leq 2$

$x_1 + x_2 \leq 2$

Non neagative constarints:

$x_1, x_2 \geq 0$

The above equations can be written as,

$\dfrac{x_1}{2} \leq 1$

$\dfrac{x_2}{2} \leq 1$

$\frac{x_1}{2} + \frac{x_2}{2} \leq 1$

Plot the above equations on $x_1 - x_2$ graph and find out the solution space.

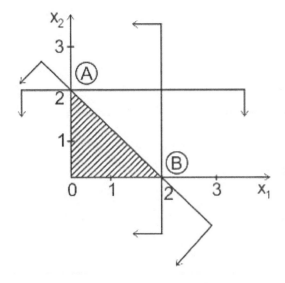

Now, find out the value of the objective function at every extreme point of solution space.

$Z = x_1 + 2x_2$

$Z_0 = 0 + 2 \times 0 = 0$

$Z_A = 0 + 2 \times 2 = 4$

$Z_B = 2 + 2 \times 0 = 2$

Since the value of the objective function is maximum at A. There $A(0,2)$ is the optimal solution.

Hence, the correct option is (B).

18. Given,

$2y + 5x - 2 = 0$ ...(i)

Passing points $(x_1, y_1) = (-1, 3)$

The general form of equation of straight line $y = mx + c$

Where slope of line is m and c is the constant.

Let m_1 and m_2 be the slope of two lines.

On converting equation into general form we get,

$2y = -5x + 2$

$y = \frac{-5}{2}x + 1$ ...(ii)

On comparing equation (ii) with general equation

$m_1 = \frac{-5}{2}$

We know that when two lines are parallel to each other, their slopes are equal

$m_1 = m_2$

$m_2 = \frac{-5}{2}$

The equation of the required line is: $y - y_1 = m(x - x_1)$

$y - 3 = \frac{-5}{2}(x - (-1))$

$\Rightarrow 2y - 6 = -5x + 5(-1)$

$\Rightarrow 2y + 5x - 6 + 5 = 0$

$\Rightarrow 2y + 5x - 1 = 0$

Hence, the correct option is (B).

19. Given,

Lines are:

$x - 2y = 5 \ldots\ldots\ldots (i)$

and $y - 2x = 5 \ldots\ldots\ldots (ii)$

Let m_1 and m_2 are the slope of the given lines

From equation (i),

$x - 5 = 2y$

$\Rightarrow y = \frac{x}{2} - \frac{5}{2}$

on comparing general equation of the line ($y = mx + c$) we get,

$m_1 = \frac{1}{2}$

From equation (ii),

$y = 2x + 5$

$m_2 = 2$

Now,

Angle between the two lines is given by:

$\tan\theta = \left|\frac{(m_1 + m_2)}{1 + m_1 \times m_2}\right|$

$\Rightarrow \tan\theta = \left|\frac{\left(\frac{1}{2} + 2\right)}{\{1 + \left(\frac{1}{2}\right) \times 2\}}\right|$

$\Rightarrow \tan\theta = \left|\frac{\left(\frac{5}{2}\right)}{(1+1)}\right|$

$\Rightarrow \tan\theta = \left|\frac{\left(\frac{5}{2}\right)}{2}\right|$

$\Rightarrow \tan\theta = \frac{5}{4}$

$\Rightarrow \theta = \tan^{-1}\left(\frac{5}{4}\right)$

Hence, the correct option is (C).

20. Given,

The length of the perpendicular from the origin to a line is 7 and the line makes an angle of 150 degrees with the positive direction of the x-axis.

We know that, If p is the length of the normal from origin to a line and α is the angle made by the normal with the positive direction of x-axis then the equation of the line is given by:

$$x\cos\alpha + y\sin\alpha = p$$

Now, the equation of a line is

$$x \times \cos 150° + y \times \sin 150° = 7$$

$\Rightarrow x \times \cos(180° - 30°) + y \times \sin(180° - 30°) = 7 \quad (\because \cos(180° - \theta) = \cos\theta, \sin(180° - \theta) = \sin\theta)$

$\Rightarrow x \times \cos 30° + y \times \sin 30° = 7$

$\Rightarrow \frac{\sqrt{3}x}{2} + \frac{y}{2} = 7 \quad (\because \cos 30° = \frac{\sqrt{3}}{2} \text{ and } \sin 30° = \frac{1}{2})$

$\Rightarrow \sqrt{3}x + y = 7 \times 2$

$\Rightarrow \sqrt{3}x + y = 14$

Hence, the correct option is (C).

21. Given:

$= \cos\frac{\pi}{5}\cos\frac{2\pi}{5}\cos\frac{4\pi}{5}\cos\frac{8\pi}{5}$

$= \frac{1}{2\sin\frac{\pi}{5}}\left(2\sin\frac{\pi}{5}\cos\frac{\pi}{5}\cos\frac{2\pi}{5}\cos\frac{4\pi}{5}\cos\frac{8\pi}{5}\right)$ (Multiplying and dividing by $\frac{1}{2\sin\frac{\pi}{5}}$)

$= \frac{1}{2\sin\frac{\pi}{5}}\left(\sin\frac{2\pi}{5}\cos\frac{2\pi}{5}\cos\frac{4\pi}{5}\cos\frac{8\pi}{5}\right)$ ($\sin 2A = 2\sin A\cos A$)

$= \frac{1}{4\sin\frac{\pi}{5}}\left(2\sin\frac{2\pi}{5}\cos\frac{2\pi}{5}\cos\frac{4\pi}{5}\cos\frac{8\pi}{5}\right)$ (Multiplying and dividing by 2)

$= \frac{1}{4\sin\frac{\pi}{5}}\left(\sin\frac{4\pi}{5}\cos\frac{4\pi}{5}\cos\frac{8\pi}{5}\right)$

$= \frac{1}{8\sin\frac{\pi}{5}}\left(2\sin\frac{4\pi}{5}\cos\frac{4\pi}{5}\cos\frac{8\pi}{5}\right)$ (Multiplying and dividing by 2)

$= \frac{1}{16\sin\frac{\pi}{5}}\left(2\sin\frac{8\pi}{5}\cos\frac{8\pi}{5}\right)$ (Multiplying and dividing by 2)

$= \frac{\sin\frac{16\pi}{5}}{16\sin\frac{\pi}{5}}$

$= \frac{\sin\left(3\pi+\frac{\pi}{5}\right)}{16\sin\frac{\pi}{5}}$

$= \frac{-\sin\frac{\pi}{5}}{16\sin\frac{\pi}{5}} [\sin(3\pi + \theta) = -\sin\theta]$

$= \frac{-1}{16}$

Hence, the correct option is (D).

22. Given:

$3\hat{\imath} + 4\hat{\jmath} - \hat{k}$ and $-2\hat{\imath} + \lambda\hat{\jmath} + 10\hat{k}$ are perpendicular.

If vectors $\vec{a}$ and $\vec{b}$ are perpendicular then $\vec{a} \cdot \vec{b} = 0$

$\vec{a} \cdot \vec{b} = (3\hat{\imath} + 4\hat{\jmath} - \hat{k}) \cdot (-2\hat{\imath} + \lambda\hat{\jmath} + 10\hat{k}) = -6 + 4\lambda - 10 = 4\lambda - 16$

$\because 3\hat{\imath} + 4\hat{\jmath} - \hat{k}$ and $-2\hat{\imath} + \lambda\hat{\jmath} + 10\hat{k}$ are perpendicular.

$4\lambda - 16 = 0$

$\Rightarrow \lambda = 4$

Hence, the correct option is (C).

23. The point that divides $5\hat{\imath}$ and $5\hat{\jmath}$ in the ratio of $k:1$ is:

By division formula: $\frac{mx_1 + nx_2}{m+n}$

$\Rightarrow \frac{(5\hat{\jmath})k + (5\hat{\imath})\cdot 1}{k+1}$

$\therefore \vec{b} = \frac{5\hat{\imath} + 5k\hat{\jmath}}{k+1}$

also $\left|\vec{b}\right| \leq \sqrt{37}$

$\Rightarrow \frac{1}{k+1}\sqrt{25 + 25k^2} \leq \sqrt{37}$

$\Rightarrow 5\sqrt{1+k^2} \leq \sqrt{37}(k+1)$

Squaring both sides,

$25(1+k^2) \leq 37(k^2 + 2k + 1)$

$\Rightarrow 6k^2 + 37k + 6 \geq 0$

$\Rightarrow (6k+1)(k+6) \geq 0$

$k \in (-\infty, -6) \cup \left[-\frac{1}{6}, \infty\right)$

Hence, the correct option is (B).

24. Given,

$\sqrt{\frac{1+\cos\theta}{1-\cos\theta}}$

$\Rightarrow \sqrt{\frac{1+\cos\theta}{1-\cos\theta}} = \sqrt{\frac{(1+\cos\theta) \times (1+\cos\theta)}{(1-\cos\theta) \times (1+\cos\theta)}}$ (By rationalization)

Mathematics : Mock Test - 4

$\Rightarrow \sqrt{\frac{1+\cos\theta}{1-\cos\theta}} = \sqrt{\frac{(1+\cos\theta)^2}{1-\cos^2\theta}}$

$\Rightarrow \sqrt{\frac{1+\cos\theta}{1-\cos\theta}} = \sqrt{\frac{(1+\cos\theta)^2}{\sin^2\theta}}$ $(\because 1 - \cos^2 x = \sin^2 x)$

$\Rightarrow \sqrt{\frac{1+\cos\theta}{1-\cos\theta}} = \sqrt{\left(\frac{1+\cos\theta}{\sin\theta}\right)^2}$

$\Rightarrow \sqrt{\frac{1+\cos\theta}{1-\cos\theta}} = \frac{1+\cos\theta}{\sin\theta}$

$\Rightarrow \sqrt{\frac{1+\cos\theta}{1-\cos\theta}} = \frac{1}{\sin\theta} + \frac{\cos\theta}{\sin\theta}$

$\Rightarrow \sqrt{\frac{1+\cos\theta}{1-\cos\theta}} = cosec\theta + \cot\theta$ $\left(\because cosec x = \frac{1}{\sin x}, \cot x = \frac{\cos x}{\sin x}\right)$

Hence, the correct option is (B).

25. Given,

$1 + \cot^2\theta$

$= 1 + \frac{\cos^2\theta}{\sin^2\theta}$ $\left(\because \cot\theta = \frac{\cos\theta}{\sin\theta}\right)$

$= \frac{\sin^2\theta + \cos^2\theta}{\sin^2\theta}$ $(\because \sin^2\theta + \cos^2\theta = 1)$

$= \frac{1}{\sin^2\theta}$

$= cosec^2\theta$

Hence, the correct option is (C).

26. Given,

$xdy = ydx + y^2 dy$

$1 = \frac{4}{x} \cdot \frac{dx}{dy} + \frac{y^2}{x}$

$\frac{dx}{dy} + x = \frac{x}{y}$

$\frac{dx}{dy} - \frac{x}{y} = -y$

$P = -\frac{1}{y}, Q = -y$

Integrating factor $= e^{\int P dy} = e^{-\log y} = \frac{1}{y}$

$\frac{1}{y}\frac{dx}{dy} - \frac{x}{y^2} = -1$

Multiply the equation with Integrating factor

$\frac{x}{y} = \int \frac{1}{y}(-y)dy + c$

$\frac{x}{y} = \int -1 dy + C$

$\frac{x}{y} = -y + c$

$y(1) = 1$

$\frac{1}{1} = -1 + c; c = 2$

$\frac{1}{y} = -y + 2; x = -y^2 + 2y$

$y(-3); -3 = -y^2 + 2y$

$y^2 - 2y - 3 = 0$

$y = \frac{+2 \pm \sqrt{4+12}}{2} = \frac{2 \pm 4}{2}$

$y = 3, -1$

$y = 3$, since $y > 0$

Hence, the correct option is (A).

27. $x^2 dy - y^2 dx = xy(x - y)(ydy)$

let $\frac{dy}{dx} = y'$

$x^2 y' - y^2 = xy(x - y)(yy')$

It appears that we need and subtract the terms to manage because u can see on the RHS iyt is obtained by some ln function resulting with terms xy, (x–y)

$x^2 y' - y^2 + xyy' - xyy' + xy - xy = xyy' - xy - y^2 + xy - xyy' + x^2 y' =$

$xy(y' - 1) - (y - x)(y + xy')$

$\int \left[\frac{xy}{x-y} \times \frac{xy(1-y') - (x-y)(y+xy')}{(xy)^2}\right] dx = \int y' dx$

$\ln\left|\frac{x-y}{xy}\right| = \frac{y^2}{2} - c$

Hence, the correct option is (A).

28. Given:

$\lim_{x \to -1} \frac{f(x)+1}{x^2 - 1} = -\frac{3}{2}$

Denominator becomes zero on putting the limits.

∴ The numerator must also be zero to have a certain value of the given limit,

i.e., $\lim_{x \to -1} [f(x) + 1] = 0$

$\lim_{x \to -1} \frac{f(x)+1}{x^2 - 1} = -\frac{3}{2}$

$\Rightarrow \frac{\lim_{x \to -1}(f(x)+1)}{\lim_{x \to -1}(x^2-1)} = \frac{3}{2}$

$\Rightarrow \lim_{x \to -1}(f(x) + 1) = \frac{3}{2}\lim_{x \to -1}(x^2 - 1)$

$\Rightarrow \lim_{x \to -1}(f(x) + 1) = \frac{3}{2}((-1)^2 - 1)$

$\Rightarrow \lim_{x \to -1}(f(x) + 1) = \frac{3}{2} \times 0$

$\Rightarrow \lim_{x \to -1} f(x) + \lim_{x \to -1} 1 = 0$

$\Rightarrow \lim_{x \to -1} f(x) + 1 = 0$

$\therefore \lim_{x \to -1} f(x) = -1$

Hence, the correct option is (B).

29. Total number of ice cream $= 6 + a + b$

Let the ice cream of vanilla flavor be a.

Let the ice cream of blueberry flavor be b.

Probability (Selecting one vanilla ice cream) $= \dfrac{\text{Number of vanilla ice-cream}}{\text{Total ice cream}}$

$\Rightarrow$ Probability (Selecting one vanilla ice cream) $= \dfrac{a}{(6+a+b)}$

$\Rightarrow \dfrac{1}{2} = \dfrac{a}{(6+a+b)}$ ....(i)

Probability (Selecting one blue berry ice cream) $= \dfrac{\text{Number of blue berry ice-cream}}{\text{Total ice cream}}$

$\Rightarrow \dfrac{2}{7} = \dfrac{b}{(6+a+b)}$ ... (ii)

Solving equation (i) and (ii), we get

$\Rightarrow a = 14$ and $b = 8$

$\Rightarrow$ Total number of ice cream $= 6 + 14 + 8 = 28$

$\therefore$ Total number of ice cream in the trunk is 28.

Hence, the correct option is (C).

30. Let, $f(x) = 3x^4 - 8x^3 + 12x^2 - 48x + 1$ be a function defined on the interval $[1,4]$.

First we have to find $f'(x)$

$f'(x) = 12x^3 - 24x^2 + 24x - 48$

Now let's find the roots of the equation $f'(x) = 0$ $12x^3 - 24x^2 + 24x - 48 = 0 \Rightarrow 12 \cdot (x^3 - 2x^2 + 2x - 4) = 0 \Rightarrow 12 \cdot (x^2 + 2) \cdot (x - 2) = 0 \Rightarrow x - 2 = 0$ $[\because (x^2 + 2) \neq 0$ as we are dealing with real valued functions] $\Rightarrow x = 2$

Now let's find out $f''(x)$ i.e., $\dfrac{d^2(f(x))}{dx^2}$

$f''(x) = 36x^2 - 48x + 24$

Now evaluate the value of $f''(x)$ at $x = 2$, we get:

$f''(2) = 72 > 0$

As we know that according to second derivative test if $f''(c) > 0$ then $x = c$ is a point of local minima

So, $x = 2$ is a point of local minima

So $f(2) = -63$

Let's calculate $f(0)$ and $f(3)$

$f(0) = 1$ and $f(3) = -8$

As we know that if a function is defined in the closed interval $[a, b]$ then the minimum value of $f(x)$ on $[a, b]$ is the smallest of $m, f(a)$ and $f(b)$.

So, the minimum value of the given function on the interval $[0,3]$ is -63.

Hence, the correct option is (D).

31. Given: $f(x) = \log(\sin x)$

Let's examine the function $f(x)$ on the interval $\left(0, \dfrac{\pi}{2}\right)$

So, first let's calculate $f'(x)$

$f'(x) = \dfrac{1}{\sin x} \cdot \dfrac{d(\sin x)}{dx} = \cot x$

As we know that $\cot x > 0 \forall x \in \left(0, \dfrac{\pi}{2}\right)$

$f'(x) > 0 \forall x \in \left(0, \dfrac{\pi}{2}\right)$

As we know that for a strictly increasing function $f'(x) > 0$ for all $x \in (a, b)$ So, the given function $f(x)$ is a strictly increasing function on $\left(0, \dfrac{\pi}{2}\right)$

$\therefore$ Option (A) is true

Now let's the function $f(x)$ on the interval $\left(0, \dfrac{\pi}{2}\right)$

As we know that, $f'(x) = \cot x$ and $\cot x < 0 \forall x \in \left(0, \dfrac{\pi}{2}\right)$

$f'(x) < 0 \forall x \in \left(0, \dfrac{\pi}{2}\right)$

As we know that for a strictly decreasing function $f'(x) < 0$ for all $x \in (a, b)$ So, the given function $f(x)$ is a strictly decreasing function on $\left(\dfrac{\pi}{2}, \pi\right)$

$\therefore$ Option (B) is true.

Hence, the correct option is (D).

32. The slope of the tangent to the curve:

The slope of curve $y = f(x)$ at some point $P(x_1, y_1)$ means the slope of the tangent to the curve at $P(x_1, y_1)$.

The slope is given as m, where $m = \dfrac{dy}{dx}$ at (x_1, y_1).

Given: $2x^3 + 3y = 2y^3 + 3x$

Differentiating with respect to x

$2(3x^2) + 3\dfrac{dy}{dx} = 2\left(3y^2 \dfrac{dy}{dx}\right) + 3(1)$

$6x^2 + 3\frac{dy}{dx} = 6y^2\frac{dy}{dx} + 3$

Taking $\frac{dy}{dx}$ on one side, we get:

$6x^2 - 3 = (6y^2 - 3)\frac{dy}{dx}$

$\frac{dy}{dx} = \frac{6x^2-3}{6y^2-3}$

Hence, the correct option is (B).

33. Given:

The circumference of a circle is 66 cm.

Circumference of circle $= 2\pi r$

According to the question:

$66 = 2\pi r$

$r = 10.5$cm

Hence, the correct option is (B).

34. $I = \int_0^{\frac{\pi}{2}} \frac{(\sin x+\cos x)^2}{\sqrt{1+\sin 2x}} dx$

$= \int_0^{\frac{\pi}{2}} \frac{(\sin x+\cos x)^2}{\sqrt{(\sin x+\cos x)^2}} dx$,

$\sin 2x = 2\sin x.\cos x, \sin^2 x + \cos^2 x = 1$

$= \int_0^{\frac{\pi}{2}} \frac{(\sin x+\cos x)^2}{\sin x+\cos x} dx$

$= \int_0^{\frac{\pi}{2}} (\sin x + \cos x) dx$

$= \int_0^{\frac{\pi}{2}} \sin x\, dx + \int_0^{\frac{\pi}{2}} \cos x\, dx$

$= \cos x \big|_0^{\frac{\pi}{2}} - \sin x \big|_0^{\frac{\pi}{2}}$

$= \left(\cos(0) - \cos\left(\frac{\pi}{2}\right)\right) + \left(\sin\left(\frac{\pi}{2}\right) - \sin(0)\right)$

$= 2$

Hence, the correct option is (C).

35. $I = \int \frac{e^x}{e^{2x}+1} dx$

Let, $e^x = t \Rightarrow e^x dx = dt$

$I = \int \frac{1}{t^2+1} dt = \tan^{-1}t + c$

$= \tan^{-1}e^x + c$

Hence, the correct option is (C).

36. $\int \frac{1}{x^2}(2x+1)^3 dx = \int \frac{(8x^3+1+12x^2+6x)}{x^2} dx$

$= \int \left(8x + 12 + \frac{6}{x} + \frac{1}{x^2}\right) dx$

$= 4x^2 + 12x + 6\log x - \frac{1}{x} + c$

Hence, the correct option is (A).

37. A binomial distribution is a common probability distribution that occurs in practice. It arises in the following situation:

- There are n independent trials.
- Each trial results in a "success" or "failure"
- The probability of success in each and every trial is equal to 'p'.

If the random variable X counts the number of successes in the n trials, then X has a binomial distribution with parameters n and p.

Properties of Binomial distribution:

If $X \sim$ Bin (n, p), then the probability mass function of the binomial distribution is

$f(x) = P(X = x) = {}^nC_r p^x(1-p)^{n-x}$

for $x = 0,1,2,3,...,n$

Mean $E(X) = \mu = np$.

Variance $(\sigma^2) = np(1-p)$

- ${}^nC_r = \frac{n!}{x!(n-x)!}$
- $\sum_{x=0}^{n} {}^nC_r p^x(1-p)^{n-x} = 1$

Let $X_1, X_2, ..., X_m$ be independent random variables such that X_i has a BIn (n_i, p) distribution, for $i = 1,2,...,m$. Let

$Y = \sum_{i=1}^{m} X_i$

Then, $Y \sim Bin(\sum_{i=1}^{m} n_i, p)$.

Hence, the correct option is (D).

38. We know Binomial distribution is:

$(q+p)^n = \sum n_{C_r} q^n p^{n-r}$

where $p + q = 1$

p is the probability of getting success and q is the probability of failure

- Mean of Binomial distribution is np
- Variance is npq.
- Standard deviation is given by the square root of the variance, as:

$S.D. = \sqrt{Variance} = \sqrt{npq}$

Hence, the correct option is (A).

39. Given:

$(1 + 4x + 4x^2)^5$

As we know,

$(a+b)^2 = (a^2 + b^2 + 2ab)$

$(1 + 4x + 4x^2) = [(1 + 2x)^2]^5$
$= (1 + 2x)^{2 \times 5}$
$= (1 + 2x)^{10}$

For Middle term: $r = \frac{10}{2} = 5$

As we know,

$^nC_r(p)^n(q)^{n-r}$

After putting the value,

$p = 1, q = 2x, r = 5$

Middle Term $= {}^{10}C_5 (1)^{10} (2x)^5$

$= \frac{10!}{5!5!} \times 32x^5$

$= \frac{10 \times 9 \times 8 \times 7 \times 6 \times 5!}{5! \times 5!}$

$= \frac{10 \times 9 \times 8 \times 7 \times 6}{5 \times 4 \times 3 \times 2!}$

$= 36 \times 7 \times 32x^5$

$= 252 \times 32x^5$

$= 8064x^5$

∴ The coefficient of the middle term in the expansion of $(1 + 4x + 4x^2)^5$ is 8064

Hence, the correct option is (A).

40. Concept:

If the equation of a line is $\frac{x-x_1}{a_1} = \frac{y-y_1}{b_1} = \frac{z-z_1}{c_1}$ and the equation of the plane is $a_2x + b_2y + c_2z + d = 0$

Then the angle between line and plane can be obtained by:

$\sin\theta = \left|\frac{a_1a_2 + b_2b_2 + c_1c_2}{\sqrt{a_1^2+b_1^2+c_1^2}\sqrt{a_2^2+b_2^2+c_2^2}}\right|$, Where (a_1, b_1, c_1) and (a_2, b_2, c_2) are d.r's of line and normal to the plane.

Given:

$\frac{x+1}{1} = \frac{y-1}{2} = \frac{z-2}{2}$

Direction ratio of line $= (1, 2, 2)$

Equation of plane is $2x - y + \sqrt{\lambda}z + 4 = 0$

Direction ratio of normal to the plane $= (2, -1, \sqrt{\lambda})$

$\sin\theta = \frac{1}{3}$

Now,

$\sin\theta = \left|\frac{1 \times 2 + 2 \times -1 + 2 \times \sqrt{\lambda}}{\sqrt{1^2+2^2+2^2}\sqrt{2^2+(-1)^2+(\sqrt{\lambda})^2}}\right|$

$\Rightarrow \frac{1}{3} = \left|\frac{2\sqrt{\lambda}}{3 \times \sqrt{5+\lambda}}\right|$

$\Rightarrow |\sqrt{5+\lambda}| = |2\sqrt{\lambda}|$

Squaring both sides, we get

$\Rightarrow 5 + \lambda = 4\lambda$

$\Rightarrow 3\lambda = 5$

$\therefore \lambda = \frac{5}{3}$

Hence, the correct option is (D).

41. Since $f(x)$ is given to be continuous at $x = 0$,

$\lim_{x \to 0} f(x) = f(0)$

Also, $\lim_{x \to a^+} f(x) = \lim_{x \to a^-} f(x)$ because $f(x)$ is same for $x > 0$ and $x < 0$.

$\therefore \lim_{x \to 0} f(x) = f(0)$

We know that,

$\lim_{x \to 0} \frac{\sin x}{x} = 1$

$\lim_{x \to 0} \frac{e^x - 1}{x} = 1$

Therefore,

$\lim_{x \to 0} \frac{\sin 3x}{e^{2x} - 1} = k - 2$

Multiplying and dividing by $3x$ in numerator and by $2x$ in denominator,

We get,

$\lim_{x \to 0} \frac{\frac{\sin 3x}{3x} \times 3x}{\frac{e^{2x}-1}{2x} \times 2x} = k - 2$

$\Rightarrow \frac{3}{2} = k - 2$

$\Rightarrow k = \frac{7}{2}$

Hence, the correct option is (D).

42. Given:

$g(x) = \int f(x)dx$

$f(x) = e^{-x-e^{-x}}$

$g(x) = \int e^{-x-e^{-x}} dx$

$= \int \frac{e^{-x}}{e^{c-x}} dx$

Substitute $e^{-x} = t$

$-e^{-x} dx = dt$

$g(x) = \int -\frac{dt}{e^t}$

$= \int -e^{-t} dt$

$g(x) = e^{-t}$

$g(x) = e^{-e^{-x}}$

Hence, the correct option is (B).

43. Given Integral:

$\int e^{\sin^{-1}x} \frac{1}{\sqrt{1-x^2}} dx$

Let, $\sin^{-1}x = t \Rightarrow \frac{1}{\sqrt{1-x^2}} dx = dt$ as we know the derivative of $\sin^{-1}x = \frac{1}{\sqrt{1-x^2}}$

Now the equation reduces to

$\int e^t dt \Rightarrow$ we know $\int e^x dx = e^x + c$

$\therefore \int e^t dt = e^t + c$, as $t = \sin^{-1}x$ our equation becomes $e^{\sin^{-1}x} + c$

$\therefore \int e^{\sin^{-1}x} \frac{1}{\sqrt{1-x^2}} dx = e^{\sin^{-1}x} + c$

Hence, the correct option is (C).

44. Concept:

For Integration with modulus, first we have to find the point where the sign of the value of the function gets change.

Given:

$\int_0^1 |5x - 3| dx$

$f(x) = 5x - 3 = 0$

$x = \frac{3}{5}$

$\therefore$ from 0 to $\frac{3}{5}$ the function is negative and $\frac{3}{5}$ to 1 the function is positive.

$\int_0^1 |5x - 3| dx = -\int_0^{\frac{3}{5}}(5x - 3) dx + \int_{\frac{3}{5}}^1 (5x - 3) dx$

$= \left(-\frac{5}{2}x^2 + 3x\right)_0^{\frac{3}{5}} + \left(\frac{5x^2}{2} - 3x\right)_{\frac{3}{5}}^1$

$= \left(-\frac{9}{10} + \frac{9}{5}\right) + \left[\left(\frac{5}{2} - 3\right) - \left(\frac{9}{10} - \frac{9}{5}\right)\right]$

$= \frac{9}{10} + \left(\frac{-1}{2} + \frac{9}{10}\right) = \frac{13}{10}$

Hence, the correct option is (B).

45. Here, $m_1 = m_2^2 \Rightarrow m_2^2 + m_2 = \frac{-2h}{b}$ ... (i)

And,

$m_2^2 m_2 = \frac{a}{b} \Rightarrow m_2 = \left(\frac{a}{b}\right)^{\frac{1}{3}}$ ... (ii)

Putting this value of m² in equation (i), we get

$\left\{\left(\frac{a}{b}\right)^{\frac{1}{3}}\right\}^2 + \left(\frac{a}{b}\right)^{\frac{1}{3}} = \frac{-2h}{b}$

On cubing both sides, we get,

$\left(\frac{a}{b}\right)^2 + \frac{a}{b} + 3\left(\frac{a}{b}\right)^{\frac{2}{3}} \cdot \left(\frac{a}{b}\right)^{\frac{1}{3}} \cdot \left\{\left(\frac{a}{b}\right)^{\frac{2}{3}} + \left(\frac{a}{b}\right)^{\frac{1}{3}}\right\} = \frac{-8h^3}{b^3}$

$\left(\frac{a}{b}\right)^2 + \frac{a}{b} - \frac{6ah}{b^2} = \frac{-8h^3}{b^3}$

$\left\{\because \left(\frac{a}{b}\right)^{\frac{2}{3}} + \left(\frac{a}{b}\right)^{\frac{1}{3}} = \frac{-2h}{b}\right\}$

$ab(a + b) - 6abh + 8h^3 = 0$.

Hence, the correct option is (A).

46. Given,

$\lim_{x \to 2} \frac{\sin(e^{x-2}-1)}{\log(x-1)}$ ...... (i)

We know that,

$\lim_{x \to a^-} f(x) = \lim_{x \to a^+} f(x) = l = \lim_{x \to a} f(x)$

On substituting, $h = x - 2$ in (i),

We get,

$\lim_{h \to 0} \frac{\sin(e^h - 1)}{\log(1+h)}$

This can be rearranged as,

$= \lim_{h \to 0} \frac{\sin(e^h - 1)}{e^h - 1} \cdot \frac{e^h - 1}{h} \cdot \frac{h}{\log(1+h)}$

$= 1 \cdot 1 \cdot 1$

$= 1$

And, $f(2) = k$

And, $f(2) = k$

$\therefore$ For the function to be continuous the value of the function $f(x)$ at $x = 2$ must equal the limiting value of 1, i.e., $k = 1$

Hence, the correct option is (D).

47. Option 1: $\forall x \exists y R(x,y) \mapsto \exists y \forall x R(x,y)$

$\forall x \exists y R(x,y)$ is not equivalent to $\exists y \forall x R(x,y)$.

Let $R(x,y)$ represent $x > x$ for the set of numbers as the universe

Example:

$\forall x \exists y R(x,y)$ means for every number x, there exist a number y that is less than x which is true.

While $\exists y \forall x R(x,y)$ means there is a number that is less than every number. Which is false

Onption 2: $(\forall x (\exists y R(x,y) \to S(x,y)]) \to \forall x \exists y S(x,y)$

This option is not a tautology. It is a false expression because two predicates can't be equivalent to single predicate on right side.

Qtion 4: $\forall x \forall y P(x,y) \to \forall x \forall y P(y,x)$

Consider $P(x,y)$ as $x < y$

then $\forall x \forall y P(x,y)$ represents for every number x, all y are greater than x.

$\forall x \forall y P(y,x)$, it means for every number y, there is every x which is greater than y.

These two statements are not equivalent at the same time. So, it is not a tautology.

Option 3:

$[\forall x \exists y (P(x,y) \to R(x,y)] \mapsto [\forall x \exists y (\neg P(x,y) \lor R(x,y)]$

As, we know that $P \to R = \neg P + R$

Here, it is the same statement as that of implication, so it is a tautology.

Hence, the correct option is (C).

48. Concept:

Hypothetical syllogism,

If $p \to q$ and $q \to r$ then $p \to r$

Formula:

$p \to q \equiv \neg q \to \neg p \equiv \neg p \lor q$

C(x): x is known to be corrupt

E(x): x will be elected

K(x): x is kind

Statement S1 can be written as:

$S1 \equiv C(x) \to \neg E(x)$

S2 can be written as:

$S2 \equiv K(x) \to E(x) \equiv \neg E(x) \to \neg K(x)$

By using hypothetical syllogism,

From S1 and S2, the conclusion is

$C(x) \to \neg K(x) \equiv K(x) \to \neg C(x)$

If a person is kind, then he is not known to be corrupt.

Hence, the correct option is (C).

49. Derivative of $g_x(z)$ at $z = 1$ gives the expectation $E(X)$.

When $gy(z)$ is expanded, it results in a binomial distribution form and mean of a binomial distribution is in the form of $N \times p$.

$g_x(z) = \sum_{j=0}^{N} p_j z^j$

$g'_x(z) = \sum_{j=1}^{N} j p_j z^{j-1} = \sum_{j=1}^{N} j p_j = E(X)$

Similarly, take the derivate of $g_y(z)$ at $z=1$.

$E(Y) = g'_y(z)\big|_{z=1}$

$= ((1 - \beta + \beta z)^N)'\big|_{z=1}$

$= N\beta(1 - \beta + \beta z)^{N-1}\big|_{z=1}$

$= N\beta(1 - \beta + \beta z)^{N-1}$

$E(Y) = N\beta$

Hence, the correct option is (B).

50. Given:

Probability mass function $= (1-p)^{k-1} p$

Concept:

Mode is the value of x for which $f(x)$ is the maximum. It can be obtained by equating the first derivative of $f(x)$ to zero and checking that the second derivative of $f(x)$ is negative i.e. $f'(x) = 0$ and $f''(x) < 0$

Calculation:

This Probability mass function is in geometric expression and the mode of geometric distribution is 1.

∴ Mode of x is 1.

Hence, the correct option is (A).

Mathematics : Mock Test 05

Q.1 What is the number of different messages that can be represented by three a's and two b's?

A. 7   B. 8   C. 9   D. 10

Q.2 A box contains 100 round discs, 50 square-shaped discs and 30 triangular discs. All the discs are made up of iron and have an equal probability of getting attracted by a magnet. If a magnet which can attract only one disc in one pass and the disc is passed over them twice. What is the probability that both times a triangular disc is attracted? The disc attracted in one pass does not fall into box again, however each time a square shaped disc is kept into the box.

A. $\frac{29}{180}$ B. $\frac{29}{1074}$ C. $\frac{1}{36}$ D. $\frac{29}{1080}$

Q.3 Order of $\begin{bmatrix} 2 & 7 & 4 \\ 3 & 1 & 0 \end{bmatrix} \begin{bmatrix} 5 \\ 4 \\ 3 \end{bmatrix}$ is:

A. 3×1   B. 2×1   C. 2×3   D. 3×3

Q.4 If $\begin{bmatrix} 2x+y & 4x \\ 5x-7 & 4x \end{bmatrix} = \begin{bmatrix} 7 & 7y-13 \\ y & x+6 \end{bmatrix}$, then $x + y =$

A. 3   B. 4   C. 5   D. 6

Q.5 Find the value of $y - x$ from the following equation:
$2\begin{bmatrix} x & 5 \\ 7 & y-3 \end{bmatrix} + \begin{bmatrix} 3 & -4 \\ 1 & 2 \end{bmatrix} = \begin{bmatrix} 7 & 6 \\ 15 & 14 \end{bmatrix}$

A. 7   B. -7   C. 6   D. -6

Q.6 In this figure PQ ⊥ RS and RT ∥ PQ. if ∠PST = 68° then find reflexive ∠RTS.

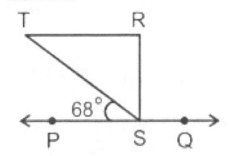

A. 134°   B. 292°   C. 234°   D. 102°

Q.7 The solution of differential equation $dy = (4 + y^2)dx$ is:

A. $y = 2\tan(x + C)$
B. $y = 2\tan(2x + C)$
C. $2y = \tan(2x + C)$
D. $2y = 2\tan(x + C)$

Q.8 The differential form of the equation $y^2 + (x-b)^2 = c$:

A. $y\frac{d^2y}{dx^2} + \left(\frac{dy}{dx}\right)^2 - 1 = 0$

B. $y\frac{d^2y}{dx^2} + \frac{dy}{dx} + 1 = 0$

C. $y\frac{d^2y}{dx^2} + \left(\frac{dy}{dx}\right)^2 + 1 = 0$

D. $\frac{d^2y}{dx^2} + \left(\frac{dy}{dx}\right)^2 - 1 = 0$

Q.9 The solution of the differential equation $\frac{dy}{dx} = \sec\left(\frac{y}{x}\right) + \frac{y}{x}$ is:

A. $\cos\left(\frac{y}{x}\right) = \log(cx)$
B. $\sin\left(\frac{x}{y}\right) = \log(cx)$
C. $\sin\left(\frac{y}{x}\right) = \log(cx)$
D. None of these

Q.10 In a binomial distribution, the mean is $\frac{2}{3}$ and variance is $\frac{5}{9}$. What is the probability that random variable $D = 2$?

[UPSC NDA, 2021]

A. $\frac{5}{36}$ B. $\frac{25}{36}$ C. $\frac{25}{54}$ D. $\frac{25}{216}$

Q.11 Let the random variables X follow $B(6, p)$ If $16P(X = 4) = P(X = 2)$, then what is the value of p:

A. $\frac{1}{3}$ B. $\frac{1}{4}$ C. $\frac{1}{5}$ D. $\frac{1}{6}$

Q.12 A binomial distribution has a mean of 5 and variance 4. The number of trials is:

A. 18   B. 17   C. 25   D. 27

Q.13 Graphic location of mode is done with reference to:

A. Cumulative frequency curve
B. Frequency Polygon
C. Frequency Curve
D. Histogram

Q.14 If $\lim_{x \to \infty}\left(\frac{x^2+x+1}{x+1} - px - q\right) = -3$, then p and q is:

A. p = 1, q = 3   B. p = 2, q = 3
C. p = 3, q = 1   D. p = 3, q = 2

Q.15 What is the area of the parabola $x^2 = y$ bounded by the line $y = 1$?

A. $\frac{1}{3}$ square unit   B. $\frac{2}{3}$ square unit
C. $\frac{4}{3}$ square units   D. 2 square units

Q.16 What is the area of the parabola $y^2 = x$ bounded by its latus rectum?

A. $\frac{1}{12}$ sq. unit   B. $\frac{1}{6}$ sq. unit
C. $\frac{1}{3}$ sq. unit   D. $\frac{1}{15}$ sq. unit

Q.17 The area of the region bounded by the curve $y = x^2$ and the line $y = 16$ is:

A. $\frac{32}{3}$ sq.units   B. $\frac{256}{3}$ sq.units

Mathematics : Mock Test - 5

C. $\frac{64}{3}$ sq.units **D.** $\frac{128}{3}$ sq.units

Q.18 The total number of subsets of a finite set A has 56 more elements than the total number of subsets of another finite set B. What is the number of elements in set A?

[BITSAT, 2014]

A. 5 **B.** 6 **C.** 7 **D.** 8

Q.19 Find $\frac{z_1}{z_2}$, when $z_1 = 6 + 2i$ and $z_2 = 2 - i$.

A. $(1+i)$ **B.** $2(1+i)$ **C.** $2+i$ **D.** $(1-i)$

Q.20 Maximam value of : $Z = 10x + 25$ y Subject to : $x \leq 3, y \leq 3, x + y \leq 5, x \geq 0, y \geq 0$ at:

A. 95 **B.** 90 **C.** 85 **D.** 80

Q.21 Solve the following using graphical method:
Minimize: $Z = 3x + 5$ y subject to $2x + 3y \geq 12, -x + y \leq 3, x \leq 4, y \geq 3, x \geq 0, y \geq 0$.

A. $-\frac{93}{2}$ **B.** $\frac{93}{2}$ **C.** $-\frac{39}{2}$ **D.** $\frac{39}{2}$

Q.22 Solve the linear programming problem by graphical method:
Minimize $Z = 3x + 2y$ Subject to the constraints $x + y \geq 8, 3x + 5y \leq 15$ and $x \geq 0, y \leq 15$.

A. 1 common region **B.** 0 common region
C. 3 common region **D.** 2 common region

Q.23 The angle between the lines $x + y - 3 = 0$ and $x - y + 3 = 0$ is α and the acute angle between the lines $x - \sqrt{3}y + 2\sqrt{3} = 0$ and $\sqrt{3}x - y + 1 = 0$ is β. Which one of the following is correct?

A. $\alpha = \beta$ **B.** $\alpha > \beta$ **C.** $\alpha < \beta$ **D.** $\alpha = 2\beta$

Q.24 The equation of the locus of a point equidistant from the point A(1, 3) and B(-2, 1) is:

A. $6x - 4y = 5$ **B.** $6x + 4y = 5$
C. $6x + 4y = 7$ **D.** $6x - 4y = 7$

Q.25 Find the equation of the line passing through $(-3,5)$ and perpendicular to the line through the points $(2,5)(-3,6)$.

A. $x + y + 20 = 0$ **B.** $x - y + 20 = 0$
C. $x + 5y + 20 = 0$ **D.** $5x - y + 20 = 0$

Q.26 A line passes through $(1,1)$ and is perpendicular to the line $3x + y = 7$. Its x-intercept is:

A. -2 **B.** 2 **C.** $\frac{2}{3}$ **D.** $\frac{-2}{3}$

Q.27 Cards numbered from 107 to 1006 are put in a bag. A card is drawn from it at random. Find the probability that the number on the card is not divisible both by 11 and 37?

A. 0.988 **B.** 0.998 **C.** 0.978 **D.** 0.968

Q.28 It is known from past experience that in a certain plant there are on the average 4 industrial accidents per month.

Find the probability that there will be less than 4 accidents in a given month. Given: $(e^{-4} = 0.0183)$

A. 0.423 **B.** 0.433 **C.** 0.443 **D.** 0.453

Q.29 In the following trigonometry expression, find the value of (MN).

$\frac{(1+\cos x)}{(1-\sin x)}(\sin x + \cos x - 1)^2 = M\sin^N x$

A. 3 **B.** 6 **C.** 4 **D.** 2

Q.30 If $\vec{a} = \hat{\imath} + 2\hat{\jmath} - 3\hat{k}, \vec{b} = 3\hat{\imath} - \hat{\jmath} + 2\hat{k}$ then the angle between $\vec{a} + \vec{b}, \vec{a} - \vec{b}$ is:

A. 0° **B.** 180° **C.** 90° **D.** $-180°$

Q.31 Let $\vec{a} = a_1\hat{\imath} + a_2\hat{\jmath} + a_3\hat{k}, \vec{b} = b_1\hat{\imath} + b_2\hat{\jmath} + b_3\hat{k}$ be three non-zero vectors such that $\vec{c}$ is a vector perpendicular to both $\vec{a}$ and $\vec{b}$. If the angle between $\vec{a}$ and $\vec{b}$ is $\frac{\pi}{6}$ then $\begin{vmatrix} a_1 & b_1 & c_1 \\ a_2 & b_2 & c_2 \\ a_3 & b_3 & c_3 \end{vmatrix} = ?$

A. 0
B. 1
C. $\frac{1}{4}(a_1^2 + a_2^2 + a_3^2)(b_1^2 + b_2^2 + b_3^2)$
D. $\frac{3}{4}(a_1^2 + a_2^2 + a_3^2)(b_1^2 + b_2^2 + b_3^2)(c_1^2 + c_2^2 + c_3^2)$

Q.32 The value of the $\sin 1° + \sin 2° + \cdots + \sin 359°$ is equal to:

A. 180 **B.** -1 **C.** 1 **D.** 0

Q.33 Value of $\cos(-1230°) \times \cot(-315°)$ is:

A. $\frac{-\sqrt{3}}{2}$ **B.** $\frac{2}{\sqrt{3}}$ **C.** $\frac{1}{2}$ **D.** $-\frac{1}{2}$

Q.34 If $\sin x + \sin 3x + \sin 5x = 0$, then the solution is:

A. $x = \frac{2n\pi}{3}, n \epsilon I$ **B.** $\frac{n\pi}{3}, n \epsilon I$
C. $(3n \pm 1)\frac{\pi}{3} n \epsilon I$ **D.** None of these

Q.35 The value of k which makes $f(x) = \begin{cases} \sin x, x \neq 0 \\ k, x = 0 \end{cases}$ continuous at $x = 0$, is:

A. 2 **B.** 1 **C.** -1 **D.** 0

Q.36 If, $y = 9\sqrt{x + \sqrt{x + \sqrt{x + \ldots \infty}}}$ find $\left(\frac{dy}{dx}\right)$ at a point where y = 3.

A. 3 **B.** -3 **C.** -6 **D.** -9

Q.37 Consider the following statements:

1. If $y = \ln(\sec x + \tan x)$, then $\frac{dy}{dx} = \sec x$.

2. If $y = \ln(\csc x - \cot x)$, then $\frac{dy}{dx} = \csc x$.

Which of the above is / are correct?

A. 1 only **B.** 2 only

C. Both 1 and 2   D. Neither 1 nor 2

Q.38 If the line $y = 4x + c$ is a tangent to the circle $x^2 + y^2 = 9$ then find the value possible values of c?
A. $\pm 3\sqrt{17}$
B. $\pm 2\sqrt{17}$
C. $\pm 5\sqrt{17}$
D. None of these

Q.39 Find the equation of tangent of $y = x^2$ at $x = 1$
A. $y = 2x - 1$
B. $y = 2x + 1$
C. $y = x - 1$
D. $y = x + 1$

Q.40 Find the approximate value of $f(3.01)$, where $f(x) = 3x^2 + 3$.
A. 30.18   B. 30.018   C. 30.28   D. 30.08

Q.41 A circle with center $(4, -5)$ is tangent to the y-axis in the standard (x, y) coordinate plane. What is the radius of this circle?
A. 4   B. 5   C. $\sqrt{41}$ D. 16

Q.42 What is the value of $\int_4^9 \frac{1}{\sqrt{x}} dx$?
A. 1   B. -2 C. 2   D. -1

Q.43 What is $\int_1^e x \ln x \, dx$ equal to?
A. $\frac{e+1}{4}$
B. $\frac{e^2+1}{4}$
C. $\frac{e-1}{4}$
D. $\frac{e^2-1}{4}$

Q.44 Find $\int_0^2 (x^2 + 1) \, dx$ as the limit of a sum :
A. $\frac{4}{3}$
B. $\frac{14}{3}$
C. $\frac{14}{5}$
D. None of these

Q.45 What is $\int \frac{dx}{x \ln x}$ equal to?
Where c is the constant of integration.
A. $\ln(\ln x) + c$
B. $\ln x + c$
C. $(\ln x)^2 + c$
D. None of the above

Q.46 What is $\int_0^a \frac{f(a-x)}{f(x)+f(a-x)} dx$ equal to?
[UPSC NDA, 2021]
A. a   B. 2a   C. 0   D. $\frac{a}{2}$

Q.47 Evaluate $\int x \ln x \, dx$.
A. $\frac{x^2}{2} \ln x - x \ln x + 2x - C$
B. $\frac{x^2}{2} \ln x + x \ln x + x + C$
C. $\frac{x^2}{2} \ln x - x \ln x - x + C$
D. $\frac{x^2}{2} \ln x - \frac{x^2}{4} + C$

Q.48 Direction: Below given a question and three statements numbered I, II and III. You have to decide whether the data provided in the statements are sufficient to answer the question. Read all the statements and give answer:
A person can purchase three articles in Rs. 49. What is the price of costliest article?

Statement I: The cost price of two articles each is Rs. 1 less than the cost price of costliest article.
Statement II: The cost price of two articles is same.
Statement III: The cost price of costliest article is 6.25% more than the cost price of cheapest article.

A. Either statement I alone or statements II and III together are sufficient.
B. Only statement III is sufficient.
C. Only statement I and II together are sufficient.
D. Only statement I and III together are sufficient.

Q.49 Direction: Below given a question and three statements numbered I, II and III. You have to decide whether the data provided in the statements are sufficient to answer the question. Read all the statements and give answer:
A metal block of density 'D' and mass 'M', in the form of a cuboid, is beaten into a thin square sheet of thickness 't', and rolled to form a cylinder of the same thickness. Find the inner radius of the cylinder –

Statement I: Cuboid has dimensions 10cm x 5 cm x 12 cm
Statement II: Thickness 't' = 1.5cm
Statement III: Mass of block, M = 216kg

A. Either statement III alone or statements I and II together are sufficient.
B. Only statement III is sufficient.
C. Statement I and Statement II together are sufficient.
D. Only statement I, II, and III together are sufficient.

Q.50 Find the value of m for which the line $\vec{r} = (\hat{i} + 2\hat{k}) + \lambda(2\hat{i} - m\hat{j} - 3\hat{k})$ is parallel to the plane $\vec{r} \cdot (m\hat{i} + 3\hat{j} + \hat{k}) = 4$?
A. 2   B. -2   C. 3   D. -3

// Smart Answer Sheet //

Correct — Indicates percentage of students who answered questions correctly.

Skipped — Indicates percentage of students who skipped questions.

Q.	Ans.	Correct / Skipped	Q.	Ans.	Correct / Skipped	Q.	Ans.	Correct / Skipped	Q.	Ans.	Correct / Skipped	Q.	Ans.	Correct / Skipped
1	D	47.83 % / 4.34 %	11	C	52.17 % / 4.35 %	21	D	34.78 % / 4.35 %	31	C	43.48 % / 4.35 %	41	A	43.48 % / 4.35 %
2	D	21.74 % / 4.35 %	12	C	69.57 % / 4.34 %	22	B	56.52 % / 0.0 %	32	D	65.22 % / 4.35 %	42	C	78.26 % / 4.35 %
3	B	86.96 % / 4.34 %	13	D	34.78 % / 4.35 %	23	B	47.83 % / 4.34 %	33	A	60.87 % / 4.35 %	43	B	52.17 % / 4.35 %
4	C	82.61 % / 4.35 %	14	A	39.13 % / 4.35 %	24	B	56.52 % / 4.35 %	34	D	21.74 % / 4.35 %	44	C	0 % / 100 %
5	A	78.26 % / 4.35 %	15	C	26.09 % / 4.34 %	25	D	56.52 % / 4.35 %	35	D	47.83 % / 4.34 %	45	A	69.57 % / 4.34 %
6	B	52.17 % / 4.35 %	16	B	43.48 % / 4.35 %	26	A	39.13 % / 4.35 %	36	B	47.83 % / 4.34 %	46	D	34.78 % / 4.35 %
7	B	65.22 % / 4.35 %	17	B	39.13 % / 4.35 %	27	B	52.17 % / 4.35 %	37	C	52.17 % / 4.35 %	47	D	65.22 % / 4.35 %
8	C	56.52 % / 4.35 %	18	B	52.17 % / 4.35 %	28	B	39.13 % / 4.35 %	38	A	56.52 % / 4.35 %	48	A	34.78 % / 4.35 %
9	C	21.74 % / 4.35 %	19	B	82.61 % / 4.35 %	29	C	39.13 % / 4.35 %	39	A	78.26 % / 4.35 %	49	C	34.78 % / 4.35 %
10	D	39.13 % / 4.35 %	20	A	73.91 % / 4.35 %	30	C	65.22 % / 4.35 %	40	A	56.52 % / 4.35 %	50	D	39.13 % / 4.35 %

Performance Analysis	
Avg. Score (%)	45.0%
Toppers Score (%)	92.0%
Your Score	

Mathematics : Mock Test - 5

//Hints and Solutions//

1. We know that:

Suppose a set of n objects has n_1 of one kind of object, n_2 of a second kind, n_3 of a third kind, and,

So, on with $n = n_1 + n_2 + n_3 + \cdots + n_k$ then the number of distinguishable permutations of the n objects is:

$$= \frac{n!}{n_1! \times n_2! \times n_3! \ldots \ldots n_k!}$$

Given: Three a's and two b's

| a | a | a | b | b |

Total number $= 3 + 2 = 5$

In the set of 5 words has 3 words of one kind and 2 words of the second kind.

Therefore, number of different messages that can be represented by three a's and two b's,

$$= \frac{5!}{3! 2!} = 10$$

Hence, the correct option is (D).

2. Given:

A box contains 100 round discs, 50 square-shaped discs and 30 triangular discs.

$$\text{Probability} = \frac{\text{Number of observation}}{\text{Total number of observation}}$$

Total number of discs $= 180$

Total number of triangular discs $= 30$

The probability that in first pass a triangular disc is attracted $= \frac{30}{180}$

$$= \frac{1}{6}$$

The first disc is kept aside and one square disc is kept inside.

The probability that in second pass a triangular disc is attracted

$$= \frac{29}{180}$$

Required Probability $= \frac{1}{6} \times \frac{29}{180}$

$$= \frac{29}{1080}$$

∴ Required Probability is $\frac{29}{1080}$

Hence, the correct option is (D).

3. Given,

First matrix $= \begin{bmatrix} 2 & 7 & 4 \\ 3 & 1 & 0 \end{bmatrix}$

Number of rows $(m_1) = 2$
Number of columns $(n_1) = 3$

So, order of first matrix $= 2 \times 3$

And second matrix $= \begin{bmatrix} 5 \\ 4 \\ 3 \end{bmatrix}$

Number of rows $(m_2) = 3$
Number of columns $(n_2) = 1$

So, order of first matrix $= 3 \times 1$

As we know,
Multiplication of matrices is possible if
Number of column (n_1) in the first matrix $=$ Number of rows (m_2) in the second matrix

i.e., $n_1 = m_2$

∴ $n_1 = m_2 = 3$

So, $\begin{bmatrix} 2 & 7 & 4 \\ 3 & 1 & 0 \end{bmatrix} \begin{bmatrix} 5 \\ 4 \\ 3 \end{bmatrix}$ is possible.

As we know,
Multiplication of matrices is possible if the order of the new matrix is a row of the first matrix and column of the second matrix.

i.e., $m_1 \times n_2$

Now,

Order of new matrix formed by multiplication $= m_1 \times n_2 = 2 \times 1$

Hence, the correct option is (B).

4. As we know,

When two matrices are equal, all the corresponding elements must be equal.

Given,

$$\begin{bmatrix} 2x + y & 4x \\ 5x - 7 & 4x \end{bmatrix} = \begin{bmatrix} 7 & 7y - 13 \\ y & x + 6 \end{bmatrix}$$

Comparing two elements of first column,

$2x + y = 7$

$\Rightarrow y = 7 - 2x \ldots(1)$

$5x - 7 = y \ldots(2)$

Compairing value of y from equation (1) and (2) we get,

$7 - 2x = 5x - 7$

$\Rightarrow 7 + 7 = 5x + 2x$

$\Rightarrow 14 = 7x$

∴ $x = 2$

Putting value of x in equation (1), we get

$y = 7 - 2 \times 2$

$\Rightarrow y = 7 - 4$

$\Rightarrow y = 3$

Now,

$x + y = 2 + 3 = 5$

So, the value of $x + y$ is 5.

Hence, the correct option is (C).

5. Given,

$2\begin{bmatrix} x & 5 \\ 7 & y-3 \end{bmatrix} + \begin{bmatrix} 3 & -4 \\ 1 & 2 \end{bmatrix} = \begin{bmatrix} 7 & 6 \\ 15 & 14 \end{bmatrix}$

$\Rightarrow \begin{bmatrix} 2x & 10 \\ 14 & 2y-6 \end{bmatrix} + \begin{bmatrix} 3 & -4 \\ 1 & 2 \end{bmatrix} = \begin{bmatrix} 7 & 6 \\ 15 & 14 \end{bmatrix}$

$\Rightarrow \begin{bmatrix} 2x+3 & 6 \\ 15 & 2y-4 \end{bmatrix} = \begin{bmatrix} 7 & 6 \\ 15 & 14 \end{bmatrix}$

As we know that,

If two matrices A and B are equal then their corresponding elements are also equal.

$\therefore 2x + 3 = 7$

$\Rightarrow 2x = 7 - 3$

$\Rightarrow 2x = 4$

$\Rightarrow x = 2$

And $2y - 4 = 14$

$\Rightarrow 2y = 14 + 4$

$\Rightarrow 2y = 18$

$\Rightarrow y = 9$

Now,

$y - x = 9 - 2 = 7$

So, the value of $y - x$ is 7.

Hence, the correct option is (A).

6. Given:

PQ ⊥ RS

RT ∥ PQ

∠PST = 68°

Calculation:

RT ∥ PS

⇒ ∠PST = ∠RTS = 68° (Alternative angles)

Reflexive ∠RTS = 360° - ∠RTS

⇒ 360° - 68° = 292°

∴ Reflexive ∠RTS is 292°

Hence, the correct option is (B).

7. Concept:

$\int \frac{1}{a^2+x^2} dx = \frac{1}{a} \tan^{-1} \frac{x}{a}$

Given: $dy = (4 + y^2)dx$

$\Rightarrow \frac{dy}{4+y^2} = dx$

Integrating both sides, we get

$\int \frac{dy}{2^2+y^2} = \int dx$

$\Rightarrow \frac{1}{2} \tan^{-1} \frac{y}{2} = x + c$

$\Rightarrow \tan^{-1} \frac{y}{2} = 2x + C$

$y = 2\tan(2x + C)$

Hence, the correct option is (B).

8. Given,

$y^2 + (x - b)^2 = c$

There are two constants b and c so differentiate two times

Differentiating w.r.t x

We get,

$2y \frac{dy}{dx} + 2(x - b) = 0$

$\Rightarrow y \frac{dy}{dx} = b - x$

Differentiating again w.r.t x

We get,

$\left(\frac{dy}{dx}\right)^2 + y \frac{d^2y}{dx^2} = -1$

$\Rightarrow y \frac{d^2y}{dx^2} + \left(\frac{dy}{dx}\right)^2 + 1 = 0$

Hence, the correct option is (C).

9. Given,

$\frac{dy}{dx} = \sec\left(\frac{y}{x}\right) + \frac{y}{x} \quad \dots \dots (1)$

Let,

$\frac{y}{x} = t$

$\Rightarrow y = xt$

Differentiating with respect to x, we get

$\frac{dy}{dx} = x \times \frac{dt}{dx} + t \times \frac{d}{dx}x$

We known that:

$\frac{d}{dx}xy = y \times \frac{d}{dx}x + x \times \frac{d}{dx}y$

So,

$\frac{dy}{dx} = x \times \frac{dt}{dx} + t$

Now, Putting these value in equation (1), we get

$x \frac{dt}{dx} + t = \sec t + t$

Mathematics : Mock Test - 5

$\Rightarrow x \dfrac{dt}{dx} = \sec t$

$\Rightarrow \dfrac{dt}{\sec t} = \dfrac{dx}{x}$

Integrating both sides, we get

$\int \dfrac{dt}{\sec t} = \int \dfrac{dx}{x}$

$\Rightarrow \int \cos t \, dt = \int \dfrac{dx}{x}$

$\Rightarrow \sin t = \log x + \log c$

$\Rightarrow \sin t = \log(cx) \quad (\because \log m + \log n = \log(mn))$

$\therefore \sin\left(\dfrac{y}{x}\right) = \log(cx)$

Hence, the correct option is (C).

10. Concept:
- Mean = np
- Variance = npq

Where n is the total number of cases, p is probability of favorable cases and q is probability of unfavorable cases(1 - p)

Given mean $= np = \dfrac{2}{3}$ ... (i)

And variance $= npq = \dfrac{5}{9}$ ... (ii)

On dividing equation (i) and (ii)

$\dfrac{\text{variance}}{\text{mean}} = \dfrac{5/9}{2/3}$

$q = \dfrac{5}{6}$

$p = 1 - q = \dfrac{1}{6}$

$np = \dfrac{2}{3}$

$n = 4$

$\therefore$ The probability that random variable $D = 2$

$P = {}^nC_2 \, p^2 q^{n-2}$

$P = {}^4C_2 \times \left(\dfrac{1}{6}\right)^2 \times \left(\dfrac{5}{6}\right)^2$

$P = 6 \times \dfrac{1}{36} \times \dfrac{25}{36}$

$P = \dfrac{25}{216}$

Hence, the correct option is (D).

11. Binomial distribution: If a random variable X has binomial distribution as B (n, p) with n and p as parameters, then the probability of random variable is given as:

$P(X = k) = \binom{n}{k} p^k (1-p)^{n-k}$

Where, n is number of observations, p is the probability of success.

Formula:

Calculate combination:

$\binom{n}{k} = \dfrac{n!}{(n-k)!k!}$

Factorial:

$n! = 1 \times 2 \times 3 \times \ldots \times (n-1) \times n$

Given: $16P(X = 4) = P(X = 2)$

To find the value of p

Calculating probabilities of random variable X,

$P(X = 4) = \binom{6}{4} p^4 (1-p)^2$

$P(X = 2) = \binom{6}{2} p^2 (1-p)^4$

Given,

$16P(X = 4) = P(X = 2)$

$\Rightarrow 16 \binom{6}{4} p^4 (1-p)^2 = \binom{6}{2} p^2 (1-p)^4$

$\Rightarrow 16 \times \dfrac{6!}{2!4!} p^4 (1-p)^2 = \dfrac{6!}{2!4!} p^2 (1-p)^4$

$\Rightarrow 16p^2 = (1-p)^2$

$\Rightarrow \pm 4p = 1 - p$

$\Rightarrow p = \dfrac{1}{5}$ or $p = -\dfrac{1}{3}$

So, $p = \dfrac{1}{5}$.

Hence, the correct option is (C).

12. Concept:
- Mean $= \mu = np$
- Standard deviation $= \sigma = \sqrt{npq}$

Where n = number of trials; p = probability of success; q = (1 - p) = probability of failure

Given: Mean $= \mu = np = 5$

Variance $= \sigma^2 = npq = 4$

$\Rightarrow 4 = np(1-p)$

$\Rightarrow 4 = 5(1-p)$

$\Rightarrow \dfrac{4}{5} = (1-p)$

$\Rightarrow p = 1 - \dfrac{4}{5}$

73

$\therefore p = \frac{1}{5}$

Again; $\mu = np = 5$

$\therefore n = \frac{5}{p} = 5 \times 5 = 25$

Hence, the correct option is (C).

13. Graphic location of mode is done with reference to histogram.

Mode is a positional average it can be located graphically by the various process.

- A histogram of the frequency distribution is drawn.
- In the histogram, the highest rectangle represents the model class.
- The top left corner of the highest rectangle is joined with the top left corner of the following rectangle and the top right corner of the highest rectangle is joined with the top right corner of the preceding rectangle respectively.

Hence, the correct option is (D).

14. Given:

$\lim\limits_{x \to \infty} \left(\frac{x^2+x+1}{x+1} - px - q \right) = -3$

On simplifying, we get:

$\Rightarrow \lim\limits_{x \to \infty} \left(\frac{x^2+x+1-px^2-px-qx-q}{x+1} \right) = -3$

$\Rightarrow \lim\limits_{x \to \infty} \left(\frac{x^2(1-p)+x(1-p-q)+1-q}{x+1} \right) = -3$

As we can see limit gives finite value. So, this is possible only when the coefficient of higher degree term will be zero.

Therefore,

$(1 - p) = 0$

Or, $p = 1$

$\Rightarrow \lim\limits_{x \to \infty} \left(\frac{x(1-p-q)+1-q}{x+1} \right) = -3 \quad ....(1)$

Dividing and multiplying by x in both numerator and denominator, we get:

$\Rightarrow \lim\limits_{x \to \infty} \left(\frac{x\left[(1-p-q)+\frac{(1-q)}{x}\right]}{x\left[1+\frac{1}{x}\right]} \right) = -3$

$\Rightarrow \lim\limits_{x \to \infty} \left(\frac{\left[(1-p-q)+\frac{(1-q)}{x}\right]}{\left[1+\frac{1}{x}\right]} \right) = -3$

$\Rightarrow \left(\frac{[(1-p-q)+0]}{[1+0]} \right) = -3$

$\Rightarrow (1-p-q) = -3$

$\Rightarrow (1-1-q) = -3 \quad (\because p = 1)$

$\therefore q = 3$

Hence, the correct option is (A).

15. Concept:

The area under the curve $y = f(x)$ between $x = a$ and $x = b$, is given by:

$\text{Area} = \int_a^b y\, dx$

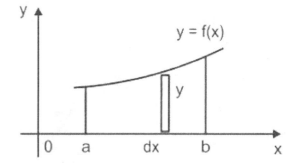

Calculation:

Here,

$x^2 = y$ and line $y = 1$ cut the parabola

$\therefore x^2 = 1$

$\Rightarrow x = 1$ and -1

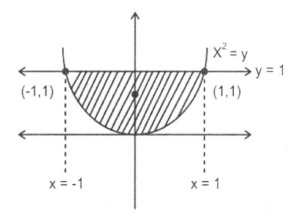

$\text{Area} = \int_{-1}^{1} y\, dx$

Here, the area is symmetric about the y-axis, we can find the area on one side and then multiply it by 2, we will get the area,

$\text{Area}_1 = \int_0^1 y\, dx$

$\text{Area}_1 = \int_0^1 x^2\, dx$

$= \left[\frac{x^3}{3} \right]_0^1 = \frac{1}{3}$

This area is between $y = x^2$ and the positive x-axis.

To get the area of the shaded region, we have to subtract this area from the area of square i.e.

$(1 \times 1) - \frac{1}{3} = \frac{2}{3}$

Total Area $= 2 \times \frac{2}{3} = \frac{4}{3}$ square units.

Hence, the correct option is (C).

16. Concept:

Equation of parabola along X-axis:

$(y)^2 = \pm 4ax$, focus $(\pm a, 0)$

Calculation:

Here, parabola $y^2 = x = 4\left(\frac{1}{4}\right)x$

Hence $a = \frac{1}{4}$,

Now focus $= (a, 0)$

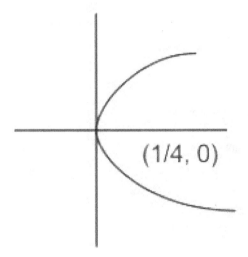

$y^2 = x$

$y = \sqrt{x}$

x from 0 to $\frac{1}{4}$

$\therefore$ Area $2 \int_0^{\frac{1}{4}} y\, dx$

$= 2 \int_0^{\frac{1}{4}} \sqrt{x}\, dx$

$\left(= 2 \left[\frac{2}{3} x^{\frac{3}{2}}\right]_0^{\frac{1}{4}}\right.$

$= 2 \left[\frac{2}{3} \left(\frac{1}{4}\right)^{\frac{3}{2}}\right]$

$= \frac{4}{3} \left(\frac{1}{4}\right)\left(\frac{1}{2}\right)$

$= \frac{1}{6}$ sq. unit

Hence, the correct option is (B).

17. Given equation of curves are

$y = x^2$ ⋯ (1)

$y = 16$ ⋯ (2)

By solving both equation (1) and (2),

$x^2 = 16$

$x = 4, -4$

$\therefore$ Points of intersection are $(4, 16)$ and $(-4, 16)$.

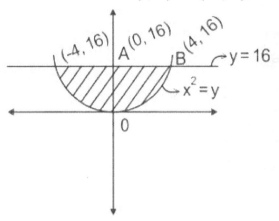

From the figure we have,

Required Area $= \int_{-4}^{4} (16 - x^2)\, dx$

By using Integral property,

$A = 2 \int_0^4 (16 - x^2)\, dx$

$= 2 \left[16x - \frac{x^3}{3}\right]_0^4$

$= 2 \left[16x - \frac{x^3}{3}\right]_0^4$

$= 2 \left[64 - \frac{64}{3}\right]$

$= 2 \times 64 \times \frac{2}{3}$

$A = \frac{256}{3}$ sq.units

Hence, the correct option is (B).

18. Let set A and B have mm and n elements, respectively.

$2^m - 2^n = 56$

$2^n(2^{m-n} - 1) = 56 = 8 \times 7 = 2^3 \times 7$

Comparing both sides, we get

$2^n = 2^3$ and $2^{m-n} = 7$

$\Rightarrow$ n = 3 and 2^{m-n} = 8

$\Rightarrow 2^{m-n} = 2^3 \Rightarrow$ m-n = 3

$\Rightarrow$ m-3 = 3 $\Rightarrow$ m = 6

Number of the elements in A is 6.

Hence, the correct option is (B).

19. Given,

$z_1 = 6 + 2i$ ...(1)

$z_2 = 2 - i$ ...(2)

On dividing equation (1) and (2), we get

$\dfrac{z_1}{z_2} = \dfrac{6+2i}{2-i}$

Multiplying by $(2 + i)$ in numerator and denominator, we get

$\dfrac{z_1}{z_2} = \dfrac{6+2i}{2-i} \times \dfrac{2+i}{2+i}$

$\Rightarrow \dfrac{z_1}{z_2} = \dfrac{12+6i+4i+2i^2}{2^2-i^2}$

$\Rightarrow \dfrac{z_1}{z_2} = \dfrac{12+10i+2\times(-1)}{4-(-1)}$ $[\because i^2 = -1]$

$\Rightarrow \dfrac{z_1}{z_2} = \dfrac{12+10i-2}{4+1}$

$\Rightarrow \dfrac{z_1}{z_2} = \dfrac{10+10i}{5}$

$\Rightarrow \dfrac{z_1}{z_2} = \dfrac{10(1+i)}{5}$

$\Rightarrow \dfrac{z_1}{z_2} = 2(1 + i)$

Hence, the correct option is (B).

20. Given:

$Z = 10x + 25y$

Subject to: $x \leq 3, y \leq 3, x + y \leq 5, x \geq 0, y \geq 0$

First we draw the lines AB, CD and EF whose equations are x = 3, y = 3 and x + y = 5 respectively.

Line	Equation	Point on the X-axis	Point on the Y-axis	Sign	Region
AB	x = 3	A(3,0)	-	≤	origin side of line AB
CD	y = 3	-	D(0,3)	≤	origin side of line CD
EF	x + y = 5	E(5,0)	F(0,5)	≤	origin side of line EF

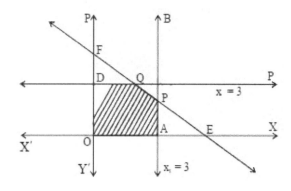

The feasible region is OAPQDO which is shaded in the figure.
The vertices of the feasible region are O (0,0), A (3, 0), P, Q and D (0, 3)
P is the point of intersection of the lines x + y = 5 and x = 3
Substituting x = 3 in x + y = 5, we get,

3+ y=5

y = 2
P= (3, 2)
Q is the point of intersection of the lines x + y = 5 and y = 3
Substituting y = 3 in x + y = 5, we get,
x + 3 = 5

x = 2

Q = (2,3)
The values of the objective function z = 10x + 25y at these vertices are

Z(O) = 10(0)+ 25(0)= 0
Z(A) = 10(3) + 25(0) = 30
Z(P) = 10(3) + 25(2) = 30 + 50 = 80
Z(Q) = 10(2) + 25(3) = 20 + 75 = 95
Z(D) = 10(0) + 25(3) =75

Z has max imumvalue 95, when x = 2 and y = 3.

Hence, the correct option is (A).

21. Given:

Min $Z = 3x + 5y$

$2x + 3y \geq 12$ .... (i)

$-x + y \leq 3$ .... (ii)

$x \leq 4, y \geq 3, x \geq 0, y \geq 0$

Taking equation (i)

$2x + 3y = 12$

Putting $x = 0, y = 4$ Let the point is $(0,4)$.

Now putting $y = 0, x = 6$ Let the point is $(6,0)$.

Now taking equation (ii)

$-x + y = 3$

Putting $x = 0, y = 3 (0,3)$

Putting $y = 0, x = -3(-3, 0)$

The graph is as follows:

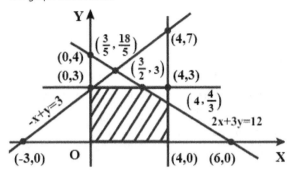

ABCDA be the feasible region bounded by these lines Now we find the coordinates of A, B, C and D for A, Solving the equations $2x + 3y = 12$ and $-xy = 3$. We get:

$x = \frac{+3}{5}$ and $y = \frac{18}{5}$

For coordinate of $A\left(\frac{+3}{5}, \frac{18}{5}\right)$

Now

$Z = 3 \times \left(+\frac{3}{5}\right) + 5 \times \frac{18}{5}$

$= \frac{+9}{5} + \frac{90}{5} = \frac{90}{5}$

For coordinate of B:

Solving the equations:

$2x + 3y = 12$ and $y = 3$

We get $x = \frac{3}{2}, y = 3$

∴ Coordinate of $B\left(\frac{3}{2}, 3\right)$

Now $Z = 3 \times \frac{3}{2} + 5 \times 3$

$= \frac{9}{2} + 15 = \frac{39}{2}$

For coordinate of C:

Solving the equations:

$x = 4$ and $y = 3$

∴ Coordinate of $C(4, 3)$

Now $Z = 3 \times 4 + 5 \times 3$

$= 12 + 1 = 27$

For coordinate of D:

Solving the equations:

$-x + y = 3$ and $x = 4$

We get $x = 4, y = 7$

Now $Z = 3 \times 4 + 5 \times 7$

$= 12 + 35 = 47$

$MinZ = \frac{39}{2}$, for $x = \frac{3}{2}, y = 3$

Hence, the correct option is (D).

22. Given:

$Z = 3x + 2y$ Subject to the constraints $x + y \geq 8, 3x + 5y \leq 15$ and $x \geq 0, y \leq 15$

Converting the given In equations Into the equations:

$x + y = 8$ ...(1)

$3x + 5y = 15$ (2)

$y = 15$ ...(3)

Region represented by $x + y \geq 8$:

The line $x + y = 8$ meets the coordinate axis at $C(8, 0)$ and $D(0, 8)$.

Table for $x + y = 8$

| X | 8 | 0 |
| y | 0 | 8 |

$A(8, 0); B(0, 8)$

Join the points C and D to obtain the line.

We find that the point $(0, 0)$ does not satisfy the in equation $x + y > 8$

So, the region opposite to the origin represents the solution set to the in equation.

Region represented by $3x + 5y \leq 15$:

The line $3x + 5y = 15$ meets the coordinate axis at $C(5, 0)$ and $D(0, 3)$

Table for $3x + 5y = 15$

| X | 5 | 0 |
| y | 0 | 3 |

$C(5, 0); D(0, 3)$

Join the points C and D to obtain the line.

Clearly $(0, 0)$ satisfies the in equation $3x + 5y \leq 15$.

So, the region containing the origin represents the solution set of this in equation.

Region represented by $y \leq 15$:

Line $y = 15$ is parallel to x-axis, its each point will satisfy the in equation in first quadrant.

So, its solution region will be towards origin.

Region represented by $x \geq 0$ and $y \geq 0$:

Since every point in the first quadrant satisfies these in equations.

So the first quadrant is the region represented by the in equations $x \geq 0$ and $y \geq 0$.

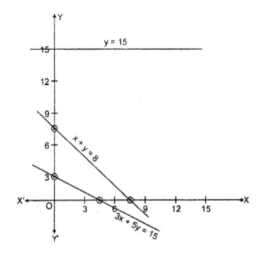

There is no any common region for solution.

Hence, the correct option is (B).

23. Given:

Angle between the lines $x + y - 3 = 0$ and $x - y + 3 = 0$ is α.

Angle between the lines $x - \sqrt{3}y + 2\sqrt{3} = 0$ and $\sqrt{3}x - y + 1 = 0$ is β.

The angle θ between the lines having slope m_1 and m_2 is given by $\tan\theta = \left|\frac{m_2 - m_1}{1 + m_1 m_2}\right|$

Let's find the slope,

Slope of line $x + y - 3 = 0$ is m_1 and slope of line $x - y + 3 = 0$ is m_2

$m_1 = -1$ and $m_2 = 1$

Therefore,

$\tan\alpha = \left|\frac{1-(-1)}{1+(-1)\times 1}\right| = \infty$

$\alpha = 90°$

Slope of line $x - \sqrt{3}y + 2\sqrt{3} = 0$ is m_1 and $\sqrt{3}x - y + 1 = 0$ is m_2

$m_1 = \left(\frac{1}{\sqrt{3}}\right)$ and $m_2 = \sqrt{3}$

$\tan\beta = \left|\frac{\sqrt{3} - \frac{1}{\sqrt{3}}}{1 + \left(\sqrt{3}\times\frac{1}{\sqrt{3}}\right)}\right| = \frac{1}{\sqrt{3}}$

$\beta = 30°$

$\alpha > \beta$

Hence, the correct option is (B).

24. Let $P(h, k)$ be any point on the locus which is equidistant from the point A(1, 3) and B(-2, 1).

According to question,

$PA = PB$

$\sqrt{(h-1)^2 + (k-3)^2} = \sqrt{(h+2)^2 + (k-1)^2}$ ...(i)

Squaring both side in equation (i) we get,

$\Rightarrow (h-1)^2 + (k-3)^2 = (h+2)^2 + (k-1)^2$

$(\because (a \pm b)^2 = a^2 + b^2 \pm 2ab)$

$\Rightarrow h^2 - 2h + 1 + k^2 - 6k + 9 = h^2 + 4h + 4 + k^2 - 2k + 1$

$\Rightarrow -2h - 6k + 10 = 4h - 2k + 5$

$\Rightarrow 6h + 4k = 5$

∴ The locus of (h, k) is $6x + 4y = 5$.

Hence, the correct option is (B).

25. The equation of the line passing through (x_1, y_1) with the slope m is:

$(y - y_1) = m(x - x_1)$

The slope of line passing through the points (x_1, y_1) and (x_2, y_2) is:

$= \frac{y_2 - y_1}{x_2 - x_1}$

The slope of line passing through the points $(2,5)(-3,6)$ is

$= \frac{6-5}{-3-2}$

$\Rightarrow m_1 = \frac{1}{-5} = \frac{-1}{5}$

The two non-vertical lines are perpendicular to each other only if and only if their slopes are negative reciprocals of each other.

The slope of perpendicular to the line through the points $(2,5)(-3,6)$ is $m_2 = \frac{-1}{m_1}$

$\Rightarrow m_2 = 5$

The equation of the line passing through $(x_1, y_1) = (-3,5)$ and perpendicular to the line through the points $(2,5)(-3,6)$ is:

$(y - y_1) = m(x - x_1)$

$\Rightarrow (y - 5) = 5(x + 3)$

$\Rightarrow 5x - y + 20 = 0$

Hence, the correct option is (D).

26. Concept:

Slope intercept form of line: y = mx + c, Where 'm' is the slope of the line and 'c' is the y-intercept.

The "point-slope" form of the equation of a straight line is: $y - y_1 = m(x - x_1)$

When two lines are perpendicular, the product of their slope is -1.

If m is the slope of a line, then the slope of a line perpendicular to it is $-\frac{1}{m}$.

Given,

$3x + y = 7$

$\Rightarrow y = -3x + 7$

Then the slope of a line perpendicular

The slope of line $= m = -3$

Then the slope of a line perpendicular to it is $\frac{-1}{m} = \frac{1}{3}$

The equation of line passing through $(1,1)$ with slope $\frac{1}{3}$ is,

$y - 1 = \left(\frac{1}{3}\right)(x - 1)$

$\Rightarrow 3y - 3 = x - 1$

$\Rightarrow 3y = x + 2$

$\Rightarrow 3y - x = 2$

For x-intercept, $y = 0$

$\therefore x = -2$

So, the x-intercept of line is -2

Hence, the correct option is (A).

27. Given,

Number between 107 to $1006 = 900$

Number of possible outcomes $= n(S) = 900$

Numbers from 107 to 1006 divisible by 11 and 37 both $= \{407, 814\}$

$= 2$

Numbers on cards not divisible by both 11 and 37 $n(E) = 900 - 2$

$= 898$

$\therefore$ Probability $= \frac{n(E)(\text{Favourable Events})}{n(S)(\text{Possible outcomes})}$

$= \frac{898}{900}$

$= 0.998$

Hence, the correct option is (B).

28. Given:

$m = 4$

The probability distribution is given by:

$p(x) = \frac{(e^{-m} \times m^x)}{x!}$

Calculation:

According to the formula,

$\Rightarrow p(x) = \frac{(e^{-4} \times 4^x)}{x!}$

Now, the probability that in a given month there will be less than 4 accidents

$= p(0) + p(1) + p(2) + p(3)$

$= \frac{\sum_{x=0}^{x=3} e^{-4} 4^x}{x!}$

$= e^{-4} \left[(1 + 4 + 8) + \frac{32}{3}\right]$

$= e^{-4}[(13) + \frac{32}{3}]$

$= 0.0183 \times \frac{71}{3}$

$= 0.0183 \times 23.666$

$= 0.433$

$\therefore$ The probability that in a given month there will be less than 4 accidents is 0.433.

Hence, the correct option is (B).

29. Given:

$\frac{(1+\cos x)}{(1-\sin x)}(\sin x + \cos x - 1)^2 = M\sin^N x$

Formula:

$(\sin x + \cos x - 1)^2 = 2(1 - \sin x)(1 - \cos x)$

According to the question:

$\Rightarrow \frac{(1+\cos x)}{(1-\sin x)} \times 2(1 - \sin x)(1 - \cos x) = M\sin^N x$

$\Rightarrow 2(1 + \cos x)(1 - \cos x) = M\sin^N x$

$\Rightarrow 2(1 - \cos^2 x) = M\sin^N x$

$\Rightarrow 2\sin^2 x = M\sin^N x$

Comparing both sides, we have

$\Rightarrow MN = (2 \times 2) = 4$

Hence, the correct option is (C).

30. Given:

$\vec{a} = \hat{i} + 2\hat{j} - 3\hat{k}$

$\vec{b} = 3\hat{i} - \hat{j} + 2\hat{k}$

So,

$(\vec{a} + \vec{b}) = \hat{i} + 2\hat{j} - 3\hat{k} + 3\hat{i} - \hat{j} + 2\hat{k}$

$(\vec{a} + \vec{b}) = (\hat{i} + \hat{3i}) + (\hat{2j} - \hat{j}) + (\widehat{-3k + 2k})$

$\vec{a} + \vec{b} = 4\hat{i} + \hat{j} - \hat{k}$

$(\vec{a} - \vec{b}) = \hat{i} + 2\hat{j} - 3\hat{k} - 3\hat{i} - \hat{j} + 2\hat{k}$

$(\vec{a} - \vec{b}) = (\hat{i} - \hat{3i}) + (\hat{2j} - \widehat{(-j)}) + (\widehat{-3k - 2k})$

$\Rightarrow \vec{a} - \vec{b} = -2\hat{i} + 3\hat{j} - 5\hat{k}$

Then,

$(\vec{a} + \vec{b}) \cdot (\vec{a} - \vec{b}) = (4\hat{i} + \hat{j} - \hat{k}) \cdot (-2\hat{i} + 3\hat{j} - 5\hat{k})$

$(\vec{a} + \vec{b}) \cdot (\vec{a} - \vec{b}) = -8 + 3 + 5 = 0$

If $(\vec{a} + \vec{b}) \cdot (\vec{a} - \vec{b}) = 0$

Then angle between two vectors is $90°$.

Hence, the correct option is (C).

31. Given:

$\vec{a} = a_1\hat{i} + a_2\hat{j} + a_3\hat{k}, \vec{b} = b_1\hat{i} + b_2\hat{j} + b_3\hat{k}$ be three non-zero vectors such that $\vec{c}$ is a vector perpendicular to both $\vec{a}$ and $\vec{b}$.

Angle between $\vec{a}$ and $\vec{b} = \frac{\pi}{6}$

We know that $\begin{vmatrix} a_1 & b_1 & c_1 \\ a_2 & b_2 & c_2 \\ a_3 & b_3 & c_3 \end{vmatrix} = [(\vec{a} \times \vec{b}) \cdot \vec{c}]^2$

So,

$= [|\vec{a} \times \vec{b}||\vec{c}|\cos 0°]^2$

($\because \vec{a} \times \vec{b}$ is parellel to vector $\vec{c}$ as $\vec{c}$ is perpendicular to both $\vec{a}$ and $\vec{b}$)

$= \left(|\vec{a}||\vec{b}|\sin\frac{\pi}{6}\right)^2$

$= |\vec{a}|^2 |\vec{b}|^2 \left(\frac{1}{2}\right)^2$

$= \frac{1}{4}|\vec{a}|^2 |\vec{b}|^2$

We know that,

$|\vec{a}|^2 = (a_1^2 + a_2^2 + a_3^2)$

$|\vec{b}|^2 = (b_1^2 + b_2^2 + b_3^2)$

So,

$\frac{1}{4}|\vec{a}|^2 |\vec{b}|^2 = \frac{1}{4}[(a_1^2 + a_2^2 + a_3^2)(b_1^2 + b_2^2 + b_3^2)]$

Hence, the correct option is (C).

32. Given,

$\sin 1° + \sin 2° + \cdots + \sin 359°$

We know that,

$\sin(180 - \theta) = \sin\theta$ .....(i)

$\sin(180 + \theta) = -\sin\theta$ .....(ii)

Therefore, Rewrite the given expression in terms of $(180 - \theta)$ and $(180 + \theta)$ we get,

$\sin 1° + \sin 2° + \cdots + \sin(180°) + \sin(180° + 1°) + \sin(180° + 2°) + \cdots + \sin(180° + 179°)$

$= \sin 1° + \sin 2° + \cdots + \sin(179°) + \sin(180°) - \sin(1°) - \sin(2°) + \cdots - \sin(179°)$

$= \sin 180°$

$= 0$

Hence, the correct option is (D).

33. Given:

$\cos(-1230°) \times \cot(-315°)$

Concept:

$\cos(-\theta) = \cos\theta$

$\cos(2n\pi + \theta) = \cos(\theta)$

$\cos(\pi - \theta) = -\cos(\theta)$

$\cot(-\theta) = -\cot(\theta)$

$\cot(2n\pi - \theta) = -\cot(\theta)$

According to the ques,

$\cos(-1230°) = \cos(1230°)$ $(\because \cos(-\theta) = \cos\theta)$

$= \cos(3 \times 360° + 150)$ $(\because \cot(2n\pi - \theta) = -\cot(\theta))$

$= \cos(150°)$

$= \cos(180° - 30°) = -\cos 30°$ $(\because \cos(\pi - \theta) = -\cos(\theta))$

$= \frac{-\sqrt{3}}{2}$

Now,

$\cot(-315°) = -\cot(315°)$ $(\because \cot(-\theta) = -\cot(\theta))$

$= -\cot(360° - 45°)$

$= \cot 45°$ $(\because \cot(2n\pi - \theta) = -\cot(\theta))$

$= 1$

$\cos(-1230°) \times \cot(-315°) = \frac{-\sqrt{3}}{2}$

Hence, the correct option is (A).

34. Given,

$\sin x + \sin 3x + \sin 5x = 0$

$\Rightarrow (\sin 5x + \sin x) + \sin 3x = 0$

$\Rightarrow 2\sin 3x \cos 2x + \sin 3x = 0$ $(\because \sin A + \sin B = 2\sin\frac{A+B}{2}\cos\frac{A-B}{2})$

$\Rightarrow \sin 3x(2\cos 2x + 1) = 0$

$\sin 3x = 0$ or $2\cos 2x + 1 = 0$

$\sin 3x = 0$ or, $\cos 2x = -\frac{1}{2}$

Now, $\sin 3x = 0$

$\Rightarrow 3x = n\pi$

$\Rightarrow x = \frac{n\pi}{3}, n \in Z$

And, $\cos 2x = -\frac{1}{2}$

$\cos 2x = \cos\frac{2\pi}{3}$

$2x = 2m\pi \pm \frac{2\pi}{3}, m \in Z$

$x = m\pi \pm \frac{\pi}{3}, m \in Z$

∴ The general solution of the given equation is: $x = \frac{n\pi}{3}$ or, $x = m\pi \pm \frac{\pi}{3}$, where $m, n \in Z$.

Hence, the correct option is (D).

35. $f(x)$ is Continuous at $x = 0$

$\Rightarrow \lim_{x \to 0^+} f(x) = \lim_{x \to 0^-} f(x) = f(0)$

$\Rightarrow \lim_{x \to 0^+} \sin x = \lim_{x \to 0^-} \sin x = k$

$\Rightarrow \lim_{h \to 0}\sin(0 + h) = \lim_{h \to 0}\sin(0 - h) = k$

$\Rightarrow k = 0$

Hence, the correct option is (B).

36. $y^2 = 9(x + y)$

$2y\left(\frac{dy}{dx}\right) = 9 + 9\left(\frac{dy}{dx}\right)$

$\left(\frac{dy}{dx}\right) = \frac{9}{2y-9}$

Now putting y = 3

we get $\left(\frac{dy}{dx}\right) = -3$

Hence, the correct option is (B).

37. Concept:

$y = \ln x$ then $\frac{dy}{dx} = \frac{1}{x}$

$y = \tan x$ then $\frac{dy}{dx} = \sec^2 x$

$y = \sec x$ then $\frac{dy}{dx} = \sec x \cdot \tan x$

$y = cosec x$ then $\frac{dy}{dx} = -cosec x \cdot \cot x$

$y = \cot x$ then $\frac{dy}{dx} = -cosec^2 x$

Let, $y = \ln(\sec x + \tan x)$

$\Rightarrow \frac{dy}{dx} = \frac{1}{\sec x + \tan x} \times (\sec x \cdot \tan x + \sec^2 x)$

$\Rightarrow \frac{dy}{dx} = \frac{\sec x}{\sec x + \tan x} \times (\tan x + \sec x)$

$\Rightarrow \frac{dy}{dx} = \sec x$

Statement (1) is true.

Now, $y = \ln(cosec x - \cot x)$,

$\Rightarrow \frac{dy}{dx} = \frac{1}{cosec x - \cot x} \times (-cosec x \cdot \cot x + cosec^2 x)$

$\Rightarrow \frac{dy}{dx} = \frac{cosec x}{cosec x - \cot x} \times (cosec x. - \cot x)$

$\Rightarrow \frac{dy}{dx} = \cosec x$

Statement (2) is true.

Hence, the correct option is (C).

38. Given: Equation of line is $y = 4x + c$ and the line is tangent to the circle $x^2 + y^2 = 9$ Here, we have to find the value of c.

As we know that, if the line $y = mx + c$ is a tangent to the circle $x^2 + y^2 = a^2$ then $c^2 = a^2(1 + m^2)$

By comparing the given equation of line and circle with $y = mx + c$ and $x^2 + y^2 = a^2$ respectively, we get:

$m = 4, a^2 = 9$

$\because m = 4$

$\Rightarrow m^2 = 16$

$\because c^2 = a^2(1 + m^2)$

By substituting $m^2 = 16$ and $a^2 = 9$ in the above equation we get,

$\Rightarrow c^2 = 9 \times (1 + 16) = 9 \times 17$

$\Rightarrow c = \pm 3\sqrt{17}$

Hence, the correct option is (A).

39. Given: $y = x^2$ and $x = 1$

As we know that equation of tangent is $\frac{y - f(a)}{x - a} = f'(a)$ for the function $y = f(x)$ at $x = a$

First find $f(a)$ and $f'(a)$

$f(1) = 1$

$\Rightarrow f'(x) = 2x$ and $f'(1) = 2$

As we know that equation of tangent is $\frac{y - f(a)}{x - a} = f'(a)$ for the function $y = f(x)$ at $x = a$

$\frac{y - 1}{x - 1} = 2$

$\Rightarrow y = 2x - 1$

So, the equation of tangent is $y = 2x - 1$.

Hence, the correct option is (A).

40. Let, small charge in x be Δx and the corresponding change in y is Δy.

$\Delta y = \frac{dy}{dx} \Delta x = f'(x) \Delta x$

Now that $\Delta y = f(x + \Delta x) - f(x)$

Therefore, $f(x + \Delta x) = f(x) + \Delta y$

Given: $f(x) = 3x^2 + 3$

Let, $x + \Delta x = 3.01 = 3 + 0.01$

Therefore, $x = 3$ and $\Delta x = 0.01$

$f(x + \Delta x) = f(x) + \Delta y$

$\Rightarrow f(x + \Delta x) = f(x) + f'(x) \Delta x$

$\Rightarrow f(3.01) = 3x^2 + 3 + (6x) \Delta x$

$\Rightarrow f(3.01) = 3(3)^2 + 3 + (6 \cdot 3)(0.01)$

$\Rightarrow f(3.01) = 30 + 0.18$

$\Rightarrow f(3.01) = 30.18$

Hence, the correct option is (A).

41. Equation of circle with center at (h, k) and radius r units is given by: $(x - h)^2 + (y - k)^2 = r^2$

Here $(h, k) = (4, -5)$ and let the radius be r units. The equation of the required circle is: $(x - 4)^2 + (y + 5)^2 = r^2$.

$\because$ y-axis is the tangent to the circle $(x - 4)^2 + (y + 5)^2 = r^2$.

So the co-ordinates of the point common to circle $(x - 4)^2 + (y + 5)^2 = r^2$ and the tangent y-axis is $(0, -5)$.

$\therefore$ The point $(0, -5)$ will satisfy the equation of circle.

$\Rightarrow (0 - 4)^2 + (-5 + 5)^2 = r^2$

$\Rightarrow r = 4$

So, the radius of the circle is 4 units.

Hence, the correct option is (A).

42. $\int \frac{1}{\sqrt{x}} dx = \int x^{-\frac{1}{2}} dx$

$= \frac{x^{-\frac{1}{2}+1}}{-\frac{1}{2}+1} + C$

$= 2\sqrt{x} + C$

$\therefore \int_4^9 \frac{1}{\sqrt{x}} dx = [2\sqrt{x}]_4^9 = 2[\sqrt{9} - \sqrt{4}] = 2(3 - 2) = 2$

Hence, the correct option is (C).

43. Integration by parts: Integration by parts is a method to find integrals of products.

The formula for integrating by parts is given by;

$\int uv dx = u \int v dx - \int \left(\frac{du}{dx} \int v dx\right) dx$

We have to find the value of $\int_1^e x \ln x dx$

$\Rightarrow \int_1^e (\ln x) x dx = \left[\ln x \left(\frac{x^2}{2}\right)\right]_1^e - \int_1^e \frac{1}{x}\left(\frac{x^2}{2}\right) dx$

$\Rightarrow \left[\ln x \left(\frac{x^2}{2}\right)\right]_1^e - \frac{1}{2}\int_1^e x\,dx$

$\Rightarrow \left[\ln x \left(\frac{x^2}{2}\right)\right]_1^e - \frac{1}{2}\left[\frac{x^2}{2}\right]_1^e$

$\Rightarrow \left[\ln e \frac{e^2}{2} - \ln 1 \frac{1^2}{2}\right] - \frac{1}{4}[e^2 - 1]$ ($\because \log e = 1$)

$\Rightarrow \left[\frac{e^2}{2} - 0\right] - \frac{1}{4}[e^2 - 1]$

$\Rightarrow \frac{e^2+1}{4}$

Hence, the correct option is (B).

44. We know that:

$\int_a^b f(x)dx = (b-a)\lim_{n\to\infty}\frac{1}{n}(f(a) + f(a+h) + \ldots + f(a+(n-1)h))$

Putting $a = 0$, $b = 2$, $h = \frac{b-a}{n} = \frac{2-0}{n} = \frac{2}{n}$

in $\int_0^2 x^2 + 1\,dx$

$I = (2-0)\lim_{n\to\infty}\frac{1}{n}(f(0) + f(n) + f(2n) + \ldots + f(n-1)h$

$f(0) = 1$

$f(h) = h^2 + 1$

$= \left(\frac{4}{n^2}\right) + 1$

$f((n-1)h) = (n-1)^2 \times \frac{4}{n^2} + 1$

$\therefore I = 2\lim_{n\to\infty}\frac{1}{n}$

$\left((1+1+\ldots n \text{ times}) + \left(0 + \frac{4}{n^2} + \frac{16}{n^2} + \ldots + \frac{(n-1)^2}{n^2}\right)\right)$

$= 2\lim_{n\to\infty}\frac{1}{n}\left(n + \frac{4}{n}\frac{(n-1)n(2n-1)}{6}\right)$

$= 2\lim_{n\to\infty}\left(1 + \frac{2}{3}\left(1 - \frac{1}{n}\right)\left(2 - \frac{1}{n}\right)\right)$

$= 2 \times \left(1 + \frac{4}{3}\right)$

$= \frac{14}{3}$

Hence, the correct option is (C).

45. Concept:

$\int \frac{dx}{x} = \ln x + c$

Calculation:

Let $I = \int \frac{dx}{x\ln x}$

Let $\ln x = t$

Differentiating with respect to x, we get

$\Rightarrow \frac{1}{x}dx = dt'$

$1 = \int \frac{dt}{t}$

$= \ln t + c$

$= \ln(\ln x) + c$

Hence, the correct option is (A).

46. As we know that $\int_a^b f(x)dx = \int_a^b f(a+b-x)dx$

$I = \int_0^a \frac{f(a-x)}{f(x)+f(a-x)}dx \ldots\ldots (1)$

So, we have lower limit $a = 0$, upper limit $b = a$

$\Rightarrow I = \int_0^a \frac{f[(0+a)-(a-x)]}{f[(a+0)-x]+f[(a+0)-(a-x)]}dx$

$\Rightarrow I = \int_0^a \frac{f(x)}{f(a-x)+f(x)}dx \ldots\ldots (2)$

Now adding equation (1) and equation (2),

$\Rightarrow 2I = \int_0^a \frac{f(a-x)}{f(x)+f(a-x)}dx + \int_0^a \frac{f(x)}{f(a-x)+f(x)}dx$

$\Rightarrow 2I = \int_0^a 1\,dx$

$\Rightarrow 2I = a$

$\therefore I = \frac{a}{2}$

Hence, the correct option is (D).

47. Integration by parts:

The formula for integrating by parts is given by;

$\Rightarrow \int uv\,dx = u\int v\,dx - \int \left(\frac{du}{dx}\int v\,dx\right)dx$

Where u is the function u(x) and v is the function v(x)

In the given function $u = x$ and $v = \ln x\,dx$.

Integrate by parts as follows:

$\int x\ln x\,dx = \ln x \int x\,dx - \int \frac{1}{x}\frac{x^2}{2}dx$

$= \frac{x^2}{2}\ln x - \int \frac{x}{2}dx$

$= \frac{x^2}{2}\ln x - \frac{x^2}{4} + C$

Hence, the correct option is (D).

48. Let the CP of each of two cheapest articles = x and the CP of costliest article = x + 1

Then, x + x + x + 1 = 49,

x = 16

therefore, the CP of costliest article = 16 + 1 = 17

From the Statement II, we can say that the cost price of two articles is same

i.e., the cost price of first article = cost price of second article= x

And from Statement III, we can say that the cost price of costliest article is 6.25% more than the cost price of cheapest article

Therefore, the cost price of costliest article $= x + x \times 6.25\%$

$= 1.0625x$

According to question,

$x + x + 1.0625x = 49$

$x = 16$

Therefore, cost price of costliest article $= 1.0625x$

$= 1.0625 \times 16 = 17$

Therefore, by combining both the statement we can also get our answer.

Hence, the correct option is (A).

49. If we have the dimensions, from Statement a,

Volume of cuboid $= 10 \times 5 \times 12 = 600 cm^3$

If thickness is ' t ' and let side of square sheet be S, then,

$600 = (S^2) \times (t)$

If $t = 1.5 cm$ is taken from Statement II,

$\frac{600}{1.5} = (S^2) = 400$

$S = 20 cm$

Height of cylinder $= S = 20 cm$ [As square sheet is rolled so the side of the cylinder will be equal to side of square]

Outer circumference $= S = 20 cm = 2\pi r$

Or, $r = \frac{10}{\pi} \approx 3.185$

Thickness taken, $t = 1.5 cm$

So inner radius $= 3.185 - 1.5 = 1.685 cm$

Whereas Statement III has no significance anywhere.

But none of the statement alone can answer the question individually.

So, answer is using statement I and II together is sufficient

Hence, the correct option is (C).

50. Given: Equation of line $\vec{r} = (\hat{i} + 2\hat{k}) + \lambda(2\hat{i} - m\hat{j} - 3\hat{k})$ and equation of plane $\vec{r} \cdot (m\hat{i} + 3\hat{j} + \hat{k}) = 4$

It is given that the given line is parallel to the given plane,

As we know that, if the line $\vec{r} = \vec{a} + \lambda\vec{b}$ is parallel to the plane $\vec{r} \cdot \vec{n} = q$ then $\vec{b} \cdot \vec{n} = 0$

Here, $\vec{b} = 2\hat{i} - m\hat{j} - 3\hat{k}$ and $\vec{n} = m\hat{i} + 3\hat{j} + \hat{k}$

$\Rightarrow \vec{b} \cdot \vec{n} = 2m - 3m - 3 = 0$

$\Rightarrow m = -3$

Hence, the correct option is (D).

Mathematics : Mock Test 06

Q.1 There are 20 cricket players, out of which 5 players can bowl. In how many ways can a team of 11 players be selected so, to include 4 bowlers?
A. $^5C_4 \times {}^{15}C_7$
B. $^5C_3 \times {}^{15}C_8$
C. $^5C_5 \times {}^{15}C_6$
D. $^5C_2 \times {}^{15}C_9$

Q.2 If $A = \begin{bmatrix} 1 & -1 & 0 \\ 3 & 2 & -1 \end{bmatrix}$ and $B = \begin{bmatrix} 1 \\ 3 \\ 5 \end{bmatrix}$, find $(AB)^T$.
A. $\begin{bmatrix} -2 \\ 4 \end{bmatrix}$
B. $[-2 \quad 4]$
C. $\begin{bmatrix} 2 \\ -4 \end{bmatrix}$
D. $[-2 \quad -4]$

Q.3 If $A = \begin{bmatrix} \cos 2\theta & -\sin 2\theta \\ \sin 2\theta & \cos 2\theta \end{bmatrix}$ and $A + A^T = I$ Where I is the unit matrix of 2×2 and A^T is the transpose of A, then the value of θ is equal to:
A. $\frac{3\pi}{2}$
B. π
C. $\frac{\pi}{3}$
D. $\frac{\pi}{6}$

Q.4 If $A = \begin{bmatrix} \cos\alpha & \sin\alpha \\ -\sin\alpha & \cos\alpha \end{bmatrix}$ then AA^T is equal to: (where A^T is the transpose of A)
A. Null matrix
B. Identify matrix
C. A
D. -A

Q.5 What is the sum of the measures of the angles ∠A, ∠B, ∠C, ∠D, ∠E, and ∠F in the given figure?

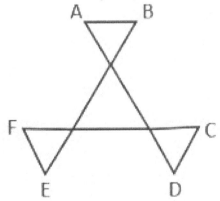

A. 180°
B. 360°
C. 540°
D. 720°

Q.6 Form the differential equation of $y = ae^{3x}\cos(x + b)$ Where $y' = \frac{dy}{dx}$ and $y^n = \frac{d^2y}{dx^2}$?
A. $y'' - 6y' + 10y = 0$
B. $y'' - 6y' - 10y = 0$
C. $y'' + 6y' - 10y = 0$
D. $y'' + 6y' + 10y = 0$

Q.7 General solution of $(x^2 + y^2)dx - 2xy dy = 0$ is:
A. $y^2 + x^2 = cx^2$
B. $x^2 - y^2 = cx$
C. $x^2 = cx(x^2 - y^2)$
D. None of these

Q.8 The integrating factor of the differential equation $2y\frac{dx}{dy} + x = 5y^2$ is, $(y \neq 0)$:
A. $\sqrt{y}$
B. y^2
C. y
D. $\frac{1}{\sqrt{y}}$

Q.9 If 7^{103} is divided by 25, then the remainder is:
A. 20
B. 16
C. 18
D. 15

Q.10 The value of the term independent of x in the expansion of $\left(x^2 - \frac{1}{x}\right)^9$ is:
A. 9
B. 18
C. 48
D. 32

Q.11 The 4th term in the expansion of $\left(\sqrt{x} + \frac{1}{x}\right)^{12}$ is:
A. $220x^2$
B. $220x^3$
C. $220x^{\frac{3}{2}}$
D. $110x^{\frac{3}{2}}$

Q.12 The following table gives the weights of one hundred persons. Copute the coefficient of dispersion by the method of limits.

Class-interval	40-45	45-50	50-55	55-60	60-65	65-70	70-75	75-80	80-85	85-90
No. of persons	4	13	8	14	9	16	17	9	8	2

A. 0.387
B. 0.385
C. 0.384
D. 0.380

Q.13 What is the area of the region bounded by the curve $f(x) = 1 - \frac{x^2}{4}, x \in [-2,2]$ and the x-axis?
A. $\frac{8}{3}$ square units
B. $\frac{4}{3}$ square units
C. $\frac{2}{3}$ square units
D. $\frac{1}{3}$ square units

Q.14 Calculate the area under the curve $y = 2\sqrt{x}$ and included between the lines $x = 0, x = 4$.
A. $\frac{32}{5}$
B. $\frac{32}{3}$
C. $\frac{31}{2}$
D. $\frac{3}{2}$

Q.15 Find the area of the curve $y = 4x^3$ between the end points $x = [-2,3]$
A. 97
B. 65
C. 70
D. 77

Q.16 If $n = 100!$, then what is the value of the following?
$\frac{1}{\log_2 n} + \frac{1}{\log_3 n} + \frac{1}{\log_4 n} + \cdots + \frac{1}{\log_{100} n}$
[UPSC NDA, 2021]
A. 0
B. 1
C. 2
D. 3

Q.17 Find the value of $\sqrt{(5 + 12i)}$, where $i = \sqrt{-1}$.

A. ±(2 + 3i) B. ±(3 + 2i)
C. ±(2 − 3i) D. ±(1 + 2i)

Q.18 The minimum of the objective function $Z = 2x + 10y$ for linear constraints $x - y \geq 0, x - 5y \leq -5, x \geq 0, y \geq 0$, is:
A. 15 B. 16 C. 17 D. 18

Q.19 The point which does not belong to the feasible region of the LPP:

Minimize: $Z = 60x + 10y$
subject to $3x + y \geq 18$
$2x + 2y \geq 12$
$x + 2y \geq 10$
$x, y \geq 0$ is:
A. (0,8) B. (4,2) C. (6,2) D. (10,0)

Q.20 Maximize $Z = 4x + 9y$, subject to the constraints $x = 0, y = 0, x + 5y \leq 200, 2x + 3y \leq 134$.
A. 359 B. 856 C. 382 D. 756

Q.21 Find the equation of the line perpendicular to the line $x - 3y + 5 = 0$ and passes through the point $(2, -4)$.
A. $3x + y - 2 = 0$ B. $3x - y - 10 = 0$
C. $x - 3y - 14 = 0$ D. $x + 3y + 10 = 0$

Q.22 What is the equation of the straight line which passes through the point of intersection of the straight lines $x + 2y = 5$ and $3x + 7y = 17$ and is perpendicular to the straight line $3x + 4y = 10$?
A. $4x + 3y + 2 = 0$ B. $4x - y + 2 = 0$
C. $4x - 3y - 2 = 0$ D. $4x - 3y + 2 = 0$

Q.23 If $f(x)$ and $g(x)$ are two probability density functions,

$$f(x) = \begin{cases} \frac{x}{a} + 1 & : -a \leq x < 0 \\ -\frac{x}{a} + 1 & 0 \leq x \leq a \\ 0 & \text{otherwise} \end{cases}$$

$$g(x) = \begin{cases} -\frac{x}{a} & : -a \leq x \leq 0 \\ \frac{x}{a} & : 0 \leq x \leq a \\ 0 & : \text{otherwise} \end{cases}$$

Which one of the following statements is true?

A. Mean of $f(x)$ and $g(x)$ are same; Variance of $f(x)$ and $g(x)$ are same
B. Mean of $f(x)$ and $g(x)$ are same; Variance of $f(x)$ and $g(x)$ are different
C. Mean of $f(x)$ and $g(x)$ are different; Variance of $f(x)$ and $g(x)$ are same
D. Mean of $f(x)$ and $g(x)$ are different; Variance of $f(x)$ and $g(x)$ are different

Q.24 Find the maximum value of 15sin θ + 20cos θ.
A. 25 B. 35 C. 30 D. 5

Q.25 If $\vec{OA} = \vec{a}$ and $\vec{OB} = \vec{b}$, then $\vec{BA}$ is:
[UPSESSB TGT Mathematics, 2013]
A. $\vec{a} + \vec{b}$ B. $\vec{a}$ C. $\vec{b}$ D. $\vec{a} - \vec{b}$

Q.26 Find the position vector of the midpoint of the vector joining the points $P(2,3,4)$ and $Q(4,1,-2)$.
A. $3\hat{i} + 2\hat{j} + \hat{k}$ B. $-3\hat{i} - 2\hat{j} - \hat{k}$
C. $-5\hat{i} - 3\hat{j} - 8\hat{k}$ D. $5\hat{i} - 3\hat{j} + 8\hat{k}$

Q.27 If $\sec^2\theta + \tan^2\theta = 3$ then find the value of $\cot\theta$.
A. 0 B. 1 C. 2 D. $\sqrt{3}$

Q.28 Suppose $\sin 2\theta = \cos 3\theta$, here $0 < \theta < \frac{\pi}{2}$ then what is the value of $\cos 2\theta$?
A. $\frac{1+\sqrt{5}}{4}$ B. $\frac{1-2\sqrt{5}}{8}$ C. $\frac{-1+\sqrt{5}}{4}$ D. $\frac{-1-\sqrt{5}}{4}$

Q.29 $\frac{\sin 7x + 6\sin 5x + 17\sin 3x + 12\sin x}{\sin 6x + 5\sin 4x + 12\sin 2x}$ equals:
A. $\sin x$ B. $2\sin x$ C. $\cos x$ D. $2\cos x$

Q.30 The value of $\frac{d}{dx} x^{2x} =$
A. $2x^2 \log x$ B. $\frac{x^2}{2(1+\log x)}$
C. x^{2x} D. $2x^{2x}[1 + \log x]$

Q.31 Find the value $f'(x)$, if $f(x) = \sin^{-1}(1 - x^2)$
A. $\frac{1}{\sqrt{1-x^2}}$ B. $\frac{2}{\sqrt{2-x^2}}$ C. $\frac{-2}{\sqrt{2-x^2}}$ D. $\frac{-1}{\sqrt{1-x^2}}$

Q.32 What is the value of expression after solving limits: $\lim_{x \to \infty} \left(\frac{x^2+5x+3}{x^2+x+3}\right)^x$
A. e^4 B. e^2 C. e^3 D. 1

Q.33 There are 7 Men and 6 Women. In how many ways can we select 5 members in which at least 3 men should be there:
[TISS NET, 2019]
A. 836 B. 256 C. 495 D. 756

Q.34 $\vec{A} \times \vec{B} = \frac{1}{2} AB$, what is the angle between A and B?
A. Zero B. 30° C. 60° D. 90°

Q.35 Find the centre and radius of $x^2 + y^2 + 6y = 0$.
A. (0,3), 3 B. (−3,0), 3
C. (3,0), 3 D. (0, −3), 3

Q.36 Find the value of k if $\lim_{x \to 2}(3x^2 + 5x - 1) = k$
A. 21 B. 18 C. 32 D. -6

Q.37 Find the equation of the normal to the curve $y = 3x^2 + 1$, which passes through $(2,13)$.
A. $x + 12y + 158 = 0$ B. $x - 12y - 156 = 0$
C. $12x + y - 156 = 0$ D. $x + 12y - 158 = 0$

Q.38 Find the equation of tangent to the curve $y = \sqrt{5x-3} - 2$, which is parallel to the line $4x - 2y + 3 = 0$?

A. $80x - 40y + 103 = 0$
B. $80x + 40y + 103 = 0$
C. $80x + 40y - 103 = 0$
D. $80x - 40y - 103 = 0$

Q.39 The maximum value of $\dfrac{\ln x}{x}$ is:

A. e B. $\dfrac{1}{e}$ C. $\dfrac{2}{e}$ D. 1

Q.40 Direction: Each of the questions below consists of a question and three statements numbered I, II and III given below it. You have to decide whether the data provided in the statements are sufficient to answer the question. Read all the statements and give answer:

On a recent journey Aman drove from City A to city B to city C. His average speed for the whole journey was 60 km/hr. Find the average speed on his journey from city B to city C.

Statement I: Average speed during the journey from city A to city B is 48 km/hr
Statement II: Total time taken for the entire journey is 3 hours
Statement III: Ratio of distance travelled while going from A to B and B to C is 2 : 3

A. Either statement III alone or statements I and II together are sufficient.
B. Only statement III is sufficient.
C. Statement I and Statement II together are sufficient.
D. Statement I and Statement II together are sufficient.

Q.41 Direction: Each of the questions below consists of a question and three statements numbered I, II and III given below it. You have to decide whether the data provided in the statements are sufficient to answer the question. Read all the statements and give answer:

How much profit did the company earn in the year 2002?

Statement I: The company earned 40% more profit in the year 2003 than that in the year 2001.
Statement II: The company earned a total profit of Rs. 20 crores in the years 2001 and 2002 taken together.
Statement III: In the year 2003, the company earned 80% of the profit earned in 2002.

A. Either statement III alone or statements I and II together are sufficient.
B. Only statement III is sufficient.
C. Statement I and Statement II together are sufficient.
D. Only statement I, II, and III together are sufficient.

Q.42 Evaluate $\int_0^{\frac{\pi}{2}} \dfrac{\cos x}{1+\sin^2 x}\,dx$:

A. $90°$
B. $45°$
C. $\tan^{-1}\left(\dfrac{1}{\sqrt{2}}\right)$
D. $-\tan^{-1}\left(\dfrac{1}{\sqrt{2}}\right)$

Q.43 What is $\int_{-\frac{\pi}{6}}^{\frac{\pi}{6}} \dfrac{\sin^5 x \cos^3 x}{x^4}\,dx$ equal to?

A. $\dfrac{\pi}{2}$ B. $\dfrac{\pi}{4}$ C. $\dfrac{\pi}{8}$ D. 0

Q.44 Evaluate: $\int \dfrac{x^2+1}{(x+1)^2}\,dx$:

A. $x - 2\log|x+1| - \dfrac{2}{x+1} + C$
B. $x + 2\log|x+1| - \dfrac{2}{x+1} + C$
C. $x + 2\log|x+1| + \dfrac{2}{x+1} + C$
D. None of these

Q.45 Evaluate: $\int \dfrac{\cot x}{\log(\sin x)}\,dx$:

A. $\log|\log(\cos x)| + C$
B. $\log|\log(\sin x)| + C$
C. $\log|\log(\cot x)| + C$
D. None of these

Q.46 If $\int \dfrac{x^2+1}{x(x+1)^2}\,dx = A\ln|x| + \dfrac{B}{1+x} + C$, where C is the constant of integration, then $A + B =$

A. 5   B. 4   C. 3   D. 2

Q.47 The point of intersection of diagonals of a square ABCD is at the origin and one of its vertices is at A(4, 2). What is the equation of the diagonal BD?

[UPSC NDA, 2021]

A. 2x + y = 0
B. 2x - y = 0
C. x + 2y = 0
D. x - 2y = 0

Q.48 The equation of the line passing through (0, 0) and perpendicular to the line 2x + 3y + 5 = 0, is:

A. 2x - 3y = 0
B. 3x - 2y = 0
C. 3x + 2y = 0
D. 2x + 3y = 0

Q.49 What is the equation of line passing through (0, 1) and making an angle with the y-axis equal to the inclination of the line x - y = 4 with x-axis?

A. y = x + 1
B. x = y + 1
C. 2x = y + 2
D. 2x = y - 2

Q.50 For a standard normal probability distribution, the mean (μ) and the standard deviation (s) are:

A. μ = 0, s = 1
B. μ = 16, s = 4
C. μ = 25, s = 5
D. μ = 100, s = 10

// Smart Answer Sheet //

Correct Indicates percentage of students who answered questions correctly.

Skipped Indicates percentage of students who skipped questions.

Q.	Ans.	Correct / Skipped	Q.	Ans.	Correct / Skipped	Q.	Ans.	Correct / Skipped	Q.	Ans.	Correct / Skipped	Q.	Ans.	Correct / Skipped
1	A	66.67 % / 11.11 %	11	D	0 % / 100 %	21	A	61.11 % / 5.56 %	31	C	61.11 % / 5.56 %	41	D	33.33 % / 5.56 %
2	B	44.44 % / 5.56 %	12	C	33.33 % / 5.56 %	22	D	66.67 % / 5.55 %	32	A	22.22 % / 11.11 %	42	B	61.11 % / 5.56 %
3	D	72.22 % / 11.11 %	13	A	33.33 % / 5.56 %	23	B	27.78 % / 5.55 %	33	D	44.44 % / 11.12 %	43	D	55.56 % / 5.55 %
4	B	72.22 % / 11.11 %	14	B	72.22 % / 5.56 %	24	A	72.22 % / 5.56 %	34	C	22.22 % / 11.11 %	44	A	33.33 % / 5.56 %
5	B	61.11 % / 5.56 %	15	A	16.67 % / 11.11 %	25	D	55.56 % / 5.55 %	35	D	72.22 % / 5.56 %	45	B	66.67 % / 5.55 %
6	C	5.56 % / 5.55 %	16	B	66.67 % / 5.55 %	26	A	72.22 % / 11.11 %	36	A	83.33 % / 5.56 %	46	C	27.78 % / 11.11 %
7	C	38.89 % / 11.11 %	17	B	38.89 % / 5.55 %	27	B	72.22 % / 5.56 %	37	D	61.11 % / 5.56 %	47	A	33.33 % / 5.56 %
8	A	38.89 % / 5.55 %	18	A	50.0 % / 5.56 %	28	A	44.44 % / 11.12 %	38	D	50.0 % / 5.56 %	48	B	55.56 % / 5.55 %
9	C	50.0 % / 5.56 %	19	B	50.0 % / 11.11 %	29	D	27.78 % / 5.55 %	39	B	72.22 % / 5.56 %	49	A	77.78 % / 5.55 %
10	D	5.56 % / 5.55 %	20	C	38.89 % / 5.55 %	30	D	61.11 % / 11.11 %	40	D	5.56 % / 5.55 %	50	A	55.56 % / 5.55 %

Performance Analysis	
Avg. Score (%)	38.0%
Toppers Score (%)	94.0%
Your Score	

//Hints and Solutions//

1. Given that:

There are 20 cricket players, out of which 5 players can bowl.

We have to make a team of 11 players so to include 4 bowlers.

So, we select 4 bowlers out of 5 players and the remaining 7 players must be selected from 15 players, i.e.,

Total ways $= {}^5C_4 \times {}^{15}C_7$

Hence, the correct option is (A).

2. Given,

$A = \begin{bmatrix} 1 & -1 & 0 \\ 3 & 2 & -1 \end{bmatrix}$ and $B = \begin{bmatrix} 1 \\ 3 \\ 5 \end{bmatrix}$

$\Rightarrow AB = \begin{bmatrix} 1 & -1 & 0 \\ 3 & 2 & -1 \end{bmatrix} \times \begin{bmatrix} 1 \\ 3 \\ 5 \end{bmatrix}$

$\Rightarrow AB = \begin{bmatrix} 1 - 3 + 0 \\ 3 + 6 - 5 \end{bmatrix}$

$\Rightarrow AB = \begin{bmatrix} -2 \\ 4 \end{bmatrix}$

As we know,

The new matrix obtained by interchanging the rows and columns of the original matrix is called as the transpose of the matrix. It is denoted by A' or A^T.

$\therefore (AB)^T = [-2 \quad 4]$

Hence, the correct option is (B).

3. Given,

$A = \begin{bmatrix} \cos 2\theta & -\sin 2\theta \\ \sin 2\theta & \cos 2\theta \end{bmatrix}$

$A + A^T = 1$

The transpose of matrix A is given by,

$A^T = \begin{bmatrix} \cos 2\theta & \sin 2\theta \\ -\sin 2\theta & \cos 2\theta \end{bmatrix}$

As, $A + A^T = I$

$\begin{bmatrix} \cos 2\theta & -\sin 2\theta \\ \sin 2\theta & \cos 2\theta \end{bmatrix} + \begin{bmatrix} \cos 2\theta & \sin 2\theta \\ -\sin 2\theta & \cos 2\theta \end{bmatrix} = I$

$\Rightarrow \begin{bmatrix} 2\cos 2\theta & 0 \\ 0 & 2\cos 2\theta \end{bmatrix} = \begin{bmatrix} 1 & 0 \\ 0 & 1 \end{bmatrix}$

As we know that,

If two matrices A and B are equal then their corresponding elements are also equal.

$\therefore 2\cos 2\theta = 1$

$\Rightarrow \cos 2\theta = \frac{1}{2}$

$\Rightarrow \cos 2\theta = \cos 60°$

$\Rightarrow 2\theta = \frac{\pi}{3}$ $[\because \cos 60° = \frac{\pi}{3}]$

$\therefore \theta = \frac{\pi}{6}$

So, the value of θ is $\frac{\pi}{6}$.

Hence, the correct option is (D).

4. Given,

$A = \begin{bmatrix} \cos\alpha & \sin\alpha \\ -\sin\alpha & \cos\alpha \end{bmatrix}$

The transpose of matrix A is given by,

$A^T = \begin{bmatrix} \cos\alpha & -\sin\alpha \\ \sin\alpha & \cos\alpha \end{bmatrix}$

Now,

$AA^T = \begin{bmatrix} \cos\alpha & \sin\alpha \\ -\sin\alpha & \cos\alpha \end{bmatrix} \times \begin{bmatrix} \cos\alpha & -\sin\alpha \\ \sin\alpha & \cos\alpha \end{bmatrix}$

$\Rightarrow AA^T =$

$\begin{bmatrix} \cos^2\alpha + \sin^2\alpha & -\cos\alpha\sin\alpha + \cos\alpha\sin\alpha \\ -\cos\alpha\sin\alpha + \cos\alpha\sin\alpha & \sin^2\alpha + \cos^2\alpha \end{bmatrix}$

$\Rightarrow AA^T = \begin{bmatrix} 1 & 0 \\ 0 & 1 \end{bmatrix}$

$\Rightarrow AA^T = I$

So, AA^T is a identify matrix.

Hence, the correct option is (B).

5. Given:

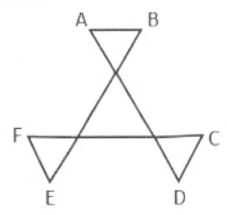

Calculation:

As, the given figure is

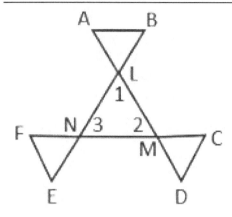

Here, in Δ LMN, ∠1 + ∠2 + ∠3 = 180°   ----(i) (Sum of interior angles of a triangle = 180°)

As, ∠BLM is the exterior angle for Δ ABL,

So, ∠A + ∠B = (∠BLM Sum of two interior angle is equal to the exterior angle)

⇒ ∠A + ∠B = 180° - ∠1   ----(ii)

Similarly, ∠CML and ∠FNL are the exterior angles of Δ CDM and Δ FEN,

So, ∠C+ ∠D = 180° - ∠2   ----(iii)

And, ∠E + ∠F = 180° - ∠3   ----(iv)

Adding equations (ii), (iii) and (iv) we get

∠A + ∠B + ∠C + ∠D + ∠E + ∠F = 180° × 3 - (∠1 + ∠2 + ∠3)   ----(v)

From (i) and (v), we get

∠A + ∠B + ∠C + ∠D + ∠E + ∠F = 180° × 3 - 180°

⇒ ∠A + ∠B + ∠C + ∠D + ∠E + ∠F = 360°

∴ The sum of the measures of the angles ∠A, ∠B, ∠C, ∠D, ∠E, and ∠F in the given figure is 360°.

Hence, the correct option is (B).

6. Given,

$y = ae^{3x}\cos(x+b)$

There are two constants a and b so differentiate two times Differentiating wr.t x,

We get,

$y' = 3ae^{3x}\cos(x+b) - ae^{3x}\sin(x+b)$

⇒ $y' = 3y - ae^{3x}\sin(x+b)$

⇒ $ae^{3x}\sin(x+b) = 3y - y'$

Differentiating again w.r.t x,

We get,

$3ae^{3x}\sin(x+b) + ae^{3x}\cos(x+b) = 3y' - y''$

⇒ $3(3y - y') + y - 3y' - y'' = 0$

⇒ $9y - 3y' + y - 3y' - y'' = 0$

⇒ $y'' + 6y' - 10y = 0$

Hence, the correct option is (C).

7. Given,

$(x^2 + y^2)dx = 2xydy$

$\frac{dy}{dx} = \frac{(x^2+y^2)}{2xy}$ is homogeneous.

Put, $y = vx$

$\frac{dy}{dx} = v + \frac{xdv}{dx}$

⇒ $v + x\frac{dv}{dx} = \frac{x^2+v^2x^2}{2vx^2} = \frac{x^2(1+v^2)}{2vx^2}$

⇒ $x\frac{dv}{dx} = \frac{1+v^2}{2v} - v = \frac{1-v^2}{2v}$

⇒ $\frac{2v}{1-v^2}dv = \frac{1}{x}dx$

By integrating both sides we get,

$\int \frac{2v}{1-v^2}dv = \int \frac{1}{x}dx \ldots\ldots (1)$

Now, we integrate $\int \frac{2v}{1-v^2}dv$

Let, $1 - v^2 = a$

On differentiating both sides w.r.t. v, we get

$\frac{d}{dv}(1 - v^2) = \frac{d}{dv}a$

$-2v = \frac{da}{dv}$

$dv = -\frac{da}{2v}$

Now, putting these values on equation (1), we get

$\int \frac{2v}{a} \times -\frac{da}{2v} = \int \frac{1}{x}dx$

⇒ $\int -\frac{da}{a} = \int \frac{1}{x}dx$

We know that,

$\int \frac{1}{x}dx = \log x$

Now,

$-\log(1 - v^2) = \log x + \log c$

⇒ $\log\left[\frac{1}{(1-v^2)}\right] = \log x + \log c$

⇒ $\left[\frac{1}{(1-v^2)}\right] = cx$

$\Rightarrow \left[\dfrac{1}{\left(1-\dfrac{y^2}{x^2}\right)}\right] = cx$

$\Rightarrow \left[\dfrac{x^2}{(x^2-y^2)}\right] = cx$

$\Rightarrow x^2 = cx(x^2 - y^2)$ is the general solution of the differential equation.

Hence, the correct option is (C).

8. Given,

$2y\dfrac{dx}{dy} + x = 5y^2$ ... (i)

Equation (i) can be simplified as,

$\dfrac{dx}{dy} + \dfrac{x}{2y} = \dfrac{5}{2}y$

On comparing eqn (i) with standard eqn,

$\dfrac{dx}{dy} + Px = Q$,

We get

$P = \dfrac{1}{2y}$ and $Q = \dfrac{5}{2}y$

Therefore,

$IF = e^{\int P dy} = e^{\int \tfrac{1}{2y} dy}$

$\Rightarrow IF = e^{\tfrac{1}{2}\log y} = e^{\log y^{\tfrac{1}{2}}}$

$\Rightarrow IF = \sqrt{y}$ $(\because e^{a\log x} = x^a)$

Hence, the correct option is (A).

9. We have,

$7^{103} = 7(49)^{51} = 7(50-1)^{51}$

$= 7(50^{51} - {}^{51}C_1 50^{50} + {}^{51}C_2 50^{49} - \cdots - 1)$

$= 7(50^{51} - {}^{51}C_1 50^{50} + {}^{51}C_2 50^{49} - \cdots) - 7 + 18 - 18$

$= 7(50^{51} - {}^{51}C_1 50^{50} + {}^{51}C_2 50^{49} - \cdots) - 25 + 18$

$= k + 18$(say) where k is divisible by 25,

$\therefore$ remainder is 18.

Hence, the correct option is (C).

10. Concept:

In the binomial expansion of $(a+b)^n$, the term which does not involve any variable is said to be an independent term.

The general term in the binomial expansion of $(a+b)^n$ is given by: $T_{r+1} = {}^nC_r \times a^{n-r} \times b^r$

Given: $\left(x^2 - \dfrac{1}{x}\right)^9$

Let $(r+1)^{th}$ be the independent term in the expansion of $\left(x^2 - \dfrac{1}{x}\right)^9$.

We know that the general term in the binomial expansion of $(a+b)^n$ is given by:

$T_{r+1} = {}^nC_r \times a^{n-r} \times b^r$

Here, $a = x^2, n = 9$ and $b = \dfrac{1}{x}$.

$\Rightarrow T_{r+1} = {}^9C_r \times x^{2(9-r)} \times \left(\dfrac{1}{x}\right)^r = {}^9C_r \times x^{18-3r}$

$\because$ The $(r+1)^{th}$ term is the independent term in the expansion of $\left(x^2 - \dfrac{1}{x}\right)^9 \Rightarrow x^{18-3r} = x^0$

$\Rightarrow 18 - 3r = 0 \Rightarrow r = 6$

$\Rightarrow 7^{th}$ term in the expansion of $\left(x^2 - \dfrac{1}{x}\right)^9$ is the independent term.

We have to find the value of the 7th term in the expansion of $\left(x^2 - \dfrac{1}{x}\right)^9$

$\Rightarrow T_7 = {}^9C_6 \times 1 = 84$

Hence, the correct option is (D).

11. Concept:

We have
$(x+y)^n = {}^nC_0 x^n + {}^nC_1 x^{n-1} \cdot y + {}^nC_2 x^{n-2} \cdot y^2 + \cdots + {}^nC_n y^n$

General term: General term in the expansion of $(x+y)^n$ is given by $T_{(r+1)} = {}^nC_r \times x^{n-r} \times y^r$

In the binomial expansion of $(x+y)^n$, the rth term from end is $(n-r+2)^{th}$ term. ${}^nC_r = \dfrac{n!}{r!(n-r)!}$

We have to find 4 th term in the expansion of $\left(\sqrt{x} + \dfrac{1}{x}\right)^{12}$

We know that, $T_{(r+1)} = {}^nC_r \times x^{n-r} \times y^r$

$\Rightarrow T_4 = T_{(3+1)} = {}^{12}C_3 \times (\sqrt{x})^{12-3} \times \left(\dfrac{1}{x}\right)^3$

$= {}^{12}C_3 \times (x)^{\tfrac{9}{2}} \times \dfrac{1}{x^3}$

$= \dfrac{12!}{3!(12-3)!} \times (x)^{\tfrac{9}{2}-3}$

$= 220 x^{\tfrac{3}{2}}$

Hence, the correct option is (D).

12. Given,

Upper limit of the Highest Class Interval (H) = 90

Lower limit of the Lowest Class Interval (L) = 40

Range = Highest Value − Lowest Value

i.e., R = H − L

Substituting the given values in the formula.

R = 90 − 40 = 50

Coefficeint of Range = $\frac{H-L}{H+L}$

= $\frac{90-40}{90+40}$

= $\frac{50}{130}$

= 0.384

So, range of the above series is 50 kg and coefficient of range is 0.384

Hence, the correct option is (C).

13. We know that:

The area of the region bounded by the curve $f(x), x \in [-a, a]$ and the x-axis is given by:

$A = \int_{-a}^{a} f(x)dx$

Therefore,

The area of the region bounded by the curve $f(x) = 1 - \frac{x^2}{4}, x \in [-2,2]$ and the x-axis will be:

$A = \int_{-2}^{2} \left(1 - \frac{x^2}{4}\right)dx$

$\Rightarrow A = \left[x - \frac{x^3}{12}\right]_{-2}^{2}$

$\Rightarrow A = [2 - (-2)] - \left[\frac{8}{12} - \frac{-8}{12}\right]$

$\Rightarrow A = 4 - \frac{4}{3}$

$\Rightarrow A = \frac{8}{3}$

Therefore, the area of the region bounded by the curve $f(x) = 1 - \frac{x^2}{4}, x \in [-2,2]$ and the x-axis is $\frac{8}{3}$ square units.

Hence, the correct option is (A).

14. Given here,

$y = 2\sqrt{x}$

$\therefore y^2 = 4x \quad (x \geq 0)$

We need to determine area under curve $y^2 = 4x(x \geq 0)$ included between the lines $x = 0, x = 4$ as:

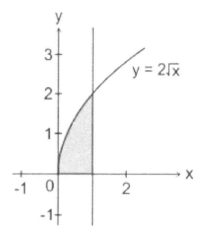

So, the area under curve will be given as:

= $\int_0^4 2\sqrt{x}dx$

= $2\int_0^4 x^{\frac{1}{2}} dx$

We know that:

$\int x^n dx = \frac{x^{n+1}}{n+1}$

$x^{m+n} = (x^m)(x^n)$

Therefore,

$2\int_0^4 x^{\frac{1}{2}} dx$

= $2\left[\frac{x^{1+\frac{1}{2}}}{1+\left(\frac{1}{2}\right)}\right]_0^4$

= $2\left[\frac{x^{1+\left(\frac{1}{2}\right)}}{\frac{3}{2}}\right]_0^4$

= $2\left[\frac{2}{3}\left((4)^{1+\left(\frac{1}{2}\right)} - 0\right)\right]$

= $2\left[\frac{2}{3}\left((4)^1(4)^{\frac{1}{2}}\right)\right]$

= $\frac{(2)(2)(4)(2)}{3}$

= $\frac{32}{3}$ sq units

Hence, the correct option is (B).

15. Let $f(x) = y = 4x^3$

Given the end points are:

$x_1 = -2, x_2 = 3$

Therefore,

Area of the curve $(A) = \left|\int_{-2}^{3} 4x^3 dx\right|$

$\Rightarrow A = \left|\int_{-2}^{0} 4x^3 dx\right| + \left|\int_{0}^{3} 4x^3 dx\right|$

$\Rightarrow A = \left|4\left[\frac{x^4}{4}\right]_{-2}^{0}\right| + \left|4\left[\frac{x^4}{4}\right]_{0}^{3}\right|$

$\Rightarrow A = |[0 - 2^4]| + |[3^4 - 0]|$

$\Rightarrow A = |-16| + |81|$

$\Rightarrow A = 97$

Hence, the correct option is (A).

16. Given:

$\frac{1}{\log_2 n} + \frac{1}{\log_3 n} + \frac{1}{\log_4 n} + \cdots + \frac{1}{\log_{100} n}$

$= \log_n 2 + \log_n 3 + \log_n 4 + \cdots + \log_n 100$

$= \log_n [2 \times 3 \times 4 \times \ldots \times 100]$

$= \log_n 100!$

$= \log_{100!} 100!$

$= 1$

Hence, the correct option is (B).

17. Let,

$\sqrt{(5 + 12i)} = x + iy$

On squaring both sides we get,

$5 + 12i = (x + iy)^2$

$\Rightarrow 5 + 12i = x^2 + (iy)^2 + 2(x)(iy)$

$\Rightarrow 5 + 12i = x^2 + i^2 y^2 + 2xyi$

As we know,

$i^2 = -1$

$\Rightarrow 5 + 12i = x^2 + (-1)y^2 + 2xyi$

$\Rightarrow 5 + 12i = (x^2 - y^2) + (2xy)i$

Comparing real and imaginary parts on both sides, we get

$x^2 - y^2 = 5$ and $2xy = 12$

$\therefore xy = 6$

$\Rightarrow y = \frac{6}{x}$

Now, $(x^2 - y^2) = 5$

Putting value of y in above equation, we get

$x^2 - \left(\frac{6}{x}\right)^2 = 5$

$\Rightarrow x^2 - \frac{36}{x^2} = 5$

$\Rightarrow \frac{x^4 - 36}{x^2} = 5$

$\Rightarrow x^4 - 36 = 5x^2$

$\Rightarrow x^4 - 5x^2 - 36 = 0$

$\Rightarrow x^4 - 9x^2 + 4x^2 - 36 = 0$

$\Rightarrow x^2(x^2 - 9) + 4(x^2 - 9) = 0$

$\Rightarrow x^2 - 9 = 0$ or $x^2 + 4 = 0$

$\Rightarrow x^2 = 9$ or $x^2 = -4$

$\Rightarrow x = \pm 3$ (we know that x^2 is always greater than zero so, we neglect $x^2 = -4$

Now, $x^2 - y^2 = 5$

$\therefore 9 - y^2 = 5$

$\Rightarrow y^2 = 4$

$\Rightarrow y = \pm 2$

So, $\sqrt{(5 + 12i)} = \pm(3 + 2i)$

Hence, the correct option is (B).

18. Given:

Minimize $Z = x + 4y$

$x + 3y \geq 3, 2x + y \geq 2, x \geq 0, y \geq 0$

To draw the feasible region, construct table as follows:

Inequality	$x + 3y \geq 3$	$2x + y \geq 2$
Corresponding equation (of line)	$x + 3y = 3$	$2x + y = 2$
Intersection of line with X-axis	$((3,0)$	$(1,0)$
Intersection of line with Y-axis	$(0,1)$	$(0,2)$
Region	Non-origin side	Non-origin side

Shaded portion XABCY is the feasible region, whose vertices are $A(3,0), B$ and $C(0,2)$ B is the point of intersection of the lines $2x + y = 2$ and $x + 3y = 3$

$\therefore B \equiv \left(\frac{3}{5}, \frac{4}{5}\right)$

Here, the objective function is

$Z = x + 4y$

$\therefore Z$ at $A(3,0) = 3 + 4(0)$

$= 3$

Z at $B\left(\frac{3}{5},\frac{4}{5}\right) = \frac{3}{5} + 4\left(\frac{4}{5}\right)$

$= \frac{19}{5}$

$= 3 \times 8$

Z at $C(0,2) = 0 + 4(2) = 8$

$\therefore Z$ has minimum value 3 at $x = 3$ and $y = 0$.

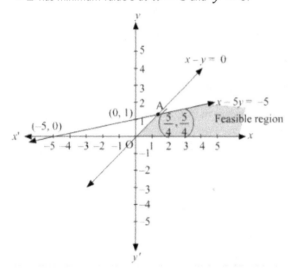

Hence, the correct option is (A).

19. Given:

Minimize: $Z = 60x + 10y$

subject to $3x + y \geq 18$

$2x + 2y \geq 12$

$x + 2y \geq 10$

$x, y \geq 0$

We test whether the inequalitiies are satisfied or not
$(0,8), 3(0) + 8 \geq 88 \geq 8$ is true.

$2(0) + 2(8) = 16 \geq 12$ is true. $0 + 2(8) = 16 \geq 10$ is true.

$\therefore (0,8)$ is in the feasible region.

$(4,2), 3(4) + 2 = 14 \geq 8$

$2(4) + 2(2) = 16 \geq 12$

$4 + 2(2) = 8 \geq 10$ is not true

$\therefore (4,2)$ is not a point in the feasible region

Hence, the correct option is (B).

20. Given:

$Z = 4x + 9y$, subject to the constraints $x = 0, y = 0, x + 5y \leq 200, 2x + 3y \leq 134$.

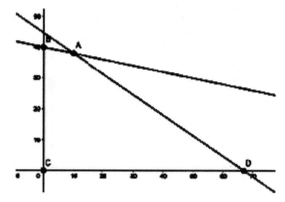

The corner points of feasible region are
$A(10,38), B(0,40), C(0,0), D(67,0)$.

The values of Z at the following points is

Corner Point	$Z = 4x + 9y$	
$A(10,38)$	382	Maximum
$B(0,40)$	360	
$C(0,0)$	0	
$D(67,0)$	268	

The maximum value of Z is 382 at point $A(10,38)$.

Hence, the correct option is (C).

21. Given,

Line $x - 3y + 5 = 0$

The general equation of a line is $y = mx + c$

Where m is the slope and c is any constant

- The slope of parallel lines is equal.
- The slope of the perpendicular line have their product $= -1$

$\Rightarrow y = \frac{1}{3}x + \frac{5}{3}$

$\Rightarrow$ Slope $(m_1) = \frac{1}{3}$ and $c_1 = \frac{5}{3}$

Now for the slope of the perpendicular line m_2

$m_1 \times m_2 = -1$

$\Rightarrow \frac{1}{3} \times m_2 = -1$

$\Rightarrow m_2 = -3$

Perpendicular line has the slope -3 and passes through $(2, -4)$

$\therefore$ Equation of the perpendicular line is

Mathematics : Mock Test - 6

$(y - y_1) = m(x - x_1)$

$\Rightarrow y - (-4) = -3(x - 2)$

$\Rightarrow y + 3x - 2 = 0$

Hence, the correct option is (A).

22. Given,

$x + 2y = 5$ ...(i)

$3x + 7y = 17$ ...(ii)

Solving equation (i) and (ii), we get

$x = 1$ and $y = 2$

Point of intersection: $(x, y) = (x_1, y_1) = (1, 2)$

Let slope of the straight line $3x + 4y = 10$ is m_1

Slope $(m_1) = \dfrac{-3}{4}$

We know that when two lines are perpendicular, the product of their slope is -1.

Slope of perpendicular line $m = \dfrac{-1}{m_1} = \dfrac{4}{3}$

Equation of line: $(y - y_1) = m(x - x_1)$

$\Rightarrow y - 2 = \dfrac{4}{3}(x - 1)$

$\Rightarrow 3y - 6 = 4x - 4$

$\therefore 4x - 3y + 2 = 0$

Hence, the correct option is (D).

23. Mean of $f(x)$:

$E(x) = \int_{-a}^{0} X\left(\dfrac{X}{a} + 1\right) dx + \int_{0}^{a} X\left(\dfrac{-X}{a} + 1\right) dx$

$= \left(\dfrac{X^3}{3a} + \dfrac{X^2}{2}\right)_{-a}^{0} + \left(\dfrac{-X^3}{3a} + \dfrac{X^3}{3}\right)_{0}^{a} = 0$

$= \int_{-a}^{0} X^2\left(\dfrac{X}{a} + 1\right) dx + \int_{0}^{a} X^2\left(\dfrac{-X}{a} + 1\right) dx$

$\left(\dfrac{X^4}{4a} + \dfrac{X^3}{3}\right)_{-a}^{0} + \left(\dfrac{-X^4}{4a} + \dfrac{X^3}{3}\right)_{0}^{a} = \dfrac{a^3}{6}$

$\Rightarrow$ Variance $= \dfrac{a^3}{6}$

Mean of $g(x)$:

$E(x) = \int_{-a}^{0} x\left(\dfrac{-x}{a}\right) dx + \int_{0}^{a} x \times \left(\dfrac{x}{a}\right) dx = 0$

Variance of $g(x)$ is $E(x^2) - \{E(X)\}^2$,

Where $E(X^2) = \int_{-a}^{0} X^2 \left(\dfrac{-X}{a}\right) dX + \int_{0}^{a} X^2 \left(\dfrac{X}{a}\right) dx =$ $\dfrac{a^3}{2}$

$\Rightarrow$ Variance $= \dfrac{a^3}{2}$

$\therefore$ Mean of $f(x)$ and $g(x)$ are same but variance of $f(x)$ and $g(x)$ are different.

Hence, the correct option is (B).

24. Given: 15sin θ + 20cos θ

Here a = 15 and b = 20

Then the maximum value $= \sqrt{15^2 + 20^2}$

$= \sqrt{225 + 400}$

$= \sqrt{(625)}$

$= 25$

∴ The maximum value of 15sin θ + 20cos θ is 25.

Hence, the correct option is (A).

25. If $\vec{OA}$ is the position vector of A and $\vec{OB}$ is position vector of B then-

$\vec{AB} =$ Position Vector of $B -$ Position Vector of A
......(I)

$\vec{BA} =$ Position Vector of $A -$ Position Vector of B
......(II)

Given, $\vec{OA} = \vec{a}$ and $\vec{OB} = \vec{b}$

Then, by equation (II)

$\vec{BA} =$ position vector of $A -$ position vector of B

$\vec{BA} = \vec{OA} - \vec{OB}$

$\vec{BA} = \vec{a} - \vec{b}$

Hence, the correct option is (D).

26. Given:

The position vector of point $P = 2\hat{i} + 3\hat{j} + 4\hat{k}$

Position Vector of point $Q = 4\hat{i} + \hat{j} - 2\hat{k}$

As we know,

The position vector of $A(x_1, y_1, z_1)$ is given by

$\vec{OA} = x_1\hat{i} + y_1\hat{j} + z_1\hat{k}$ Compute the position vector of the midpoint of P and Q using the formula:

If $C(x, y, z)$ is the midpoint of segment $\vec{AB}$, then we have the position vector of $C = \vec{OC} = \dfrac{\vec{OA} + \vec{OB}}{2}$

95

$$= \left(\frac{x_1+x_2}{2}, \frac{y_1+y_2}{2}, \frac{z_1+z_2}{2}\right)$$

The position vector of R which divides PQ in half is given by:

$$\vec{r} = \frac{2\hat{\imath}+3\hat{\jmath}+4\hat{k}+4\hat{\imath}+\hat{\jmath}-2\hat{k}}{2}$$

$$\vec{r} = \frac{2\hat{\imath}+3\hat{\jmath}+4\hat{k}+4\hat{\imath}+\hat{\jmath}-2\hat{k}}{2}$$

$$\vec{r} = \frac{6\hat{\imath}+4\hat{\jmath}+2\hat{k}}{2}$$

$$= 3\hat{\imath}+2\hat{\jmath}+\hat{k}$$

Hence, the correct option is (A).

27. Given,

$$\sec^2\theta + \tan^2\theta = 3 \quad \text{...(i)}$$

Subtracting 1 from both sides in equation (i) we get,

$\sec^2\theta + \tan^2\theta - 1 = 3 - 1$ ($\because \sec^2\theta - 1 = \tan^2\theta$)

$\Rightarrow \tan^2\theta + \tan^2\theta = 2$

$\Rightarrow 2\tan^2\theta = 2$

$\Rightarrow \tan^2\theta = 1$

$\Rightarrow \tan\theta = 1$

Now,

$$\cot\theta = \frac{1}{\tan\theta}$$

$= 1$

Hence, the correct option is (B).

28. Given:

$$\sin2\theta = \cos3\theta, 0 < \theta < \frac{\pi}{2}$$

As we know that, $\sin2\theta = 2\sin\theta\cos\theta$ and $\cos3\theta = 4\cos^3\theta - 3\cos\theta$

$\Rightarrow 2\sin\theta\cos\theta = 4\cos^3\theta - 3\cos\theta$

$\Rightarrow 2\sin\theta = 4\cos^2\theta - 3$

$\Rightarrow 2\sin\theta = 4(1-\sin^2\theta) - 3 = 4 - 4\sin^2\theta - 3$

$\Rightarrow 4\sin^2\theta + 2\sin\theta - 1 = 0$

Comparing the above equation with quadratic equation $ax^2 + bx + c = 0$, $a = 4, b = 2$ and $c = -1$

Now substituting the values in the quadratic formula $x = \frac{-b \pm \sqrt{b^2 - 4ac}}{2a}$ we get,

$$\sin\theta = \frac{-2 \pm \sqrt{-2^2 - 4(4)(-1)}}{2(4)}$$

$$= \frac{-2 \pm \sqrt{4+16}}{8}$$

$$= \frac{-2 \pm \sqrt{20}}{8}$$

$$= \frac{-1 \pm \sqrt{5}}{4}$$

Thus, $\sin\theta = \frac{-1 \pm \sqrt{5}}{4}$

Since, $0 < \theta < \frac{\pi}{2} \Rightarrow \theta$ lies between $0°$ to $90° \Rightarrow$ all ratios are positive.

$$\Rightarrow \sin\theta = \frac{-1+\sqrt{5}}{4}$$

As we know that, $\cos2\theta = \cos^2\theta - \sin^2\theta$

$= 1 - 2\sin^2\theta$

$$\Rightarrow \cos2\theta = 1 - 2\left(\frac{-1+\sqrt{5}}{4}\right)^2$$

$$= \frac{1+\sqrt{5}}{4}$$

$\therefore$ The the value of $\cos2\theta$ is $\frac{1+\sqrt{5}}{4}$

Hence, the correct option is (A).

29. Given,

$$\frac{\sin7x+6\sin5x+17\sin3x+12\sin x}{\sin6x+5\sin4x+12\sin2x}$$

$$= \frac{\sin7x+\sin5x+5\sin5x+5\sin3x+12\sin3x+12\sin x}{\sin6x+5\sin4x+12\sin2x}$$

By using, $\sin x + \sin y = 2\sin\left(\frac{x+y}{2}\right)\cos\left(\frac{x-y}{2}\right)$

Therefore,

$$= \frac{(2\sin(\frac{7x+5x}{2})\cos(\frac{7x-5x}{2})+5\times(2\sin(\frac{5x+3x}{2})\cos(\frac{5x-3x}{2}))+12\times(2\sin(\frac{3x+x}{2})\cos(\frac{3x-x}{2}))}{(\sin6x+5\sin4x+12\sin2x)}$$

$$= \frac{2\sin6x\cos x+10\sin4x\cos x+24\sin2x\cos x}{(\sin6x+5\sin4x+12\sin2x)}$$

$$= \frac{2\cos x(\sin6x+5\sin4x+12\sin2x)}{(\sin6x+5\sin4x+12\sin2x)}$$

$= 2\cos x$

Hence, the correct option is (D).

30. Given:

$$\frac{d}{dx}x^{2x}$$

Concept:

$\log x^n = n\log x$

$\frac{d}{dx}[\log x] = \frac{1}{x}$

Let, $y = x^{2x}$

Taking log on both the sides, we get

$\log y = \log(x^{2x}) = 2x \log x$

$(\because \log x^n = n \log x)$

Now, taking derivatives,

$\frac{d}{dx}[\log y] = 2\left\{\frac{d}{dx}[x]\log x + \frac{d}{dx}[\log x]x\right\}$

$\frac{1}{y}\frac{dy}{dx} = 2\left[\log x + x \cdot \frac{1}{x}\right]$

$\left(\because \frac{d}{dx}[\log x] = \frac{1}{x}\right)$

$\Rightarrow \frac{dy}{dx} = 2y[1 + \log x]$

$\Rightarrow \frac{dy}{dx} = 2x^{2x}[1 + \log x]$

$(\because y = x^{2x})$

Hence, the correct option is (D).

31. Concept:

$\frac{d}{dx}\sin^{-1}x = \frac{1}{\sqrt{1-x^2}}$

$\frac{d}{dx}\tan^{-1}x = \frac{1}{1+x^2}$

Let $u = 1 - x^2$

$\frac{du}{dx} = -2x$

$y = \sin^{-1}(1-x^2) = \sin^{-1}u$

$\frac{dy}{dx} = \frac{dy}{du} \times \frac{du}{dx}$

$\frac{dy}{dx} = \frac{d}{du}\sin^{-1}u \times (-2x)$

$\frac{dy}{dx} = \frac{1}{\sqrt{1-u^2}} \times (-2x)$

$\frac{dy}{dx} = \frac{-2x}{\sqrt{1-(1-x^2)^2}}$

$\frac{dy}{dx} = \frac{-2x}{\sqrt{2x^2 - x^4}}$

$\frac{dy}{dx} = \frac{-2}{\sqrt{2-x^2}}$

Hence, the correct option is (C).

32. $\lim_{x \to \infty} \left(\frac{x^2+5x+3}{x^2+x+2}\right)^x = \lim_{x \to \infty} \left(1 + \frac{4x+1}{x^2+x+2}\right)^x$

$= \lim_{x \to \infty}\left[\left(1 + \frac{4x+1}{x^2+x+2}\right)^{\frac{x^2+x+2}{4x+1}}\right]^{\frac{(4x+1)x}{x^2+x+2}}$

$= e^{\lim_{x \to \infty}\frac{4x^2+x}{x^2+x+2}} \left[\because \lim_{x \to \infty}(1+\lambda x)^{\frac{1}{x}} = e^{\lambda}\right]$

$= e^{\lim_{x \to \infty}\frac{4+\frac{1}{x}}{1+\frac{1}{x}+\frac{2}{x^2}}} = e^4$

Hence, the correct option is (A).

33. There will be 3 cases for calculating the number of ways to form a committee is as follows,

Case 1: 3 Men, 2 Women

For selecting 3 men out of 7 and 2 women out of 6 to form the 5 people committee, we can use the formulas given in the hint as follows,

$= {}^7C_3 \times {}^6C_2$

$= 35 \times 15$

$= 525$

Case 2: 4 Men, 1 Woman

For selecting 4 men out of 7 and 1 woman out of 6 to form thee 5 people committee, we can use the formulas given in the hint as follows

$= {}^7C_4 \times {}^6C_1$

$= 35 \times 6$

$= 210$

Case 3: 5 Men, 0 Women

For selecting 5 men out of 7 and 0 women out of 6 to form thee 5 people committee, we can use the formulas given in the hint as follows,

$= {}^7C_5 \times {}^6C_0$

$= 21 \times 1$

$= 21$

Total $= 525 + 210 + 21 = 756$

Hence, the correct option is (D).

34. Using Dot Product principle: $A \times B = AB\cos(\$)$
Here, $\$$, means the angle between vector A and B
Angle of arbitrary vectors A, B, is defined in range $(0°, 180°)$
Then, factor AB dissolved on both sides of equation. We will get

$\cos(\$) = \frac{1}{2}$

Finally referring to the above range, you can get only one answer: 60°

Hence, the correct option is (C).

35. Given,

$x^2 + y^2 + 6y = 0$

$\Rightarrow x^2 + y^2 + 6y + 9 - 9 = x^2 + (y+3)^2 - 9 = 0$

$\Rightarrow x^2 + (y+3)^2 = 9$

Standard equation of the circle with radius r and centre (h, k) is given by

$(x - h)^2 + (y - k)^2 = r^2$

By comparing, we get

$h = 0, k = -3, r = 3$

∴ Centre $= (0, -3)$, Radius $= 3$

Hence, the correct option is (D).

36. As we know that, if $\lim_{x \to a} f(x)$ does not result into indeterminate form, then we use direct substitution in order to find the limits.

Here, also we can see that, $\lim_{x \to 2}(3x^2 + 5x - 1)$ does not result into any indeterminate form.

So, we can substitute $x = 2$ in the expression $3x^2 + 5x - 1$ in order to find the value of k.

$\Rightarrow \lim_{x \to 2}(3x^2 + 5x - 1) = k$

$\Rightarrow 3 \times 2^2 + 5 \times 2 - 1 = k$

$\Rightarrow 21 = k$

or, $k = 21$

Hence, the correct option is (A).

37. The slope of the tangent to the curve $= \frac{dy}{dx}$

The slope of normal to the curve $= \frac{-1}{\left(\frac{dy}{dx}\right)}$

Point-slope is the general form: $y - y_1 = m(x - x_1)$, Where $m =$ slope

Here, $y = 3x^2 + 1$

$\frac{dy}{dx} = 6x$

$\left.\frac{dy}{dx}\right|_{x=2} = 12$

Slope of normal to the curve $= \frac{-1}{\left(\frac{dy}{dx}\right)} = \frac{-1}{12}$

Equation of normal to curve passing through $(2, 13)$ is:

$y - 13 = \frac{-1}{12}(x - 2)$

$\Rightarrow 12y - 156 = -x + 2$

$\Rightarrow x + 12y - 158 = 0$

Hence, the correct option is (D).

38. Given: Equation of curve is $y = \sqrt{5x - 3} - 2$ and the tangent to the curve $y = \sqrt{5x - 3} - 2$ is parallel to the line $4x - 2y + 3 = 0$

The given line $4x - 2y + 3 = 0$ can be re-written as:

$y = 2x + \left(\frac{3}{2}\right) = 0$

Now by comparing the above equation of line with $y = mx + c$ we get,

$m = 2$ and $c = \frac{3}{2}$

∵ The line $4x - 2y + 3 = 0$ is parallel to the tangent to the curve $y = \sqrt{5x - 3} - 2$

As we know that if two lines are parallel then their slope is same.

So, the slope of the tangent to the curve $y = \sqrt{5x - 3} - 2$ is $m = 2$

Let, the point of contact be (x_1, y_1)

As we know that slope of the tangent at any point say (x_1, y_1) to a curve is given by:

$m = \left[\frac{dy}{dx}\right]_{(x_1, y_1)}$

$\Rightarrow \frac{dy}{dx} = \frac{1}{2} \cdot \frac{1}{\sqrt{5x-3}} \cdot 5 - 0 = \frac{5}{2\sqrt{5x-3}}$

$\Rightarrow \left[\frac{dy}{dx}\right]_{(x_1, y_1)} = \frac{5}{2\sqrt{5x_1-3}}$

∵ Slope of tangent to the curve $y = \sqrt{5x - 3} - 2$ is $m = 2$

$\Rightarrow 2 = \frac{5}{2\sqrt{5x_1-3}}$

By squaring both the sides of the above equation we get:

$4 = \frac{25}{4 \cdot (5x_1 - 3)}$

$\Rightarrow x_1 = \frac{73}{80}$

∵ (x_1, y_1) is point of conctact i.e., (x_1, y_1) will satisfy the equation of curve:

$y = \sqrt{5x - 3} - 2$

$\Rightarrow y_1 = \sqrt{5x_1 - 3} - 2$

By substituting $x_1 = \frac{73}{80}$ in the above equation we get:

$y_1 = -\frac{3}{4}$

So, the point of contact is: $\left(\frac{73}{80}, -\frac{3}{4}\right)$

As we know that equation of tangent at any point say (x_1, y_1) is given by:

$$y - y_1 = \left[\frac{dy}{dx}\right]_{(x_1,y_1)} \cdot (x - x_1)$$

$$\Rightarrow y + \frac{3}{4} = 2 \cdot \left(x - \frac{73}{80}\right)$$

$$\Rightarrow 80x - 40y - 103 = 0$$

So, the equation of tangent to the given curve at the point $\left(\frac{73}{80}, -\frac{3}{4}\right)$ is $80x - 40y - 103 = 0$

Hence, the correct option is (D).

39. Given: Let $f(x) = \frac{\ln x}{x}$

Differentiating both sides, we get:

$$f'(x) = \frac{d}{dx}\left(\frac{\ln x}{x}\right)$$

$$= \frac{\frac{1}{x}(x) - 1(\ln x)}{x^2}$$

$$\Rightarrow f'(x) = \frac{1 - \ln x}{x^2}$$

$$f''(x) = \frac{d}{dx}(f'(x))$$

$$= \frac{d}{dx}\left(\frac{1 - \ln x}{x^2}\right)$$

$$= \frac{x^2 \frac{d}{dx}(1 - \ln x) - (1 - \ln x)\frac{d}{dx}(x^2)}{(x^2)^2}$$

$$= \frac{x^2\left(-\frac{1}{x}\right) - (1 - \ln x)(2x)}{x^4}$$

$$\Rightarrow \frac{-x - 2x + 2x(\ln x)}{x^4}$$

$$\Rightarrow \frac{x(-3 + 2(\ln x))}{x^4}$$

$$\Rightarrow f''(x) = \frac{-(3 - 2\ln x)}{x^3}$$

To find the value of x

$f'(x) = 0$

$$\Rightarrow \frac{1 - \ln x}{x^2} = 0$$

$\Rightarrow 1 - \ln x = 0$

$\Rightarrow \ln x = 1$

$\Rightarrow x = e^1 = e$ $(\ln_a b = c \Rightarrow b = a^c)$

Now, at $x = e$,

$$f''(e) = \frac{-(3 - 2\ln e)}{e^3}$$

$$= \frac{-3 + 2}{e^3}$$

$$= \frac{-1}{e^3} < 0$$

At $x = e$, maximum value of $f(x)$ obtain

$$\therefore f(x = e) = \frac{\ln x}{x}$$

$$= \frac{\ln e}{e}$$

$$= \frac{1}{e} \quad (\because \ln e = 1)$$

Hence, the correct option is (B).

40. Given, on a recent journey Aman drove from City A to city B to city C. His average over the whole journey was $60 km/hr$.

From statement I, average speed during journey from city A to city B is $48 km/hr$.

From statement II, total journey time is 3 hours

From statement III, ratio of distance travelled while going from A to B and B to C is $2:3$.

Thus, statement I and II and III or I and III are not sufficient to answer the question.

From statement III,

Let the distances to be covered be $2x$ and $3x$ respectively.

Total distance covered $= 2x + 3x = 5x$

Average speed $= \dfrac{\text{total distance}}{\text{total time}}$

$$\Rightarrow \frac{5x}{3} = 60$$

$\Rightarrow x = 36 km$

Now, distance travelled from city A to city $B = 2x = 72 km$

Let the time of this journey be 't'

$\dfrac{72}{t} = 48$

$\Rightarrow t = 1.5$ hours

Thus, time taken for journey from city B to city $C = 3 - 1.5 = 1.5$ hours

Distance travelled in this journey $= 3x = 108 km$

Average speed on the journey from city B to city $C = \dfrac{108}{1.5} = 72 km/hr$

Thus, statement I, II and III are together sufficient

Hence, the correct option is (D).

41. Taking all statement together,

Let the profit earned by company in $2001 = $ Rs. x and in $2002 = $ Rs. y

Profit earned in $2003 = 1.4x$

$x + y = $ Rs. 20 crore ..... (i)

From statement (III),

$1.4x = y \times \dfrac{80}{100}$

$x = \dfrac{4}{5} \times \dfrac{1}{1.4} y$

$x = \dfrac{4}{7} y$ .... (ii)

From equation (i) and (ii), we can get the required profit.

So all the statements are required to find profit in the year 2002.

Hence, the correct option is (D).

42. Substitution method: If the function cannot be integrated directly substitution method is used. To integration by substitution is used in the following steps:

- A new variable is to be chosen, say "t"
- The value of dt is to is to be determined.
- Substitution is done and integral function is then integrated.
- Finally, initial variable t, to be returned.

Let $\sin x = t \Rightarrow \cos x \, dx = dt$

$\Rightarrow 1 = \int \dfrac{\cos x}{1+\sin^2 x} dx$

$\Rightarrow 1 = \int \dfrac{1}{1+t^2} dt$

$\Rightarrow 1 = \tan^{-1} t + c$

$\Rightarrow 1 = \tan^{-1}(\sin x) + c$

Putting the limits,

$\Rightarrow 1 = [\tan^{-1}(\sin 90°) + c] - [\tan^{-1}(\sin 0°) + c]$

$\Rightarrow 1 = \tan^{-1}(1)$

$\Rightarrow I = 45°$ or $\dfrac{\pi}{4}$

Hence, the correct option is (B).

43. Concept:

If $f(x)$ is even function then $f(-x) = f(x)$

If $f(x)$ is odd function then $f(-x) = -f(x)$

Properties of definite integral,

If $f(x)$ is even function then $\int_{-a}^{a} f(x) dx = 2 \int_{0}^{a} f(x) dx$

If $f(x)$ is odd function then $\int_{-a}^{f} f(x) dx = 0$

Let $I = \int_{-\frac{\pi}{6}}^{\frac{\pi}{6}} \dfrac{\sin^5 x \cos^3 x}{x^4} dx$

And, $f(x) = \dfrac{\sin^5 x \cos^3 x}{x^4}$

Replaced x by $-x_s$

$\Rightarrow f(-x) = \dfrac{\sin^5(-x)\cos^3(-x)}{(-x)^4}$

As we know $\sin(-\theta) = -\sin\theta$ and $\cos(-\theta) = \cos\theta$

$= \dfrac{-\sin^5 x \cos^3 x}{x^4}$

$\Rightarrow f(-x) = -f(x)$

So, $f(x)$ is odd function

Therefore, $I = 0$.

Hence, the correct option is (D).

44. Here we have to find the value of $\int \dfrac{x^2+1}{(x+1)^2} dx$

As we can see that the given integrand is not a proper rational function, So by division algorithm.

$\Rightarrow \dfrac{x^2+1}{(x+1)^2} = 1 - \dfrac{2x}{(x+1)^2}$

$\Rightarrow \int \dfrac{x^2+1}{(x+1)^2} dx = \int dx - \int \dfrac{2x}{(x+1)^2} dx \cdots$ (1)

Let's find the value of $\int \dfrac{2x}{(x+1)^2} dx$

Let $\dfrac{2x}{(x+1)^2} = \dfrac{A}{(x+1)} + \dfrac{B}{(x+1)^2}$

$\Rightarrow 2x = A(x+1) + B$

On equating the coefficients of x in the above equation we get A = 2

On equating the constant terms, we get A + B = 0

$\therefore A = 2 \Rightarrow B = -2$

$\Rightarrow \dfrac{2x}{(x+1)^2} = \dfrac{2}{(x+1)} - \dfrac{2}{(x+1)^2}$

$\Rightarrow \int \dfrac{2x}{(x+1)^2} dx = 2\int \dfrac{dx}{x+1} - 2\int \dfrac{dx}{(x+1)^2}$

As we know that,

$\int \dfrac{dx}{x} = \log|x| + C$ and $\int x^n dx = \dfrac{x^{n+1}}{n+1} + C$ where C is a constant

$\Rightarrow \int \dfrac{2x}{(x+1)^2} dx = 2\log|x+1| + \dfrac{2}{x+1}$

By substituting the value of $\int \frac{2x}{(x+1)^2} dx$ in equation (1) we get

$\Rightarrow \int \frac{x^2+1}{(x+1)^2} dx = x - 2\log|x+1| - \frac{2}{x+1} + C$.

Hence, the correct option is (A).

45. Concept:

$\int \frac{dx}{x} = \log|x| + C$, where C is a constant

$\int [f(x) \pm g(x)]dx = \int f(x)dx \pm \int g(x)dx$

Given: $\int \frac{\cot x}{\log(\sin x)} dx$

Let $\log(\sin x) = t$

Now by differentiating the above equation we get,

$\Rightarrow \frac{d(\log(\sin x))}{dx} = \frac{dt}{dx}$

$\Rightarrow \frac{1}{\sin x} \cdot \cos x = \frac{dt}{dx}$

$\Rightarrow \cot x \, dx = dt$

$\Rightarrow \int \frac{\cot x}{\log(\sin x)} dx = \int \frac{dt}{t}$

As we know that, $\int \frac{dx}{x} = \log|x| + C$

$\Rightarrow \int \frac{dt}{t} = \log|t| + C$

Now by substituting $\log(\sin x) = t$ in the above equation we get,

$\Rightarrow \int \frac{\cot x}{\log(\sin x)} dx = \log|\log(\sin x)| + C$

Hence, the correct option is (B).

46. Given:

$\int \frac{x^2+1}{x(x+1)^2} dx = A\ln|x| + \frac{B}{1+x} + C$

$\int \frac{x^2+1}{x(x+1)^2}$

$= \int \frac{(x+1)^2 - 2x}{x(x+1)^2}$

$= \int \left(\frac{1}{x} - \frac{2}{(1+x)^2} dx\right)$

$= \ln|x| - 2\frac{(1+x)^{-1}}{-1} + C$

$= \ln|x| + \frac{2}{1+x} + C$

Comparing with the RHS,

$A = 1, B = 2$

$\therefore A + B = 3$.

Hence, the correct option is (C).

47. Concept:

The equation of a line passing through the point (x_1, y_1) and having the slope 'm' is given as:

$y - y_1 = m \cdot (x - x_1)$

Given: The point of intersection of diagonals of a square ABCD is at the origin and one of its vertices is at A(4, 2).

So, the diagonal AC passes through the origin,

As we know that, the slope of the line joining the points (x_1, y_1) and (x_2, y_2) is: $m = \frac{y_2 - y_1}{x_2 - x_1}$

The slope of line AC is given by

$\frac{2-0}{4-0} = \frac{1}{2}$

In square $ABCD$, the diagonals AC and BD are perpendicular to each other.

$\Rightarrow$ Slope of $AC \times$ slope of $BD = -1$

So, the slope of BD is - 2 .

As we know that, the equation of a line passing through the point (x_1, y_1) and having the slope 'm' is given as:

$y - y_1 = m \cdot (x - x_1)$

The equation of BD whose slope is - 2 and passes through origin is given by:

$y - 0 = (-2) \cdot (x - 0)$

$\Rightarrow 2x + y = 0$

Hence, the correct option is (A).

48. Concept:

The product of the slopes of a pair of perpendicular lines is -1.

The slope of the line $2x + 3y + 5 = 0$ is $m = -\frac{2}{3}$.

$\therefore$ The slope of the line perpendicular to it, must be $n = \frac{3}{2}$.

So, let the equation of the required line be $y = \frac{3}{2}x + c$.

Since this line passes through $(0,0)$, we must have:

$0 = 0 + c$

$\Rightarrow c = 0$

$\therefore$ The required equation of the line is $y = \frac{3}{2}x$; which can also be written as $3x - 2y = 0$.

Hence, the correct option is (B).

49. Concept:

The equation of line is y = mx + c, where m is slope.

Given equation of line is x - y = 4

$\Rightarrow y = x - 4$ which is equal to $y = mx + c$, where m is slope of the line

$\Rightarrow m = 1$

$\Rightarrow m = \tan\theta = 1$

$\Rightarrow \theta = 45°$

So, the equation of line $x - y = 4$ makes angle $\theta_1 = 45°$ with X-axis.

The required line makes an angle $\theta_2 = 45°$ with Y-axis. and makes an angle $45°$ with X-axis also. The line passing through the point $(0,1)$.

Slope of the required line is $m = \tan\theta = 1$

Equation of line is,

y = mx+c

⇒ y = x + c.

Since, the line passing through the point (0,1) ,put x = 0 and y = 1 to find c.

⇒ 1 = 0 + c

⇒ c = 1.

Equation of line is y = x + 1

Hence, the equation of line passing through (0, 1) and making an angle with the y-axis equal to the inclination of the line x - y = 4 with x-axis is y = x + 1.

Hence, the correct option is (A).

50. The simplest case of a normal distribution is known as the standard normal distribution. This is a special case when μ = 0 and σ = 1, and it is described by this probability density function:

$\phi(x) = \frac{1}{\sqrt{2\pi}} e^{-\frac{1}{2}x^2}$

Here, the factor $\frac{1}{\sqrt{2\pi}}$ ensures that the total area under the curve $\phi(x)$ is equal to one.

The factor $\frac{1}{2}$ in the exponent ensures that the distribution has unit variance (i.e., variance being equal to one), and therefore also unit standard deviation.

This function is symmetric around $x = 0$, where it attains its maximum value $\frac{1}{\sqrt{2\pi}}$ and has inflection points at $x = +1$ and $x = -1$.

Hence, the correct option is (A).

Mathematics : Mock Test 07

Q.1 What is the number of diagonals of a heptagon?
A. 14   B. 16   C. 9   D. 18

Q.2 Consider the experiment of throwing a die, if a multiple of 3 comes up, throw the die again and if any other number comes, toss a coin. Find the conditional probability of the event 'the coin shows a tail', given that at least one die shows as 3.
A. 0   B. 1   C. 3   D. 5

Q.3 If B = $\begin{vmatrix} 1 & 4 \\ 2 & k \end{vmatrix}$ is a singular matrix, then value of k = _____.
A. 2   B. 27   C. -27   D. 8

Q.4 The system of equations:
2x + y - 3z = 5
3x - 2y + 2z = 5 and
5x - 3y - z = 16
A. Is inconsistent
B. Is consistent, with a unique solution
C. Is consistent, with infinitely many solutions
D. Has its solution lying along x - axis in three - dimensional space

Q.5 If $A = \begin{bmatrix} 1 & 1 \\ 1 & 1 \end{bmatrix}$, then $A^{100} = $
A. 2^{100} A   B. 2^{99} A
C. 2^{101} A   D. None of these

Q.6 In the given figure rays P || Q || R || S and the ray l || m. find θ_1 and θ_2 respectively.

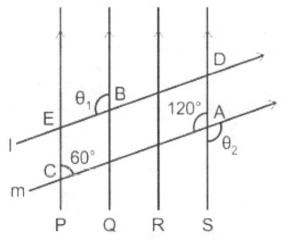

A. 120°, 140°   B. 120°, 120°
C. 160°, 150°   D. 60°, 120°

Q.7 The differential equation of the family of curves $y = c_1 e^x + c_2 e^{-x}$ is:
A. $\frac{d^2y}{dx^2} + y = 0$ B. $\frac{d^2y}{dx^2} - y = 0$
C. $\frac{d^3y}{dx^3} + y = 0$ D. $\frac{d^4y}{dx^4} - 1 = 0$

Q.8 Form the differential equation of the following $y^2 = a(b^2 - x^2)$:
A. $yy' - xyy'' + x(y')^2 = 0$
B. $yy' + xyy'' + x(y')^2 = 0$
C. $yy' + yy'' - x(y')^2 = 0$
D. $yy' - xyy'' - x(y')^2 = 0$

Q.9 Solve the differential equation:
$xdy - 2ydx = 0$
A. $y^2x = c$ B. $xy = c$ C. $y = x^2c$ D. $yx^2 = c$

Q.10 Calculate range and coefficient of range of the following series, which gives the monthly expenditure (in Rs.) of seven students: 22,35,32,45,42,48,39.
A. 27, 0.30   B. 26, 0.37   C. 25, 0.40   D. 24, 0.47

Q.11 Find the area between the curve $y = x^2$ and $y = x$.
A. $\frac{5}{6}$ sq. unit   B. $\frac{1}{3}$ sq. unit
C. $\frac{1}{2}$ sq. unit   D. $\frac{1}{6}$ sq. unit

Q.12 Find the area of the region (in square unit) bounded by the curve $y = x - 2$ and $x = 0$ to $x = 4$.
A. 2 sq. unit   B. 4 sq. unit
C. 3 sq. unit   D. 6 sq. unit

Q.13 Find the area bounded between the curve $y = x^2$ and $y = x^3$.
A. $\frac{1}{2}$ B. $\frac{1}{12}$ C. 1   D. $\frac{1}{24}$

Q.14 Consider the following.
1. $z\bar{z} = |z|^2$
2. $z^{-1} = \frac{z}{|z|^2}$, where z = complex number
Which of the above statement is/are correct?
A. Only 1   B. Only 2
C. Both 1 and 2   D. Neither 1 nor 2

Q.15 Minimize $Z = 7x + y$ subject to $5x + y \geq 5, x + y \geq 3, x \geq 0, y \geq 0$.
A. 4   B. 6   C. 3   D. 5

Q.16 Region represented by the in equation system $x + y \leq 3, y \leq 6$ and $x \geq 0, y \geq 0$ is:
A. Unbounded in first quadrant
B. Unbounded in first and second quadrant
C. Bounded in first quadrant
D. None of the these

Q.17 Determine graphically the minimum value of the objective function. $Z = -50x + 20y$

Mathematics : Mock Test - 7

Subject to constraints
$2x - y \geq -5$
$3x + y \geq 3$
$2x - 3y \leq 12$
$x \geq 0, y \geq 0$

A. No minimum
B. 3 minimum
C. 2 minimum
D. 1 minimum

Q.18 Find the values of k for which the length of the perpendicular from the point $(4,1)$ on the line $3x - 4y + k = 0$ is 2 units?

A. 18
B. -2
C. -18
D. None of these

Q.19 What is the acute angle between the lines represented by the equations $y - \sqrt{3}x - 5 = 0$ and $\sqrt{3}y - x + 6 = 0$?

A. 30°
B. 45°
C. 60°
D. 75°

Q.20 Find the value of x so that the inclination of the line joining the points $(x, -3)$ and $(2,5)$ is 135°?

A. −5
B. 5
C. 10
D. −10

Q.21 Find the acute angle between the lines $6x + 9y + 15 = 0$ and $12x + 18y + 30 = 0$.

A. 0°
B. 90°
C. 45°
D. None of these

Q.22 Consider a Poisson distribution for the tossing of a biased coin. The mean for this distribution is μ. The standard deviation for this distribution is given by _____.

A. $\sqrt{\mu}$
B. μ^2
C. μ
D. $\frac{1}{\mu}$

Q.23 Jobs arrive at a facility at an average rate of 5 in an 8 hour shift. The arrival of the jobs follows Poisson distribution. The average service time of a job on the facility is 40 minutes. The service time follows exponential distribution. Idle time (in hours) at the facility per shift will be _____.

A. $\frac{5}{7}$
B. $\frac{14}{3}$
C. $\frac{7}{5}$
D. $\frac{10}{3}$

Q.24 Write unit vector in the direction of the sum of vectors: $\vec{a} = 2\hat{i} - \hat{j} + 2\hat{k}$ and $\vec{b} = -\hat{i} + \hat{j} + 3\hat{k}$

A. $[\frac{1}{\sqrt{26}}, 0, \frac{5}{\sqrt{26}}]$
B. $[\frac{2}{\sqrt{26}}, 1, \frac{5}{\sqrt{26}}]$
C. $[\frac{1}{\sqrt{26}}, -1, \frac{4}{\sqrt{26}}]$
D. $[\frac{1}{\sqrt{23}}, 3, \frac{5}{\sqrt{26}}]$

Q.25 Find the angle between two vectors $(\vec{a} = 2\hat{i} + \hat{j} - 3\hat{k})$ and $(\vec{b} = 3\hat{i} - 2\hat{j} - \hat{k})$.

A. −160°
B. −60°
C. 160°
D. 60°

Q.26 If $6\sin^2 x - 2\cos^2 x = 4$, then find the value of $\tan x$.

A. $\sqrt{3}$
B. $\sqrt{2}$
C. $\sqrt{5}$
D. 0

Q.27 If $\cos^{-1}\left(\frac{p}{a}\right) + \cos^{-1}\left(\frac{q}{b}\right) = \alpha$, then $\frac{p^2}{a^2} + k\cos\alpha + \frac{q^2}{b^2} = \sin^2\alpha$ where k is equal to:

A. $-\frac{2pq}{ab}$
B. $\frac{2pq}{ab}$
C. $-\frac{pq}{ab}$
D. $\frac{pq}{ab}$

Q.28 What is the value of following?
$\cot\left[\sin^{-1}\frac{3}{5} + \cot^{-1}\frac{3}{2}\right]$

A. $\frac{6}{17}$
B. $\frac{7}{16}$
C. $\frac{16}{7}$
D. $\frac{17}{6}$

Q.29 The value of $\int_0^{\frac{\pi}{4}} \sqrt{\tan x}\, dx + \int_0^{\frac{\pi}{4}} \sqrt{\cot x}\, dx$ is equal to

A. $\frac{\pi}{4}$
B. $\frac{\pi}{2}$
C. $\frac{\pi}{2\sqrt{2}}$
D. $\frac{\pi}{\sqrt{2}}$

Q.30 If $2x^3 - 3y^2 = 7$, what is $\frac{dy}{dx}$ equal to $(y \neq 0)$:

A. $\frac{x^2}{2y}$
B. $\frac{x}{2y}$
C. $\frac{x^2}{y}$
D. None of the above

Q.31 Which of these is a second-order differential equation?

A. $y' + x = y^2$
B. $y'y'' + y = \sin x$
C. $y'''y'' + y = 0$
D. None of these

Q.32 The value of $\sqrt{24.99}$ is:

A. 4.999
B. 4.899
C. 5.001
D. 4.897

Q.33 If the radius of a sphere is measured as 6 m with an error of 0.02 m, then find the approximate error in calculating its surface area.

A. 0.48 square meters
B. 0.96 square meters
C. 1.20 square meters
D. 0.72 square meters

Q.34 The value of $(242)^{\frac{1}{5}}$ is.

A. 2.997
B. 2.0997
C. 2.00997
D. 2.000997

Q.35 The length of the tangent drawn to a circle of radius 4 cm from a point 5 cm away from the center of the circle is.

A. 3 cm
B. $4\sqrt{2}$ cm
C. $5\sqrt{2}$ cm
D. 4cm

Q.36 Find the value of k if $\lim_{x \to 7} g(x) = k$ where $g(x) = \sqrt{8x - 7}$

A. 3
B. 6
C. 7
D. None of these

Q.37 If $f(x) = |x - 1|$ and $g(x) = \tan x$ then $fog\left(\frac{3\pi}{4}\right)$

A. 2
B. 0
C. 1
D. None of these

Q.38 Consider the function $f(x) = |x|$ in the interval $-1 \leq x \leq 1$. At the point $x = 0, f(x)$ is:

A. Continuous and differentiable
B. Non - continuous and differentiable

104

C. Continuous and non - differentiable
D. Neither continuous nor differentiable

Q.39 $\int_{-3}^{3} \cot^{-1} x \, dx$ is equal to:

A. 3π B. 0 C. 6π D. 3

Q.40 $\int_{-5}^{5} |x+2| \, dx$ is equal to:

A. 28 B. 30 C. 29 D. 27

Q.41 $\int_{0}^{\pi} \sin^6 x \cos^5 x \, dx$ is equal to?

A. 2π
B. π
C. 0
D. None of these

Q.42 Find the integration of $\frac{x^4 + 3x^2 - x + 5}{x}$:

A. $\frac{x^4}{4} + \frac{3x^2}{2} + x + \log x^5 + c$
B. $\frac{x^4}{4} + \frac{3x^2}{2} - x + \log x^5 + c$
C. $\frac{x^4}{4} + \frac{5x^2}{2} + x + \log x^5 + c$
D. $\frac{x^5}{5} + \frac{3x^2}{2} - x + \log x^5 + c$

Q.43 Determine $f(x)$ for $f'(x) = 4x^3 - 2\frac{1}{\sqrt{x}} + e^{-4x}$, and $f(0) = \frac{3}{4}$:

A. $x^4 - 4\sqrt{x} - \frac{e^{-4x}}{4} + 1$
B. $x^4 - 4\sqrt{x} + \frac{e^{-4x}}{4} + 1$
C. $x^4 - \sqrt{x} - \frac{e^{-4x}}{4} + 1$
D. $x^4 - 4\sqrt{x} + e^{-4x} + 1$

Q.44 What is $\int \frac{e^x(1+x)}{\cos^2(xe^x)} dx$ equal to?

Where c is a constant of integration.

A. $xe^x + c$
B. $\cos(xe^x) + c$
C. $\tan(xe^x) + c$
D. $x \cosec(xe^x) + c$

Q.45 The mean and variance of a binomial distribution are 8 and 4 respectively, then $p(x = 1)$ is equal to:

A. $\frac{1}{2^{12}}$ B. $\frac{1}{2^4}$ C. $\frac{1}{2^6}$ D. $\frac{1}{2^8}$

Q.46 The acute angle between the planes $2x - y + z = 6$ and $x + y + 2z = 7$ is:

A. π B. $\frac{2\pi}{3}$ C. $\frac{\pi}{2}$ D. $\frac{\pi}{3}$

Q.47 Let $p, q,$ and r be propositions and the expression $(p \to q) \to r$ be a contradiction. Then the expression $(r \to p) \to q$ is:

A. A tautology
B. A contradiction
C. Always true when p is false
D. Always true when q is true

Q.48 If T(x) denotes is a trigonometric function, P(x) denotes x is a periodic function and C(x) denotes x is a continuous function then the statement "It is not the case that some trigonometric functions are not periodic" can be logically represented as:

A. $\neg \exists x[T(x) \land \neg P(x)]$
B. $\neg \exists x[T(x) \lor \neg P(x)]$
C. $\neg \exists x[\neg T(x) \land \neg P(x)]$
D. $\neg \exists x[T(x) \land P(x)]$

Q.49 If $\sin(\alpha + \beta) = 6\sin(\alpha - \beta)$ and $k = \frac{\tan \alpha}{\tan \beta}$, then, what is the value of k?

A. $\frac{3}{5}$ B. $\frac{6}{5}$ C. $\frac{4}{5}$ D. $\frac{7}{5}$

Q.50 If $f(x) = [x]$ is a smallest integer function and $g(x) = x^2$ then find the value of $gof\left(\frac{-9}{2}\right)$

A. -16 B. 16 C. -9 D. 9

Mathematics : Mock Test - 7

// Smart Answer Sheet //

Correct — Indicates percentage of students who answered questions correctly.

Skipped — Indicates percentage of students who skipped questions.

Q.	Ans.	Correct / Skipped
1	A	47.37 % / 5.26 %
2	A	26.32 % / 15.79 %
3	D	73.68 % / 15.79 %
4	B	42.11 % / 15.78 %
5	B	42.11 % / 15.78 %
6	B	68.42 % / 15.79 %
7	B	47.37 % / 15.79 %
8	D	26.32 % / 15.79 %
9	C	57.89 % / 15.79 %
10	B	63.16 % / 15.79 %
11	D	47.37 % / 15.79 %
12	B	57.89 % / 15.79 %
13	B	63.16 % / 15.79 %
14	A	47.37 % / 15.79 %
15	D	36.84 % / 15.79 %
16	C	47.37 % / 15.79 %
17	A	26.32 % / 15.79 %
18	C	26.32 % / 15.79 %
19	A	57.89 % / 15.79 %
20	C	57.89 % / 21.06 %
21	A	57.89 % / 15.79 %
22	A	52.63 % / 15.79 %
23	B	42.11 % / 15.78 %
24	A	73.68 % / 15.79 %
25	D	52.63 % / 15.79 %
26	A	68.42 % / 15.79 %
27	A	21.05 % / 21.06 %
28	A	31.58 % / 15.79 %
29	D	26.32 % / 15.79 %
30	C	68.42 % / 15.79 %
31	B	57.89 % / 21.06 %
32	A	63.16 % / 15.79 %
33	B	42.11 % / 15.78 %
34	A	52.63 % / 21.05 %
35	A	36.84 % / 21.05 %
36	C	84.21 % / 15.79 %
37	A	42.11 % / 15.78 %
38	C	26.32 % / 15.79 %
39	A	21.05 % / 15.79 %
40	C	42.11 % / 15.78 %
41	C	31.58 % / 15.79 %
42	B	78.95 % / 15.79 %
43	A	36.84 % / 15.79 %
44	C	47.37 % / 26.31 %
45	A	63.16 % / 15.79 %
46	D	57.89 % / 15.79 %
47	D	21.05 % / 15.79 %
48	A	31.58 % / 15.79 %
49	D	47.37 % / 15.79 %
50	B	36.84 % / 15.79 %

Performance Analysis	
Avg. Score (%)	48.0%
Toppers Score (%)	96.0%
Your Score	

//Hints and Solutions//

1. Given:

The polygon given is a heptagon.

Therefore, the no. of sides of the given polygon $n = 7$.

As we know that, no. of diagonals that can be drawn by joining the angular points of a polygon having n sides is given by:

$$^nC_2 - n = \frac{n \times (n-3)}{2}$$

No. of diagonals $= \frac{7(7-3)}{2}$

Therefore,

No. of diagonal of heptagon $= 14$

Hence, the correct option is (A).

2. The sample space of the experiment is,

$S = \{(1, H), (1, T), (2, H), (2, T), (3, 1), (3, 2), (3, 3), (3, 4), (3, 5), (3, 6), (4, H), (4, T), (5, H), (5, T, (6, 1), (6, 2), (6, 3), (6, 4), (6, 5), (6, 6)\}$

Let A be the event that the coin shows a tail and B be the event that at least one die shows 3.

$A = \{(1, T), (2, T), (4, T) \cdot (5, T)\}$

$B = \{(3,1), (3,2), (3,3), (3,4), (3,5), (3,6), (6,3)\}$

$\Rightarrow A \cap B - \phi$

$\therefore P(A \cap B) - D$

Then,

$P(B) = P(\{3, 1\}) + P(\{3, 2\}) + P(\{3, 3\}) + P(\{3, 4\}) + P(13, 5\}) + P(\{3, 6\}) + P(\{6, 3\})$

$= \frac{1}{36} + \frac{1}{36} + \frac{1}{36} + \frac{1}{36} + \frac{1}{36} + \frac{1}{36} + \frac{1}{36}$

$= \frac{7}{36}$

Probability of the event that the coin shows a tail, given that at least one die shows 3 is given by,

$P\left(\frac{A}{B}\right) = \frac{P(A \cap B)}{P(B)}$

$= \frac{0}{\left(\frac{7}{36}\right)}$

$= 0$

Hence, the correct option is (A).

3. A matrix is said to be singular if its determinant is zero.

i.e. for matrix A to be singular, $|A| = 0$.

The determinant of a square matrix of order two:

If $A = \begin{bmatrix} a_{11} & a_{12} \\ a_{21} & a_{22} \end{bmatrix}$ is a square matrix of order 2 then the determinant is given by:

$\det(A) = |A|$

$= \Delta$

$= \begin{vmatrix} a_{11} & a_{12} \\ a_{21} & a_{22} \end{vmatrix}$

$= a_{11}a_{22} - a_{12}a_{21}$

Given:

$B = \begin{vmatrix} 1 & 4 \\ 2 & k \end{vmatrix}$ is a singular matrix

Therefore, $|B| = 0$

$\Rightarrow (k - 8) = 0$

$\therefore k = 8$

Hence, the correct option is (D).

4. Given:

The system of equations

$2x + y - 3z = 5$

$3x - 2y + 2z = 5$ and

$5x - 3y - z = 16$

So,

$A = \begin{bmatrix} 2 & 1 & -3 \\ 3 & -2 & 2 \\ 5 & -3 & -1 \end{bmatrix}$

det (A) = |A| = 2 × {(- 2 × - 1) - (- 3 × 2)} - 1 × {(3 × - 1) - (2 × 5)} + (- 3) × {(3 × - 3) - (5 × - 2)}

$\Rightarrow |A| = 2 \times (2 + 6) - 1 \times (- 3 - 10) - 3 \times (- 9 + 10)$

$\Rightarrow |A| = 16 + 13 - 3 = 26$

$\therefore |A| \neq 0$

So, system is consistent having unique solution.

Hence, the correct option is (B).

5. Given:

$A = \begin{bmatrix} 1 & 1 \\ 1 & 1 \end{bmatrix}$

$A^2 = A.A = \begin{bmatrix} 1 & 1 \\ 1 & 1 \end{bmatrix}\begin{bmatrix} 1 & 1 \\ 1 & 1 \end{bmatrix}$

$= \begin{bmatrix} 1+1 & 1+1 \\ 1+1 & 1+1 \end{bmatrix}$

$= \begin{bmatrix} 2 & 2 \\ 2 & 2 \end{bmatrix}$

Mathematics : Mock Test - 7

$$= 2\begin{bmatrix} 1 & 1 \\ 1 & 1 \end{bmatrix} = 2A$$

$$A^3 = A^2 \cdot A = \begin{bmatrix} 2 & 2 \\ 2 & 2 \end{bmatrix}\begin{bmatrix} 1 & 1 \\ 1 & 1 \end{bmatrix}$$

$$= \begin{bmatrix} 2+2 & 2+2 \\ 2+2 & 2+2 \end{bmatrix}$$

$$= \begin{bmatrix} 4 & 4 \\ 4 & 4 \end{bmatrix}$$

$$= 4\begin{bmatrix} 1 & 1 \\ 1 & 1 \end{bmatrix}$$

$$= 2^2 \begin{bmatrix} 1 & 1 \\ 1 & 1 \end{bmatrix} = 2^2 A$$

Observing the pattern here

$$A^n = 2^{n-1} \cdot A$$

$$\Rightarrow A^{100} = 2^{99} A$$

Hence, the correct option is (B).

6. Given:

Rays P || Q || R || S and the ray l || m.

Calculation:

We are given that, ∠ECA = 60°

So, ∠IBQ = 60° (Opposite angles in a parallelogram are equal)

Now, ∠IBQ + θ₁ = 180° (Linear pairs)

⇒ θ₁ = 180° - 60°

⇒ θ₁ = 120°

Now, we know that vertically opposite angles are equal

∴ ∠CAD = θ₂ = 120°

∴ θ₁ = 120° and θ₂ = 120°

Hence, the correct option is (B).

7. Given,

$y = c_1 e^x + c_2 e^{-x}$

Differentiating w.r.t. x

We get,

$$\frac{dy}{dx} = \frac{d}{dx} c_1 e^x + \frac{d}{dx} c_2 e^{-x}$$

$$\Rightarrow \frac{dy}{dx} = c_1 e^x - c_2 e^{-x}$$

$$\Rightarrow \frac{d}{dx}\left(\frac{dy}{dx}\right) = \frac{d}{dx}(c_1 e^x - c_2 e^{-x})$$

$$\Rightarrow \frac{d^2 y}{dx^2} = c_1 e^x + c_2 e^{-x} = y$$

$$\Rightarrow \frac{d^2 y}{dx^2} - y = 0$$

Hence, the correct option is (B).

8. Given,

$y^2 = a(b^2 - x^2)$

Differentiating w.r.t x

We get,

$2yy' = a(-2x)$

$\Rightarrow yy' = -ax$ .....(i)

Differentiating w.r.t x again

$yy'' + (y')^2 = -a$ .....(ii)

From (i) and (ii), we get,

$yy' = x(yy'' + (y')^2)$

$\Rightarrow yy' - xyy'' - x(y')^2 = 0$

Hence, the correct option is (D).

9. Given,

$xdy - 2ydx = 0$

$xdy = 2ydx$

On separating variable,

$$\frac{dy}{y} = 2\frac{dx}{x}$$

Integrating both sides we get,

$$\int \frac{dy}{y} = 2\int \frac{dx}{x}$$

$\Rightarrow \log y = 2\log x + \log c$ $[\because \int \frac{1}{x} dx = \log x]$

$\Rightarrow \log y = \log x^2 + \log c$ $[\because n \log n = \log n^m]$

$\Rightarrow \log y - \log x^2 = \log c$

$\Rightarrow \log \frac{y}{x^2} = \log c$ $[\because \log n - \log m = \log \frac{m}{x}]$

$\therefore y = x^2 c$

Hence, the correct option is (C).

10. Given:

Highest Value $(H) = 48$

Lowest Value $(L) = 22$

Range = Highest Value − Lowest Value

i.e $R = H - L$

Substituting the given values in the formula.

$R = 48 - 22 = 26$

Coefficient of Range

$= \frac{H-L}{H+L}$

$= \frac{48-22}{48+22}$

$= \frac{26}{70}$

$= 0.37$

Thus, range is 26 and coefficient of range is 0.37

Hence, the correct option is (B).

11. Given:

Curve 1: $y = x^2 = f(x)$ (say)

Curve 2: $y - x = 0$

$\Rightarrow y = x = g(x)$ (say)

The curve can be drawn as:

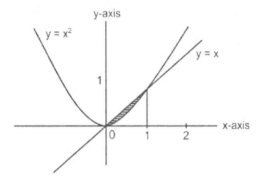

To find the intersections (or limits of the area) putting value of y from curve 1

$\Rightarrow x^2 - x = 0$

$\Rightarrow x(x-1) = 0$

$\Rightarrow x = 0, x = 1$

Now the required area (A) is:

$A = \left|\int_{x_1}^{x_2}[f(x) - g(x)]dx\right|$

$\Rightarrow A = \left|\int_0^1 [x^2 - x]\, dx\right|$

$\Rightarrow A = \left|\left[\frac{x^3}{3} - \frac{x^2}{2}\right]_0^1\right|$

$\Rightarrow A = \left|\frac{1}{3} - \frac{1}{2} - (0)\right|$

$\Rightarrow A = \frac{1}{6}$ sq. unit

Hence, the correct option is (D).

12. Given curve and lines are:

$y = x - 2$ and $x = 0$ to $x = 4$

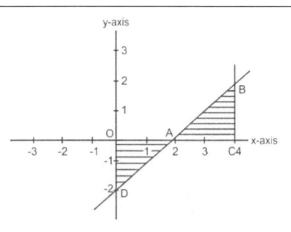

In figure $\triangle ABC$ and $\triangle AOD$ is similar.

So, Area of the region $= 2 \times$ (Area of $\triangle ABC$)

For the area of $\triangle ABC$

We know that:

$= \int_{x_1}^{x_2} |y_2 - y_1|\, dx$

$= \int_2^4 (x - 2)\, dx$

$= \left[\frac{x^2}{2} - 2x\right]_2^4$

$= \frac{4^2}{2} - 2(4) - \left(\frac{2^2}{2} - 2 \times 2\right)$

$= 8 - 8 - 2 + 4$

$= 2$ sq. unit

So,

Area of the region $= 2 \times$ (Area of $\triangle ABC$)

$= 2 \times 2$

$= 4$ sq. unit

Hence, the correct option is (B).

13. Given:

$y = x^3$ and $y = x^2$

Finding a point of intersection:

$\Rightarrow x^3 - x^2 = 0$

$\Rightarrow x^2(x - 1) = 0$

$\Rightarrow x = 0, 1$

Let us draw the graph of the curve $y = x^2$ and $y = x^3$

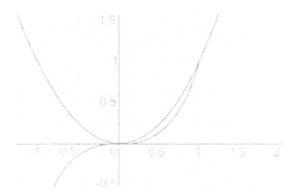

Let the required area be A.

Using the formula of the area under the curve,

$$A = \left|\int_a^b f(x) - g(x)dx\right|$$

$$\Rightarrow A = \left|\int_0^1 (x^3 - x^2)\,dx\right|$$

$$= \left|\left[\frac{x^4}{4} - \frac{x^3}{3}\right]_0^1\right|$$

Substitute the limit to evaluate the area:

$$\Rightarrow A = \left|\frac{1}{4} - \frac{1}{3} - 0 + 0\right|$$

$$= \frac{1}{12}$$

Hence, the correct option is (B).

14. Let,

Complex number, $z = a + ib$

Conjugate of complex number $= \bar{z} = a - ib$

So, $z\bar{z} = (a + ib)(a - ib)$

$\Rightarrow z\bar{z} = a^2 - (ib)^2$

$\Rightarrow z\bar{z} = a^2 - i^2(b)^2$

$\Rightarrow z\bar{z} = a^2 - (ib)^2$

$\Rightarrow z\bar{z} = a^2 + b^2$ ...(1) $(\because i^2 = -1)$

As we know,

Modulus of complex number is given by,

$|z| = \sqrt{(a^2 + b^2)}$

On squaring both sides, we get

$|z|^2 = \left(\sqrt{a^2 + b^2}\right)^2$

$\therefore |z|^2 = a^2 + b^2$ ...(2)

Comparing equation (1) and (2), we get

$z\bar{z} = |z|^2$

Now,

$z^{-1} = \frac{1}{z} = \frac{1}{a+ib}$

$\Rightarrow z^{-1} = \frac{1}{a+ib} \times \frac{a-ib}{a-ib}$

$\Rightarrow z^{-1} = \frac{1}{a+ib} \times \frac{a-ib}{a-ib}$

$\Rightarrow z^{-1} = \frac{a-ib}{a^2-(ib)^2}$

$\Rightarrow z^{-1} = \frac{a-ib}{a^2-i^2b^2}$

$\Rightarrow z^{-1} = \frac{a-ib}{a^2-(-1)b^2}$ $[\because i^2 = -1]$

$\Rightarrow z^{-1} = \frac{a-ib}{a^2+b^2}$

$\therefore z^{-1} = \frac{\bar{z}}{|z|^2} \neq \frac{z}{|z|^2}$

So, only statement 1 is correct.

Hence, the correct option is (A).

15. Given:

$Z = 7x + y$ subject to $5x + y \geq 5, x + y \geq 3, x \geq 0, y \geq 0$

First we draw the lines AB and CD whose equations are $5x + y = 5$ and $x + y = 3$ respectively.

Line	Inequation	Point x	Points on y	Sign	Feasible region
AB	$5x + y = 5$	$A(1, 0)$	$B(0, 5)$	$\geq$	Non-origin side AB
CD	$x + y = 3$	$C(3, 0)$	$D(0, 3)$	$\geq$	Non-origin side of line CD

1 unit $= 1\ cm$ both axis

Mathematics : Mock Test - 7

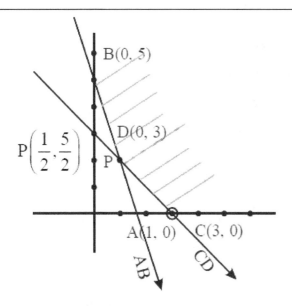

common feasible region BPC

Points   Minimize $z = 7x + y$
$B(0,5)$ $Z(B) = 7(0) + 5 = 5$
$P\left(\frac{1}{2}, \frac{5}{2}\right)$ $Z(P) = 7 \times \frac{1}{2} + \frac{5}{2} = 6$
$C(3,0)$ $Z(C) = 7 \times (3) + 0 = 21$

Z is minimum at $x = 0, y = 5$ and $\min(Z) = 5$

Hence, the correct option is (D).

16. Given:

$x + y \leq 3, y \leq 6$ and $x \geq 0, y \geq 0$

Converting the given in equations into equations

$x + y = 3$ ....(1)

$y = 6$ ....(2)

Reglon represented by $x + y \leq 3$:

The line $x + y = 3$ meets the coordinate axes are $A(3,0)$ and $B(0,3)$ respectively,

$x + y = 3$

| x | 3 | 0 |
| y | 0 | 3 |

$A(3,0); B(0,3)$

Join points A and B to obtain the line.

Clearly, $(0,0)$ satisfies the in equation $x + y \leq 3$.

So, the region containing the origin represent the solution set of the in equation.

Reglon represented by $y \leq 6$:

The line $y = 6$ is parallel to x-axis and its every point will satisfy the in equation in first, quadrant, region containing the origin represents the solution set of this in equation.

Reglon represented by $x \geq 0$ and $y \geq 0$:

Since every point in first quadrant satisfy the in equations, so the first quadrant is the solution set of these in equations.

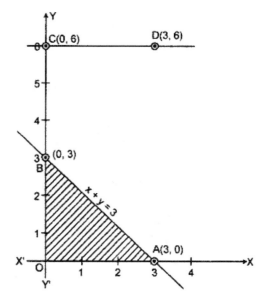

The shaded region is the common region of in equations. This is feasible region of solution which is bounded and is in first quadrant.

Hence, the correct option is (C).

17. Given,

Objective function is $Z = -50x + 20y$.

We have to minimize Z on given constraints

$2x - y \geq -5$

$3x + y \geq 3$

$2x - 3y \leq 12$

$x \geq 0, y \geq 0$

After plotting all the constraints we get the common region (Feasible region) as shown in the image.

There are four corner points $(0,5), (0,3), (1,0)$ and $(6,0)$

Now, at corner points value of Z are as follows:

Corner Point	Value of $Z = -50x + 20y$
(0,5)	100
(0,3)	60
(1,0)	-50
(6,0)	-300 (minimum)

111

Since common region is unbounded. So, value of Z may be minimum at $(6,0)$ and minimum value may be -300.

Now to check if this minimum is correct or not, we have to draw region $-50x + 20y \leq -300$

Since, there are some common region with feasible region(See image). So, -300 will not be minimum value of Z.

So, Z has no minimum value.

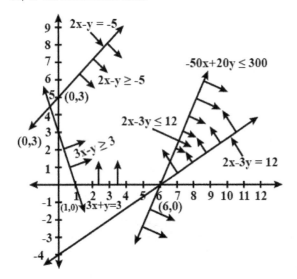

Hence, the correct option is (A).

18. Given,

The length of the perpendicular from the point $(4,1)$ on the line $3x - 4y + k = 0$ is 2 units.

The perpendicular distance d from $P(x_1, y_1)$ to the line $ax + by + c = 0$ is given by

$$d = \left|\frac{ax_1 + by_1 + c}{\sqrt{a^2 + b^2}}\right| \quad \text{......(i)}$$

Let $P = (4,1)$

Here $x_1 = 4, y_1 = 1, a = 3, b = -4$ and $d = 2$

Now substitute $x_1 = 4$ and $y_1 = 1$ in the equation (i) we get,

$\Rightarrow d = \left|\frac{3 \times x_1 - 4 \times y_1 + k}{\sqrt{3^2 + (-4)^2}}\right| = 2$

$\Rightarrow d = \left|\frac{3 \times 4 - 4 \times 1 + k}{\sqrt{25}}\right| = 2$

$\Rightarrow \left|\frac{8+k}{5}\right| = 2$

$\Rightarrow |8+k| = 10$

$\Rightarrow k = 2 \text{ or } -18$

Hence, the correct option is (C).

19. Given,

$y - \sqrt{3}x - 5 = 0$

$\sqrt{3}y - x + 6 = 0$

$y - \sqrt{3}x - 5 = 0$

$\Rightarrow y = \sqrt{3}x + 5$

So, slope of line, $m_1 = \sqrt{3}$

$\sqrt{3}y - x + 6 = 0$

$\Rightarrow y = \frac{x}{\sqrt{3}} - \frac{6}{\sqrt{3}}$

So, slope of the line, $m_2 = \frac{1}{\sqrt{3}}$

Let θ be the acute angle between the lines.

The angle θ between the lines having slope m_1 and m_2 is given by:

$\tan\theta = \left|\frac{m_1 - m_2}{1 + m_1 m_2}\right|$

$\Rightarrow \tan\theta = \left|\frac{\sqrt{3} - \frac{1}{\sqrt{3}}}{1 + \sqrt{3} \times \frac{1}{\sqrt{3}}}\right|$

$\Rightarrow \tan\theta = \left|\frac{\frac{2}{\sqrt{3}}}{2}\right|$

$\Rightarrow \tan\theta = \frac{1}{\sqrt{3}}$

$\Rightarrow \theta = 30°$

Hence, the correct option is (A).

20. Given,

The inclination of the line joining the points $(x, -3)$ and $(2,5)$ is $135°$

Here, we have to find the value of x.

As we know that, the slope of a line is given by $\tan \alpha$ and it is denoted by m where $\alpha \neq \frac{\pi}{2}$ and it represents the angle which a given line makes with respect to the $X-$ axis in the positive direction.

$m = \tan(135°) = \tan(180° - 135°)$

$= -\tan 45°$

$= -1$

As we know that, the slope of the line joining the points (x_1, y_1) and (x_2, y_2) is:

$m = \frac{y_2 - y_1}{x_2 - x_1}$

Here, $x_1 = x, y_1 = -3, x_2 = 2, y_2 = 5$ and $m = -1$.

$-1 = \frac{5-(-3)}{2-x}$

$\Rightarrow -2 + x = 8$

$\Rightarrow x = 10$

Hence, the correct option is (C).

21. Given lines are

$6x + 9y + 15 = 0$ ....(1)

$12x + 18y + 30 = 0$ ....(2)

compare eq (1) with $a_1 x + b_1 y + c_1 = 0$ and eq (2) with $a_2 x + b_2 y + c_2 = 0$

$a_1 = 6, b_1 = 9, c_1 = 15$ and $a_2 = 12, b_2 = 18, c_2 = 30$

$\frac{a_1}{a_2} = \frac{1}{2}, \frac{b_1}{b_2} = \frac{1}{2}, \frac{c_1}{c_2} = \frac{1}{2}$

$\frac{a_1}{a_2} = \frac{b_1}{b_2} = \frac{c_1}{c_2}$

Lines are parallel.

So, Angle between lines is zero.

Hence, the correct option is (A).

22. Poisson distribution formula,

$P(x) = \frac{e^{-\lambda} \lambda^x}{x!}$

where λ = mean value of occurrence within an interval
$P(x)$ = probability of x occurrence within an interval For Poisson Distribution we have

Mean = Variance = (Standard Deviation)^2

∴ Standard Deviation = $\sqrt{\text{Mean}} = \sqrt{\mu}$

Hence, the correct option is (A).

23. Given:

Arrival rate $(\lambda) = \frac{5 \text{ Jobs}}{8 \text{ Hour}}$

Service time for one job is 40 min

Therefore, Service rate $(\mu) = \frac{3 \text{ Jobs}}{2 \text{ Hour}}$

Utilization factor $\rho = \frac{\lambda}{\mu}$

Idle time $= 1 - \rho$

$\lambda = \frac{5 \text{ Jobs}}{8 \text{ Hour}}$

$\mu = \frac{3 \text{ Jobs}}{2 \text{ Hour}}$

$\rho = \frac{\lambda}{\mu} = \frac{\frac{5}{8}}{\frac{3}{2}} = \frac{5}{12}$

Idle time $= 1 - \rho$

$= 1 - \frac{5}{12}$

$= \frac{7}{12}$ hour

Therefore, Idle time for 8 hour shift $= \frac{7}{12} \times 8$

$= \frac{14}{3}$ hours.

Hence, the correct option is (B).

24. Given:

Vectors $\vec{a} = 2\hat{i} - \hat{j} + 2\hat{k}$ and $\vec{b} = -\hat{i} + \hat{j} + 3\hat{k}$

By writing them in the component form that is:

$\vec{a} = (2, -1, 2)$ and $\vec{b} = (-1, 1, 3)$

Then the sum of the vectors can be computed as follows:

$(2-1)\hat{i} + (-1+1)\hat{j} + (2+3)\hat{i}$

$= \hat{i} + 0\hat{j} + 5\hat{k}$

$= (1, 0, 5)$

Now the unit vector can be obtained as:

$\| \vec{a} + \vec{b} \| = \sqrt{(1)^2 + (0)^2 + (5)^2}$

$= \sqrt{1 + 25} = \sqrt{26}$

Unit Vector: $\frac{i}{\sqrt{26}} + \frac{5\hat{k}}{\sqrt{26}}$

Hence, the correct option is (A).

25. Given:

$\vec{a} = 2\hat{i} + \hat{j} - 3\hat{k}$ and $\vec{b} = 3\hat{i} - 2\hat{j} - \hat{k}$

$\vec{a} \cdot \vec{b} = (2\hat{i} + \hat{j} - 3\hat{k})(3\hat{i} - 2\hat{j} - \hat{k})$

$= 6 - 2 + 3 = 7$ ..... (1)

$|\vec{a}| = \sqrt{2^2 + 1^2 + (-3)^2} = \sqrt{14}$ ... (2)

$|\vec{b}| = \sqrt{3^2 + (-2)^2 + (-1)^2} = \sqrt{14}$ ..... (3)

$\cos\theta = \frac{\vec{a} \cdot \vec{b}}{|\vec{a}| \cdot |\vec{b}|}$

Put the values from (1), (2) amnd (3) in above equation:

$= \frac{7}{\sqrt{14} \cdot \sqrt{14}}$

$= \frac{1}{2}$

$\cos\theta = \cos 60°$

$\theta = 60°$

Hence, the correct option is (D).

26. Given,

$6\sin^2 x - 2\cos^2 x = 4$

$\Rightarrow 6\sin^2 x - 2\cos^2 x = 4 \times 1$

As we know that,

$\sin^2 x + \cos^2 x = 1$

$\Rightarrow 6\sin^2 x - 2\cos^2 x = 4(\sin^2 x + \cos^2 x)$

$\Rightarrow 6\sin^2 x - 2\cos^2 x = 4\sin^2 x + 4\cos^2 x$

$\Rightarrow 6\sin^2 x - 4\sin^2 x = 4\cos^2 x + 2\cos^2 x$

$\Rightarrow 2\sin^2 x = 6\cos^2 x$

$\Rightarrow \tan^2 x = 3$

$\therefore \tan x = \sqrt{3}$

Hence, the correct option is (A).

27. Given,

$\frac{p^2}{a^2} + k\cos\alpha + \frac{q^2}{b^2} = \sin^2\alpha \ldots(i)$

$\cos^{-1}\left(\frac{p}{a}\right) + \cos^{-1}\left(\frac{q}{b}\right) = \alpha$

As we know,

$\cos^{-1}x + \cos^{-1}y = \cos^{-1}\left(xy - \sqrt{1-x^2}\cdot\sqrt{1-y^2}\right)$

$\cos^{-1}\left(\frac{pq}{ab} - \sqrt{1-\frac{p^2}{a^2}}\sqrt{1-\frac{q^2}{b^2}}\right) = \alpha$

$\cos\alpha = \left(\frac{pq}{ab} - \sqrt{1-\frac{p^2}{a^2}}\sqrt{1-\frac{q^2}{b^2}}\right)$

$\frac{pq}{ab} - \cos\alpha = \sqrt{1-\frac{p^2}{a^2}}\sqrt{1-\frac{q^2}{b^2}}$

Squaring both sides, we get

$\left(\frac{pq}{ab} - \cos\alpha\right)^2 = \left(\sqrt{1-\frac{p^2}{a^2}}\sqrt{1-\frac{q^2}{b^2}}\right)^2$

$\frac{(pq)^2}{(ab)^2} + \cos^2\alpha - 2\frac{pq}{ab}\cos\alpha = \left(1-\frac{p^2}{a^2}\right)\left(1-\frac{q^2}{b^2}\right)$

$\frac{(pq)^2}{(ab)^2} + \cos^2\alpha - 2\frac{pq}{ab}\cos\alpha = 1-\frac{p^2}{a^2}-\frac{q^2}{b^2}+\frac{(pq)^2}{(ab)^2}$

$\sin^2\alpha = \frac{p^2}{a^2} + \frac{q^2}{b^2} - 2\frac{pq}{ab}\cos\alpha \ldots(ii)$

Comparing equation (i) and (ii), we get

$k = -\frac{2pq}{ab}$

Hence, the correct option is (A).

28. Given,

$\cot\left[\sin^{-1}\frac{3}{5} + \cot^{-1}\frac{3}{2}\right] \ldots(i)$

Let $a = \cot^{-1}\left(\frac{3}{2}\right)$

$\Rightarrow \cot a = \frac{3}{2} = \frac{\text{Base}}{\text{Perpendicular}}$

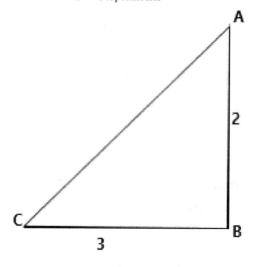

$AC^2 = AB^2 + BC^2$

$\Rightarrow AC^2 = 2^2 + 3^2$

$\Rightarrow AC^2 = 13$

$\Rightarrow AC = \sqrt{13}$

$\sin a = \frac{\text{Perpendicular}}{\text{Hypotenuse}}$

$\Rightarrow \sin a = \frac{2}{\sqrt{13}}$

$\Rightarrow a = \sin^{-1}\left(\frac{2}{\sqrt{13}}\right)$

From equation (i), we get

$\cot\left[\sin^{-1}\frac{3}{5} + \sin^{-1}\frac{2}{\sqrt{13}}\right]$

$= \cot\left[\sin^{-1}\left\{\left(\frac{3}{5}\right)\sqrt{1-\left(\frac{4}{13}\right)} + \left(\frac{2}{\sqrt{13}}\right)\sqrt{1-\left(\frac{9}{25}\right)}\right\}\right]$

$= \cot\left[\sin^{-1}\left(\frac{17}{5\sqrt{13}}\right)\right]$

$= \cot\left[\cot^{-1}\left(\frac{6}{17}\right)\right]$

$= \frac{6}{17}$

Hence, the correct option is (A).

29. Given,

$= \int_0^{\frac{\pi}{4}} \sqrt{\tan x}\, dx + \int_0^{\frac{\pi}{4}} \sqrt{\cot x}\, dx$

$= \int_0^{\frac{\pi}{4}} (\sqrt{\tan x} + \sqrt{\cot x})\, dx$

$= \int_0^{\frac{\pi}{4}} \frac{(\sin x + \cos x)}{\sqrt{\sin x} \times \sqrt{\cos x}}\, dx$

$= \sqrt{2} \int_0^{\frac{\pi}{4}} \frac{(\sin x + \cos x)}{\sqrt{1 - (\sin^2 x + \cos^2 x - 2\sin x \cos x)}}\, dx$

= Put $\sin x - \cos x = t$; $(\cos x + \sin x)dx = dt$

= When $x = 0, t = -1$ and $x = \frac{\pi}{4}, t = 0$

$= \sqrt{2}[\sin^{-1}(0) - \sin^{-1}(-1)]$

$= \sqrt{2}\left[0 - \left(-\frac{\pi}{2}\right)\right] = \frac{\pi}{\sqrt{2}}$

Hence, the correct option is (D).

30. Given,
$2x^3 - 3y^2 = 7$

Differentiating w.r.t. x, we get

$6x^2 - 6y\frac{dy}{dx} = 0$

$\Rightarrow x^2 - y\frac{dy}{dx} = 0$

$\Rightarrow \frac{dy}{dx} = \frac{x^2}{y}$

Hence, the correct option is (C).

31. The order of a differential equation is the order of the highest order derivative.

So, $y''y' + y = \sin x$ has order 2.

Hence, the correct option is (B).

32. Let, small charge in x be Δx and the corresponding change in y is Δy.

Therefore, $\Delta y = \frac{dy}{dx} \Delta x$

We have to find the value of $\sqrt{24.99}$

Let, $x + \Delta x = 24.99 = 25 - 0.01$

Therefore, $x = 25$ and $\Delta x = -0.01$

Assume, $y = x^{\frac{1}{2}}$

Differentiating with respect to x, we get:

$\frac{dy}{dx} = \frac{1}{2}x^{-\frac{1}{2}} = \frac{1}{2\sqrt{x}}$

At $x = 25$

$\left[\frac{dy}{dx}\right]_{x=25} = \frac{1}{10}$ and $y = (25)^{\frac{1}{2}} = 5$

As we know $\Delta y = \frac{dy}{dx} \Delta x$

So, $\Delta y = \frac{1}{10} \times (-0.01) = -0.001$

Therefore, approximate value of $\sqrt{24.99} = (24.99)^{\frac{1}{2}} = y + \Delta y = 5 - 0.001 = 4.999$

Hence, the correct option is (A).

33. Let, the radius of a sphere is r meters.

The surface area of Sphere $(A) = 4\pi r^2$

Given: Radius of a sphere $= 6m$ and $\Delta r = 0.02m$

Now, the volume of the sphere is given by,

$A = 4\pi r^2$

Differentiating with respect to r, we get:

$\frac{dS}{dr} = 8\pi r$

$\Rightarrow dS = 8\pi r \cdot dr$

$\Rightarrow dS = 8\pi \cdot 6 \cdot (0.02)$

$\Rightarrow dS = 0.96$ square meters

Hence, the correct option is (B).

34. Let, small charge in x be Δx and the corresponding change in y is Δy.

Therefore, $\Delta y = \frac{dy}{dx} \Delta x$

We have to find the value of $(242)^{\frac{1}{5}}$

Let, $x + \Delta x = 242 = 243 - 1$

Therefore, $x = 243$ and $\Delta x = -1$

Assume, $y = x^{\frac{1}{5}}$

Differentiating with respect to x, we get:

$\frac{dy}{dx} = \frac{1}{5}x^{-\frac{4}{5}} = \frac{1}{5(x)^{\frac{4}{5}}}$

At $x = 243$

$\left[\frac{dy}{dx}\right]_{x=243} = \frac{1}{405}$ and $y = (243)^{\frac{1}{5}} = 3$

As we know $\Delta y = \frac{dy}{dx} \Delta x$

So, $\Delta y = \frac{1}{405} \times (-1) = 0.0024$

Therefore, approximate value of $(242)^{\frac{1}{5}} = y + \Delta y = 3 - 0.0024 = 2.997$

Hence, the correct option is (A).

35. According to the question,

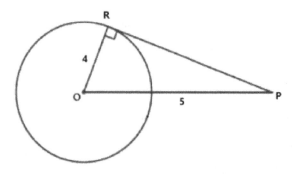

Triangle ORP is a right angle triangle,

By, using Pythagoras theorem,

$\Rightarrow OP^2 = OR^2 + RP^2$

$\Rightarrow (5)^2 = (4)^2 + (RP)^2$

$\Rightarrow 25 = 16 + (RP)^2$

$\Rightarrow (RP)^2 = 25 - 16$

$\Rightarrow (RP)^2 = 9$

$RP = 3\ cm$

Hence, the correct option is (A).

36. Given:

$\lim\limits_{x \to 7} g(x) = k$

where, $g(x) = \sqrt{8x - 7}$

As we know that, if $\lim\limits_{x \to a} f(x)$ does not result into indeterminate form, then we use direct substitution in order to find the limits.

Here, also we can see that $\lim\limits_{x \to 7} g(x)$ does not result into any indeterminate form.

So, we can substitute $x = 7$ in the expression $g(x) = \sqrt{8x - 7}$ in order to find the value of k.

$\lim\limits_{x \to 7} g(x) = k$, where $g(x) = \sqrt{8x - 7}$, i.e.,

$\Rightarrow \lim\limits_{x \to 7} \sqrt{8x - 7} = k$

$\Rightarrow \sqrt{(8 \times 7) - 7} = k$

$\Rightarrow \sqrt{49} = k$

$\Rightarrow 7 = k$

or, $k = 7$

Hence, the correct option is (C).

37. Given:

$f(x) = |x - 1|$ and $g(x) = \tan x$

As we know that,

if $f: A \to B$ and $g: B \to C$ are functions then $fog(x) = f(g(x)$ is a function from A to C.

$\Rightarrow fog\left(\frac{7\pi}{4}\right) = f\left(g\left(\frac{3\pi}{4}\right)\right)$

$\Rightarrow g\left(\frac{3\pi}{4}\right) = \tan\left(\frac{3\pi}{4}\right) = \tan\left(\frac{\pi}{2} + \frac{\pi}{4}\right))$

As we know that,

$\tan\left(\frac{\pi}{2} + \theta\right) = -\tan\theta$

$\Rightarrow g\left(\frac{3\pi}{4}\right) = -\tan\left(\frac{\pi}{4}\right) = -1$

$\Rightarrow fog\left(\frac{7\pi}{6}\right) = f(-1)$

$\because f(x) = |x - 1| so, f(-1) = |-1 - 1| = |-2|$

So, $fog\left(\frac{3\pi}{4}\right) = 2$

Hence, the correct option is (B).

38. Given,

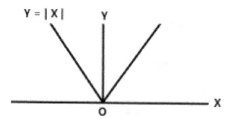

$f(x) = |x|$

$|x| = x$ for $x \geq 0$

$|x| = -x$ for $x < 0$

At $x = 0$

Left limit $= 0$, Right limit $= 0, f(0) = 0$

AS

Left limit = Right limit = Function value $= 0$

∴ $|x|$ is continuous at $x = 0$.

Now

Left derivative (at $x = 0$) = -1

Right derivative (at $x = 0$) = 1

Left derivative $\neq$ Right derivative

∴ $|x|$ is not differentiable at $x = 0$

Hence, the correct option is (C).

39. Given,

$\int_{-3}^{3} \cot^{-1} x \, dx$

Let us consider $\cot^{-1} x = u$.

On differentiating u on both sides we get, $-\frac{1}{1+x^2} dx = du$.

Therefore, we integrate the given function as follows:

$\int \cot^{-1} x \, dx = x \cot^{-1} x + \int \frac{x}{1+x^2} dx$

$= x \cot^{-1} x + \frac{1}{2} \ln(1 + x^2) + C$

Now as the given integral is definite we will remove the constant of integration and put the limits.

$= \left[3 \cot^{-1} 3 + \frac{1}{2} \ln(10)\right] - \left[-3 \cot^{-1}(-3) + \frac{1}{2} \ln(10)\right]$

$= 3\left(\cot^{-1}(3) + \cot^{-1}(-3)\right)$

$= 3\left(\cot^{-1}(3) + \pi - \cot^{-1}(3)\right)$

$= 3\pi$

Therefore, $\int_{-3}^{3} \cot^{-1} x \, dx = 3\pi$.

Hence, the correct option is (A).

40. Given,

$\int_{-5}^{5} |x + 2| \, dx$

Consider $|x + 2|$

$|x + 2| = x + 2$ for $x \geq -2$

$|x + 2| = -x - 2$ for $x < -2$

Now,

$\int_{-5}^{5} |x + 2| \, dx$

$= \int_{-5}^{-2}(-x - 2) \, dx + \int_{-2}^{5}(x + 2) \, dx$

$= \left[\frac{-x^2}{2} - 2x\right]_{-5}^{-2} + \left[\frac{x^2}{2} + 2x\right]_{-2}^{5}$

$= \left(\frac{-4}{2} + 4\right) - \left(\frac{-25}{2} + 10\right) + \left(\frac{25}{2} + 10\right) - \left(\frac{4}{2} - 4\right)$

$= 29$

∴ $\int_{-5}^{5} |x + 2| \, dx$ is equal to 29.

Hence, the correct option is (C).

41. Given,

$\int_0^{\pi} \sin^6 x \cos^5 x \, dx$

Let $I = \int_0^{\pi} \sin^6 x \cos^5 x \, dx$

Using property $\int_a^b f(x) dx = \int_a^b f(a + b - x) dx$

$I = \int_0^{\pi} \sin^6(\pi - x) \cos^5(\pi - x) dx$

As we know, $\sin(\pi - x) = \sin x$ and $\cos(\pi - x) = -\cos x$

$I = -\int_0^{\pi} \sin^6 x \cos^5 x \, dx$

$I = -I$

$2I = 0$

∴ $I = 0$

∴ $\int_0^{\pi} \sin^6 x \cos^5 x \, dx$ is equal to 0.

Hence, the correct option is (C).

42. Given,

$\frac{x^4 + 3x^2 - x + 5}{x}$

$= \frac{x^4}{x} + \frac{3x^2}{x} - \frac{x}{x} + \frac{5}{x}$

$= x^3 + 3x - 1 + \frac{5}{x}$

Now,

$I = \int \frac{x^4 + 3x^2 - x + 5}{x} dx$

$= \int \left(x^3 + 3x - 1 + \frac{5}{x}\right) dx$

$= \int x^3 dx + 3\int x \, dx - \int 1 \, dx + \int \frac{5}{x} dx$

$= \frac{x^4}{4} + 3\frac{x^2}{2} - x + 5 \log x + c$

$= \frac{x^4}{4} + \frac{3x^2}{2} - x + \log x^5 + c$

∴ The integration of $\frac{x^4 + 3x^2 - x + 5}{x}$ is $\frac{x^4}{4} + \frac{3x^2}{2} - x + \log x^5 + c$.

Hence, the correct option is (B).

43. Given,

$f'(x) = 4x^3 - 2\frac{1}{\sqrt{x}} + e^{-4x}$

$f(x) = \int f(x)dx$

$\Rightarrow f(x) = \int 4x^3 - 2\frac{1}{\sqrt{x}} + e^{-4x} dx$

$\Rightarrow f(x) = 4\left[\frac{x^4}{4}\right] - 2\left[\frac{x^{\frac{1}{2}}}{\frac{1}{2}}\right] + \left[\frac{e^{-4x}}{4}\right]$

$\Rightarrow f(x) = x^4 - 4\sqrt{x} - \frac{e^{-4x}}{4} + C$

Now,

$f(0) = \frac{3}{4}$

$\Rightarrow 0^4 - 4\sqrt{0} - \frac{e^{-4(0)}}{4} + C = \frac{3}{4}$

$\Rightarrow C - \frac{1}{4} = \frac{3}{4}$

$\Rightarrow C = 1$

$f(x) = x^4 - 4\sqrt{x} - \frac{e^{-4x}}{4} + 1$

Hence, the correct option is (A).

44. Given,

$\int \frac{e^x(1+x)}{\cos^2(xe^x)} dx$

Consider,

$I = \int \frac{e^x(1+x)}{\cos^2(xe^x)} dx$

Put $xe^x = t$

Differentiating with respect to x, we get

$xe^x + e^x = \frac{dt}{dx}$

$e^x(x+1)dx = dt$

Integration (1) becomes, we get

$I = \int \frac{1}{\cos^2(t)} dt$

$I = \int \sec^2 t \, dt$

$I = \tan t + c$

Re-substitute the value of t, we get

$I = \tan(xe^x) + c$

$\therefore \int \frac{e^x(1+x)}{\cos^2(xe^x)} dx$ equal to $\tan(xe^x) + c$.

Hence, the correct option is (C).

45. Given,

Mean $\mu = np = 8$

Variance $\sigma^2 = npq = 4$

Dividing equation (2) by (1), we get

$q = \frac{1}{2}$

As we know, $p + q = 1$

$p = 1 - q = \frac{1}{2}$

Put the value of n in equation (1), we get

$n = 16$

Now,

$P(x = 1) = {}^{16}C_1 \left(\frac{1}{2}\right)^1 \times \left(\frac{1}{2}\right)^{16-1}$

$= 16 \times \frac{1}{2^{16}}$

$= 2^4 \times \frac{1}{2^{16}}$

$= \frac{1}{2^{12}}$

$\therefore p(x = 1)$ is equal to $\frac{1}{2^{12}}$.

Hence, the correct option is (A).

46. Given,

$2x - y + z = 6$ and $x + y + 2z = 7$

That means,

$a_1 = 2, b_1 = -1, c_1 = 1$ and $a_2 = 1, b_2 = 1, c_2 = 2$

Formula for angle between the plane:

$\cos\theta = \frac{a_1 a_2 + b_1 b_2 + c_1 c_2}{\sqrt{(a_1^2+b_1^2+c_1^2)(a_2^2+b_2^2+c_2^2)}}$

$\cos\theta = \frac{2\times 1 + 1\times(-1) + 1\times 2}{\sqrt{(2^2+(-1)^2+1^2)(1^2+1^2+2^2)}}$

$\cos\theta = \frac{3}{\sqrt{6\times 6}} = \frac{1}{2}$

$\theta = 60°$

$\therefore$ The acute angle between the planes $2x - y + z = 6$ and $x + y + 2z = 7$ is $\frac{\pi}{3}$.

Hence, the correct option is (D).

47. $(p \rightarrow q) \rightarrow r$ is a contradiction which is possible only when r is false and $(p \rightarrow q)$ is true.

Now, from here we can clearly say that option 4 is correct as $(r \to p) \to q$ means $\neg(r \to p) \vee q$.

Since r is false, $(r \to p)$ is true and $\neg(r \to p)$ becomes false.

So, it becomes (false $\vee$ q).

Now it totally depends on q. Whenever q is true, this value will always be true.

Hence, the correct option is (D).

48. Statement: "It is not the case that some trigonometric functions are not periodic"

"some trigonometric functions are not periodic" means

There exist some trigonometric functions which are also not periodic.

∃x [T(x) ∧ ¬ P(x)]

The negation of it.

"It is not the case that some trigonometric functions are not periodic"

¬ ∃x[T(x) ∧ ¬ P(x)]

Hence, the correct option is (A).

49. Given,

$\sin(\alpha + \beta) = 6\sin(\alpha - \beta)$ and $k = \dfrac{\tan\alpha}{\tan\beta}$

$\sin(\alpha + \beta) = 6\sin(\alpha - \beta)$

$\Rightarrow \sin\alpha\cos\beta + \cos\alpha\sin\beta = 6\sin\alpha\cos\beta - 6\cos\alpha\sin\beta$

$\Rightarrow \cos\alpha\sin\beta + 6\cos\alpha\sin\beta = 6\sin\alpha\cos\beta - \sin\alpha\cos\beta$

$\Rightarrow 7\cos\alpha\sin\beta = 5\sin\alpha\cos\beta$

$\Rightarrow \dfrac{\sin\alpha}{\cos\alpha} = \dfrac{7}{5} \times \dfrac{\sin\beta}{\cos\beta}$

$\Rightarrow \tan\alpha = \dfrac{7}{5} \times \tan\beta$

$\Rightarrow k = \dfrac{\tan\alpha}{\tan\beta} = \dfrac{7}{5}$

∴ The value of k is $\dfrac{7}{5}$

Hence, the correct option is (D).

50. Given:

$f(x) = [x]$ is a smallest integer function and $g(x) = x^3$

Here, we have to find the value of $gof\left(\dfrac{-9}{2}\right)$

$gof\left(\dfrac{-9}{2}\right) = g\left(f\left(\dfrac{-9}{2}\right)\right)$

∵ $f(x) = [x]$ is a smallest integer function i.e $f\left(\dfrac{-9}{2}\right) = -4$

$gof\left(\dfrac{-17}{5}\right) = g(-4)$

$g(x) = x^2$

So, $g(-4) = (-4)^2 = 16$

Therefore, $gof\left(\dfrac{-9}{2}\right)$ is equal to 16.

Hence, the correct option is (B).

Mathematics : Mock Test 08

Q.1 12 points are marked on a circle. How many octagon can be formed joining these points.
A. 495   B. 520   C. 545   D. 675

Q.2 If matrix $A = \begin{bmatrix} 1 & -2 \\ -6 & 4 \end{bmatrix}$ and $B = \begin{bmatrix} 2 & -1 \\ 1 & 3 \end{bmatrix}$, that $A(B^T)$ is:
A. $\begin{bmatrix} 4 & -5 \\ -16 & 6 \end{bmatrix}$ B. $\begin{bmatrix} 0 & -7 \\ 8 & 12 \end{bmatrix}$
C. $\begin{bmatrix} 0 & 7 \\ -8 & 18 \end{bmatrix}$ D. $\begin{bmatrix} 0 & -7 \\ -8 & 12 \end{bmatrix}$

Q.3 If $A = \begin{bmatrix} 1 & 3+x & 2 \\ 1-x & 2 & y+1 \\ 2 & 5-y & 3 \end{bmatrix}$ is a symmetric matrix, then $3x + y$ is equal to:
[UPSESSB TGT Mathematics, 2019]
A. -1   B. 0
C. 1   D. None of these

Q.4 If $A = \begin{bmatrix} 2 & 3 \\ -1 & 2 \end{bmatrix} = \frac{1}{2}(P+Q)$ where P is symmetric and Q is skew symmetric matrix then P and Q are:
A. $P = \begin{bmatrix} 4 & 2 \\ 2 & 4 \end{bmatrix}$ and $Q = \begin{bmatrix} 0 & 4 \\ 4 & 0 \end{bmatrix}$
B. $P = \begin{bmatrix} 4 & 2 \\ 2 & 4 \end{bmatrix}$ and $Q = \begin{bmatrix} 0 & 4 \\ -4 & 0 \end{bmatrix}$
C. $P = \begin{bmatrix} 4 & 2 \\ 2 & 4 \end{bmatrix}$ and $Q = \begin{bmatrix} 0 & -4 \\ -4 & 0 \end{bmatrix}$
D. None of these

Q.5 In the given figure, AB || CD, ∠APQ = 50° and ∠PRD = 127°, find the value of y − x?

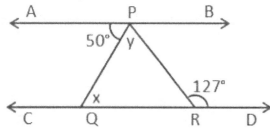

A. 41°   B. 37°   C. 27°   D. 31°

Q.6 If $\frac{dy}{dx} = e^{-3y}, y = 0$ when $x = 5$, value of x for $y = 5$ is:
A. $\frac{e^{15}+14}{3}$ B. $\frac{e^{15}-14}{3}$ C. 0   D. $e - \frac{3y}{5}$

Q.7 Integrating factor of $(1-x^2)\frac{dy}{dx} - xy = 1$ is:
A. $1-x^2$ B. $\frac{1}{1-x^2}$ C. $\frac{1}{\sqrt{1-x^2}}$ D. $\sqrt{1-x^2}$

Q.8 Solve the differential equation $\sin x \frac{dy}{dx} + \frac{y}{\sin x} = x \sin x e^{\cot x}$:

A. $ye^{-\cot x} = \frac{x^2}{2} + c$ B. $ye^{\cot x} = \frac{x^2}{2} + c$
C. $ye^{-\cot x} = x + c$ D. $ye^{\cot x} = x + c$

Q.9 For a distribution, the coefficient of variation is 22.5% and mean is 7.5. Calculate standard deviation.
A. 1.96   B. 1.69   C. 2.18   D. 4.96

Q.10 Find the area of the region bounded by the curves $y = x^3 + 4x + 2$, the line $x = 0, x = 4$ and the x-axis.
A. 104 sq. units   B. 92 sq. units
C. 84 sq.units   D. 96 sq. units

Q.11 Find the area between $y = 2x^2$ and $y + 6x - 8 = 0$.
A. $\frac{125}{2}$ B. $\frac{125}{3}$ C. $\frac{115}{3}$ D. $\frac{195}{2}$

Q.12 Find the area bounded by the curves $y \geq x^2$ and $y = |x|$.
A. $\frac{17}{6}$ square units   B. $\frac{8}{3}$ square units
C. 2 square units   D. $\frac{1}{3}$ square units

Q.13 If $x + iy = \frac{3+4i}{2-i}$ where $i = \sqrt{-1}$, then what is the value of y?
A. $\frac{9}{5}$ B. $\frac{11}{5}$ C. $\frac{2}{5}$ D. $\frac{13}{5}$

Q.14 Solve the linear programming problem by graphical method:
Minimize $Z = 3x + 5y$ Subject to the constraints $x + 3y \geq 3, x + y \geq 2$ and $x \geq 0, y \geq 0$.
A. 7   B. +12   C. +13   D. -13

Q.15 Maximize: $z = 3x + 5y$
Subject to: $x + 4y \leq 24$
$3x + y \leq 21$
$x + y \leq 9$
$x \geq 0, y \geq 0$
A. $(x,y) = \left(\frac{65}{11}, \frac{51}{61}\right), z = \frac{435}{21}$
B. $(x,y) = \left(\frac{60}{11}, \frac{51}{11}\right), z = \frac{435}{11}$
C. $(x,y) = \left(\frac{6}{11}, \frac{51}{6}\right), z = \frac{5}{21}$
D. $(x,y) = \left(\frac{63}{121}, \frac{51}{6}\right), z = \frac{95}{21}$

Q.16 Maximize $Z = x + 2y$, subject to the constraints
$x + 2y \geq 100$
$2x - y \leq 0$
$2x + y \leq 200$
$x, y \geq 0$ by graphical method.

A. 356   B. 659   C. 298   D. 400

Q.17 The equation of the line which passes through (1, 2) and is parallel to the line passing through (3, 4) and (4, 5), is:
A. x + y + 1 = 0
B. x + y - 1 = 0
C. x - y + 1 = 0
D. None of these.

Q.18 The angle between the two planes $3x - 4y + 5z = 20$ and $4x + 3y + 5z = 25$, is:
A. $0°$ B. $\frac{\pi}{2}$ C. $\frac{\pi}{3}$ D. $\frac{\pi}{6}$

Q.19 Let X be a binomial random variable with mean 1 and variance $\frac{3}{4}$. The probability that X takes the value of 3 is:
A. $\frac{3}{64}$ B. $\frac{3}{16}$ C. $\frac{27}{64}$ D. $\frac{3}{4}$

Q.20 What is the probability of getting a sum 9 from two throws of a dice?
A. $\frac{1}{9}$ B. $\frac{1}{4}$ C. $\frac{2}{3}$ D. $\frac{3}{4}$

Q.21 Find the value of x if $\tan 3x = \sin 45° \cos 45° + \sin 30°$
A. $15°$ B. $30°$ C. $10°$ D. $20°$

Q.22 If $\vec{a} = 3\hat{i} + 4\hat{j} + 5\hat{k}$ and $\vec{\beta} = 2\hat{i} + \hat{j} - 4\hat{k}$, The sum of two vectors such that one is parallel to $\vec{a}$ and other is perpendicular to $\vec{a}$. Then $\vec{\beta}$:
A. $-2\hat{i} - \hat{j} + 4\hat{k}$
B. $2\hat{i} - \hat{j} - 4\hat{k}$
C. $-4\hat{i} - \hat{j} + 7\hat{k}$
D. $-7\hat{i} - \hat{j} + 9\hat{k}$

Q.23 The vector $a = \alpha i + 2j + \beta k$ lies in the plane of the vectors $b = i + j$ and $c = i + k$ and bisects the angle between b and c. Then, which one of the following gives possible values of α and β is:
A. $\alpha = 1, \beta = 1$
B. $\alpha = 2, \beta = 2$
C. $\alpha = 1, \beta = 2$
D. $\alpha = 2, \beta = 1$

Q.24 The value of $\cos 20° + \cos 100° + \cos 140°$ is:
A. 0   B. $\frac{1}{\sqrt{2}}$ C. $\frac{1}{2}$ D. 1

Q.25 Find the value of $\cot\left(22\frac{1°}{2}\right)$.
A. $1 + \sqrt{2}$ B. $1 - \sqrt{2}$ C. $2 + \sqrt{2}$ D. $2 - \sqrt{2}$

Q.26 If $\sin x + \cos x = \sqrt{2}$, then what is $\cos^2(2x)$ equal to?
A. 1   B. $\sqrt{2}$ C. 0   D. -1

Q.27 If $x = \sin^2 t$ and $y = \cos^2 t$ then find the value of $\frac{dy}{dx}$.
A. 1
B. $\frac{1}{2}$
C. 1
D. None of these

Q.28 Evaluate $\lim_{x \to 2} \frac{\sqrt{3-x}-1}{2-x}$.

A. 0   B. ∞ C. $\frac{1}{2}$ D. $\frac{-1}{2}$

Q.29 When a coin is tossed 8 times getting ahead is a success. Then the probability that at least 2 heads will occur is:
A. $\frac{247}{265}$ B. $\frac{73}{256}$ C. $\frac{247}{256}$ D. $\frac{27}{256}$

Q.30 The value of $\sqrt{36.01}$ is:
A. 6.0833   B. 6.00833
C. 6.000833   D. 6.0000833

Q.31 It is given that at $x = 2$, the function $x^3 - 12x^2 + kx - 8$ attains its maximum value, on the interval $[0,3]$. Find the value of k.
A. 23   B. 34   C. 36   D. 35

Q.32 The maximum value of $\sin\left(x + \frac{\pi}{6}\right) + \cos\left(x + \frac{\pi}{6}\right)$ in the interval $\left(0, \frac{\pi}{2}\right)$ is attained at:
A. $\frac{\pi}{12}$ B. $\frac{\pi}{6}$ C. $\frac{\pi}{3}$ D. $\frac{\pi}{2}$

Q.33 If $f(x) = 2^{|x|}$ and $g(x) = [x]$ where [.] denotes greatest integer function then find the value of $fog\left(\frac{-17}{2}\right)$?
A. $\frac{1}{512}$ B. $\frac{1}{256}$ C. 256   D. 512

Q.34 $\int x \cos x^2 dx = ?$
A. $\frac{1}{2}\sin x + C$
B. $-\frac{1}{2}\cos x^2 + C$
C. $\frac{1}{2}\cos x^2 + C$
D. $\frac{1}{2}\sin x^2 + C$

Q.35 Evaluate: $\int e^{\log x} \sin x dx$
A. $-x\sin x + \cos x + c$
B. $x\sin x + \cos x + c$
C. $-x\cos x + \sin x + c$
D. $x\cos x + \sin x + c$

Q.36 Find the $\int \frac{2}{\sin 2x \cdot \log(\tan x)}$
A. $\log(\sin x) + c$ B. $\log(\cos x) + c$
C. $\log(\tan x) + c$ D. $\log[\log(\tan x)] + c$

Q.37 Evaluate: $\int \frac{e^{2x}}{e^{2x}+1} dx$
A. $(e^{2x} + 1) + c$
B. $\frac{1}{2}(e^{2x} + 1) + c$
C. $\ln(e^{2x} + 1) + c$
D. $\frac{1}{2}\ln(e^{2x} + 1) + c$

Q.38 Evaluate: $\int_1^4 (5x^2 - 8x + 5) dx$
A. 45   B. 50   C. 60   D. 32

Q.39 $\int_1^3 |x - 2| dx$ equal to?
A. 3   B. 4   C. 2   D. 1

Q.40 Evaluate: $\int_0^1 x \tan^{-1} x dx$
A. $\frac{\pi}{4} + \frac{1}{2}$ B. $\frac{\pi}{4} - \frac{1}{2}$
C. $\frac{1}{2} + \frac{\pi}{4}$ D. $-\frac{\pi}{4} - \frac{1}{2}$

Q.41 What is the radius and the center of the circle $2y^2 + 2x^2 + 12y = 32$

A. 5 and (3,0)
B. 3 and (0,−3)
C. 5 and (0,−3)
D. 3 and (−3,0)

Q.42 Find the foot of the perpendicular of the point $(4,5,4)$ on the plane $x + 2y + z = 2$.

A. $(-1,-1,-1)$
B. $(-2,1,1)$
C. $\left(\frac{4}{3}, \frac{-1}{3}, \frac{4}{3}\right)$
D. $(-1,-2,1)$

Q.43 The solution of differential equation $\frac{dy}{dx} = \frac{2+y}{x}$ is:

A. $2 + y = x + c$
B. $2 + y = cx$
C. $2 + y = \log x + c$
D. None of these

Q.44 The minimum number of times a die must be thrown so that there is better than even chances of getting a 4 is:

A. 4
B. 8
C. 5
D. 6

Q.45 The mean and standard deviation of a binomial distribution are 16 and 3 respectively. What is the number of trails?

A. 36
B. 48
C. 18
D. 60

Q.46 In a binomial distribution, the mean is $\frac{2}{3}$ and variance is $\frac{5}{9}$. What is the probability that random variable $D = 3$?

A. $\frac{5}{36}$
B. $\frac{25}{36}$
C. $\frac{25}{54}$
D. $\frac{5}{324}$

Q.47 Which one of the following options is correct given three positive integers x, y and z, and a predicate P(x)= -(x = 1) ∧ ∀ y(∃z(x=y*z) ⇒ (y = x) ∨ (y = 1))

A. P(x) being true means that x is a prime number
B. P(x) being true means that x is a number other than 1
C. P(x) is always true irrespective of the value of x
D. P(x) being true means that x has exactly two factors other than 1 and x

Q.48 The function $f(x)$ is defined as:

$f(x) = \begin{cases} bx^2 - a, & \text{if } x < -1 \\ ax^2 - bx - 2, & \text{if } x \geq -1 \end{cases}$

If $f(x)$ is differentiable everywhere, the equation whose roots are a and b is:

A. $x^2 + 3x - 2 = 0$
B. $x^2 - 3x + 2 = 0$
C. $x^2 + 3x + 2 = 0$
D. $x^2 - 5x + 6 = 0$

Q.49 $\int_{-1}^{1} x|x|dx$ is equal to:

A. 0
B. $\frac{2}{3}$
C. 2
D. −2

Q.50 The XY-plane divides the line segment joining the points $(-1,3,4)$ and $(2,-5,6)$:

A. Internally in the ratio 2: 3
B. Internally in the ratio 3: 2
C. Externally in the ratio 2: 3
D. Internally in the ratio 2: 1

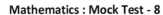

// Smart Answer Sheet //

Correct — Indicates percentage of students who answered questions correctly.

Skipped — Indicates percentage of students who skipped questions.

Q.	Ans.	Correct / Skipped	Q.	Ans.	Correct / Skipped	Q.	Ans.	Correct / Skipped	Q.	Ans.	Correct / Skipped	Q.	Ans.	Correct / Skipped
1	A	32.91 % / 4.18 %	11	B	16.03 % / 3.24 %	21	A	47.05 % / 1.13 %	31	C	63.32 % / 1.84 %	41	C	82.63 % / 0.0 %
2	A	77.56 % / 0.0 %	12	D	62.53 % / 1.86 %	22	B	24.12 % / 4.35 %	32	A	57.44 % / 1.5 %	42	C	16.25 % / 4.07 %
3	A	29.47 % / 3.59 %	13	B	44.71 % / 1.16 %	23	A	30.06 % / 4.33 %	33	D	51.9 % / 1.01 %	43	B	45.68 % / 1.21 %
4	B	22.39 % / 3.7 %	14	A	23.78 % / 3.74 %	24	A	49.59 % / 1.55 %	34	D	53.81 % / 1.74 %	44	A	29.41 % / 3.59 %
5	C	61.02 % / 1.37 %	15	B	27.47 % / 3.95 %	25	A	66.93 % / 1.21 %	35	C	89.22 % / 0.0 %	45	B	69.26 % / 1.19 %
6	A	24.14 % / 3.7 %	16	D	55.97 % / 1.24 %	26	C	22.06 % / 4.03 %	36	D	83.08 % / 0.0 %	46	D	48.75 % / 1.88 %
7	D	15.6 % / 3.22 %	17	C	68.85 % / 1.33 %	27	C	64.56 % / 1.88 %	37	D	54.5 % / 1.71 %	47	A	69.72 % / 1.08 %
8	A	62.76 % / 1.9 %	18	C	59.1 % / 1.4 %	28	C	43.86 % / 1.69 %	38	C	43.82 % / 1.03 %	48	B	41.83 % / 1.44 %
9	B	85.7 % / 0.0 %	19	A	61.79 % / 1.65 %	29	C	31.17 % / 3.44 %	39	D	59.5 % / 1.25 %	49	A	43.82 % / 1.48 %
10	A	54.3 % / 1.33 %	20	A	78.73 % / 0.0 %	30	C	14.71 % / 4.75 %	40	B	60.48 % / 1.16 %	50	C	63.91 % / 1.27 %

Performance Analysis	
Avg. Score (%)	41.0%
Toppers Score (%)	56.0%
Your Score	

Mathematics : Mock Test - 8

//Hints and Solutions//

1. We know that:

The number of ways to select r things out of n things is given by ^nC_r

$$^nC_r = \frac{n!}{(n-r)! \times (r)!} = \frac{n \times (n-1) \times ... (n-r+1)}{r!}$$

$$^nC_r = {}^nC_{n-r}$$

Given,

Here, the number of points $= 12$

Octagon is formed by 8 points.

∴ Number of octagon = Number of ways of selecting 8 points out of 12

$= {}^{12}C_8$

$= {}^{12}C_4 \quad (\because {}^nC_r = {}^nC_{n-r})$

$= \frac{12!}{4! 8!}$

$= \frac{12 \times 11 \times 10 \times 9}{4 \times 3 \times 2 \times 1}$

$= 495$

Hence, the correct option is (A).

2. Given,

$A = \begin{bmatrix} 1 & -2 \\ -6 & 4 \end{bmatrix}$ and $B = \begin{bmatrix} 2 & -1 \\ 1 & 3 \end{bmatrix}$

Transpose of matrix $B = (B^T) = \begin{bmatrix} 2 & 1 \\ -1 & 3 \end{bmatrix}$

Now,

$A(B^T) = \begin{bmatrix} 1 & -2 \\ -6 & 4 \end{bmatrix} \times \begin{bmatrix} 2 & 1 \\ -1 & 3 \end{bmatrix}$

$\Rightarrow A(B^T) = \begin{bmatrix} 2+2 & 1-6 \\ -12-4 & -6+12 \end{bmatrix}$

$\Rightarrow A(B^T) = \begin{bmatrix} 4 & -5 \\ -16 & 6 \end{bmatrix}$

Hence, the correct option is (A).

3. Given,

$A = \begin{bmatrix} 1 & 3+x & 2 \\ 1-x & 2 & y+1 \\ 2 & 5-y & 3 \end{bmatrix}$

As we know,

Any real square matrix $A = (a_{ij})$ is said to be a symmetric matrix if $a_{ij} = a_{ji}$ or in other words if A is a real square matrix such that $A = A^t$ then A is said to be a symmetric matrix.

$A = A^t$

∴ $a_{ij} = a_{ji}$

∴ $A^t = \begin{bmatrix} 1 & 1-x & 2 \\ 3+x & 2 & 5-y \\ 2 & y+1 & 3 \end{bmatrix} = \begin{bmatrix} 1 & 3+x & 2 \\ 1-x & 2 & y+1 \\ 2 & 5-y & 3 \end{bmatrix} = A$

On comparing, we get

$3 + x = 1 - x$

$\Rightarrow x + x = 1 - 3$

$\Rightarrow 2x = -2$

$\Rightarrow x = -1$

And, $y + 1 = 5 - y$

$\Rightarrow y + y = 5 - 1$

$\Rightarrow 2y = 4$

$\Rightarrow y = 2$

Now,

$3x + y = 3 \times (-1) + 2$

$\Rightarrow 3x + y = -3 + 2$

$\Rightarrow 3x + y = -1$

Hence, the correct option is (A).

4. Given,

$A = \begin{bmatrix} 2 & 3 \\ -1 & 2 \end{bmatrix} = \frac{1}{2}(P + Q)$

Where P is symmetric and Q is a skew-symmetric matrix.

As we know,

Any square matrix can be be expressed as the sum of the symmetric and skew-symmetric matrix. i.e If A is a square matrix then A can be expressed as where $A + A'$ is symmetric and $A - A'$ is skew-symmetric matrix.

On comparing $A = \begin{bmatrix} 2 & 3 \\ -1 & 2 \end{bmatrix} = \frac{1}{2}(P + Q)$ with $A = \frac{1}{2}(A + A') + \frac{1}{2}(A - A')$ we get,

$P = A + A'$ and $Q = A - A'$

As, $A = \begin{bmatrix} 2 & 3 \\ -1 & 2 \end{bmatrix}$

∴ $A' = \begin{bmatrix} 2 & -1 \\ 3 & 2 \end{bmatrix}$

So, $P = \begin{bmatrix} 2 & 3 \\ -1 & 2 \end{bmatrix} + \begin{bmatrix} 2 & -1 \\ 3 & 2 \end{bmatrix}$

$\Rightarrow P = \begin{bmatrix} 4 & 2 \\ 2 & 4 \end{bmatrix}$

Similarly,

$Q = \begin{bmatrix} 2 & 3 \\ -1 & 2 \end{bmatrix} - \begin{bmatrix} 2 & -1 \\ 3 & 2 \end{bmatrix}$

$\Rightarrow Q = \begin{bmatrix} 0 & 4 \\ -4 & 0 \end{bmatrix}$

So,

$P = \begin{bmatrix} 4 & 2 \\ 2 & 4 \end{bmatrix}$ and $Q = \begin{bmatrix} 0 & 4 \\ -4 & 0 \end{bmatrix}$

Hence, the correct option is (B).

5. Given:

AB || CD

∠APQ = 50°

∠PRD = 127°

Calculation:

∠APQ = ∠x   ---- (Alternate angles are equal)

⇒∠x = 50° ------ (1)

∠APR = ∠PRD = 127°   ---- (Alternate angles are equal)

Since, ∠APR = ∠APQ + ∠y

⇒∠APQ + ∠y = 127°

⇒ 50° + ∠y = 127°

⇒ ∠y = 127° - 50°

⇒ ∠y = 77° ------(2)

So, from (1) & (2) we get,

∠y - ∠x = 77° - 50° = 27°

∴ The value of y – x is 27°.

Hence, the correct option is (C).

6. Given,

$\frac{dy}{dx} = e^{-3y}$

⇒ $\frac{dy}{e^{-3y}} = dx$

⇒ $e^{3y} dy = dx$

On integrating both side

We get,

$\int e^{3y} dy = \int dx$

⇒ $\frac{e^{3y}}{3} = x + C \ldots \ldots (i)$

⇒ $\frac{e^{2(0)}}{3} = 5 + C \quad (\because e^0 = 1)$

⇒ $C + 5 = \frac{1}{3}$

⇒ $C = \frac{1}{3} - 5$

⇒ $C = \frac{-14}{3}$

Substituting $y = 5$ and $C = \frac{-14}{5}$,

We get,

$\frac{e^{15}}{3} = x - \frac{14}{3}$

∴ $x = \frac{e^{15} + 14}{3}$

Hence, the correct option is (A).

7. Given,

$(1 - x^2)\frac{dy}{dx} - xy = 1 \ldots (i)$

Dividing both sides in equation (i) by $1 - x^2$, we will be able to get it in the standard form.

$\frac{dy}{dx} + \left(\frac{-x}{1-x^2}\right)y = \frac{1}{1-x^2}$

$P = \frac{-x}{1-x^2} \ldots (ii)$

Now,

On calculating $\int P dx$

$\int P dx = \int \frac{-x}{1-x^2} dx$

Substituting $1 - x^2 = t$ in equation (ii),

So that $-2x dx = dt$,

We get:

$\int P dx = \frac{1}{2} \int \frac{1}{t} dt$

Using $\int \frac{1}{x} dx = \log x + C$ and ignoring the constant C,

We get,

$\int P dx = \frac{1}{2} \log t \ldots (iii)$

By substituting $1 - x^2 = t$ in equation (iii) we get,

$\int P dx = \frac{1}{2} \log(1 - x^2)$

⇒ $\int P dx = \log\sqrt{1 - x^2}$

Now, the integrating factor will be:

$F = e^{\int P dx}$

⇒ $F = e^{\log\sqrt{1-x^2}}$

⇒ $F = \sqrt{1 - x^2}$, which is the required integrating factor.

Hence, the correct option is (D).

8. Given,

$\sin x \frac{dy}{dx} + \frac{y}{\sin x} = x \sin x e^{\cot x}$

$\frac{dy}{dx} + \frac{y}{\sin^2 x} = x \cdot e^{\cot x}$

It is form of $\frac{dy}{dx} + Py = Q$

I. $F. = e^{\int p dx}$

I. $F. = e^{\int \csc^2 x dx}$

$= e^{-\cot x}$

The solution of the linear equation is given by,

$y(I.F) = \int Q(I.F \cdot)dx + c$

$\Rightarrow ye^{-cotx} = \int xe^{cotx} \cdot e^{-cotx} dx + c$

$\Rightarrow ye^{-cotx} = \int x \, dx + c$

$\Rightarrow ye^{-cotx} = \frac{x^2}{2} + c$

Hence, the correct option is (A).

9. Given,

Coefficient of variation $= 22.5\%$

Mean, $\overline{X} = 7.5$

Now,

Coefficient of Variation $= \frac{\sigma}{\overline{X}} \times 100$

$\Rightarrow 22.5 = \frac{\sigma}{7.5} \times 100$

$\Rightarrow \frac{22.5 \times 7.5}{100} = \sigma$

$\Rightarrow \sigma = \frac{168.75}{100}$

$\Rightarrow \sigma = 1.687$

$\Rightarrow \sigma = 1.69$ approx

So, standard deviation is 1.69
Hence, the correct option is (B).

10. Here, we have to find the area of the region bounded by the curves $y = x^3 + 4x + 2$, the line $x = 0, x = 4$ and the x-axis.

So, the area enclosed by the given curves is given by:

$\int_0^4 (x^3 + 4x + 2) \, dx$

As we know that,

$\int x^n dx = \frac{x^{n+1}}{n+1} + C$

$\Rightarrow \int_0^4 (x^3 + 4x + 2) \, dx$

$= \left[\frac{x^4}{4} + \frac{4x^2}{2} + 2x\right]_0^4$

$= \frac{1}{4}(256) + \frac{64}{2} + (2 \times 4)$

$= 104$ sq. units

Hence, the correct option is (A).

11. Given:

Curve 1: $y = 2x^2 = f(x)$ (say)

Curve 2: $y + 6x - 8 = 0$

$\Rightarrow y = 8 - 6x = g(x)$ (say)

To find the intersections (or limits of the area) putting value of y from curve 1

$\Rightarrow 2x^2 = 8 - 6x$

$\Rightarrow 2x^2 + 6x - 8 = 0$

$\Rightarrow 2x^2 + 6x - 8 = 0$

$\Rightarrow (2x - 2)(x + 4) = 0$

$\Rightarrow x_1 = -4, x_2 = 1$

Now the required area (A) is:

$A = \left|\int_{x_1}^{x_2}[f(x) - g(x)]dx\right|$

$\Rightarrow A = \left|\int_{-4}^{1}[2x^2 - (8 - 6x)] \, dx\right|$

$\Rightarrow A = \left|\int_{4}^{1}[2x^2 - 8 + 6x] \, dx\right|$

$\Rightarrow A = \left|\left[\frac{2x^3}{3} - 8x + \frac{6x^2}{2}\right]_{-4}^{1}\right|$

$\Rightarrow A = \left|\frac{2}{3} - 8 + 3 - \left(\frac{2(-4)^3}{3} - 8(-4) + 3(-4)^2\right)\right|$

$\Rightarrow A = \left|\frac{-13}{3} - \frac{(-128)}{3} - 32 - 48\right|$

$\Rightarrow A = \left|\frac{(-125)}{3}\right|$

$\Rightarrow A = \frac{125}{3}$

Hence, the correct option is (B).

12. As we know:

Area between two curves: Let curves are f(x) and g(x)

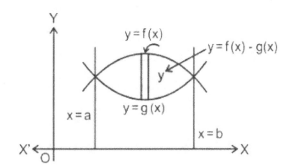

Area $= \int_a^b [f(x) - g(x)]dx = \int_a^b [\text{Top} - \text{bottom}]dx$

$y = |x| = \begin{cases} -x, x < 0 \\ x, x \geq 0 \end{cases}$

$y = x^2$ and $y = \pm x$ solving these two equation, we get intersection points.

$\Rightarrow y = x^2 = \pm x$

$\Rightarrow x^2 \pm x = 0$

$\Rightarrow x(x \pm 1) = 0$

$\therefore x = 0, \pm 1$

Put the value of x in $y = x^2$

x	0	-1	1
y	0	1	1

The point of intersection of the given curves are $(0,0), (-1,1)$ and $(1,1)$

The area bounded by the curves $y \geq x^2$ and $y = |x|$ is represented by the shaded region.

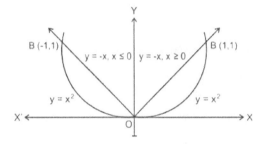

It is clearly observed that, the required area is symmetrical about y- axis.

$\therefore$ Required area $=$ Area between parabola $(y = x^2)$ and line $(y = x)$ between limits $x = 0$ and $x = 1$

Area $= 2 \times \int_0^1 [$ Top $-$ bottom $]dx$

$= 2 \int_0^1 [x - x^2] \, dx$

$= 2 \left[\frac{x^2}{2} - \frac{x^3}{3}\right]_0^1$

$= 2 \left[\frac{1}{2} - \frac{1}{3}\right]$

$= \frac{1}{3}$ sq. unit

Hence, the correct option is (D).

13. Given,

$x + iy = \frac{3+4i}{2-i}$

Multiplying the numerator and denominator with $(2 + i)$, we get

$x + iy = \frac{3+4i}{2-i} \times \frac{2+i}{2+i}$

$\Rightarrow x + iy = \frac{6+11i+4i^2}{4-i^2}$

Given,

$i = \sqrt{-1}$

$\therefore i^2 = -1$

$\Rightarrow x + iy = \frac{6+11i+4\times(-1)}{4-(-1)}$

$\Rightarrow x + iy = \frac{2+11i}{5}$

$\Rightarrow x + iy = \frac{2}{5} + i\frac{11}{5}$

Comparing real and imaginary parts, we get

$x = \frac{2}{5}$ and $y = \frac{11}{5}$

Hence, the correct option is (B).

14. Given:

$Z = 3x + 5y$

$x + 3y \geq 3, x + y \geq 2$ and $x \geq 0, y \geq 0$

Converting the given in equations into equations

$x + 3y = 3$

$x + y = 2$

Reglon represented by $x + 3y \geq 3$:

The line $x + 3y = 3$ meets the coordinate axis at $A(3,0)$ and $B(0,1)$

$x + 3y = 3$

| x | 3 | 0 |
| y | 0 | 1 |

$A(3,0); B(0,1)$

Join the points A to 5 to obtain a line.

Clearly $(0,0)$ does not satisfy the in equation $x + 3y \geq 3$.

So the region opposite to the origin, represents the solution set of the in equation.

Reglon represented by $x + y \geq 2$:

The line $x + y = 2$ meets the coordinate axis at points $C(2,0)$ and $D(0,2)$. $x + y = 2$

| x | 2 | 0 |
| y | 0 | 2 |

$C(2,0); D(0,2)$

Join the points C to D to obtain the line.

Clearly $(0,0)$ does not satisfy the in equation $x + y \geq 2$

So the region opposite to origin, represents the solution set of the in equation.

Reglon represented by $x \geq 0, y \geq 0$:

Since every point in the first quadrant satisfies these in equations.

So the first quadrant is the region represented by the equations $x \geq 0, y \geq 0$.

The point of intersection of lines $x + 3y = 3$ and $x + y = 2$ is $E\left(\frac{3}{2}, \frac{1}{2}\right)$

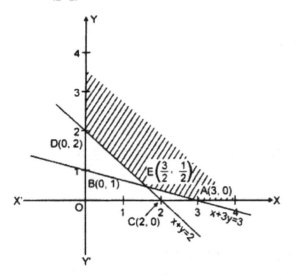

The shaded region A ED is an open and common region of given in equations. This is the proper solution of the given linear programming problem.

The coordinates of the shaded region are $A(3,0)$, $E\left(\frac{3}{2}, \frac{1}{2}\right)$ and $D(0,2)$.

The values of the objective function of these points are given in following table:

Point	x-coordinate	y-coordinate	Objective function $Z = 3x + 5y$
A	3	0	$Z_A = 3 \times 3 + 5(0) = 9$
E	$\frac{3}{2}$	$\frac{1}{2}$	$Z_E = 3\left(\frac{3}{2}\right) + 5\left(\frac{1}{2}\right) = 7$
D	0	2	$Z_D = 3(0) + 5(2) = 10$

Clearly Z is minimum at $x = \frac{3}{2}$ and $y = \frac{1}{2}$

Therefore $x = \frac{3}{2}$ and $y = \frac{1}{2}$ is the required solution of the L.P. problem and the minimum value of Z is 7.

Hence, the correct option is (A).

15. The maximize: $z = 3x + 5y$ Given subjective to,

$x + 4y \leq 24$

$3x + y \leq 21$

$x + y \leq 9, \quad x \geq 0, y \geq 0$

Consider,

$x + 4y = 24$ .....(1)

$3x + y = 21$ .....(2)

$x + y = 9$ .....(3)

On solving equation (1) and (2), we get $y = \frac{51}{11}$

From equation (1),

$x = \frac{60}{11}$

Therefore, $(x, y) = \left(\frac{60}{11}, \frac{51}{11}\right)$ and $z = 3x + 5y = \frac{435}{11} = 39.54$

Now,

On solving equation (2) and (3), we get $x = 6$

From equation (3),

$y = 3$

Therefore, $(x, y) = (6, 3)$

and $z = 3x + 5y = 33$

Now,

On solving equation (1) and (3), we get $y = 5$

From equation (3),

$x = 4$

Therefore, $(x, y) = (4, 5)$

and $z = 3x + 5y = 37$

So, $(x, y) = \left(\frac{60}{11}, \frac{51}{11}\right), z = \frac{435}{11}$

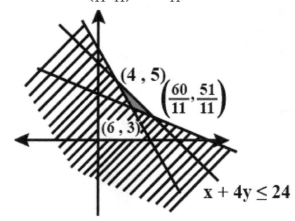

Hence, the correct option is (B).

16.

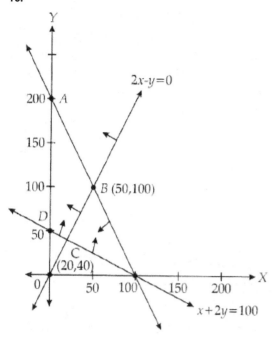

Given:

Maximize $Z = x + 2y$

$x + 2y \geq 100$

$2x - y \leq 0$

$2x + y \leq 200$

$x, y \geq 0$

On solving equations $2x - y = 0$ and $x + 2y = 100$ we get point $B(20,40)$

On solving $2x - y = 0$ and $2x + y = 200$ we get $C(50,100)$

∴ Feasible region is shown by ABCDA

The corner points of the feasible region are:

$A(0,50), B(20,40), C(50,100), D(0,200)$

Let us evaluate the objective function Z at each corner points:

At $A(0,50)$, $Z = 0 + 100 - 100$

At $B(20,40), Z = 20 + 80 = 100$

At $C(50,100), Z = 50 + 200 = 250$

At $D(0,200), Z = 0 + 400 = 400$

So, Maximum value of Z is 400.

Hence, the correct option is (D).

17. As we know,

Straight Lines:

The general equation of a line is $y = mx + c$, where m is the slope of the line.

Parallel Lines: If two lines are parallel, then their slopes are equal.

Let the equation of the line passing through $(3,4)$ and $(4,5)$ be $y = mx + c$.

∴ We must have:

$4 = 3m + c$ ... (1)

And, $5 = 4m + c$ ... (2)

Subtracting equation (1) from equation (2), we get:

$1 = m$.

Let the equation of the line passing through the point $(1,2)$ be $y = nx + d$.

Since this line is parallel to the above line, we must have $n = m = 1$.

Also, $2 = 1(1) + d$.

$\Rightarrow d = 1$.

The required equation is, therefore:

$y = x + 1$

Hence, the correct option is (C).

18. Given that,

Two equations of the plane are:

$3x - 4y + 5z = 20$

and, $4x + 3y + 5z = 25$

As we know,

The angle θ between two planes $A_1 x + B_1 y + C_1 z + D_1 = 0$ and $A_2 x + B_2 y + C_2 z + D_2 = 0$ is given by:

$\cos\theta = \left| \dfrac{A_1 A_2 + B_1 B_2 + C_1 C_2}{\sqrt{A_1^2 + B_1^2 + C_1^2} \sqrt{A_2^2 + B_2^2 + C_2^2}} \right|$

From the given equations of the planes, we have:

$A_1 = 3, B_1 = -4, C_1 = 5$

$A_2 = 4, B_2 = 3, C_2 = 5$

Using the formula for the angle between two planes, we get:

$\cos\theta = \left| \dfrac{(3)(4) + (-4)(3) + (5)(5)}{\sqrt{(3)^2 + (-4)^2 + (5)^2} \sqrt{(4)^2 + (3)^2 + (5)^2}} \right|$

$\Rightarrow \cos\theta = \dfrac{25}{\sqrt{50}\sqrt{50}} = \dfrac{1}{2}$

$\Rightarrow \theta = \frac{\pi}{3}$

Hence, the correct option is (C).

19. Given:

Mean $= np = 1$

Variance $= npq = \frac{3}{4}$

$\Rightarrow p = \frac{1}{4}, q = \frac{3}{4}, n = 4$

Binomial distribution $P(X = r) = {}^nC_r p^r q^{n-r}$

$P(X = 3) = {}^4C_3 \left(\frac{1}{4}\right)^3 \left(\frac{3}{4}\right)^{4-3}$

$P(X = 3) = \frac{4 \times 3 \times 2 \times 1}{3 \times 2 \times 1} \times \frac{1}{64} \times \frac{3}{4}$

$P(X = 3) = 4 \times \frac{1}{64} \times \frac{3}{4}$

$= \frac{3}{64}$

Hence, the correct option is (A).

20. Given:

In two throws of a dice, total chances $n(S) = (6 \times 6) = 36$

Let E is the event of getting a sum 9

$\therefore E = \{(3,6), (4,5), (5,4), (6,3)\}$

$\Rightarrow n(E) = 4$

$\therefore P(E) = \frac{n(E)}{n(S)}$

$= \frac{4}{36}$

$= \frac{1}{9}$

Hence, the correct option is (A).

21. We have, $\tan 3x = \sin 45° \cos 45° + \sin 30°$

$\Rightarrow \tan 3x = \frac{1}{\sqrt{2}} \times \frac{1}{\sqrt{2}} + \frac{1}{2}$

$\Rightarrow \tan 3x = \frac{1}{2} + \frac{1}{2}$

$\Rightarrow \tan 3x = 1$

$\Rightarrow \tan 3x = \tan 45°$

$\Rightarrow 3x = 45°$

$\Rightarrow x = 15°$

$\therefore$ The value of x is $15°$.

Hence, the correct option is (A).

22. Given:

$\vec{a} = 3\hat{i} + 4\hat{j} + 5\hat{k}$

$\vec{\beta} = 2\hat{i} + \hat{j} - 4\hat{k}$

Let $\beta = \beta_1 + \beta_2$

So, $\beta_1 = \lambda \vec{a}$ and $\beta_2 \cdot \vec{a} = 0$

Now,

$\beta_1 = \lambda(3\hat{i} + 4\hat{j} + 5\hat{k})$

$\beta_1 = 3\lambda\hat{i} + 4\lambda\hat{j} + 5\lambda\hat{k}$

Now,

$\beta_2 = \beta - \beta_1$

$\beta_2 = (2 - 3\lambda)\hat{i} + (1 - 4\lambda)\hat{j} + (-4 - 5\lambda)\hat{k}$

Since, $\beta_2 \cdot \vec{a} = 0$

So, $3(2 - 3\lambda) + 4(1 - 4\lambda) + 5(-4 - 5\lambda) = 0$

$\Rightarrow 6 - 9\lambda + 4 - 16\lambda - 20 - 25\lambda = 0$

$\Rightarrow -10 - 50\lambda = 0$

$\Rightarrow 50\lambda = -10$

$\Rightarrow \lambda = \frac{-1}{5}$

So, $\beta_1 = \frac{-1}{5}(3\hat{i} + 4\hat{j} + 5\hat{k})$

$= \frac{-3}{5}\hat{i} - \frac{4}{5}\hat{j} - \hat{k}$

And,

$\beta_2 = \frac{13}{5}\hat{i} + \frac{9}{5}\hat{j} - 3\hat{k}$

So,

$\beta = \left(\frac{-3}{5}\hat{i} - \frac{4}{5}\hat{j} - \hat{k}\right) + \left(\frac{13}{5}\hat{i} + \frac{9}{5}\hat{j} - 3\hat{k}\right)$

$\beta = \beta_1 + \beta_2$

$= 2\hat{i} - \hat{j} - 4\hat{k}$

Hence, the correct option is (B).

23. Given:

$b = i + j$ and $c = j + k$

The equation of bisector of b and c is:

$r = \lambda(b + c)$

$= \lambda\left(\frac{i+j}{\sqrt{2}} + \frac{j+k}{\sqrt{2}}\right)$

$= \frac{\lambda}{\sqrt{2}}(i + 2j + k)$ .....(i)

Since, vector a lies in plane of b and c.

$\therefore a = b + \mu c$

Put the given values in above equation:

$\frac{\lambda}{\sqrt{2}}(i + 2j + k) = (i + j) + \mu(j + k)$

On equating the coefficient of i both sides, we get:

$\frac{\lambda}{\sqrt{2}} = 1$

$\Rightarrow \lambda = \sqrt{2}$

On putting $\lambda = \sqrt{2}$ in Eq. (i), we get:

$r = i + 2j + k$

Since the given vector a represents the same bisector equation r.

$\therefore \alpha = 1$ and $\beta = 1$

Hence, the correct option is (A).

24. Given,

$\cos 20° + \cos 100° + \cos 140°$

$= 2\cos\frac{20°+100°}{2}\cos\frac{100°-20°}{2} + \cos 140°$

$\left(\because \cos A + \cos B = 2\cos\frac{A+B}{2}\cos\frac{A-B}{2}\right)$

$= 2\cos 60°\cos 40° + \cos 140°$

$= 2 \times \frac{1}{2}\cos 40° + \cos 140°$

$= \cos 40° + \cos 140°$

$= 2\cos\frac{140°+40°}{2}\cos\frac{140°-40°}{2}$ $\left(\because \cos A + \cos B = 2\cos\frac{A+B}{2}\cos\frac{A-B}{2}\right)$

$= 2\cos 90°\cos 50°$ $(\because \cos 90° = 0)$

$= 2 \times 0 \times \cos 50°$

$= 0$

Hence, the correct option is (A).

25. Given,

$\cot\left(22\frac{1}{2}°\right)$

We know that, $\cot x = \frac{\cos x}{\sin x}$

$\Rightarrow \cot\left(22\frac{1}{2}°\right) = \frac{\cos\left(22\frac{1}{2}°\right)}{\sin\left(22\frac{1}{2}°\right)}$

$\Rightarrow \sin\left(\frac{45°}{2}\right) = \pm\sqrt{\frac{1-\cos(45°)}{2}}$ $\left(\because \sin\frac{A}{2} = \pm\sqrt{\frac{1-\cos A}{2}}\right)$

As we know that, $0° < \frac{A}{2} < 90°$ where all trigonometric ratios are positive.

$\Rightarrow \sin\left(\frac{45°}{2}\right) = \sqrt{\frac{\sqrt{2}-1}{2\sqrt{2}}}$ ......(i)

$\Rightarrow \cos\left(\frac{45°}{2}\right) = \pm\sqrt{\frac{1+\cos(45°)}{2}}$ $\left(\because \cos\frac{A}{2} = \pm\sqrt{\frac{1+\cos A}{2}}\right)$ ......(ii)

As we know that, $0° < \frac{A}{2} < 90°$ where all trigonometric ratio's are positive.

$\Rightarrow \cos\left(\frac{45°}{2}\right) = \sqrt{\frac{\sqrt{2}+1}{2\sqrt{2}}}$

So, from equation (i) and (ii), we get

$\Rightarrow \cot\left(22\frac{1}{2}°\right) = \frac{\sqrt{\frac{\sqrt{2}+1}{2\sqrt{2}}}}{\sqrt{\frac{\sqrt{2}-1}{2\sqrt{2}}}}$

$= 1 + \sqrt{2}$

$\Rightarrow \sqrt{\frac{\sqrt{2}+1}{\sqrt{2}-1}}$

Rationalization above the equation

$\Rightarrow \sqrt{\frac{\sqrt{2}+1}{\sqrt{2}-1} \times \frac{\sqrt{2}+1}{\sqrt{2}+1}}$

$\Rightarrow \sqrt{\frac{(\sqrt{2}+1)^2}{(\sqrt{2})^2-(1)^2}}$ $(\because a^2 - b^2 = (a+b)(a-b))$

$\Rightarrow \sqrt{\frac{(\sqrt{2}+1)^2}{2-1}}$

$-1 + \sqrt{2}$

Hence, the correct option is (A).

26. Given,

$\sin x + \cos x = \sqrt{2}$ ....(i)

By squaring both the sides in equation (i), we get

$(\sin x + \cos x)^2 = (\sqrt{2})^2$

$\Rightarrow \sin^2 x + \cos^2 x + 2\sin x \cos x = (\sqrt{2})^2$
$(\because (a+b)^2 = a^2 + b^2 + 2ab)$

As we know that, $\sin^2 x + \cos^2 x = 1$ and $\sin 2x = 2\sin x \cos x$

$1 + \sin 2x = 2$

$\Rightarrow \sin 2x = 1$ ....(ii)

As we know that, $\sin^2 x + \cos^2 x = 1$

Therefore,

$\sin^2 2x + \cos^2 2x = 1$

$\Rightarrow \cos^2 2x = 1 - \sin^2 2x$

By using equation (ii) we get,

$\Rightarrow \cos^2 2x = 1 - 1^2$

$\Rightarrow \cos^2 2x = 0$

Hence, the correct option is (C).

27. Given,

$x = \sin^2 t$ and $y = \cos^2 t$

As we know that, x and y are parametric functions of t. So first we have to find out the derivative of x and y with respect to t.

As we know that, $\frac{d(\sin x)}{dx} = \cos x$ and $\frac{d(\cos x)}{dx} = -\sin x$.

$\Rightarrow \frac{dx}{dt} = \frac{d(\sin^2 t)}{dt} = 2 \cdot \sin t \cdot \cos t$

$\Rightarrow \frac{dy}{dt} = \frac{d(\cos^2 t)}{dt} = 2 \cdot \cos t \cdot (-\sin t)$

As we know that,

$\frac{dy}{dx} = \frac{dy}{dt} \times \frac{dt}{dx}$

$\Rightarrow \frac{dy}{dx} = \frac{\frac{dy}{dt}}{\frac{dx}{dt}}$

$= \frac{-2 \cdot \cos t \cdot \sin t}{2 \cdot \sin t \cdot \cos t} = -1$

Hence, the correct option is (C).

28. $\lim_{x \to 2} \frac{\sqrt{3-x}-1}{2-x}$

At $x = 2$, the value is $\frac{0}{0}$, so limit is of an indeterminate form $\left(\frac{0}{0}, \frac{\infty}{\infty}, 0 \times \infty, 0^0, 1^\infty, \infty^0\right)$.

To avoid indeterminate form, rationalizing the numerator

$\frac{\sqrt{3-x}-1}{2-x} = \frac{\sqrt{3-x}-1}{2-x} \times \frac{\sqrt{3-x}+1}{\sqrt{3-x}+1}$

$= \frac{(\sqrt{3-x})^2 - 1}{(2-x)(\sqrt{3-x}+1)} = \frac{3-x-1}{(2-x)(\sqrt{3-x}+1)}$

$= \frac{1}{\sqrt{3-x}+1}$

$\therefore \lim_{x \to 2} \frac{\sqrt{3-x}-1}{2-x} = \lim_{x \to 2} \frac{1}{\sqrt{3-x}+1} = \frac{1}{1+1} = \frac{1}{2}$

Hence, the correct option is (C).

29. Let x be number a discrete random variable which denotes the number of heads obtained in n

n = 8

The general form for the probability of random variable x is,

P(X = x) = $^nC_x \times p^x \times q^{n-x}$

Now, in the question, we want at least two heads,

Now, p = q = $\frac{1}{2}$

So, $P(X \geq 2) = {}^8C_2 \times \left(\frac{1}{2}\right)^2 \times \left(\frac{1}{2}\right)^{8-2}$

$\Rightarrow P(X \geq 2) = {}^8C_2 \times \left(\frac{1}{2}\right)^2 \times \left(\frac{1}{2}\right)^6$

$\Rightarrow 1 - P(X < 2) = {}^8C_0 \times \left(\frac{1}{2}\right)^0 \times \left(\frac{1}{2}\right)^8 + {}^8C_1 \times \left(\frac{1}{2}\right)^1 \times \left(\frac{1}{2}\right)^{8-1}$

$\Rightarrow 1 - P(X < 2) = \left(\frac{1}{2}\right)^8 + 8 \times \left(\frac{1}{2}\right)^1 \times \left(\frac{1}{2}\right)^7$

$\Rightarrow 1 - P(X < 2) = \frac{1}{256} + 8 \times \left(\frac{1}{2}\right)^8$

$\Rightarrow 1 - P(X < 2) = \frac{1}{256} + \frac{8}{256}$

$\Rightarrow 1 - P(X < 2) = \frac{9}{256}$

$\Rightarrow P(X < 2) = 1 - \frac{9}{256}$

$\Rightarrow P(X < 2) = \frac{(256-9)}{256}$

$\Rightarrow P(X < 2) = \frac{247}{256}$

Hence, the correct option is (C).

30. Let, small change in x be Δx and the corresponding change in y is Δy.

Therefore, $\Delta y = \frac{dy}{dx} \Delta x$

We have to find the value of $\sqrt{36.01}$

Let, $x + \Delta x = 36.01 = 36 + 0.01$

Therefore, $x = 36$ and $\Delta x = -0.01$

Assume, $y = x^{\frac{1}{2}}$

Differentiating with respect to x, we get:

$\frac{dy}{dx} = \frac{1}{2} x^{-\frac{1}{2}} = \frac{1}{2\sqrt{x}}$

At $x = 36$

$\left[\frac{dy}{dx}\right]_{x=36} = \frac{1}{12}$ and $y = (36)^{\frac{1}{2}} = 6$

As we know $\Delta y = \dfrac{dy}{dx}\Delta x$

So, $\Delta y = \dfrac{1}{12} \times (0.01) = 0.000833$

Therefore, approximate value of
$\sqrt{36.01} = (36.01)^{\frac{1}{2}} = y + \Delta y = 6 + 0.00083 = 6.00083$

Hence, the correct option is (C).

31. Following steps to finding maxima and minima using derivatives.

Find the derivative of the function. Set the derivative equal to 0 and solve. This gives the values of the maximum and minimum points. Now we have to find the second derivative.

$f'(x)$ is less than 0 then the given function is said to be maxima

If $f'(x)$ Is greater than 0 then the function is said to be minima

Let, $f(x) = x^3 - 12x^2 + kx - 8$

Differentiating with respect to x, we get:

$f'(x) = 3x^2 - 24x + k$

It is given that function attains its maximum value of the interval $[0,3]$ at $x = 2$

$\therefore f'(2) = 0$

$3 \times 2^2 - (24 \times 2) + k = 0$

$\therefore k = 36$

Hence, the correct option is (C).

32. Following steps to finding maxima and minima using derivatives.

Find the derivative of the function.

Set the derivative equal to 0 and solve. This gives the values of the maximum and minimum points.

Now we have find second derivative.

$f'(x)$ is less than 0 then the given function is said to be maxima

If $f'(x)$ Is greater than 0 then the function is said to be minima

Let, $f(x) = \sin\left(x + \dfrac{\pi}{6}\right) + \cos\left(x + \dfrac{\pi}{6}\right)$

Differentiate with respect to x, we get:

$f'(x) = \cos\left(x + \dfrac{\pi}{6}\right) - \sin\left(x + \dfrac{\pi}{6}\right)$

Again differentiate with respect to x,

$f''(x) = -\sin\left(x + \dfrac{\pi}{6}\right) - \cos\left(x + \dfrac{\pi}{6}\right) = -\left[\sin\left(x + \dfrac{\pi}{6}\right) + \cos\left(x + \dfrac{\pi}{6}\right)\right]$

For maximum value $f'(x) = 0$

$\cos\left(x + \dfrac{\pi}{6}\right) - \sin\left(x + \dfrac{\pi}{6}\right) = 0$

$\Rightarrow \cos\left(x + \dfrac{\pi}{6}\right) = \sin\left(x + \dfrac{\pi}{6}\right)$

$\Rightarrow \tan\left(x + \dfrac{\pi}{6}\right) = 1$

$\therefore x + \left(\dfrac{\pi}{6}\right) = \left(\dfrac{\pi}{4}\right)$

$\Rightarrow x = \dfrac{\pi}{12}$

At $x = \dfrac{\pi}{12}, f''(x) < 0$

So, function is maximum at $x = \dfrac{\pi}{12}$

Hence, the correct option is (A).

33. Given,

$f(x) = 2^{|x|}$ and $g(x) = [x]$ where [.] denotes greatest integer function

Here, we have to find out the value of $fog\left(\dfrac{-3}{2}\right)$

$fog\left(\dfrac{-17}{2}\right) = f\left(g\left(\dfrac{-17}{2}\right)\right)$

$\because g(x) = [x]$,

So, $g\left(\dfrac{-17}{2}\right) = \left[\dfrac{-17}{2}\right] = -9$

$fog\left(\dfrac{-17}{2}\right) = f(-9)$

$\because f(x) = 2^{|x|}$

So, $f(-9) = 2^{|-9|}$

$= 2^9$

$= 512$

So, $fog\left(\dfrac{-17}{2}\right) = 512$

Hence, the correct option is (D).

34. Given,

$\int x\cos x^2 \, dx$

Let $t = x^2$

By differentiating the above equation with respect to x, we get

$\Rightarrow dt = 2x\,dx$

$\Rightarrow \dfrac{dt}{2} = x\,dx$

$\Rightarrow \int x\cos x^2 \, dx = \dfrac{1}{2}\int \cos t\, dt$

As we know that,

$\int \cos x \, dx = \sin x + C$ where C is a constant

$\int x \cos x^2 \, dx = \frac{1}{2} \sin t + C$

By substituting $t = x^2$ in the above equation we get

$\int x \cos x^2 \, dx = \frac{1}{2} \sin x^2 + C$

Hence, the correct option is (D).

35. Given,

$\int e^{\log x} \sin x \, dx$

Let $I = \int e^{\log x} \sin x \, dx$

$= \int x \sin x \, dx \quad (\because e^{\log x} = x)$

Using by parts formula,

$= x \int \sin x \, dx - \int \frac{dx}{dx} \times \{\int \sin x \, dx\} dx$

$= -x \cos x + \int \cos x \, dx$

$= -x \cos x + \sin x + c$

Hence, the correct option is (C).

36. Let $I = \int \frac{2}{\sin 2x \cdot \log(\tan x)} \, \ldots(i)$

Take $\log(\tan x) = t$

$\frac{1}{\tan x}(\sec^2 x) dx = dt$

$\Rightarrow \frac{\cos x}{\sin x \cdot \cos^2 x} dx = dt$

$\Rightarrow \frac{1}{\sin x \cdot \cos x} dx = dt$

$\Rightarrow dx = \sin x \cdot \cos x \, dt$

Putting the value of $\log(\tan x)$ and dx in equation (i)

Now, $I = \int \frac{2}{2 \sin x \cdot \cos x \cdot t} \sin x \cdot \cos x \, dt$

$= \int \frac{1}{t} dt$

$= \log t + c$

$= \log[\log(\tan x)] + c$

Hence, the correct option is (D).

37. Given,

$\int \frac{e^{2x}}{e^{2x}+1} dx$

$I = \int \frac{e^{2x}}{e^{2x}+1} dx$

Let $t = e^{2x} + 1$

Differentiating with respect to x, we get

$dt = 2e^{2x} dx$

$I = \frac{1}{2} \int \frac{2e^{2x}}{e^{2x}+1} dx$

$= \frac{1}{2} \int \frac{dt}{t}$

$= \frac{1}{2} \ln t$

$= \frac{1}{2} \ln(e^{2x} + 1) + c$

Hence, the correct option is (D).

38. Given,

$\int_1^4 (5x^2 - 8x + 5) dx$

Let, $I = \int_1^4 (5x^2 - 8x + 5) dx$

$I = \int_1^4 (5x^2) dx - \int_1^4 8x \, dx + \int_1^4 5 \, dx$

Using, $\int^n dx = \frac{1}{n+1} x^{n+1} + c$

$I = 5 \int_1^4 x^2 \, dx - 8 \int_1^4 x \, dx + 5 \int_1^4 dx$

$I = 5 \left[\frac{x^3}{3}\right]_1^4 - 8 \left[\frac{x^2}{2}\right]_1^4 + 5[x]_1^4$

$I = 5 \left[\frac{4^3 - 1^3}{3}\right] - 8 \left[\frac{4^2 - 1^2}{2}\right] + 5[4 - 1]$

$= 5 \times \frac{63}{3} - 8 \times \frac{15}{2} + 5 \times 3$

$= 60$

Hence, the correct option is (C).

39. Given,

$\int_1^3 |x - 2| \, dx$

Now,

$f(x) = |x - 2|$

$\Rightarrow f(x) = \begin{cases} -(x - 2), & 1 \leq x < 2 \\ x - 2, & 2 \leq x \leq 3 \end{cases}$

$\int_1^3 |x - 2| dx = \int_1^2 -(x - 2) dx + \int_2^3 (x - 2) dx$

$\int_1^3 |x - 2| dx = \int_1^2 (2 - x) dx + \int_2^3 (x - 2) dx$

$= \left[2x - \frac{x^2}{2}\right]_1^2 + \left[\frac{x^2}{2} - 2x\right]_2^3$

$= \left[\left(4 - \frac{4}{2}\right) - \left(2 - \frac{1}{2}\right)\right] + \left[\left(\frac{9}{2} - 6\right) - \left(\frac{4}{2} - 4\right)\right]$

$= 2 - \frac{3}{2} - \frac{3}{2} + 2$

Mathematics : Mock Test - 8

$= 4 - 3 = 1$

Hence, the correct option is (D).

40. Given,

$\int_0^1 x \tan^{-1} x \, dx$

Let $I = \int_0^1 x \tan^{-1} x \, dx$

Apply by parts rule,

$= \left[\tan^{-1} x \cdot \int x \, dx\right]_0^1 - \int_0^1 \left\{\frac{d(\tan^{-1} x)}{dx} \cdot \int x \, dx\right\} dx$

$= \left[\tan^{-1} x \cdot \frac{x^2}{2}\right]_0^1 - \int_0^1 \frac{1}{1+x^2} \cdot \frac{x^2}{2} dx$

$= \left[\tan^{-1} x \cdot \frac{x^2}{2}\right]_0^1 - \frac{1}{2}\int_0^1 \frac{1+x^2-1}{1+x^2} dx$

$= \left[\tan^{-1} x \cdot \frac{x^2}{2}\right]_0^1 - \frac{1}{2}\int_0^1 \left[1 - \frac{1}{1+x^2}\right] dx$

$= \left[\tan^{-1} x \cdot \frac{x^2}{2}\right]_0^1 - \frac{1}{2}[x - \tan^{-1} x]_0^1$

$= \left[\tan^{-1} 1 \cdot \frac{1^2}{2}\right] - \frac{1}{2}[1 - \tan^{-1} 1]$

$= \frac{\pi}{4} \times \frac{1}{2} - \frac{1}{2} + \frac{1}{2} \times \frac{\pi}{4}$

$= \frac{\pi}{4} - \frac{1}{2}$

Hence, the correct option is (B).

41. Given,

$2y^2 + 2x^2 + 12y = 32$

$2y^2 + 2x^2 + 12y - 32 = 0$

Comparing to the general equation of a circle

$ax^2 + ay^2 + 2gx + 2fy + c = 0$

$a = 2, g = 0, f = 6, c = -32$

$\therefore$ Center $= \left(-\frac{g}{a}, -\frac{f}{a}\right) = (0, -3)$

Radius $= \sqrt{\left(\frac{g}{a}\right)^2 + \left(\frac{f}{a}\right)^2 - \left(\frac{c}{a}\right)}$

$\Rightarrow R = \sqrt{\left(\frac{0}{2}\right)^2 + \left(\frac{6}{2}\right)^2 - \left(\frac{-32}{2}\right)}$

$\Rightarrow R = \sqrt{\left(\frac{0}{2}\right)^2 + \left(\frac{6}{2}\right)^2 + \left(\frac{32}{2}\right)}$

$\Rightarrow R = \sqrt{(9 + 16)}$

$R = 5$

$\therefore$ Radius and center of the circle $2y^2 + 2x^2 + 12y = 32$ are 5 and $(0, -3)$ respectively.

Hence, the correct option is (C).

42. Let $A(a, b, c)$ is foot of perpendicular of point $P(4,5,4)$

Given plane is $x + 2y + z = 2$.

So,

PA will be normal to the given plane, so direction ratios of PA will be proportional to $(1,2,1)$.

PA passes from $(4,5,4)$ and have direction ratios $(1,2,1)$.

Equation of line $PA = \frac{x-4}{1} = \frac{y-5}{2} = \frac{z-4}{1} = r$ (say)

So, point $A(a, b, c)$ in the form of r is $(r + 4, 2r + 5, r + 4)$

Since $A(a, b, c)$, lies on the given plane, so,

Plane $x + 2y + z = 2$

$1.(r + 4) + 2.(2r + 5) + r + 4 - 2 = 0$

$\therefore r = \frac{-8}{3}$

So, foot of perpendicular $A(r + 4, 2r + 5, r + 4)$ will be $\left(\frac{4}{3}, \frac{-1}{3}, \frac{4}{3}\right)$

Hence, the correct option is (C).

43. Given:

$\frac{dy}{dx} = \frac{2+y}{x}$

It is a first-order differential equation,

We can solve this by separating variables,

$\Rightarrow \frac{dy}{dx} = \frac{2+y}{x}$

$\Rightarrow \frac{dy}{2+y} = \frac{dx}{x}$

Integrating both sides, we get

$\Rightarrow \int \frac{dy}{2+y} = \int \frac{dx}{x}$

$\Rightarrow \log(2 + y) = \log x + \log c$

$\Rightarrow \log(2 + y) = \log cx$ ($\because \log m + \log n = \log mn$)

$\therefore 2 + y = cx$

Hence, the correct option is (B).

44. The questions is indirectly asking that number of time die must be thrown so that probability of getting '4' atleast once ≥ 0.5

Let 'n' be the number of time die is thrown

Probability of atleast one $4 = 1$ - Probability of no 4

Using Binomial Distribution

Probability of not even single $4 = nC_0 \left(\frac{1}{6}\right)^0 \left(\frac{5}{6}\right)^n = \left(\frac{5}{6}\right)^n$

$0.5 \geq 1 - \left(\frac{5}{6}\right)^n$

$\left(\frac{5}{6}\right)^n \geq 0.5$

$n\log_{10}\left(\frac{5}{6}\right) \geq \log_{10}(0.5)$

$n \geq 3.8$

$n \approx 4$

Hence, the correct option is (A).

45. Given,

Mean $= \mu = np = 16$

Standard deviation $= \sigma = \sqrt{npq} = 3$

$\therefore$ Variance $= \sigma^2 = npq = 9$

$\Rightarrow 9 = np(1-p) = 16(1-p)$

$\Rightarrow \frac{9}{16} = (1-p)$

$\Rightarrow (1-p) = \frac{3}{4}$

$\Rightarrow p = 1 - \frac{3}{4}$

$\therefore p = \frac{1}{4}$

Again;

$\mu = np = 16$

$\therefore n = \frac{16}{p} = 16 \times \left(\frac{4}{1}\right) = 48$

Hence, the correct option is (B).

46. Given,

Mean $= np = \frac{2}{3}$ and variance $= npq = \frac{5}{9}$

$\frac{\text{Variance}}{\text{Mean}} = \frac{\frac{5}{9}}{\frac{2}{3}}$

$q = \frac{5}{6}$

$p = 1 - q = \frac{1}{6}$

$np = \frac{2}{3}$

$n = 4$

$\therefore$ The probability that random variable $D = 3$

$P = {}^nC_3 p^3 q^{n-3}$

$P = {}^4C_3 \times \left(\frac{1}{6}\right)^3 \times \left(\frac{5}{6}\right)^1$

$P = 4 \times \frac{1}{216} \times \frac{5}{6}$

$P = \frac{5}{324}$

Hence, the correct option is (D).

47.

Precedence of logical operators	
Operators	Precedence
¬ NOT	1
∧ AND	2
∨ OR	3
⇒ conditional	4
⇔ bi-conditional	5

The given predicate is,

P(x)= -(x = 1) ∧ ∀ y(∃z(x=y*z) ⇒ (y = x) ∨ (y = 1))

If x is a prime number then (x ≠ 1 and the only divisors of x are x and 1)

∴P(x) is true means x is a prime number.

Hence, the correct option is (A).

48. A function $f(x)$ is differentiable at a point $x = a$ in its domain if its derivative is continuous at a.

This means that $f'(a)$ must exist, or equivalently:

$\lim_{x \to a^+} f'(x) = \lim_{x \to a^-} f'(x) = \lim_{x \to a} f'(x) = f'(a)$

If a function is differentiable at a point, it will be continuous as well.

Since the given function is differentiable, we can write:

$\lim_{x \to -1^-} f'(x) = \lim_{x \to -1^+} f'(x)$

$\lim_{x \to -1^-} (2bx) = \lim_{x \to -1^+} (2ax - b)$

$-2b = -2a - b$

$-b = -2a$

$2a = b - (1)$

Since $f(x)$ will also be continuous, we can write:

$\lim_{x \to -1^-} (bx^2 - a) = \lim_{x \to -1^+} (ax^2 - bx - 2)$

$b - a = a + b - 2$

$2a = 2$

$a = 1$

Using Equation (1):

$b = 2$

These are the roots of the equation:

$x^2 - 3x + 2 = 0$

Hence, the correct option is (B).

49. Given,

$\int_{-1}^{1} x|x|dx$

Let $I = \int_{-1}^{1} x|x|dx = \int_{-1}^{1} x|x|dx$

$= \int_{-1}^{0} x|x|dx + \int_{0}^{1} x|x|dx$

$\left(\because \int_{a}^{b} f(x) = \int_{a}^{c} f(x) + \int_{c}^{b} f(x)\right)$

$= \int_{-1}^{0} x(-x)dx + \int_{0}^{1} x(x)dx$

$= \int_{-1}^{0} -x^2 dx + \int_{0}^{1} x^2 dx$

$= -\left[\frac{x^3}{3}\right]_{-1}^{0} + \left[\frac{x^3}{3}\right]_{0}^{1}$

$= -\left[0 - \left(-\frac{1}{3}\right)\right] + \left[\frac{1}{3}\right]$

$= -\frac{1}{3} + \frac{1}{3} = 0$

Hence, the correct option is (A).

50. Let XY-plane divides the line joining the points $A(-1,3,4)$ and $B(2,-5,6)$ in the ratio $k:1$ at point P.

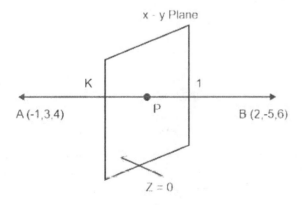

Therefore, by using section formula, co-ordinates of P are:

$P(x, y, z) = \left(\frac{2k-1}{k+1}, \frac{-5k+3}{k+1}, \frac{6k+4}{k+1}\right)$

Since in the XY-plane, $z = 0$.

$\Rightarrow \frac{6k+4}{k+1} = 0$

$\Rightarrow 6k + 4 = 0$

$\Rightarrow k = -\frac{2}{3}$

∴ The ratio is $2:3$ externally.

Hence, the correct option is (C).

Mathematics : Mock Test 09

Q.1 What is $C(n,r) + 2C(n,r+1) + C(n,r+2)$ equal to?
A. C(n + 1, r)
B. C(n + 1, r + 2)
C. C(n + 2, r + 2)
D. C(n + 2, r + 3)

Q.2 The inverse of a diagonal matrix is a:
A. Symmetric matrix
B. Skew-symmetric matrix
C. Diagonal matrix
D. None of the above

Q.3 If $A = \begin{bmatrix} 0 & 1 \\ 1 & 0 \end{bmatrix}$, then the matrix A is a/an:
A. Singular matrix
B. Involuntary matrix
C. Nilpotent matrix
D. Idempotent matrix

Q.4 For any square matrix P, defined matrices $Q = P + P^T, R = P - P^T$, then:
A. Both Q and R are anti-symmetric
B. R is anti-symmetric and Q is symmetric
C. Both are symmetric
D. None of the above is true

Q.5 The difference between two complementary angles is 15°. Find the ratio of greater and smaller angles.
A. 7 : 5
B. 6 : 5
C. 7 : 6
D. 5 : 4

Q.6 If $\frac{dy}{dx} - 4y = 0$, find the solution of the differential equation if, $y(0) = 1$
A. $y = 4e^x$
B. $y = e^{4x}$
C. $y = e^{-4x}$
D. $y = e^{x+4}$

Q.7 Consider the following statements in respect of the differential equation
$\frac{d^2y}{dx^2} + \cos\left(\frac{dy}{dx}\right) = 0$
1. The degree of the differential equation is not defined.
2. The order of the differential equation is 2
Which of the above statements is correct?
A. 1 only
B. 2 only
C. Both 1 and 2
D. Neither 1 nor 2

Q.8 The solution of the differential equation $\frac{dy}{dx} = \frac{y(1-3x^2)}{}$ is:
A. e^{x^3-1}
B. Ce^{x^3-1}
C. $e^{x(1-x^2)}$
D. $Ce^{x(1-x^2)}$

Q.9 Find range and coefficient of range from the weekly wage (in Rs.) of 10 workers of a factory:
310, 350, 420, 105, 115, 290, 245, 450, 300, 375.
A. 345, 0.62
B. 245, 0.50
C. 145, 0.52
D. 445, 0.42

Q.10 Find the area under the curve between $y = x$ and $y = 2x + 6$.
A. 72
B. 18
C. 36
D. 54

Q.11 Find the area between the lines $y = |x - 2|$ and $y = 5 - |x + 1|$.
A. 10
B. 8
C. 6
D. 4

Q.12 The area enclosed within the curve |x| + |y| = 1 (in square units) is:
A. $\sqrt{2}$
B. 1
C. $\frac{1}{\sqrt{2}}$
D. 2

Q.13 The number of real solutions of the equation $1 + \sin x \cdot \sin^2 \frac{x}{2} = 0$ in $[-\pi, \pi]$ is:
[UPSESSB TGT Mathematics, 2016]
A. 0
B. 1
C. 2
D. 3

Q.14 What is the modulus of $\frac{1+7i}{(2-i)^2}$?
A. $2\sqrt{2}$
B. 2
C. $\sqrt{2}$
D. 3

Q.15 Find the middle terms in the expansion of $\left(2x + \frac{1}{x}\right)^8$
A. $^8C_4 \times 2^4$
B. $^8C_4 \times 2^5$
C. $^8C_4$
D. None of the above

Q.16 Solve the following in equations $\frac{2x+4}{x-1} \geq 5$
A. (1, 2]
B. (1, 3)
C. (1, 3]
D. (1, 4]

Q.17 The greatest coefficient in the expansion of $(1 + x)^{2n+4}$ is
A. $^{2n+4}C_{n+1}$
B. $^{2n+4}C_{n+2}$
C. $^{2n+4}C_n$
D. $^{2n+4}C_{n+5}$

Q.18 Find the equation of line passing through $(h, 0)$ and $(0, k)$ and divided by the point $(1,2)$ in the ratio $2:3$ is:
A. 3x + 4y = 10
B. 3x + 3y = 20
C. x + 4y = 20
D. 3x + y = 5

Q.19 The perpendicular distance between the straight lines $6x + 8y + 15 = 0$ and $3x + 4y + 9 = 0$ is
A. $\frac{3}{2}$ units
B. $\frac{3}{10}$ unit
C. $\frac{3}{4}$ unit
D. $\frac{2}{7}$ unit

Q.20 The angle between x = y + 8, and x + y = 5 is:
A. 0°
B. 30°
C. 90°
D. None of these

Q.21 If the straight lines $x - 2y = 0$ and $kx + y = 1$ intersect at the point $\left(1, \frac{1}{2}\right)$, then what is the value of k?
A. 1
B. 2
C. $\frac{1}{2}$
D. $\frac{-1}{2}$

Q.22 If x is a Poisson random variate with mean 3, then $P\{|x-3|<1\}$ will be _____.

A. $\left(\frac{99}{8}\right)e^{-3}$
B. $\left(\frac{9}{2}\right)e^{-3}$
C. $\left(\frac{3}{2}\right)e^{-3}$
D. $\left(\frac{1}{3}\right)e^{-3}$

Q.23 If calls arrive at a telephone exchange such that the time of arrival of any call is independent of the time of arrival of earlier or future calls, the probability distribution function of the total number of calls in a fixed time interval will be:

A. Poisson
B. Gaussian
C. Exponential
D. Gamma

Q.24 The longest period of 3sin x - 4sin³ x is?

A. 2π
B. $\frac{\pi}{3}$
C. $\frac{2\pi}{3}$
D. None of the above

Q.25 The vector $-\hat{i}+\hat{j}+\hat{k}$ bisects the angle between the vectors $\vec{c}$ and $3\hat{i}+4\hat{j}$. Then unit vector in the direction of $\vec{c}$ is:

A. $\frac{1}{15}(-11\hat{i}+10\hat{j}-2\hat{k})$
B. $\frac{1}{15}(11\hat{i}-10\hat{j}+2\hat{k})$
C. $\frac{1}{15}(-11\hat{i}-10\hat{j}-2\hat{k})$
D. $\frac{1}{15}(11\hat{i}+10\hat{j}+2\hat{k})$

Q.26 If the vectors $\alpha\hat{i}+\alpha\hat{j}+\gamma\hat{k}, \hat{i}+\hat{k}$ and $\hat{\gamma}+\gamma\hat{j}+\beta\hat{k}$ lie on a plane, where α, β and γ are distinct non-negative numbers, then y is:

A. Arithmetic mean of α and β
B. Geometric mean of α and β
C. Harmonic mean of α and β
D. None of the above

Q.27 If $3\sin\alpha = 5\sin\beta$ then $\frac{\tan\frac{\alpha+\beta}{2}}{\tan\frac{\alpha-\beta}{2}}$ equals to:

A. 1
B. 2
C. 3
D. 4

Q.28 Find the value of $\sqrt{2+\sqrt{2+2\cos 4\theta}}$.

A. $2\sin\theta$
B. $2\cos\theta$
C. $\sin\theta$
D. $\cos\theta$

Q.29 Find the value of
$\sin[(n+1)A]\sin[(n+2)A]+\cos[(n+1)A]\cos[(n+2)A]$

A. $\sin(A+B)$
B. $\cos(A+B)$
C. $\cos A$
D. $\sin A$

Q.30 If $f(x) = x\sin x$, then $f'(0) =$?

A. -1
B. 0
C. 1
D. ∞

Q.31 What is the value of $\frac{dy}{dx}$, if $y^2 + x^2 + 3x + 5 = 0$ at $(0,-3)$?

A. 1
B. 1.5
C. 2
D. 0.5

Q.32 Solve: $\lim\limits_{x\to 0}\tan x =$

A. 0
B. 1
C. -1
D. None of these

Q.33 A card is drawn from a well-shuffled pack of 52 cards. A gambler bets that it is either a heart or an ace. What are the odds against his winning this bet?

A. 9:4
B. 4:9
C. 35:52
D. 1:3

Q.34 Area of a circle is 81π and the equations of the normal to the circle are $2y+3x-5=0$ and $2y-3x+5=0$. Find the equation of the circle.

A. $\left(x-\frac{5}{3}\right)^2 + y^2 = 9$
B. $\left(x-\frac{5}{3}\right)^2 + y^2 = 81$
C. $\left(x+\frac{5}{3}\right)^2 + y^2 = 81$
D. $\left(x+\frac{5}{3}\right)^2 + y^2 = 9$

Q.35 Evaluate $\lim\limits_{x\to 0}\frac{\log(1+2x)}{\tan 2x}$

A. -1
B. 1
C. 2
D. 4

Q.36 Amongst all the pairs of positive numbers with sum 24, find those whose product is maximum?

A. 10 and 14
B. 12 and 12
C. 2 and 22
D. None of these

Q.37 The maximum and minimum values of the function |cos 2x + 7| are:

A. 9, 5
B. 10, 4
C. 8, 6
D. 8, 7

Q.38 Find the minimum value of $3x^4 - 8x^3 + 12x^2 - 48x + 1$ on the interval $[1,4]$ and $x \in R$?

A. -25
B. -39
C. -75
D. None of these

Q.39 What is $\int_{-1}^{1}\left\{\frac{d}{dx}\left(\tan^{-1}\frac{1}{x}\right)\right\}dx$ equal to?

A. 0
B. $-\frac{\pi}{4}$
C. $-\frac{\pi}{2}$
D. $\frac{\pi}{2}$

Q.40 What is $\int_{e^{-1}}^{e^2}\left|\frac{\ln x}{x}\right|dx$ equal to?

A. $\frac{3}{2}$
B. $\frac{5}{2}$
C. 3
D. 4

Q.41 What is $\int_{-a}^{a}(x^2+\sin x)\,dx$ equal to?

A. a
B. 0
C. $\frac{2a^2}{3}$
D. $\frac{2a^3}{3}$

Q.42 Evaluate:
$\int \sin^{-1}(3x-4x^3)dx$

A. $3x(\sin^{-1}x) + 3\sqrt{1+x^2} + C$
B. $3x(\sin^{-1}x) - 3\sqrt{1-x^2} + C$
C. $3x(\sin^{-1}x) + 3\sqrt{1-x^2} + C$
D. $3x(\sin^{-1}x) - 3\sqrt{1+x^2} + C$

Q.43 What is $\int\left(e^{\log x} + \sin x\right)\cos x\,dx$ equal to?

[UPSC NDA, 2020]

A. $\sin x + x\cos x + \frac{\sin^2 x}{2} + c$
B. $\sin x - x\cos x + \frac{\sin^2 x}{2} + c$
C. $x\sin x + \cos x + \frac{\sin^2 x}{2} + c$
D. $x\sin x - x\cos x + \frac{\sin^2 x}{2} + c$

Q.44 What is $\int (x\cos x + \sin x)dx$ equal to?
Where c is an arbitrary constant.

A. $x\sin x + c$
B. $x\cos x + c$
C. $-x\sin x + c$
D. $-x\cos x + c$

Q.45 For the linear programming problem:
Maximum $Z = 3X_1 + 2X_2$
Subject to:
$-2X_1 + 3X_2 \leq 9$
$x_1 - 5x_2 \geq -20$
$X_1, X_2 \geq 0$
The above problem has:
A. Unbounded solution
B. Infeasible solution
C. Alternative optimum solution
D. Degenerate solution

Q.46 The minimum of the objective function $Z = 2x + 10y$ for linear constraints $x - y \geq 0, x - 5y \leq -5, x \geq 0 y \geq 0$, is:

A. 15   B. 16   C. 17   D. 18

Q.47 Consider the following Linear Programming Problem (LPP):
Maximize $Z = 3x_1 + 2x_2$
Subject to:
$x_1 \leq 4$
$x_2 \leq 6$
$3x_1 + 2x_2 \leq 18$
$x_1 \geq 0, x_2 \geq 0$
A. The LPP has a unique optimal solution
B. The LPP is infeasible
C. The LPP is unbounded
D. The LPP has multiple optimal solutions

Q.48 Evaluate $\left(\cos\frac{\pi}{16} + i\sin\frac{\pi}{16}\right)^8 = ?$

A. 0   B. 1   C. i D. $-i$

Q.49 Square root of $4 + 3i$ is:

A. $\pm\left(\frac{1}{\sqrt{2}} + i\frac{3}{\sqrt{2}}\right)$
B. $\pm\left(\frac{3}{\sqrt{2}} - i\frac{1}{\sqrt{2}}\right)$
C. $\pm\left(\frac{5}{\sqrt{2}} + i\frac{3}{\sqrt{2}}\right)$
D. $\pm\left(\frac{3}{\sqrt{2}} + i\frac{1}{\sqrt{2}}\right)$

Q.50 If $z \neq 0$ and $2 + \cos\theta + i\sin\theta = \frac{3}{z}$, then the value of $2(z + \bar{z}) - |z|^2$ equals:

A. 3   B. 2   C. 1   D. 4

Mathematics : Mock Test - 9

// Smart Answer Sheet //

Correct — Indicates percentage of students who answered questions correctly.

Skipped — Indicates percentage of students who skipped questions.

Q.	Ans.	Correct / Skipped	Q.	Ans.	Correct / Skipped	Q.	Ans.	Correct / Skipped	Q.	Ans.	Correct / Skipped	Q.	Ans.	Correct / Skipped
1	C	28.99 % / 3.89 %	11	B	32.65 % / 3.22 %	21	C	87.66 % / 0.0 %	31	D	41.52 % / 1.88 %	41	D	21.42 % / 3.04 %
2	C	53.87 % / 1.62 %	12	D	68.32 % / 1.49 %	22	B	42.13 % / 1.69 %	32	A	55.76 % / 1.41 %	42	C	46.01 % / 1.48 %
3	B	20.92 % / 4.95 %	13	A	46.72 % / 1.07 %	23	A	83.62 % / 0.0 %	33	A	19.63 % / 4.85 %	43	C	50.67 % / 1.16 %
4	B	50.17 % / 1.42 %	14	C	68.76 % / 1.96 %	24	C	47.95 % / 1.96 %	34	B	67.09 % / 1.01 %	44	A	86.5 % / 0.0 %
5	A	25.68 % / 3.77 %	15	A	60.61 % / 1.05 %	25	C	29.95 % / 3.07 %	35	B	61.52 % / 1.25 %	45	A	88.95 % / 0.0 %
6	B	69.21 % / 1.94 %	16	C	47.14 % / 1.21 %	26	B	76.86 % / 0.0 %	36	B	83.01 % / 0.0 %	46	A	54.5 % / 1.8 %
7	C	44.73 % / 1.23 %	17	B	52.42 % / 1.99 %	27	D	16.47 % / 4.62 %	37	C	77.92 % / 0.0 %	47	D	53.11 % / 1.51 %
8	D	59.74 % / 1.09 %	18	D	89.66 % / 0.0 %	28	B	86.44 % / 0.0 %	38	D	27.81 % / 3.79 %	48	C	46.06 % / 1.72 %
9	A	69.56 % / 1.16 %	19	B	47.52 % / 1.87 %	29	C	41.1 % / 1.29 %	39	C	18.61 % / 3.22 %	49	D	69.99 % / 1.15 %
10	B	50.06 % / 1.42 %	20	C	79.42 % / 0.0 %	30	B	76.64 % / 0.0 %	40	B	49.96 % / 1.69 %	50	A	10.74 % / 3.65 %

Performance Analysis	
Avg. Score (%)	45.0%
Toppers Score (%)	65.0%
Your Score	

Mathematics : Mock Test - 9

//Hints and Solutions//

1. The given problem can be written as,

$${}^nC_r + {}^nC_{r+1} + {}^nC_{r+1} + {}^nC_{r+2}$$

We know that:

$${}^nC_r = \frac{n!}{r!(n-r)!}$$

Therefore,

$${}^nC_r + {}^nC_{r+1} + {}^nC_{r+1} + {}^nC_{r+2}$$

$$= \frac{n!}{r!(n-r)!} + \frac{n!}{(r+1)!(n-r-1)!} + \frac{n!}{(r+1)!(n-r-1)!} + \frac{n!}{(r+2)!(n-r-2)!}$$

$$= \frac{n!}{r!(n-r-1)!}\left[\frac{1}{(n-r)} + \frac{1}{(r+1)}\right] + \frac{n!}{(r+1)!(n-r-2)!}\left[\frac{1}{(n-r-1)} + \frac{1}{(r+2)}\right]$$

$$= \frac{n!}{r!(n-r-1)!}\left[\frac{r+1+n-r}{(n-r)(r+1)}\right] + \frac{n!}{(r+1)!(n-r-2)!}\left[\frac{r+2+n-r-1}{(n-r-1)(r+2)}\right]$$

$$= \frac{n! \times (n+1)}{r! \times (r+1) \times (n-r-1) \times (n-r)} + \frac{n!}{(r+1)!(n-r-2)!} \times \frac{(n+1)}{(n-r-1)(r+2)}$$

$$= \frac{(n+1)!}{(r+1)!(n-r)!} + \frac{n! \times (n+1)}{(r+2)(r+1) \times (n-r-1)(n-r-2)}$$

$$= \frac{(n+1)!}{(r+1)!(n-r)!} + \frac{(n+1)!}{(r+2)!(n-r-1)!}$$

$$= \frac{(n+1)!}{(r+1)!(n-r-1)!}\left[\frac{1}{n-r} + \frac{1}{r+2}\right]$$

$$= \frac{(n+1)!}{(r+1)!(n-r-1)!}\left[\frac{n-r+r+2}{(r+2)(n-r)}\right]$$

$$= \frac{(n+2)(n+1)!}{(r+2)(r+1)!(n-r)(n-r-1)!}$$

$$= \frac{(n+2)!}{(r+2)!(n-r)!}$$

$$= {}^{n+2}C_{r+2}$$

$$= C(n+2, r+2)$$

Hence, the correct option is (C).

2. The inverse of a diagonal matrix is obtained by replacing each element in the diagonal with its reciprocal.

We know, a square matrix in which every element except the principal diagonal elements is zero is called a Diagonal Matrix.

The inverse of a diagonal matrix is obtained by replacing each element in the diagonal with its reciprocal which is again a diagonal matrix as well as a symmetric matrix.

Consider a diagonal matrix

$$D = \begin{bmatrix} 1 & 0 & 0 \\ 0 & 2 & 0 \\ 0 & 0 & 3 \end{bmatrix}$$

Its inverse is obtained by replacing each element in the diagonal with its reciprocal.

$$\Rightarrow D^{-1} = \begin{bmatrix} \frac{1}{1} & 0 & 0 \\ 0 & \frac{1}{2} & 0 \\ 0 & 0 & \frac{1}{3} \end{bmatrix}$$

which is again diagonal matrix and the symmetric matrix also.

Hence, the correct option is (C).

3. Singular Matrix: Any square matrix of order n is said to be singular if |A| = 0.

Involuntary Matrix: Any square matrix of order n is said to be an involuntary matrix if $A^2 = I$, where I is the identity matrix of order n.

Nilpotent Matrix: Any square matrix of order n is said to be nilpotent matrix if there exist least positive integer m such that $A^m = O$, where O is the null matrix of order n.

Idempotent Matrix: Any square matrix of order n is said to be an idempotent matrix if $A^2 = A$.

Given: $A = \begin{bmatrix} 0 & 1 \\ 1 & 0 \end{bmatrix}$,

$$\Rightarrow A^2 = \begin{bmatrix} 0 & 1 \\ 1 & 0 \end{bmatrix} \times \begin{bmatrix} 0 & 1 \\ 1 & 0 \end{bmatrix}$$

$$= \begin{bmatrix} 1 & 0 \\ 0 & 1 \end{bmatrix} = I$$

Hence, A is an involuntary matrix as $A^2 = I$.

Hence, the correct option is (B).

4. If A is symmetric then $A^T = A$ and if is anti-symmetric then $A^T = -A$

We can start with finding the transpose of given expressions like,

$$\Rightarrow (P + P^T)^T = P^T + P \text{ and}$$

$$\Rightarrow (P - P^T)^T = P^T - P$$

$$\Rightarrow (P - P^T)^T = -(P - P^T)$$

Hence we can say that,

$Q = P + P^T$ and $R = P - P^T$ are symmetric and anti-symmetric respectively.

Hence, the correct option is (B).

5. Given:

The difference between two complementary angles is 15°

Calculation:

Let two complementary angles be ∠x and ∠y respectively.

∠x - ∠y = 15°   ----(i) (given)

∠x + ∠y = 90°   ----(ii) (Sum of complementary angles is 90°)

From (i), ∠y = 15 + ∠x   ----(iii)

From (ii), ∠y = 90 - ∠x   ----(iv)

On comparing the values of ∠y from (iii) & (iv) we get,

15 + ∠x = 90 - ∠x

⇒ 2∠x = 75

⇒ ∠x = 37.5

So, ∠y = 90 - 37.5 = 52.5

Since, ∠x = 37.5 and ∠y = 52.5

Therefore, Greater angle : Smaller angle = ∠y : ∠x

⇒ 52.5 : 37.5 = 7 : 5

∴ Required ratio is 7 : 5

Hence, the correct option is (A).

6. Given,

$\frac{dy}{dx} - 4y = 0$

⇒ $\frac{dy}{y} = 4dx$

Integrating both sides,

$\int \frac{dy}{y} = \int 4dx$

⇒ $\log y = 4x + c \left[\because \int \frac{1}{x} dx = \log x \right]$

⇒ $y = e^{4x+c}$

Now,

$y(0) = 1$

⇒ $1 = e^{0+c}$

⇒ $c = 0$

∴ $y = e^{4x}$

Hence, the correct option is (B).

7. $\frac{d^2y}{dx^2} + \cos\left(\frac{dy}{dx}\right) = 0$

1. As the given differential equation is not a polynomial equation in derivatives, the degree of this equation is not defined

So, this statement is true

2. Here Highest derivative: $\frac{d^2y}{dx^2}$

∴ Order = 2

Hence, the correct option is (C).

8. The given equation is,

$\frac{dy}{dx} = y(1 - 3x^2)$

⇒ $\frac{dy}{y} = (1 - 3x^2)dx$

Integrating both side, we get,

$\int \frac{dy}{y} = \int (1 - 3x^2)dx$

We know that,

$\int \frac{dx}{x} = \log x$ and $\int x^n dx = \frac{x^{n+1}}{n+1}$

∴ $\log y = x - x^3 + c$

We also know that,

If $\log x = n$ then $x = e^n$

∴ $y = e^{x - x^3 + c}$

⇒ $y = e^{x - x^3} \cdot e^c$

⇒ $y = Ce^{x(1-x^2)}$ [Let $e^c = C$]

Hence, the correct option is (D).

9. Given:

Highest Value $(H) = 450$

Lowest Value $(L) = 105$

Range = Highest Value − Lowest Value

i.e $R = H - L$

Substituting the given values in the formula.

$R = 450 - 105 = 345$

Coefficient of Range

$= \frac{H-L}{H+L}$

$= \frac{450-105}{450+105}$

$= \frac{345}{555}$

$= 0.62$

Thus, range is 345 and coefficient of range is 0.62

Hence, the correct option is (A).

10. Given:

$y = x$ and $y = 2x + 6$

Finding a point of intersection:

⇒ $x = 2x + 6$

⇒ $x = -6$

Thus, y = - 6.

Let us draw the graph of the curve $y = x$ and $y = 2x + 6$.

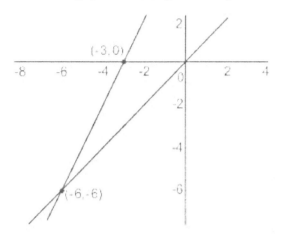

Let the enclosed area be A.

Using the formula of the area under the curve,

$A = \left| \int_a^b f(x) - g(x) dx \right|$

$\Rightarrow A = \left| \int_{-6}^{0} (2x + 6 - x) \, dx \right|$

$= \left| \int_{-6}^{0} (x + 6) \, dx \right|$

$= \left| \left[\frac{x^2}{2} + 6x \right]_{-6}^{0} \right|$

Substitute the limit to evaluate the area:

$\Rightarrow A = \left| 0 + 0 - \frac{36}{2} + 36 \right|$

$= 18$

Hence, the correct option is (B).

11. Shaded area has to be calculated:

Curve 1: $y = |x - 2|$

$\Rightarrow y = 2 - x$ for $x < 2$

$\Rightarrow y = x - 2$ for $x \geq 2$

Curve 2: $y = 5 - |x + 1|$

$\Rightarrow y = 5 + x + 1 = x + 6$ for $x < -1$

$\Rightarrow y = 5 - x - 1 = 4 - x$ for $x \geq -1$

It can be drawn as:

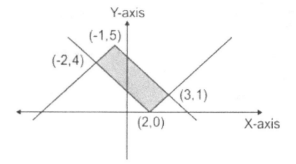

Area enclosed $(A) = \int_{x_1}^{x_2} (y_1 - y_2) \, dx$

$\Rightarrow A = \int_{-1}^{2} (5 - |x + 1|) - (|x - 2|) dx$

$\Rightarrow A = \int_{-2}^{-1} x + 6 - (2 - x) dx + \int_{-1}^{2} 4 - x - (2 - x) dx + \int_{2}^{3} 4 - x - (x - 2) dx$

$\Rightarrow A = \int_{-2}^{-1} (2x + 4) dx + \int_{-1}^{2} 2 dx + \int_{2}^{3} (6 - 2x) dx$

$\Rightarrow A = \left| [x^2 + 4x]_{-2}^{-1} \right| + \left| [2x]_{-1}^{2} \right| + \left| [6x - x^2]_{2}^{3} \right|$

$\Rightarrow A = |[-3 + 4(1)]| + |[2(3)]| + |[6(1) - (5)]|$

$\Rightarrow A = 1 + 6 + 1$

$\Rightarrow A = 8$ sq. units

Hence, the correct option is (B).

12. Let's make a list of the different equations for different combinations of $x, y \geq 0$ and $x, y < 0$.

Cases	Equation
x ≥ 0 AND y ≥ 0	x + y = 1
x ≥ 0 AND y < 0	x - y = 1
x < 0 AND y ≥ 0	- x + y = 1
x < 0 AND y< 0	- x - y = 1

The graph of the curve |x| + |y| = 1 will look like this:

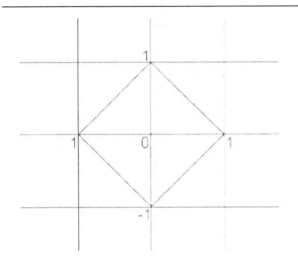

The area of the above figure will be:

4 × Area of the small triangle.

$= 4 \times \left(\frac{1}{2} \times 1 \times 1\right)$

= 2 square units.

Hence, the correct option is (D).

13. Given, $1 + \sin x \cdot \sin^2 \frac{x}{2} = 0$

$\Rightarrow 2 + 2\sin x \cdot \sin^2 \frac{x}{2} = 0$

$\Rightarrow 2 + \sin x(1 - \cos x) = 0$

$\Rightarrow 4 + 2\sin x(1 - \cos x) = 0$

$\Rightarrow 4 + 2\sin x - \sin 2x = 0$

$\Rightarrow \sin 2x = 2\sin x + 4$

Above is not possible for any value of x as LHS has maximum value 1 and RHS has minimum value 2.

Hence, the correct option is (A).

14. As we know,

If $z = x + iy$...(1) be any complex number, then its modulus is given by,

$|z| = \sqrt{x^2 + y^2}$

Let,

$z = \frac{1+7i}{(2-i)^2}$

$= \frac{1+7i}{2^2 + i^2 - 4i}$

$= \frac{1+7i}{4-1-4i}$

$= \frac{1+7i}{3-4i}$

$= \frac{1+7i}{3-4i} \times \frac{3+4i}{3+4i}$

$= \frac{3+4i+21i+28i^2}{3^2-(4i)^2}$

$= \frac{3+25i-28}{9+16}$

$= \frac{-25+25i}{25}$

$\therefore z = -1 + i$...(2)

Comparing equation (1) and (2), we get

$x = -1$ or $y = 1$

As, $|z| = \sqrt{x^2 + y^2}$

$\therefore |z| = \sqrt{(-1)^2 + 1^2}$

$\Rightarrow |z| = \sqrt{1+1}$

$\Rightarrow |z| = \sqrt{2}$

So, the modulus of $\frac{1+7i}{(2-i)^2}$ is $\sqrt{2}$.

Hence, the correct option is (C).

15. General term: General term in the expansion of $(x+y)^n$ is given by

$T_{(r+1)} = {}^nC_r \times x^{n-r} \times y^r$

Middle terms: The middle terms is the expansion of $(x+y)^n$ depends upon the value of n.

- If n is even, then total number of terms in the expansion of $(x+y)^n$ is $n+1$. So there is only one middle term i.e. $\left(\frac{n}{2}+1\right)$ th term is the middle term.

- If n is odd, then total number of terms in the expansion of $(x+y)^n$ is $n+1$. So there are two middle terms i.e. $\left(\frac{n+1}{2}\right)^{th}$ and $\left(\frac{n+3}{2}\right)^{th}$ are two middle terms.

Here, we have to find the middle terms in the expansion of $\left(2x + \frac{1}{x}\right)^8$

Here $n = 8$ (n is even number)

Middle term $= \left(\frac{n}{2}+1\right) = \left(\frac{8}{2}+1\right) = 5$ th term

$T_5 = T_{(4+1)} = {}^8C_4 \times (2x)^{(8-4)} \times \left(\frac{1}{x}\right)^4$

$T_5 = {}^8C_4 \times 2^4$

Hence, the correct option is (A).

16. Rules for Operations on Inequalities:

Adding the same number to each side of an inequality does not change the direction of the inequality symbol.

Subtracting the same number from each side of an inequality does not change the direction of the inequality symbol.

Multiplying each side of an inequality by a positive number does not change the direction of the inequality symbol.

Multiplying each side of an inequality by a negative number reverses the direction of the inequality symbol.

Dividing each side of an inequality by a positive number does not change the direction of the inequality symbol.

Dividing each side of an inequality by a negative number reverses the direction of the inequality symbol.

Given:

$\frac{2x+4}{x-1} \geq 5$

$\Rightarrow \frac{2x+4}{x-1} - 5 \geq 0$

$\Rightarrow \frac{2x+4-5(x-1)}{x-1} \geq 0$

$\Rightarrow \frac{2x+4-5x+5}{x-1} \geq 0$

$\Rightarrow \frac{9-3x}{x-1} \geq 0$

$\Rightarrow \frac{-3(x-3)}{x-1} \geq 0$

Multiplying each side of an inequality by a negative number $\left(\frac{-1}{3}\right)$ reverses the direction of the inequality symbol.

$\Rightarrow \frac{(x-3)}{x-1} \leq 0$, Here $x - 1 \neq 0 \Rightarrow x \neq 1$

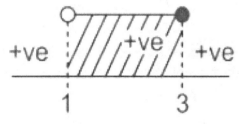

So the solution set of the given in equations is (1, 3]

Hence, the correct option is (C).

17. The greatest coefficient will be of the middle term.

General term: General term in the expansion of $(x+y)^n$ is given by $T_{(r+1)} = {}^nC_r \times x^{n-r} \times y^r$

Middle terms: The middle terms is the expansion of $(x+y)^n$ depends upon the value of n.

1. If n is even, then the total number of terms in the expansion of $(x+y)^n$ is $n+1$.

So there is only one middle term i.e., $\left(\frac{n}{2}+1\right)$ th term is the middle term.

2. If n is odd, then the total number of terms in the expansion of $(x+y)^n$ is $n+1$.

So there are two middle terms i.e., $\left(\frac{n+1}{2}\right)^{th}$ and $\left(\frac{n+3}{2}\right)^{th}$ are two middle terms.

We have to find the greatest coefficient in the expansion of $(1+x)^{2n+4}$

As we know the greatest coefficient will be of the middle term of the expansion.

Here, $(2n+4)$ is even, there will be only one middle term.

Middle term $= \left(\frac{2n+4}{2}+1\right)$ th term $= (n+2+1)^{th}$ term $= (n+3)^{th}$ term

General term in the expansion of $(x+y)^3$ is given by $T_{(r+1)} = {}^nC_r \times x^{n-r} \times y^r$

$\therefore T_{(n+3)} = T_{(n+2)+1} = {}^{2n+4}C_{n+2} x^{n+2}$

Hence, the correct option is (B).

18. Here,
$m : n = 2 : 3, (x, y) = (1, 2), (x_1, y_1) = (0, k), (x_2, y_2) = (h, 0)$

Using section formula,

$\therefore x = \frac{mx_2+nx_1}{m+n}$

$\Rightarrow 1 = \frac{3(h)+2(0)}{2+3}$

$\Rightarrow 1 = \frac{3h}{5}$

$\Rightarrow 3h = 5$

$\Rightarrow h = \frac{5}{3}$

$y = \frac{my_2+ny_1}{m+n}$

$\Rightarrow 2 = \frac{2(k)+3(0)}{2+3}$

$\Rightarrow 2k = 10$

$\Rightarrow k = 5$

Therefore, x and y intercept are $\frac{5}{3}$ and 5.

Hence, required equation

$\left(\frac{x}{\frac{5}{3}}\right) + \left(\frac{y}{5}\right) = 1$

$\Rightarrow 3x + y = 5$

$\therefore$ Required equation is $3x + y = 5$

Hence, the correct option is (D).

19. Given lines are $6x + 8y + 15 = 0$ and $3x + 4y + 9 = 0$

$\Rightarrow 6x + 8y + 15 = 0$

Take 2 common from above equation, we get

$\Rightarrow 3x + 4y + \frac{15}{2} = 0$ ....(i)

And $3x + 4y + 9 = 0$ .....(ii)

Equation (i) and (ii) are parallel to each other.

$\therefore$ The distance between the parallel lines are given by, $\frac{|c_2-c_1|}{\sqrt{a^2+b^2}}$

$= \frac{\left|\frac{15}{2}-9\right|}{\sqrt{3^2+4^2}} = \frac{\left(\frac{3}{2}\right)}{5} = \frac{3}{10}$

Hence, the correct option is (B).

20. Given,

$x = y + 8$

$\Rightarrow y = x - 8$

$x + y = 5$

$\Rightarrow y = -x + 5$

As we know,

Equation of straight line is $y = mx + c$.

$\therefore$ Slope of line $y = x - 8$ is $m_1 = 1$

Also, Slope of line $y = -x + 5$ is $m_2 = -1$.

Now, $\theta = \tan^{-1}\left|\frac{m_2-m_1}{1+m_1 m_2}\right|$

$\Rightarrow \theta = \tan^{-1}\left|\frac{-1-1}{1+(-1)(1)}\right|$

$\Rightarrow \theta = \tan^{-1}\left|\frac{-2}{1-1}\right|$

$\Rightarrow \theta = \tan^{-1}(\infty) = 90°$

$(\because \tan 90° = \infty \Rightarrow \tan^{-1}\infty = 90°)$

Hence, the correct option is (C).

21. As we know,

The point (x, y) that lies on the line will satisfy the equation of a line.

Given,

The straight lines $x - 2y = 0$ and $kx + y = 1$ intersect at the point $\left(1, \frac{1}{2}\right)$.

The point $\left(1, \frac{1}{2}\right)$ lies on the line $kx + y = 1$.

The point $\left(1, \frac{1}{2}\right)$ is satisfying the equation of line $kx + y = 1$.

$\therefore k(1) + \frac{1}{2} = 1$

$\Rightarrow k = 1 - \frac{1}{2}$

$\Rightarrow k = \frac{1}{2}$

So, the value of k is $\frac{1}{2}$.

Hence, the correct option is (C).

22. Concept:

Poisson distribution formula,

$P(x) = \frac{e^{-\lambda}\lambda^x}{x!}$

where λ = mean value of occurrence within an interval

$P(x)$ = probability of x occurrence within an interval

Calculation:

Mean $(\lambda) = 3, x = 3$

We need to find $P\{|x - 3| < 1\}$,

After simplifying we get $P(2 < x < 4)$

So between 2 and 4, only one integer value possible is 3.

$\Rightarrow P\{|x - 3| < 1\} = P(3)$

$P(x) = \frac{e^{-\lambda}\lambda^x}{x!}$

$\Rightarrow P(3) = \frac{e^{-3}3^3}{3!}$

$= \frac{e^{-3}(3\times 3\times 3)}{3\times 2\times 1}$

$= \left(\frac{9}{2}\right)e^{-3}$

Hence, the correct option is (B).

23. Concept:

Poisson distribution is applied when the number of trials is very large and the probability of success is small.

Calculation:

Let's say we have an event E such that the success of the event is "Ringing a call at a time t_0" and failure is "Not ringing a call at time t_0".

Since the total number of success or failure of the event is unknown.

Therefore, we can say that the event is a random variable.

1 hour = 3600 sec = 3600000 msec = $3.6 \times 10^9 \mu$ sec

The event can occur a large number of times for any given time interval and the probability of success is very less.

This property corresponds to Poisson distribution.

Hence, the correct option is (A).

24. Period of $3\sin x - 4\sin^3 x$

As we know $3\sin x - 4\sin^3 x = \sin 3x$

Period of $\sin x$ is 2π

Therefore, the Period of $\sin 3x$ is $\dfrac{2\pi}{3}$

Hence, the correct option is (C).

25. Given:

The vector $-\hat{\imath} + \hat{\jmath} + \hat{k}$ bisects the angle between the vectors $\vec{c}$ and $3\hat{\imath} + 4\hat{\jmath}$.

Let $\hat{c} = x\hat{\imath} + y\hat{\jmath} + z\hat{k}$

where $x^2 + y^2 + z^2 = 1$ ...... (1)

Unit vector along $3\hat{\imath} + 4\hat{\jmath} = \dfrac{3\hat{\imath}+4\hat{\jmath}}{\sqrt{3^2+4^2}}$

$= \dfrac{3\hat{\imath}+4\hat{\jmath}}{5}$

The bisectors of these two is given by:

$r = t(\hat{a} + \hat{b})$

$r = t\left(x\hat{\imath} + y\hat{\jmath} + x\hat{k} + \dfrac{3\hat{\imath}+4\hat{\jmath}}{5}\right)$

$r = \dfrac{t}{5}[(5x+3)\hat{\imath} + (5y+4)\hat{\jmath} + 5z\hat{k}]$ ...... (2)

But the bisector is given by $-\hat{\imath} + \hat{\jmath} - \hat{k}$ ....(3)

Comparing (2) and (3), we get

$\dfrac{t}{5}(5x+3) = -1$

$\Rightarrow x = -\dfrac{5+3t}{5t}$

$\dfrac{t}{5}(5y+4) = 1$

$\Rightarrow y = \dfrac{5-4t}{5t}$

$\dfrac{t}{5}(5z) = -1$

$\Rightarrow z = -\dfrac{1}{t}$

Put all the values in equation (1), we get

$\left(-\dfrac{5+3t}{5t}\right)^2 + \left(\dfrac{5-4t}{5t}\right)^2 + \left(-\dfrac{1}{t}\right)^2 = 1$

$\Rightarrow \dfrac{25+9t^2+30t+25+16t^2-40t+25}{25t^2} = 1$

$\Rightarrow 25t^2 - 10t + 75 = 25t^2$

$\Rightarrow t = 7.5$

Thus,

$x = -\dfrac{5+3\times 7.5}{5\times 7.5} = -\dfrac{11}{15}$

$y = \dfrac{5-4\times 7.5}{5\times 7.5} = -\dfrac{10}{15}$

$z = -\dfrac{1}{7.5} = -\dfrac{2}{15}$

$\hat{c} = x\hat{\imath} + y\hat{\jmath} + z\hat{k}$

So, $\hat{c} = \dfrac{1}{15}(-11\hat{\imath} - 10\hat{\jmath} - 2\hat{k})$

Hence, the correct option is (C).

26. Given:

Vectors $\alpha\hat{\imath} + \alpha\hat{\jmath} + \gamma\hat{k}, \hat{\imath} + \hat{k}$ and $\hat{\gamma} + \gamma\hat{\jmath} + \beta\hat{k}$ lie on a plane Vectors lie on the same plane so vectors are coplanar.

Condition for coplanarity: $\vec{a} \cdot (\vec{b} \times \vec{c}) = \begin{vmatrix} a_1 & b_1 & c_1 \\ a_2 & b_2 & c_2 \\ a_3 & b_3 & c_3 \end{vmatrix} = 0$

Therefore, $\begin{vmatrix} \alpha & \alpha & \gamma \\ 1 & 0 & 1 \\ \gamma & \gamma & \beta \end{vmatrix} = 0$

On expanding, we get:

$\alpha[0 - \gamma] - \alpha[\beta - y] + \gamma[y - 0] = 0$

$\Rightarrow -\alpha y - \alpha\beta + \alpha y + y^2 = 0$

$\Rightarrow y^2 = \alpha\beta$

$\therefore \alpha, \beta, \gamma$ are in G.P.

Hence, the correct option is (B).

27. Given,

$3\sin\alpha = 5\sin\beta$

$\Rightarrow \dfrac{\sin\alpha}{\sin\beta} = \dfrac{5}{3}$

As we know that componendo and dividendo rule is given as,

If $\dfrac{a}{b} = \dfrac{c}{d}$

Then $\dfrac{a+b}{a-b} = \dfrac{c+d}{c-d}$

Then applying this rule, we get

$\Rightarrow \dfrac{\sin\alpha+\sin\beta}{\sin\alpha-\sin\beta} = \dfrac{5+3}{5-3} = 4$

As we know,

$\sin C + \sin D = 2\sin\left(\frac{C+D}{2}\right)\cos\left(\frac{C-D}{2}\right)$

$\sin C - \sin D = 2\sin\left(\frac{C-D}{2}\right)\cos\left(\frac{C+D}{2}\right)$

$\Rightarrow \dfrac{2\sin\frac{\alpha+\beta}{2}\cos\frac{\alpha-\beta}{2}}{2\cos\frac{\alpha+\beta}{2}\sin\frac{\alpha-\beta}{2}} = 4$

$\Rightarrow \dfrac{\tan\frac{\alpha+\beta}{2}}{\tan\frac{\alpha-\beta}{2}} = 4$

$\therefore \dfrac{\tan\frac{\alpha+\beta}{2}}{\tan\frac{\alpha-\beta}{2}}$ equals to 4.

Hence, the correct option is (D).

28. Given,

$y = \sqrt{2 + \sqrt{2 + 2\cos 4\theta}}$

$y = \sqrt{2 + \sqrt{2(1 + \cos 4\theta)}}$

$\because 1 + \cos 2\theta = 2\cos^2\theta$

$\Rightarrow y = \sqrt{2 + \sqrt{2(2\cos^2 2\theta)}}$

$\Rightarrow y = \sqrt{2(1 + \cos 2\theta)}$

$\Rightarrow y = \sqrt{2 \cdot 2\cos^2\theta}$

$\Rightarrow y = 2\cos\theta$

Hence, the correct option is (B).

29. Let,

$y = \sin[(n+1)A]\sin[(n+2)A] + \cos[(n+1)A]\cos[(n+2)A]$

$\Rightarrow y = \cos[(n+1)A]\cos[(n+2)A] + \sin[(n+1)A]\sin[(n+2)A]$

$\because \cos(A - B) = \cos A \cdot \cos B - \sin A \cdot \sin B$

$\Rightarrow y = \cos[(n+1)A - (n+2)A]$

$\Rightarrow y = \cos(-A)$

$\because \cos(-\theta) = \cos\theta$

$\Rightarrow y = \cos A$

Hence, the correct option is (C).

30. $f(x) = x\sin x$

As we know that,

$D(uv) = uv' + vu'$

So,

$f'(x) = x(\cos x) + \sin x(1)$

$= x\cos x + \sin x$

By putting $x = 0$, we have

$f'(0) = 0 + \sin(0)$ ($\because \sin(0) = 1$)

$= 0$

Hence, the correct option is (B).

31. Chain Rule (Differentiation by substitution): If y is a function of u and u is a function of x.

$\dfrac{dy}{dx} = \dfrac{dy}{du} \times \dfrac{du}{dx}$

Given,

$y^2 + x^2 + 3x + 5 = 0$

Differentiating with respect to x, we get

$2y\dfrac{dy}{dx} + 2x + 3(1) + 0 = 0$

$\Rightarrow 2y\dfrac{dy}{dx} + 2x + 3 = 0$

$\Rightarrow 2y\dfrac{dy}{dx} = -(2x + 3)$

$\Rightarrow \dfrac{dy}{dx} = -\dfrac{2x+3}{2y}$

Now at $(0, -3)$

$\Rightarrow \dfrac{dy}{dx} = -\dfrac{2(0)+3}{2(-3)}$

$\Rightarrow \dfrac{dy}{dx} = -\dfrac{3}{(-6)}$

$\therefore \dfrac{dy}{dx} = \dfrac{1}{2} = 0.5$

Hence, the correct option is (D).

32. $\lim_{x \to 0} \tan x = \lim_{x \to 0}\left(\dfrac{\sin x}{\cos x}\right)$

$\Rightarrow \lim_{x \to 0} \tan x = \dfrac{\lim_{x \to 0} \sin x}{\lim_{x \to 0} \cos x}$

$\Rightarrow \lim_{x \to 0} \tan x = \dfrac{0}{1}$

$\Rightarrow \lim_{x \to 0} \tan x = 0$

Hence, the correct option is (A).

33. Let S be a sample space and E be an event such that $n(S) = n, n(E) = m$ and each outcome is equally likely.

Then $P(E) = \dfrac{n(E)}{n(S)} = \dfrac{m}{n} = \dfrac{\text{Number of favourable outcomes of }E}{\text{Total number of possible outcomes}}$

If A and B are two events associated with a random experiment, then $P(A \cup B) = P(A) + P(B) - P(A \cap B)$

Let A: Heart is drawn from a pack of cards.

Let B: An ace is drawn from a pack of cards.

As we know that, probability of an event is given by: $P(E) = \dfrac{n(E)}{n(S)}$

So, probability of winning the bet is given $P(A \text{ or } B)$ i.e., $P(A \cup B)$

$\Rightarrow P(A) = \frac{13}{52}, P(B) = \frac{4}{52}$ and $P(A \cap B) = \frac{1}{52}$

As we know that, $P(A \cup B) = P(A) + P(B) - P(A \cap B)$

$\Rightarrow P(A \text{ or } B) = P(A \cup B) = \frac{13}{52} + \frac{4}{52} - \frac{1}{52} = \frac{4}{13}$

∴ Probability of losing the bet $= 1 - \frac{4}{13} = \frac{9}{13}$

∴ Odds against winning the bet is $\frac{9}{13} : \frac{4}{13} = \frac{9}{4}$

Hence, the correct option is (A).

34. Given normal to the circle are:

$2y - 3x + 5 = 0$ .....(i)

$2y + 3x - 5 = 0$ .....(ii)

Substracting (ii) from (i)

$-6x + 10 = 0$

$\Rightarrow x = \frac{5}{3}$

From equation (ii)

$2y + 3\left(\frac{5}{3}\right) - 5 = 0$

$\Rightarrow y = 0$

∴ Coordinates of the centre are $\left(\frac{5}{3}, 0\right)$

Given the area of circle $= 81\pi$

$\pi r^2 = 81\pi$

$\Rightarrow r^2 = 81$

The equation of circle is:

$(x - h)^2 + (y - k)^2 = R^2$

$\Rightarrow \left(x - \frac{5}{3}\right)^2 + (y - 0)^2 = 81$

$\Rightarrow \left(x - \frac{5}{3}\right)^2 + y^2 = 81$

Hence, the correct option is (B).

35. Given:

$\lim_{x \to 0} \frac{\log(1+2x)}{\tan 2x}$

Dividing and multiplying the numerator and denominator by $2x$, we get:

$= \lim_{x \to 0} \frac{\frac{\log(1+2x)}{2x} \times 2x}{\frac{\tan 2x}{2x} \times 2x}$

We know that:

$\lim_{x \to a} \left[\frac{f(x)}{g(x)}\right] = \frac{\lim_{x \to a} f(x)}{\lim_{x \to a} g(x)}$, provided $\lim_{x \to a} g(x) \neq 0$

$= \frac{\lim_{x \to 0} \frac{\log(1+2x)}{2x}}{\lim_{x \to 0} \frac{\tan 2x}{2x}}$

As we know that:

$\lim_{x \to 0} \frac{\tan x}{x} = 1$

and, $\lim_{x \to 0} \frac{\log(1+x)}{x} = 1$

Therefore,

$\lim_{x \to 0} \frac{\tan 2x}{2x} = 1$

and, $\lim_{x \to 0} \frac{\log(1+2x)}{2x} = 1$

Therefore,

$\lim_{x \to 0} \frac{\log(1+2x)}{\tan 2x} = \frac{1}{1} = 1$

Hence, the correct option is (B).

36. Let, the pairs of positive numbers with sum 24 be: x and $24 - x$.

Then, let $f(x)$ denotes the product of such pairs

i.e., $f(x) = x \times (24 - x) = 24x - x^2$

Here we have to find that pair of number for which $f(x)$ is maximum.

First we have to find $f'(x)$

$f'(x) = 24 - 2x$

Now let's find the roots of the equation $f'(x) = 0$

$2x = 24$

$\Rightarrow x = 12$

Now let's find out $f''(x)$ i.e., $\frac{d^2(f(x))}{dx^2}$

$f''(x) = -2$

Now evaluate the value of $f''(x)$ at $x = 12$

$f''(12) = -2 < 0$

As we know that according to second derivative test if $f''(c) < 0$ then $x = c$ is a point of maxima

So, $x = 12$ is a point of maxima

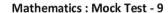

So, when $x = 12$ then $24 - x = 12$

Thus, the required numbers are 12 and 12

Hence, the correct option is (B).

37. Minimum and maximum value of cos x is -1 and 1

$-1 \leq \cos x \leq 1$

So, the minimum and maximum value of cos 2x is -1 and 1

$-1 \leq \cos 2x \leq 1$

Maximum value of |cos 2x + 7|

Here, cos 2x = 1

|1+7| = |8| = 8

Minimum value of |cos 2x + 7|

Here, cos 2x = -1

|(-1)+7| = |6| = 6

Maximum value = 8, Minimum value = 6

Hence, the correct option is (C).

38. Let, $f(x) = 3x^4 - 8x^3 + 12x^2 - 48x + 1$ be a function defined on the interval $[1,4]$

First we have to find $f'(x)$

$f'(x) = 12x^3 - 24x^2 + 24x - 48$

Now let's find the roots of the equation $f'(x) = 0$

$12x^3 - 24x^2 + 24x - 48 = 0$

$\Rightarrow 12 \cdot (x^3 - 2x^2 + 2x - 4) = 0$

$\Rightarrow 12 \cdot (x^2 + 2) \cdot (x - 2) = 0$

$\Rightarrow x - 2 = 0$ $\quad [\because (x^2 + 2) \neq 0$ as we are dealing with real valued functions]

$\Rightarrow x = 2$

Now let's find out $f''(x)$ i.e., $\frac{d^2(f(x))}{dx^2}$

$f''(x) = 36x^2 - 48x + 24$

Now evaluate the value of $f''(x)$ at $x = 2$, we get:

$f''(2) - 72 > 0$

As we know that according to second derivative test if $f''(c) > 0$ then $x = c$ is a point of local minima

So, $x = 2$ is a point of local minima

So $f(2) = -63$

Let's calculate $f(0)$ and $f(3)$

$f(0) = 1$ and $f(3) = -8$

As we know that if a function is defined in the closed interval $[a, b]$ then the minimum value of $f(x)$ on $[a, b]$ is the smallest of $m, f(a)$ and $f(b)$.

So, the minimum value of the given function on the interval $[0,3]$ is -63.

Hence, the correct option is (D).

39. We have to find the value of $\int_{-1}^{1} \left\{ \frac{d}{dx}\left(\tan^{-1}\frac{1}{x}\right) \right\} dx$

Let $I = \int_{-1}^{1} \left\{ \frac{d}{dx}\left(\tan^{-1}\frac{1}{x}\right)\right\} dx = \int_{-1}^{1} \left(\frac{d}{dx}\cot^{-1}x\right) dx$
$= \int_{-1}^{1} \frac{-1}{1+x^2} dx$

Let $f(x) = \frac{-1}{1+x^2}$

Now, $f(-x) = \frac{-1}{1+(-x)^2} = \frac{-1}{1+x^2}$

$\Rightarrow f(-x) = f(x)$

$\Rightarrow f(x)$ is even function

According to the concept used

$\Rightarrow I = \int_{-1}^{1} \frac{-1}{1+x^2} dx = 2\int_{0}^{1} \frac{-1}{1+x^2} dx = -2\int_{0}^{1} \frac{1}{1+x^2} dx$

$\Rightarrow I = -2[\tan^{-1}x]_0^1$

$\Rightarrow I = -2[\tan^{-1}(1) - \tan^{-1}(0)]$

$\Rightarrow I = -2\left(\frac{\pi}{4}\right) = \frac{-\pi}{2}$

$\therefore$ The value of the integral $\int_{-1}^{1} \left\{\frac{d}{dx}\left(\tan^{-1}\frac{1}{x}\right)\right\} dx$ is $\frac{-\pi}{2}$.

Hence, the correct option is (C).

40. To find: $\int_{e^{-1}}^{e^2} \left|\frac{\ln x}{x}\right| dx$

Using property, $\int_{-a}^{a} |f(x)| dx = \int_{-a}^{0} -f(x) dx + \int_{0}^{a} f(x) dx$, where $f(x) < 0$ for all $x < 0$.

$\int_{e^{-1}}^{e^2} \left|\frac{\ln x}{x}\right| dx = \int_{e^{-1}}^{e^0} -\frac{\ln x}{x} dx + \int_{e^0}^{e^2} \frac{\ln x}{x} dx$

Put $\ln x = t$

Differentiating both sides

$\frac{dx}{x} = dt$

$\int_{e^{-1}}^{0} -\frac{\ln x}{x} dx + \int_{e^0}^{e^2} \frac{\ln x}{x} dx = \int_{-1}^{0} -t\,dt + \int_{0}^{2} t\,dt$

$= \left[-\frac{t^2}{2}\right]_{-1}^{0} + \left[\frac{t^2}{2}\right]_{0}^{2}$

$= \frac{1}{2} + 2$

$= \frac{5}{2}$

Hence, the correct option is (B).

41. Let $I = \int_{-a}^{a}(x^2 + \sin x)\,dx$

$= \int_{-a}^{a} x^2\,dx + \int_{-a}^{a} \sin x\,dx$

$= I_1 + I_2$

Now,

$I_1 = \int_{-a}^{a} x^2\,dx$

Here $f(x) = x^2$

Replace x by $-x$, we get

$\Rightarrow f(-x) = (-x)^2 = x^2$

$\Rightarrow f(-x) = f(x)$

So, $f(x)$ is even function.

As we know, If $f(x)$ even function then $\int_{-a}^{a} f(x)\,dx = 2\int_{0}^{a} f(x)\,dx$

Therefore, $I_1 = 2\int_{0}^{a} x^2\,dx$

$= 2 \times \left[\dfrac{x^3}{3}\right]_{0}^{a}$

$= 2 \times \left[\dfrac{a^3}{3} - 0\right] = \dfrac{2a^3}{3}$

Now,

$I_2 = \int_{-a}^{a} \sin x\,dx$

Here $f(x) = \sin x$

Replace x by $-x$, we get

$\Rightarrow f(-x) = \sin(-x) = -\sin x$ $(\because \sin(-\theta) = -\sin\theta)$

$\Rightarrow f(-x) = -f(x)$

So, $f(x)$ is odd function.

As we know, If $f(x)$ even function then $\int_{-a}^{a} f(x)\,dx = 0$

$I = I_1 + I_2 = \dfrac{2a^3}{3} + 0 = \dfrac{2a^3}{3}$

Hence, the correct option is (D).

42. Here, we have to find the value of $\int \sin^{-1}(3x - 4x^3)\,dx$

Let $x = \sin t \Rightarrow t = \sin^{-1} x$

By differentiating $x = \sin t$ with respect to x we get,

$\Rightarrow dx = \cos t\,dt$

$\Rightarrow \int \sin^{-1}(3x - 4x^3)\,dx = \int \sin^{-1}(3\sin t - 4\sin^3 t)\cdot \cos t\,dt$

As we know that, $\sin 3x = 3\sin x - 4\sin^3 x$

$\Rightarrow \int \sin^{-1}(3x - 4x^3)\,dx = 3\int t\cdot \cos t\,dt \cdots (1)$

Now by applying integration by parts(ILATE Rule) over $\int t\cdot \cos t\,dt$ we get

Here, $u(t) = t$ and $v(t) = \cos t$

$\Rightarrow \int t \cdot \cos t\,dt = t\cdot \int \cos t\,dt - \int \left\{\dfrac{d(t)}{dt}\cdot \int \cos t\,dt\right\}dt$

As we know that, $\int \cos x\,dx = \sin x + C$ where C is a constant $\int t\cdot \cos t\,dt = t\cdot \sin t - \int 1\cdot \sin t\,dt$

As we know that, $\int \sin x\,dx = -\cos x + C$ where C is a constant

$\int t\cdot \cos t\,dt = t\cdot \sin t + \cos t$

By substituting the value of $\int t\cdot \cos t\,dt$ in the equation (1), we get $\Rightarrow \int \sin^{-1}(3x - 4x^3)\,dx = 3t\cdot \sin t + 3\cos t + C$ where C is a constant

By substituting $x = \sin t \Rightarrow t = \sin^{-1} x$ in the above equation and $\because x = \sin t \Rightarrow \cos t = \sqrt{1 - x^2}$

$\Rightarrow \int \sin^{-1}(3x - 4x^3)\,dx = 3x\left(\sin^{-1} x\right) + 3\sqrt{1 - x^2} + C$

where C is a constant

Hence, the correct option is (C).

43. Given,

$\int \left(e^{\log x} + \sin x\right)\cos x\,dx$

Let $I = \int \left(e^{\log x} + \sin x\right)\cos x\,dx$

$\Rightarrow \int (x\cos x + \sin x\cos x)\,dx$ $(\because e^{\log x} = x)$

$\Rightarrow \int x\cos x\,dx + \int \sin x\cos x\,dx$

$\Rightarrow I = I_1 + I_2 \ldots (1)$

Now,

$I_1 = \int x\cos x\,dx$

Applying by parts, we get

$\Rightarrow x\int \cos x\,dx - \int \left(\dfrac{dx}{dx}\int \cos x\,dx\right)dx$

$\Rightarrow x\sin x - \int \sin x\,dx + c$

$\Rightarrow x\sin x + \cos x + c$

Now,

$I_2 = \int \sin x \cos x \, dx$

Let $\sin x = t$

Differentiating with respect to x, we get

$\Rightarrow \cos x \, dx = dt$

$\Rightarrow I_2 = \int t \, dt = \dfrac{t^2}{2} + c$

$\Rightarrow \dfrac{\sin^2 x}{2} + c$

Put the value of I_1 and I_2 in equation (1), we get

$\therefore$ The required integral (I) is $x\sin x + \cos x + \dfrac{\sin^2 x}{2} + c$.

Hence, the correct option is (C).

44. Given,

$\int (x\cos x + \sin x) dx$

Let $I = \int (x\cos x + \sin x) dx$

$= \int x\cos x \, dx + \int \sin x \, dx$

Applying by parts, we get

$= x \int \cos x \, dx - \int \left(\dfrac{dx}{dx} \int \cos x \, dx\right) dx + \int \sin x \, dx$

$= x\sin x - \int \sin x \, dx + \int \sin x \, dx + c$

$= x\sin x + c$

Hence, the correct option is (A).

45. Unbounded Solution: If the feasible region is not bounded, it is possible that the value of the objective function goes on increasing without leaving the feasible region. This is known as an unbounded solution.

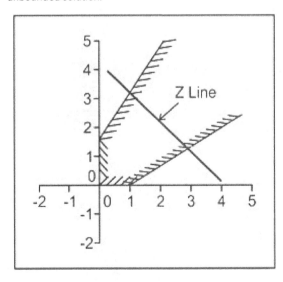

Plotting the graph for the given constraints as shown in figure. From figure we can see that LPP has unbounded solution.

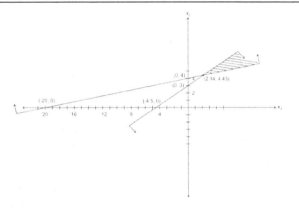

Hence, the correct option is (A).

46. Given:

Minimize $Z = x + 4y$

$x + 3y \geq 3, 2x + y \geq 2, x \geq 0, y \geq 0$

To draw the feasible region, construct table as follows:

Inequality	$x + 3y \geq 3$	$2x + y \geq 2$
Corresponding equation (of line)	$x + 3y = 3$	$2x + y = 2$
Intersection of line with X-axis	(3,0)	(1,0)
Intersection of line with Y-axis	(0,1)	(0,2)
Region	Non-origin side	Non-origin side

Shaded portion XABCY is the feasible region, whose vertices are $A(3,0), B$ and $C(0,2)$ B is the point of intersection of the lines $2x + y = 2$ and $x + 3y = 3$

$\therefore B \equiv \left(\dfrac{3}{5}, \dfrac{4}{5}\right)$

Here, the objective function is

$Z = x + 4y$

$\therefore Z$ at $A(3,0) = 3 + 4(0)$

$= 3$

Z at $B\left(\dfrac{3}{5}, \dfrac{4}{5}\right) = \dfrac{3}{5} + 4\left(\dfrac{4}{5}\right)$

$= \dfrac{19}{5}$

$= 3 \times 8$

Z at $C(0,2) = 0 + 4(2) = 8$

$\therefore Z$ has minimum value 3 at $x = 3$ and $y = 0$.

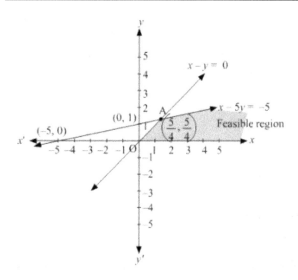

Hence, the correct option is (A).

47.

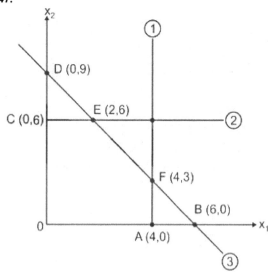

$Z_{max} = 3x_1 + 2x_2$

Subjected to:

$x_1 \leq 4$ ..... (i)

$x_2 \leq 6$ ... (ii)

$3x_1 + 2x_2 \leq 18$ ... (iii)

and $x_1, x_2 \geq 0$

Now the intersections of the lines are denoted by E, F

For $E, 3x_1 + 2x_2 = 18$

$x_2 = 6$

So,

$3x_1 + (2 \times 6) = 18$

$x_1 = 2$

$E(2,6)$

$x_1 = 4$

$(3 \times 4) + 2x_2 = 18$

$x_2 = 3$

$F(4,3)$

So the feasible points are $(0,0), (4,0), (4,3), (2,6), (0,6)$

$Z(0,0) = 0$

$Z(4,0) = 12$

$Z(4,3) = (3 \times 4) + (2 \times 3) = 18$

$Z(2,6) = (3 \times 2) + (2 \times 6) = 18$

$Z(0,6) = 12$

So the objective function has multiple solution.

Hence, the correct option is (D).

48. Given,

$\left(\cos\frac{\pi}{16} + i\sin\frac{\pi}{16}\right)^8$

As we know that,

$e^{i\cdot\theta} = \cos\theta + i\sin\theta$

$\Rightarrow \left(\cos\frac{\pi}{16} + i\sin\frac{\pi}{16}\right)^a = \left[e^{\frac{i\cdot\pi}{16}}\right]^8 = e^{\frac{i\cdot\pi}{2}}$

$\Rightarrow e^{\frac{i\cdot\pi}{2}} = \cos\frac{\pi}{2} + i\sin\frac{\pi}{2} = i$

Hence, the correct option is (C).

49. Given,

$4 + 3i$

Comparing with standard form $a + bi$, we get

$a = 4, b = 3$

$\Rightarrow \sqrt{a + ib} = \pm\left(\sqrt{\frac{\sqrt{a^2+b^2}+a}{2}} + i\sqrt{\frac{\sqrt{a^2+b^2}-a}{2}}\right)$

$\Rightarrow \sqrt{4 + 3i} = \pm\left(\sqrt{\frac{\sqrt{4^2+3^2}+4}{2}} + i\sqrt{\frac{\sqrt{4^2+3^2}-4}{2}}\right)$

$\Rightarrow \pm\left(\sqrt{\frac{\sqrt{25}+4}{2}} + i\sqrt{\frac{\sqrt{25}-4}{2}}\right)$

$\therefore \sqrt{4 + 3i} = \pm\left(\frac{3}{\sqrt{2}} + i\frac{1}{\sqrt{2}}\right)$

Hence, the correct option is (D).

50. Given,

$2 + \cos\theta + i\sin\theta = \frac{3}{z}$ .....(1)

$\Rightarrow 2 + \cos\theta - i\sin\theta = \frac{3}{\bar{z}}$ ...(2)

Adding (1) and (2) we get,

$4 + 2\cos\theta = \frac{3}{z} + \frac{3}{\bar{z}}$ ....(3)

Also, $|2 + \cos\theta + i\sin\theta|^2 = \left|\frac{3}{z}\right|^2$

$\Rightarrow (2 + \cos\theta)^2 + \sin^2\theta = \frac{9}{|z|^2}$

$\Rightarrow 4 + 4\cos\theta + \cos^2\theta + \sin^2\theta = \frac{9}{|z|^2}$

$\Rightarrow 5 + 4\cos\theta = \frac{9}{|z|^2}$ ...(4)

Multiplying equation (3) by 2 and subtracting from (4), we get:

$-3 = \frac{9}{|z|^2} - 6\left(\frac{1}{z} + \frac{1}{\bar{z}}\right)$

$\Rightarrow -3 = \frac{9}{|z|^2} - 6\left(\frac{z+\bar{z}}{z\bar{z}}\right)$

$\Rightarrow -3 = \frac{9}{|z|^2} - 6\left(\frac{z+\bar{z}}{|z|^2}\right)$

$\Rightarrow -3|z|^2 = 9 - 6(z + \bar{z})$

$\Rightarrow 2(z + \bar{z}) - |z|^2 = 3$

$\therefore 2(z + \bar{z}) - |z|^2$ is equal to 3.

Hence, the correct option is (A).

Mathematics : Mock Test 10

Q.1 If $^{2n}C_3 : {}^nC_3 = 17:2$, find n.
A. 50   B. 26   C. 24   D. 52

Q.2 A box contains 20 electric bulbs, out of which 4 are defective. Two bulbs are chosen at random from this box. The probability that at least one of these is defective is:
A. $\frac{7}{19}$ B. $\frac{6}{19}$ C. $\frac{5}{19}$ D. $\frac{4}{19}$

Q.3 If $A = \begin{bmatrix} 4 & -3 \\ 1 & 0 \end{bmatrix}$ then $A + A^T$ is equal to:
A. $\begin{bmatrix} 4 & -2 \\ -3 & 0 \end{bmatrix}$ B. $\begin{bmatrix} 8 & -2 \\ -3 & 0 \end{bmatrix}$
C. $\begin{bmatrix} 8 & -2 \\ -2 & 0 \end{bmatrix}$ D. $\begin{bmatrix} 8 & -2 \\ -2 & 3 \end{bmatrix}$

Q.4 Consider the following statements in respect of the matrix
$A = \begin{bmatrix} 0 & 1 & 2 \\ -1 & 0 & -3 \\ -2 & 3 & 0 \end{bmatrix}$

1) The matrix A is skew-symmetric.
2) The matrix A is symmetric.
3) The matrix A is invertible.

Which of the above statements is/are correct?
A. 1 only   B. 3 only   C. 1 and 3   D. 2 and 3

Q.5 If $A = \begin{bmatrix} 4 & x+2 \\ 2x-3 & x+1 \end{bmatrix}$ is symmetric, then x is equal to:
A. 2   B. 3   C. -1   D. 5

Q.6 Find the angle between the line $\vec{r} = (\hat{i} + 2\hat{j} - \hat{k}) + \lambda(\hat{i} - \hat{j} + \hat{k})$ and the plane $\vec{r} \cdot (2\hat{i} - \hat{j} + \hat{k}) = 6$?
A. $\sin^{-1}\left(\frac{2\sqrt{2}}{3}\right)$ B. $\sin^{-1}\left(\frac{\sqrt{2}}{3}\right)$
C. $\cos^{-1}\left(\frac{2}{3}\right)$ D. $\sin^{-1}\left(\frac{1}{3}\right)$

Q.7 The differential equation representing the family of curves $y = a\sin(\lambda x + a)$ is:
A. $\frac{d^2y}{dx^2} + \lambda^2 y = 0$ B. $\frac{d^2y}{dx^2} - \lambda^2 y = 0$
C. $\frac{d^2y}{dx^2} + \lambda y = 0$ D. None of these

Q.8 The solution of $x^2 \frac{dy}{dx} = x^2 + xy + y^2$ will be:
A. $\log x = \tan^{-1}\frac{y}{x} + c$
B. $\log x = \tan^{-1}\frac{x}{y} + c$
C. $\log y = \tan^{-1}\frac{x}{y} + c$
D. $\log y = \tan^{-1}\frac{y}{x} + c$

Q.9 Solve: $x\frac{dy}{dx} - y = x^2$ for $y(2)$, given $y(1) = 1$
A. 1   B. 2   C. 3   D. 4

Q.10 Find the value of coefficient for the given data:

Marks (more than)	0	10	20	30	40	50	60
No. of students	200	180	150	100	40	15	5

A. 0.39   B. 0.49   C. 0.89   D. 0.93

Q.11 The area under the curve $y = x^4$ and the lines $x = 1, x = 5$ and x-axis is:
A. $\frac{3124}{3}$ sq. units   B. $\frac{3124}{7}$ sq. units
C. $\frac{3124}{5}$ sq. units   D. $\frac{3124}{9}$ sq. units

Q.12 The area under the curve $y = x^2$ and the lines $x = -1, x = 2$ and x-axis is:
A. 3 sq. units   B. 5 sq. units
C. 7 sq. units   D. 9 sq. units

Q.13 The area of the region bounded by the curves $y = x^2$ and $y = 2x + 3$ equals:
A. $\frac{9}{2}$ sq. unit   B. $\frac{32}{3}$ sq. units
C. $\frac{13}{2}$ sq. units   D. $\frac{16}{3}$ sq. units

Q.14 If (x) is an odd periodic function with period 2, then f(4) equal to:
[BITSAT, 2014]
A. -4   B. 4   C. 2   D. 0

Q.15 What is the modulus in $\frac{\sqrt{2}+i}{\sqrt{2}-i}$ where $i = \sqrt{-1}$?
A. 3   B. $\frac{1}{2}$
C. 1   D. None of the above

Q.16 Consider the following Linear Programming Problem (LPP).
Maximise $Z = x_1 + 2x_2$
Subject to:
$x_1 \leq 2$
$x_2 \leq 2$
$x_1 + x_2 \leq 2$
$x_1, x_2 \geq 0$ (i.e. +ve decision variables)
What is the optimal solution to the above LPP?
A. 2,2   B. 0,2   C. 2,0   D. 0,0

Q.17 In an Linear programming problem, the restrictions or limitations under which the objective function is to be optimised are called_____.
A. Constraints   B. Objective function
C. Decision variables   D. None of the above

Mathematics : Mock Test - 10

Q.18 While solving a linear programming model, if a redundant constraint is added, then what will be its effect on existing solution?
A. There will be no effect
B. The solution space will get further constrained
C. The solution space becomes concave
D. The problem no longer remains solvable

Q.19 If $A(-4,2), B(1,-3)$ and $C(-5,1)$ are three points, find the angle between BA and BC.
A. $\theta = \tan^{-1}\left(\frac{4}{11}\right)$
B. $\theta = \tan^{-1}\left(\frac{(-1)}{5}\right)$
C. $\theta = \tan^{-1}\left(\frac{1}{11}\right)$
D. $\theta = \tan^{-1}\left(\frac{5}{11}\right)$

Q.20 If the straight lines $2x + 3y - 3 = 0$ and $x + ky + 7 = 0$ are perpendicular, then the value of k is:
A. $\frac{-3}{2}$
B. $\frac{-2}{3}$
C. $\frac{3}{2}$
D. $\frac{-1}{3}$

Q.21 Find the derivative of $x^{\sin x}$ with respect to x?
A. $\frac{(\sin x - x \times \cos x \times \log x)}{x}$
B. $\frac{(\sin x + x \times \cos x \times \log x)}{x}$
C. $\frac{x^{\sin x}(\sin x + x \times \cos x \times \log x)}{x}$
D. $\frac{x^{\sin x}(\sin x - x \times \cos x \times \log x)}{x}$

Q.22 Find the values of k so the line $\frac{2x-2}{2k} = \frac{4-y}{3} = \frac{z+2}{-1}$ and $\frac{x-5}{1} = \frac{y}{k} = \frac{z+6}{4}$ are at right angles
A. 0
B. -2
C. 2
D. 1

Q.23 Let $X \in \{0,1\}$ and $Y \in \{0,1\}$ be two independent binary random variables. If $P(X = 0) = p$ and $P(Y = 0) = q$, then $P(X + Y) \geq 1$ is equal to:
A. $pq + (1-p)(1-q)$
B. pq
C. $p(1-q)$
D. $1 - pq$

Q.24 Let X and Y be two Gaussian random variables with mean $\mu_x = 6, \mu_y = -2$ and variable $\sigma_x = \sigma_y = 4$ respectively. The respected value of XY is $E[XY] = -22$. If a random variable is defined as $Z = X + 3Y$, what will be the probability density function of Z?
A. $\frac{1}{\sqrt{200\pi}} e^{\frac{-z^2}{200}}$
B. $\frac{1}{\sqrt{200\pi}} e^{\frac{z^2}{200}}$
C. $\frac{1}{\sqrt{2\pi}} e^{\frac{-z^2}{2}}$
D. $\frac{1}{\sqrt{2\pi}} e^{\frac{z^2}{2}}$

Q.25 When $0° \leq \theta \leq 90°$, then solution of $\cos^2\theta + \sin\theta - 2 = 0$ is:
A. $\theta = 30°$
B. $\theta = 60°$ or $45°$
C. $\theta = 45°$ or $90°$
D. $\theta = 60°$ or $90°$

Q.26 The cross product of two parallel vectors is:
A. 0
B. 1
C. Parallel
D. Perpendicular

Q.27 What is the value of λ for which the vectors $2\hat{i} - 5\hat{j} - \hat{k}$ and $-\hat{i} + 4\hat{j} + \lambda\hat{k}$ are perpendicular?
A. 21
B. -18
C. -22
D. 22

Q.28 If $\sin^{-1}x - \cos^{-1}x = \frac{\pi}{6}$. Find the value of x.
A. $\frac{1}{2}$
B. $\frac{\sqrt{3}}{2}$
C. $-\frac{1}{2}$
D. $-\frac{\sqrt{3}}{2}$

Q.29 Find the value of $\cosec(\sin^{-1}\cos\sin^{-1}x + \cos^{-1}\sin\cos^{-1}x)$.
A. $\sqrt{2}$
B. $\frac{2}{\sqrt{3}}$
C. 1
D. 2

Q.30 If $\tan\beta = \cos\theta \cdot \tan\alpha$, then find the value of $\tan^2\left(\frac{\theta}{2}\right)$.
A. $\frac{\sin(\alpha+\beta)}{\sin(\alpha-\beta)}$
B. $\frac{\cos(\alpha-\beta)}{\cos(\alpha+\beta)}$
C. $\frac{\sin(\alpha-\beta)}{\sin(\alpha+\beta)}$
D. $\frac{\cos(\alpha+\beta)}{\cos(\alpha-\beta)}$

Q.31 If $f(x) = \frac{\sin(e^{x-2}-1)}{\log(x-1)}, x \neq 2$ and $f(x) = k$ For $x = 2$, then value of k for which f is continuous is:
A. -2
B. -1
C. 0
D. 1

Q.32 Differentiate $2x\sin x^2$ with respect to x^2.
A. $\frac{\sin x^2 + 2x\cos x^2}{x}$
B. $\frac{\sin x^2}{x} + 2x\cos x^2$
C. $2\sin x^2 + 4x^2\cos x^2$
D. $\frac{\sin x^2}{x} - \cos x^2$

Q.33 The derivative of $\log_{10} x$ with respect to x^2 is:
A. $\frac{1}{2x^2}\log_e 10$
B. $\frac{2}{x^2}\log_{10} e$
C. $\frac{1}{2x^2}\log_{10} e$
D. None of these

Q.34 If $y = \left(x + \sqrt{1+x^2}\right)^n$, then $(1+x^2)\frac{d^2y}{dx^2} + x\frac{dy}{dx}$
A. n^2y
B. $-n^2y$
C. $-y$
D. $2x^2y$

Q.35 Which of the following equation has y = c_1e^x + c_2e^{-x} as the general solution ?
A. $\frac{d^2y}{dx^2} + y = 0$
B. $\frac{d^2y}{dx^2} - y = 0$
C. $\frac{d^2y}{dx^2} + 1 = 0$
D. $\frac{d^2y}{dx^2} - 1 = 0$

Q.36 Find the value of x for which $y = [x(x-2)]^2$ is an increasing function:
A. $0 < x < 1$
B. $x > 2$
C. Both A and B
D. Neither A nor B

Q.37 What is the value of $\lim_{x \to 0} \frac{(1-\cos 2x)^2}{x^4}$?
A. 1
B. 8
C. 4
D. 0

Q.38 The equation of a plane containing the line of intersection of the planes $2x - y - 4 = 0$ and $y + 2z - 4 = 0$ and passing through the point $(1,1,0)$ is:
A. $x - 3y - 2z = -2$
B. $2x - z = 2$

C. $x - y - z = 0$
D. $x + 3y + z = 4$

Q.39 The coefficient of x^n in the expansion of $\left(\frac{1+x}{1-x}\right)^2$, is:

A. $^{n+1}C_n + {^nC_{n-1}} + {^{n-1}C_{n-2}}$
B. $^{n+1}C_n + 2^n C_{n-1} + {^{n-1}C_{n-2}}$
C. $^{n+1}C_n + {^{n+2}C_{n-1}} + {^{n+3}C_{n-2}}$
D. $^{n+1}C_n + 2 \times {^nC_{n-1}} + {^{n-1}C_{n-2}}$

Q.40 In a Binomial Distribution (BD) the mean is 15 and variance is 10, then parameter n (number of trials) is

A. 28 B. 16 C. 45 D. 25

Q.41 Let x denote the number of times heads occur in n tosses of a fair coin, If $P(x = 4)$, $P(x = 5)$ and $P(x = 6)$ are in AP, then the value of n is:

A. 7 B. 10 C. 12 D. 15

Q.42 Find $a + 3b$ if $\int (x^2 - 1) dx = \frac{x^3}{a} + bx + C$ where C is integration constant?

A. 2
B. 0
C. 1
D. None of the above

Q.43 $\int \frac{dx}{1+x+x^2+x^3}$ is equal to:

A. $\frac{1}{2}\left[\log\frac{(x+1)^2}{x^2+1} + \tan^{-1}x\right]$
B. $\frac{1}{4}\left[\log\frac{(x+1)^2}{x^2+1} + 2\tan^{-1}x\right]$
C. $\frac{1}{2}\left[\log\frac{(x+1)^2}{x^2+1} - 2\tan^{-1}x\right]$
D. None of these

Q.44 $\int \frac{1}{(x+1)\sqrt{1-2x-x^2}} dx$ is equal to:

A. $\sqrt{2}\cosh^{-1}\left(\frac{\sqrt{2}}{1+x}\right)$
B. $\frac{1}{\sqrt{2}}\cosh^{-1}\left(\frac{\sqrt{2}}{1+x}\right)$
C. $-\sqrt{2}\cosh^{-1}\left(\frac{\sqrt{2}}{1+x}\right)$
D. $\frac{-1}{\sqrt{2}}\cosh^{-1}\left(\frac{\sqrt{2}}{1+x}\right)$

Q.45 The value of the integral $\int_0^{\frac{\pi}{2}} \frac{\sqrt{\tan x}}{1+\sqrt{\tan x}} dx$ is:

A. $\frac{\pi}{2}$
B. $\frac{\pi}{4}$
C. $\frac{\pi}{6}$
D. None of these

Q.46 What is $\int_{-\frac{\pi}{6}}^{\frac{\pi}{6}} \frac{\sin^5 x \cos^3 x}{x^4} dx$ equal to?

A. $\frac{\pi}{2}$ B. $\frac{\pi}{4}$ C. $\frac{\pi}{8}$ D. 0

Q.47 Evaluate $\int_0^{\frac{\pi}{2}} \log \cot x \, dx$?

A. 0 B. 1 C. $\frac{\pi}{4}$ D. -1

Q.48 Which one of the following predicate formulae is NOT logically valid?
Note that W is a predicate formula without any free occurrence of x.

A. ∀x(p(x) ∨ W) ≡ ∀x p(x) ∨ W
B. ∃x(p(x) ∧ W) ≡ ∃x p(x) ∧ W
C. ∀x(p(x) → W) ≡ ∀x p(x) → W
D. ∃x(p(x) → W) ≡ ∀x p(x) → W

Q.49 Consider the first order predicate formula φ:
∀x [(∀z z|x ⇒ z = x) ∨ (z = 1) ⇒ ∃w (w > x) ∧ (∀z z|w ⇒ w = z) ∨ (z = 1)]
Here 'a|b' denotes that 'a divides b', where a and b are integers.
Consider the following sets:
S1. {1,2,3, ... , 100}
S2. Set of all positive integers
S3. Set of all integers
Which of the above sets satisfy φ?

A. S1 and S2
B. S1 and S3
C. S2 and S3
D. S1, S2 and S3

Q.50 Find the equation of circle with center at $(2,5)$ and radius 5 units.

A. $x^2 + y^2 + 4x - 10y + 4 = 0$
B. $x^2 + y^2 - 4x - 10y + 4 = 0$
C. $x^2 + y^2 + 4x + 10y + 4 = 0$
D. $x^2 + y^2 + 4x - 10y - 4 = 0$

Mathematics : Mock Test - 10

// Smart Answer Sheet //

Correct Indicates percentage of students who answered questions correctly.

Skipped Indicates percentage of students who skipped questions.

Q.	Ans.	Correct / Skipped	Q.	Ans.	Correct / Skipped	Q.	Ans.	Correct / Skipped	Q.	Ans.	Correct / Skipped	Q.	Ans.	Correct / Skipped
1	B	22.98 % / 3.49 %	11	C	42.68 % / 1.76 %	21	C	19.43 % / 4.82 %	31	D	69.46 % / 1.93 %	41	A	18.69 % / 3.1 %
2	A	29.0 % / 3.51 %	12	A	66.01 % / 1.93 %	22	B	14.06 % / 4.31 %	32	B	55.0 % / 1.93 %	42	B	43.73 % / 1.85 %
3	C	87.13 % / 0.0 %	13	B	47.88 % / 1.6 %	23	D	84.44 % / 0.0 %	33	C	51.53 % / 1.98 %	43	B	22.03 % / 3.06 %
4	A	44.29 % / 1.08 %	14	D	13.65 % / 3.4 %	24	A	21.59 % / 3.83 %	34	A	48.54 % / 1.58 %	44	D	57.4 % / 1.71 %
5	D	89.39 % / 0.0 %	15	C	50.07 % / 1.48 %	25	A	40.77 % / 1.47 %	35	B	41.31 % / 1.68 %	45	B	65.9 % / 1.62 %
6	A	54.08 % / 1.88 %	16	B	18.68 % / 3.38 %	26	A	47.26 % / 1.68 %	36	C	20.88 % / 4.57 %	46	D	79.54 % / 0.0 %
7	A	65.91 % / 1.13 %	17	A	77.51 % / 0.0 %	27	C	40.74 % / 1.11 %	37	C	83.5 % / 0.0 %	47	A	88.09 % / 0.0 %
8	A	59.69 % / 1.93 %	18	A	62.93 % / 1.93 %	28	B	46.66 % / 1.06 %	38	C	26.61 % / 3.61 %	48	C	64.89 % / 1.5 %
9	D	21.13 % / 4.73 %	19	B	29.87 % / 3.03 %	29	C	60.43 % / 1.64 %	39	D	48.02 % / 1.64 %	49	C	42.91 % / 1.73 %
10	A	86.12 % / 0.0 %	20	B	46.93 % / 1.79 %	30	C	12.63 % / 4.94 %	40	C	50.58 % / 1.67 %	50	B	81.19 % / 0.0 %

Performance Analysis	
Avg. Score (%)	50.0%
Toppers Score (%)	58.0%
Your Score	

Mathematics : Mock Test - 10

//Hints and Solutions//

1. We know that:

$$^nC_r = \frac{n \times (n-1) \times \ldots \times (n-r+1)}{r!}$$

Given,

$$^{2n}C_3 : ^nC_3 = 17 : 2$$

$$\Rightarrow \frac{2n(2n-1)(2n-2)}{3!} : \frac{n(n-1)(n-2)}{3!} = 17 : 2$$

$$\Rightarrow \frac{2n(2n-1)(2n-2)}{n(n-1)(n-2)} = \frac{17}{2}$$

$$\Rightarrow \frac{4(n-1)(2n-1)}{(n-1)(n-2)} = \frac{17}{2}$$

$$\Rightarrow \frac{4(2n-1)}{(n-2)} = \frac{17}{2}$$

$$\Rightarrow 2 \times 4(2n-1) = 17 \times (n-2)$$

$$\Rightarrow 16n - 8 = 17n - 34$$

$$\Rightarrow n = 26$$

Hence, the correct option is (B).

2. We know that maximum portability is 1.

So we can get the total probability of non-defective bulbs and subtract it from 1 to get the total probability of defective bulbs.

Total cases of non defective bulbs $= (^{16}C_2)$

As we know,

$$^nC_r = \frac{n!}{r!(n-r)!}$$

$$= \frac{16 \times 15}{2 \times 1}$$

$$= 120$$

Total cases $= ^{20}C_2$

$$= \frac{20 \times 19}{2 \times 1}$$

$$= 190$$

Total probability of non-defective bulbs $= \frac{120}{190}$

$$= \frac{12}{19}$$

The probability that at least one of these is defective $= 1 - \frac{12}{19}$

$$= \frac{7}{19}$$

Hence, the correct option is (A).

3. Given,

$$A = \begin{bmatrix} 4 & -3 \\ 1 & 0 \end{bmatrix}$$

As we know,
If the transpose of matrix is equal to it, the matrix is known as symmetric matrix.
If the transpose of matrix is equal to the negative of itself, the matrix is said to be skew symmetric matrix.
If the determinant of a square matrix $n \times n$ is zero, then A is not invertible.
Here, transpose of A is negative of A, so matrix A is a skew symmetric matrix.

The transpose of a matrix A is given by, $A^T = \begin{bmatrix} 4 & 1 \\ -3 & 0 \end{bmatrix}$

Now,

$$A = \begin{bmatrix} 4 & -3 \\ 1 & 0 \end{bmatrix}$$

$$A + A^T = \begin{bmatrix} 4 & -3 \\ 1 & 0 \end{bmatrix} + \begin{bmatrix} 4 & 1 \\ -3 & 0 \end{bmatrix}$$

$$= \begin{bmatrix} 4+4 & -3+1 \\ 1+(-3) & 0+0 \end{bmatrix}$$

$$= \begin{bmatrix} 8 & -2 \\ -2 & 0 \end{bmatrix}$$

Hence, the correct option is (C).

4. Given,

$$A = \begin{bmatrix} 0 & 1 & 2 \\ -1 & 0 & -3 \\ -2 & 3 & 0 \end{bmatrix}$$

The transpose of matrix A is given by,

$$A^T = \begin{bmatrix} 0 & -1 & -2 \\ 1 & 0 & 3 \\ 2 & -3 & 0 \end{bmatrix}$$

As we know,
If the transpose of matrix is equal to it, the matrix is known as symmetric matrix.
If the transpose of matrix is equal to the negative of itself, the matrix is said to be skew symmetric matrix.
If the determinant of a square matrix $n \times n$ is zero, then A is not invertible.
Here, transpose of A is negative of A, so matrix A is a skew symmetric matrix.

$$A = \begin{bmatrix} 0 & 1 & 2 \\ -1 & 0 & -3 \\ -2 & 3 & 0 \end{bmatrix}$$

$$\text{Det } A = 0 - 1(0-6) + 2(-3-0)$$

$$= 6 - 6$$

$$= 0$$

So, The matrix A is skew-symmetric.
Hence, the correct option is (A).

5. Given,

$$A = \begin{bmatrix} 4 & x+2 \\ 2x-3 & x+1 \end{bmatrix}$$

A real square matrix $A = (a_{ij})$ is said to be symmetric, if $A = A^T$
Where A^T = transpose of matrix A

$$A^T = \begin{bmatrix} 4 & 2x-3 \\ x+2 & x+1 \end{bmatrix}$$

$$\therefore A = A^T$$

$$\Rightarrow \begin{bmatrix} 4 & x+2 \\ 2x-3 & x+1 \end{bmatrix} = \begin{bmatrix} 4 & 2x-3 \\ x+2 & x+1 \end{bmatrix}$$

On comparing elements of both matrix, we get

$x + 2 = 2x - 3$

$\Rightarrow 2 + 3 = 2x - x$

$\therefore x = 5$

Hence, the correct option is (D).

6. Given:

Equation of line $\vec{r} = (\hat{i} + 2\hat{j} - \hat{k}) + \lambda(\hat{i} - \hat{j} + \hat{k})$ and equation of plane $\vec{r} \cdot (2\hat{i} - \hat{j} + \hat{k}) = 6$

Here, we have to find the angle between the given line and the plane.

As we know that, if θ is the angle between the line $\vec{r} = \vec{a} + \lambda \vec{b}$ and the plane $\vec{r} \cdot \vec{n} = q$ is given by $\sin\theta = \frac{\vec{b} \cdot \vec{n}}{|\vec{b}||\vec{n}|}$

Here, $\vec{b} = \hat{i} - \hat{j} + \hat{k}$ and $\vec{n} = 2\hat{i} - \hat{j} + \hat{k}$

$\Rightarrow \vec{b} \cdot \vec{n} = 2 + 1 + 1 = 4$

$|\vec{b}| = \sqrt{1^2 + (-1)^2 + 1^2} = \sqrt{3}$ and $|\vec{n}| = \sqrt{2^2 + (-1)^2 + (1)^2} = \sqrt{6}$

By substituting the above-given values in $\sin\theta = \frac{\vec{b} \cdot \vec{n}}{|\vec{b}||\vec{n}|}$, we get

$\Rightarrow \sin\theta = \frac{4}{\sqrt{3} \times \sqrt{6}} = \frac{2\sqrt{2}}{3}$

$\Rightarrow \theta = \sin^{-1}\left(\frac{2\sqrt{2}}{3}\right)$

Hence, the correct option is (A).

7. Given,

$y = a\sin(\lambda x + a) \ldots (i)$

Now,

Differentiating both sides of equation (i) we get,

$\Rightarrow \frac{dy}{dx} = a\cos(\lambda x + a) \times \frac{d}{dx}(\lambda x + \alpha)$

$\Rightarrow \frac{dy}{dx} = a\lambda \cos(\lambda x + \alpha)$

Again differentiating both sides we get,

$\frac{d^2y}{dx^2} = -a\lambda^2 \sin(\lambda x + a)$

From equation (i) we get,

$\frac{d^2y}{dx^4} = -\lambda^2 y$

$\therefore \frac{d^2y}{dx^2} + \lambda^2 y = 0$

Hence, the correct option is (A).

8. Given,

$x^2 \frac{dy}{dx} = x^2 + xy + y^2$

$\Rightarrow \frac{dy}{dx} = 1 + \frac{y}{x} + \left(\frac{y}{x}\right)^2 \ldots (i)$

Substituting, $\frac{y}{x} = v$

$\Rightarrow y = vx$

Then,

Differentiate W.r.t x, we get,

$\frac{dy}{dx} = v \times x\frac{dv}{dx} + x \times v\frac{d}{dx}$

$\Rightarrow \frac{dy}{dx} = v + x\frac{dv}{dx}$

Now, putting these values in eq (i),

We get,

$v + x\frac{dv}{dx} = 1 + v + v^2$

$\Rightarrow x\frac{dv}{dx} = 1 + v^2$

$\Rightarrow \frac{dx}{x} = \frac{dv}{1+v^2}$

On integrating both sides we get,

$\int \frac{dx}{x} = \int \frac{dv}{1+v^2}$

$\Rightarrow \log x = \tan^{-1} v + c, c =$ constant of integration

Putting the value of v we get,

$\therefore \log x = \tan^{-1}\frac{y}{x} + c$

Hence, the correct option is (A).

9. Given,

$y(1) = 1$

$x\frac{dy}{dx} - y = x^2$

$\Rightarrow \frac{dy}{dx} - \frac{y}{x} = x$

It is linear differential equation is of first order.

$IF = e^{\frac{-1}{x}dx}$

$\Rightarrow IF = e^{-\ln x}$

$\Rightarrow IF = \frac{1}{x}$

Now,

$y \times (IF) = \int Q(IF)dx$

$\Rightarrow y \times \frac{1}{x} = \int x \times \frac{1}{x} dx$

$\Rightarrow \frac{y}{x} = \int dx$

Integrating,

$\frac{y}{x} = x + c$ (where c is integration constant)

$\Rightarrow \frac{1}{1} = 1 + c$

$\Rightarrow c = 0$

$\frac{y}{x} = x$ Or $y = x^2$

For $y(2)$

$y = 2^2$

$\Rightarrow y = 4$

Hence, the correct option is (D).

10.

Marks (X)	Frequency (f)	Mid-Values (m)	fm	$\|d_{\bar{x}}\| = \|m - \bar{X}\| = \|m - 29.5\|$	$f \times \|d\bar{x}\| = f\|d_{\bar{x}}\|$
0 – 10	20	5	100	24.5	490
10 – 20	30	15	450	14.5	435
20 – 30	50	25	1250	4.5	225
30 – 40	60	35	2100	5.5	330
40 – 50	25	45	1125	15.5	387.5
50 – 60	10	55	550	25.5	255
60 – 70	5	65	325	35.5	177.5
	$\sum f = 200$		$\sum fm = 5900$		$\sum f\|d_{\bar{x}}\| = 2300$

Given,

$\sum fm = 5900$,

$\sum f = 200$,

$\sum f|d\bar{x}| = 2300$

Now,

Mean, $\bar{X} = \frac{\sum fm}{\sum f}$

$= \frac{5900}{200}$

$= 29.5$ marks

And,

Mean deviation (M.D. $_{\bar{x}}$) $= \frac{\sum f|d\bar{x}|}{\sum f}$

$= \frac{2300}{200}$

$= 11.5$ marks

So,

Coefficient of M. D. $= \frac{M.D._{\bar{x}}}{\bar{X}}$

$= \frac{11.5}{29.5}$

$= 0.39$

Hence, the correct option is (A).

11. The area under the function $y = f(x)$ from $x = a$ to $x = b$ and the x-axis is given by the definite integral

$\left|\int_a^b f(x)dx\right|$

This is for curves that are entirely on the same side of the x-axis in the given range.

If the curves are on both sides of the x-axis, then we calculate the areas of both sides separately and add them.

Definite integral: If $\int f(x)dx = g(x) + c$, then $\int_a^b f(x)dx = [g(x)]_a^b = g(b) - g(a)$.

$\int x^n dx = \frac{x^{n+1}}{n+1} + C$

$\int x^4 dx = \frac{x^5}{5} + C$

Using the above concept for area of a curve, we can say that the required area is:

Mathematics : Mock Test - 10

$I = \int_1^5 x^4 \, dx$

$= \left[\dfrac{x^5}{5}\right]_1^5$

$= \dfrac{5^5}{5} - \dfrac{1^5}{5}$

$= \dfrac{3125 - 1}{5}$

$= \dfrac{3124}{5}$ sq. units

Hence, the correct option is (C).

12. Concept:

The area under a Curve by Integration:

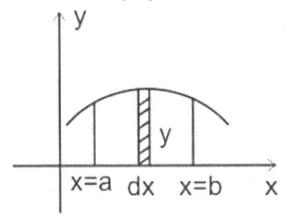

In this case, we find the area is the sum of the rectangles, heights $y = f(x)$ and width dx.

$\therefore$ Area $= \int_a^b y \, dx = \int_a^b f(x) \, dx$

Calculation:

Here, we have to find the area of the region bounded by the curves $y = x^2$, x-axis and ordinates $x = -1$ and $x = 2$

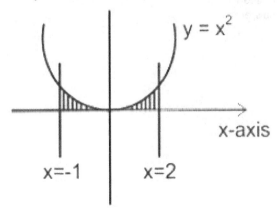

So, the area enclosed by the given curves is given by

$\int_{-1}^2 x^2 \, dx$

As we know that, $\int x^n dx = \dfrac{x^{n+1}}{n+1} + C$

Area $= \int_{-1}^2 x^2 \, dx$

$= \left[\dfrac{x^3}{3}\right]_{-1}^2$

$= \left[\dfrac{8}{3} - \dfrac{-1}{3}\right] = \dfrac{9}{3} = 3$

Area $= 3$ sq. units.

Hence, the correct option is (A).

13. Concept:

$\int x^n dx = \dfrac{x^{n+1}}{n+1} + C$

Calculation:

Equation of curve $\Rightarrow y = x^2$

Equation of line $\Rightarrow y = 2x + 3$

Line intersect the curve

$\therefore x^2 = 2x + 3$

$\Rightarrow x^2 - 2x - 3 = 0$

$\Rightarrow x^2 - 3x + x - 3 = 0$

$\Rightarrow x(x - 3) + 1(x - 3) = 0$

$\Rightarrow (x - 3)(x + 1) = 0$

$\Rightarrow x = 3; 1$

So the line cut the curve at $x = 3$ and $x = -1$

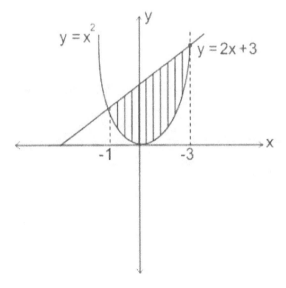

Now area of the region bounded by curve $=$ area below the line $-$ area below curve

∴ Area $= \int_{-1}^{3}(2x + 3 - x^2)$

$= \left[\frac{2x^2}{2} + 3x - \frac{x^3}{3}\right]_{-1}^{3} =$
$\left[3^2 + 3(3) - \frac{3^3}{3} - \left((-1)^2 - 3 - \left(\frac{-1}{3}\right)\right)\right]$

$= \left[9 + 9 - 9 - 1 + 3 - \frac{1}{3}\right]$

$= \left[8 + \frac{8}{3}\right]$

$= \frac{32}{3}$ sq. units

Hence, the correct option is (B).

14. Since f(x) is an odd periodic function with period 2.

∴ $f(-x) = -f(x)$ and $f(x + 2) = f(x)$

∴ $f(2) = f(0 + 2) = f(0)$

and $f(-2) = f(-2 + 2) = f(0)$

Now, $f(0) = f(-2) = -f(2) = -f(0)$

$\Rightarrow 2f(0) = 0$, i.e., $f(0) = 0$

∴ $f(4) = f(2 + 2) = f(2) = f(0) = 0$

Thus, $f(4) = 0$

Hence, the correct option is (D).

15. As we know,

If $z = x + iy$...(1) be any complex number, then its modulus is given by,

$|z| = \sqrt{x^2 + y^2}$

Let,

$z = \frac{\sqrt{2}+i}{\sqrt{2}-i}$

Multiplying by $(\sqrt{2} + i)$ in numerator and denominator, we get

$z = \frac{\sqrt{2}+i}{\sqrt{2}-i} \times \frac{\sqrt{2}+i}{\sqrt{2}+i}$

$\Rightarrow z = \frac{2+2\sqrt{2}i+i^2}{2-i^2}$

$\Rightarrow z = \frac{2+2\sqrt{2}i-1}{2-(-1)}$ [∵ $i^2 = -1$]

$\Rightarrow z = \frac{1+2\sqrt{2}i}{3}$

$\Rightarrow z = \frac{1}{3} + i\frac{2\sqrt{2}}{3}$...(2)

Comparing equation (1) and (2), we get

$x = \frac{1}{3}$ and $y = \frac{2\sqrt{2}}{3}$

As, $|z| = \sqrt{x^2 + y^2}$

∴ $|z| = \sqrt{\left(\frac{1}{3}\right)^2 + \left(\frac{2\sqrt{2}}{3}\right)^2}$

$\Rightarrow |z| = \sqrt{\frac{1}{9} + \frac{8}{9}}$

$\Rightarrow |z| = 1$

So, the modulus of $\frac{\sqrt{2}+i}{\sqrt{2}-i}$ is 1.

Hence, the correct option is (C).

16. Given

Objective function

Maximize, $Z = X_1 + 2X_2$

Constraints:

$X_1 \leq 2$ ......(1)

$X_2 \leq 2$ ......(2)

$X_1 + X_2 \leq 2$ ......(3)

Non neagative constarints

$X_1, X_2 \geq 0$

The above equations can be written as

$\frac{X_1}{2} \leq 1$ (4)

$\frac{X_2}{2} \leq 1$ (5)

$\frac{X_1}{2} + \frac{X_2}{2} \leq 1$ (6)

Plot the above equations on $X_1 - X_2$ graph and find out the solution space,

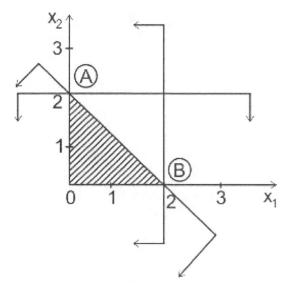

Now, find out the value of the objective function at every extreme point of solution space.

$Z_0 = 0 + 2 \times 0 = 0$

$Z_A = 0 + 2 \times 2 = 4$

$Z_B = 2 + 2 \times 0 = 2$

Since the value of the objective function is maximum at A. There $A(0,2)$ is the optimal solution.

Hence, the correct option is (B).

17. In an Linear programming problem, the restrictions or limitations under which the objective function is to be optimised are called Constraints.

Constraints:

- These are the restrictions on the variables of an linear programming problem are called as linear constraints.
- The final solution of the objective function must satisfy these constraints.

Hence, the correct option is (A).

18. While solving a linear programming model, if a redundant constraint is added, then there will be no effect on the existing solution.

Linear programming (LP) in industrial engineering is used for the optimization of our limited resources when there is a number of alternate solutions possible for the problem. The real-life problems can be written in the form of a linear equation by specifying the relation between its variables.

The general LP problem calls for optimizing a linear function for variables called the "objective function" subjected to a set of linear equations and inequalities called the constraints or restriction.

A redundant constraint is a constraint that can be removed from a system of linear constraints without changing the feasible region.

Hence, the correct option is (A).

19. To find the angle between two lines we have to find the slopes of the given points.

Slope of two points $= \dfrac{(y_2 - y_1)}{(x_2 - x_1)}$

Slope of $B(1, -3)$ $A(-4, 2)$:

$m_1 = \dfrac{(2-(-3))}{(-4-1)}$

$= \dfrac{(5)}{-5}$

$= -1$

Slope of $B(1, -3)$ $C(-5, 1)$:

$m_2 = \dfrac{(1-(-3))}{(-5-1)}$

$= \dfrac{(4)}{(-6)}$

$= -\dfrac{2}{3}$

Angle between two lines,

$\theta = \tan^{-1}\left|\dfrac{(m_1 - m_2)}{1 + m_1 m_2}\right|$

$= \tan^{-1}\left|\dfrac{\left(\frac{-1}{1} - \frac{-2}{3}\right)}{1 + \left(\frac{-1}{1}\right)\left(\frac{-2}{3}\right)}\right|$

$= \tan^{-1}\left|\dfrac{\frac{-1}{3}}{1 + \frac{2}{3}}\right|$

$= \tan^{-1}\left(-\dfrac{1}{5}\right)$

Hence, the correct option is (B).

20. Let the one line has slope m_1 and the second line has slope m_2.

If two straight lines are perpendicular then the multiplication of their slopes will be -1, that is $"m_1 m_2 = -1"$.

Compare both the given equation with the standard form, $y = mx + c$

The slope, m_1 for the line, $2x + 3y - 3 = 0$ is, $-\dfrac{2}{3}$

The slope, m_2 for the line, $x + ky + 7 = 0$ is, $-\dfrac{1}{k}$

As both the equations are perpendicular, so $m_1 m_2 = -1$

$\left(-\dfrac{2}{3}\right)\left(-\dfrac{1}{k}\right) = -1$

$\Rightarrow \dfrac{2}{3k} = -1$

$\Rightarrow k = -\frac{2}{3}$

Hence, the correct option is (B).

21. Derivative of $\log x$ with respect to x is $\frac{1}{x}$

Derivative of $\sin x$ with respect to x is $\cos x$

Product rule: $(uV)' = uV' + vu'$

Given function is $y = x^{\sin x}$

By taking log on both sides we get,

$\Rightarrow \log y = \sin x \times \log x$

We differentiate the function with respect to x

$\Rightarrow \frac{1}{y}\frac{dy}{dx} = \sin x \times (\log x)' + (\sin x)' \times \log x$

$\Rightarrow \frac{1}{y}\frac{dy}{dx} = \sin x \times \frac{1}{x} + \cos x \times \log x$

$\Rightarrow \frac{1}{y}\frac{dy}{dx} = \frac{\sin x + x \times \cos x \times \log x}{x}$

$\Rightarrow \frac{dy}{dx} = \frac{y(\sin x + x \times \cos x \times \log x)}{x}$

$\because y = x^{\sin x}$

$\Rightarrow \frac{dy}{dx} = \frac{x^{\sin x}(\sin x + x \times \cos x \times \log x)}{x}$

Hence, the correct option is (C).

22. Given lines are $\frac{2x-2}{2k} = \frac{4-y}{3} = \frac{z+2}{-1}$ and $\frac{x-5}{1} = \frac{y}{k} = \frac{z+6}{4}$

Write the above equation of a line in the standard form of lines

$\Rightarrow \frac{2(x-1)}{2k} = \frac{-(y-4)}{3} = \frac{z+2}{-1} \Leftrightarrow \frac{(x-1)}{k} = \frac{y-4}{-3} = \frac{z+2}{-1}$

So, the direction ratio of the first line is $(k, -3, -1)$

$\frac{x-5}{1} = \frac{y}{k} = \frac{z+6}{4}$

So, direction ratio of second line is $(1, k, 4)$

Lines are perpendicular,

$\therefore (k \times 1) + (-3 \times k) + (-1 \times 4) = 0$

$\Rightarrow k - 3k - 4 = 0$

$\Rightarrow -2k - 4 = 0$

$\therefore k = -2$

Hence, the correct option is (B).

23. Concept:

1) $P(X = 0) + P(X = 1) = 1$

2) If $Z = X + Y$, then $pdf(Z)$ = convolution of pdf (x) and pdf (y)

Application:

Given:

$P(X = 0) = p$

$\therefore P(X = 1) = 1 - p$

Also Given: $P(Y = 0) = q$

$\therefore P(Y = 1) = 1 - q$

$P(X+Y \geq 1) = P(X=0) \cdot P(Y=1) + P(X=1) \cdot P(Y=0) + P(X=1) \cdot P(Y=1)$

$= p \cdot (1-q) + (1-p) \cdot q + (1-p) \cdot (1-q) = 1 - pq$

Hence, the correct option is (D).

24. $\overline{X} = \mu_X = 6, \overline{Y} = \mu_y = -2$

The variance of the random variables is given as $\sigma_x = \sigma_y = 4$

The expected value is 22, i.e.

$E[XY] = \overline{XY} = -22$

Random variable is defined as $Z = X + 3Y$

Since X and Y are Gaussian random variables and Z is a linear combination of two, Z will be also a Gaussian random variable.

The mean of random variable Z is obtained as:

$\overline{Z} = \overline{X + 3Y} = \overline{X} + 3\overline{Y}$

$= 6 + 3 \times (-2)$

$= 0$

Again, the variance of Z is obtained as:

$\sigma_Z^2 = \overline{Z^2} - \overline{Z}^2 = \overline{Z^2}$

$= \overline{(X+3Y)^2} = \overline{X^2 + 9Y^2 + 6XY}$

$= \overline{X}^2 + 9\overline{Y}^2 + 6\overline{XY}$

$= \left(\sigma_X^2 + \overline{X}^2\right) + 9\left(\sigma_Y^2 + \overline{Y}^2\right) + 6\overline{XY}$

$= (16 + 36) + 9(16 + 4) + 6(-22) = 100$

Thus, the PDF of Z is given by:

$f_Z(Z) = \frac{1}{\sqrt{2\pi\sigma_Z^2}} e^{-\frac{(Z-m_Z)^2}{2\sigma_Z^2}}$

$= \frac{1}{\sqrt{200\pi}} e^{-\frac{(Z-0)^2}{2 \times 100}}$

$f_z(z) = \frac{1}{\sqrt{200\pi}} e^{\frac{-z^2}{e^{200}}}$

Hence, the correct option is (A).

25. Given:

$\cos^2\theta + \sin\theta - 2 = 0$

$\Rightarrow (1 - \sin^2\theta) + \sin\theta - 2 = 0$

$\Rightarrow -\sin^2\theta + \sin\theta - 1 = 0$

$\Rightarrow \sin^2\theta - \sin\theta + 1 = 0$

$Put x = \sin\theta$

Equation (1) becomes,

$\Rightarrow x^2 - x + 1 = 0$ which is of the type $ax^2 + bx + c = 0$

Its solution is given by $x = \frac{-b \pm \sqrt{b^2 - 4ac}}{2n}$

$\Rightarrow x = \frac{1 \pm \sqrt{(-1)^2 - 4(1)(1)}}{2(1)}$

$\Rightarrow x = \frac{1 \pm \sqrt{-3}}{2}$

$\Rightarrow x = \frac{1}{2} \pm i\frac{\sqrt{3}}{2}$ [$\because i^2 = -1$]

$\Rightarrow \sin\theta = \frac{1}{2} \pm i\frac{\sqrt{3}}{2}$

Comparinng real parts,

$\Rightarrow \sin\theta = \frac{1}{2}$

$\Rightarrow \theta = 30°$

When $0° \leq \theta \leq 90°$, then solution of $\cos^2\theta + \sin\theta - 2 = 0$ is $30°$.

Hence, the correct option is (A).

26. Let two vectors are $\vec{A}$ and $\vec{B}$.

As we know,

$\vec{A} \times \vec{B} = |A| \times |B| \times \sin\theta \times \hat{n}$

It two vectors are parallel then the angle between them must be $0°$.

$\vec{A} \times \vec{B} = |A| \times |B| \times \sin 0° \times \hat{n} = 0$

Hence, the correct option is (A).

27. Given,

$2\hat{i} - 5\hat{j} - \hat{k}$ and $-\hat{i} + 4\hat{j} + \lambda\hat{k}$ are perpendicular.

Let $\vec{a} = 2\hat{i} - 5\hat{j} - \hat{k}$ and $\vec{b} = -\hat{i} + 4\hat{j} + \lambda\hat{k}$

We know that,

If vectors $\vec{a}$ and $\vec{b}$ are perpendicular, then

$\vec{a} \cdot \vec{b} = 0$

$\Rightarrow (2\hat{i} - 5\hat{j} - \hat{k}) \cdot (-\hat{i} + 4\hat{j} + \lambda\hat{k}) = 0$

$\Rightarrow -2 - 20 - \lambda = 0$

$\Rightarrow -22 - \lambda = 0$

$\therefore \lambda = -22$

Hence, the correct option is (C).

28. Given,

$\sin^{-1}x - \cos^{-1}x = \frac{\pi}{6}$

As we know,

$\sin^{-1}x + \cos^{-1}x = \frac{\pi}{2}$

$\cos^{-1}x = \sin^{-1}x - \frac{\pi}{2}$

Then,

$\sin^{-1}x - \frac{\pi}{2} + \sin^{-1}x = \frac{\pi}{6}$

$2\sin^{-1}x = \frac{2\pi}{3}$

$\sin^{-1}x = \frac{\pi}{3}$

$x = \sin\frac{\pi}{3} = \frac{\sqrt{3}}{2}$

Hence, the correct option is (B).

29. Given,

$cosec(\sin^{-1}\cos\sin^{-1}x + \cos^{-1}\sin\cos^{-1}x)$

Let $y = \cos(\sin^{-1}x)$

Also

$\Rightarrow y = \sin(\cos^{-1}x)$

$= cosec(\sin^{-1}y + \cos^{-1}y)$

As we know,

$\sin^{-1}y + \cos^{-1}y = \frac{\pi}{2}$

$= cosec\frac{\pi}{2} = 1$

Hence, the correct option is (C).

30. Given,

$\tan\beta = \cos\theta \cdot \tan\alpha$

$\cos\theta = \frac{\tan\beta}{\tan\alpha}$ ....(i)

As we know that,

$$\cos\theta = \frac{1-\tan^2\frac{\theta}{2}}{1+\tan^2\frac{\theta}{2}} \ldots(ii)$$

From equation (i) and (ii), we get

$$\frac{1-\tan^2\frac{\theta}{2}}{1+\tan^2\frac{\theta}{2}} = \frac{\tan\beta}{\tan\alpha}$$

$$\tan\frac{2}{2} = \frac{\tan\alpha - \tan\beta}{\tan\alpha + \tan\beta}$$

$$= \frac{\sin\alpha\cos\beta - \cos\alpha\sin\beta}{\sin\alpha\cos\beta + \cos\alpha\sin\beta}$$

$$= \frac{\sin(\alpha-\beta)}{\sin(\alpha+\beta)}$$

Hence, the correct option is (C).

31. $\lim_{x\to 2} \frac{\sin(e^{x-2}-1)}{\log(x-1)}$

$= \lim_{h\to 0} \frac{\sin(e^h-1)}{\log(1+h)}$

On substituting $h = x - 2$

$= \lim_{h\to 0} \frac{\sin(e^h-1)}{e^h-1} \cdot \frac{e^h-1}{h} \cdot \frac{h}{\log(1+h)}$

$= 1 \cdot 1 \cdot 1$

$= 1$

Hence, the correct option is (D).

32. Let $f(x) = 2x\sin x^2$ and $g(x) = x^2$

$\frac{df(x)}{dx} = 2\sin x^2 + 2x\cos x^2 (2x)$

$\frac{df(x)}{dx} = 2\sin x^2 + 4x^2\cos x^2$

Also

$\frac{dg(x)}{dx} = 2x$

Now differentiation of $f(x)$ with respect to $g(x)$ is

$\frac{df(x)}{dg(x)} = \frac{\frac{df(x)}{dx}}{\frac{dg(x)}{dx}}$

$\frac{df(x)}{dg(x)} = \frac{2\sin x^2 + 4x^2\cos x^2}{2x}$

$\frac{df(x)}{dg(x)} = \frac{\sin x^2}{x} + 2x\cos x^2$

Hence, the correct option is (B).

33. Let $u = \log_{10} x$ and $v = x^2$

Then,

$\Rightarrow \frac{du}{dx} = \frac{d}{dx}\log_{10} x$

$\frac{du}{dx} = \frac{1}{x\log_e 10} \left[\because \frac{d}{dx}\log_a x = \frac{1}{x\log_e a}\right]$

$\Rightarrow \frac{dv}{dx} = \frac{d}{dx}x^2$

$\frac{dv}{dx} = 2x$

$\therefore \frac{du}{dv} = \frac{\frac{du}{dx}}{\frac{dv}{dx}}$

$\Rightarrow \frac{du}{dv} = \frac{\frac{1}{x\log_e 10}}{2x}$

$\Rightarrow \frac{du}{dv} = \frac{1}{2x^2}\log_{10} e$

Hence, the correct option is (C).

34. Given:

$y = \left(x + \sqrt{1+x^2}\right)^n$

$\Rightarrow \frac{dy}{dx} = n\left(x + \sqrt{1+x^2}\right)^{n-1} \left(1 + \frac{1}{2}(1+x^2)^{-1/2} \cdot 2x\right)$

$\Rightarrow \frac{dy}{dx} = n\left(x + \sqrt{1+x^2}\right)^{n-1} \frac{(\sqrt{1+x^2}+x)}{\sqrt{1+x^2}}$

$\Rightarrow \frac{dy}{dx} = \frac{n\left(\sqrt{1+x^2}+x\right)^n}{\sqrt{1+x^2}}$

or,

$\Rightarrow \sqrt{1+x^2}\frac{dy}{dx} = ny$

or,

$\Rightarrow \sqrt{1+x^2}y_1 = ny,$ let $\left(y_1 = \frac{dy}{dx}\right)$

Squaring both side,

$\Rightarrow (1+x^2)y_1^2 = n^2 y^2$

Differentiating both side,

$\Rightarrow (1+x^2)2y_1 y_2 + y_1^2 \cdot 2x = n^2 \cdot 2yy_1,$ $\left(y_2 = \frac{dy_1}{dx}\right)$

or,

$\Rightarrow (1+x^2)y_2 + xy_1 = n^2 y$

Hence, the correct option is (A).

35. Given:

$y = c_1 e^x + c_2 e^{-x}$

Differentiating with respect to x,

$\frac{dy}{dx} = c_1 e^x - c_2 e^{-x}$

Again, Differentiating with respect to x, we get

$\frac{d^2y}{dx^2} = c_1 e^x + c_2 e^{-x}$

$\frac{d^2y}{dx^2} = y$

$\frac{d^2y}{dx^2} - y = 0$

This is the required differential equation of the given equation of curve.

Hence, the correct option is (B).

36. Given:

$y = [x(x-2)]^2 = [x^2 - 2x]^2$

Diff. w.r.t. to x,

$\frac{dy}{dx} = y = 2(x^2 - 2x)(2x - 2) = 4x(x-2)(x-1)$

$\frac{dy}{dx} = 0$

$x = 0, x = 2$ and $x = 1$

The points $x = 0, x = 1$ and $x = 2$ divide the real line into four disjoint intervals i.e., $(-\infty, 0), (0,1), (1,2)(2, \infty)$

In intervals $(-\infty, 0)$ and $(1,2)$ $\frac{dy}{dx} < 0$: y is strictly decreasing in intervals $(-\infty, 0)$ and $(1,2)$ However, in intervals $(0,1)$ and $(2, \infty)$, $\frac{dy}{dx} > 0$

∴ y is strictly Increasing in intervals $(0,1)$ and $(2, \infty)$

∴ y is the strictly increasing intervals $0,2$

Hence, the correct option is (C).

37. Given:

$\lim_{x \to 0} \frac{(1-\cos 2x)^2}{x^4}$

We know that:

$1 - \cos 2\theta = 2\sin^2 \theta$

$\lim_{x \to 0} \frac{\sin x}{x} = 1$

$= \lim_{x \to 0} \frac{(2\sin^2 x)^2}{x^4}$

$= \lim_{x \to 0} \frac{4\sin^4 x}{x^4}$

$= \lim_{x \to 0} 4 \times \left(\frac{\sin x}{x}\right)^4$

$= 4 \times 1 = 4$

Hence, the correct option is (C).

38. Any plane passing through the intersection line of the two given planes be, $P_1 + \lambda P_2 = 0$

$(2x - y - 4) + \lambda(y + 2z - 4) = 0 \quad \ldots(1)$

It also passes through $(1,1,0)$

$(2 \times 1 - 1 - 4) + \lambda(1 + 0 - 4) = 0$

$-3 - 3\lambda = 0$

$\Rightarrow 1 + \lambda = 0$

$\Rightarrow \lambda = -1$

Substitute $\lambda = -1$ in equation (1)

$(2x - y - 4) - 1(y + 2z - 4) = 0$

$2x - y - 4 - y - 2z + 4 = 0$

$2x - 2y - 2z = 0$

Thus, the required equation of plane is $x - y - z = 0$

Hence, the correct option is (C).

39. The expression $\left(\frac{1+x}{1-x}\right)^2$ can be written as:

$= (1+x)^2 \times (1-x)^{-2}$

$= (1 + 2x + x^2)$
$(1 + {}^2C_1 x + {}^3C_2 x^2 + \ldots {}^{2+(n-1)}C_n x^n + \ldots)$

$= (1 + 2x + x^2)$
$(1 + {}^2C_1 x + {}^3C_2 x^2 + \ldots + {}^{n-1}C_{n-2}x^{n-2} + {}^nC_{n-1}x^{n-1} + {}^{n+1}C_n x^n + \ldots)$

x^n will be obtained by multiplying $(1$ and ${}^{n+1}C_n x^n)$ and $(2x$ and ${}^nC_{n-1}x^{n-1})$ and $(x^2$ and ${}^{n-1}C_{n-2}x^{n-2})$.

∴ Coefficient of x^n will be: $(1 \times {}^{n+1}C_n) + (2 \times {}^nC_{n-1}) + (1 \times {}^{n-1}C_{n-2})$

$= {}^{n+1}C_n + 2 \times {}^nC_{n-1} + {}^{n-1}C_{n-2}$

Hence, the correct option is (D).

40. Mean of the distribution $(\mu_x) = n \times p$

The variance $(\sigma_x^2) = n \times p \times (1-p)$

Standard deviation $(\sigma_x) = \sqrt{np(1-p)}$

Given:

mean of $BD = np = 15$

And variance of $BD = npq = 10$

$\Rightarrow np(1-p) = 10 \quad (\because p + q = 1)$

$\Rightarrow 1 - p \frac{10}{15} = \frac{2}{3}$

$\Rightarrow P = 1 - \frac{2}{3}$

$\Rightarrow p = \frac{1}{3}$

$\therefore n = \frac{15}{1/3}$

$= 15 \times 3 = 45$

Hence, the correct option is (C).

41. Clearly, x is a binomial variate with parameters n and $p = \frac{1}{2}$ such that

$P(x = r) = {}^nC_r p^r q^{n-r}$

$= {}^nC_r \left(\frac{1}{2}\right)^r \left(\frac{1}{2}\right)^{n-r}$

$= {}^nC_r \left(\frac{1}{2}\right)$

Now, $P(x = 4), P(x = 5)$ and $P(x = 6)$ are in AP.

If a, b, c are in AP then $2b = a + c$

$\therefore 2P(x = 5) = P(x = 4) + P(x = 6)$

$\Rightarrow 2 \cdot {}^nC_5 \left(\frac{1}{2}\right)^n = {}^nC_4 \left(\frac{1}{2}\right)^n + {}^nC_6 \left(\frac{1}{2}\right)^n$

$\Rightarrow 2 \cdot {}^nC_5 = {}^nC_4 + {}^nC_6$

$\Rightarrow 2 \frac{n!}{(n-5)!5!} = \frac{n!}{(n-4)!4!} + \frac{n!}{(n-6)!6!}$

$\Rightarrow \frac{2}{5(n-5)} = \frac{1}{(n-4)(n-5)} + \frac{1}{6 \times 5}$

$\Rightarrow n^2 - 21n + 98 = 0$

$\Rightarrow (n-7)(n-14) = 0$

$\therefore n = 7$ or 14

Hence, the correct option is (A).

42. Given:

$\int (x^2 - 1) dx = \frac{x^3}{a} + bx + C$

As we know that,

$\int [f(x) \pm g(x)] dx = \int f(x) dx \pm \int g(x) dx \Rightarrow \int (x^2 - 1) dx = \int x^2 dx - \int dx$

$\int x^n dx = \frac{x^{n+1}}{n+1} + C$

$\Rightarrow \int (x^2 - 1) dx = \frac{x^3}{3} - x + C$

Now, by comparing the above equation with $\int (x^2 - 1) dx = \frac{x^3}{a} + bx + C$ we get

$\Rightarrow a = 3$ and $b = -1$

$\Rightarrow a + 3b = 0$

Hence, the correct option is (B).

43. Let $I = \int \frac{dx}{1+x+x^2+x^3} = \int \frac{dx}{(1+x)(1+x^2)}$

Let $\frac{1}{(1+x)(1+x^2)} = \frac{A}{1+x} + \frac{Bx+C}{1+x^2}$

$1 = A(1 + x^2) + (Bx + C)(1 + x)$

Comparing the coefficients of x^2, x, and constant terms,

$\Rightarrow A + B = 0, B + C = 0, C + A = 1$

Solving these equations, we get

$\Rightarrow A = \frac{1}{2}, B = -\frac{1}{2}, C = \frac{1}{2}$

$I = \frac{1}{2} \int \frac{dx}{(1+x)} - \frac{1}{2} \int \frac{(x-1)}{(1+x^2)} dx$

$= \frac{1}{2} \log(1+x) - \frac{1}{4} \log(x^2+1) + \frac{1}{2} \tan^{-1} x$

$= \frac{1}{4} \left[\log \frac{(x+1)^2}{x^2+1} + 2\tan^{-1} x \right]$

Hence, the correct option is (B).

44. Let Integral I as

$I = \int \frac{1}{(x+1)\sqrt{1-2x-x^2}} dx$

Put $x + 1 = \frac{1}{t} \Rightarrow dx = \frac{-1}{t^2} dt$

$\Rightarrow I = \int \frac{\frac{-1}{t^2} dt}{\frac{1}{t}\sqrt{1-2\left(\frac{1}{t}-1\right)-\left(\frac{1}{t}-1\right)^2}}$

$= -\int \frac{dt}{\sqrt{2t^2-1}}$

$= -\frac{1}{\sqrt{2}} \int \frac{dt}{\sqrt{t^2-\left(\frac{1}{\sqrt{2}}\right)^2}}$

$= -\frac{1}{\sqrt{2}} \cosh^{-1}\left(\frac{t}{y\sqrt{2}}\right)$

$= -\frac{1}{\sqrt{2}} \cosh^{-1}\left(\frac{\sqrt{2}}{x+1}\right)$

Hence, the correct option is (D).

45. Here, we have to find the value of the integral $\int_0^{\frac{\pi}{2}} \frac{\sqrt{\tan x}}{1+\sqrt{\tan x}}$

Let $I = \int_0^{\frac{\pi}{2}} \frac{\sqrt{\tan x}}{1+\sqrt{\tan x}} dx$ .... (1)

As we know that, $\int_a^b f(x) dx = \int_a^b f(a+b-x) dx$

$\Rightarrow I = \int_0^{\frac{\pi}{2}} \frac{\sqrt{\cot x}}{1+\sqrt{\cot x}} dx$ ..... (2)

Adding equation (1) and (2), we get

$\Rightarrow 2I = \int_0^{\frac{\pi}{2}} \left[\frac{\sqrt{\tan x}}{1+\sqrt{\tan x}} + \frac{\sqrt{\cot x}}{1+\sqrt{\cot x}} \right] dx$

$\Rightarrow 2I = \int_0^{\frac{\pi}{2}} dx = \frac{\pi}{2}$

$\Rightarrow I = \frac{\pi}{4}$

Hence, the correct option is (B).

46. Let $I = \int_{-\frac{\pi}{6}}^{\frac{\pi}{6}} \frac{\sin^5 x \cos^3 x}{x^4} dx$

Let $f(x) = \frac{\sin^5 x \cos^3 x}{x^4}$

Replaced x by $-x$,

$\Rightarrow f(-x) = \frac{\sin^5(-x)\cos^3(-x)}{(-x)^4}$

As we know $\sin(-\theta) = -\sin\theta$ and $\cos(-\theta) = \cos\theta$

$= \frac{-\sin^5 x \cos^3 x}{x^4}$

$\Rightarrow f(-x) = -f(x)$

So, $f(x)$ is odd function

Therefore, $I = 0$

Hence, the correct option is (D).

47. Let, $I = \int_0^{\frac{\pi}{2}} \log \cot x \, dx$ ... (1)

Now using property, $\int_0^a f(x) dx = \int_0^a f(a-x) dx$

$I = \int_0^{\frac{\pi}{2}} \log \cot \left(\frac{\pi}{2} - x \right) dx$

$I = \int_0^{\frac{\pi}{2}} \log \tan x \, dx$ ... (2)

Adding eq. (1) and (2), we get

$\Rightarrow 2I = \int_0^{\frac{\pi}{2}} (\log \cot x + \log \tan x) \, dx$

$\Rightarrow 2I = \int_0^{\frac{\pi}{2}} \log(\tan x \times \cot x) dx \quad [\because \log m + \log n = \log mn]$

$\Rightarrow 2I = \int_0^{\frac{\pi}{2}} \log 1 \, dx$

$\Rightarrow 2I = 0 \quad [\because \log 1 = 0]$

$\Rightarrow I = 0$

Hence, the correct option is (A).

48. Option(A):

∀x(p(x) ∨ W) ≡ ∀x p(x) ∨ W

This is logically valid. Because, W is free of any quantifier so, ∀x would be associated with p(x) only and hence L.H.S and R.H.S are equal.

Option(B):

∃x(p(x) ∧ W) ≡ ∃x p(x) ∧ W

This also logically valid. Because, W is free of any quantifier so, ∃x would be associated with p(x) only and hence L.H.S and R.H.S are equal.

Option(C):

∀x(p(x) → W) ≡ ∀x p(x) → W

This is logically NOT valid.

L.H.S: ∀x(p(x) → W)

= ∀x(¬ p(x) ∨ W)

= ∀x (¬ p(x)) ∨ W

= ¬ ∃x p(x) ∨ W

= ∃x p(x) → W.

This is not equal to R.H.S

Option(D):

∃x(p(x) → W) ≡ ∀x p(x) → W

This is logically valid.

L.H.S: ∃x(p(x) → W)

= ∃x(¬ p(x) ∨ W)

= ∃x(¬ p(x)) ∨ W

= ¬ ∀x p(x) ∨ W

= ∀x p(x) → W = R.H.S

Only option (C) predicate formulae is NOT logically valid.

Hence, the correct option is (C).

49. Given:

∀x [(∀z z|x ⇒ z =x) ∨ (z=1) ⇒ ∃w (w > x) ∧ (∀z z|w ⇒w=z) ∨ (z=1)]

Let, X ≡ (∀z z|x ⇒ z =x) ∨ (z=1)

Y ≡ ∃w (w > x)

Z ≡ (∀z z|w ⇒ w = z) ∨ (z=1

∀x [X ⇒ Y ⇒ Z]

X is true: If x is prime number

Y is true: If there exist a w which is greater than x

Z is true. If w is prime

S1 = {1,2,3, ... , 100}

Let x = 97

z = 97

∴ z|x ⇒ (z = 1) ≡ T ⇒ T ≡ T

prime number greater than 97 is 101

But S1 is not included in set. Hence there doesn't exist w which is greater than x

T ⇒ F.Z ≡ T ⇒ F ≡ F

Therefore, S1 does not satisfy ϕ

S2. Set of all positive integers satisfy ϕ

S3. Set of all integers

If x is negative, X ≡ T

F ⇒ Y.Z ≡ T

Also, set of all positive integers satisfy ϕ.

Hence, the correct option is (C).

50. Equation of circle with center at (a, b) and radius r units is
$(x - a)^2 + (y - b)^2 = r^2$

So, equation of circle is $(x - 2)^2 + (y - 5)^2 = 5^2$

$\Rightarrow x^2 + y^2 - 4x - 10y + 4 = 0$.

Hence, the correct option is (B).

Physics & Chemistry : Mock Test 01

Physics

Q.1 The displacement of a particle executing simple harmonic motion is given by $y = A_0 + A\sin\omega t + B\cos\omega t$. Then the amplitude of its oscillation is given by:

[NEET UG, 2019]

A. $A_0 + \sqrt{A^2 + B^2}$
B. $\sqrt{A^2 + B^2}$
C. $\sqrt{A_0^2 + (A+B)^2}$
D. $(A + B)$

Q.2 Average velocity of a particle executing SHM in one complete vibration is :

[NEET UG, 2019]

A. $\frac{A\omega}{2}$
B. $A\omega$
C. $\frac{A\omega^2}{2}$
D. Zero

Q.3 A force F = 20 + 10 y acts on a particle in y-direction where F is in newton and y in meter. Work done by this force to move the particle from y = 0 to y = 1 m is:

[NEET UG, 2019]

A. 30 J
B. 5 J
C. 25 J
D. 20 J

Q.4 What is the emissive power of sun when its temperature is doubled?

A. 2 times
B. 4 times
C. 8 times
D. 16 times

Q.5 If two unit masses are placed at unit distance apart the force of attraction between them is equal to ____.

A. Acceleration due to gravity
B. Gravitational potential
C. Universal gravitational constant
D. Gravitational field strength

Q.6 What is the ratio of the wavelength of photon released when the electron jumps from 5th to 4th orbit of a hydrogen atom and then from 4th to the ground state?

A. 3 : 125
B. 4 : 81
C. 81 : 4
D. 125 : 3

Q.7 Calculate the wavelength of radiation emitted when He⁺ makes a transition from the state n = 4 to the state n = 3.

A. 164 nm
B. 468 nm
C. 250 nm
D. 125 nm

Q.8 Calculate the Bohr radius of 3rd orbit of Be³⁺.

A. 0.83 nm
B. 3.50 nm
C. 0.12 nm
D. 1.70 nm

Q.9 For what condition wave speed in sine wave is greater than the maximum speed of particle:

A. $A < \frac{\lambda}{2\pi}$
B. $A > \frac{\lambda}{2\pi}$
C. $A > \frac{\lambda}{\pi}$
D. $A < \frac{\lambda}{\pi}$

Q.10 Light of wavelength 4000 Å is incident on a metal plate whose function is 2eV. The maximum kinetic energy of emitted photoelectron will be:

A. 12.01 eV
B. 21.22 eV
C. 23.12 eV
D. 10.37 eV

Q.11 In an n-type silicon, which of the following statements is true ?

A. Electrons are majority carriers and trivalent atoms are the dopants
B. Electrons are minority carriers and pentavalent atoms are the dopants
C. Holes are minority carriers and pentavalent atoms are the dopants
D. Holes are majority carriers and trivalent atoms are the dopants

Q.12 The scale of temperature in which the temperature is only positive is:

A. Farenheit
B. Celcius
C. Kelvin
D. Reaumur

Q.13 _____ developed the corpuscular theory of light.

A. Newton
B. Huygen
C. Foucault
D. Maxwell

Q.14 Select the correct statement regarding plane mirror:

A. The laws of reflection of light is only true for the plane mirror
B. The plane mirror always forms real images
C. The plane mirror may form a virtual image
D. The virtual image is always erect

Q.15 An electron and a proton are allowed to fall through the separation between the plates of a parallel plate capacitor of voltage $5\ V$ and separation distance $h = 1\ mm$. Calculate the time of flight for both electron and proton:

A. 63.45×10^{-7}
B. 64.15×10^{-7}
C. 63.25×10^{-9}
D. 65.15×10^{-9}

Q.16 The rms value of an ac current of $50\ Hz$ is $10 amp$. The time taken by the alternating current in reaching from zero to maximum value and the peak value of current will be:

A. 2×10^{-2} sec and $14.14 amp$
B. 1×10^{-2} sec and 7.07 amp
C. 5×10^{-3} sec and $7.07 amp$
D. 5×10^{-3} sec and $14.14 amp$

Q.17 A coil having 100 turns and area of $0.001 m^2$ is free to rotate about an axis. The coil is placed perpendicular to magnetic field of $1.0 wb/m^2$. The resistance of the coil is 10. If the coil is rotated rapidly through an angle of $180°$, how much charge will flow through the coil?

A. 0.02 coulomb
B. 0.04 coulomb
C. 0.08 coulomb
D. 0.07 coulomb

Q.18 A circular coil of radius $10\ cm$, 500 turns and resistance 2Ω is placed with its plane perpendicular to the horizontal component of the earth's magnetic field. It is rotated about its vertical diameter through $180°$ in $0.25\ s$. Estimate the magnitudes of the emf and current induced in the coil. Horizontal component of the earth's magnetic field at the place is $3.0 \times 10^{-5}\ T$:

173

A. $1.5 \times 10^{-3}\ A$ B. $1.9 \times 10^{-3}\ A$
C. $1.4 \times 10^{-3}\ A$ D. $1.2 \times 10^{-3}\ A$

Q.19 The function $\sin^2(\omega t)$ represents :

A. A simple harmonic motion with a period $\frac{2\pi}{\omega}$
B. A simple harmonic motion with a period $\frac{\pi}{\omega}$
C. A periodic, but not a simple harmonic motion with a period $\frac{2\pi}{\omega}$
D. A periodic, but not simple harmonic motion with a period $\frac{\pi}{\omega}$

Q.20 In a p-n-p transistor, working as a common base amplifier, the current gain is 0.96 and the emitter current is 7.2 mA. The base current is:

A. 0.20 mA   B. 0.36 mA   C. 0.29 mA   D. 0.45 mA

Q.21 In the given circuit, the potential difference across PQ will be nearest to

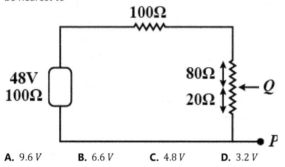

A. 9.6 V   B. 6.6 V   C. 4.8 V   D. 3.2 V

Q.22 What is the direction of force of friction acting on a body moving on a fixed surface?

A. Along the different of motion
B. Opposite to the direction of motion
C. Independent of Motion
D. Both (A) and (B)

Q.23 A geyser heats water flowing at the rate of 3.0 litres per minute from $27°C$ to $77°C$. If the geyser operates on a gas burner, what is the rate of consumption of the fuel if its heat of combustion is $4.0 \times 10^4 J/g$?

A. $4.0 \times 10^4 J/g$ B. $1.0 \times 10^4 J/g$
C. $4.0 \times 10^{-8} J/g$ D. $5.0 \times 10^5 J/g$

Q.24 What amount of heat must be supplied to $2.0 \times 10^{-2} kg$ of Nitrogen (at room temperature) to raise its temperature by $45°C$ at constant pressure? (Molecular mass of $N_2 = 28; R = 8.3 J mol^{-1} K^{-1}$.)

A. 773.38J   B. 933.38J   C. 903.28J   D. 900.38J

Q.25 "Heat cannot by itself flow from a body at a lower temperature to a body at a higher temperature"- the statement is which of the following?

A. First law of thermodynamics
B. Conservation of mass
C. Conservation of momentum
D. Second law of thermodynamics

Q.26 Hydraulic machines work under the Principle of:

A. Newton's Law   B. Joules Law
C. Pascal's Law   D. Floatation Law

Q.27 The viscosity of liquid:

A. Increases with increase in temperature
B. Decreases with increase in temperature
C. Decreases with decrease in temperature
D. Remains constant regardless of any change in the temperature

Q.28 The potential inside a charged hollow sphere is _____.

A. Zero
B. Same as that on the surface
C. Less than that on the surface
D. None of these

Q.29 According to Gauss's law, if E is _____, the charge density in the ideal conductor is zero.

A. Positive   B. Negative   C. Zero   D. Unity

Q.30 A point charge $+10\mu C$ is at a distance of $5cm$ directly above the centre of a square of side $10cm$, as shown in Figure. What is the magnitude of the electric flux through the square? (Hint: Think of the square as one face of a cube with edge $10cm$).

A. $1.88 \times 10^5 Nm^2 C^{-1}$
B. $2.90 \times 10^5 Nm^2 C^{-1}$
C. $1.52 \times 10^5 Nm^2 C^{-1}$
D. $3.2 \times 10^5 Nm^2 C^{-3}$

Q.31 If a unit positive charge is placed inside a sphere of radius r, then the electric flux through the sphere will be:

A. $\varepsilon_o r$ B. $\frac{\varepsilon_o}{r}$ C. ε_o^{-1} D. ε_o

Q.32 Ria needs to calculate the number of turns that a solenoid should have, in order to induce a voltage of $50V$ provided that the magnetic flux in its cavity changes from 70 mWb to 20 mWb per time 0.20 s. What will be her answer?

A. 50   B. 2   C. 20   D. 200

Q.33 A solid cylindrical conductor of radius R has a uniform current density I. The magnetic field H inside the conductor at distance r from the axis of the conductor is:

A. $\frac{I}{2\pi r}$ B. $\frac{I}{4\pi r}$ C. $\frac{Ir}{2\pi R^2}$ D. $\frac{Ir}{4\pi R^2}$

Q.34 Which of the following does not affect the apparent frequency in doppler effect?

A. Speed of source
B. Speed of observer
C. Frequency of source
D. Distance between source and observer

Q.35 Two spherical bodies of masses $'M'$ and $'5M'$ and radii $'R'$ and $'2R'$, respectively, are released in free space with initial separation between their centres equal to $'12R'$. If they attract each other due to gravitational force only, then

what is the distance covered by the smaller body just before collision?
A. 1.5R   B. 2.5R   C. 4.5R   D. 97.5R

Q.36 Two masses m_1 and m_2 are suspended together by a mass-less spring of spring constant K. When the masses are in equilibrium, m_1 is removed without disturbing the system. The angular frequency and amplitude of oscillation of m_2 are

A. $\sqrt{\frac{K}{m_2}}, \frac{m_1 g}{K}$
B. $\sqrt{\frac{K}{m_1}}, \frac{m_1 g}{K}$
C. $\sqrt{\frac{K}{m_1}}, \frac{m_2 g}{K}$
D. $\sqrt{\frac{K}{m_2}}, \frac{m_2 g}{K}$

Q.37 A man of height $'h'$ walks along a straight path towards a lamp post of height H with a uniform velocity $'u'$. The velocity of the edge of the shadow on the ground will be:

A. $\frac{hu}{(H-h)}$ B. $\frac{hu}{(H+h)}$ C. $\frac{(H+h)}{hu}$ D. $\frac{(H-h)}{hu}$

Q.38 Which Semiconductors are created by doping an intrinsic semiconductor with acceptor impurities?
A. p -type
B. n -type
C. Both (A) and (B)
D. None of them

Q.39 In an n-type silicon, which of the following statement is true:
A. Electrons are majority carriers and trivalent atoms are the dopants.
B. Electrons are minority carriers and pentavalent atoms are the dopants.
C. Holes are minority carriers and pentavalent atoms are the dopants.
D. Holes are majority carriers and trivalent atoms are the dopants.

Q.40 At what temperature is the root mean square speed of an atom in an argon gas cylinder equal to the rms speed of a helium gas atom at $-20°C$? (Atomic mass of $Ar = 39.9u$ and $He = 440u$)
A. $2.52 \times 10^3\ K$ B. $2.52 \times 10^2\ K$
C. $4.03 \times 10^3\ K$ D. $4.03 \times 10^2\ K$

Q.41 A simple pendulum of length l and having a bob of mass M is suspended in a car. The car is moving on a circular track of radius R with a uniform speed v. If the pendulum makes small oscillations in a radial direction about its equilibrium position, what will be its time period?

A. $2\pi \sqrt{\frac{1}{g^2 - \frac{v^4}{R^2}}}$
B. $2\pi \sqrt{\frac{1}{g^2 + \frac{v^4}{R^2}}}$
C. $2\pi \sqrt{g^2 - \frac{v^4}{R^2}}$
D. $2\pi \sqrt{g^2 + \frac{v^4}{R^2}}$

Q.42 The property of the sound waves that determines the pitch of the sound is its:
A. Frequency   B. Amplitude
C. Wave length   D. Intensity

Q.43 Which one of the following types of radiation has the shortest wavelength?

A. Radio waves   B. Visible light
C. Infrared (IR)   D. Ultraviolet (UV)

Q.44 In a periscope, the two plane mirrors are kept
A. parallel to each other
B. perpendicular to each other
C. at an angle of 60° with each other
D. at an angle of 45° with each other

Q.45 The relationship between torque and angular momentum is analogous to:
A. Speed and velocity
B. Velocity and acceleration
C. Force and linear momentum
D. Energy and work

Q.46 An object is rotating about a fixed point. The kinetic energy of the object is E and its angular momentum is L. Then which of the following is true?
A. $L \propto E^{\frac{1}{3}}$
B. $L \propto E$
C. $L \propto E^{-1}$
D. $L \propto \sqrt{E}$

Q.47 The instantaneous voltage across a pure resistor is _____ with current.
A. Leads   B. Out of phase
C. Lags   D. In- phase

Q.48 When an inductive load is connected, the power factor is:
A. Unity   B. Infinite   C. Lagging   D. Leading

Q.49 Two waves are represented by $y_1 = a \cdot \sin(\omega t), and\ y_2 = a.\cos\omega t$. If both the waves are superimposed then the resultant amplitude will be:
A. $\sqrt{2}a$ B. $\sqrt{3}a$
C. $2a$ D. None of these

Q.50 Which of the following is correct for the constructive interference of the two harmonic waves?
A. The amplitude of the resultant wave is equal to the sum of the amplitudes of individual waves
B. The Intensity of the resultant wave is equal to the sum of the intensities of individual waves
C. Both (A) and (B)
D. None of these

Chemistry

Q.51 Which is the only non-metallic element that is in liquid state at room temperature?
A. Francium   B. Helium
C. Bromine   D. Mercury

Q.52 Choose the correct statement from the below options.
A. Metallic character decreases on moving from left to right in a period
B. Metallic character increases on moving from left to right in a period
C. Metallic character remains constant on moving from left to right in a period
D. None of these

Q.53 Consider the reaction (which is not balanced):
$NO_2(g) \to NO(g) + O_2(g)$.
Find the power to which concentration of NO is raised in the equilibrium constant equation.
A. 2   B. 0   C. 4   D. 1

Q.54 A buffer solution is prepared by mixing 'a' moles of CH_3COONa and 'b' moles of CH_3COOH such that $(a+b) = 1$, into water to make $1\,L$ buffer solution. If the buffer capacity of this buffer solution is plotted against moles of salt CH_3COONa (with a) then the plot obtained will be (to the scale) approximately.

A.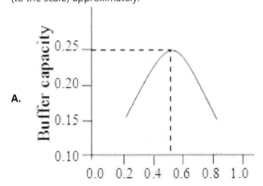

B.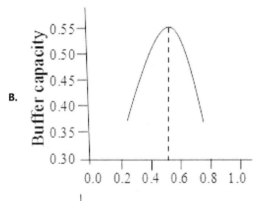

C.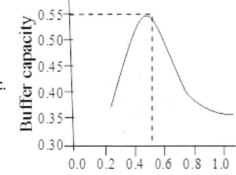

D.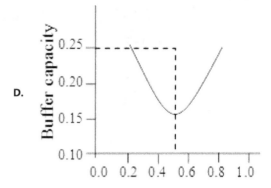

Q.55 Arrange the following in increasing order of their boiling points:
I. Ethylmethylamine
II. Propylamine
III. Trimethylamine
A. II < I < III   B. III < I < II
C. III < II < I   D. I < III < II

Q.56 The statement "atom is indivisible" was proposed by:
A. Rutherford   B. Dalton
C. Bohr   D. Einstein

Q.57 Iron is extracted from iron oxide using carbon monoxide as shown.
iron oxide + carbon monoxide → iron + carbon dioxide
Which statement is correct?
A. Carbon monoxide is oxidised to carbon dioxide
B. Carbon monoxide is reduced to carbon dioxide
C. Iron is oxidised to iron oxide
D. Iron oxide is oxidised to iron

Q.58 The rate of a first order reaction is $1.5 \times 10^{-2} M\,min^{-1}$ at $0.5M$ concentration of the reactant. The half-life of the reaction is:
A. 0.383 min   B. 23.1 min
C. 8.73 min   D. 7.53 min

Q.59 For a 1st order reaction, if the concentration is doubled then the rate of reaction becomes:
A. Double   B. Half
C. Four times   D. Remain same

Q.60 The rate constant for a first order reaction is $4.606 \times 10^{-3}\,s^{-1}$. The time required to reduce $2.0g$ of the reactant to $0.2g$ is:
A. 200 s   B. 500 s   C. 1000 s   D. 100 s

Q.61 An aqueous solution of hydrochloric acid:
A. Obeys Raoult's law
B. Shows negative deviation from Raoult's law
C. Shows positive deviation from Raoult's law
D. Obeys Henry's law at all compositions

Q.62 Exactly $1\,g$ of urea dissolved in $75\,g$ of water gives a solution that boils at $100.114°C$ at 760 torr. The molecular weight of urea is 60.1. The boiling point elevation constant for water is:

A. 1.02 B. 0.51 C. 3.06 D. 1.51

Q.63 At a particular temperature, the vapour pressures of two liquids A and B are 120 mm and 180 mm of mercury respectively. If 2 moles of A and 3 moles of B are mixed to form an ideal solution, the vapour pressure of the solution at the same temperature will be: (in mm of mercury)

A. 156 B. 145 C. 150 D. 108

Q.64 Which of the following defect, if present, lowers the density of the crystal?

A. Frenkel defect
B. Schottky defect
C. Substitutional impurity defect
D. Interstitial impurity defect

Q.65 Ammonium chloride crystallizes in a body centred cubic lattice with edge length of unit cell of 390 pm. If the size of chloride ion is 180 pm, the size of ammonium ion would be:

A. 174 pm B. 158 pm C. 142 pm D. 126 pm

Q.66 A crystal of lead (II) sulphide has NaCl structure. In this crystal the shortest distance between a Pb^{2+} ion and S^{2-} ion is 297 pm. What is the volume of unit cell in lead sulphide?

A. $209.6 \times 10^{-24}\ cm^3$
B. $209.6 \times 10^{-25}\ cm^3$
C. $209.6 \times 10^{-23}\ cm^3$
D. $209.6 \times 10^{-22}\ cm^3$

Q.67 The law, which states that at constant temperature, the volume of a given mass of gas is inversely proportional is pressure, is known as:

A. Boyles law B. Charles law
C. Combine gas law D. Avogadros law

Q.68 Which of the following metal is not an alkali metal?

A. Magnesium B. Rubidium
C. Sodium D. Caesium

Q.69 Which of the following scientist proposed that a 'vital force' was responsible for the formation of organic compounds?

A. Berzilius B. Wohler
C. Berthelot D. Kolbe

Q.70 Up to which element, the Law of Octaves was found applicable?

A. Oxygen B. Calcium
C. Cobalt D. Potassium

Q.71 Which of the following is an example of absorption?

A. Water on silica gel
B. Oxygen on metal surface
C. Water on calcium chloride
D. None of these

Q.72 The bond length between hybridized carbon atom and other carbon atom is minimum in:

A. Propane B. Butane C. Propene D. Propyne

Q.73 The enthalpy of vaporisation of a substance is $8400\ J\ mol^{-1}$ and its boiling point is $-173.15°C$. The entropy change for vaporisation is:

A. $84\ Jmol^{-1}\ K^{-1}$ B. $21\ Jmol^{-1}\ K^{-1}$
C. $49\ Jmol^{-1}\ K^{-1}$ D. $12\ Jmol^{-1}\ K^{-1}$

Q.74 If ΔH is the change in enthalpy and ΔE, the change in internal energy accompanying a gaseous reaction, then

A. ΔH is always greater than ΔE.
B. $\Delta H < \Delta E$ only if the number of moles of the products is greater than the number of moles of the reactants.
C. ΔH is always less than ΔE.
D. $\Delta H < \Delta E$ only if the number of moles of products is less than the number of moles of the reactants.

Q.75 Calculate the number of protons, neutrons and electrons in $^{80}_{35}Br$.

A. 35,45,35 B. 30,35,45
C. 45,35,45 D. 35,45,45

Q.76 Which among the following is an example of a saturated carbon compound?

A. Ethane
B. Ethene
C. Ethyne
D. All options are correct

Q.77 Match the list-I with List-II

	List-I (Electrode)		List-II (Type)
1.	Calomel	P.	Reference
2.	Glass	Q.	Redox
3.	Hydrogen	R.	Membrane
4.	Quinhydrone	S.	Gas

A. 1-P, 2-R, 3-S, 4-Q B. 1-Q, 2-P, 3-S, 4-R
C. 1-R, 2-Q, 3-P, 4-S D. 1-S, 2-P, 3-R, 4-Q

Q.78 Calculate e.m.f of the following cell at $298\ K$:

$$2Cr(s) + 3Fe^{2+}(0.1M) \rightarrow 2Cr^{3+}(0.01M) + 3Fe(s)$$

Given: $E°(Cr^{3+}\ |\ Cr) = -0.74 V$ $E°(Fe^{2+}\ |\ Fe) = -0.44\ V$

A. 0.31V B. 0.27V C. 0.34V D. 0.43V

Q.79 For the following cell, calculate the emf:

$$\frac{Al}{Al^{+3}}(0.01M)\ ||\ \frac{Fe^{+2}(0.02M)}{Fa}$$

Given: $E°_{Al} + \frac{3}{Al} = -1.66\ V$

A. 1.11V B. 2.22V C. 1.22V D. 1.232V

Q.80 A complex has the molecular formula $Co.5NH_3.NO_2.Cl_2$. One mole of this complex produces three moles of ions in an aqueous solution. On reacting this solution with excess of $AgNO_3$ solution, we get 2 moles of white ppt. The complex is:

A. $[Co(NH_3)_4(NO_2)Cl](NH_3Cl)$
B. $[Co(NH_3)_5Cl](ClNO_2)$

C. $[Co(NH_3)_5NO_2]Cl_2$
D. $[Co(NH_3)_5NO_2 \cdot Cl_2]$

Q.81 The co-ordination number and oxidation state of Cr in $K_3[Cr(C_2O_4)_3]$ are respectively:
A. 6 and +3 B. 3 and 0 C. 4 and +2 D. 3 and +3

Q.82 Which of the following compounds is expected to exhibit optical isomerism? [en = ethylenediamine]
A. cis-[Co(en) $_2Cl_2$]
B. cis-[$Pt(NH_3)_2Cl_2$]
C. trans-[Co(en) $_2Cl_2$]
D. trans- $[Pt(NH_3)_2Cl_2]$

Q.83 Which has a smell of oil of wintergreen?
A. Ethyl salicylate B. Methyl salicylate
C. Benzaldehyde D. Phenyl salicylate

Q.84 What is the name of the following compound?
CH_3CH_2COCl
A. Butanoyl chloride B. Propanoyl chloride
C. 1 chloro propanone D. None of these

Q.85 Toluene reacts with halogen in presence of iron(III) chloride giving ortho and para halo compounds, the reaction is?
A. Nucleophilic substitution reaction
B. Free radical addition reaction
C. Electrophilic elimination reaction
D. Electrophilic substitution reaction

Q.86 What is the structural formula of Haloalkane?
A. X-R-X B. R-F C. R-X-X D. R-X

Q.87 Which of the following Aldehydes is also known as formalin?
A. Acetaldehyde B. Acrolein
C. Acetone D. Formaldehyde

Q.88 When a primary amine reacts with chloroform in alcoholic KOH. the product is:
A. An isocyanide B. An Aldehyde
C. A cyanide D. An alcohol

Q.89 A nucleotide is formed by:
A. Nitrogen base, sugar and phosphate
B. Pyrimidine, sugar and phosphate
C. Purine, sugar and phosphate
D. Purine, pyrimidine and phosphate

Q.90 Glycogen is a polymer of:
A. Glucose B. Sucrose
C. Galactose D. Fructose

Q.91 The materials used for making non-stick utensils of kitchens is:
A. PVC B. Polyether
C. Teflon D. Rayon

Q.92 Natural rubber is a polymer of:

[Bihar PSC, 2019]
A. Isoprene B. Styrene
C. Vinyl acetate D. Propene

Q.93 What is the formula of hematite?
A. Fe_3O_4 B. $FeSO_4 \cdot 7H_2O$
C. Fe_2O_3 D. $FeCl_3$

Q.94 Which of the following is Baeyer'sreagent?
A. CrO B. Cr_2O_3 C. CrO_5 D. CrO_3

Q.95 Isopropyl chloride undergoes hydrolysis by:
A. SN^1 mechanism
B. SN^2 mechanism
C. Neither SN^1 or SN^2 mechanism
D. Either SN^1 or SN^2 mechanism

Q.96 Which of the following reaction occur when urea is added to soil as a fertilizer?
A. $NH_2CONH_2 \rightarrow HNCO + NH_3$
B. $NH_2CONH_2 + H_2O \rightarrow 2NH_3 + CO_2$
C. $2NH_2CONH_2 \rightarrow H_2NCONHCONH_2 + NH_3$
D. Both (A) and (B)

Q.97 The current synthesis of poly-carbonate is an application of:
A. Green revolution B. Green chemistry
C. Waste management D. None of the above

Q.98 An organic compound A on reduction gives compound B, which on reaction with trichloro methane and caustic potash forms C. The compound 'C' on catalytic reduction gives N-methyl benzenamine, the compound 'A' is :
A. Nitrobenzene B. Nitromethane
C. Methanamine D. Benzenamine

Q.99 Haloforms are trihalogen derivatives of:
A. Ethane B. Methane C. Propane D. Benzene

Q.100 Helium gas is used in gas balloons instead of hydrogen gas because it is:
[Territorial Army Officer, 2019]
A. Lighter than hydrogen
B. More abundant than hydrogen
C. Non-combustible
D. More stable

Physics & Chemistry : Mock Test - 1

// Smart Answer Sheet //

Correct — Indicates percentage of students who answered questions correctly.

Skipped — Indicates percentage of students who skipped questions.

Q.	Ans.	Correct / Skipped	Q.	Ans.	Correct / Skipped	Q.	Ans.	Correct / Skipped	Q.	Ans.	Correct / Skipped	Q.	Ans.	Correct / Skipped
1	B	22.5 % / 17.5 %	17	A	30.0 % / 25.0 %	33	C	22.5 % / 30.0 %	49	A	42.5 % / 27.5 %	65	B	20.0 % / 20.0 %
2	D	37.5 % / 27.5 %	18	B	30.0 % / 27.5 %	34	D	42.5 % / 27.5 %	50	A	22.5 % / 27.5 %	66	A	22.5 % / 20.0 %
3	C	42.5 % / 27.5 %	19	D	10.0 % / 25.0 %	35	D	5.0 % / 27.5 %	51	C	42.5 % / 15.0 %	67	A	45.0 % / 20.0 %
4	D	40.0 % / 27.5 %	20	C	22.5 % / 27.5 %	36	A	17.5 % / 27.5 %	52	A	67.5 % / 17.5 %	68	A	52.5 % / 20.0 %
5	C	45.0 % / 20.0 %	21	D	25.0 % / 25.0 %	37	A	20.0 % / 27.5 %	53	A	47.5 % / 20.0 %	69	A	20.0 % / 20.0 %
6	D	32.5 % / 27.5 %	22	B	60.0 % / 27.5 %	38	A	30.0 % / 30.0 %	54	B	27.5 % / 17.5 %	70	B	55.0 % / 15.0 %
7	B	15.0 % / 27.5 %	23	A	20.0 % / 27.5 %	39	C	30.0 % / 27.5 %	55	B	45.0 % / 17.5 %	71	C	40.0 % / 20.0 %
8	C	27.5 % / 27.5 %	24	B	25.0 % / 27.5 %	40	A	32.5 % / 25.0 %	56	B	55.0 % / 20.0 %	72	D	57.5 % / 20.0 %
9	A	17.5 % / 27.5 %	25	D	42.5 % / 27.5 %	41	B	30.0 % / 27.5 %	57	A	50.0 % / 20.0 %	73	A	32.5 % / 17.5 %
10	D	22.5 % / 27.5 %	26	C	57.5 % / 27.5 %	42	B	22.5 % / 27.5 %	58	B	42.5 % / 17.5 %	74	D	17.5 % / 20.0 %
11	C	32.5 % / 27.5 %	27	B	52.5 % / 27.5 %	43	D	35.0 % / 27.5 %	59	A	50.0 % / 17.5 %	75	A	65.0 % / 20.0 %
12	C	45.0 % / 27.5 %	28	B	15.0 % / 27.5 %	44	A	15.0 % / 27.5 %	60	B	55.0 % / 17.5 %	76	A	70.0 % / 15.0 %
13	A	40.0 % / 27.5 %	29	C	50.0 % / 27.5 %	45	C	62.5 % / 27.5 %	61	B	30.0 % / 20.0 %	77	A	22.5 % / 17.5 %
14	D	45.0 % / 27.5 %	30	A	12.5 % / 27.5 %	46	D	30.0 % / 27.5 %	62	B	25.0 % / 20.0 %	78	A	30.0 % / 17.5 %
15	C	22.5 % / 27.5 %	31	C	30.0 % / 30.0 %	47	D	45.0 % / 27.5 %	63	A	40.0 % / 17.5 %	79	D	2.5 % / 20.0 %
16	D	30.0 % / 27.5 %	32	D	25.0 % / 27.5 %	48	C	42.5 % / 27.5 %	64	B	55.0 % / 20.0 %	80	C	32.5 % / 20.0 %

Physics & Chemistry : Mock Test - 1

Q.	Ans.	Correct / Skipped
81	A	37.5 % / 17.5 %
82	A	32.5 % / 20.0 %
83	B	37.5 % / 20.0 %
84	B	45.0 % / 20.0 %
85	D	27.5 % / 20.0 %
86	D	72.5 % / 20.0 %
87	D	62.5 % / 20.0 %
88	A	32.5 % / 20.0 %
89	A	45.0 % / 20.0 %
90	A	65.0 % / 17.5 %
91	C	72.5 % / 20.0 %
92	A	65.0 % / 17.5 %
93	C	40.0 % / 17.5 %
94	B	30.0 % / 20.0 %
95	D	30.0 % / 17.5 %
96	B	27.5 % / 17.5 %
97	B	45.0 % / 20.0 %
98	A	32.5 % / 20.0 %
99	B	45.0 % / 20.0 %
100	C	32.5 % / 17.5 %

Performance Analysis

Avg. Score (%)	36.0%
Toppers Score (%)	91.0%
Your Score	

Physics & Chemistry : Mock Test - 1

//Hints and Solutions//

1. Given,

$y = A_0 + A\sin\omega t + B\sin\omega t$

Equation of SHM

$y' = y - A_0 = A\sin\omega t + B\cos\omega t$

Resultant amplitude,

$R = \sqrt{A^2 + B^2 + 2AB\cos 90°}$

$= \sqrt{A^2 + B^2}$

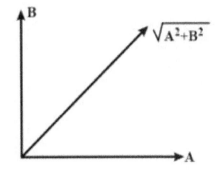

Hence, the correct option is (B).

2. In one complete vibration, displacement is zero. So, average velocity in one complete vibration:

$= \dfrac{\text{Displacement}}{\text{Time interval}} = \dfrac{y_f - y_i}{T} = 0$

Hence, the correct option is (D).

3. Given:

Force $F = 20 + 10y$

Particles moves from y = 0 to y = 1m

So, work done on a particle is given as:

$W = \int_0^1 F \cdot dy = \int_0^1 20 + 10y$

$\therefore W = \left[20y + \dfrac{10y^2}{2}\right]_0^1$

$= 20 + 5 = 25 J$

Hence, the correct option is (C).

4. Stefan's Law: According to it the radiant energy emitted by a perfectly black body per unit area per sec (i.e. emissive power of black body) is directly proportional to the fourth power of its absolute temperature i.e.

$E \propto T^4$

$\Rightarrow E = \sigma T^4$

Where, is a constant called Stefan's constant.

The value of Stefan's constant is $5.67 \times 10^{-8} \ W/m^2 \ K^4$.

Stefan's Law is used to accurately find the temperature Sun, Stars, and the earth. A black body is an ideal body that absorbs or emits all types of electromagnetic radiation.

Mathematically, Stefan's law can be written as:

$\Rightarrow E = \sigma T^4$

When the temperature is doubled i.e., $T_1 = 2T$

$\Rightarrow E_1 = \sigma(T_1)^4$

$\Rightarrow E_1 = \sigma(2T)^4 = 16\sigma T^4 \quad [\because E = \sigma T^4]$

$\Rightarrow E_1 = 16E$

The emissive power of the sun will increase by 16 times when its temperature is doubled.

Hence, the correct option is (D).

5. If two unit masses are placed at unit distance apart the force of attraction between them is equal to universal gravitational constant.

Therefore, the force of attraction between two unit point massess separated by a unit distance is called universal gravitational constant.

Hence, the correct option is (C).

6. Given:

$n_1 = 4$ and $n_2 = 5$

The wavelength of the radiations emitted from the hydrogen atom is given by:

$\dfrac{1}{\lambda_1} = R\left[\dfrac{1}{(4)^2} - \dfrac{1}{(5)^2}\right]$

$= R\left[\dfrac{1}{16} - \dfrac{1}{25}\right] = \dfrac{9R}{400}$ .....(1)

When electrons jump from 4th to 1st orbit, then the wavelength of the radiations emitted from the hydrogen atom is given by:

$\dfrac{1}{\lambda_2} = R\left[\dfrac{1}{(1)^2} - \dfrac{1}{(4)^2}\right]$

$= R\left[\dfrac{1}{1} - \dfrac{1}{16}\right] = \dfrac{15R}{16}$ .....(2)

Divide equation (1) and (2), we get,

$\dfrac{\lambda_1}{\lambda_2} = \dfrac{400 \times 15R}{9R \times 16}$

$= \dfrac{125}{3}$

$= 125 : 3$

Hence, the correct option is (D).

7. Given:

$n_1 = 3$ and $n_2 = 4$

As we know,

When an electron jumps from n_2 orbit to the n_1 orbit $(n_2 > n_1)$, the energy of the atom changes from En_2 to En_1. This extra energy $(En_2 - En_1)$ is emitted as a photon of electromagnetic radiation. This corresponding wavelength is given as,

$$\frac{1}{\lambda} = RZ^2 \left(\frac{1}{n_1^2} - \frac{1}{n_2^2}\right) \quad \text{......(i)}$$

Where, Rydberg constant $(R) = 1.0973 \times 10^7 \, m^{-1}$, $Z = 2$, for He^+ ion

Put all the given values in (i),

$$\frac{1}{\lambda} = 4R\left(\frac{1}{9} - \frac{1}{16}\right)$$

$$= 4R \times \frac{7}{144}$$

$$= \frac{7}{36}R$$

$$\Rightarrow \lambda = \frac{36}{7R}$$

$$= \frac{36}{7 \times 1.0973 \times 10^7}$$

$$= 468 \, nm$$

Hence, the correct option is (B).

8. Given:

$Be^{3+} \rightarrow$ The atomic number of beryllium is 4 i.e., $z = 4$

3rd orbit $(n) = 3$

Radius of orbit is given by:

$$r = \frac{n^2 h^2}{4\pi^2 m e^2} \times \frac{1}{Z} = 0.529 \times \frac{n^2}{Z}$$

Put the given values in above formula,

$$= 0.529 \times 10^{-10} \times \frac{3^2}{4}$$

$$= 1.19 \times 10^{-10} \, m$$

$$= 0.119 \times 10^{-9} \, m \approx 0.12 \, nm$$

Hence, the correct option is (C).

9. Let the equation of wave is given by $y = A \sin(\omega t - kx)$

Where, A is amplitude

ω is angular frequency

k is wave number

Now,

Velocity of wave $(v) = \frac{\omega}{k}$ ...(1)

Maximum velocity of particle $(v_p) = A\omega$ ...(2)

Comparing both equation, we get

$$A\omega = \frac{\omega}{k}$$

$$\Rightarrow A = \frac{1}{k} \quad \text{...(3)}$$

but, $k = \frac{2\pi}{\lambda}$

by substituting value of k in (3),

$$A = \frac{1}{\frac{2\pi}{\lambda}}$$

$$\Rightarrow A = \frac{\lambda}{2\pi}$$

Therefore, $A < \frac{\lambda}{2\pi}$

Hence, the correct option is (A).

10. Given:

The wavelength of the incident light $= 4000 \, \text{Å}$

$= 4000 \times 10^{-10} m$

and the value of the work function is 2eV.

As we know,

Work function $\phi = hf - KE$

Where hf the incident energy of the light and KE is the kinetic energy of the ejected photoelectron.

Therefore, $KE = hf - \phi$

We know that $f = \frac{c}{\lambda}$

Thus, $KE = \frac{hc}{\lambda} - \phi$ ....(i)

We know that:

$c = 3 \times 10^8$ m/s, $h = 606 \times 10^{-34}$, $\phi = 2$

Put the given values in equation (i),

$$= \frac{6.6 \times 10^{-34} \times 3 \times 10^8}{4000 \times 10^{-10} \times 1.6 \times 10^{-19}} - 2 \quad (1.6 \times 10^{-19} \text{ is used to get the value in terms of eV})$$

$\Rightarrow KE = 10.37 eV$

Therefore, the value of the kinetic energy of the ejected photoelectron is $10.37 eV$.

Hence, the correct option is (D).

11. An n-type semiconductor is obtained by doping a semiconductor with a pentavalent impurity. The impurity so added produces free electrons. Therefore, in an n-type semiconductor, the electrons are majority carriers and holes are minority carriers and pentavalent atoms are the dopants.

Hence, the correct option is (C).

12. Since the absolute zero temperature is 0 Kelvin. Below this temperature, we can't measure in kelvin scale.

So the Kelvin scale of temperature is only positive.

The freezing point and boiling point of water at different temperature scales are:

Scale	Freezing Point	Boiling Point
Centigrade ($0°C$)	$0°C$	$100°C$
Fahrenheit ($°F$)	$32°F$	$212°F$
Kelvin (K)	$273K$	$373K$
Reaumur ($0°R$)	$0°R$	$80°R$

Hence, the correct option is (C).

13. The corpuscular theory was largely developed by Sir Isaac Newton.

It stated that light is made up of small discrete particles called corpuscles which travel in a straight line with a finite velocity and possess impetus.

Newton's corpuscular theory is based on the following points:

- Light consists of very thin particles called corpuscles.
- These corpuscles after emission travel in a straight line and at a very high velocity.
- When these particles enter the eyes they cause a sensation of vision.
- Corpuscles of different colors have different sizes.

Hence, the correct option is (A).

14. Plane Mirror: A plane mirror is a mirror with a flat (planar) reflective surface.

The characteristics of an image formed in a plane mirror:

- The image formed by the plane mirror is virtual and erect i.e., image cannot be projected or focused on a screen.
- The distance of the image 'behind' the mirror is the same as the distance of the object in front of the mirror.
- The size of the image formed is the same as the size of the object.
- The image is laterally inverted, i.e., left hand appears to be the right hand when seen from the plane mirror.
- If the object moves towards (or away from) the mirror at a certain rate, the image also moves towards (or away from) the mirror at the same rate.
- The laws of reflection are true for both plane mirrors as well as spherical mirrors.
- The plane mirror always forms the virtual and erect images.

Hence, the correct option is (D).

15. Given:

$m_p = 1.6 \times 10^{-27}\ kg, g = 10\ ms^{-2}$

$m_e = 9.1 \times 10^{-27} Kg$

$h = 1\ mm = 10^{-3}\ m$

$V = 5\ V$

Time of flight of electron $t_e = \sqrt{\dfrac{2h}{a}}$ (ignoring gravity)

We know that $F = ma$

Similarly $F = eE$

$\therefore a = \dfrac{eE}{m}$ [also $E = \dfrac{V}{d} = \dfrac{5}{10^{-3}} = 5000 Vm^{-1}$]

$\therefore t_e = \sqrt{\dfrac{2hm_e}{eE}} = \sqrt{\dfrac{2 \times 10^{-3} \times 9.1 \times 10^{-31}}{1.6 \times 10^{-19} \times 5000}}$

$= \left[\dfrac{2 \times 9.1 \times 10^{-34}}{1.6 \times 5 \times 10^{-16}}\right]^{\frac{1}{2}} = [2.275 \times 10^{-18}]^{\frac{1}{2}}$

$t_e \simeq 1.5 \times 10^{-9}\ S$ or $\simeq 1.5\ ns$

Time flight for proton is:

$t_p = \sqrt{\dfrac{2hm_p}{eE}}$

$= \sqrt{\dfrac{2 \times 10^{-3} \times 1.6 \times 10^{-27}}{1.6 \times 10^{-19} \times 5000}} = \left[\dfrac{2 \times 10^{-30}}{5 \times 10^{-16}}\right]^{\frac{1}{2}}$

$= [0.4 \times 10^{-14}]^{\frac{1}{2}}$

$= [4000 \times 10^{-18}]^{\frac{1}{2}}$

$= 63.25 \times 10^{-9}$

$t_p = 63.25\ ns$

Hence, the correct option is (C).

16. $I = 10\ A$
$f = 50\ Hz$
$I_{rms} = \left(\dfrac{I_m}{\sqrt{2}}\right)$

where I_m is peak value $I_m = \sqrt{2} \cdot I_{rms}$

$\therefore I_m = 10\sqrt{2}A = 10 \times 1.41 = 14.1\ A$

Time taken to reach form 0 to I_m is $\left[\left(\dfrac{T}{4}\right) - 0\right] = \left(\dfrac{T}{4}\right)$

$t = \left(\dfrac{T}{4}\right) = \left(\dfrac{1}{4f}\right)$

$\therefore t = \left[\dfrac{1}{\{4 \times 50\}}\right] = \left[\dfrac{1}{200}\right] sec$

$\therefore t = 0.5 \times 10^{-2} sec$

$t = 5 \times 10^{-3} sec$

Hence, the correct option is (D).

17. $\varnothing = nAB\cos\theta = nAB\cos 0° = nAB$

$[\theta = 0°] \, d\phi = nAB - (-nAB) = 2nAB$

Again the charge induced is:

$\frac{d\phi}{R} = \frac{2nAB}{R2} \times 100 \times 0.001 \times \frac{1}{10} = 0.02$ coulomb

Hence, the correct option is (A).

18. Initial flux through the coil,

$\Phi_{B \text{ (initial)}} = BA\cos\theta$

$= 3.0 \times 10^{-5} \times (\pi \times 10^{-2}) \times \cos 0°$

$= 3\pi \times 10^{-7} \, Wb$

Final flux after the rotation,

$\Phi_{B(\text{final})} = 3.0 \times 10^{-5} \times (\pi \times 10^{-2}) \times \cos 180°$

$= -3\pi \times 10^{-7} \, Wb$

Therefore, estimated value of the induced emf is,

$\varepsilon = N \frac{\Delta\Phi}{\Delta t}$

$= 500 \times \frac{(6\pi \times 10^{-7})}{0.25}$

$= 3.8 \times 10^{-3} \, V$

$I = \frac{\varepsilon}{R}$

$= 1.9 \times 10^{-3} \, A$

Hence, the correct option is (B).

19. As given,

$y = \sin^2 \omega t$

$\Rightarrow y = \frac{1 - \cos 2\omega t}{2}$

$\Rightarrow y = \frac{1}{2} - \frac{\cos 2\omega t}{2}$

It is a periodic motion but it is not SHM.

∴ Angular speed $= 2\omega$

∴ Period $T = \frac{2\pi}{\text{angular speed}}$

$\Rightarrow T = \frac{2\pi}{2\omega}$

$\Rightarrow T = \frac{\pi}{\omega}$

Hence, the correct option is (D).

20. Current gain $= \frac{I_C}{I_B}$

$I_C =$ collector current

$I_E =$ emitter current

So, $I_C = 96 \times 7.2 = 6.912$

As $I_E = I_B + I_C$

So, $I_B = I_E - I_C$

$= (7.2 - 6.912)$ mA

$= 288$ mA

≈ 0.29 mA

Hence, the correct option is (C).

21. The potential difference across PQ

i.e., potential difference across the resistance of 20Ω which is $V = i \times 20$

$i = \frac{48}{100 + 100 + 80 + 20}$

$= 0.16 \, A$

$V = 0.16 \times 20$

$= 3.2 \, V$

Hence, the correct option is (D).

22. When we try to slide a body on a surface, the motion of the body is opposed by a force called the force of friction. The frictional force arises due to intermolecular interaction.

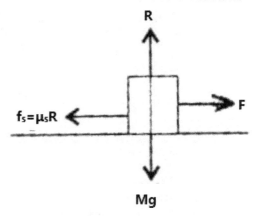

When an external force (F) is applied to move the body and the body does not move, then the frictional force acts opposite to applied force F and is equal to the applied force i.e., $F - f = 0$. When the body remains at rest, the frictional force is called the static friction. Static friction is a self-adjusting force.

Friction force, $f_s = \mu mg$

Where,

$\mu_s =$ coefficient of friction.

Thus, friction force act opposite to the direction of motion.

Hence, the correct option is (B).

23. It is given that,

Water flows at a rate of 3.0 litre $/min = 3 \times 10^{-3} m^3/min$

Density of water, $\rho = 10^3 kg/m^3$.

Clearly, mass of water flowing per minute $= 3 \times 10^{-3} \times 10^3 kg/min = 3 kg/min$

The geyser heats the water, raising the temperature from $27°C$ to $77°C$.

Initial temperature, $T_1 = 27°C$

Final temperature, $T_2 = 77°C$

Thus, rise in temperature,

$\Delta T = T_2 - T_1$

$\Delta T = 77°C - 27°C$

$\Delta T = 50°C$

Now, heat of combustion $= 4 \times 10^4 J/g = 4 \times 10^7 J/kg$

Specific heat of water $= 4.2 J/g°C$

It is known that total heat used, $\Delta Q = mc\Delta T$

$\Delta Q = 3 \times 4.2 \times 10^3 \times 50$

$\Delta Q = 6.3 \times 10^5 J/min$

Now, consider $m kg$ of fuel to be used per minute.

Thus, the heat produced $= m \times 4 \times 10^7 J/min$

However, the heat energy taken by water $=$ heat produced by fuel

Thus, equating both the sides,

$\Rightarrow 6.3 \times 10^5 = m \times 4 \times 10^7$

$\Rightarrow m = \frac{6.3 \times 10^5}{4 \times 10^4}$

$\Rightarrow m = 15.75 g/min$

Clearly, the rate of consumption of the fuel when its heat of combustion is $4.0 \times 10^4 J/g$ supposing the geyser operates on a gas burner is $15.75 g/min$.

Hence, the correct option is (A).

24. Given that,

Mass of Nitrogen, $m = 2.0 \times 10^{-2} kg = 20g$.

Rise in temperature, $\Delta T = 45°C$.

Molecular mass of $N_2, M = 28$

Universal gas constant, $R = 8.3 J mol^{-1} K^{-1}$

Number of moles, $n = \frac{m}{M}$

$n = \frac{2 \times 10^{-2} \times 10^3}{28}$

$n = 0.714$

Now, molar specific heat at constant pressure for nitrogen,

$C_p = \frac{7}{2} R$

$C_p = \frac{7}{2} \times 8.3$

$C_p = 29.05 J mol^{-1} K^{-1}$

The total amount of heat to be supplied is given by the relation:

$\Delta Q = n C_p \Delta T$

$\Delta Q = 0.714 \times 29.05 \times 45$

$\Delta Q = 933.38 J$

Clearly, the amount of heat to be supplied is $933.38 J$.

Hence, the correct option is (B).

25. In physics, the second law of thermodynamics says that heat flows naturally from an object at a higher temperature to an object at a lower temperature, and heat doesn't flow in the opposite direction of its own.

Hence, the correct option is (D).

26. Pascal's Law:

"Any force applied to a confined fluid is transmitted uniformly in all directions throughout the fluid regardless of the shape of the container".

The main applications of the hydraulic system are as follows:

- Industrial: Automated production lines, machine tool industries, Paper industries.
- Mobile hydraulics: Material handling equipment, commercial vehicles, tunnel boring equipment.
- Automobiles: It is used in the systems like breaks, shock absorbers, steering system.
- Marine applications: It mostly covers ocean-going vessels, fishing boats, and naval equipment.

Hence, the correct option is (C).

27. The viscosity of liquids decreases with an increase in temperature while it increases in the case of gases.

Viscosity is a measure of resistance to flow which arises due to the internal friction between layers of fluid. This resistance to fluid motion is like internal friction analogous to friction when a solid moves on a surface.

Strong intermolecular forces between molecules hold them together and resist the movement of layers past one another.

When a liquid is heated, the kinetic energy of its molecules increases and the intermolecular attraction becomes weaker. Hence, the viscosity of a liquid decreases with increase in its temperature.

Hence, the correct option is (B).

28. Electric field intensity is zero inside the hollow spherical charged conductor. So no work is done in moving a test charge inside the conductor and on its surface. Therefore there is no potential difference between any two points inside or on the surface of the conductor.

Hence, the correct option is (B).

29. The Electric Field for a uniformly distributed spherical charge is given by

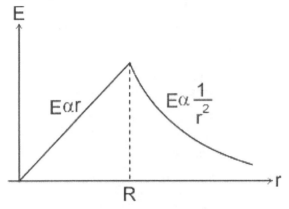

Gauss' law states that the electric flux through any closed surface is equal to the total charge inside divided by ε_0.

Charges are the source and sinks of the electric field. Since in a conducting material the electric field is everywhere zero, the divergence of E is zero, and by Gauss law, the charge density in the interior of the conductor must be zero.

Hence, the correct option is (C).

30. Let us assume that the charge $q = \pm 10\mu C = 10^{-5} C$ is placed at a distance of $5 cm$ from the square $ABCD$ of each side $10 cm$. The square $ABCD$ can be considered as one of the six faces of a cubic Gaussian surface of each side $10 cm$.

Now, the total electric flux through the faces of the cube as per the Gaussian theorem:

$$\phi = \frac{q}{\epsilon_0}$$

Therefore, the total electric flux through the square $ABCD$ will be:

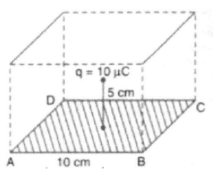

$$\phi_E = \frac{1}{6} \times \phi$$

$$= \frac{1}{6} \times \frac{q}{\epsilon_0}$$

$$= \frac{1}{6} \times \frac{10^{-5}}{8.854 \times 10^{-12}} \quad (\because \epsilon_0 = 8.854 \times 10^{-12})$$

$$= 1.88 \times 10^5 Nm^2 C^{-1}$$

Hence, the correct option is (A).

31. Given:

$Q = 1$, and $r =$ radius of the sphere

By the Gauss law, if the total charge enclosed in a closed surface is Q, then the total electric flux associated with it will be given as,

$$\Rightarrow \phi = \frac{Q}{\varepsilon_0} \quad \cdots (1)$$

By equation 1 the total flux linked with the sphere is given as,

$$\Rightarrow \phi = \frac{Q}{\varepsilon_0}$$

$$\Rightarrow \phi = \frac{1}{\varepsilon_0}$$

$$\Rightarrow \phi = \varepsilon_0^{-1}$$

Hence, the correct option is (C).

32. Concept:

According to Faraday's law of electromagnetic induction, the induced emf is equal to the rate of change of flux multiplied by the number of turns.

$$E = -N \frac{d\phi}{dt}$$

The negative sign is due to Lenz's law.

Calculation:

Given voltage is $50\ V$, $d\phi = 70 - 20 = 50$ mWb, $dt = 0.2\ s$

Total number of turns is:

$$N = \frac{|E|}{|d\phi|} |dt|$$

$$N = \frac{50}{50 \times 10^{-3}} 0.2$$

$$N = 200$$

Hence, the correct option is (D).

33. Concept:

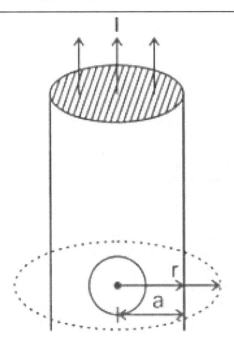

The magnetic field inside (for $r < a$) solid conducting cylindrical wire carrying current I is given by Amperes law

$$\oint H.dl = I_{enclosed}$$

$$H = \frac{Ir}{2\pi a^2}$$

For $r = a$

$$H = \frac{I}{2\pi a}$$

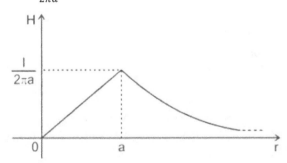

Analysis:

Radius $= R$

Distance from axis $= r$

$\because r < R$

$\oint H.dl = I_{enclosed}$

$H = \dfrac{Ir}{2\pi R^2}$

Hence, the correct option is (C).

34. When sound waves are emitted by a moving source, or when the observer of the sound is moving, the apparent frequency of the sound can change. The shift in frequency due to motion of the sound wave source or of the observer is called the Doppler effect. The distance between the source and observer does not affect the apparent frequency in Doppler effect.

Hence, the correct option is (D).

35. Distance between their surfaces
$= 12R - R - 2R = 9R$
Since,
$P \propto mass$
$a \propto mass$
We know that,
$Distance \propto acceleration$
So, we can write
$\dfrac{a_1}{a_2} = \dfrac{m}{5m} = \dfrac{s_1}{s_2}$
$\dfrac{s_1}{s} = 51$
$5s\, s_1 = s_2\, \ldots\ldots (i)$
$s_1 + s_2 = 9R \ldots\ldots (ii)$
On solving these equations;
$s_1 = 1.5R$
$s_2 = 7.5R$
Since smaller ball have more acceleration in same time interval, smaller ball will cover more distance.
Hence, the correct option is (D).

36. Angular Frequency: $\omega = \sqrt{\dfrac{k}{m_2}}$

Amplitude : $y = A\sin\sqrt{\dfrac{k}{m_2}}$

Step-by-step explanation:

Mass $1 = m_1$

Mass $2 = m_2$

Spring constant $= k$

Angular frequency $= ?$

Amplitude $= ?$

Solution:

As it is given that masses are in equilibrium so initially there is no motion which means that there will be no angular velocity in the start

when m_1 is removed equilibrium will be disturbed and an angular velocity is produced and it will revolve in a circle

We know the formula for angular frequency of an object

$$\omega = \sqrt{\dfrac{k}{m}}$$

Where k is spring constant and m is the mass of object so for the given

Angular frequency will be

$$\omega = \sqrt{\dfrac{k}{m_2}}$$

Now for amplitude we know the formula

$y = A\sin\omega t$

Here t is the time period, A is amplitude and ω is angular frequency

Putting the value of ω here,

$$y = A\sin\left(\sqrt{\frac{k}{m_2}}\right)t$$

Hence, the correct option is (A).

37. Let in same time t, distances covered by man and edge of image be respectively x and y.

$$\tan\theta = \frac{H-h}{x} = \frac{H}{x+y}$$

$$\Rightarrow Hx = Hx + Hy - hx + hy$$

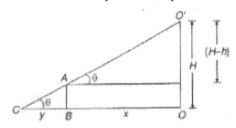

$$\Rightarrow \frac{x}{y} = \frac{(H-h)}{h} \quad \ldots\ldots(i)$$

Now $x = ut$

And $y = vt$

$$\Rightarrow \frac{x}{y} = \frac{u}{v} \quad \ldots\ldots(ii)$$

So, $\frac{u}{v} = \frac{(H-h)}{h}$

$$\Rightarrow v = \frac{hu}{(H-h)}$$

Hence, the correct option is (A).

38. When a suitable trivalent impurity (also called acceptor impurities as these accept electrons from the covalent bond of intrinsic semiconductor) is added to pure semiconductor crystal, we get an extrinsic semiconductor known as a p-type semiconductor.
Hence, the correct option is (A).

39. In an n-type silicon, the electrons are the majority carriers, while the holes are the minority carriers. An n-type semiconductor is obtained when pentavalent atoms, such as phosphorus, are doped in silicon atoms.
Hence, the correct option is (C).

40. Let 1 and 2 represent for Argon atom and Helium atom.

rms speed of Argon, $v_{rms_1} = \sqrt{\frac{3RT_1}{M_1}}$

rms speed of Helium, $v_{rms_2} = \sqrt{\frac{3RT_2}{M_2}}$

According to question,

$v_{rms_1} = v_{rms_2}$

$$\therefore \sqrt{\frac{3RT_1}{M_1}} = \sqrt{\frac{3RT_2}{M_2}}$$

or $\frac{T_1}{M_1} = \frac{T_2}{M_2}$

or $T_1 = \frac{T_2}{M_2} \times M_1 = \frac{253}{4} \times 39.9 = 2.52 \times 10^3 \, K$

Hence, the correct option is (A).

41. The bob of the simple pendulum will experience the acceleration due to gravity and the centripetal acceleration provided by the circular motion of the car.

Acceleration due to gravity $= g$

Centripetal acceleration $= \frac{v^2}{R}$

Where,

v is the uniform speed of the car

R is the radius of the track

Effective acceleration (a_{eff}) is given as:

$$a_{eff} = \sqrt{g^2 + \left(\frac{v^2}{R}\right)^2}$$

Time period, $T = 2\pi\sqrt{\frac{l}{a_{eff}}}$

Where, l is the length of the pendulum

$$\therefore \text{Time period, } T = 2\pi\sqrt{\frac{l}{g^2 + \frac{v^4}{R^2}}}$$

Hence, the correct option is (B).

42. The property of the sound waves that determines the pitch of the sound is its frequency.

The higher the frequency of a sound, the higher pitch. Amplitude is the maximum displacement of vibrating particles of the medium from their mean position. When sound travels from one medium to another, both its velocity and wavelength undergo changes.

Hence, the correct option is (B).

43. Ultraviolet has the shortest wavelength among the given options.

Gamma rays have the shortest wavelength and highest energy in the electromagnetic spectrum.

Radio waves have the highest wavelength and least energy. Radio waves consist of Radar, Amplitude Modulated (AM), Frequency Modulation, and TV.

Electromagnetic spectrum (in order of increasing wavelength) gamma rays, x-rays, ultraviolet, visible light (VIBGYOR), infrared, microwaves, radio waves

Hence, the correct option is (D).

44. In a periscope, the two plane mirrors are kept parallel to each other.

A periscope is an instrument used for observing over an obstacle or object which is prevented by a direct line of sight. When light falls on one of the mirrors, it gets reflected back and the reflected rays fall on the other mirror which further gets reflected towards the observer's eyes. In a periscope, the two plane mirrors are kept parallel to each other. The mirrors are at 45° to the horizontal plane.

Hence, the correct option is (A).

45. The relationship between torque and angular momentum is analogous to force and linear momentum.

Torque = rate of change of angular momentum

Force = rate of change of linear momentum

Hence, the correct option is (C).

46. Angular momentum,

$L = I \times \omega$ ----(1)

Rotational kinetic energy,

$E = \frac{1}{2}I\omega^2$

$\Rightarrow \omega = \sqrt{\frac{2E}{I}}$ ---(2)

Substituting (2) in (1) we get

$L = I \times \sqrt{\frac{2E}{I}}$

$= \sqrt{2EI}$

Therefore, $L \propto \sqrt{E}$

Hence, the correct option is (D).

47. In purely resistive circuits, the current and applied voltage are in phase with each other.

In purely inductive circuits, the current lags the applied voltage by 90°.

In purely capacitive circuits, the current leads the applied voltage by 90°.

Hence, the correct option is (D).

48. When an inductive load is connected, the power factor is lagging.

The overall power factor is defined as the cosine of the angle between the phase voltage and phase current. In AC circuits, the power factor is also defined as the ratio of the real power flowing to the load to the apparent power in the circuit.

In a purely inductive circuit, the current lags the voltage by 90° and the power factor is zero lagging.

In a purely capacitive circuit, the current leads the voltage by 90° and the power factor is zero leading.

Hence, the correct option is (C).

49. Given: $y_1 = a \cdot \sin(\omega t)$, and $y_2 = a \cdot \cos\omega t$

$\Rightarrow y_2 = a\cos(\omega t) = a\sin\left(\omega t + \frac{\pi}{2}\right)$

The resultant amplitude of the wave after superposition of two waves:

$\Rightarrow A = \sqrt{a^2 + b^2 + 2a \times b \times \cos\phi}$

Where, $a =$ amplitude of wave $1, b =$ amplitude of wave 2, and $\phi =$ phase difference

Here, $a = a, b = a$ and $\phi = \frac{\pi}{2} - 0 = \frac{\pi}{2}$

$\Rightarrow A = \sqrt{a^2 + a^2 + 2a \times a \times \cos\frac{\pi}{2}}$

$\Rightarrow A = \sqrt{2a^2}$

$\Rightarrow A = \sqrt{2}a$

Hence, the correct option is (A).

50. 'The amplitude of the resultant wave is equal to the sum of the amplitudes of individual waves' is correct for the constructive interference of the two harmonic waves.

When two or more waves come together at some point in space then the resultant disturbance wave is the vector sum of disturbance of the individual waves.

When two waves superimpose then the resultant amplitude of the wave at that point is the vector sum of amplitudes of each individual wave. This phenomenon is called the interference of waves.

If two waves superimpose with each other in the same phase, the amplitude of the resultant is equal to the sum of the amplitudes of individual waves resulting in the maximum intensity of light, this is known as constructive interference.

Hence, the correct option is (A).

51. Bromine the only non-metallic element that is in a liquid state at room temperature. It is a member of the halogen elements (Group 17) of the periodic table. Bromine is found in nature dispersed throughout Earth's crust only in compounds as soluble and insoluble bromides.

Hence, the correct option is (C).

52. 'Metallic character decreases on moving from left to right in a period' is the correct statement.

When we take a look at the modern form of the periodic table we see that metals are placed on the left side and non-metals are placed on the right side and metalloids find a place in between the metals and the non-metals. As we move from left to right, the atomic number keeps increasing and so the valence electrons. So, as we move right in the period the valence electrons increase and the metallic character decreases.

Hence, the correct option is (A).

53. The equilibrium constant should be written after balancing the equation.

Thus, the equation becomes:

$2NO_2(g) \rightarrow 2NO(g) + O_2(g)$.

We know that:

In a reaction at equilibrium, the equilibrium concentrations of all reactants and products can be measured. The equilibrium constant (K_c) is a mathematical relationship that shows how the concentrations of the products vary with the concentration of the reactants in a reversible chemical reaction at a given temperature.

Therefore, the equilibrium constant becomes:

$K_c = \dfrac{[NO]^2[O_2]}{[NO_2]^2}$

Hence, the correct option is (A).

54. We know that:

Buffer capacity $= 2.303 \dfrac{as}{(a+s)}$

Given that:

$a + s = 1$

Buffer capacity $= 2.303$ as,

Graph of buffer capacity vs addition salt, keeping $a + s = 1$ can be draw as,

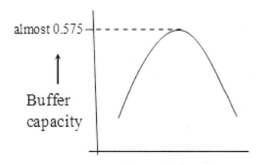

$Max B.C. = 2.303(0.5 \times 0.3)$

$= 0.575$

Mini $B.C. = 2.303(0.01 \times 0.99)$

$= 0.022$

Hence, the correct option is (B).

55. The boiling point of a given compound is as follows:

I. Ethylmethylamine - 33 to 34 °C

II. Propylamine - 49 °C

III. Trimethylamine - 2.9 °C

Hence, the correct option is (B).

56. The statement "atom is indivisible" was proposed by Dalton.

John Dalton considered that "all matter is composed of small particle called the atom."

According to Dalton:

- Atom is the smallest indivisible part of matter which takes part in the chemical reaction.
- Atom is neither created nor be destroyed.

Hence, the correct option is (B).

57. Oxygen of iron oxide is removed and added to carbon monoxide to form carbon dioxide.

The reaction takes place as follows:

$Fe_2O_3(s) + 3CO(g) \xrightarrow{\Delta} 2Fe(l) + 3CO_2(g)$

Carbon mono oxide : oxidation

Iron oxide : reduction

Hence, the correct option is (A).

58. We know that for a first order reaction:-

Rate = k[R]

$\therefore 1.5 \times 10^{-2} M\text{min}^{-1} = k[0.5M]$

$\Rightarrow k = \dfrac{1.5 \times 10^{-2} M/\text{min}}{0.5M}$

$\Rightarrow k = 0.03 \text{ min}^{-1}$

We also know that, half life of a first order reaction:

$t_{\frac{1}{2}} = \dfrac{\ln(2)}{k}$

$= \dfrac{0.693}{k}$

$= \dfrac{0.693}{0.03 \text{ min}^{-1}}$

$= 23.1$ min

Hence, the correct option is (B).

59. For a first-order reaction,

rate=K[A]

When the concentration of A is doubled,

New rate = K[2A]

= 2 × rate

The rate of reaction becomes double.

Hence, the correct option is (A).

60. Given,

$[A]_0 = 2$ g

$[A]_t = 0.2$ g

The rate constant for a first order reaction, K= $4.606 \times 10^{-3} \, s^{-1}$

Physics & Chemistry : Mock Test - 1

For a first order reaction,

$$K = \frac{2.303}{t} \log \frac{[A]_0}{[A]_t}$$

Where,

K = First order rate constant

$[A]_0$ = Initial concentration

$[A]_t$ = Concentration at time 't'

$$\Rightarrow t = \frac{2.303}{4.606 \times 10^{-3}} \log \frac{2}{0.2}$$

$$\Rightarrow t = \frac{1000}{2} \log 10$$

As we know,

$\log 10 = 1$

$\Rightarrow t = 500\ s$

Hence, the correct option is (B).

61. An aqueous solution of hydrochloric acid shows negative deviation from Raoult's law.

Raoult's law states that the vapor pressure of a solvent above a solution is equal to the vapor pressure of the pure solvent at the same temperature scaled by the mole fraction of the solvent present, i.e.,

$[P_{solution} = X_{solvent} P°_{solvent}]$

If the attraction between different molecules, for example between HCl and H_2O molecules, is stronger, the escaping tendency from the solution to the vapour phase will be smaller, then the partial vapour pressure will be smaller than predicted by Raoult's law and the system exhibits a negative deviation.

Hence, the correct option is (B).

62. Given:

Weight of solute $(w) = 1\ g$

Weight of solvent $(W) = 75\ g$

Boiling point of solution $= 100.114°C$

Boiling point of solvent $= 100°C$

Therefore,

$\Delta T = 100.114 - 100 = 0.114°C$

Molecular weight of solute $(m) = 60.1$

Boiling point elevation constant $(K) = ?$

We know that:

$$m = \frac{1000 \times K \times w}{\Delta T \times W}$$

or, $K = \frac{m \times \Delta T \times W}{1000 \times w}$

$$= \frac{60.1 \times 0.114 \times 75}{1000 \times 1}$$

$$= \frac{513.8}{1000}$$

$K = 0.513$

Hence, the correct option is (B).

63. Given:

Vapour pressure of liquid A,

$P_A = 120\ mm$

Vapour pressure of liquid B,

$P_B = 180\ mm$

Number of moles of liquid A,

$n_A = 2$

Number of moles of liquid B,

$n_B = 3$

Therefore,

Mole fraction of liquid A,

$$X_A = \frac{n_A}{n_A + n_B}$$

$$= \frac{2}{5}$$

Mole fraction of liquid B,

$$X_B = \frac{n_B}{n_A + n_B}$$

$$= \frac{3}{5}$$

We know that:

Vapor Pressure of solution,

$P = X_A P_A + X_B P_B$

$= \frac{2}{5} \times 120 + \frac{3}{5} \times 180$

$= 48 + 108$

$P = 156\ mm\ Hg$

Hence, the correct option is (A).

64. In ionic solids the vacancies are produced due to absence of cations and anions in stoichiometric proportions resulting in defect called Schottky defect.

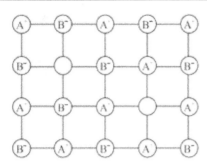

Schottky defect

The density is less than expected due to missing spaces.

Hence, the correct option is (B).

65. Given:

$a = 390 \, pm$

For bcc structure:

Interionic distance $= r^+ + r^- = \dfrac{\sqrt{3}}{2} a$

where, a: edge length

$r^+_{NH_4^+} + r^-_{Cl^-} = \dfrac{\sqrt{3}}{2} a$

$r^+_{NH_4^+} + 180 = \dfrac{\sqrt{3}}{2} \times 390$

$r^+_{NH_4^+} + 180 = 338$

$r^+_{NH_4^+} = 338 \, pm - 180 \, pm$

$r^+_{NH_4^+} = 158 \, pm$

Hence, the correct option is (B).

66. Given:

Distance between a Pb²⁺ ion and S²⁻ ion is 297 pm.

$\Rightarrow (r + r') = 297 pm = 297 \times 10^{-10} cm$

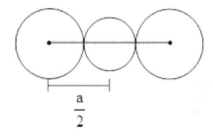

$NaCl$ structure - fcc structure

$\Rightarrow Pb^{2+}$ occupies O^- voids at edge centers.

We know that:

$a = 2(r + r')$

$\dfrac{a}{2} = 297 \times 10^{-10} \, cm$

$a = 297 \times 2 \times 10^{-10} \, cm$

Volume $= a^3 = 209584584 \times 10^{-30} \, cm^3$

$= 209.58 \times 10^{-24} \, cm^3$

Hence, the correct option is (A).

67. The law, which states that at constant temperature, the volume of a given mass of gas is inversely proportional is pressure, is known as Boyles law. As per Boyle's law, any change in the volume occupied by a gas (at constant quantity and temperature) will result in a change in the pressure exerted by it. In other words, the product of the initial pressure and the initial volume of a gas is equal to the product of its final pressure and final volume (at constant temperature and number of moles). This law can be expressed mathematically as follows:

$P_1 V_1 = P_2 V_2$

Where,

- P_1 is the initial pressure exerted by the gas
- V_1 is the initial volume occupied by the gas
- P_2 is the final pressure exerted by the gas
- V_2 is the final volume occupied by the gas

Hence, the correct option is (A).

68. Alkali metals are the elements of group 1. The outer shell configuration of group 1 elements is ns^1, where n is the number of it's period. Magnesium is not an alkali metal because it's outer shell configuration is ns^2.

Hence, the correct option is (A).

69. This theory was given by Berzelius in 1809. According to this theory, the organic living compounds are not formed from inorganic compounds but from a vital force. The German Scientist contradicted the theory and prepared Urea through ammonium chloride and Potassium Cyanate.

Hence, the correct option is (A).

70. The law of octaves was found to be applicable till calcium. After calcium, the properties of the next elements were not synchronous as per the law of octaves. Law of octaves, in chemistry, the generalization made by the English chemist J.A.R. Newlands in 1865 that, if the chemical elements are arranged according to increasing atomic weight, those with similar physical and chemical properties occur after each interval of seven elements.

Hence, the correct option is (B).

71. Water on calcium chloride is an example of absorption. During absorption, the adsorbate molecules penetrate the bulk of the adsorbent. This is because water is added to the calcium carbonate, water goes in the bulk of the calcium carbonate.

Hence, the correct option is (C).

72. $C - C$ bond length $= 1.54 \overset{\circ}{A}$

$C = C$ bond length $= 1.34 \overset{\circ}{A}$

$C \equiv C$ bond length $= 1.20 \overset{\circ}{A}$

$$H - C \equiv C - \underset{\underset{H}{|}}{\overset{\overset{H}{|}}{C}} - H$$

Since propyne has a triple bond, therefore it has minimum bond length.

Hence, the correct option is (D).

73. Given: Enthalpy of vaporisation of a substance is: $8400 \, J \, mol^{-1}$

Temperature or boiling point of substance is: $-173.15°C$

We have Kelvin = temperature

= Celsius temperature+ $273.15°C$

$= -173.15°C + 273.15°C$

$= 100 \, K$

Now, we know,

Change in entropy, $\Delta S = \frac{q_{rev}}{T}$

$= \left(\frac{8400}{100}\right)$

$= 84 \, Jmol^{-1}K^{-1}$

Hence, the correct option is (A).

74. $\Delta H < \Delta E$ only if the number of moles of products is less than the number of moles of the reactants.

If $n_p < n_r; \Delta n_g = n_p - n_r = -$ ve. where, n_p = No. of moles of products

n_r = No. of moles of reactants, n_g = No. of moles of gas

Therefore, $\Delta H < \Delta E$

Hence, the correct option is (D).

75. In this case, $^{80}_{35}Br$,

$Z = 35$

$A = 80$

Number of protons = number of electrons = $Z = 35$

Number of neutrons = $80 - 35 = 45$

Hence, the correct option is (A).

76. Ethane is an example of a saturated carbon compound. Saturated hydrocarbons are carbon compound that contains only single bonds between carbon atoms. Ethane is a colorless, odorless gas. Ethane is isolated on an industrial scale from natural gas and as a petrochemical by-product of petroleum refining. The chemical formula of Ethane is C_2H_6.

Ethane can be found underground in liquid form in rock formations.

Other details:

Ethene	C_2H_4
Acetylene systematic name is ethyne	C_2H_2
Ethanol (simple alcohol)	C_2H_5OH

Hence, the correct option is (A).

77.

	List-I (Electrode)		List-II (Type)
1.	Calomel	P.	Reference
2.	Glass	Q.	Membrane
3.	Hydrogen	R.	Gas
4.	Quinhydrone	S.	Redox

Hence, the correct option is (A).

78. The balanced chemical reaction can be written as follows:

$2Cr(s) + 3Fe^2 + (0.1M) \rightarrow 2Cr^3 + (0.01M) + 3Fe(s)$

Given

$E^o_{\frac{Cr^{3+o}}{Cr}} = -0.74V$

$E^o_{\frac{Fe^{2+o}}{Fe}} = -0.44 \, V$

The cell can be represented as follows:

$Cr|Cr^{3+}(0.01M)||Fe^{2+}(0.1M)|Fe(s)$

E^o_{Cell} can be calculated as follows:

$E^o_{Cell} = E_{\frac{Fe^{2+o}}{Fe}} - E_{\frac{Cr^{3+o}}{Cr}}$

$E^o_{Cell} = -0.44 - (-0.74) = 0.30 \, V$

$E_{Cell} = E^o_{Cell} - \frac{2.303RT}{nF} \log\left(\frac{[Cr^3]^2}{[Fe^{2+}]^3}\right)$

Putting all the values of the constants, we get,

$E_{Cell} = 0.30 - \frac{0.0591}{6} \log\left(\frac{(0.01)^2}{(0.1)^2}\right)$

$E_{Cell} = 0.30 + 0.01$

$E_{Cell} = 0.31 \, V$

Hence, the correct option is (A).

79. We know the cell reaction

$E^o_{cell} = E^o_{Cathode} - E^o_{anode}$

Here Fe is cathode and A is anode

$$\therefore E^0_{cell} = -0.44 - (-1.66)$$

$$= -0.44 + 1.66$$

Cell reaction $= +1.22\ V$

$2A - 6e^- \rightarrow 2Al^{3+}$ At anode

$3Fe^{2+} + 6e^- \rightarrow 3Fe$ At cathode

$2Al + 3Fe^{2+} \rightarrow 2Al^{3+} + 3Fe$ Cell reaction

Here

$n = 6$ (Number of electron in cell reaction)

$$E^0_{cell} = E^0_{cell} + \frac{0.059}{n}\log\frac{[Fe^{2+}]^3}{[A]^{3+}]^2}$$

$$= 1.22 + \frac{0.059}{6}\log\frac{[0.02]^3}{[0.01]^2}$$

$$= 1.22 + 9.8 \times 10^{-3}\log\left[\frac{8\times 10^{-6}}{1\times 10^{-4}}\right]$$

$$= 1.22 + 9.8 \times 10^{-3} \times 1.25$$

$$= 1.22 + 0.0122$$

$$= 1.232\ V$$

Hence, the correct option is (D).

80. A complex has the molecular formula $Co.5NH_3.NO_2.Cl_2$. One mole of this complex produces three moles of ions in an aqueous solution. On reacting this solution with excess of $AgNO_3$ solution, we get 2 moles of white ppt. The complex is $[Co(NH_3)_5NO_2]Cl_2$.

$[Co(NH_3)_5NO_2]Cl_2$ can form three ions, one $[Co(NH_3)_5NO_2]^{2+}$ and two Cl^- ions.

As 1 mole of complex gives 2 moles of Cl^- ions, 2 moles of AgCl will be precipitated.

Hence, the correct option is (C).

81. The co-ordination number and oxidation state of Cr in $K_3[Cr(C_2O_4)_3]$ are 6 and +3 respectively.

Co-ordination number of Cr^{3+} ion is six because chromium ion is surrounded by three bidentate ligands.

For oxidation state of central metal ion $3 + x - 6 = 0$

[where x is the oxidation state of central metal ion]

As oxalate is a bidentate ligand, coordination number of Cr is 6.

Since the overall charge on the complex is 0, the sum of oxidation states of all elements in it should be equal to 0

Let the oxidation number of Cr be x.

Therefore, 3+x+3×(−2)=0

x=+3

Hence, the correct option is (A).

82. cis-[Co(en)$_2Cl_2$] compounds is expected to exhibit optical isomerism.

Compound 'a' does not have an element of symmetry and thus exhibits optical isomerism.

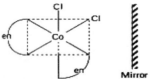

Hence, the correct option is (A).

83. Methyl salicylate has a smell of oil of wintergreen.

- Methyl salicylate (oil of wintergreen or wintergreen oil) is an organic compound with the formula $C_6H_4(OH)(CO_2CH_3)$.
- It is produced by many species of plants, particularly wintergreens.
- It is also produced synthetically.
- It is used as a fragrance, in foods and beverages, and in liniments.

Hence, the correct option is (B).

84. Given: CH_3CH_2COCl

Numbering the carbon atoms as:

$\overset{3}{C}H_3\overset{2}{C}H_2\overset{1}{C}OCl$

- This is an acid chloride.
- It consists of three carbon atoms in the parent chain and chloroformyl group $(-COCl)$.
- In the IUPAC name, the suffix "oyl chloride" is added. Therefore, the IUPAC name will be propanoyl chloride.

Hence, the correct option is (B).

85. Toluene reacts with halogen in presence of iron(III) chloride giving ortho and para halo compounds, the reaction is electrophilic substitution reaction.

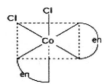

The H atom or aromatic nucleus is replaced with Cl atom. The electrophile in this reaction is Cl^+ ion obtained by the reaction of Cl_2 with $AlCl_3$.

Hence, the correct option is (D).

86. Structural formula of Haloalkane is R-X.

It was derived from alkanes containing a halogens or more.

They are used as flame retardants, fire extinguishers, refrigerants, propellants, solvents, and medicinal items.

"RX" in which R is an alkyl or alkyl substituted group and X is a halogen (F, Cl, Br, I).

Haloalkanes are commonly used in organic synthesis as synthonous alternatives to alkyl cation (R+).

Hence, the correct option is (D).

87. Formaldehyde is also known as formalin.

It is an organic compound which occurs naturally with formula CH_2O (H–CHO).

It is an effective precursor for many other chemicals and compounds.

This is primarily used in industrial resin processing, e.g. for particle boards and coatings.

Acetaldehyde and Acrolein are the Aldehydes while Acetone is the Ketones.

Hence, the correct option is (D).

88. When a primary amine reacts with chloroform in alcoholic KOH, the product is an isocyanide.

Carbylamine reaction:

- Primary amines when treated with chloroform and ethanolic KOH gives carbylamines or isocyanides.
- The reaction occurs via carbene intermediate,
- Chloroform reacts with KOH to give chloro carbene: CCl_2.

The general form of the reaction is:

$$\underset{\text{Primary amine}}{R-NH_2} + \underset{\text{Chloroform}}{CHCl_3} + \underset{\text{Potassium hydroxide}}{3KOH(alc.)} \xrightarrow{\Delta}$$
$$\underset{\text{Carbylamine}}{R-NC} + 3KCl + 3H_2O$$

For example,

$$\underset{\text{Methanmine}}{CH_3-NH_2} + CHCl_3 + 3KOH(alc.) \xrightarrow{\Delta}$$
$$\underset{\text{Methyl carblylamine or methyl isocyanide}}{CH_3-NC} + 2KCl + 3H_2O$$

Hence, the correct option is (A).

89. A nucleotide is formed of nitrogen base, sugar and phosphate.

A nucleotide is composed of three distinctive chemical sub-units: a five-carbon sugar molecule, a nucleobase, (the two of which together are called a nucleoside) and one phosphate group. With all three joined, a nucleotide is also termed a "nucleoside mono-phosphate", "nucleoside di-phosphate" or "nucleoside tri-phosphate", depending on how many phosphates make up the phosphate group. The nucleobase molecule, also known as a nitrogenous base.

Hence, the correct option is (A).

90. Glycogen is a polymer of glucose. Glycogen is a substance which is deposited in body tissues in the form of carbohydrates and it is broken down in the form of glucose which provides an instant source of energy to muscles by the process of glycolysis. It is accumulated in response to insulin and it is broken down into glucose in response to glucagon and it is mainly stored in the liver and the muscles. It provides the body with an instant source of energy when the blood glucose level decreases. It maintains blood glucose level and it is really important because glucose is the only fuel used by the brain virtually.

Hence, the correct option is (A).

91. The materials used for making non-stick utensils of kitchens is teflon.

Teflon:

- Teflon is short for tetrafluoroethylene, also known as PTFE.
- It is used to make non-stick cookware, pans because it is unreactive in nature and has non-stick properties.

Rayon:

- Rayon is a synthetic fibre whose properties are similar to that of silk.
- Rayon is obtained from a natural source like wood pulp.

PVC:

- PVC stands for Poly Vinyl Chloride.
- It is a plastic that gets deformed easily when heated and can be moulded again into other forms.

Polyether:

- It is a synthetic polymer made by joining polymers that have an ester linkage between them.
- It falls in a class of compounds called polyurethanes.

Hence, the correct option is (C).

92. Natural rubber is an added polymer from a tropical rubber tree that is collected as a milky white fluid known as latex.

The monomer isoprene (2-methyl-1,3-butadiene) produces natural rubber. As isoprene has two double bonds, after the polymerization response, it still retains one of them. The cis structure for the methyl groups is natural rubber.

Rubber is an example of a polymer of the elastomer kind where, after being stretched or deformed, the polymer has the ability to return to its original form. When in a resting state, the rubber polymer is coiled. The elastic properties derive from the ability to stretch the chains apart but the chains snap back to the initial position when the stress is released.

Thus, natural rubber is a polymer of isoprene.

Hence, the correct option is (A).

93. Ferric oxide (Fe_2O_3) occurs in nature as haematite. It is a red powder, insoluble in H_2O and not acted upon by air or

H_2O. It is amphoteric in nature and reacts with acids and alkalis and used as a catalyst in the oxidation of CO to CO_2 in the Bosch process.

Hence, the correct option is (C).

94. Cr_2O_3 is amphoteric.

Chromium(atomic no. 24, symbol-Cr) forms many oxides. Some of its common oxidation states are $+2, +3$ and $+6$. Chromium (III) oxide (green in colour) is amphoteric, i.e., it can react as both acid and base. Its formula is Cr_2O_3.

Hence, the correct option is (B).

95. Isopropyl chloride undergoes hydrolysis by either SN^1 or SN^2 mechanism because it is secondary alkyl halide, can undergo SN^1 or SN^2 depending on solvent and nucleophile.

Hence, the correct option is (D).

96. Urea is a major fertilizer used worldwide. It provides nitrogen to the soil by decomposing to ammonia and CO_2 when acted on by urease, an enzyme in soils. Then, ammonia is taken by the plants.

$NH_2CONH_2 + H_2O \rightarrow 2NH_3 + CO_2$

Hence, the correct option is (B).

97. The family of polycarbonates contains very important polymers which are used where high optical properties combined with strength are needed. The polycarbonate is manufactured by a condensation reaction between bisphenol A and either carbonyl chloride or diphenyl carbonate. Carbonyl chloride is a very poisonous gas. On the other hand, diphenyl carbonate is produced from dimethyl carbonate, which is readily manufactured from methanol, carbon monoxide and oxygen in the liquid phase, in presence of copper(II) chloride, $CuCl_2$.

Hence, the correct option is (B).

98. The compound 'A' is nitrobenzene. On reduction it gives aniline (compound B), which on reaction with trichloro methane and caustic potash forms isocyanobenzene (or phenyl isocyanide, compound (C), Hoffmann's carbylamine test). The compound 'C' on catalytic reduction gives N-methyl benzenamine.

Hence, the correct option is (A).

99. Haloforms are trihalogen derivatives of methane. Haloform compounds with the formula CHX_3, where X is a halogen atom. Example : Chloroform $CHCl_3$

$$CH_4 \xrightarrow[+3X]{-3H} CHX_3 (X = Cl, Br, I)$$

Hence, the correct option is (B).

100. Helium gas is used in gas balloons instead of hydrogen gas because it is non-combustible.

Hydrogen and helium are the most commonly used lift gases.

Although helium is twice as heavy as (diatomic) hydrogen, they are both so much lighter than air that this difference is inconsequential.

Helium is the second lightest gas. For that reason, it is an attractive gas for lifting as well.

Hence, the correct option is (C).

Physics & Chemistry : Mock Test 02

Physics

Q.1 A block of mass m is placed on a smooth table. Its two sides are attached to fixed walls by means of collinear horizontal springs of spring constants k_1 and k_2 $(k_1 > k_2)$ as shown in the figure. The block is made to oscillate horizontally along the line of two springs. The frequency of its oscillation is:

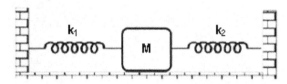

A. $\frac{1}{2\pi}\left(\frac{k_1+k_2}{m}\right)$
B. $\frac{1}{2\pi}\sqrt{\frac{k_1+k_2}{m}}$
C. $\frac{1}{2\pi}\sqrt{\frac{m}{k_1+k_2}}$
D. $\frac{1}{2\pi}\sqrt{\frac{m}{k_1 k_2}}$

Q.2 A body executing Simple Harmonic Motion has its velocity 10 cm/s and 7 cm/s when its displacement from the mean position is 3 cm and 4 cm, respectively. The length of the path is:

A. 10 cm **B.** 9.52 cm **C.** 4 cm **D.** 11.36 cm

Q.3 In a resonance tube experiment, the first and the second resonance with a given tuning fork were observed at 16.7 cm and 51.7 cm respectively. The wavelength as deduced from the data is:

A. 70.0 cm **B.** 66.8 cm
C. 68.8 cm **D.** None of these

Q.4 The silvering in thermos flasks is done to avoid heat transfer by:
A. Convection
B. Conduction
C. Radiation
D. Both convection and conduction

Q.5 The work function of Cesium is 2.27eV. The cut-off voltage which stops the emission of electrons from a cesium cathode irradiated with light of 600nm wavelength is:
A. 0.5eV **B.** -0.2eV
C. 0.2eV **D.** 2.06785 eV

Q.6 Consider an excited hydrogen atom in state n moving with a velocity v (v<< c). It emits a photon in the direction of its motion and changes its state to a lower state m. Apply momentum and energy conservation principle to calculate the frequency v of the emitted radiation. Compare this with the frequency v_0 emitted if the atom were at rest.

A. $v_0 = v\left(1-\frac{v}{c}\right)$
B. $v_0 = v\left(1+\frac{v}{c}\right)$
C. $v = v_0\left(1-\frac{v}{c}\right)$
D. $v = v_0\left(1+\frac{v}{c}\right)$

Q.7 Carbon, silicon, and germanium have four valence electrons each. These are characterised by valence and conduction bands separated by energy bandgap respectively equal to $(Eg)_C, (Eg)_{Si}$ and $(Eg)_{Ge}$. Which of the following statements is true?
A. $(Eg)_{Si} < (Eg)_{Ge} < (Eg)_C$
B. $(Eg)_C < (Eg)_{Ge} > (Eg)_{Si}$
C. $(Eg)_C > (Eg)_{Si} > (Eg)_{Ge}$
D. $(Eg)_C = (Eg)_{Si} = (Eg)_{Ge}$

Q.8 "Good absorber of heat is good radiator of heat also" is:
A. Stefan's law **B.** Kirchhof's law
C. Plank's law **D.** Wien's law

Q.9 In the Radioactive transformation $Z \xrightarrow{\alpha} y \xrightarrow{\beta} X \xrightarrow{\beta} R$: the nuclei of R and Z are:
A. Isobars **B.** Isotopes **C.** Isomers **D.** Isotones

Q.10 Wavelengths of extreme lines of Paschen series for hydrogen is:
A. 2.27 μm and 7.43 μm
B. 1.45 μm and 4.04 μm
C. 0.818 μm and 1.89 μm
D. 0.365 μm and 0.656 μm

Q.11 What is the energy of an electron that is revolving in the second orbit of the hydrogen?
A. - 1.51 eV **B.** - 3.4 eV
C. - 13.6 eV **D.** - 15.1 eV

Q.12 The time required for the light to pass through a glass slab (refractive index $= 1.5$) of thickness 4 mm is:
($c = 3 \times 10^8$ m/sec, speed of light in free space)
A. 10^{-11} sec **B.** 2×10^{-11} sec
C. 2×10^{-12} sec **D.** 2×10^{-5} sec

Q.13 A convex lens of focal length 50 cm and a concave lens of focal length 25 cm are placed in contact with each other. Then the equivalent focal length of the combination will be:
A. 50 cm **B.** −25 cm **C.** −50 cm **D.** 25 cm

Q.14 A spherical source of power 4 W and frequency 800 Hz is emitting sound waves. The intensity of waves at a distance 200 m is:
A. 8×10^{-6} W/m^2
B. 2×10^{-4} W/m^2
C. 1×10^{-4} W/m^2
D. 4×10^5 W/m^2

Q.15 A bullet of mass 20 g has an initial speed of 1 ms^{-1}, just before it starts penetrating a mud wall of thickness 20 cm. If the wall offers a mean resistance of 2.5×10^{-2} N, the speed of the bullet after emerging from the other side of the wall is close to:

A. $0.3\ ms^{-1}$
B. $0.4\ ms^{-1}$
C. $0.1\ ms^{-1}$
D. $0.7\ ms^{-1}$

Q.16 A stream of electrons is moving along the line AB lying in the same plane as a circular conducting loop. Select the correct options from the following.

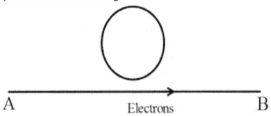

A. A current will be induced in a clockwise direction as seen from above
B. A current will be induced in an anticlockwise direction as seen from above
C. No current will be induced in the coil
D. A current will be induced and will change direction as electrons move towards and away from the coil

Q.17 A cylinder with a movable piston contains 3 moles of hydrogen at standard temperature and pressure. The walls of the cylinder are made of a heat insulator, and the piston is insulated by having a pile of sand on it. By what factor does the pressure of the gas increase if the gas is compressed to half its original volume?
A. 2.666
B. 3.656
C. 2.639
D. None of the above

Q.18 Which of the following process is used to do maximum work done on the ideal gas if the gas is compressed to half of its initial volume?
A. Isothermal
B. Isochoric
C. Isobaric
D. Adiabatic

Q.19 What happens when a gas expands adiabatically?
A. No energy is needed for expansion
B. Law of conservation of energy is inapplicable
C. Energy is needed and comes from the wall of the gas's container
D. Internal energy of the gas is used in doing work

Q.20 If a person travels from the equator to the poles, he finds that the value of acceleration due to gravity (g) ____
A. Decreases
B. Increases
C. Remains constant
D. Decrease upto a certain latitude, becomes zero and then it increases

Q.21 Which one of the following affects the efficiency of oil transportation through pipeline?
A. Surface Tension
B. Stress
C. Viscosity
D. Strain

Q.22 Some insects like water strider is able to walk on the surface of water due to:
A. Gravitational force
B. Surface tension
C. Viscosity
D. Capilariy rise

Q.23 A uniformly charged conducting sphere of $2.4m$ diameter has a surface charge density of $80.0\mu C/m^2$. What is the total electric flux leaving the surface of the sphere?
A. $1.3 \times 10^8 Nm^2/C$
B. $1.6 \times 10^5 Nm^3/C$
C. $2.5 \times 10^8 Nm^2/C$
D. $1.6 \times 10^8 Nm^2/C$

Q.24 A circuit has a section AB as shown in the figure. The emf of the source equals $E = 10V$, the capacitor capacitances are equal to $C_1 = 1.0\mu F$ and $C_2 = 2.0\mu F$ and the potential difference $V_A - V_B = 5.0V$. Find the voltage across each capacitor.

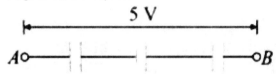

A. 10 and 5 Volt
B. 15 and 25 Volt
C. 10 and 15 Volt
D. 17 and 34 Volt

Q.25 Find the capacitance of the infinite ladder between points X and Y in the following figure:

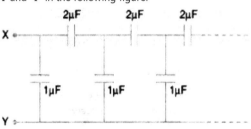

A. $1\mu F$
B. $2\mu F$
C. $3\mu F$
D. $5\mu F$

Q.26 What is the force between two small charged sphere having charges of $2 \times 10^{-7}C$ and $3 \times 10^{-7}C$ placed $30cm$ apart in air?
A. $6.5 \times 10^{-3} N$
B. $7 \times 10^{-13} N$
C. $1.5 \times 10^3 N$
D. $6 \times 10^{-3} N$

Q.27 Find the electric charge Q_1 on plates of capacitor C_1, shown in Figure below:

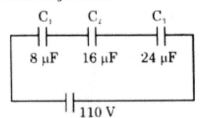

A. $50 \times 10^{-5}C$
B. $48 \times 10^{-5}C$
C. $52 \times 10^{-5}C$
D. $48 \times 12^{-5}C$

Q.28 The total electric flux through a closed surface in which a certain amount of charge is placed depends on the:
A. Shape of the surface
B. Size of the surface

C. Both shape and size of the surface
D. None of these

Q.29 An infinitely long uniform solid wire of radius a carries a uniform dc current of density $\vec{J}$.
The magnetic field at a distance r from the center of the wire is proportional to:
A. r for $r < a$ and $\frac{1}{r^2}$ for $r > a$
B. 0 for $r < a$ and $\frac{1}{r}$ for $r > a$
C. r for $r < a$ and $\frac{1}{r}$ for $r > a$
D. 0 for $r < a$ and $\frac{1}{r^2}$ for $r > a$

Q.30 The work done on moving a charge particle of -5 C in an electric field is 100 J. Find the potential difference.
A. 20 volt   B. -20 volt   C. 10 volt   D. -10 volt

Q.31 The wavelength associated with a moving particle depends upon power p of its mass m, q th power of its velocity v and r th power of Planck's constant h. Then the correct set of values of p, q and r is:
A. $p = 1, q = -1, r = 1$
B. $p = 1, q = 1, r = 1$
C. $p = -1, q = -1, r = -1$
D. $p = -1, q = -1, r = 1$

Q.32 The temperature at which the speed of sound in the air becomes double of its value at $27°C$, is-
A. $-123°C$ B. $927°C$ C. $327°C$ D. $54°C$

Q.33 Interference proves:
[UPSESSB TGT Science, 2016]
A. Transverse nature of a wave
B. Longitudinal nature of wave
C. Wave nature
D. Particle nature

Q.34 Light can be polarized by:
[UPSESSB TGT Science, 2016]
A. Reflection   B. Refraction
C. Scattering   D. All the above

Q.35 Light is polarized to the maximum when it is incident on a glass surface at an angle of incidence:
[UPSESSB TGT Science, 2016]
A. 57°   B. 67°   C. 53°   D. 37°

Q.36 A boatman can row with a speed of $10 kmh^{-1}$ in still water. If the river flows steadily at $5 kmh^{-1}$, in which direction should the boatman row in order to reach a point on the other bank directly opposite to the point from where he started? (The width of the river is $2\ km$):
A. Along the flow
B. 60° in NW
C. 90° to the flow of the river
D. 120° with the direction of flow

Q.37 Which of the following is used primarily in semiconductors?
A. Alkali metals
B. Alkaline earth metals
C. Metalloids
D. Halogens

Q.38 What is the need for doping?
A. To increase the conductivity of semiconductor
B. To decrease the conductivity of semiconductor
C. To increase the temperature of semiconductor
D. To decrease the temperature of semiconductor

Q.39 An ideal gas is enclosed in a cylinder at pressure of 2 atm and temperature, $300\ K$. The mean time between two successive collisions is $6 \times 10^{-8}\ s$. If the pressure is doubled and temperature is increased to $500\ K$, the mean time between two successive collisions will be close to:
A. $0.5 \times 10^{-8}\ s$ B. $2 \times 10^{-7}\ s$
C. $3 \times 10^{-6}\ s$ D. $4 \times 10^{-8}\ s$

Q.40 One kg of a diatomic gas is at a pressure of $8 \times 10^4\ N/m^2$. The density of the gas is $4\ kg/m^3$. What is the energy of the gas due to its thermal motion?
A. $3 \times 10^4\ J$ B. $5 \times 10^4\ J$
C. $6 \times 10^4\ J$ D. $7 \times 10^4\ J$

Q.41 $1 kWh = $ _____ J
A. $3.6 \times 10^4 J$ B. $3.6 \times 10^5 J$
C. $3.6 \times 10^6 J$ D. $3.6 \times 10^3 J$

Q.42 Heating effect produced by current is due to the _____.
A. Collision of electrons
B. Movement of electrons
C. Resistance in electrons
D. Lose of energy

Q.43 Two waves $y_1 = a \cdot \sin(\omega t)$ and $y_2 = a \cdot \sin(\omega t + \phi)$ are moving in the same direction, if both the waves are superimposed then the amplitude of the resultant wave is:
A. $2a. \sin\left(\frac{\phi}{2}\right)$ B. $2a. \cos\left(\frac{\phi}{2}\right)$
C. $2a$ D. None of these

Q.44 When two wave pulses overlap each other, the displacement of the resultant wave is the:
A. Algebric sum of the displacement due to each pulse
B. Vector sum of the displacement due to each pulse
C. Product of the displacement due to each pulse
D. None of these

Q.45 Magnetic field at a distance r from an infinitely long straight conductor carrying a steady current varies as:
A. $\frac{1}{r^2}$ B. $\frac{1}{r}$ C. $\frac{1}{r^3}$ D. $\frac{1}{\sqrt{r}}$

Q.46 Radius of a current carrying circular coil is R at a distance $x(x >> R)$ on the axis of circular coil the magnetic field produced B is proportional to:

A. $B \propto \frac{1}{x^{\frac{3}{2}}}$
B. $B \propto \frac{1}{x^2}$
C. $B \propto \frac{1}{x^3}$
D. $B \propto \frac{1}{x^{-\frac{1}{2}}}$

Q.47 The expression $\frac{1}{2}I\omega^2$ represents Rotational:

A. Kinetic energy
B. Angular momentum
C. Torque
D. Power

Q.48 The radius of gyration of a rod of length 'L' rotating about an axis perpendicular to the rod at its mid-point is _____.

A. $\frac{L}{3}$
B. $\frac{L}{4\sqrt{3}}$
C. $\frac{L}{12}$
D. $\frac{L}{2\sqrt{3}}$

Q.49 In a purely capacitive circuit -

A. e.m.f. is ahead of current by $\frac{\pi}{2}$
B. Current is ahead of e.m.f. by $\frac{\pi}{2}$
C. Current lags behind e.m.f. by π
D. e.m. f is lags of e.m.f. by π

Q.50 If A.C. voltage is applied to a pure capacitor, then voltage across the capacitor _____.

A. Leads the current by phase angle $\left(\frac{\pi}{2}\right)$ rad
B. Leads the current by phase angle (π) rad
C. Lags behind the current by phase angle $\left(\frac{\pi}{2}\right)$ rad
D. Lags behind the current by phase angle (π) rad.

Chemistry

Q.51 Heavy water is _____.

A. Monoterium oxide
B. Polyterium oxide
C. Deuterium oxide
D. Tritium oxide

Q.52 Which of the following given elements is the least reactive among all other elements?

A. Ag
B. Hg
C. Au
D. Al

Q.53 Solid $Ba(NO_3)_2$ is gradually dissolved in a $1.0 \times 10^{-4} M\, Na_2CO_3$ solution. At which concentration of Ba^{2+}, precipitate of $BaCO_3$ begins to form? $(K_{sp}$ for $BaCO_3 = 5.1 \times 10^{-9})$

A. $5.1 \times 10^{-5} M$
B. $7.1 \times 10^{-5} M$
C. $4.1 \times 10^{-5} M$
D. $8.1 \times 10^{-7} M$

Q.54 The pH of a 10 ml aqueous solution of HCl is 4. The amount of water to be added to this solution in order to change its pH from 4 to 5 is:

A. 30 ml
B. 60 ml
C. 90 ml
D. 120 ml

Q.55 The increasing order of basicity of the following compounds is:

[JEE Main Advanced, 2018]

A. (b) < (a) < (c) < (d)
B. (b) < (a) < (d) < (c)
C. (d) < (b) < (a) < (c)
D. (a) < (b) < (c) < (d)

Q.56 Which of the following is not a homologous series?

A. CH_4
B. C_2H_6
C. C_4H_9
D. C_3H_8

Q.57 In which of the following does sulphur has the lowest oxidation state?

A. H_2SO_4
B. SO_2
C. H_2SO_3
D. H_2S

Q.58 Two different first order reactions have rate constants k_1 and k_2 at $T_1 (k_1 > k_2)$. If temperature is increased from T_1 to T_2, then new constants become k_3 and k_4 respectively. Which among the following relations is correct?

A. $k_1 > k_2 = k_3 = k_4$
B. $k_1 < k_3$ and $k_2 < k_4$
C. $k_1 = k_3 = k_4$
D. $k_1 > k_2 > k_3 > k_4$

Q.59 In the presence of a catalyst, the heat evolved or absorbed during the reaction _____.

A. Increases
B. Decreases
C. Remains unchanged
D. May increase or decrease

Q.60 A catalyst is added to a reaction to increase the rate of reaction. Which of the following statements is correct?

A. A catalyst increases the activation energy between reactants and products and hence, lowers the potential energy barrier.
B. A catalyst provides an alternate pathway or reaction mechanism.
C. A catalyst alters G, Gibbs energy of reaction.
D. A catalyst changes the equilibrium constant of a reaction.

Q.61 $12\, g$ of urea is present in 1 litre of solution and $68.4\, g$ of sucrose is separately dissolved in 1 litre of another sample of solution. The lowering of vapour pressure of first solution is:

A. Equal to that of second solution
B. Greater than that of second solution
C. Less than that of second solution
D. Double that of seconds solution

Q.62 If $1.202\, g\, mL^{-1}$ is the density of 20% aqueous KI, determine the molality of KI.

A. 1.51 m
B. 2.53 m
C. 3.54 m
D. 2.55 m

Q.63 A solution is obtained by mixing 300 g of 25% solution and 400 g of 40% solution by mass. Calculate the mass percentage of the solvent in resulting solution.
A. 68.40%   B. 65.53%   C. 66.43%   D. 67.42%

Q.64 The unit cell length of sodium chloride crystal is 564 pm. Its density would be:
A. $1.082\ g\ cm^{-3}$ B. $2.165\ g\ cm^{-3}$
C. $3.247\ g\ cm^{-3}$ D. $4.330\ g\ cm^{-3}$

Q.65 Which of the following is a molecular solid?
A. I_2 B. Solid NH_3
C. Ice   D. All of these

Q.66 In a hexagonal closed packing lattice, coordination number of an atom in a unit cell is:
A. 12   B. 6   C. 18   D. 3

Q.67 The arrangement of elements in the Modem Periodic Table is based on their:
A. Increasing atomic mass in the period
B. Increasing atomic number in the horizontal rows
C. Increasing atomic number in the vertical columns
D. Increasing atomic mass in the group

Q.68 Carbon belongs to the second period and Group 14. Silicon belongs to the third period and Group 14. If atomic number of carbon is 6, the atomic number of silicon is:
A. 7   B. 14   C. 21   D. 24

Q.69 Identify the element with the atomic number 10.
A. Neon   B. Calcium   C. Nitrogen   D. Silicon

Q.70 The melting point of alkali metal is _____.
A. Depends on the atmosphere
B. Low
C. High
D. Zero

Q.71 First organic compound to be synthesised was_____.
A. Urea   B. Cane sugar
C. Methane   D. Acetic acid

Q.72 A person living in Shimla observed that cooking food without using pressure cooker takes more time. The reason for this observation is that at high altitude:
A. Pressure increases
B. Temperature decreases
C. Pressure decreases
D. Temperature increases

Q.73 How does the surface tension of a liquid vary with increase in temperature?
A. Remains same
B. Decreases
C. Increases
D. No regular pattern is followed

Q.74 A poisonous gas is adsorbed at activated charcoal. The activated charcoal is:
A. Absorber   B. Adsorbate

C. Absorbate   D. Adsorbent

Q.75 Among the following the maximum covalent character is shown by the compound:
A. $MgCl_2$ B. $FeCl_2$ C. $SnCl_2$ D. $AlCl_3$

Q.76 The tendency of a reaction to take place spontaneously is greatest when the reaction is:
A. Exothermic and randomness increases
B. Endothermic & randomness increases
C. Exothermic and randomness decreases
D. Endothermic & randomness decreases

Q.77 The enthalpy and entropy change for the reaction:
$Br_2(l) + Cl_2(g) \rightarrow 2BrCl(g)$ are $30 kJ mol^{-1}$ and $105 J K^{-1} mol^{-1}$ respectively.
The temperature at which the reaction will be in equilibrium is:
A. $273K$ B. $450K$ C. $300K$ D. $285.7K$

Q.78 The number of electrons, protons and neutrons in a species are equal to $18,\ 16$ and 16 respectively. Assign the proper symbol to the species.
A. $^{32}_{18}S^{2-}$ B. $^{32}_{16}Ca^{2-}$ C. $^{32}_{16}P^{2-}$ D. $^{32}_{16}S^{2-}$

Q.79 If we assume that one-sixth the mass of an atom of ^{12}C isotope is taken as the reference, the mass of one molecule of oxygen will:
A. Be double its original value
B. Be half its original value
C. Be the same
D. Increase by four fold

Q.80 On electrolysis of dilute sulphuric acid using Platinum (Pt) electrode, the product obtained at anode will be:
[NEET UG, 2020], [MPPEB Sub Engineer (Mechanical), 2020]
A. Hydrogen gas   B. Oxygen gas
C. H₂S gas   D. SO₂ gas

Q.81 If a Zn^{2+}/Zn electrode is diluted 100 times, then the emf will show:
A. An increase of $59\ mV$
B. A decrease of $59\ mV$
C. An increase of $29.5\ mV$
D. A decrease of $29.5\ mV$

Q.82 Electrolysis of dilute aqueous $NaCl$ solution was carried out by passing 10 milli ampere current. The time required to liberate 0.01 mol of H_2 gas at the cathode is: (1 Faraday $= 96500 C mol^{-1}$)
A. 9.65×10^4 sec   B. 19.3×10^4 sec
C. 28.95×10^4 sec   D. 38.6×10^4 sec

Q.83 Hybridization of Fe in $K_3[Fe(CN)_6]$ is:
A. sp^3 B. d^2sp^3 C. sp^3d^2 D. dsp^3

Q.84 Transition metal compounds are usually coloured. This is due to the electronic transition:
A. from p orbital to s-orbital

B. from d orbital to s-orbitals
C. from d orbital to p-orbital
D. within the d-orbitals

Q.85 In nitroprusside ion, the iron and NO exist as Fe(II) and NO^+ rather than Fe(III) and NO. These forms can be distinguished by:
A. estimating the concentration of iron
B. measuring the concentration of CN^-
C. measuring the solid-state magnetic moment
D. thermally decomposing the compound

Q.86 Which statement is correct?
A. Fumaric acid is stronger than Maleic acid
B. Maleic acid is stronger than fumaric acid
C. Both (A) and (B)
D. None of the above

Q.87 What is the name of the above reaction?

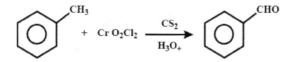

A. Williamson's synthesis
B. Gatterman-Koch process
C. Etard reaction
D. Hoffmann elimination reaction

Q.88 The correct order of increasing acidic strength is:
A. Phenol < Ethanol < Chloroacetic acid < Acetic acid
B. Ethanol < Phenol < Chloroacetic acid < Acetic acid
C. Ethanol < Phenol < Acetic acid < Chloroacetic acid
D. Chloroacetic acid < Acetic acid < Phenol < Ethanol

Q.89 Functional group -CHO is present in which of the following?
A. Ketone
B. Aldehyde
C. Alcohol
D. Carboxylic acid

Q.90 Molecules: General formula. (n represents the number of carbon atoms in chain)
1. Aldehydes: $C_nH_{2n}O$
2. Carboxylic acids: $C_nH_{2n}O_2$
3. Cycloalkanes: C_nH_{2n}
4. Alkanes: C_nH_{2n+2}
Which of the above matching is correct? Choose from the options given below:
A. 1 and 2 only
B. 1 and 4 only
C. 1, 2 and 4 only
D. All are correct

Q.91 Which of the following compounds give(s) positive test with Tollens' reagent?
A. Carboxylic acid
B. Alcohol
C. Alpha hydroxy ketones
D. Aldehydes

A. A and B
B. B and C
C. A, B and D
D. C and D

Q.92 Most abundant organic compound on earth is _____.
A. Proteins
B. Steroids
C. Cellulose
D. Lipids

Q.93 Protein synthesis in a cell takes place _____.
A. Only on ribosomes attached to the nuclear envelope
B. In the nucleolus as well as in cytoplasm
C. In cytoplasm as well as in mitochondria
D. Only in the cytoplasm

Q.94 Match column A with column B:

Column A	Column B
1. Rayon	a. Coating of non-stick
2. Teflon	b. Handles and Switches
3. Bakelite	c. Pipes
4. PVC	d. Clothes

A. 1-a, 2-d, 3-b, 4-c
B. 1-d, 2-a, 3-b, 4-c
C. 1-d, 2-a, 3-c, 4-b
D. 1-c, 2-a, 3-b, 4-d

Q.95 A high molecular weight compound formed by combining large numbers of small molecules of low molecular weight is called:
A. Polymer
B. Alkali
C. Acid
D. Direct Dyes

Q.96 Plastic used to preserve yogurts is replaced with a polymer called polylactic acid is an example of _____.
A. Green chemistry
B. Waste management
C. Green revolution
D. None of above

Q.97 Sustainable development focuses on more use of _____.
A. Renewable Resources
B. Abiotic Resources
C. Agriculture Resources
D. Natural Resources

Q.98 Which of the following is Baeyer's reagent?
A. Acidified $KMnO_4$
B. Alkaline $KMnO_4$
C. Acidified $K_2Cr_2O_7$
D. Aqueous $KMnO_4$

Q.99 The monohalogen derivatives of alkanes are called?
A. Alkene halide
B. Haloalkanes
C. Halogen alkyl
D. None of the above

Q.100 All alkali metals are good dash agents?
A. Oxidizing
B. Reducing
C. Both oxidising and reducing
D. Neither oxidizing not reducing

// Smart Answer Sheet //

Correct — Indicates percentage of students who answered questions correctly.

Skipped — Indicates percentage of students who skipped questions.

Q.	Ans.	Correct / Skipped	Q.	Ans.	Correct / Skipped	Q.	Ans.	Correct / Skipped	Q.	Ans.	Correct / Skipped	Q.	Ans.	Correct / Skipped
1	B	42.42 % / 12.13 %	17	C	21.21 % / 30.31 %	33	C	57.58 % / 27.27 %	49	B	48.48 % / 27.28 %	65	D	57.58 % / 18.18 %
2	B	30.3 % / 30.31 %	18	D	24.24 % / 27.28 %	34	D	42.42 % / 30.31 %	50	C	39.39 % / 30.31 %	66	A	48.48 % / 21.22 %
3	A	21.21 % / 30.31 %	19	D	45.45 % / 30.31 %	35	A	30.3 % / 27.28 %	51	C	54.55 % / 21.21 %	67	B	69.7 % / 21.21 %
4	C	36.36 % / 30.31 %	20	B	42.42 % / 30.31 %	36	D	33.33 % / 30.31 %	52	C	48.48 % / 21.22 %	68	B	69.7 % / 21.21 %
5	D	21.21 % / 30.31 %	21	C	60.61 % / 30.3 %	37	C	57.58 % / 30.3 %	53	A	42.42 % / 21.22 %	69	A	78.79 % / 21.21 %
6	A	9.09 % / 27.27 %	22	B	63.64 % / 30.3 %	38	A	60.61 % / 30.3 %	54	C	21.21 % / 21.21 %	70	B	45.45 % / 21.22 %
7	C	30.3 % / 30.31 %	23	D	30.3 % / 30.31 %	39	D	18.18 % / 30.3 %	55	B	15.15 % / 21.21 %	71	A	45.45 % / 21.22 %
8	B	51.52 % / 30.3 %	24	A	12.12 % / 30.3 %	40	B	18.18 % / 30.3 %	56	C	69.7 % / 21.21 %	72	C	54.55 % / 21.21 %
9	B	33.33 % / 27.28 %	25	B	27.27 % / 30.31 %	41	C	48.48 % / 30.31 %	57	D	63.64 % / 21.21 %	73	B	48.48 % / 21.22 %
10	C	30.3 % / 30.31 %	26	D	54.55 % / 30.3 %	42	A	36.36 % / 30.31 %	58	B	54.55 % / 21.21 %	74	D	39.39 % / 21.22 %
11	B	60.61 % / 30.3 %	27	B	51.52 % / 30.3 %	43	B	36.36 % / 30.31 %	59	C	45.45 % / 18.19 %	75	D	36.36 % / 21.22 %
12	B	51.52 % / 30.3 %	28	D	18.18 % / 30.3 %	44	B	60.61 % / 30.3 %	60	B	36.36 % / 21.22 %	76	A	51.52 % / 21.21 %
13	C	21.21 % / 30.31 %	29	C	21.21 % / 27.27 %	45	B	39.39 % / 30.31 %	61	A	24.24 % / 21.21 %	77	D	30.3 % / 21.22 %
14	A	18.18 % / 30.3 %	30	B	54.55 % / 30.3 %	46	C	27.27 % / 30.31 %	62	A	12.12 % / 21.21 %	78	D	39.39 % / 21.22 %
15	D	18.18 % / 27.27 %	31	D	27.27 % / 30.31 %	47	A	51.52 % / 30.3 %	63	C	30.3 % / 18.18 %	79	C	27.27 % / 21.21 %
16	B	21.21 % / 27.27 %	32	B	45.45 % / 30.31 %	48	D	39.39 % / 30.31 %	64	B	36.36 % / 21.22 %	80	B	18.18 % / 21.21 %

Q.	Ans.	Correct / Skipped
81	B	27.27 % / 21.21 %
82	B	30.3 % / 21.22 %
83	B	48.48 % / 21.22 %
84	D	60.61 % / 21.21 %
85	C	27.27 % / 21.21 %
86	B	42.42 % / 21.22 %
87	C	51.52 % / 21.21 %
88	C	54.55 % / 21.21 %
89	B	69.7 % / 21.21 %
90	D	48.48 % / 21.22 %
91	D	39.39 % / 21.22 %
92	C	48.48 % / 21.22 %
93	C	15.15 % / 21.21 %
94	B	63.64 % / 21.21 %
95	A	75.76 % / 21.21 %
96	A	54.55 % / 21.21 %
97	A	66.67 % / 21.21 %
98	B	33.33 % / 21.22 %
99	B	78.79 % / 21.21 %
100	B	54.55 % / 21.21 %

Performance Analysis	
Avg. Score (%)	41.0%
Toppers Score (%)	96.0%
Your Score	

Physics & Chemistry : Mock Test - 2

//Hints and Solutions//

1. When a block of mass m is displaced from its position. One spring gets compressed and the other one gets extended by the same distance x. As x is the same for both the springs, they act in parallel.

Two springs are connected in parallel, so, the equivalent force constant.

$k_{eq} = k_1 + k_2$

So, the frequency of oscillation is,

$f = \frac{1}{2\pi}\sqrt{\frac{k_1+k_2}{m}}$

Hence, the correct option is (B).

2. We know that velocity is given by:

$v = \omega\sqrt{A^2 - x^2}$ cm/sec

$v_1 = 10$ cm/sec

$v_2 = 7$ cm

$x_1 = 3$ cm

$x_2 = 4$

$v_1 = \omega\sqrt{A^2 - x_1^2}$

$v_2 = \omega\sqrt{A^2 - x_2^2}$

$\therefore \frac{10}{7} = \frac{\omega\sqrt{A^2-3^2}}{\omega\sqrt{A^2-4^2}}$

$\Rightarrow \frac{100}{49} = \frac{A^2-9}{A^2-16}$

$\Rightarrow 51A^2 = 1600 - (9 \times 49)$

$\therefore A = 4.76$ cm

Length of the path is $2A = 2 \times 4.76 = 9.52$ cm

Hence, the correct option is (B).

3. By using end correction-

$n_1 = \frac{v}{4(l_1+e)}$

$n_2 = \frac{3v}{4(l_2+e)}$

$n_1 = n_2 = n$

So, $\frac{3v}{4(l_2+e)} = \frac{v}{4(l_1+e)}$

$\Rightarrow l_2 + e = 3(l_1 + e)$

$\Rightarrow 51.7 + e = 3(16.7 + e)$

$\Rightarrow 51.7 + e = 50.1 + 3e$

$\Rightarrow 2e = 1.6$

$\Rightarrow e = \frac{1.6}{2} = 0.8$

As we know,

$\lambda = 4(l_1 + e)$

$\lambda = 4(16.7 + 0.8)$

$\lambda = 70.0$ cm

Hence, the correct option is (A).

4. In a thermos flask, we have two walls and the space between them is made a vacuum. Due to this vacuum, there is less chance of heat transfer of heat.

As the glass is a bad conductor of heat that's why silver coated glass wall is used so that the heat transfer via radiation can be reduced.

Hence, the correct option is (C).

5. Given:

$\lambda = 600 \, nm$

We know that

$c = 3 \times 10^8 \, m/s$

$h = 4.1357 \times 10^{-15} eV$

The energy of the photon with a wavelength lambda is given by

$E = \frac{hc}{\lambda}$

Where h is the planck's constant

c is the speed of light

λ is the wavelength

Put the values in formula given above.

$E = \frac{4.1357 \times 10^{-15} \times 3 \times 10^8}{600 \times 10^{-9}}$

$= \frac{4.1357 \times 3}{6}$

$= 2.06785 \, eV$

Hence, the correct option is (D).

6. Let E_n and E_m be the energies of electron in n^{th} and m^{th} states.

Then, $E_n - E_m = hv_0$ ... (1)

In the second case when the atom is moving with a velocity v. Let v' be the velocity of atom after emitting the photon. Applying conservation of linear momentum,

$mv = mv' + \frac{hv}{c}$ (m = mass of hydrogen atom)

$\Rightarrow v' = \left(v - \frac{hv}{mc}\right) \ldots (2)$

Applying conservation of energy

$E_n + \frac{1}{2}mv^2 = E_m + \frac{1}{2}mv'^2 + hv$

$\Rightarrow hv = (E_n - E_m) + \frac{1}{2}m(v^2 - v'^2)$

From equation (1) and (2)

$= hv_0 + \frac{1}{2}m\left[v^2 - \left(v - \frac{hv}{mc}\right)^2\right]$

$= hv_0 + \frac{1}{2}m\left[v^2 - v^2 - \frac{h^2v^2}{m^2c^2} + \frac{2hvv}{mc}\right]$

$= hv_0 + \frac{hvv}{c} - \frac{h^2v^2}{2mc^2}$

Here the term is $\frac{h^2v^2}{2mc^2}$ is very small. So, can be neglected.

$\therefore hv = hv_0 + \frac{hvv}{c}$

$\Rightarrow v = v_0 + \frac{vv}{c}$

$\Rightarrow v_0 = v\left(1 - \frac{v}{c}\right)$

Hence, the correct option is (A).

7. The energy band gap is maximum for carbon and silicon and least for germanium out of the given three elements. The energy band gap of the these elements are related as: $(E_g)_C > (E_g)_{Si} > (E_g)_{Ge}$

Hence, the correct option is (C).

8. "Good absorber of heat is good radiator of heat also" is kirchhof's law.

Kirchhoff's Radiation Law: For any arbitrary body emitting and absorbing thermal radiation in thermodynamic equilibrium, the emissivity is equal to absorptivity.

A black body is an example of a good absorber of heat as well as a good emitter of heat. The ease with which a black body can absorb a photon is the reverse process of emitting the one. This entire cycle takes place because of the number of transitions that are associated with the EM field.

Hence, the correct option is (B).

9. Alpha particle emission reduces the atomic number by 2. So, Atomic Number of Y = Atomic Number of $Z - 2$

Beta emission increases the atomic number by 1. So, Atomic Number of X is that of $Y + 1$ Similarly, Atomic number of R is Atomic Number of $X + 1$, which is Same as $Y + 2$ so, R has same atomic number as Z, but different mass numbers. i.e., R and Z are isotopes.

Hence, the correct option is (B).

10. Paschen series: When an electron in a Hydrogen atom transit from higher energy orbit to 3rd orbit. (outer orbit n_2 = n > 3 to the orbit n_1 = 3) known as Paschen Series.

So the empirical formula for the observed wavelengths (λ) for hydrogen (Z = 1) is,

$R_\infty = 1.1$

$\frac{1}{\lambda} = R_\infty \left(\frac{1}{n_1^2} - \frac{1}{n_2^2}\right) \ldots (i)$

For λ_{min}, $n_1 = 3$ and $n_2 = \infty$

Put above values in (i),

$\frac{1}{\lambda_{min}} = R_\infty \left(\frac{1}{3^2} - 0\right)$

$\Rightarrow \frac{1}{\lambda_{min}} = 1.1 \times 10^7 \left(\frac{1}{3^2}\right)$

$\Rightarrow \lambda_{min} = 0.818 \mu m$

For λ_{max}, $n_1 = 3$ and $n_2 = 4$

Put above values in (i),

$\frac{1}{\lambda_{max}} = R_\infty \left(\frac{1}{3^2} - \frac{1}{4^2}\right)$

$\Rightarrow \frac{1}{\lambda_{max}} = 1.1 \times 10^7 \left(\frac{1}{3^2} - \frac{1}{4^2}\right)$

$\Rightarrow \lambda_{max} = 1.89 \mu m$

$\lambda_{min} = 0.818 \mu m$ and $\lambda_{max} = 1.89 \mu m$

Hence, the correct option is (C).

11. Given:

The electron is in 2nd orbit so $n = 2$.

The energy of an electron at n^{th} orbit is given by:

$E = -\frac{13.6}{n^2} eV$

So, the energy of an electron at the 2nd orbit will be:

$E = -\frac{13.6}{2^2}$

$= -3.4 eV$

Hence, the correct option is (B).

12. Given:

The thickness of the slab = Distance travelled = 4 mm = 4×10^{-3} m;

Refractive index $\mu = 1.5$

$c = 3 \times 10^8$ m/sec

So, Time to pass through the glass slab

$t = \dfrac{\text{Distance travelled}}{\text{speed inside slab}}$

$t = \dfrac{4 \times 10^{-3}}{\frac{3 \times 10^8}{1.5}}$

$= \dfrac{4 \times 10^{-3} \times 1.5}{3 \times 10^8}$

$= 2 \times 10^{-11}$ sec

Hence, the correct option is (B).

13. Given:

$f_1 = 50$ cm (convex lens)

$f_2 = -25$ cm (concave lens)

We know that:

The focal length of the combination:

$\dfrac{1}{f} = \dfrac{1}{f_1} + \dfrac{1}{f_2}$

$\dfrac{1}{f} = \dfrac{1}{50} + \dfrac{-1}{25}$

$f = -50$ cm

Hence, the correct option is (C).

14. Given:

Power $(P) = 4\,W$, Distance $(r) = 200\,m$

We know that,

Intensity $(I) = \dfrac{P}{4\pi r^2}$

$= \dfrac{4}{4\pi \times (200)^2}$

$= 7.9 \times 10^{-6}\,W/m^2$

$\approx 8 \times 10^{-6}\,W/m^2$

Hence, the correct option is (A).

15. Given,

$m = 20\,g = 20 \times 10^{-3}\,kg$

Initial speed $m = 1\,ms^{-1}$

Thickness, $s = 20\,cm = 20 \times 10^{-2}\,m$

Resistance offered by the wall, $F = -2.5 \times 10^{-2}\,N$

So, deacceleration of bullet,

$F = ma$

$a = \dfrac{F}{m}$

$= \dfrac{-2.5 \times 10^{-2}}{20 \times 10^{-3}}$

$= -\dfrac{5}{4}\,ms^{-2}$

Now, using the equation of motion,

$v^2 = u^2 + 2as$

$v^2 = 1 + 2\left(-\dfrac{5}{4}\right)(20 \times 10^{-2})$

$v^2 = \dfrac{1}{2}$

$v = \dfrac{1}{\sqrt{2}} = 0.7\,ms^{-1}$

Hence, the correct option is (D).

16. Stream of flowing electrons can be considered as current whose direction is opposite to the flow of direction of electrons. As electrons are flowing from A to B, it means current is flowing from B to A. Due to this current, there will be a change in magnetic flux through the coil, so a current will be induced in the coil which opposes the change in flux.
If we observe the coil from above then the direction of current induced in the coil will be in an anticlockwise direction.
Hence, the correct option is (B).

17. Here, the cylinder is said to be completely insulated from its neighbourhood. As a result, no heat gets exchanged between the system (cylinder) and its neighbourhood. Clearly, the process turns out to be adiabatic.

Now, consider:

Final pressure inside the cylinder $= P_2$

Initial volume inside the cylinder $= V_1$

Final volume inside the cylinder $= V_2$

Ratio of specific heats, $\gamma = 1.4$

For an adiabatic process, it is known that $P_1 V_1^{\gamma} = P_2 V_2^{\gamma}$.

Also, the final volume is compressed to half of its initial volume.

$\Rightarrow V_2 = \dfrac{V_1}{2}$

Thus,

$\Rightarrow P_1 V_1^{\gamma} = P_2 \left(\dfrac{V_2}{2}\right)^{\gamma}$

$\Rightarrow \dfrac{P_2}{P_1} = \dfrac{V_1^{\gamma}}{\left(\frac{V_1}{2}\right)^{\gamma}}$

$\Rightarrow \dfrac{P_2}{P_1} = 2^{\gamma} = 2^{1.4} = 2.639$

Clearly, the pressure rises by a factor of 2.639.

Hence, the correct option is (C).

18. The $P-V$ diagram of adiabatic process, isothermal process and isobaric process.

Work done in process= area enclosed by $P-V$ diagram with volume axis. Since area under the curve is maximum for adiabatic process, so work done on the gas will be maximum for adiabatic process.

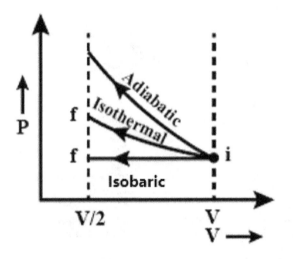

Hence, the correct option is (D).

19. An adiabatic expansion has less work done and no heat flow, thereby a lower internal energy comparing to an isothermal expansion which has both heat flow and work done. For an adiabatically expanding ideal monatomic gas which does work on its environment (W is positive), internal energy of the gas should decrease.

Hence, the correct option is (D).

20. If a person travels from the equator to the poles, he finds that the value of acceleration due to gravity (g) increases.

Value of effective g increases as we move from equator to north pole because on equator its value is less due to earth's rotational motion and consequent centrifugal force. Moreover, the equator of the earth is at a larger distance from the centre of the earth as compared to the poles. This is another reason why g is greater on the pole than the equator.

Hence, the correct option is (B).

21. Viscosity is a measure of resistance to flow which arises due to the internal friction between layers of fluid.

Most of the fluids offer some resistance to motion. This resistance to fluid motion is like internal friction analogous to friction when a solid moves on a surface.

Strong intermolecular forces between molecules hold them together and resist the movement of layers past one another. Hence, to deliver a large volume of oil in lesser time, viscosity must be as low as possible.

The SI unit of viscosity is poiseiulle (Pl).

Its other units are N s m⁻² or Pa s.

1 poise = 1 g cm⁻¹s⁻¹ = 10⁻¹kg m⁻¹s⁻¹.

Hence, the correct option is (C).

22. Some insects like water strider is able to walk on the surface of water due to surface tension

Water striders are able to walk on top of water due to a combination of several factors. Water striders use the high surface tension of water and long, hydrophobic legs to help them stay above water. Water striders use this surface tension to their advantage through their highly adapted legs and distributed weight.

Hence, the correct option is (B).

23. Given,

Diameter of the sphere $= 2.4m$

$\therefore$ Radius of sphere, $r = \frac{2.4}{2} = 1.2m$

Surface charge density of conducting sphere,

$\sigma = 80 \times 10^{-6} C/m^2$

Therefore,

Charge on sphere will be:

$q = \sigma A = \sigma 4\pi r^2$

$q = 80 \times 10^{-6} \times 4 \times 3.14 \times (1.2)^2$

$q = 1.45 \times 10^{-3} C$

Then, the total electric flux leaving the surface of the sphere will be calculated using the gauss formula, i.e.,

$\phi = \frac{q}{\varepsilon_0}$

$\phi = \frac{1.45 \times 10^{-3}}{8.854 \times 10^{-12}}$ ($\because \epsilon_0 = 8.854 \times 10^{-12}$)

$\phi = 1.6 \times 10^8 Nm^2/C$

Hence, the correct option is (D).

24. Let the charge distribution be as shown in the figure:

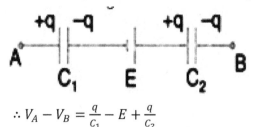

$\therefore V_A - V_B = \frac{q}{C_1} - E + \frac{q}{C_2}$

or, $(V_A - V_B) + E = q\left(\frac{1}{C_1} + \frac{1}{C_2}\right)$

$(V_A - V_B) + E = \frac{q(C_2+C_1)}{C_1 C_2}$

$$\therefore q = \frac{[(V_A-V_B)+E]C_1C_2}{C_1+C_2}$$

Voltage across C_1 is $V_1 = \frac{q}{C_1}$

$$= \frac{[(V_A-V_B)+E]C_2}{C_1+C_2}$$

$$= \frac{(5+10)2.0}{1.0+2.0}$$

$$= 10 \text{ Volt}$$

Voltage across C_2 is $V_2 = \frac{q}{C_2}$

$$= \frac{[(V_A-V_B)+E]C_1}{C_1+C_2}$$

$$= \frac{(5+10)1.0}{1.0+2.0}$$

$$= 5 \text{ Volt}$$

Hence, the correct option is (A).

25. Let C be the capacitance of the infinite ladder.

As the ladder is infinite, the addition of one more element of two capacitors ($1\mu F$ and $2\mu F$) across the points X and Y should not change the total capacitance.

Therefore, the total capacity of the arrangement shown in the figure must remain C only.

In figure, $2\mu F$ capacitor is in series with capacitance C.

$\therefore$ Their combined capacity $= \frac{2 \times C}{2+C}$

This combination is in parallel with $1\mu F$ capacitor.

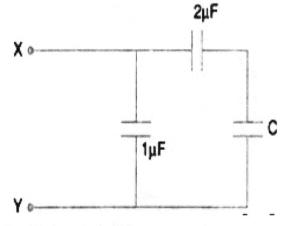

The equivalent capacity of the arrangement is

$$1 + \frac{2C}{2+C} = C$$

or, $C^2 + 2C = 2 + 3C$

or, $C^2 - C - 2 = 0$

$\therefore C = 2, -1$

As capacitance cannot be negative.

$\therefore C = 2\mu F$

Hence, the correct option is (B).

26. Charge on the first sphere, $Q_1 = 2 \times 10^{-7} C$

Charge on the second sphere, $Q_2 = 3 \times 10^{-7} C$

Distance between the spheres is, $r = 30cm, r = 0.3m$

The electrostatic force between two charges is given by the formula, $F = \frac{kQ_1Q_2}{r^2}$

Where $k = \frac{1}{4\pi\varepsilon} = 9 \times 10^9$

$$F = \frac{9 \times 10^9 \times 2 \times 10^{-7} \times 3 \times 10^{-7}}{(0.3)^2}$$

$$= 6 \times 10^{-3} N$$

Hence, the correct option is (D).

27. Let,

Effective capacitance $= C$

Then:

$$\frac{1}{C} = \frac{1}{C_1} + \frac{1}{C_2} + \frac{1}{C_3}$$

$$= \frac{1}{8} + \frac{1}{16} + \frac{1}{24}$$

$$= \frac{6+3+2}{48}$$

$$C = \frac{48}{11} \mu F$$

Potential difference, $V = 110V$

We know that:

Charge, $Q = CV$

$$Q = \frac{48}{11} \times 10^{-6} \times 110$$

$$= 480 \times 10^{-6}$$

$$= 48 \times 10^{-5}$$

Since the capacitors are in series each capacitor has the same charge i.e., $48 \times 10^{-5} C$.

Hence, the correct option is (B).

28. Gauss's law:

According to Gauss law, the total electric flux linked with a closed surface called Gaussian surface is $\frac{1}{\varepsilon_o}$ the charge enclosed by the closed surface.

So if the total charge enclosed in a closed surface is Q, then the total electric flux associated with it will be given as,

$$\Rightarrow \phi = \frac{Q}{\varepsilon_o} \quad \ldots\ldots (1)$$

By equation (1) it is clear that the total flux linked with the closed surface in which a certain amount of charge is placed does not depend on the shape and size of the surface.

Hence, the correct option is (D).

29. Magnetic flux density at a distance ' r ' from the wire is

$$\left|\vec{B}\right| = \frac{\mu_o \cdot I}{2\pi r}$$

For $r < a, I = J.\pi r^2 \ldots\ldots$ (uniform current density)

$$\Rightarrow \left|\vec{B}\right| = \frac{\mu_o \cdot J \pi a^2}{2\pi r}$$

$$\Rightarrow \left|\vec{B}\right| = \frac{\mu_o J a^2}{2} \cdot \frac{1}{r}$$

$$\Rightarrow \left|\vec{B}\right| \propto \frac{1}{r}$$

For $r > a$

Hence, the correct option is (C).

30. Given:

Charge $(q) = -5$ C

Work done $(W) = 100$ J

Electric potential $(V) = \frac{W}{q}$

$= \frac{100}{-5}$

$= -20$ volt

Hence, the correct option is (B).

31. Wavelength associated with a moving particle $\lambda = m^p v^q h^r$

$[M^0 L T^0] = [M^p][LT^{-1}]^q[ML^2\ T^{-1}]^r$

$[M^0 L T^0] = [M^{p+r}\ L^{q+2r}\ T^{-q-r}]$

$\therefore p + r = 0, q + 2r = 1, -q - r = 0$

After solving we get,

$p = -1, q = -1, r = 1$

Hence, the correct option is (D).

32. From the formula for the speed of sound in air

$$\frac{v_1}{v_2} = \sqrt{\left(\frac{T_1}{T_2}\right)}$$

$$\frac{v_1}{2v_1} = \sqrt{\left(\frac{273+27}{T_2}\right)}$$

$$\frac{1}{2} = \sqrt{\left(\frac{300}{T_2}\right)}$$

Squaring both sides:

$$\frac{1}{4} = \frac{300}{T_2}$$

$T_2 = 300 \times 4 = 1200\ K$

$= 1200 - 273 = 927°C$

Hence, the correct option is (B).

33. The wave theory of light was first demonstrated by Thomas Young in 1801 through Young's double-slit experiment.

This experiment shows that the observed pattern of interference occurs due to the superposition of light waves which proves the wave nature of light.

In this experiment, two narrow slits that are close to each other, are illuminated by a monochromatic light source.

The two slits are responsible for the production of two different wavefronts which then superimpose on a screen forming the definite interference pattern.

For two coherent sources S_1 and S_2, the resultant intensity at some point p is given by:

$$I = I_1 + I_2 + 2\sqrt{I_1 I_2}\cos\phi$$

Thus, interference proves wave nature.

Hence, the correct option is (C).

34. Lightwave that is vibrating in more than one plane is referred to as unpolarized light. Light emitted by the sun, by a lamp in the classroom, or by a candle flame is unpolarized light.

A light wave is known to vibrate in a multiple directions.

A light wave is vibrating in vertical and in horizontal plane

It is possible to transform unpolarized light into polarized light. Polarized light waves are light waves in which the vibrations occur in a single plane. The process of transforming unpolarized light into polarized light is known as polarization. There are a variety of methods of polarizing light.

The four methods discussed on this page are:

- Polarization by Transmission
- Polarization by Reflection
- Polarization by Refraction

- Polarization by Scattering
- Polarization by Selective absorption
- Polarization by Double refraction

Hence, the correct option is (D).

35. The angle of incidence at which a beam of unpolarized light falling on a transparent surface is reflected as a beam of completely plane polarised light is called polarising or Brewster angle. It is denoted by i_P.

Brewster's law: It states that when a ray is passed through some transparent medium having refractive index μ at any particular angle of incidence, the reflected ray is completely polarized; and the angle between reflected and refracted ray is $90°$.

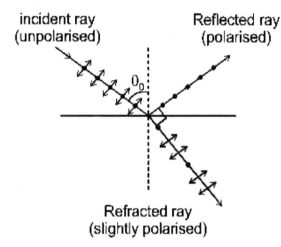

$\mu = \tan\theta_B$

Where μ = refractive index and θ_B is Brewster's angle or polarizing angle (i_p).

Given that:

The light is incident on the glass.

The refractive index of glass $(\mu) = \frac{3}{2}$

The angle of incidence $(i_p) = ?$

$\frac{3}{2} = \tan\theta$

$\Rightarrow \theta = \tan^{-1}\left(\frac{3}{2}\right)$

$\Rightarrow \theta = 56.30° \approx 57°$

Hence, the correct option is (A).

36.

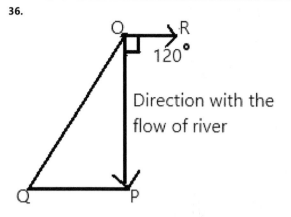

Suppose OR represents the direction of flow of the river. O is the starting point and P is the point where boatman wants to reach. Vector PQ represents the direction in which boatman must row to reach the point P. Vector OP shows the direction of the flow of the river.

Then,

$OQ = 10 kmh^{-1}$

$QP = 5\ km\ h^{-1}$

$\sin\theta = \frac{QP}{OR} = \frac{5}{10} = \frac{1}{2} = \sin 30°$

Or, $\theta = 30°$ or $\angle POQ = 30°$

Thus, $\angle QOP = +\angle POQ + \angle POR$

$= 30° + 90° = 120°$

Thus, the boatman must row making an angle of $120°$ with the direction of flow of the river.

Hence, the correct option is (D).

37. A metalloid is any chemical element which has properties in between those of metals and nonmetals, or that has a mixture of them. Metalloids are semiconductors because they are neither good nor poor conductors. All the elements commonly recognized as metalloids have been used in the semiconductor or solid-state electronic industries.

Hence, the correct option is (C).

38. In order to increase the conductivity of pure semiconductors and to overcome their other limitations, a small amount, say, 1 part per million (ppm), of impurity atoms having valency different from 4, is added to the purr semiconductor.

Hence, the correct option is (A).

39. Given:
$T_1 = 300K$ and $T_2 = 500K$
Mean time $\tau_1 = 6 \times 10^{-8}$
$\tau_2 = ?$

$\tau = \frac{1}{(\sqrt{2}\pi\eta d^2 V_{Avg})}$

$$\eta = \left(\frac{\text{No. of molecules}}{\text{volume}}\right) = \frac{N}{V}$$

$$\tau = \frac{V}{\sqrt{2}\pi N d^2 V_{Avg}}$$

$$V_{Avg} = \sqrt{\frac{2RT}{MW}}$$

$$\tau \alpha \frac{V}{\sqrt{T}}$$

$$\tau \alpha \frac{\sqrt{T}}{p}$$

$$\frac{\tau_1}{\tau_2} = \sqrt{\frac{T_1}{T_2}}\left(\frac{p_2}{p_1}\right)$$

$$\tau_2 = (6 \times 10^{-8})\sqrt{\frac{T_2}{T_1}}\left(\frac{p_1}{p_2}\right)$$

$$\tau_2 = (6 \times 10^{-8})\sqrt{\frac{500}{300}}\left(\frac{p}{2p}\right)$$

$$\tau_2 = (3 \times 10^{-8})\sqrt{\frac{5}{3}}$$

$$\tau_2 = 4 \times 10^{-8} \text{ sec.}$$

Hence, the correct option is (D).

40. Given:

Density $= 4 Kg/m^3$

$P = 8 \times 10^4 N/m^2$

$U = \frac{5}{2}\mu RT$

For diatomic gases. (5 is the degrees of freedom as the gas is diatomic)

But $PV = \mu RT$

So,

$U = \frac{5}{2}PV$

$V = \frac{\text{mass}}{\text{density}}$

$= \frac{1\ kg}{4\ kg/m^3}$

$= \frac{1}{4} m^3$

$P = 8 \times 10^4\ N/m^2$

$\therefore U = \frac{5}{2} \times 8 \times 10^4 \times \frac{1}{4}$

$= 5 \times 10^4\ J$

Hence, the correct option is (B).

41. 1 unit of electric energy: When one-kilowatt load works for 1 hour then the energy consumed is called 1 unit of electricity.

1 Unit of electricity $= 1KWh = 1000$ Watt-hour $= 3.6 \times 10^6 J$

1 Kilo-watt $= 1000$ Watt

1 Watt: The energy consumption rate of 1 joule per second is called 1 watt.

Since $1hr = 3600$ sec

1 Kilo-watt $= 1000$ Watt

$1KWh = 1000$ Watt-hour $= 1000 \times 3600$ W.s $= 3.6 \times 10^6$ J

Hence, the correct option is (C).

42. Heating effect produced by current is due to the collision of electrons.

- When a potential difference is applied across the ends of a conductor, its free electrons get accelerated in the opposite direction of the applied field.
- But the speed of the electrons does not increase beyond a constant drift speed. This is because, during the course of their motion, the electrons collide frequently with the positive metal ions.
- The kinetic energy gained by the electrons during the intervals of free acceleration between collisions is transferred to the metal ions at the time of the collision.
- The metal ions begin to vibrate about their mean positions more and more violently.

Hence, the correct option is (A).

43. If two waves are given as,

$\Rightarrow y_1 = a.\sin(\omega t)$

$\Rightarrow y_2 = a.\sin(\omega t + \phi)$

By the principle of superposition, the resultant wave is given by,

$\Rightarrow y = y_1 + y_2$

$\Rightarrow y = a \cdot \sin(\omega t) + a \cdot \sin(\omega t + \phi)$

$\Rightarrow y = 2a \cdot \cos\frac{\phi}{2}\sin\left(\omega t + \frac{\phi}{2}\right)$ ---(1)

By equation (1) the amplitude of the resultant wave is given as,

$\Rightarrow A = 2a.\cos\frac{\phi}{2}$

Hence, the correct option is (B).

44. When two wave pulses overlap each other, the displacement of the resultant wave is the Vector sum of the displacement due to each pulse.

According to the principle of superposition of waves, when two or more waves come together at some point in space then the resultant disturbance wave is the vector sum of disturbance of the individual waves.

Hence, the correct option is (B).

45. At distance r from an infinitely long straight current carrying conductor, magnetic field is:

$B = \frac{\mu_0 I}{2\pi r}$

Where B is the magnetic field, μ_0 permeability of the medium I is the current in the wire, and r is the distance from the wire to that point.

So, $B \propto \frac{1}{r}$

Hence, the correct option is (B).

46. The magnetic field due to a circular coil of radius R at distance x from the center is given by:

$\Rightarrow B = \frac{\mu_0 I R^2}{2(R^2+x^2)^{\frac{3}{2}}}$

At a distance $x(x \gg R)$ on the axis of the circular coil we can ignore R in the above equation, then the above equation can be written as:

$\Rightarrow B = \frac{\mu_0 I R^2}{2(x^2)^{\frac{3}{2}}}$

$\Rightarrow B = \frac{\mu_0 I R^2}{2x^3}$

$\Rightarrow B \propto \frac{1}{x^3}$

Hence, the correct option is (C).

47. The expression $\frac{1}{2}I\omega^2$ represents Rotational Kinetic energy.

The energy, which a body has by virtue of its rotational motion, is called rotational kinetic energy. A body rotating about a fixed axis possesses kinetic energy because its constituent particles are in motion, even though the body as a whole remains in place.

Mathematically rotational kinetic energy can be written as -

$KE = \frac{1}{2}I\omega^2$

Where I = moment of inertia and ω = angular velocity

Hence, the correct option is (A).

48. Given: L = length of rod, r = Radius of gyration,

The moment of inertia of any uniform rod of length L and Mass M about the axis is given by:

$\rightarrow I = \frac{ML^2}{12}$ -----(1)

If r is the radius of the thin rod axis, then the equation of moment of inertia is given by:

$\Rightarrow I = Mr^2$ --------(2)

On equating above two-equation, we get

$\Rightarrow Mr^2 = \frac{ML^2}{12}$

$\Rightarrow r = \sqrt{\frac{L^2}{12}} = \frac{L}{\sqrt{4 \times 3}}$

$\Rightarrow r = \frac{L}{2\sqrt{3}}$

So, the radius of gyration of the rod is $r = \frac{L}{2\sqrt{3}}$

Hence, the correct option is (D).

49. Alternating emf in the circuit is:

$e = e_o \sin \omega t$

Current in the inductive circuit is:

$I = I_o \sin\left(\omega t + \frac{\pi}{2}\right)$

From above it is clear that current leads the voltage by $\frac{\pi}{2}$.

Hence, the correct option is (B).

50. In a capacitor, as the voltage applied is increased, there is current going into the capacitor. Now, as the applied voltage reaches the positive peak, the charging (in flow of current) stops. As the voltage starts to reduce, current flows out of the capacitor and continues until the voltage reaches the negative peak and discharging stops.

If we trace this out on a graph we will see that the current is leading the voltage by 90°, reaching zero current at the peaks of the voltage and maximum current as the voltage is going through zero. Hence, the voltage across the capacitor lags behind current by the phase angle $\left(\frac{\pi}{2}\right) rad$.

Hence, the correct option is (C).

51. Heavy water (D_2O), also called deuterium oxide.

Heavy water is used as a moderator in some reactors because it slows down neutrons effectively and also has a low probability of absorption of neutrons.

Hence, the correct option is (C).

52. Au i.e Gold is the least reactive from the given elements.

Reactivity is defined as the rate at which a chemical substance tends to undergo a chemical reaction.

Hence, the correct option is (C).

53. Given that:

Concentration of $Na_2CO_3 = 1.0 \times 10^{-4} M$

$\therefore [CO_3^-] = 1.0 \times 10^{-4} M$

i.e., $s = 1.0 \times 10^{-4} M$

At equilibrium:

$[Ba^{++}][CO_3^{--}] = K_{sp}$ of $BaCO_3$

$[Ba^{++}] = \frac{K_{sp}}{[CO_3^{--}]}$

$= \dfrac{5.1 \times 10^{-9}}{1.0 \times 10^{-4}}$

$= 5.1 \times 10^{-5} M$

Hence, the correct option is (A).

54. On dilution, milli equivalent of the solute remains constant.

Intially pH of $HCl = 4$

So, normality of $HCl = 10^{-4}\ N$

After dilution pH of $HCl = 5$

So, normality of HCl will be $= 10^{-5}\ N$

$N_1 V_1 = N_2 V_2$

$10^{-4} \times 10 = 10^{-5} \times V$

$V = 100\ mL$

So, the amount of water to be added to this solution in order to change its pH from 4 to 5 is $= 100 - 10 = 90$

Thus, 90 mL of water should be added for this pH change.

Hence, the correct option is (C).

55. Order of base nature depends on electron donation tendency.

In compound nitrogen ⌃⌃NH is sp2 hybridized so least basic among all given compounds. the

compound ⌃=NH₂ ⌃NH is very strong nitrogenous organic base as lone pair of one nitrogen delocalize in resonance and make another nitrogen negatively charged and conjugate acid have two equivalent resonating structure.

Thus it is most basic in given compounds.

⌃NHCH₃ (secondary amine) more basic than ⌃NH₂ (primary amine)

Hence, the correct option is (B).

56. C₄H₉ does not belongs to homologous series.

Homologous series is a series of compounds with similar chemical properties and some functional groups differing from the successive member by CH₂.

Carbon chains of varying length have been observed in organic compounds having the same general formula.

Alkanes with general formula CₙH₂ₙ₊₂, alkenes with general formula CₙH₂ₙ and alkynes with general formula CₙH₂ₙ₋₂ form the most basic homologous series in organic chemistry.

Hence, the correct option is (C).

57. (D) $H_2 S$

Let oxidation number of sulphur in $H_2 S$ be x.

$\therefore 2 + x = 0$

$x = -2$

(A) $H_2 SO_4$

Let oxidation number of sulphur in $H_2 SO_4$ be x.

$\therefore 2 + x - 4(2) = 0$

$x = +6$

(B) SO_2

Let oxidation number of sulphur in SO_2 be x.

$x + (2 \times -2) = 0$

$x - 4 = 0$

$x = +4$

(C) $H_2 SO_3$

Let oxidation number of sulphur in $H_2 SO_3$ be x.

$\therefore 2 + x + (3)(-2) = 0$

$x = 4$

Hence, the correct option is (D).

58. As given, the temperature is increased from T_1 to T_2, then new constants become k_3 and k_4 respectively.

Rate constant increases with increase in temperature.

So, $k_1 < k_3$ and $k_2 < k_4$

Hence, the correct option is (B).

59. In the presence of a catalyst, the heat evolved or absorbed during the reaction remains unchanged. The enthalpy change value of the reaction will not be affected by a catalyst. A catalyst will only lower the required activation energy for the reactions. Since it will lower the activation energy for both the forward and reverse reactions to the same extent, the net change in enthalpy is zero.

Hence, the correct option is (C).

60. A catalyst works by providing an alternative reaction pathway to the reaction product. The rate of the reaction is increased as this alternative route has lower activation energy than the reaction route not mediated by the catalyst.

Hence, the correct option is (B).

61. Given:

Weight of Urea $= 12\ g$

And, weight of sucrose $= 68.4\ g$

We know that:

Number of moles $= \dfrac{\text{Weight}}{\text{Molar mass}}$

Therefore,

Moles of urea $= \dfrac{12}{60} = 0.2$

(Molar mass of Urea is $60 gm.$)

Moles of sucrose $= \dfrac{68.4}{342} = 0.2$

(Molar mass of sucrose is $342 gm.$)

Since, there are equal moles of solute in equal volumes of water, the mole fraction is the same.

As per Raoult's law, the relative lowering of pressure will also be the same.

Hence, the correct option is (A).

62. Molar mass of $KI = 39 + 127 = 166\ g\ mol^{-1}$

20% aqueous solution of KI means $20\ g$ of KI is present in $100\ g$ of solution.

Therefore,

Mass of $KI = 20\ g$

That is,

$20\ g$ of KI is present in $(100-20)g$ of water $= 80\ g$ of water

We know that:

Molality of the solution $= \dfrac{\text{Moles of }KI}{\text{Mass of water in }kg}$

$= \dfrac{\frac{\text{Mass of KI}}{\text{Molar Mass of KI}}}{\text{Mass of water in }kg}$

$= \dfrac{\frac{20}{166}}{0.08}\ m$

$= 1.506\ m$

$= 1.51\ m$

Hence, the correct option is (A).

63. Given that:

The solution is obtained by mixing 300 g of 25% solution and 400 g of 40% solution by mass.

Therefore,

Total amount of solute present in the mixture will be given by,

$300 \times \dfrac{25}{100} + 400 \times \dfrac{40}{100}$

$= 75 + 160$

$= 235\ g$

Total amount of solution $= 300 + 400 = 700\ g$

Therefore,

Mass percentage of the solute in the resulting solution $= \dfrac{\text{Total amount of solute}}{\text{Total amount of solution}} \times 100$

$= \dfrac{235}{700} \times 100$

$= 33.57\%$

Then, mass percentage of the solvent in the resulting solution will be:

$= (100 - 33.57)\%$

$= 66.43\%$

Hence, the correct option is (C).

64. Given:

$a = 564 pm = 564 \times 10^{-10} cm$

We know that:

The density is given by the formula:

$\rho = \dfrac{zM}{a^3 N_A}$

As we know that,

Each unit cell of $NaCl$ has $4Na^-$ and $4Cl^-$ ions.

$\Rightarrow z = 4$

Avogadro's number, $N_A = 6.022 \times 10^{23}/mol$

The total mass of $NaCl$:

$M = 22.99 + 34.34 = 58.5\ g/mol$

Therefore,

Density, $\rho = \dfrac{zM}{a^3 N_A}$

$= \dfrac{4 \times 58.5}{(564 \times 10^{-10})^3 \times 6.022 \times 10^{23}}\ g\ cm^{-3}$

$= 2.165\ g\ cm^{-3}$

Hence, the correct option is (B).

65. All the mentioned compounds are examples of molecular solids:

- I_2 is an example of non polar molecular solid,
- Solid NH_3 is an example of polar molecular solid and
- Ice is an example of hydrogen bonded molecular solid.

Hence, the correct option is (D).

66. In the hexagonal closest packed (hcp) each ion has 12 neighboring ions, therefore, it has a coordination number of 12 and contains 6 atoms per unit cell.

The centre atom in layer B of HCP structure is touched with 12 other atoms of the same cell.

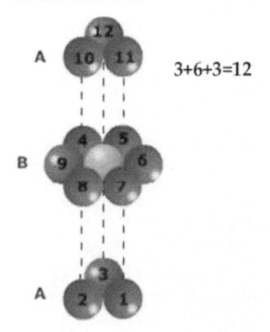

Hence, the correct option is (A).

67. The arrangement of elements in the Modern Periodic Table is based on increasing atomic number in the horizontal rows.

In 1869, Russian chemist Dmitri Mendeleev created the framework that became the modern periodic table, leaving gaps for elements that were yet to be discovered. While arranging the elements according to their atomic weight, if he found that they did not fit into the group he would rearrange them.

Hence, the correct option is (B).

68. Carbon belongs to the second period and Group 14. Silicon belongs to the third period and Group 14. If atomic number of carbon is 6, the atomic number of silicon is 14.

Silicon is a chemical element with the symbol Si and atomic number 14. It is a hard, brittle crystalline solid with a blue-grey metallic lustre, and is a tetravalent metalloid and semiconductor. It is a member of group 14 in the periodic table: carbon is above it; and germanium, tin, lead, and flerovium are below it.

Hence, the correct option is (B).

69. Neon is a chemical element with the symbol Ne and atomic number 10. It is a noble gas. Neon is a colourless, odourless, inert monatomic gas under standard conditions, with about two-thirds the density of air. It was discovered (along with krypton and xenon) in 1898 as one of the three residual rare inert elements remaining in dry air after nitrogen, oxygen, argon and carbon dioxide were removed.

Hence, the correct option is (A).

70. The melting and boiling points of alkali metals are quite low and they decrease down the group due to weakening of their metallic bonds. Francium is the only element in this group which is a liquid at room temperature.

Hence, the correct option is (B).

71. Urea was the first organic compound synthesized in a laboratory, which revolutionized and gave birth to organic chemistry.

German chemist Friedrich Wohler prepared urea in a laboratory in 1828 from ammonium cyanate. Nowadays urea is prepared commercially from liquid ammonia and liquid carbon.

Hence, the correct option is (A).

72. A person living in Shimla observed that cooking food without using pressure cooker takes more time. The reason for this observation is that at high altitude pressure decrease.

At high altitude, atmospheric pressure is low. Therefore, liquids at high altitude boil at lower temperatures in comparison to that at sea level hence pressure cooker is used for cooking food which otherwise takes more time.

Hence, the correct option is (C).

73. The surface tension of a liquid decreases with increase in temperature.

The strength of surface tension depends on intermolecular forces. As temperature increases, molecules of liquid become more active and they move more rapidly; therefore, the intermolecular forces are more instable. Surface tension decreases with increasing temperature.

Hence, the correct option is (B).

74. A poisonous gas is adsorbed at activated charcoal. The activated charcoal is adsorbent.

Adsorption is the adhesion of molecules of gas, liquid, or dissolved solid particles on to the surface. In this process a layer of the adsorbate the molecules or atoms being accumulated on the surface of the adsorbent.

Hence, the correct option is (D).

75. Covalent character in ionic compounds is governed by Fazan's Rule. $AlCl_3$ will show maximum covalent character on account of the higher polarizing power of Al^{3+} because of its having a higher positive charge and smaller size.

We know that, the extent of polarization is proportional to covalent character in ionic bonds. Fajans rule states that the polarizing power of cation increases, with an increase in the magnitude of positive charge on the cation. Therefore, polarizing power $\propto$ charge of cation. The polarizing power of a cation increases with the decrease in the size of a cation. Therefore,

Polarizing (power) $\propto \dfrac{1}{\text{(Size of cation)}}$

Here the $AlCl_3$ is satisfying the above two conditions i.e., Al is in a $+3$ oxidation state and also has a small size. So it has a more covalent character.

Hence, the correct option is (D).

76. For exothermic reaction ΔH = negative and if randomness increases it means ΔS becomes positive. Thus, according to $\Delta G = \Delta H - T\Delta S$, ΔG becomes negative so, the reaction is spontaneous.

Hence, the correct option is (A).

77. At equilibrium, Gibbs free energy change $(\Delta G°)$ is equal to zero. The following thermodynamic relation is used to show the relation of $(\Delta G°)$ with the enthalpy change $(\Delta H°)$ and entropy change $(\Delta S°)$.

$\Delta G° = \Delta H° - \Delta S°$

$0 = 30 \times 10^3 (J\ mol^{-1}) - T \times 105(J\ K^{-1})mol^{-1}$

Therefore,

$T = \frac{30 \times 10^3}{105} K = 285.71\ K$

Hence, the correct option is (D).

78. The atomic number is equal to number of protons $= 16$. The element is sulphur (S).

Atomic mass number $=$ number of protons $+$ number of neutrons

$= 16 + 16 = 32$

Species is not neutral as the number of protons is not equal to electrons. It is anion (negatively charged) with charge equal to excess electrons $= 18 - 16 = 2$

Thus symbol is $^{32}_{16}S^{2-}$.

Hence, the correct option is (D).

79. If we assume that one-sixth the mass of an atom of ^{12}C isotope is taken as the reference, the mass of one molecule of oxygen will be the same.

We know that:

$12\ g$ of Carbon $= 6.023 \times 10^{23}$ atoms

So,

$1g = \frac{6.023 \times 10^{23}}{12}$

$\therefore 6g$ of carbon $= 6 \times \frac{6.023 \times 10^{23}}{12}$

$= \frac{1}{2} \times 6.023 \times 10^{23}$

This is our new Avogadro's number according to the given conditions.

Then,

1 atomic mass unit $= \frac{1}{N_A}$

$= \frac{2}{6.023 \times 10^{23}}$

Mass of 1 mole of $O_2 = 32 \times$ Avogrado's number

$\times \frac{2}{6.023 \times 10^{23}}$

$= 32 \times \frac{6.023 \times 10^{23}}{2} \times \frac{2}{6.023 \times 10^{23}}$

$= 32g$

Therefore, there is no change in the mass number of O_2.

Hence, the correct option is (C).

80. Dissociation of sulfuric acid,

$H_2SO_4 \rightarrow 2H^+(aq) + SO_4^{-2}(aq)$

Disssociation of water,

$H_2O \rightarrow H^+(aq) + OH^-(aq)$

At Anode: $4OH^- \rightarrow 2H_2O^+(l) + O_2(g) + 4e^-$

Thus, on electrolysis of dilute sulphuric acid using Platinum (Pt) electrode, the product obtained at anode will be Oxygen gas.

Hence, the correct option is (B).

81. We know,

$E_{cell} = \frac{0.059}{2} \log \frac{1}{C}$

where, $C = 100$ times

$E_{cell} = -\frac{0.059}{2} \log \frac{1}{100}$ $\left(\because \log \frac{1}{100} = -2\right)$

$= -\frac{0.059}{2} \times -2$

$= 0.059V$

$= 59\ mV$

Thus, if the Zn^{2+}/Zn electrode is diluted to 100 times than the emf is decrease of $59\ mV$.

Hence, the correct option is (B).

82. $Q = i \times t$

$Q = 10 \times 10^{-3} \times t$

$2H_2O + 2e^- \rightarrow H_2 + 2OH^-$

To liberate 0.01 mole of H_2, 0.02 Faraday charge is required

$Q = 0.02 \times 96500C$

$\therefore 0.02 \times 96500 = 10^{-2} \times t$

$\Rightarrow t = 19.3 \times 10^4$ sec

Hence, the correct option is (B).

83. Hybridization of Fe in $K_3[Fe(CN)_6]$ is d^2sp^3.

In the given complex of Fe^{3+}, as the co-ordination number is '6', there are two possibilities. It can be d^2sp^3 or sp^3d^2. But the ligand attached with central metal ion, Fe^{3+}, is strong field ligand so it will promate inner orbital complex, d^2sp^3.

Hence, the correct option is (B).

84. Transition metal compounds are usually coloured. This is due to the electronic transition within the d-orbitals.

Transition elements (also known as transition metals) are elements that have partially filed d orbitals.

Many ionic and covalent compounds of transition elements are coloured and this colouring property is due to $d - d$ electronic excitation. The colour of the compound is complementary to the colour absorbed.

Hence, the correct option is (D).

85. In nitroprusside ion, the iron and NO exist as Fe(II) and NO^+ rather than Fe(III) and NO. These forms can be distinguished by measuring the solid-state magnetic moment.

Nitroprusside ion is $[Fe(CN)_5NO]^{2-}$. If the central atom iron is present here in Fe^{2+} form, its effective atomic number will be $26 - 2 + (6 \times 2) = 36$ and the distribution of electrons in valence orbitals (hybridised and unhybridized) of the Fe^{2+} will be

It has no unpaired electron. So this anionic complex is diamagnetic. If the nitroprusside ion has Fe^{3+} and NO, the electronic distribution will be such that it will have one unpaired electron i.e. the complex will be paramagnetic.

Thus, magnetic moment measurement establishes that in nitroprusside ion, the Fe and NO exist as F(II) and NO^+ rather than Fe(III) and NO.

Hence, the correct option is (C).

86. Maleic acid is stronger than fumaric acid.

- Maleic acid is cis-butenedioic acid whereas fumaric acid is trans-butenedioic acid.
- Maleic acid is able to lose H^+ ion and it results in the formation of intra hydrogen bond. Whereas fumaric acid being a trans isomer has strong interaction with both the oxygen atoms of each carboxylic group. Therefore, fumaric acid is unable to give hydrogen ions as compared to maleic acid.
- That is why, maleic acid is stronger than fumaric acid.

Hence, the correct option is (B).

87. Given reaction:

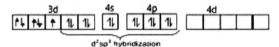

The above reaction is known as Etard reaction.

- The Etard Reaction is a chemical reaction that involves the direct oxidation of an aromatic or heterocyclic bound methyl group to an aldehyde using chromyl chloride.
- When toluene is reacted with Chromyl Chloride, then a chromium complex is formed (Etard Complex) whose hydrolysis gives Benzaldehyde.

Hence, the correct option is (C).

88. The correct order of increasing acidic strength is Ethanol < Phenol < Acetic acid < Chloroacetic acid.

- Phenol is more acidic than ethanol because in phenol, the phenoxide ion obtained on deprotonation is stabilized by resonance which is not possible in case of ethanol.
- Also carboxylic acids are more acidic than alcohols and phenols as the carboxylate ion is stabilized by resonance. Chloroacetic acid is more acidic than acetic acid due to inductive effect of chlorine atom which stabilizes the carboxylate anion.

Hence, the correct option is (C).

89. Functional group -CHO is present in Aldehydes.

Aldehyde is a class of organic compounds, in which a carbon atom shares a double bond with an oxygen atom, a single bond with a hydrogen atom, and a single bond with another atom or group of atoms (designated R in general chemical formulas and structure diagrams).

The double bond between carbon and oxygen is characteristic of all aldehydes and is known as the carbonyl group.

Aldehydes are often written in the short form as R–CHO

Aldehydes are considered the most important functional group.

Aldehydes contain the carbonyl group bonded to at least one hydrogen atom.

The IUPAC system of nomenclature assigns a characteristic suffix -al to aldehydes. For example, H2C=O is methanol.

The functional group of -OH is Alcohol.

The functional group of >C=O is Ketone.

The functional group of -COOH is Carboxylic acid.

Hence, the correct option is (B).

90. All the given options are correctly matched.

Aldehyde has C_nH_2O general formula. Example: Ethanal $-C_2H_4O, n = 2$

Carboxylic acid has $C_nH_{2n}O_2$ general formula. Example: Propionic acid $- C_3H_6O_2, n = 3$

Cycloalkane has C_nH_{2n} general formula. Example: Cyclobutane $-C_4H_8, n = 4$

Alkane also has C_nH_{2n+2} general formula. Example: Ethane $-C_2H_6, n = 2$

Hence, the correct option is (D).

91. Alpha hydroxy ketones and Aldehydes give a positive test with Tollens' reagent.

Ketones generally don't give positive test with Tollen's reagent, but alpha hydroxyl ketones are an exception. Iodoform test, Ester test, etc., are used for alcohols. The litmus test, Sodium bicarbonate test and Ester test are used for carboxylic acid.

Hence, the correct option is (D).

92. The compounds that contain carbon are known as organic compounds. Most abundant organic compound on earth is cellulose.

Carbohydrates are grouped into monosaccharides, disaccharides and polysaccharides. Cellulose, a storage form of carbohydrate found in plants that humans cannot digest, is among the most plentiful of the carbohydrates worldwide. Cellulose is a polymer of linear polysaccharide, with several monosaccharide glucose units. The acetal linkage is beta which distinguishes it from starch. Human beings are unable to digest cellulose because there are no sufficient enzymes for breaking down beta-acetal linkages.

Hence, the correct option is (C).

93. Protein synthesis in a cell takes place in cytoplasm as well as in mitochondria. Protein synthesis takes place during the translation process inside the ribosomes. The ribosome is the protein factory of the cell. Ribosomes are found in both prokaryotic and eukaryotic cells. Ribosomes are also found in association with other cell organelles like mitochondria. The ribosomes are synthesized in the nucleolus. Also, the ribosomes are found attached to the Endoplasmic Reticulum (ER) means they are found freely present in the cytoplasm. 70 S ribosomes are found in the matrix of the mitochondria of both the prokaryotic and the eukaryotic cells. This is because mitochondria are the powerhouse of the cell and the major site for aerobic respiration and ATP production.

Hence, the correct option is (C).

94. Rayon:

- Rayon is a synthetic fibre whose properties are similar to that of silk.
- Rayon is obtained from a natural source like wood pulp.
- It has a very shiny appearance and hence called artificial silk.

Teflon:

- Teflon is short for tetrafluoroethylene, also known as PTFE.
- It is used to make non-stick cookware, pans because it is unreactive in nature and has non-stick properties.
- It is a synthetic polymer.

Bakelite:

- Plastic is also a polymer like synthetic fibre.
- There are two types of plastics: thermoplastics and thermosetting plastics.
- Thermosetting plastics are the one which when moulded once cannot be softened by heating.

PVC:

- PVC stands for Poly Vinyl Chloride.
- It is a plastic that gets deformed easily when heated and can be moulded again into other forms.
- It is used to make pipes, containers, various type of toys etc.

Column A (Fibres)	Column B (Uses)
1. Rayon	d. Clothes
2. Teflon	a. Coating of non-stick
3. Bakelite	b. Handles and Switches
4. PVC	c. Pipes

The correct option is thus 1-d, 2-a, 3-b, 4-c.

Hence, the correct option is (B).

95. A high molecular weight compound formed by combining large numbers of small molecules of low molecular weight is called Polymer.

A polymer is a large molecule composed of many repeated sub units, known as monomers. Because of their broad range of properties, both synthetic and natural polymers play an essential and ubiquitous role in everyday life.

Polymers range from familiar synthetic plastics such as polystyrene to natural biopolymers such as DNA and proteins, that are fundamental to biological structure and function. Polymers, both natural and synthetic, are created via the polymerisation of many monomers.

Their large molecular mass relative to small molecular compounds produces unique physical properties, including toughness, viscoelasticity and a tendency to form glasses and semicrystalline structures rather than crystals.

Hence, the correct option is (A).

96. Plastic used to preserve yogurts is replaced with a polymer called polylactic acid is an example of green chemistry.

Since usage of petroleum-based plastic is harmful to the environment, a polymer called polylactic acid, made using microorganisms to convert cornstarch into a resin, is used to preserve yogurt. The resulting polymer is used to replace rigid petroleum-based plastic used in yogurt containers and water bottles and is environment-friendly. It is an application of green chemistry.

Hence, the correct option is (A).

97. Sustainable development focuses on more use of renewable resources.

Renewable resources are the resources which can be replenishment. Like sunlight, rainwater. The use of renewable resources favours the sustainable development. As sustainable development focuses on the meeting the need of present without hampering the future generation.

Hence, the correct option is (A).

98. Alkaline $KMnO_4$ is called Baeyer's reagent. Baeyer's reagent is an alkaline solution of cold potassium permanganate, which is a powerful oxidant making this a redox reaction. Reaction with double or triple bonds ($-C = C-$ or $-C \equiv C-$) in an organic material causes the colour to fade from purplish-pink to brown. It is a syn addition reaction.

Hence, the correct option is (B).

99. The monohalogen derivatives of alkanes are called Haloalkanes.

So, on a general basis saturated hydrocarbon is called alkanes, Generally, when one hydrogen atom of an alkane is replaced by a halogen atom, then the compound obtained is called a mono halogen derivative of alkanes. Typically they are called as alkyl halides (depending on the degree of substitution at the carbon atom carrying the halogen, alkyl halides are classified into primary, secondary and tertiary alkyl halides) or halo alkenes.

The general formula is $C_nH_{2n+1}X$

Hence, the correct option is (B).

100. All the alkali metals are good reducing agents due to their low ionization energies. The reducing character of group 1 elements follows the increasing order of Sodium, Potassium, rubidium, Caesium and lithium.

Hence, the correct option is (B).

Physics & Chemistry : Mock Test 03

Physics

Q.1 A simple wave motion represents by $y = 5(\sin 4\pi t + \sqrt{3}\cos 4\pi t)$. Its amplitude is:

[BITSAT, 2012]

A. 5 B. $5\sqrt{3}$ C. $10\sqrt{3}$ D. 10

Q.2 If k_s and k_p respectively are effective spring constant in series and parallel combination of springs as shown in figure, find $\dfrac{k_s}{k_p}$.

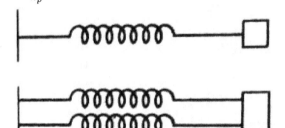

[BITSAT, 2012]

A. $\dfrac{9}{2}$ B. $\dfrac{3}{7}$ C. $\dfrac{2}{9}$ D. $\dfrac{7}{3}$

Q.3 If the displacement of the simple pendulum at any time is 0.02 m and acceleration is 2 m/s², then in this time angular velocity will be:

[BITSAT, 2012]

A. 100 rad/s B. 10 rad/s
C. 1 rad/s D. 0.1 rad/s

Q.4 A bifocal lens is used as a remedy in which of the following defects in the eyes?

A. Hyperopia B. Presbyopia
C. Astigmatism D. Myopia

Q.5 A ray of light suffers minimum deviation while passing through a prism of refractive index 1.5 and refracting angle 60°. Calculate the angle of deviation and angle of incidence? (Given: $\sin^{-1} 0.75 = 48°$)

A. 36° and 48° B. 48° and 36°
C. 45° and 30° D. 60° and 30°

Q.6 A Proton and an alpha particle both are accelerated through the same potential difference. The ratio of corresponding de-Broglie wavelengths is:

A. $2\sqrt{2}$ B. $\dfrac{1}{2\sqrt{2}}$ C. 2 D. $\sqrt{2}$

Q.7 When photons of wavelength λ_1 are incident on an isolated sphere, the corresponding stopping potential is found to be V. When photons of wavelength λ_2 are used, the corresponding stopping potential was thrice of that the above value. If light of wavelength λ_3 is used then find the stopping potential for this case:

A. $\dfrac{hc}{e}\left[\dfrac{1}{\lambda_3} - \dfrac{1}{\lambda_2} - \dfrac{1}{\lambda_1}\right]$

B. $\dfrac{hc}{e}\left[\dfrac{1}{\lambda_3} + \dfrac{1}{\lambda_2} - \dfrac{1}{\lambda_1}\right]$

C. $\dfrac{hc}{e}\left[\dfrac{1}{\lambda_3} + \dfrac{1}{2\lambda_2} - \dfrac{3}{2\lambda_1}\right]$

D. None of the above

Q.8 Suppose a pure Si crystal has 5×10^{28} atoms m^{-3}. It is doped by 1 ppm concentration of pentaralent As. Calculate the number of electrons and holes. Given that $n_i = 1.5 \times 10^{16}\ m^{-3}$.

A. $4.5 \times 10^9\ m^{-3}$ B. $5.5 \times 10^9\ m^{-3}$
C. $6.5 \times 10^9\ m^{-3}$ D. $7.5 \times 10^9\ m^{-3}$

Q.9 Water in an electric kettle becomes hot due to _____.

A. Conduction
B. Convection
C. Radiation
D. Motion of its molecules

Q.10 Which of the following spectral series of hydrogen atom is lying in visible electromagnetic wave?

A. Paschen series B. Pfund series
C. Lyman series D. Balmer series

Q.11 The Bohr model is applicable to:

A. Hydrogen atom B. He⁺ atom
C. Both (A) and (B) D. None of these

Q.12 The three stable isotopes of neon: $^{20}_{10}Ne, ^{21}_{10}Ne$ and $^{22}_{10}Ne$ have respective abundances of $90.51\%, 0.27\%$ and 9.22%. The atomic masses of the three isotopes are $19.99u, 20.99u$ and $21.99u$ respectively. Obtain the average atomic mass of neon.

A. $20.17u$ B. $2.7u$
C. $2.75u$ D. None of these

Q.13 A ball is rolling on a table without slipping. Its part of energy associated with rotational motion will be:

A. $\dfrac{2}{5}$ B. $\dfrac{2}{7}$ C. $\dfrac{3}{5}$ D. $\dfrac{3}{7}$

Q.14 The moment of inertia of a circular ring of radius 'R' and mass 'M' about diameter is:

A. $\dfrac{MR^2}{4}$ B. $\dfrac{MR^2}{2}$ C. $\dfrac{MR^2}{12}$ D. $\dfrac{2}{5}MR^2$

Q.15 In a series resonant circuit, the AC voltage across resistance R, inductor L and capacitor C, are $5\ V, 10\ V$ and $10\ V$ respectively. The AC voltage applied to the circuit will be:

A. 10V B. 25V C. 5V D. 20V

Q.16 If a current I given by $I_0 \sin[\omega t - (\frac{\pi}{2})]$ flows in an ac circuit across which an ac potential of $E = E_0 \sin \omega t$ has been applied, then the power consumption P in the circuit will be,

A. $2E_0 I_0$ B. $\sqrt{2} E_0 I_0$ C. $E_0 I_0$ D. 0

Q.17 A circular loop of radius R, carrying current I, lies in the $X - Y$ plane with its center at the origin. The total magnetic flux through the $X - Y$ plane is:
A. Directly proportional to I
B. Directly proportional to R
C. Inversely proportional to R
D. Zero

Q.18 A small square loop of wire of side l is placed inside a large square loop of wire of side $L (L \gg l)$. The loops are coplanar and their centers coincide. The mutual inductance of the system is proportional to:

A. $\frac{l}{L}$ B. $\frac{l^2}{L}$ C. $\frac{L}{l}$ D. $\frac{L^2}{l}$

Q.19 The inductance of a solenoid $0.5\ m$ long of cross-sectional area $420\ cm^2$ and with 500 turns is:
A. $26.4\ mH$ B. $2.64\ mH$
C. $25.0\ mH$ D. $0.26\ mH$

Q.20 If the ratio of the concentration of electrons to that of holes in semiconductors is $\frac{7}{5}$ and the ratio of currents is $\frac{7}{4}$, then the ratio of drift velocities is:

A. $\frac{5}{8}$ B. $\frac{4}{5}$ C. $\frac{5}{4}$ D. $\frac{4}{7}$

Q.21 The barrier potential in a $p - n$ junction is $0.3V$. The current required is $6mA$. The emf of the cell required for use in the circuit if the resistance of 200Ω is connected in series with a junction is (in V):

A. $2.0V$ B. $1.9V$ C. $1.5V$ D. $1.1V$

Q.22 When a real gas expands adiabatically against a finite pressure, its:
A. Internal energy increases
B. Internal energy decreases
C. Temperature always increases
D. Internal energy remains constant

Q.23 $ABCDA$ is a cyclic process explaining the thermodynamic process. What is the work done by the system in the cycle?

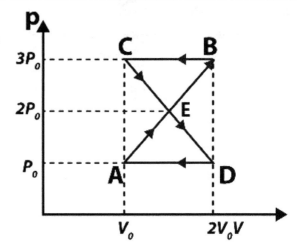

A. 0 B. $\frac{P_0 V_0}{2}$ C. $P_0 V_0$ D. $2 P_0 V_0$

Q.24 What is the ratio of $\frac{C_p}{C_v}$ for gas if the pressure of the gas is proportional to the cube of its temperature and the process is an adiabatic process?

A. $\frac{4}{3}$ B. $\frac{5}{7}$ C. $\frac{3}{2}$ D. $\frac{7}{9}$

Q.25 Newton's law of gravitation is applicable in the case of _____.
A. Planets and stars only
B. Point masses only
C. Big bodies onlyy
D. All bodies in the universe

Q.26 A smooth sphere of mass m strikes a second sphere of mass $2m$ which is at rest. After the collision their directions of motion are at right angles. Then the coefficient of restitution is:

A. 0 B. $\frac{1}{2}$ C. $-\frac{1}{2}$ D. 1

Q.27 It is easier to wash clothes in hot water because:
A. Surface tension of hot water is more
B. Surface tension of hot water is less
C. Less soap is used
D. None of these

Q.28 If a liquid does not wet glass, its angle of contact is _____.
A. Zero   B. Acute
C. Obtuse   D. Right angle

Q.29 The electrostatic force of repulsion between two positively charged ions carrying equal charge is $3.7 \times 10^{-9} N$, when they are separated by a distance of $5 \overset{\circ}{A}$. How many electrons are missing from each ion?

A. 2 B. 4 C. 6 D. 8

Q.30 Find the amount of work done in rotating a dipole of dipole moment $3 \times 10^{-3} cm$ from its position of stable equilibrium to the position of unstable equilibrium, in a uniform electric field of intensity $10^4 NC^{-1}$.

A. 50 J   B. 60 J   C. 80 J   D. 70 J

Q.31 Two charges, one of $+5\mu C$ and another of $-5\mu C$ are kept $1 mm$ apart. Calculate the dipole moment.
A. $2 \times 10^7 C - m$
B. $5 \times 10^{-9} C - m$
C. $2 \times 10^{-8} C - m$
D. $5 \times 10^8 C - m$

Q.32 An electric dipole, when held at $30°$ with respect to a uniform electric field of $10^4 N/C$ experiences a torque of $9 \times 10^{-26} Nm$. Calculate the dipole moment of the dipole.
A. $1.8 \times 10^{-29} cm$
B. $2.7 \times 10^{-18} cm$
C. $1.7 \times 10^{-14} cm$
D. $3.8 \times 10^{-20} cm$

Q.33 In figure (i) two positive charges q_2 and q_3 fixed along the y-axis, exert a net electric force in the $+x$ direction on a charge q_1 fixed along the x axis. If a positive charge Q is added at $(x, 0)$ in figure (ii), the force on q_1:

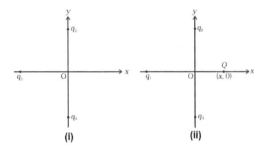

A. Shall increase along the positive x-axis.
B. Shall decrease along the positive x-axis.
C. Shall point along the negative x-axis.
D. Shall increase but the direction changes because of the intersection of Q with q_2 and qy

Q.34 What is the electric potential at a distance of 9 cm from 3 nC?
A. 270 volt   B. 3 volt   C. 300 volt   D. 30 volt

Q.35 The electric potential due to a system of charge is given by $V = 5x^2 - 2y^2 + 12$, where x, y, z are the coordinates in meter and V is in volts. The electric field intensity at $(-4,3,0)$ along X-direction is:
A. 52 V/m
B. -11 V/m
C. 2.5 V/m
D. 40 V/m

Q.36 Electrostatic potential at a distance r from a point charge q is proportional to:
A. $\frac{1}{r}$ B. $\frac{1}{r^2}$ C. r D. r^2

Q.37 A pipe of length 85 cm is closed from one end. Find the number of possible natural oscillations of air column in the pipe whose frequencies lie below $1250 Hz$. The velocity of sound in air is $340 m/s$.
A. 6   B. 4   C. 12   D. 8

Q.38 The maximum number of possible interference maxima for slit-separation equal to twice the wavelength in Young's double-slit experiment, is
A. Infinity   B. 5   C. 3   D. Zero

Q.39 What is the effect on the interference fringes in Young's double slit experiment if the width of the source slit is increased?
A. The fringe width increases.
B. The fringe width decreases.
C. The fringes become more distinct.
D. The fringes become less distinct.

Q.40 In Young's double slit experiment, if the distance between the slits and the screen is doubled and the separation between the slits is reduced to half, the fringe width:
A. Is doubled
B. Becomes four times
C. Is halved
D. Remains unchanged

Q.41 A particle is moving along x-axis has acceleration f at time t, given by $f = f_0\left(1 - \frac{t}{T}\right)$, where f_0 and T are constants. The particle at $t = 0$ has zero velocity. In the time interval between $t = 0$ and the instant when $f = 0$, the velocity (v_2) of the particle is then
A. $f_0 T$ B. $\frac{1}{2} f_0 T^2$ C. $f_0 T^2$ D. $\frac{1}{2} f_0 T$

Q.42 To obtain p-type Si semiconductor, we need to dope pure Si with:
A. Aluminium
B. Phosphorous
C. Oxygen
D. Germanium

Q.43 When an impurity is doped into an intrinsic semiconductor, the conductivity of the semiconductor:
A. Increases
B. Decreases
C. Remains the same
D. Becomes zero

Q.44 Two gases A and B have equal pressure P, temperature T, and volume V. The two gases are mixed together and the resulting mixture has the same temperature T and volume V as before. The ratio of pressure exerted by the mixture to either of the two gases is:
A. 1:1   B. 2:1   C. 3:1   D. 1:2

Q.45 An ideal gas at $27°$ is compressed adiabatically to $\frac{8}{27}$ of its original volume. The rise in its temperature is; $\left(\gamma = \frac{5}{3}\right)$
A. 225°C   B. 375°C   C. 400°C   D. 450°C

Q.46 The phase difference between two similar waves is ϕ. Both the waves are moving in the same direction and superimposed. If the resultant wave has zero displacements everywhere at all times, then the value of ϕ is:
A. 0
B. $\frac{\pi}{2}$
C. π
D. None of these

Q.47 The ratio of the intensity of two waves is $4:1$. If both the waves are superimposed in the same phase then the intensity

of the resultant wave is x and if both the waves are superimposed in the opposite phase then the intensity of the resultant wave is y. Find the ratio of x to y.

A. $3:1$
B. $9:1$
C. $4:1$
D. None of these

Q.48 The e.m.f. and the current of an a.c. circuit are $V = 100\sin(100t)$ volt and current $i = 100\sin\left(100t + \frac{\pi}{3}\right)mA$ respectively. The power dissipated in the circuit is:

A. 10 watt
B. 2.5 watt
C. 5 watt
D. 10^4 watt

Q.49 An inductor of reactance 2Ω and a resistor of 2Ω are connected in series to the terminals of a $12\ V$ (rms) a.c. source. The power dissipated in the circuit is:

A. 9 watt
B. 36 watt
C. 18 watt
D. 72 watt

Q.50 Average power in LCR circuit depends upon:

A. Current
B. Current, emf, and phase difference
C. Emf
D. Phase difference

Chemistry

Q.51 An ionic compound has a unit cell consisting of A ions at the corners of a cube and B ions on the centres of the faces of the cube. The empirical formula for this compound would be:

A. AB
B. A_2B
C. AB_3
D. A_3B

Q.52 Which of the following will show Schottky defect?

A. CaF_2
B. Zns
C. $AgCl$
D. $CsCl$

Q.53 The appearance of colour in solid alkali metal halides is generally due to:

A. Schottky defect
B. Frenkel defect
C. Interstitial position
D. F - centres

Q.54 For the reaction, $CO_{(g)} + Cl_{2(g)} \rightleftharpoons COCl_{2(g)}$, then K_p/K_c is equal to:

A. $\sqrt{RT}$
B. RT
C. $\frac{1}{RT}$
D. 1.0

Q.55 The solubility (in $molL^{-1}$) of $AgCl\,(K_{sp} = 1.0 \times 10^{-10})$ in a $0.1 M KCl$ solution will be:

A. 1.0×10^{-9}
B. 1.0×10^{-10}
C. 1.0×10^{-5}
D. 1.0×10^{-11}

Q.56 Which of the following is a set of essential amino acids?

A. Glycine, Alanine, Tyrosine, Glutamic acid
B. Glycine, Alanine, Threonine, Lysine
C. Tyrosine, Glutamic acid, Valine, Leucine
D. Leucine, Threonine, Alanine, Tyrosine

Q.57 Which of the following expression of concentration of a solution is independent of temperature?

A. Molarity
B. Normality
C. Formality
D. Molality

Q.58 In the reaction $4Fe + 3O_2 \rightarrow 4Fe^{3+} + 6O^{2-}$ which of the following statements is incorrect?

A. It is a redox reaction
B. Metallic iron is a reducing agent
C. Fe^{3+} is an oxidising agent
D. Metallic iron is reduced to Fe^{3+}

Q.59 Which of the following theory is not related to the chemical kinetics?

A. Collision theory
B. VSEPR theory
C. Absolute reaction rate
D. None of the above

Q.60 In _____, a reaction product is itself a catalyst for that reaction leading to positive feedback.

A. Autocatalysis
B. Catalysis
C. Pressure jump
D. Fast reactions

Q.61 A reaction has both ΔH and ΔS negative. The rate of reaction:

A. Increases with increase of temperature
B. Increases with decrease of temperature
C. Remains unaffected by change of temperature
D. Cannot be predicted for change in temperature

Q.62 Which of the following 0.10m aqueous solution will have the lowest freezing point?

A. $Al_2(SO_4)_3$
B. $C_5H_{10}O_8$
C. KI
D. $C_{12}H_{22}O_{11}$

Q.63 How much of sucrose is to be added to 500 g of water such that it boils at 100°C if the molar elevation constant for water is 0.52 K kg mol⁻¹ and the boiling point of water at 750 mm Hg is 99.63°C?

A. 125.60 g
B. 123.62 g
C. 124.90 g
D. 121.67 g

Q.64 To lower the melting point of $75\ g$ of acetic acid by $1.5°C$, how much mass of ascorbic acid is needed to be dissolved in the solution where $K_f = 3.9\ K\ kg\ mol^{-1}$?

A. 6.07 g
B. 7.09 g
C. 4.03 g
D. 5.08 g

Q.65 Cobalt sulphate (CoSO₄) is also known as _____.

A. Blue Vitriol
B. Red Vitriol
C. Green vitriol
D. None of the above

Q.66 What is the chemical formula of alcohol?

A. ROH
B. RCHO
C. RCOX
D. RCOOH

Q.67 Which of the following is the most reactive non-metal?

A. Chlorine
B. Hydrogen
C. Fluorine
D. Selenium

Q.68 What is the atomic number of element of period 3 and group 17 of the Periodic Table?

A. 10
B. 04
C. 17
D. 21

Q.69 Which element has three shells which are completely filled with electrons?

A. Argon B. Neon
C. Krypton D. Aluminum

Q.70 The removal of the second electron in alkali metals is _____.

A. Difficult B. Easy
C. Medium D. None of these

Q.71 Pick out the option that is not a functional group from the following.

A. Hydroxyl group
B. Benzene group
C. Aldehyde group
D. Carboxylic acid group

Q.72 The value of gas constant per degree per mole is approximately:

A. $1\ cal$ B. $2\ cal$ C. $3\ cal$ D. $4\ cal$

Q.73 The rate of diffusion of methane at a given temperature is twice that of gas X. The molecular mass of gas X is:

A. 64 B. 32 C. 4 D. 8

Q.74 Which of the following statements is true?

A. The first law of thermodynamics is not adequate in predicting the direction of the process.
B. In an exothermic reaction, the total enthalpy of the products is greater than that of reactants.
C. The standard enthalpy of a diamond is zero at $298\ K$ and $1\ atm$ pressure.
D. It is possible to calculate the value of ΔH for the reaction $H_2(g) + Br_2(\ell) \to 2HBr(g)$ from the bond enthalpy data.

Q.75 Calculate the heat required to make $6.4 Kg\ CaC_2$ from $CaO(s)$ and $C(s)$ from the reaction:

$$CaO(s) + 3C(s) \to CaC_2(s) + CO(g)$$

given that $\Delta_f H°(CaC_2) = -14.2$ kcal. $\Delta fH°(CO) = -26.4$ kcal.

A. $5624\ kcal$ B. $1.11 \times 10^4\ kcal$
C. $86.24 \times 10^3\ kcal$ D. $1100\ kcal$

Q.76 Which of these pairs of species have the same order of bond?

A. O_2^-, CN^- B. N^+, CN^+
C. CO, NO D. CN^-, NO^+

Q.77 Which among the following is an example of Adsorption?

A. Silica gel in contact with water vapours
B. Misty windows
C. Painting
D. All of the above

Q.78 The Vividh Bharati station of All India Radio, Delhi, broadcasts on a frequency of 1368 kHz. Calculate the wavelength of the electromagnetic radiation emitted by transmitter.

A. $319.3\ m$ B. $219.3\ m$ C. $200\ m$ D. $220.3\ m$

Q.79 Cooking gas (LPG) mainly consists of:

A. Ethene B. Ethyne
C. Propene D. Propane and Butane

Q.80 Assertion: The cell potential of mercury cell is $1.35\ V$, which remains constant.

Reason: In mercury cell, the electrolyte is a paste of KOH and ZnO.

A. Both Assertion and Reason are correct and Reason is the correct explanation for Assertion.
B. Both Assertion and Reason are correct but Reason is not the correct explanation for Assertion.
C. Assertion is correct but Reason is incorrect.
D. Assertion is incorrect but Reason is correct

Q.81 A current of 2 amp when passed for 5 hours through a molten salt deposits $22.2\ g$ of metal of atomic mass 177. The oxidation state of the metal in the metal salt is:

A. +1 B. +2 C. +3 D. +4

Q.82 The number of moles of electrons passed when a current of $2A$ is passed through a solution of electrolyte for 20 minutes is:

A. 4.1×10^{-4} mole B. 1.24×10^{-2} mole
C. 2.487×10^{-2} mole D. 2.487×10^{-1} mole

Q.83 According to Werner's theory of coordination compounds:

A. Primary valency is ionizable
B. Secondary valency is ionizable
C. Primary and secondary valencies are ionizable
D. Neither primary nor secondary valency is ionizable

Q.84 Ammonia acts as a very good ligand but ammonium ion does not form complexes because:

A. NH_3 is a gas while NH_4^+ is in liquid form.
B. NH_3 undergoes sp³ hybridization while NH_4^+ undergoes sp³d hybridization.
C. NH_4^+ ion does not have any lone pair of electrons.
D. NH_4^+ ion has one unpaired electron while NH_3 has two unpaired electrons.

Q.85 Which of the following is a tridentate ligand?

A. $EDTA^{4-}$ B. $(COO)_2^{2-}$
C. Dien D. NO_2^-

Q.86 Presence of unsaturation in organic compounds can be tested with:

A. Fehling's reagent B. Tollens' reagent
C. Baeyer's reagent D. Fittig's reaction

Q.87 Which among the following is most reactive to give nucleophilic addition?

A. FCH_2CHO B. $ClCH_2CHO$
C. $BrCH_2CHO$ D. ICH_2CHO

Q.88 Which of the following carboxylic acid is highly insoluble in water?

A. Propanoic acid B. Butanoic acid
C. Pentanoic acid D. Decanoic acid

Q.89 Which of the following is a functional isomer of Dimethyl ether?
A. Ethanol
B. Mthanol
C. 2 - methlyl propanol
D. None of these

Q.90 Match correctly the functional group given in List-I with the Nomenclature of that functional group given in list-II:

List I	List II
a. Aldehyde	i. Propanone
b. Halogen	ii. Propanal
c. Ketone	iii. Propanol
d. Alcohol	iv. Bromopropane

A. a-iv, b-i, c-ii, d-iii
B. a-ii, b-iv, c-i, d-iii
C. a-ii, b-i, c-iv, d-iii
D. a-ii, b-iii, c-iv, d-i

Q.91 Ether is formed when alkyl halide is heated with sodium alkoxides. This method is called:
A. Kolbe synthesis
B. Wurtz reaction
C. Perkin Reaction
D. Williamson's Synthesis

Q.92 In RNA, thymine is replaced by_____.
A. Guanine
B. Uracil
C. Both (A) and (B)
D. None of these

Q.93 Carrier ions like sodium ions facilitate the absorption of substances like:
A. Amino acids and glucose
B. Glucose and fatty acids
C. Fatty acids and glycerol
D. Fructose and some amino acids

Q.94 Which among the following is a biodegradable polymer?
A. Nylon-2-nylon-6
B. Polyvinyl chloride
C. Bakelite
D. Polythene

Q.95 The non-metal used in the vulcanization of rubber is _____.
A. Phosphorus
B. Sulphur
C. Graphite
D. Iodine

Q.96 Taking chromium and arsenic, which are toxic, out of pressure-treated wood, and using new less toxic chemicals for bleaching paper, are examples of_____.
A. Green chemistry
B. Waste management
C. Green revolution
D. None of above

Q.97 In which of the following type of nano-material, one dimension is outside the nano scale?
A. One dimensional nano material
B. Two dimensional nano material
C. Three dimensional nano material
D. Zero dimensional nano material

Q.98 Which of the following products have green chemistry approach?
A. Ibuprofen
B. Surfactant
C. Propene
D. All of the above

Q.99 Which is the correct order of decreasing bond dissociation enthalpy?
A. F2 > Cl2 > Br2 > I2 $F_2 > Cl_2 > Br_2 > I_2$
B. $I_2 > Br_2 > Cl_2 > F_2$
C. $Cl_2 > Br_2 > F_2 > I_2$
D. $Br_2 > I_2 > F_2 > Cl_2$

Q.100 Nitrogen dioxide is not produced on heating:
A. KNO_3
B. $Pb(NO_3)_2$
C. $Cu(NO_3)_2$
D. $AgNO_3$

// Smart Answer Sheet //

Correct: Indicates percentage of students who answered questions correctly.

Skipped: Indicates percentage of students who skipped questions.

Q.	Ans.	Correct / Skipped	Q.	Ans.	Correct / Skipped	Q.	Ans.	Correct / Skipped	Q.	Ans.	Correct / Skipped	Q.	Ans.	Correct / Skipped
1	D	42.31 % / 7.69 %	17	D	26.92 % / 23.08 %	33	A	38.46 % / 19.23 %	49	B	42.31 % / 19.23 %	65	B	38.46 % / 34.62 %
2	C	30.77 % / 19.23 %	18	B	23.08 % / 23.07 %	34	C	65.38 % / 23.08 %	50	B	61.54 % / 23.08 %	66	A	65.38 % / 34.62 %
3	B	53.85 % / 23.07 %	19	A	26.92 % / 26.93 %	35	D	38.46 % / 19.23 %	51	C	34.62 % / 34.61 %	67	C	46.15 % / 34.62 %
4	B	42.31 % / 26.92 %	20	C	34.62 % / 23.07 %	36	A	73.08 % / 23.07 %	52	D	34.62 % / 34.61 %	68	C	57.69 % / 34.62 %
5	A	26.92 % / 23.08 %	21	C	38.46 % / 23.08 %	37	A	34.62 % / 19.23 %	53	D	42.31 % / 34.61 %	69	A	53.85 % / 34.61 %
6	A	26.92 % / 19.23 %	22	B	30.77 % / 23.08 %	38	B	26.92 % / 26.93 %	54	C	23.08 % / 34.61 %	70	A	57.69 % / 34.62 %
7	C	30.77 % / 23.08 %	23	A	53.85 % / 23.07 %	39	D	19.23 % / 19.23 %	55	A	23.08 % / 34.61 %	71	B	57.69 % / 34.62 %
8	A	26.92 % / 23.08 %	24	C	38.46 % / 23.08 %	40	B	46.15 % / 23.08 %	56	A	19.23 % / 23.08 %	72	B	42.31 % / 34.61 %
9	B	42.31 % / 23.07 %	25	D	61.54 % / 26.92 %	41	D	15.38 % / 23.08 %	57	D	42.31 % / 34.61 %	73	A	23.08 % / 34.61 %
10	D	57.69 % / 23.08 %	26	B	30.77 % / 23.08 %	42	A	38.46 % / 19.23 %	58	D	30.77 % / 34.61 %	74	A	26.92 % / 34.62 %
11	C	50.0 % / 26.92 %	27	B	61.54 % / 23.08 %	43	A	65.38 % / 19.24 %	59	B	42.31 % / 34.61 %	75	B	26.92 % / 34.62 %
12	A	50.0 % / 26.92 %	28	C	61.54 % / 23.08 %	44	B	26.92 % / 23.08 %	60	A	46.15 % / 34.62 %	76	D	26.92 % / 34.62 %
13	B	30.77 % / 19.23 %	29	A	23.08 % / 23.07 %	45	B	26.92 % / 23.08 %	61	A	15.38 % / 34.62 %	77	D	50.0 % / 34.62 %
14	B	46.15 % / 23.08 %	30	B	53.85 % / 23.07 %	46	C	23.08 % / 23.07 %	62	A	30.77 % / 34.61 %	78	B	50.0 % / 34.62 %
15	C	30.77 % / 23.08 %	31	B	50.0 % / 23.08 %	47	B	42.31 % / 26.92 %	63	D	23.08 % / 34.61 %	79	D	46.15 % / 34.62 %
16	D	30.77 % / 23.08 %	32	A	46.15 % / 23.08 %	48	B	23.08 % / 23.07 %	64	D	19.23 % / 34.62 %	80	B	30.77 % / 34.61 %

Physics & Chemistry : Mock Test - 3

Q.	Ans.	Correct / Skipped	Q.	Ans.	Correct / Skipped	Q.	Ans.	Correct / Skipped	Q.	Ans.	Correct / Skipped	Q.	Ans.	Correct / Skipped
81	C	26.92 % / 34.62 %	85	C	26.92 % / 34.62 %	89	A	46.15 % / 34.62 %	93	A	26.92 % / 34.62 %	97	A	23.08 % / 34.61 %
82	C	57.69 % / 34.62 %	86	C	30.77 % / 34.61 %	90	B	61.54 % / 34.61 %	94	A	57.69 % / 34.62 %	98	D	46.15 % / 34.62 %
83	A	30.77 % / 34.61 %	87	A	19.23 % / 34.62 %	91	D	42.31 % / 34.61 %	95	B	50.0 % / 34.62 %	99	C	23.08 % / 34.61 %
84	C	50.0 % / 34.62 %	88	D	38.46 % / 34.62 %	92	B	50.0 % / 34.62 %	96	A	46.15 % / 34.62 %	100	A	23.08 % / 34.61 %

Performance Analysis	
Avg. Score (%)	42.0%
Toppers Score (%)	96.0%
Your Score	

Physics & Chemistry : Mock Test - 3

//Hints and Solutions//

1. We know that,

$y = a\sin\omega t + b\cos\omega t$ ....(1)

Given that,

$y = 5(\sin 4\pi t + \sqrt{3}\cos 4\pi t)$

$y = 5\sin 4\pi t + 5\sqrt{3}\cos 4\pi t$ ......(2)

$A = \sqrt{a^2 + b^2}$

On comparing equation (1) and (2) we get,

$a = 5$ and $b = 5\sqrt{3}$

$A = \sqrt{(5)^2 + (5\sqrt{3})^2}$

$= \sqrt{25 + 75}$

$= \sqrt{100}$

$= 10$

Hence, the correct option is (D).

2. The effective spring constant k_s of this arrangement is:

$\frac{1}{k_s} = \frac{1}{k} + \frac{1}{2k}$

$\frac{1}{k_s} = \frac{2+1}{2k} = \frac{3}{2k}$

$k_s = \frac{2k}{3}$

The effective spring constant k_p of this arrangement is

$k_p = k_1 + k_2$

$= k + 2k = 3k$

$\therefore \frac{k_s}{k_p} = \frac{\frac{2k}{3}}{3k} = \frac{2}{9}$

Hence, the correct option is (C).

3. In a simple pendulum,

$x = x_0 \sin(\omega t + \phi)$

$\Rightarrow a = \frac{d^2 x}{dt^2} = -\omega^2 x$

$\Rightarrow \omega = \sqrt{\frac{a}{x}} = \sqrt{\frac{2}{0.02}}$

$= 10 \, rad/s$

Hence, the correct option is (B).

4. An eye that suffers from myopia as well as from hypermetropia is said to suffer from presbyopia. A person with this defect cannot see objects distinctly placed at any distance from him. To correct this defect, a person is prescribed bifocal lens that has both types of lenses convex and concave.

Hence, the correct option is (B).

5. Given:

The angle of the prism $A = 60°$

The refractive index of the prism $(\mu) = 1.5$

$\sin^{-1} 0.75 = 48°$

The Refractive index (μ) of a prism for minimum deviation (δ_m):

$\mu = \frac{\sin\left(\frac{A+\delta_m}{2}\right)}{\sin\frac{A}{2}}$

Where, $A =$ angle of the prism

The relation between the angle of the prism A and incident angle (i):

$i = \frac{(A+\delta_m)}{2}$

From the formula of refractive index,

$1.5 = \frac{\sin\left(\frac{60°+\delta_m}{2}\right)}{\sin\left(\frac{60°}{2}\right)}$

$1.5 \times \sin 30° = \sin\left(\frac{60°+\delta_m}{2}\right)$

$1.5 \times \frac{1}{2} = \sin\left(\frac{60°+\delta_m}{2}\right)$

$0.75 = \sin\left(\frac{60°+\delta_m}{2}\right)$

$\sin^{-1} 0.75 = \frac{60°+\delta_m}{2}$

$48° = \frac{60°+\delta_m}{2}$

$\delta_m = 96° - 60°$

$\delta_m = 36°$

Angle of incidence (i)

$i = \frac{(60+36)}{2}$

$i = 48°$

So, the angle of deviation and angle of incidence is $36°$ and $48°$ respectively.

Hence, the correct option is (A).

6. The de-Broglie wavelength of a particle of mass m and moving with velocity v is given by,

$\lambda = \dfrac{h}{mv}$ $(\because p = mv)$

de-Broglie wavelength of a proton of mass m_1 and kinetic energy k is given by,

$\lambda_1 = \dfrac{h}{\sqrt{2\, m_1 k}}$ $(\because p = \sqrt{2mk})$

$\Rightarrow \lambda_1 = \dfrac{h}{\sqrt{2\, m_1 qV}}$ ..... (i) $[\because k = qV]$

For an alpha particle mass m_2 carrying charge q_0 is accelerated through potential V, then,

$\lambda_2 = \dfrac{h}{\sqrt{2\, m_2 q_0\, V}}$

$\because$ For $\alpha-$ particle $(^4_2 He)$:

$q_0 = 2q$ and $m_2 = 4\, m_1$

$\therefore \lambda_2 = \dfrac{h}{\sqrt{2 \times 4\, m_1 \times 2q \times V}}$ ..... (ii)

The ratio of corresponding wavelength, from Eqs. (i) and (ii), we get,

$\dfrac{\lambda_1}{\lambda_2} = \dfrac{h}{\sqrt{2\, m_1 qV}} \times \dfrac{\sqrt{2 \times m_1 \times 4 \times 2qV}}{h}$

$= \dfrac{4}{\sqrt{2}} \times \dfrac{\sqrt{2}}{\sqrt{2}}$

$\Rightarrow \dfrac{\lambda_1}{\lambda_2} = 2\sqrt{2}$

Hence, the correct option is (A).

7. Let us assume that the threshold frequency of the sphere is λ_0. Let the stopping potential is V' of the surface when the light of wavelength λ_3 is used. Thus according to Einstein photoelectric equation.

$\dfrac{hc}{\lambda_1} = \dfrac{hc}{\lambda_0} + eV$ .....(i)

$\dfrac{hc}{\lambda_2} = \dfrac{hc}{\lambda_0} + 3eV$ .....(ii)

$\dfrac{hc}{\lambda_3} = \dfrac{hc}{\lambda_0} + eV'$ .....(iii)

From equation (i) and (ii)

$\dfrac{hc}{\lambda_2} = \dfrac{hc}{\lambda_0} + 3\left(\dfrac{hc}{\lambda_1} - \dfrac{hc}{\lambda_0}\right)$

$\Rightarrow \dfrac{hc}{\lambda_2} = \dfrac{hc}{\lambda_0} + \dfrac{3hc}{\lambda_1} - \dfrac{3hc}{\lambda_0}$

$\Rightarrow \dfrac{hc}{\lambda_2} - \dfrac{3hc}{\lambda_1} = -\dfrac{2hc}{\lambda_0}$ ... (iv)

From equation (iii) and (iv)

$\dfrac{hc}{\lambda_2} - \dfrac{3hc}{\lambda_1} = -2\left(\dfrac{hc}{\lambda_3} - eV'\right)$

$\Rightarrow \dfrac{hc}{\lambda_2} - \dfrac{3hc}{\lambda_1} = -\dfrac{2hc}{\lambda_3} + 2eV'$

$\Rightarrow hc\left(\dfrac{1}{\lambda_2} + \dfrac{2}{\lambda_3} - \dfrac{3}{\lambda_1}\right) = 2eV'$

$\Rightarrow \dfrac{hc}{e}\left(\dfrac{1}{2\lambda_2} + \dfrac{1}{\lambda_3} - \dfrac{3}{2\lambda_1}\right) = V'$

Hence, the correct option is (C).

8. Here $n_i = 1.5 \times 10^{16}\, m^{-3}$

Doping concentration of pentavalent As atoms $= 1ppm =$ 1part per million $= 10^6$

$\therefore$ Number density of pentavalent As atoms,

$N_D = \dfrac{5 \times 10^{28}}{10^6} = 5 \times 10^{22}$ atom m^{-3}

Now, the thermally generated electrons $(n_i \propto 10^{16}\, m^{-3})$ are negligibly small as compared to those produced by doping, so

$n_e \simeq N_D = 5 \times 10^{22}\, m^{-3}$

Also,

$n_e =$ number of electrons

$n_h =$ number of holes

$n_e n_h = n_i^2$

$n_h = \dfrac{n_i^2}{n_e} = \dfrac{1.5 \times 10^{16} \times 1.5 \times 10^{16}}{5 \times 10^{22}}$

$= 4.5 \times 10^9\, m^{-3}$

Hence, the correct option is (A).

9. Water in an electric kettle becomes hot by convection. It is the process of transfer of heat by mass motion of a fluid such as water when the heated fluid is caused to move away from the source of it and carrying energy with it.

Hence, the correct option is (B).

10. When an electron in Hydrogen atom transit from higher energy orbit to 2nd orbit. (outer orbit n₂ > 2 to the orbit n₁ = 2) known as Balmer Series.

When atoms are excited they emit light of certain wavelengths that correspond to different colors. Due to the electron making transitions between two energy levels in an atom. The light emission can be seen as a series of colored lines, known as atomic spectra.

The Balmer series: It includes the lines due to transitions from an outer orbit n₂ > 2 to the orbit n₁ = 2. Four of the Balmer lines lie in the "visible" part of the spectrum. The energy released from this spectrum gives the visible part of the spectrum.

Hence, the correct option is (D).

11. Bohr model is applicable to both the Hydrogen atom and the He⁺ atom.

Hydrogenic atoms are atoms consisting of a nucleus with positive charge Ze⁺ and a single electron, where Z is the proton number. For examples are a hydrogen atom, singly ionized helium, doubly ionized lithium, and so forth. Bohr model is applicable to hydrogenic atoms. It cannot be extended even to mere two-electron atoms such as helium.

Bohr's model correctly predicts the frequencies of the light emitted by hydrogenic atoms, the model is unable to explain the relative intensities of the frequencies in the spectrum.

Hence, the correct option is (C).

12. Given:

The masses of isotopes of neon are, $19.99u, 20.99u$ and $21.99u$. Relative abundance of the isotopes are $90.51\%, 0.27\%$ and 9.22%.

Therefore, Average atomic mass of neon is,

Average atomic mass $= \sum_{i=1}^{n} \frac{(mass_{(i)})}{(Abundance_{(i)})}$

$m = \frac{90.51\% \times 19.99 + 0.27\% \times 20.99 + 9.22\% \times 21.99}{(90.51\% + 0.27\% + 9.22\%)}$

$m = \frac{90.51 \times 19.99 + 0.27 \times 20.99 + 9.22 \times 21.99}{(90.51 + 0.27 + 9.22)}$

$= \frac{1809.29 + 5.67 + 202.75}{100}$

$= \frac{2017.7}{100}$

$= 20.17u$

Hence, the correct option is (A).

13. Total kinetic energy of a rolling ball

$K.E.$ = linear $K.E.$ + rotational $K.E.$

$K.E. = \frac{1}{2}mv^2 + \frac{1}{2}I\omega^2$

$= \frac{1}{2}mv^2 + \frac{1}{2} \times \frac{2}{5}mr^2 \cdot \frac{v^2}{r^2}$

$= \left(\frac{5+2}{10}\right)mv^2 = \frac{7}{10}mv^2$

Fraction of total energy associated with rotational kinetic energy

$= \frac{\frac{1}{5}mv^2}{\frac{7}{10}mv^2}$

$= \frac{1}{5} \times \frac{10}{7} = \frac{2}{7}$

Hence, the correct option is (B).

14.

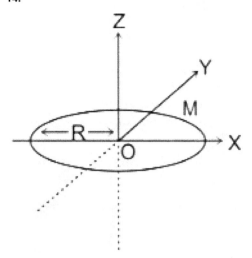

We know that moment of inertia of a ring through its center perpendicular to the ring plane is MR^2

$I_z = MR^2$

By perpendicular axis theorem

$I_z = I_x + I_y$

$MR^2 = I_x + I_y$

By symmetry $I_x = I_y = I$

$MR^2 = I + I$

$I = \frac{MR^2}{2}$

The moment of inertia of a circular ring of radius 'R' and mass 'M' about diameter is $\frac{MR^2}{2}$.

Hence, the correct option is (B).

15. Given,

Voltage across resistor, $V_R = 5V$

Voltage across inductor, $V_L = 10V$

Voltage across capacitor, $V_C = 10V$

The AC voltage applied to the circuit is given as

$V = \sqrt{V_R^2 + (V_L - V_C)^2}$

Substituting the given values, we get,

$= \sqrt{(5)^2 + (10 - 10)^2}$

$= 5V$

Hence, the correct option is (C).

16. We know that,

$I = I_0 \sin\left(\omega t - \{\frac{\pi}{2}\}\right)$

$E = E_0 \sin \omega t$

Now power consumed $= P = EI\cos\theta$

$\theta =$ angle or phase difference between E and I

Here $\theta = 90°$

$\therefore P = EI\cos 90°$

$P = 0$

Hence, the correct option is (D).

17. Since here total flux entering equals the total flux leaving and hence net flux equals zero.

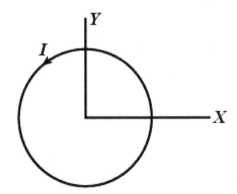

Hence, the correct option is (D).

18. Magnetic field produced by a current i in a large square loop at its centre $B \propto \frac{i}{L}$ say $B = K\frac{i}{L}$

$\therefore$ Magnetic flux linked with smaller loop,

$\phi = B.S\phi = \left(K\frac{i}{L}\right)(l^2)$

Therefore, the mutual inductance

$M = \frac{\phi}{i} = K\frac{l^2}{L}$ or $M \propto \frac{l^2}{L}$

Hence, the correct option is (B).

19. Given,

Length of solenoid, $l = 0.5\ m$

Cross-sectional area, $A = 420 \times 10^{-4}\ m^2$

Number of turns, $n = 500$

We know,

$L = \frac{\mu_0 n^2 A}{l}$

$L = \frac{(4\pi \times 10^{-7}) \times (500)^2 \times (420 \times 10^{-4})}{0.5}$

$L = \frac{0.013}{0.5} = 0.026\ H$

$L = 26.4\ mH$

Therefore, Inductance of solenoid is $26.4\ mH$.

Hence, the correct option is (A).

20. The drift velocity of charge carriers in the material of constant cross-sectional area A is given as:

$v = \frac{I}{nAq}$

(Here I is the current flowing through the material, n is the charge-carrier density, and q is the charge on the charge-carrier).

We have the ratio of I as $\frac{7}{4}$ and ratio of n as $\frac{7}{5}$.

$I = nAev_d$ or $I \propto nv_d$

$\therefore \frac{I_e}{I_h} = \frac{n_e v_e}{n_h v_h}$ or $\frac{n_e}{n_h}$

$= \frac{I_e}{I_h} \times \frac{v_h}{v_e}$

$= \frac{7}{4} \times \frac{4}{5} = \frac{7}{5}$

Hence, the correct option is (C).

21. Given that,

$V_D = 0.3V$

$I = 6mA = 0.006A$

$R = 200\Omega$

Here we can write,

$E - V_D = IR$

Where, E is the emf of battery

$E = IR + V_D$

$E = (0.006 \times 200) + 0.3$

$E = 1.2 + 0.3$

$= 1.5V$

Hence, the correct option is (C).

22. From the first law of thermodynamics,

$dU = q - W$

In adiabatic process no change of heat takes place.

So, $dU = -W$

Since, the gas is expanding, the work is done by the gas.

$dU = -W$.

Hence internal energy of the system decreases.

Again, $dU = C_v(T_2 - T_1) = W$

Since here W is negative, so $T_1 > T_2$.

So temperature will also decrease.

Hence, the correct option is (B).

23. In a cyclic process work done is equal to the area under the cycle and is positive if the cycle is clockwise and negative if anticlockwise.

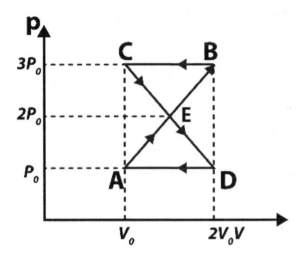

$W_{AEDA} = +$ Area of $\triangle AED = +\frac{1}{2} P_0 V_0$

$W_{BCEB} = -$ Area of $\triangle BCE = -\frac{1}{2} P_0 V_0$

The net work done by the system is:

$W_{net} = W_{AEDA} + W_{BCEB}$

$= +\frac{1}{2} P_0 V_0 - \frac{1}{2} P_0 V_0 = 0$

Hence, the correct option is (A).

24. Given,

$p \propto T^3$ ... (i)

In an adiabatic process,

$T^\gamma p^{1-\gamma} = $ constant $\left[\text{as } \gamma = \frac{C_p}{C_v} \right]$

$T \propto \frac{1}{p^{\frac{(1-\gamma)}{\gamma}}}$

$T^{\left(\frac{\gamma}{\gamma-1}\right)} \propto p$ ... (ii)

Comparing Eqs. (i) and (ii),

Since the pressure is same in both the condition, equating the powers of temperature from both sides we get,

$3\gamma - 3 = \gamma$ or $2\gamma = 3$

$\frac{C_p}{C_v} = \gamma = \frac{3}{2}$

Hence, the correct option is (C).

25. Newton's law of gravitation is applicable in the case of all bodies in the universe.

Newton's law of universal gravitation states that any two bodies in the universe attract each other with a force that is directly proportional to the product of their masses and inversely proportional to the square of the distance between them. Since any two bodies can be there so it doesn't matter whether they are small or large.

Hence, the correct option is (D).

26. Given,

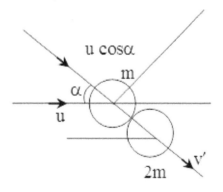

At equilibrium,

$mu\cos\alpha = 2mv'$

$\Rightarrow v' = \frac{u\cos\alpha}{2}$

$\Rightarrow \frac{1}{2} = \frac{v'}{u\cos\alpha}$ .... (1)

As we know that,

The coefficient of restitution,

$e = \frac{v'}{u\cos\alpha}$ .... (2)

From equation (1) and (2), we get

$e = \frac{1}{2}$

Hence, the correct option is (B).

27. The surface tension decreases as the temperature increases. The surface tension of hot water is very less compared to cold water and thus that makes washing clothes easier in hot water.

Hence, the correct option is (B).

28. Contact angle: The contact angle is a measure of the ability of a liquid to wet the surface of a solid.

Adhesive forces: Attractive forces between molecules of different types are called adhesive forces.

Cohesive forces: Attractive forces between molecules of the same types are called cohesive forces.

For contact angle 90° the cohesive forces and adhesive forces are in the equilibrium state.

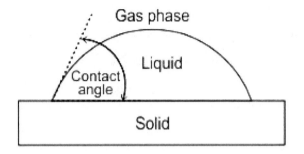

If a liquid doesn't wet the glass which means the interaction of liquid molecules is greater than the interaction between the liquid and solid molecule, these lead to an obtuse angle of contact.

Hence, the correct option is (C).

29. Given,

Electrostatic force of repulsion, $F = 3.7 \times 10^{-9} N$

Let us say charge is $q_1 = q_2 = q$

Distance between two charges, $r = 5A = 5 \times 10^{-10} m$

The number of electrons missing, $n = ?$

Using Coulomb's law,

$F = \dfrac{1}{4\pi\epsilon_0} \dfrac{q_1 q_2}{r^2}$

$3.7 \times 10^{-9} = 9 \times 10^9 \times \dfrac{q \times q}{(5 \times 10^{-10})^2}$

$q^2 = \dfrac{3.7 \times 10^{-9} \times 25 \times 10^{-20}}{9 \times 10^9}$

$q^2 = 10.28 \times 10^{-38}$

$q = 3.2 \times 10^{-19}$ Coulomb

As, we know that:

$q = ne$

$\therefore n = \dfrac{q}{e}$

$= \dfrac{3.2 \times 10^{-19}}{1.6 \times 10^{-19}}$

$= 2$

Therefore, the number of electrons missing is $n = 2$.

Hence, the correct option is (A).

30. Given,

Dipole Moment, $P = 3 \times 10^{-3} cm$

We know that:

In rotating the dipole from the position of stable equilibrium by an angle θ, the amount of work done is given by,

$W = PE(1 - \cos\theta)$

For unstable equilibrium, $\theta = 180°$

$\therefore W = PE(1 - \cos 180°) \quad [\because \cos 180° = -1]$

$= 2PE$

$= 2 \times 3 \times 10^{-3} \times 10^4 J$

$= 60 J$

Hence, the correct option is (B).

31. Given:

Charge on dipole is $\pm 5\mu C = \pm 5 \times 10^{-6} C$

Distance between the charges $= 1mm = 10^{-3} m$

We know that:

Dipole moment is given by:

$P = q(2a)$

$= 5 \times 10^{-6} \times 1 \times 10^{-3}$

$= 5 \times 10^{-9} C - m$

Hence, the correct option is (B).

32. Given,

Electric field, $E = 10^4 NC^{-1}$

Torque,

$T = 9 \times 10^{-26} Nm$

$\theta = 30°$

When electric dipole is placed at an angle θ with the direction of the electric field, torque acting on the dipole is given by,

$T = pE\sin\theta$

$p = \dfrac{T}{E\sin\theta}$

$= \dfrac{9 \times 10^{-26}}{10^4 \times \sin 30°}$

$= \dfrac{9 \times 10^{-26}}{10^4 \times 0.5}$

$= 1.8 \times 10^{-29} cm$

Hence, the correct option is (A).

33. The net electrostatic force on the charge qx by the charges q_2 and q_3 is along the positive x-direction. Therefore, the nature of force between q_1, q_2 and q_1, q_3 should be attractive. It means qx should be negative.

Obviously, due to addition of positive charge Q at $(x, 0)$, the force on $-q$ shall increase along the positive x-axis.

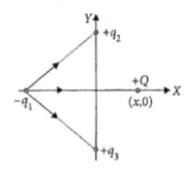

Hence, the correct option is (A).

34. Given,

$Q = 3$ nC $= 3 \times 10^{-9}$ C and $d = 9$ cm $= 0.09$ m

Electric Potential due to point charge given by the formula:

$V = \dfrac{kQ}{d}$

Where $k = 9 \times 10^9$ Nm^{2}C^{-2}, Q is the charge on the particle and d is the distance.

$V = \dfrac{9 \times 10^9 \times 3 \times 10^{-9}}{0.09}$

$V = 300$ volt

Hence, the correct option is (C).

35. Electric potential: The electric potential is also known as voltage (V), is the difference in potential energy per unit charge between two points in an electric field.

Electric field: The region around an electric charge in which it can influence other charges is known as the electric field.

The electric field intensity (E) at any location is defined as the force experienced by a unit charge placed at that location.

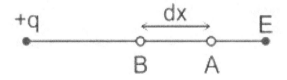

Consider two points A and B as given in the figure separated by a small distance dx in an electric field.

The electric force acting on a unit positive charge at A is equal to E.

The work done in moving a unit positive charge from A to B against the electric field is given by:

$dW = -E \times dx$

The work done is equal to the potential difference (dV) between A and B,

$dV = -E \times dx$

$\Rightarrow E = \dfrac{-dV}{dx}$

Given that:

Electric potential, $V = 5x^2 - 2y^2 + 12$

The intensity of the electric field along X-direction:

$E = \dfrac{-dV}{dx}$

$= \dfrac{-d(5x^2 - 2y^2 + 12)}{dx}$

$= -10x$

At $(-4, 3, 0)$

$E = -10(-4)$

$= 40$ V/m.

Hence, the correct option is (D).

36. Electric potential: The amount of work done to move a unit charge from a reference point to a specific point in an electric field without producing an acceleration is called electric potential. It is denoted by V.

The electric potential due to a point charge at a distance is given by:

$V = \dfrac{1}{4\pi\epsilon_0} \times \dfrac{q}{r}$

Here, $r =$ distance from the charged particle, $E =$ Electric field due to charges, $V =$ potential due to charge and $k = \dfrac{1}{(4\pi\epsilon_0)} =$ constant $= 9 \times 10^{-9}$ Nm^2/C^2

Since $V = \dfrac{1}{4\pi\epsilon_0} \times \dfrac{q}{r}$

So the electrostatic potential at a distance r from a point charge q is proportional to $\dfrac{1}{r}$.

Hence, the correct option is (A).

37. Given:

Velocity of sound $(V) = 340 \; m/s$

Length of air column $(L) = 85 \; cm = 0.85 \; m$

We know that,

Fundamental frequency of pipe closed at one end is given as,

$f = \dfrac{V}{4L}$

Where (V) is velocity of sound, (L) is length of air column.

Putting value in equation $f = \frac{V}{4L}$

$$f = \frac{340}{4 \times 0.85} = 100\ Hz$$

∴ Possible frequencies $= nf\ (n$ is odd $)$

The possible frequency is
$100\ Hz, 300\ Hz, 500\ Hz, 700\ Hz,\ 900\ Hz$ and $1100\ Hz$ below $1250\ Hz$.

Thus the number of possible natural oscillations whose frequency is below 1250 is 6.

Hence, the correct option is (A).

38. The condition for maxima in Young's double-slit experiment is $d\sin\theta = n\lambda$ where d is the separation between the slits and λ is the wavelength of light used.

The maxima that are farthest from the slits is infinitely up or infinitely down the screen and corresponds to $\theta = \frac{\pi}{2}$.

So, with the given condition, we have, $n = \frac{d\sin t(90°)}{\lambda}$

$= \frac{d}{\lambda}$

$= 2$

Thus, we have two maxima on the screen on either side of the central maxima. Thus, the maximum number of possible maxima observed are $2 + 1 + 2 = 5$.

Hence, the correct option is (B).

39. When the widths of the two slits are increased, the fringes become brighter. However, the width of each slit should be considerably smaller than the separation between the slits. When the slits become so wide that this condition is not satisfied, the interference pattern disappears i.e., The fringes become less distinct.

Hence, the correct option is (D).

40. Fringe width $\beta = \frac{D\lambda}{d}$ .....(1)

where D is the distance between slits and screen
and d is the distance between the slits.

Thus, From question $D' = 2D$ and $d' = \frac{d}{2}$

When D is doubled and d is reduced to half, then the fringe width becomes four times

$\beta' = \frac{\lambda 2D}{\left(\frac{d}{2}\right)}$

$= \frac{4\lambda D}{d}$

$= 4\beta$ from(1)

Thus, when the double slit experiment the distance between the slits and the screen is doubled and the separation between the slits is reduced to half, the fringe width becomes four times.

Hence, the correct option is (B).

41. Acceleration $f = f_0\left(1 - \frac{t}{T}\right)$

At $f = 0,\quad 0 = f_0\left(1 - \frac{t}{T}\right)$

Since f_0 is a constant,

∴ $1 - \frac{t}{T} = 0$ or $t = T$

Also, acceleration $f = \frac{dv}{dt}$

$\int_0^{v_x} dv = \int_{t=0}^{t=T} f\, dt = \int_0^T f_0\left(1 - \frac{t}{T}\right) dt$

$v_x = \left[f_0 t - \frac{f_0 t^2}{2T}\right]_0^T$

$= f_0 T - \frac{f_0 T^2}{2T} = \frac{1}{2} f_0 T$

Hence, the correct option is (D).

42. Aluminium is a trivalent impurity. Trivalent impurity atoms have 3 valence electrons. Such atoms on being added to pure semiconductor, instead of producing free electrons, accept electrons from the semiconductor. For this reason, trivalent impurity atoms are called acceptor impurity atoms. The semiconductor so produced is called p-type extrinsic semiconductor.

Hence, the correct option is (A).

43. The conductivity in an intrinsic semiconductor is due to the thermal motion of bound electrons. But extrinsic semiconductor contains more number of free electrons in case of n-type (and free holes in p-type) due to which the current flows. Thus conductivity of intrinsic semiconductor is more than that of extrinsic.

Hence, the correct option is (A).

44. Let P_1 and P_2 be the partial pressures of gases A and B, respectively. Under equal conditions of temperature and volume,

$P_1 = P_2$

Let P be the total pressure exerted by the mixture of two gases A and B. Using Dalton's law of partial pressures,

$P = P_1 + P_2$

$\Rightarrow P = 2P_1$

$\Rightarrow \frac{P}{P_1} = \frac{2}{1}$

$\Rightarrow P : P_1 = 2 : 1$

Hence, the correct option is (B).

45. Let initial volume V_1 be V

Given:

Final volume, $V_2 = \frac{8}{27}V$

Initial temperature, $T_1 = 273 + 27 = 300K$

$\gamma = \frac{5}{3}$

We have to find the rise in temperature, say T_2.

For an adiabatic process:

$TV^{\gamma-1} =$ constant

Thus,

$T_1 V_1^{\gamma-1} = T_2 V_2^{\gamma-1}$

$\Rightarrow T_2 = T_1 \left(\frac{V_1}{V_2}\right)^{\gamma-1}$

$\Rightarrow T_2 = 300 \times \left(\frac{27}{8}\right)^{\frac{5}{3}-1}$

$\Rightarrow T_2 = 300 \times \left(\frac{27}{8}\right)^{\frac{2}{3}}$

$\Rightarrow T_2 = 300 \times \frac{9}{4} = 675K$

$\Rightarrow T_2 = 675 - 273 = 402°C$

Rise in temperature $= 402°C - 27°C = 375°C$

Hence, the correct option is (B).

46. We know that if two similar waves have phase difference ϕ and both the waves are moving in the same direction and superimposed, then the resultant displacement is given as, Let two similar waves of phase difference ϕ are given as:

$y_1 = a \cdot \sin(kx - \omega t)$

$y_2 = a \cdot \sin(kx - \omega t + \phi)$

By the principle of superposition, the net displacement is given by,

$y = 2a \cdot \cos\frac{\phi}{2} \sin\left(kx - \omega t + \frac{\phi}{2}\right)$ ...(1)

If the resultant wave has zero displacements everywhere at all times, then by equation (1),

$y = 0$

$2a \cdot \cos\frac{\phi}{2} \sin\left(kx - \omega t + \frac{\phi}{2}\right) = 0$

$\phi = \pi$

Hence, the correct option is (C).

47. Given,

$\frac{I_1}{I_2} = \frac{4}{1}$

We know that when two waves are superimposed in the same phase, the intensity of the resultant wave is maximum.

Maximum intensity is given as,

$I_{max} = \left(\sqrt{I_1} + \sqrt{I_2}\right)^2$ ...(1)

We know that when two waves are superimposed in the opposite phase, the intensity of the resultant wave is minimum.

Minimum intensity is given as,

$I_{min} = \left(\sqrt{I_1} - \sqrt{I_2}\right)^2$ ...(2)

By dividing equation (1) and equation (2),

$\frac{I_{max}}{I_{min}} = \frac{x}{y} = \frac{\left(\sqrt{I_1}+\sqrt{I_2}\right)^2}{\left(\sqrt{I_1}-\sqrt{I_2}\right)^2}$

$\frac{x}{y} = \frac{\left(\sqrt{\frac{I_1}{I_2}}+1\right)^2}{\left(\sqrt{\frac{I_1}{I_2}}-1\right)^2}$

$\frac{x}{y} = \frac{9}{1}$

Hence, the correct option is (B).

48. Given,

Potential, $V = 100\sin(100t)V$, $i = 100\sin\left(100t + \frac{\pi}{3}\right)mA$

Phase difference $(\theta) = \frac{\pi}{3}$

Here Peak current $(I_0) = 100\ mA = 100 \times 10^{-3}\ A$

Peak voltage $(V_0) = 100\ V$

rms current $(I_{rms}) = \frac{I}{\sqrt{2}} = \frac{i_0}{\sqrt{2}}$

rms voltage $(V_{rms}) = \frac{V}{\sqrt{2}} = \frac{v_0}{\sqrt{2}}$

The average power dissipated in an AC circuit is given by:

$P_{avg} = V_{rms} I_{rms} Cos\theta$

$P_{avg} = \frac{V_0}{\sqrt{2}} \times \frac{I_0}{\sqrt{2}} \times Cos\frac{\pi}{3}$

$P_{avg} = \frac{v_0 i_0}{2} \times \frac{1}{2}$

$= \frac{100 \times 100 \times 10^{-3}}{4}$

$= \frac{10}{4} = 2.5\ W$

Hence, the correct option is (B).

49. Given,

Inductive reactance $X_L = 2\Omega$

Capacitive reactance $X_C = 0\Omega$

Resistance $R = 2\Omega$

Rms voltage $V_{rms} = 12V$

The impedance of the A.C. circuit is:

$$Z = \sqrt{(X_L - X_C)^2 + R^2}$$

Where Z = impedance

X_L = Inductance

X_C = Capacitance

R = Resistance.

$$Z = \sqrt{(2-0)^2 + 2^2}$$

$$\Rightarrow 2\sqrt{2}\,\Omega$$

$I_{rms} = \dfrac{V_{rms}}{Z}$

Where,

$V_{rms} = RMS$ voltage of the circuit

Z = impedance of the circuit.

$I_{rms} = \dfrac{12}{2\sqrt{2}} = \dfrac{6}{\sqrt{2}} = 3\sqrt{2}\ A$

The average power dissipated by the resistor (power is never dissipated by inductor or capacitor) of resistance R in any ac circuit with rms current I_{rms} is given by:

$$P = I_{rms}^2 R$$

Where P = power dissipated

$I_{rms} = RMS$ current in a circuit

R = resistance of a circuit.

$$P = \left(3\sqrt{2}\right)^2 \times 2 = 36 \text{ watt}$$

$P = 36$ watt

Hence, the correct option is (B).

50. The average power dissipated in an AC circuit is given by:

$$P_{avg} = V_{rms} I_{rms} \cos\theta$$

From the above equation, it is clear that the average power depends upon current, emf, and phase difference.

Hence, the correct option is (B).

51. Since A is present at the 8 corners, number of A ions per unit cell $= \dfrac{1}{8} \times 8 = 1$

Since B is present at the centre of 6 faces, number of B per unit cell $= \dfrac{1}{2} \times 6 = 3$

∴ The ratio of A and B is $1:3$, so the formula of the compound is AB_3.

Hence, the correct option is (C).

52. In ionic solids the vacancies are produced due to absence of cations and anions in stoichiometric proportions resulting in defect called Schottky defect.

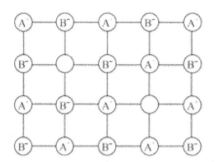

Schottky defect

This defect arises when cation and anion are of similar sizes.

CsCl shows Schottky defect.

Hence, the correct option is (D).

53. The appearance of colour in solid alkali metal halides is generally due to F - centres.

- F - centres (Farbe - centre) are generated when an electron occupies a vacancy generated by anion. This electron excites and de-excites losing photons which is of visible region in spectrum.
- Irradiations of alkali halides with gamma radiations creates anion vacancies where an electron is trapped and is responsible for the absorption of light.
- On heating the alkali halide in excess of alkali metal vapours creates vacancies in which an electron is trapped. So, there appears colour in solid alkali metal halides.

Hence, the correct option is (D).

54. Given equation is:

$$CO(g) + Cl_2(g) \rightleftharpoons COCl_2(g)$$

We know that:

$$K_p = K_p[RT]^n$$

Where,

n = Concentration of products - concentration of reactants

$n = 1 - 2 = -1$

Therefore,

$$K_p = K_c[RT]^{\Delta n};$$

$$\therefore \frac{K_p}{K_c} = [RT]^{-1}$$

$$= \frac{1}{RT}$$

Hence, the correct option is (C).

55. Solubility is defined as the maximum amount of solute that can be dissolved in a solvent at equilibrium. The solubility product constant describes the equilibrium between a solid and its constituent ions in a solution,

Let solubility of $AgCl = x$ mole/ L

$AgCl \rightleftharpoons Ag^+ + Cl^-$

i.e., $K_{sp}(AgCl) = x^2$

$KCl \to K^+ + Cl^-$

$[Cl^-]$ from $KCl = 0.1\ m$

Total $[Cl^-]$ in solution $= x + 0.1$

$K_{sp}(AgCl) = [Ag^+][Cl^-] = x(x + 0.1)$

$1.0 \times 10^{-10} = x(x + 0.1)$

$1.0 \times 10^{-10} = 0.1x$ (as $x^2 << 1$)

$x = 1.0 \times 10^{-9}\ mol/L$

Hence, the correct option is (A).

56. Humans can produce 10 of the 20 amino acids. The others must be supplied with food. Failure to obtain enough of even 1 of the 10 essential amino acids, those that we cannot make, results in degradation of the body's proteins—muscle and so forth—to obtain the one amino acid that is needed. Unlike fat and starch, the human body does not store excess amino acids for later use—the amino acids must be in the food every day.

The 10 amino acids that we can produce are alanine, asparagine, aspartic acid, cysteine, glutamic acid, glutamine, glycine, proline, serine, and tyrosine. Tyrosine is produced from phenylalanine, so if the diet is deficient in phenylalanine, tyrosine will be required as well.

Hence, the correct option is (A).

57. The expression of Molality of concentration of a solution is independent of temperature.

We know that:

$$Molality = \frac{Number\ of\ moles\ of\ solute}{Mass\ of\ solvent\ in\ kilograms}$$

Since mass is unaffected by the change in temperature, therefore, molality is independent of temperature.

Hence, the correct option is (D).

58. Given reaction,

$4Fe + 3O_2 \to 4Fe^{+3} + 6O^{2-}$

Clearly, given reaction is a redox reaction in which, Fe gets oxidised to Fe^{+3} by losing of three electrons, and O_2, gets reduced to O^{2-}.

Thus, Metallic iron (Fe) is a reducing agent and Fe^{+3} is an oxidising agent.

Hence, the correct option is (D).

59. VSEPR theory is not related to the chemical kinetics.

Valence shell electron pair repulsion (VSEPR) theory is a model used in chemistry to predict the geometry of individual molecules from the number of electron pairs surrounding their central atoms. The VSEPR theory is used to predict the shape of the molecules from the electron pairs that surround the central atoms of the molecule

Hence, the correct option is (B).

60. In autocatalysis, a reaction product is itself a catalyst for that reaction leading to positive feedback.

A single chemical reaction is said to have undergone autocatalysis, or be autocatalytic, if one of the reaction products is also a reactant and therefore a catalyst in the same or a coupled reaction. The reaction is called an autocatalytic reaction. A catalyst is a substance that accelerates the rate of a chemical reaction but remains chemically unchanged afterwards.

Hence, the correct option is (A).

61. A reaction has both ΔH and ΔS negative. The rate of reaction increases with increase of temperature.

There is no relation between spontaneity and rate of reaction as rate of reaction is the measure of how fast is the product formed and spontaneity refers whether the reaction occurs with release of free energy which is set at the specified temperature.

Spontaneity has no connection with speed of the reaction taking place. Although, in order to increase the rate of the reaction the temperature should be increased as it provides activation energy to the molecule for collision.

Hence, the correct option is (A).

62. Depression in freezing point is a colligative property which depends upon the amount of the solute.

$\Delta T_f = i \times K_f \times m$

Thus, for a given solvent and given concentration, ΔT_f is directly porportional to i (Van't Hoff factor) i.e. maximum T_f (and hence lowest freezing point) will correspond to maximum value of i.

(A) $Al_2(SO_4)_3 \xrightarrow{H_2O} 2Al^{3+} + 3SO_4^{2-}$

Here, Van't Hoff factor, i = 5

(B) $C_5H_{10}O_8 \xrightarrow{H_2O}$ No ionization

Here, Van't Hoff factor, i = 1

(C) $KI \xrightarrow{H_2O} K^+ + I^-$

Here, Van't Hoff factor, i = 2

(D) $C_{12}H_{22}O_{11} \xrightarrow{H_2O}$ No ionization

Here, Van't Hoff factor, i = 2

Therefore, $0.10M (\approx 0.10\ m)$ aqueous solution will have the lowest feezing point.

Hence, the correct option is (A).

63. Given that:

Mass of water, $w_1 = 500\ g$

Elevation constant, $K_b = 0.52\ K\ kg\ mol^{-1}$

Boiling point of sucrose = 100°C

Boiling point of water = 99.63°C

Therefore, elevation of boiling point, $\Delta T_b = (100 + 273) - (99.63 + 273)$

= 0.37 K

Molar mass of sucrose $(C_{12}H_{22}O_{11})$ will be,

$M_2 = 12 \times 12 + 22 \times 1 + 11 \times 16$

$= 342$

We know that:

$\Delta T_b = \dfrac{K_b \times 1000 \times w_2}{M_2 \times w_1}$

Or, $w_2 = \dfrac{\Delta T_b \times M_2 \times w_1}{K_b \times 1000}$

$= \dfrac{0.37 \times 342 \times 500}{0.52 \times 1000}$

$= 121.67\ g$

Hence, the correct option is (D).

64. Given that:

Mass of acetic acid $(w_1) = 75\ g$

Lowering of the melting point, $\Delta T_f = (1.5 + 273) - (0 + 273) = 1.5\ K$

Molar mass of ascorbic acid $(C_6H_8O_6)$ will be,

$M_2 = 6 \times 12 + 8 \times 1 + 6 \times 16$

$= 176\ g\ mol^{-1}$

We know that:

$\Delta T_f = \dfrac{K_f \times w_2 \times 1000}{M_2 \times w_1}$

Or, $w_2 = \dfrac{\Delta T_f \times M_2 \times w_1}{K_f \times 1000}$

$= \dfrac{1.5 \times 176 \times 75}{3.9 \times 1000}$

$= 5.08\ g$

Hence, the correct option is (D).

65. Cobalt sulphate (CoSO₄) is also known as red vitriol.

This compound is used for electroplating, in preparing drying agents, and for pasture top-dressing for agricultural use.

Hence, the correct option is (B).

66. ROH is the chemical formula of alcohol.

Alcohol is an organic compound that carries at least one functional group of hydroxyls (–OH) bound to a saturated atom.

Hence, the correct option is (A).

67. Fluorine is the most reactive non-metal.

Fluorine is the most reactive non-metal because it is the most electronegative of all of the non-metal elements of the periodic table. Due to its strong electro negativity & small size, Fluorine has a strong tendency to accept electrons from other atoms or ions. As a result, it oxidises all other substances.

Hence, the correct option is (C).

68. The Element present in third period and seventeenth group of the periodic table is Chlorine and atomic number of Chlorine is 17.

Chlorine is a chemical element with the symbol Cl and atomic number 17. The second-lightest of the halogens, it appears between fluorine and bromine in the periodic table and its properties are mostly intermediate between them. Chlorine is a yellow-green gas at room temperature.

Hence, the correct option is (C).

69. Argon element has three shells that are completely filled with electrons.

Third-most abundant gas in the Earth's atmosphere. It is produced industrially by the fractional distillation of liquid air. It is commonly used to fill incandescent light bulbs. It is used in tungsten filament. All Helium, Neon, and Argon have completely filled outermost shells. But it is asked which element have all three shells filled. So, Argon-Ar (2,8,8) has all three shells filled completely filled with electrons.

Hence, the correct option is (A).

70. The removal of the second electron in alkali metals is difficult.

The first ionization enthalpy of alkali metals is the lowest among the elements in their respective periods and increases on moving down the Group. The second ionization enthalpies of the alkali metals are very high because by releasing an electron, ions require noble gas configuration, so removal of the second electron is difficult.

Hence, the correct option is (A).

71. Benzene group is not a functional group. Functional groups can be defined as an atom or group of atoms joined in a

specified manner which is responsible for the characteristic chemical properties of the organic compound. Hydroxyl group $(-OH)$, aldehyde group $(-CHO)$, and carboxylic acid group $(-COOH)$, all cause changes in chemical properties when attached to the hydrocarbon chains.

Hence, the correct option is (B).

72. The value of gas constant per degree per mole is approximately $2\ cal$.

In the equation of state of an ideal gas $PV = nRT$, the value of universal gas constant would depend only on the units of measurement. It is independent of the nature of the gas, the pressure of the gas and the temperature of the gas.

For example,

$R = 8.314\ J/mol/K$

$R = 1.99\ cal/mol/K$

$R = 0.08206\ Latm/mol/K$

Hence, the correct option is (B).

73. We can say that the rate of diffusion of methane at a given temperature is twice that of gas X. So

we can write it as $r_{CH4} = 2r_X$. And the molar mass of methane i.e. $M_{CH4} = 16$ (approx.)

We know that the rate of diffusion in inversely proportional to the square root of its molar mass i.e.

$\frac{r_{CH4}}{r_X} = \sqrt{\frac{M_X}{M_{CH4}}}$

By putting the values we have,

$\frac{2r_X}{r_X} = \sqrt{\frac{M_X}{16}}$

now to remove the square root we will square both the sides, it gives

$(2)^2 = \left(\sqrt{\frac{M_X}{16}}\right)^2$

$4 = \frac{M_X}{16}$

So it gives us the value $M_X = 16 \times 4 = 64$.

Hence, the correct option is (A).

74. The first law of thermodynamics is not adequate in predicting the direction of a process. It is the law of conservation of energy. However, it does not predict whether the process will occur spontaneously and if so, in which direction. For example, the first law of thermodynamics does not indicate whether heat can flow from a colder end to a hotter end or not.

Hence, the correct option is (A).

75. We know,

$n = \frac{Mass}{Molecular\ weight}$ where n = No. of moles

For 1 mole of CaC_2

$\Delta H = \Delta H_f(CaC) + H_f(CO) - H_f(CaO)$

$\Rightarrow -14.2 - 26.4 + 151.6 = 111.1 kcal$

$\therefore$ For 100 moles, $\Delta H = 1.11 \times 10^4$ Kcal

Hence, the correct option is (B).

76. Species containing the same number of electrons have the same bond order.

CN^-: 14 electrons (6 from carbon, 7 from nitrogen, add 1 for negative charge)

NO^+: 14 electrons (8 from oxygen, 7 from nitrogen, subtract 1 for positive charge)

So, CN^- and NO^+ have the same bond order.

Hence, the correct option is (D).

77. Adsorption: It is the process of deposition of molecules of liquid or gases onto the surface of a solid particle.

Silica and Aluminium gels are used to adsorb moisture to reduce humidity.

Misty windows: Water molecules cling to the window glass.

Painting: molecules of liquid paint cling to wood, metals and other materials.

The chromatographic analysis is based on the phenomenon of adsorption.

Hence, the correct option is (D).

78. Given,

$v = 1368$ kHz $= 1368 \times 10^3$ Hz

As we know,

The speed of light, $c = 3 \times 10^8$ m/s

The wavelength is,

$\lambda = \frac{c}{v}$

$= \frac{3.00 \times 10^8}{1368 \times 10^3}$

$= 219.3\ m$

Hence, the correct option is (B).

79. Liquefied petroleum gas (LPG) mainly consists of propane and butane.

Ethyl Mercaptan (CH₃CH₂SH) is an organic sulphur compound. It has a distinct smell that is used to detect the leakage of otherwise odourless LPG cooking gas.

Fuel Gases	Major component	Uses

Compressed natural gas (CNG)	Methane Ethane	Can be used in place of gasoline, diesel fuel and liquefied petroleum gas (LPG)
Liquefied petroleum gas (LPG)	Butane Propane	LPG is used for cooking. An alternative to electric heating, heating oil, or kerosene. As it is odourless so Methyl Mercaptan is added to it so there may be a smell if LPG leak from its storage container.

Hence, the correct option is (D).

80. Yes, the potential of mercury cell does not change during life time beacuse no ion is involved in the reason whose concentration may change and electrolyte is a paste of KOH and ZnO in mercury cell.

Hence, the correct option is (B).

81. $W = \dfrac{ItE}{96500}$

$\therefore E = \dfrac{W \times 96500}{It}$

$= \dfrac{22.2 \times 96500}{2 \times 5 \times 3600}$

$= 59.5$

Equivalent mass $(E) = \dfrac{\text{Atomic mass}}{\text{oxidation state}}$

$\Rightarrow 59.5 = \dfrac{177}{n}$

$\Rightarrow n = \dfrac{177}{59.5}$

$\therefore n = 2.97 \approx 3$

Hence, the correct option is (C).

82. Current passed, $I = 2A$

Time for which current is passed $t = 20\ min = 20\ min \times 60s/min = 1200\ s$

So, total charge flown, $Q = It = 2A \times 1200\ s = 2400C$

Number of moles of electrons $n = \dfrac{Q}{96500} = \dfrac{2400C}{96500C/mol\ e^-} = 2.487 \times 10^{-2}$ moles

Hence, the correct option is (C).

83. Primary valency is ionizable according to Werner's theory of coordination compounds.

According to Werner's theory, a coordination compound has two different types of valency, primary and secondary. The primary valency or the ionizable valency is satisfied by the negatively charged ions in the solution.

Primary valency is ionizable and is satisfied by the negative charges whereas Secondary valency is non-ionizable and is satisfied by the positive charged or neutral species in the solution. The primary valency corresponds to the oxidation state of the metal ion. The secondary valency corresponds to the coordination number of the metal complex. The molecules or ions that satisfy the secondary valency are called ligands and they can be either negatively charged or neutral.

For example, in $[Cu(NH_3)_4]SO_4$ primary valency is 2 and secondary valency is 4. Secondary valence refers to coordination number. Since copper is coordinated to 4 ammonia ligands, secondary valence is 4. Primary valence is satisfied by anions. Since sulphate ion has -2 charge, primary valence is 2.

Hence, the correct option is (A).

84. Ammonia acts as a very good ligand but ammonium ion does not form complexes because NH_4^+ ion does not have any lone pair of electrons.

Complexes are formed by the donation of a pair of electrons from ligand to metal. In ammonia, N atom has one lone pair of electrons. So it can form complexes. Nitrogen donates this lone pair of electrons to the proton to form an ammonium ion. NH_4^+ ion does not possess any lone pair of electrons which it can donate to central metal ion therefore it does not form complexes. Thus, Ammonia can be a very good ligand but ammonium ion does not form complexes.

Hence, the correct option is (C).

85. Dien (Diethylenetriamine) has following structure:

$H_2\ddot{N} - CH_2 - CH_2 - \ddot{N}H - CH_2 - CH_2 - \ddot{N}H_2.$

In Dien, the number of donor atoms is three so it is a tridentate ligand. Each nitrogen atom is a donor atom.

$EDTA^{4-}$ is a hexadentate ligand. $(COO)_2^{2-}$ is a bidentate ligand. NO_2^- is a monodentate ligand.

Hence, the correct option is (C).

86.

$$\text{>C=C<} + MnO_4^- \longrightarrow -\underset{OH}{\underset{|}{C}}-\underset{OH}{\underset{|}{C}}-$$

Baeyer's reagent (alk. $KMnO_4$) which is pink in colour decolourises due to the presence of unsaturation.

Thus, it shows the presence of unsaturation in an organic compound.

Hence, the correct option is (C).

87. FCH_2CHO is most reactive towards nucleophilic addition since presence of most electronegative F withdraws electron from carbon of carbonyl group making it more polar.

Hence, the correct option is (A).

88. Higher carboxylic acids are insoluble in water due to the increased hydrophobic interaction of the hydrocarbon part.

- Thus, decanoic acid is highly insoluble in water, as it contains longer hydrocarbon chain.
- Decanoic acid is a ten-carbon, saturated fatty acid. It is present in palm kernel, coconut fat and in milk fat.

Hence, the correct option is (D).

89. A functional isomer of Dimethyl ether is Ethanol.

It has the same chemical formula but different functional groups attached to them. e.g C_3H_6O

It has two functional isomers i.e.,

propanal   propanone (acetone)

Hence, the correct option is (A).

90. Correctly match functional group given in List-I with the Nomenclature of that functional group given in list-II:

Functional Group	Suffix	Nomenclature
Aldehyde	-al	Propanal
Halogen	-pane	Bromopropane
Ketone	-one	Propanone
Alcohol	-ol	Propanol

Hence, the correct option is (B).

91. Ether is formed when alkyl halide is heated with sodium alkoxides. This method is called Williamson's Synthesis.

Ethers can be prepared in the laboratory by Williamson's synthesis.

In this method, when an alkyl halide is treated with sodium alkoxide, the nucleophilic substitution of the halogen atom by the alkoxide group takes place.

The general example is given below.

Williamson Ether Synthesis

R_1 — OH + Na/K ⟶ R_1 — $O^⊖Na^⊕$

Methanol   Sodium/   Sodium
           Potassium   Methoxide

R_1 — O — R_2 + NaX/KX ⟵ R_2—X $|$ −$\frac{1}{2}H_2\uparrow$

Ether   Sodium/
            Potassium Halide

Williamson's synthesis is used to prepare symmetrical as well as unsymmetrical ethers.

As the reaction is a nucleophilic substitution reaction, the alkyl halide should be primary alkyl halide, using secondary and tertiary alkyl halide will yield alkenes due to elimination reaction and not ethers.

It is preferable to take secondary or tertiary alkoxide ion and primary alkyl halide.

Hence, the correct option is (D).

92. In RNA (Ribonucleic acid), thymine is replaced by uracil.

This ribonucleic acid acts as a template for the synthesis of proteins, where it transforms the genetic material from the genes to protein synthesis components, to form the amino acids. The nitrogenous bases are purines and pyrimidines. The purines are adenine and guanine. The pyrimidines are thymine and cytosine. In RNA, the thymine is replaced by uracil. Uridylic acid is formed by the combination of uracil as a nitrogenous base, ribose sugar, and triphosphate. It is mainly found in RNA. It is an ester of phosphoric acid with the nucleoside uridine.

Hence, the correct option is (B).

93. Carrier ions like sodium ions facilitate the absorption of substances like amino acids and glucose.

Glucose and amino acids are co-transported along with sodium ions in the intestinal epithelium. The Na/Glucose co-transporter (SGLT 1) facilitates glucose-coupled sodium absorption while amino acid-coupled sodium absorption occurs through the epithelial cells with the help of sodium/amino acid co-transporters. There are specific co-transporters for different classes of amino acids.

Hence, the correct option is (A).

94. Nylon-2-nylon-6 is a biodegradable polymer.

The polymers that can be broken down rapidly by enzyme catalysis reactions are called biodegradable polymers. The enzymes are produced by micro-organisms. The carbon-carbon bonds of chain growth polymers are inert to enzyme-catalyzed reaction and they are non-biodegradable.

When we insert an ester group in the carbon chain which is hydrolyzable, the microorganisms can break them down by their enzymatic action. Some examples of the bio-degradable polymers with esteric linkage are polylactide and polyglycolide.

Polylactide   Polyglycolide

Nylon-2-nylon-6 is formed by copolymerization of Glycine and Aminocaproic acid. It is used in making bristles for toothbrushes, strings for musical instruments, etc.

Polyvinyl chloride, Bakelite and Polythene are non-biodegradable polymers.

Hence, the correct option is (A).

95. The non-metal used in the vulcanization of rubber is Sulphur.

Vulcanization of rubber is a process that improves the elasticity of rubber and strength of rubber by heating it in the presence of Sulphur.

The chemical process that converts natural rubber materials of a variety of elasticity, hardness and mechanical durability by heating is known as Sulfur vulcanization. Vulcanization of rubber was invented in the year 1839 by an American chemist Charles Good year.

Hence, the correct option is (B).

96. Since usage of petroleum-based plastic is harmful to the environment, a polymer called polylactic acid, made using micro-organisms to convert cornstarch into a resin, is used to preserve yogurt. The resulting polymer is used to replace rigid petroleum-based plastic used in yogurt containers and water bottles and is environment-friendly. It is an application of green chemistry.

Hence, the correct option is (A).

97. In one-dimensional nanomaterials (1D), one dimension is outside the nanoscale. This class includes nanotubes, nanorods, and nanowires.

Hence, the correct option is (A).

98. Surfactants are made which are readily biodegradable, and in some cases are manufactured from renewable plant-derived resources such as carbohydrates (sucrose, glucose) or plant oils.

Propene is being produced by a variety of ways from materials produced in turn from biodegradable resources, The propene is used to manufacture polypropene.

The current commercial method for producing ibuprofen has just three steps and minimal waste.

Hence, all are applications of green chemistry.

Hence, the correct option is (D).

99. The correct order of decreasing bond dissociation enthalpy is:

$Cl_2 > Br_2 > F_2 > I_2$

With an increase in size, the bond dissociation enthalpy decreases. Fluorine has exceptionally low bond dissociation enthalpy because of the high electronegativity but higher than iodine.

Bond dissociation enthalpy can be defined as the standard change in enthalpy when a bond is cleaved via homolytic fission. The products formed from the homolysis of the bond are generally radicals.

Hence, the correct option is (C).

100. Nitrogen dioxide is not produced on heating KNO_3.

Heavy metal nitrates liberate NO_2 on heating.

$2KNO_3 \xrightarrow{\Delta} 2KNO_2 + O_2$

$2\,Pb(NO_3)_2 \xrightarrow{\Delta} 2PbO + 4NO_2 + O_2$

$2Cu(NO_3)_2 \xrightarrow{\Delta} 2CuO + 4NO_2 + O_2$

$2AgNO_3 \xrightarrow{\Delta} 2Ag + 2NO_2 + O_2$

Hence, the correct option is (A).

Physics & Chemistry : Mock Test 04

Physics

Q.1 A wave executes a periodic motion $y = 2\sin\frac{\pi}{4}\left(4t + \frac{x}{2}\right)$. What is the frequency?

A. 0.5 Hz   **B.** 1.0 Hz   **C.** 0.25 Hz   **D.** 2.0 Hz

Q.2 The time period of a pendulum is 0.5 sec on earth surface. What will be the new time period when this pendulum is taken on a planet where acceleration due to gravity becomes one by twenty fourth of that of the earth and length of the pendulum rod reduced to $\frac{1}{6}$ of the original length?

A. 0.25 sec   **B.** 1 sec   **C.** 2 sec   **D.** 4 sec

Q.3 A rod of mass M and length L is pivoted about its end O as shown in the figure. Find the period of SHM.

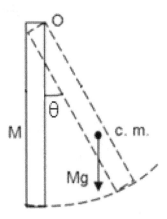

A. $2\pi\sqrt{\frac{3L}{2g}}$ **B.** $2\pi\sqrt{\frac{2L}{3g}}$ **C.** $2\pi\sqrt{\frac{E}{9}}$ **D.** $2\pi\sqrt{\frac{L}{3g}}$

Q.4 Which among the following statements is true about Huygen's principle?
A. Each point on a wavefront is a source of secondary waves
B. Each point on a wavefront is a sink of secondary waves
C. No point on a wavefront is a source of secondary waves
D. None of these

Q.5 At Kavalur in India, the astronomers using a telescope whose objective and a diameter of one metre started using a telescope of diameter 2.54 m this resulted in _____.
A. The increase in the resolving power by 2.54 times for the same λ
B. The increase in the limiting angle by 2.54 times for the same λ
C. Decrease in the resolving power
D. No effect on the limiting angle

Q.6 A laser device produces amplification in the:

A. Microwave region
B. Ultraviolet or visible region
C. Invisible region
D. None of the above

Q.7 Two photons of same frequency are produced due to the annhiliation of a proton and antiproton. Wave length of the proton so produced is:
A. 1.1×10^{-14} m   **B.** 1.3×10^{-15} m
C. 1.7×10^{-17} m   **D.** 1.9×10^{-19} m

Q.8 For a CE-transistor amplifier, the audio signal voltage across the collector resistance of $2\ k\Omega$ is $2\ V$. Suppose the current amplification factor of the transistor is 100, find the input signal voltage and base current, if the base resistance is $1 k\Omega$.
A. $0.20\ V$ and $15\mu A$ **B.** $0.50\ V$ and $50\mu A$
C. $0.01\ V$ and $10\mu A$ **D.** $0.05\ V$ and $20\mu A$

Q.9 A thermodynamic system is taken through the cycle $ABCD$ as shown in the figure. Heat rejected by the gas during the cycle is:

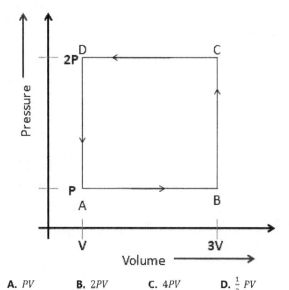

A. PV **B.** $2PV$ **C.** $4PV$ **D.** $\frac{1}{2}PV$

Q.10 Consider a spherical shell of radius R at temperature T. The black body radiation inside it can be considered as an ideal gas of photons with internal energy per unit volume $u = \frac{U}{V}\alpha T^4$ and pressure $P = \frac{1}{3}\left(\frac{U}{V}\right)$. If the shell now undergoes an adiabatic expansion the relation between T and R is:

A. $T\alpha e^{-R}$ **B.** $T\alpha e^{-3R}$ **C.** $T\alpha\frac{1}{R}$ **D.** $T\alpha\frac{1}{R^3}$

Q.11 The iron blade has a ring in which the wooden handle is fixed. The ring is slightly smaller in size than a wooden handle.

The ring is heated. When the ring cools, it _____ and tightly fits on the handle.
A. Contracts
B. Expands
C. Evaporates
D. Condenses

Q.12 In the spectrum of hydrogen, the ratio of the longest wavelength in the Lyman series to the longest wavelength in the Balmer series is:
A. $\frac{5}{27}$
B. $\frac{4}{9}$
C. $\frac{9}{4}$
D. $\frac{27}{5}$

Q.13 The ionization energy of hydrogen atom in excited state is:
A. 4 eV
B. 3.4 eV
C. 1.51eV
D. 1.9eV

Q.14 The nucleus of which of the following atoms whose atomic mass numbers ' A ' are given in the options would have the highest binding energy per nucleon?
A. 200
B. 100
C. 50
D. 20

Q.15 The moment of inertia of uniform semicircular disc of mass M and radius r about a line perpendicular to the plane of the disc through the centre is:
A. $\frac{1}{4}Mr^2$
B. $\frac{2}{5}Mr^2$
C. Mr^2
D. $\frac{1}{2}Mr^2$

Q.16 A disc of mass $2\ kg$ and diameter $2\ m$ is performing rotational motion. Find the work done, if the disc is rotating from 300 rpm to 600rpm:
A. 1479 J
B. 147.9 J
C. 14.79 J
D. 1.479 J

Q.17 A body of mass M is kept on a rough horizontal surface (friction coefficient $=\mu$). A person is trying to pull the body by applying a horizontal force but the body is not moving. The force by the surface on the body is F, where:
A. $F=Mg$
B. $F=\mu Mg$
C. $Mg \leq F \leq Mg\sqrt{1+\mu^2}$
D. $Mg \geq F \geq Mg\sqrt{1-\mu^2}$

Q.18 The mutual inductance between two planar concentric rings of radii r_1 and r_2 (with $r_1 > r_2$) placed in air is given by
A. $\frac{\mu_0\pi r^2}{2R}$
B. $\frac{\mu_0\pi_1^2}{2r_2}$
C. $\frac{\mu_0\pi(r_1+r_2)^2}{2r_1}$
D. $\frac{\mu_0\pi(r_1+r_2)^2}{2r_2}$

Q.19 A transformer is used to light a $100W$ and $110V$ lamp from $220V$ mains. If the main current is 0.5 amp, the efficiency of the transformer is approximately:
A. 50%
B. 90%
C. 10%
D. 30%

Q.20 If the flux of magnetic induction through a coil of resistance R and having N turns changes from ϕ_1 to ϕ_2, then the magnitude of the charge that passes through this coil is
A. $\frac{\phi_2-\phi_1}{R}$
B. $\frac{N(\phi_2-\phi_1)}{R}$
C. $\frac{\phi_2-\phi_1}{NR}$
D. $\frac{NR}{\phi_2-\phi_1}$

Q.21 If the speed of rotation of earth about its axis increases, then the weight of the body at the equator will _____.

A. Decrease
B. Increases
C. Remain constant
D. Sometimes increases sometimes decrease

Q.22 Which law of thermodynamics defines the concept of temperature?
A. First Law of Thermodynamics
B. Second Law of Thermodynamics
C. Zeroth Law of Thermodynamics
D. Third Law of Thermodynamics

Q.23 A tank is filled with water of density $1\frac{g}{cm^3}$ and oil of density $0.9\frac{g}{cm^3}$. The height of water layer is $100\ cm$ and that of oil layer is $400\ cm$. If $g=980\frac{cm}{s^2}$, then the velocity of efflux from an opening in the bottom of the tank will be-
A. $(952.53)\frac{cm}{s}$
B. $(940.23)\frac{cm}{s}$
C. $(949.53)\frac{cm}{s}$
D. $(939.54)\frac{cm}{s}$

Q.24 A liquid flows through pipes of different diameters. Velocity of liquid is $2\ ms^{-1}$. At the point where the diameter of the pipe is $6\ cm$. The velocity of liquid at a point where the diameter of the pipe is 3 cm will be:
A. $1\ ms^{-1}$
B. $4\ ms^{-1}$
C. $8\ ms^{-1}$
D. $16\ ms^{-1}$

Q.25 The electrostatic force between charges of $200\mu C$ and $500\mu C$ placed in free space is $5gf$. Find the distance between the two charges. Take $g=10ms^{-2}$.
A. $2.35\times 10^3 m$
B. $1.34\times 10^3 m$
C. $1.34\times 10^2 m$
D. $2.34\times 10^2 m$

Q.26 Which among the following statement is correct regarding an ideal conductor in a static electric field?
A. Static electric field intensity inside a conductor is non zero.
B. Static field intensity outside conductor is zero.
C. Static field intensity at the surface of a conductor is directly normal to the surface.
D. Static field intensity at the surface of the conductor is directly parallel to the surface.

Q.27 A charge of $10\ \mu C$ is brought from infinity to point P in an external electric field. Point P is located at a distance of 5 cm away from $5\ \mu C$ charge. Calculate the work done to bring the $10\ \mu C$ to point P from infinity?
A. 90 J
B. 9 J
C. 900 J
D. 9000 J

Q.28 What is the magnitude of emf induced in a 200 turn coil with cross-sectional area of 0.16 m 2, if the magnetic field through the coil changes from 0.1 Wb/m 2 to 0.5 Wb/m 2 at a uniform rate over a period of 0.02 seconds?
A. −520 V
B. −640 V
C. −725 V
D. −815 V

Q.29 A spherical balloon of radius a is charged. The energy density in the electric field at point P shown in the figure given below is W. If the balloon is inflated to a radius b without altering its charge, what is the energy density at P?

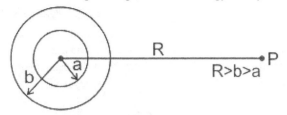

A. $W\left(\frac{b}{a}\right)^3$ **B.** $W\left(\frac{b}{a}\right)^2$ **C.** $W\left(\frac{b}{a}\right)$ **D.** W

Q.30 The speed of wave in a medium is $760 \, m/s$. If 3600 waves are passing through a point in the medium in 2 minutes, then its wavelength is:
A. $13.8 \, m$ **B.** $25.3 \, m$ **C.** $41.5 \, m$ **D.** $57.2 \, m$

Q.31 The intensity ratio of two waves is $1:9$. The ratio of their amplitudes, is
A. $3:1$ **B.** $1:3$ **C.** $1:9$ **D.** $9:1$

Q.32 Two identical wires have the same fundamental frequency of 400 Hz when kept under the same tension. If the tension in one wire is increased by 2% the number of beats produced will be:
A. 4   **B.** 2   **C.** 8   **D.** 1

Q.33 The phenomenon of sound propagation in the air is:
A. Isothermal process   **B.** Isobaric process
C. Adiabatic process   **D.** None of these

Q.34 A man travels 1 mile due east, then 5 miles due south, then 2 miles due east and finally 9 miles due north. His displacement is
A. 3 miles
B. 5 miles
C. 4 miles
D. Between 5 and 9 miles

Q.35 How are charge carriers produced in intrinsic semiconductors?
A. By pure atoms   **B.** By electrons
C. By impure atoms   **D.** By holes

Q.36 How is the resistance of semi-conductor classified?
A. High resistance
B. Positive temperature co-efficient
C. Negative temperature co-efficient
D. Low resistance

Q.37 On giving 220 V to a resistor the power dissipated is 40 watt, then the value of resistance is:
A. $1210 \, \Omega$ **B.** $2000 \, \Omega$
C. $1000 \, \Omega$ **D.** None of these

Q.38 If two bulbs, one of 200 W and the other of 100 W are connected in series with a 100 V battery, then which bulb will have more brightness:
A. 100 W bulb will have more brightness
B. 200 W bulb will have more brightness
C. Both bulb will have equal brightness
D. Can't say

Q.39 A $240 \, V, 60 \, Hz$ voltage source is connected to resistor of 60Ω. Find the value of net power consumed by resistance over a complete cycle.
A. $0 \, W$ **B.** $1000 \, W$ **C.** $960 \, W$ **D.** $540 \, W$

Q.40 Which of the following measures the power loss in AC circuit?
A. Power factor   **B.** Impedance
C. Mean current   **D.** None of the above

Q.41 The resistance of a wire is R. If the length of the wire is doubled by stretching, then the new resistance will be:
A. $2R$ **B.** $4R$ **C.** $\frac{R}{4}$ **D.** $\frac{R}{2}$

Q.42 Two similar waves 'x' and 'y' of amplitude 'a' are moving in the same direction and superimposed. If the wave 'y' is lagging behind the wave 'x' by one-fourth of the cycle, then the amplitude of the resultant wave is equal to:
A. a **B.** $\frac{a}{\sqrt{2}}$
C. $\sqrt{2}a$ **D.** None of these

Q.43 Two harmonic waves $y_1 = a \cdot \sin(kx - \omega t)$ and $y_2 = a \cdot \sin(kx - \omega t + \phi)$ are moving in the same direction, if both the waves are superimposed then the initial phase angle of the resultant wave is:
A. ϕ **B.** $\frac{\phi}{2}$
C. $\frac{\phi}{4}$ **D.** None of these

Q.44 Which of following is true for diatomic gas?
A. $C_v = \frac{3}{1}R$ **B.** $C_p = \frac{7}{2}R$
C. $C_p = \frac{5}{2}R$ **D.** $C_p C_v = R$

Q.45 If temperature of the gas is increased to three times, then its root mean square velocity become:
A. 3 times   **B.** 9 times
C. $\frac{1}{2}$ times   **D.** $\sqrt{3}$ times

Q.46 The total internal energy of a mole of a rigid diatomic gas is?
A. $\frac{3RT}{2}$ **B.** $\frac{RT}{2}$ **C.** $\frac{5RT}{2}$ **D.** $\frac{7RT}{2}$

Q.47 Below stated are some of the materials. You need to identify which of the following will not create a B-H curve?
1. Permalloy
2. Titanium
3. Lead
4. Nickel
5. Cobalt

A. 1,4 and 5   B. Only 2
C. 2 and 4   D. 2 and 3

Q.48 When the temperature exceeds the transition temperature, a ferromagnetic material becomes similar to:
A. Anti-ferromagnetic material
B. Diamagnetic material
C. Ferrimagnetic material
D. Paramagnetic material

Q.49 In the circuit shown in the figure, the input voltage V_i is $20\ V$, $V_{BE} = 0$ and $V_{CE} = 0$. The values of I_B, I_C and β are given by:

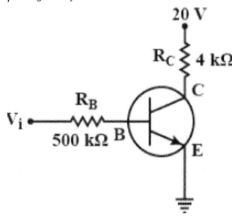

A. $I_B = 20\mu A, I_C = 5\ mA, \beta = 250$
B. $I_B = 40\mu A, I_C = 10\ mA, \beta = 250$
C. $I_B = 40\mu A, I_C = 5\ mA, \beta = 125$
D. $I_B = 25\mu A, I_C = 5\ mA, \beta = 200$

Q.50 How does the dynamic resistance of diode vary with temperature?
A. Directly proportional
B. Inversely proportional
C. Independent
D. Directly to the square of temperature

Chemistry

Q.51

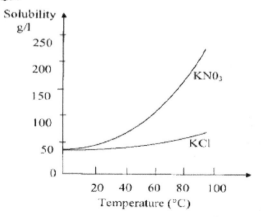

Given the solubility curves of KNO_3 and KCl, which of the following statements is not true?

A. At room temperature the solubility of KNO_3 and KCl are not equal.
B. The solubilities of both KNO_3 and KCl increase with temperature.
C. The solubility of KCl decreases with temperature.
D. The solubility of KNO_3 increases much more compared to that of KCl with increase in temperature.

Q.52 When $10ml$ of $0.2M$ solution of an acid is added to $250ml$ of a buffer solution with $pH = 6.34$, the pH of the solution becomes 6.32. The buffer capacity of the solution is:
A. 0.1   B. 0.2   C. 0.3   D. 0.4

Q.53 Which of the following is incorrect for primary amines?
A. On reaction with nitrous acid alkylamines produce alcohol
B. On reaction with nitrous acid arylamines produce phenol
C. Alkylamines are more basic than ammonia
D. Alkylamines are more basic than arylamines

Q.54 The displacement of electrons in a multiple bond in the presence of attacking reagent is called
A. Inductive effect   B. Electromeric effect
C. Resonance   D. Hyper conjugation

Q.55 The oxidation number of Cr in CrO_5 which has the following structure, is:

A. +4   B. +5   C. +6   D. +3

Q.56 In a first order reaction with time the concentration of the reactant decreases:
A. Linearly   B. Exponentially
C. No change   D. None of these

Q.57 A zero order reaction is one in which the rate of the reaction is independent of:
A. The temperature of the reaction
B. The concentration of the reactants
C. The concentration of the products
D. The volume of the vessel in which the reaction is carried out

Q.58 For an elementary reaction $2A + B \rightarrow A_2B$, if the volume of vessel is quickly reduced to half of its original volume, then what will happen to the rate of reaction?
A. Remains unchanged
B. Increases four times
C. Increases eight times
D. Decreases eight times

Q.59 During osmosis, flow of water through a semi-permeable membrane is:

A. From a solution having higher concentration only.
B. From both sides of a semi-permeable membrane with equal flow rates.
C. From both sides of a semi-permeable membrane with unequal flow rates.
D. From a solution having lower concentration only.

Q.60 If benzene in solution containing 30% by mass in carbon tetrachloride, calculate the mole fraction of benzene.
A. 0.412   B. 0.326   C. 0.529   D. 0.458

Q.61 Heptane and octane form an ideal solution. At 373 K, the vapour pressures of the two liquid components are 105.2 kPa and 46.8 kPa respectively. What will be the vapour pressure of a mixture of 26.0 g of heptane and 35 g of octane?
A. 74.3 kPa   B. 73.43 kPa
C. 76.42 kPa   D. 79.50 kPa

Q.62 Which of the following is not a thermodynamic coordinate?
A. Gas constant (R)   B. Pressure (P)
C. Volume (V)   D. Temperature (T)

Q.63 For the process to occur under adiabatic conditions, the correct condition is:
A. $\Delta T = 0$ B. $\Delta p = 0$ C. $q = 0$ D. $w = 0$

Q.64 Hess's law is applicable for the determination of heat of _____.
A. Transition   B. Formation
C. Reaction   D. All of these

Q.65 For an ionic crystal of general formula AX and co-ordination number 6, the value of radius ratio will be:
A. Greater than 0.73
B. In between 0.414 and 0.732
C. In between 0.22 and 0.41
D. Less than 0.22

Q.66 Which of the following statement is not true about amorphous solids?
A. On heating, they may become crystalline at certain temperature.
B. They may become crystalline on keeping for long time.
C. Amorphous solids can be moulded by heating.
D. They are anisotropic in nature.

Q.67 Match the following:

Column 1	Column 2
1. HCL	a. Covalent solids
2. CCl₄	b. Ionic solids
3. CaF₂	c. Polar solids
4. AlN	d. Non polar solids

A. 1-a, 2-c, 3-d, 4-b   B. 1-d, 2-b, 3-a, 4-c
C. 1-c, 2-d, 3-b, 4-a   D. 1-a, 2-b, 3-d, 4-c

Q.68 All gases except He and H_2 exhibit _____ at a lower temperature.
A. Positive deviation
B. Positive deviation then negative deviation
C. Negative deviation
D. None of the above

Q.69 When you heat a sample of gas, what happens to the particles that make up the gas?
A. The particles move faster
B. The particles break apart
C. The particles get smaller
D. The particles become more dense

Q.70 Alkali metals are strongly _____.
A. Neutral   B. Electropositive
C. Electronegative   D. Non-metallic

Q.71 The total number of ions present in 111 g of CaCl₂ is:
A. 1 Mole   B. 2 Mole   C. 3 Mole   D. 4 Mole

Q.72 The maximum number of hydrogen bonds that a molecule of water can have is:
A. 1   B. 2   C. 3   D. 4

Q.73 The stabilization of a dispersed phase in a lyophobic colloidal solution is due to:
A. The adsorption of charged substance on dispersed phase
B. The large electrokinetic potential developed in the colloid
C. The viscosity of the medium
D. The formation of an electrical layer between two phases

Q.74 The wavelength range of the visible spectrum extends from violet ($400 \, nm$) to red ($750 \, nm$). Express these wavelengths in frequencies (Hz). (1nm = $10^{-9} \, m$)
A. 7.50×10^{14} Hz, 4×10^{14} Hz
B. 5.50×10^{14} Hz, 4×10^{14} Hz
C. 6.50×10^{14} Hz, 5.00×10^{14} Hz
D. 8.50×10^{14} Hz, 3×10^{14} Hz

Q.75 A hydrocarbon has molecular formula C₂H₆. Which of the class of hydrocarbons cannot have this formula?
A. Cycloalkene   B. Bicycloalkane
C. A diene   D. None of these

Q.76 By what factor must $[H^+]$ be increased to increase the reduction potential of a hydrogen electrode, having fixed pressure of hydrogen gas, by 0.0282 V?
A. 2   B. 3   C. 4   D. 5

Q.77 At equilibrium, if $K_p = 1$, then:
A. $\Delta G^0 > 1$ B. $\Delta G^\circ < 1$
C. $\Delta G^0 = 0$ D. $\Delta G^0 = 1$

Q.78 During the electrolysis of molten sodium chloride, the time required to produce 0.10 mol of chlorine gas using a current of 3 amperes is:
A. $55 \, min$ B. $110 \, min$
C. $220 \, min$ D. $330 \, min$

Q.79 The complex $[Co(NH_3)_5(NO_2)]^{2+}$ and $[Co(NH_3)_5(ONO)]^{2+}$ are called:
A. Ionisation isomer

B. Linkage isomers
C. Coordination isomer
D. Geometrical isomer

Q.80 Which of the following is not a neutral ligand?
A. H_2O B. NH_3 C. ONO   D. CO

Q.81 The correct name of $[Pt(NH_3)_4Cl_2][PtCl_4]$ is:
A. tetraamminedichloroplatinum(IV) tetrachloroplatinate(II)
B. dichlorotetraammineplatinium(IV) tetrachloroplatinate(II)
C. tetrachloroplatinum(II) tetraammineplatinate(IV)
D. tetrachloroplatinum(II) dichlorotetraammineplatinate(IV)

Q.82 Boiling points of carbonyl compounds are higher than those of alkanes due to:
A. Hydrogen bonding
B. Dipole-dipole interactions
C. Van der Waals forces
D. All of the above

Q.83 Identify the product for the following reaction.
$CH \equiv CH + HOCl \rightarrow$
A. $CHCl_2 - CHO$
B. $CH(OH) = CHCl$
C. $ClCH_2CH_2OH$
D. CH_3COCl

Q.84 Ozonolysis of an organic compound gives formaldehyde as one of the products. This confirms the presence of:
A. Two ethylenic double bonds
B. A vinyl group
C. An isopropyl group
D. An acetylenic triple bond

Q.85 Chemical name of Gammaxane is:
A. Toluene
B. Benzene hexachloride
C. Chloro benzene
D. Aniline

Q.86 Phenol is also known as _____.
A. Carboxylic acid   B. Carbolic acid
C. Benzoic acid   D. None of the above

Q.87 Soaps are sodium or potassium salts of long chain _____.
A. Carboxylic acid   B. Alcohols
C. Aldehydes   D. Esters

Q.88 An enzyme brings about _____.
A. Decrease in reaction time
B. Increase in activation energy
C. Increase in reaction time
D. Reduction in activation energy

Q.89 The enzymes hexokinase which catalyses glucose to glucose- 6-phosphate in glycolysis is inhibited by glucose- 6-phosphate. This is an example of:
A. Feedback allosteric inhibition
B. Non-competitive inhibition
C. Competitive inhibition
D. None of these

Q.90 Which polymers occur naturally?
A. Starch and Nylon
B. Starch and Cellulose
C. Proteins and Nylon
D. Proteins and PVC

Q.91 What is Teflon?
A. $(C_2F_4)_n$ B. $(C_4F_2)_n$
C. $(k_2Cr_2O_7)_n$ D. $(CF)_n$

Q.92 Lower amines can be prepared from amines through:
A. Wurtz reaction
B. Schmidt reaction
C. Hofmann bromamide reaction
D. Mannich reaction

Q.93 Which of the following amines can be prepared by Gabriel phthalimide reaction?
[JEE Main Advanced, 2019]
A. n-butylamine   B. triethylamine
C. t-butylamine   D. neo-pentylamine

Q.94 Transitional elements exhibit variable valencies because they release electrons from the following orbits :
A. ns orbit   B. ns and np orbits
C. (n-1) d and ns orbits   D. (n-1) d orbit

Q.95 Which of the following chloride does not respond to the chromyl chloride test?
A. $NaCl$ B. $NaCl_2$ C. $AlCl_3$ D. Hg_2Cl_2

Q.96 A solution of $(-) - 2$-chloro-2-phenylethane in toluene racemises slowly in the presence of a small amount of $SbCl_5$, due to the formation of:
A. Carbene   B. Carbocation
C. Free radical   D. Carbanion

Q.97 Which of the following noble gases is not obtained via fractional distillation?
A. Krypton   B. Argon   C. Neon   D. Helium

Q.98 What is the common name of 3-Bromopropene?
A. Tert-Butyl bromide
B. Vinyl bromide
C. Allyl bromide
D. Propylidene bromide

Q.99 The melting point of particles in nano form _____.
A. Increases
B. Decreases
C. Remains same
D. Increases then decreases

Q.100 What is the general electronic configuration of the halogens?
A. ns^2np^5 B. ns^2np^2 C. ns^2np^3 D. ns^2np^4

Physics & Chemistry : Mock Test - 4

// Smart Answer Sheet //

Correct — Indicates percentage of students who answered questions correctly.

Skipped — Indicates percentage of students who skipped questions.

Q.	Ans.	Correct / Skipped	Q.	Ans.	Correct / Skipped	Q.	Ans.	Correct / Skipped	Q.	Ans.	Correct / Skipped	Q.	Ans.	Correct / Skipped
1	A	58.58 % / 1.45 %	17	C	12.82 % / 3.99 %	33	C	48.13 % / 1.05 %	49	C	46.37 % / 1.46 %	65	B	86.53 % / 0.0 %
2	B	21.74 % / 3.27 %	18	A	44.15 % / 1.04 %	34	B	49.34 % / 1.2 %	50	A	59.63 % / 1.69 %	66	D	61.78 % / 1.45 %
3	B	55.05 % / 1.1 %	19	B	69.19 % / 1.2 %	35	C	58.5 % / 1.21 %	51	C	78.97 % / 0.0 %	67	C	85.26 % / 0.0 %
4	A	68.31 % / 1.6 %	20	B	44.38 % / 1.68 %	36	C	55.75 % / 1.68 %	52	D	18.1 % / 3.91 %	68	C	20.29 % / 4.91 %
5	A	24.42 % / 3.0 %	21	A	88.04 % / 0.0 %	37	A	44.21 % / 1.88 %	53	B	60.53 % / 1.93 %	69	A	88.65 % / 0.0 %
6	B	76.12 % / 0.0 %	22	C	85.45 % / 0.0 %	38	A	67.77 % / 1.32 %	54	B	60.49 % / 1.97 %	70	B	79.96 % / 0.0 %
7	B	82.55 % / 0.0 %	23	C	60.18 % / 1.07 %	39	C	53.17 % / 1.55 %	55	C	51.0 % / 1.89 %	71	C	45.73 % / 1.62 %
8	C	43.61 % / 1.11 %	24	C	76.28 % / 0.0 %	40	A	48.23 % / 1.26 %	56	B	58.69 % / 1.78 %	72	D	86.55 % / 0.0 %
9	B	21.96 % / 3.98 %	25	C	49.05 % / 1.93 %	41	B	18.72 % / 4.86 %	57	B	69.4 % / 1.82 %	73	D	50.28 % / 1.03 %
10	C	25.0 % / 3.37 %	26	C	57.14 % / 1.35 %	42	C	56.3 % / 1.74 %	58	C	49.67 % / 1.45 %	74	A	77.36 % / 0.0 %
11	B	42.2 % / 1.91 %	27	B	68.05 % / 1.43 %	43	B	45.21 % / 1.81 %	59	D	79.73 % / 0.0 %	75	D	42.05 % / 1.7 %
12	A	62.68 % / 1.92 %	28	B	76.57 % / 0.0 %	44	B	43.55 % / 1.73 %	60	D	65.33 % / 1.17 %	76	B	23.08 % / 4.87 %
13	B	58.92 % / 1.89 %	29	D	56.29 % / 1.03 %	45	D	56.92 % / 1.32 %	61	B	23.96 % / 3.91 %	77	C	82.27 % / 0.0 %
14	B	54.09 % / 1.3 %	30	B	25.02 % / 4.08 %	46	C	64.67 % / 1.03 %	62	A	51.33 % / 1.05 %	78	B	64.87 % / 1.76 %
15	D	44.31 % / 1.49 %	31	B	47.04 % / 1.11 %	47	D	47.46 % / 1.43 %	63	C	13.01 % / 3.01 %	79	B	17.23 % / 4.16 %
16	A	57.15 % / 1.45 %	32	A	11.66 % / 3.64 %	48	D	48.38 % / 1.5 %	64	D	31.9 % / 4.87 %	80	C	86.31 % / 0.0 %

Q.	Ans.	Correct / Skipped
81	A	18.86 % / 4.77 %
82	B	30.2 % / 4.74 %
83	A	16.85 % / 4.43 %
84	B	31.42 % / 3.86 %
85	B	63.87 % / 1.22 %
86	B	79.29 % / 0.0 %
87	A	86.11 % / 0.0 %
88	D	54.79 % / 1.5 %
89	A	25.81 % / 4.39 %
90	B	52.67 % / 1.81 %
91	A	66.85 % / 1.46 %
92	C	76.22 % / 0.0 %
93	A	66.17 % / 1.07 %
94	C	45.69 % / 1.16 %
95	D	61.35 % / 1.36 %
96	B	69.36 % / 1.31 %
97	D	58.36 % / 1.14 %
98	C	46.47 % / 1.74 %
99	B	42.2 % / 1.57 %
100	A	44.08 % / 1.46 %

Performance Analysis	
Avg. Score (%)	40.0%
Toppers Score (%)	62.0%
Your Score	

//Hints and Solutions//

1. Given that:

$y = 2\sin\frac{\pi}{4}\left(4t + \frac{x}{2}\right) = 2\sin\left(\pi t + \frac{\pi x}{8}\right)$

$A = 2;\ w = \pi\ rad/s$

$\omega = 2\pi f$

$f = 0.5\ Hz$

Hence, the correct option is (A).

2. Given,

Time period on earth $= T$

$T = 2\pi\sqrt{\frac{l}{g}} = 0.5 sec$

Now on the other planet:

New length $= l' = \frac{l}{6}$ and acceleration due to gravity $= g' = \frac{g}{24}$

New time period,

$Tl = 2\pi\sqrt{\frac{ll}{gl}} = 2\pi\sqrt{\frac{l \times 24}{6 \times g}}$

$T' = 2T = 1 sec$

Hence, the correct option is (B).

3. $\tau = \frac{MgL}{2}\sin\theta$

For the small angle, $\sin\theta \approx \theta$

And we have $\tau = I\alpha = I\frac{d^2\theta}{dt^2}$

So, $\left(\frac{ML^2}{3}\right)\frac{d^2\theta}{dt^2} = -\frac{MgL}{2}\theta$

$\frac{d^2\theta}{dt^2} = -\frac{3g}{2L}\theta$

So, the angular frequency is $\omega = \sqrt{\frac{3g}{2L}}$

$\therefore T = 2\pi\sqrt{\frac{2L}{3g}}$

Hence, the correct option is (B).

4. Huygen's principle states that every point on the wavefront may be considered as a source of secondary spherical wavelets that spread out in the forward direction at the speed of light.

The new wavefront is the tangential surface of all these secondary wavelets.

- Secondary sources start making their own wavelets, these waves are similar to that of the primary source.
- It states that each point on a wavefront is a source of wavelets, which spread forward with the same speed.
- Huygens's principle states that each point on a wavefront is a source of wavelets, which spread forward with the same speed.

Hence, the correct option is (A).

5. The resolving power of a telescope is given by:

Resolving power $= \frac{D}{1.22\lambda}$

From the above equation, it is clear that the resolving power of the telescope is directly proportional to the diameter of the telescope when the wavelength is constant.

So, on using the telescope of diameter 2.54 m in place of 1 m, resolving power will increase by 2.54 times for the same λ.

Hence, the correct option is (A).

6. A laser device produces amplification in the Ultraviolet or visible region.

Laser, a device that stimulates atoms or molecules to emit light at particular wavelengths and amplifies that light, typically producing a very narrow beam of radiation. The emission generally covers an extremely limited range of visible, infrared, or ultraviolet wavelengths.

Hence, the correct option is (B).

7. Given:

Two photons of same frequency are produced due to the annhiliation of a proton and antiproton.

We know that:

$c = 3 \times 10^8$

Mass of a proton $= 1.67 \times 10^{-27}$

$E = mc^2$

Put the values in above formula.

$E = (2 \times 1.67 \times 10^{-27}) \times (3 \times 10^8)^2\ J$

$= 3.006 \times 10^{-10}\ J$

Also We know that:

$2h\nu = E$ or $2h\frac{c}{\lambda} = E$

$\therefore \lambda = \frac{2hc}{E}$

Put the values in above formula.

$= \frac{2 \times 6.62 \times 10^{-34} \times 3 \times 10^8}{3.006 \times 10^{-10}}\ m$

$= 1.323 \times 10^{-15}\ m$

Hence, the correct option is (B).

8. Given,

$R_C = 2k\Omega = 2000\Omega$, $R_B = 1k\Omega = 1000\Omega$, $\beta = 100$, $V_0 = 2\ V$

Voltage gain,

$$\frac{V_0}{V_i} = \frac{\beta R_C}{R_B}$$

or

$$\frac{2}{V_i} = 100 \times \frac{2000}{1000}$$

$V_i = 0.01\ V$

∴ Input signal voltage, $V_i = 0.01\ V$.

$$\beta = \frac{I_C}{I_B} = \frac{\frac{V_0}{R_C}}{I_B}.$$

∴ Base current,

$$I_B = \frac{V_0}{\beta R_C}$$

$$= \frac{2}{100 \times 2000} = 10^{-5}\ A = 10\mu A$$

Hence, the correct option is (C).

9. The following figure shows the cyclic process of gas. If an object returns to its initial position after one or more processes it went through.

$ABCDA$ is the cycle. The pressure at the points both D and C remain the same, which is $2P$. The volume at the point D is V and at the point C is $3V$. So, the work done by the gas from point D to point C, $W_{DC} = 2P(3V - V) = 4PV$

The pressures at the points C and B are $2P$ and P respectively. The volume at the points both C and B remain the same, which is $3V$. So, the work done by the gas from point C to point B,

$W_{CB} = P(3V - 3V) = 0$

The pressure at the points both B and A remain the same, which is P. The volume at the point B is $3V$ and at the point A is V,

So, the work done by the gas from point B to point A, $W_{BA} = P(V - 3V) = -2PV$

The pressures at the points A and D are P and $2P$ respectively. The volume at the points both A and D remain the same, which is V.

So, the work done by the gas from point A to the point D, $W_{AD} = P(V - V) = 0$

Hence the total work done in the whole cycle,

$W = 4PV - 2PV = 2PV$

We know the heat rejected from the cycle is equal to the amount of total work done by the gas, so $Q = W$

$Q = 2PV$

Hence, the correct option is (B).

10. In a spherical shell, the internal energy per unit volume is given by $\frac{U}{V} \alpha T^4$

$U = CVT^4$

Here C is a constant

Next the value of P,

$$= \frac{1}{3}\left(\frac{U}{V}\right) = \frac{1}{3}\left(\frac{CVT^4}{V}\right)$$

From adiabatic expansion, $dQ = 0$ and $dU = -dW$

$d(CVT)^4 = -PdV$

We get,

$$\Rightarrow 4VdT = -\frac{4}{3}TdV$$

$$\Rightarrow \frac{dT}{T} = \frac{dV}{3V}$$

On integrating,

$$\Rightarrow TV^{\frac{1}{3}} = C^1$$

$$\Rightarrow T\left(\frac{4}{3}\pi R^3\right)^{\frac{1}{3}} = C^1$$

$TR = $ Constant

$$\therefore T\alpha \frac{1}{R}$$

Hence, the correct option is (C).

11. When the metal heated, the length, surface area, volume of the metal also increased. The increase in temperature which results in metal expands and this expansion is termed as the thermal expansion of metal i.e. expansion in metal due to the heating effect.

So, the iron blade has a ring in which the wooden handle is fixed. The ring is slightly smaller in size than a wooden handle. When the ring is heated which is made up of metal expands, after the ring cools, it tightly fits in the wooden handle.

Hence, the correct option is (B).

12. We know that, if an electron jumps from higher energy levels $n_2 = 2, 3, 4\ldots$ to $n_1 = 1$ then the line of the spectrum is Lyman series.

$$\frac{1}{\lambda} = R\left(\frac{1}{1^2} - \frac{1}{n_2^2}\right)$$

For the longest wavelength of the Lyman series:

$$\frac{1}{\lambda_l} = R\left(\frac{1}{n_1^2} - \frac{1}{n_2^2}\right)$$

$n_1 = 1, n_2 = 2$

$$\Rightarrow \frac{1}{\lambda_l} = R\left(\frac{1}{1} - \frac{1}{4}\right)$$

$$= \frac{3R}{4} \ldots(i)$$

For the longest wavelength of the Balmer series:

$n_1 = 2, n_2 = 3$

$$\frac{1}{\lambda_b} = R\left(\frac{1}{2^2} - \frac{1}{3^2}\right)$$

$$= R\left(\frac{1}{4} - \frac{1}{9}\right)$$

$$= \frac{5R}{36} \ldots(ii)$$

From (i) and (ii),

$$\frac{\lambda_l}{\lambda_b} = \frac{\frac{5R}{36}}{\frac{3R}{4}}$$

$$\frac{\lambda_l}{\lambda_b} = \frac{\frac{5}{36}}{\frac{3}{4}}$$

$$= \frac{5}{27}$$

Hence, the correct option is (A).

13. The ionization energy of the hydrogen atom in the excited state means the atom is already in the first excited state and n = 2.

The energy of the electron in any excited state is given by,

$$E_n = -13.6 \frac{z^2}{n^2} eV$$

The above equation can be written for the excited state of the hydrogen atom as,

$$E_n = \frac{-13.6}{2^2} eV$$

$$= -3.4 eV$$

Hence, the correct option is (B).

14. The binding energy of a particle can be defined as the minimum energy required to remove nucleons (Proton or neutron) to an infinite distance from the nucleus. It can be expressed as:

$$\Delta E = (Zm_p + (A-Z)m_n - M)c^2 \times 931.5 MeV$$

This is derived by using Einstein's mass-energy relation and we can consider binding energy per nucleons as an average energy per nucleon needed to separate a nucleus into its individual nucleons.

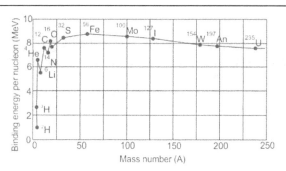

According to the graph of binding energy per nucleons vs the atomic mass number of atoms, we can see that,

Iron (Fe) is most stable element since binding energy needed to remove 1 nucleon is highest for iron and as we increase atomic mass the binding energy needed to remove 1 nucleon decreases because of coloumbic repulsion between protons inside nucleus which makes it less stable. So among the give option ^{100}Mo is most stable. i.e., among all option atom with an atomic mass number of 100 will have the highest binding energy per nucleon.

Hence, the correct option is (B).

15. A circular disc will have 2 times the mass of the semicircular disc.

Moment of inertia of circular disc of mass $2M$ is:

$$I_{\text{circular disc}} = \frac{1}{2}(2M)r^2 = Mr^2$$

Moment of inertia of semi-circular disc is half of the Moment of inertia of circular disc due to symmetry,

$$\therefore I_{\text{semicircular disc}} = \frac{1}{2} I_{\text{circular disc}}$$

$$= \frac{1}{2} Mr^2$$

Hence, the correct option is (D).

16. The rotational kinetic energy is given by,

$$E = \frac{1}{2} I \omega^2$$

Where I is the moment of inertia of the object about the axis of rotation and ω is the angular velocity of the

Now, the disc is rotating about its center. So, the moment of inertia of the disc about the axis of rotation is,

$$I = \frac{mr^2}{2}$$

Where r is the radius of the disc and m is the mass of the disc.

Now, radius of the disc is $r = \frac{d}{2} = \frac{2}{2} = 1m$

So, $I = \frac{2 \times 1^1}{2} = 1 kgm^{-2}$

Now, the initial angular velocity of the disc is,

$$\omega_i = 300 rpm = \frac{300 \times 2\pi}{60} = 10\pi$$

Again, the final angular velocity of the disc is,

$\omega_f = 600 rpm = \frac{600 \times 2\pi}{60} = 20\pi$

Now, the initial rotational kinetic energy of the disc is,

$E_i = \frac{1}{2} I \omega_i^2 = \frac{1}{2} \times 1 \times (10\pi)^2 = 493.48 J$

The final rotational kinetic energy of the disc is,

$E_f = \frac{1}{2} I \omega_f^2 = \frac{1}{2} \times 1 \times (20\pi)^2 = 1973.92 J$

So, work done,

$W = E_f - E_i$

$W = 1973.92 - 393.48$

$W = 1480.44 J$

$W \approx 1479 J$

Hence, the correct option is (A).

17. Free body diagram is given as,

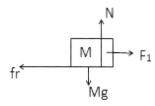

If $F_1 = 0$

So contact force will only have Normal which is equal to Mg.

So F will be Mg.

Now as F_1 increases f_r keeps increasing till it reaches limiting value i.e., $\mu N = \mu mg$.

So, in that case, contact force F will be,

$\sqrt{N^2 + f_r^2} = \sqrt{(Mg)^2 + (\mu Mg)^2}$

$F = Mg\sqrt{1 + \mu^2}$

This means contact force F will lie between $Mg \leq F \leq Mg\sqrt{1 + \mu^2}$.

Hence, the correct option is (C).

18. Given, two circular coils one of radius 'r' and the other of radius 'R' placed coaxially with their centers coinciding. Suppose a current I_2 flows through the outer circular coil. The magnetic field at the centre of the coil is

$B_2 = \frac{\mu_0 I_2}{2R}$

Magnetic field B_2 may be considered constant over the cross-sectional area of the inner smaller coil.

$\phi = B.A$

$\phi_1 = \pi r^2 B_2$

$= \frac{\mu_0 \pi r^2 I_2}{2R}$

$= M I_2$

$M = \frac{\phi_1}{I_2} = \frac{\mu_0 \pi r^2}{2R}$

Hence, the correct option is (A).

19. Given,

Output power $P = 100W$

Voltage across primary $V_p = 220V$

Current in the primary $I_p = 0.5A$

Efficiency of a transformer

$\eta = \frac{\text{output power}}{\text{input power}} \times 100$

$= \frac{P}{V_p I_p} \times 100$

$= \frac{100}{220 \times 0.5} \times 100 = 90\%$

Hence, the correct option is (B).

20. Change in flux, $\Delta\phi = \phi_2 - \phi_1$

Induced emf, $e = \frac{-N\Delta\phi}{t} = \frac{N(\phi_2 - \phi_1)}{t}$

$\Rightarrow |e| = N \left| \frac{-\Delta\phi}{t} \right|$

$= \frac{N(\phi_2 - \phi_1)}{t}$

Induced current, $i = \frac{|e|}{R} = \frac{N(\phi_2 - \phi_1)}{R \cdot t}$

Charge passes through the coil, $q = it$

$q = \frac{N(\phi_2 - \phi_1) \cdot t}{R \cdot t}$

$q = \frac{N(\phi_2 - \phi_1)}{R}$

Hence, the correct option is (B).

21. If the speed of rotation of the earth about its axis In the weight of the body at the equator will decrease.

This is due to the gravity's force is resolved into a centripetal force that acts parallel to the equator. Thus, at the Poles, apparent weight is the same as mg.

At the equator, apparent weight will be $mg' = m(g - R\omega^2)$

Where, ω is the angular velocity.

Hence, the correct option is (A).

22. Zeroth Law of Thermodynamics defines the concept of temperature.

The First Law of Thermodynamics tells us about the concept of internal energy.

The Second Law of Thermodynamics tells us that some form of energy gets lost whenever energy is transferred or transformed.

The Third Law of Thermodynamics tells us about the concept of entropy.

Hence, the correct option is (C).

23. Let $d(w)$ and $d(o)$ be densities of water and oil resp, then the pressure at the bottom of the tank will be

$= h(w) \times d(w) \times g + h(o) \times d(o) \times g$

Let this pressure be equivalent to pressure due to water of height h

$h \times d(w) \times g = h(w) \times d(w) \times g + h(o) \times d(o) \times g$

$h = h(w) + [h(o) \times \frac{d(0)}{d(w)}]$

$h = 100 + [\frac{400(0.9)}{1}]$

$h = 100 + 360 = 460 \; cm$

According to Toricelli's theorem

$v = \sqrt{2ghv}$

$= \sqrt{2 \times 980 \times 460}v$

$= \sqrt{920 \times 980}v$

$= \sqrt{901600}$

Velocity of efflux $= 949.53 \frac{cm}{s}$

Hence, the correct option is (C).

24. According to the principle of continuity,

$A_1 V_1 = A_2 V_2$

$\Rightarrow \frac{\pi d_1^2}{u} V_1 = \frac{\pi d_2^2}{u} V_2$

$\Rightarrow d_1^2 V_1 = d_2^2 V_2$

$\Rightarrow 36 \times 2 = 9 \times V_2$

$V_2 = 8 \; m/sec$

Hence, the correct option is (C).

25. Given:

Charge, $q_1 = 200 \times 10^{-6} C = 2 \times 10^{-4} C$

Charge, $q_2 = 500 \times 10^{-6} C = 5 \times 10^{-4} C$

Electrostatic force, $F = 5gf = 5 \times 10^{-3} kgf = 5 \times 10^{-3} \times 10 N = 5 \times 10^{-2} N$

We have to find the distance between two charges i.e., r

Using the formula:

$F = \frac{1}{4\pi\varepsilon_0} \frac{q_1 q_2}{r^2}$

$5 \times 10^{-2} = \frac{9 \times 10^9 \times 2 \times 10^{-4} \times 5 \times 10^{-4}}{r^2}$

$r = 1.34 \times 10^2 m$

Hence, the correct option is (C).

26. Static field intensity at the surface of a conductor is directly normal to the surface this statement is correct regarding an ideal conductor in a static electric field.

Under the static condition, the electric field inside the solid perfect conductor is zero in electrostatic equilibrium even if it is isolated, charged, and present in the external electrostatic field.

Now, it is known that a perfect solid conductor is an equipotential body. The potential inside the conductor is the same as the potential at the surface. Since the surface of the solid conductor is an equipotential surface hence the electric field will be perpendicular or in other words normal to the perfectly solid conductor surface.

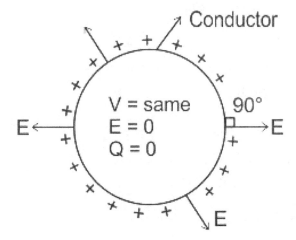

Hence, the correct option is (C).

27. The electrostatic potential is given by:

$V = \frac{W}{q}$

The electrostatic potential due to a point charge is given by:

$V = \frac{Kq}{r} \quad [\because K = \frac{1}{4\pi\epsilon_0}]$

Where $W =$ Work, $q =$ charge and $r =$ distance

Given:

$q_1 = 5 \mu C$

$r = 5$ cm $= 5 \times 10^{-2}$ m

$q_2 = 10 \mu C$

The electric potential due to $5 \mu C$ at a distance of 5 cm away from it is

$V = \dfrac{9 \times 10^9 \times 5 \times 10^{-6}}{5 \times 10^{-2}} = 9 \times 10^5 V$

The work done in moving the charge of $10 \mu C$ from infinity to P is:

$W = V \times q$

$= 9 \times 10^5 \times 10 \times 10^{-6}$

$= 9$ J

Hence, the correct option is (B).

28. Given:

$N = 200, a = 0.16$ m 2

Change in magnetic flux density $(dB) = 0.5 - 0.1 = 0.4$ Wb/m 2

$t = 0.02$ sec

Induced emf $e = \dfrac{-Nd\phi}{dt}$

$d\phi = (dB) \cdot a$

$= 0.4 \times 0.16$

$= 0.064$ Wb

$e = \dfrac{-200 \times (0.064)}{0.02}$

$= -640$ V

Hence, the correct option is (B).

29. The energy density at P is W.

Explanations is given as:

Gauss Law states that the net electric flux through a closed surface enclosing a volume equals the charge enclosed by it.

$\oint_s \vec{E} \cdot \vec{ds} = \dfrac{Q}{\varepsilon_o}$

Since $\vec{D} = \varepsilon_o \vec{E}$, we can write:

$\oint_s \vec{D} \cdot \vec{ds} = Q$

$\vec{D}$ is the electric flux density.

Observations:

1) For a Gaussian sphere around point P, the net charge enclosed by it will not change with a change in radius.

2) Since the net outward electric field through any closed surface is equal to the charge enclosed by it, the electric field outside the spherical balloon will not change with the change in its radius.

3) So, the energy density at point P will be the same as W for the inflated radius b of the balloon.

Hence, the correct option is (D).

30. Given,

Speed $(v) = 760 \ m/s$

Number of Waves $(n) = 3600$

Time $(t) = 2 \times 60$ sec $= 120$ sec

$f(frequency) = \dfrac{n}{time} = \dfrac{3600}{2 \times 60} = 30 \ Hz$

The relation between frequency (f), wavelength (λ) and speed (v) is given by:

$v = \lambda f$

$\Rightarrow \lambda = \dfrac{v}{f}$

$\Rightarrow \lambda = \dfrac{760}{30} = 25.3 \ m$

Hence, the correct option is (B).

31. Intensity $\propto$ (amplitude) ^{2}

$\therefore \dfrac{I_1}{I_2} = \dfrac{a_1^2}{a_2^2}$

$\Rightarrow \dfrac{1}{9} = \dfrac{a_1^2}{a_2^2}$

$\Rightarrow \dfrac{a_1}{a_2} = \dfrac{1}{3}$

$\Rightarrow a_1 : a_2 = 1 : 3$

Hence, the correct option is (B).

32. We know that,

$n \propto \sqrt{T}$

$\dfrac{\Delta n}{n} = \dfrac{1}{2} \dfrac{\Delta T}{T}$

Where, $T =$ Tension

$n =$ Frequency

Beat frequency

$$\Delta n = \left(\frac{1}{2}\frac{\Delta T}{T}\right)n$$

$$\Delta n = \frac{1}{2} \times \frac{2}{100} \times 400$$

$$\Delta n = 4$$

Hence, the correct option is (A).

33. Sound is a mechanical wave. It requires a medium for transmission. There is no transmission of sound in a vacuum. The transmission of sound in the air is in the form of a longitudinal wave. The transmission of sound in the air is in the form of compression and deceleration caused by the vibration of air particles. So, the phenomenon of sound propagation in the air is also an adiabatic process.

Hence, the correct option is (C).

34.

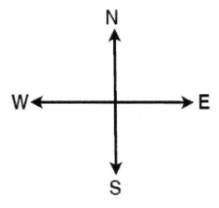

Consider the initial position is at the origin, and North is $+Y$ axis, South being negative Y axis, East is positive X-axis and west is the negative X-axis.

Then starting from origin,

After 1 miles due east, his coordinates are $(1,0)$

After 5 miles due south, his coordinates become $(1,-5)$

After 2 miles due east, his coordinates are ($1+2,-5$) i.e $(3,-5)$

After 9 miles due north , his coordinates are $(3,-5+9)$ i.e $(3,4)$

Hence, distance from the initial position is $\sqrt{3^2+4^2}=5$
Hence, the correct option is (B).

35. Impure semiconductors in which the charge carriers are produced due to impurity atoms are called extrinsic semiconductors. They are obtained by doping an intrinsic semiconductor with impurity atoms.
Hence, the correct option is (C).

36. Semiconductors have negative temperature co-efficient. The reason for this is, when the temperature is increased, a large number of charge carriers are produced due to the breaking of covalent bonds and hence these electrons move freely and gives rise to conductivity.
Hence, the correct option is (C).

37. Given:

Potential difference $(V) = 220V$

Power of the bulb $(P) = 40W$

We know that:

The rate at which electrical energy is dissipated into other forms of energy is called electrical power i.e.,

$$P = \frac{W}{t} = VI = I^2R = \frac{V^2}{R}$$

Where, $V =$ Potential difference, $R =$ Resistance and $I =$ current.

The resistance can be calculated as,

$$R = \frac{V^2}{P} = \frac{(220)^2}{40} = 1210\Omega$$

Hence, the correct option is (A).

38. Given:

$P_1 = 200W$

$P_2 = 100W$

$V = 100V$

We know that:

The rate at which the electric energy is dissipated or consumed is termed as electric power.

The electric power is given as,

$$P = IV = I^2R = \frac{V^2}{R}$$

Where, $P =$ electric power, $V =$ voltage, $I =$ current and $R =$ resistance

$$R = \frac{V^2}{P}$$

$R \propto \frac{1}{P}$ ... (1)

For an electric bulb, the resistance of the bulb is inversely proportional to the power of the bulb.

So, the bulb which has more power will have low resistance, therefore the $100W$ bulb will have more resistance compared to the $200W$ bulb.

The heat dissipated by the bulb is given as,

$$H = I^2R$$

Both the bulbs are connected in series so the current in both the bulbs will be equal. So the heat dissipated will be more in the bulb which has more resistance.

Since the resistance of the $100W$ bulb is more, so the heat dissipation of the $100W$ bulb will be more.

The brightness of the bulb depends on the heat dissipation by the bulb, so the $100W$ bulb will have more brightness.

Hence, the correct option is (A).

39. Given,

$V = 240\ V$ and $R = 60\Omega$

Power consumed by resistance is given by:

$P = V \times I$

Current flowing through the circuit is given by,

$\Rightarrow I = \dfrac{V}{R}$

$\Rightarrow I = \dfrac{240}{60}$

$I = 4\ A$

Net power consumed by resistor

$P = 240 \times 4 = 960\ W$

Hence, the correct option is (C).

40. Power factor is the amount by which the power delivered in the circuit is less than the theoretical maximum of the circuit due to voltage and current being out of phase. So, the power factor is a measure of power loss in AC circuits.

Power factor of an AC circuit is defined as the ratio of the real power consumed by a circuit to the apparent power consumed by the same circuit.

Power factor $= \dfrac{\text{Real Power}}{\text{Apparent Power}}$

$= \dfrac{\text{watt}}{\text{volt-ampere}}$

$= \dfrac{VI\cos\phi}{VI}$

$= \cos\phi$

Hence, the correct option is (A).

41. Given,

$R_1 = R$ and $l_2 = 2l_1$

As we know that the resistance of the wire is,

$R = \dfrac{\rho l}{A}$

When the wire is stretched then, then its area will decrease automatically. But the volume of wire will be the same.

So,

Volume of original wire $=$ Volume of new wire

$A_1 l_1 = A_2 l_2$

$\Rightarrow A_1 l_1 = A_2 2l_1$

$\Rightarrow A_2 = \dfrac{A_1}{2}$

The resistance of the wire in 1st case

$R_1 = R = \dfrac{\rho l_1}{A_1}$

The resistance of the wire in 1st case

$R_2 = \dfrac{\rho l_2}{A_2} = \dfrac{\rho 2l_1}{\frac{A_1}{2}} = \dfrac{4\rho l_1}{A_1}$

Divide equation (1) and (2), we get

$\dfrac{R}{R_2} = \dfrac{\frac{\rho l_1}{A_1}}{\frac{4\rho l_1}{A_1}} = \dfrac{1}{4}$

$R_2 = 4R$

Hence, the correct option is (B).

42. Given,

$a_x = a_y = a$, and $\phi = \dfrac{\pi}{2}$

We know that when two similar waves are superimposed, the amplitude of the resultant wave is given as,

$\Rightarrow A = 2a \cdot \cos\dfrac{\phi}{2}$

$\Rightarrow A = 2a \cdot \cos\dfrac{\pi}{4}$

$A = \sqrt{2}a$

Hence, the correct option is (C).

43. Two harmonic waves are,

$y_1 = a \cdot \sin(kx - \omega t)$

$y_2 = a \cdot \sin(kx - \omega t + \phi)$

Where $\phi =$ phase difference between y_1 and y_2.

By the principle of superposition, the net displacement is given by,

$y = 2a \cdot \cos\dfrac{\phi}{2} \sin\left(kx - \omega t + \dfrac{\phi}{2}\right)\quad \cdots (1)$

By equation (1) it is clear that the initial phase angle of the resultant wave is $\dfrac{\phi}{2}$.

Hence, the correct option is (B).

44. As we know,

$C_v = \dfrac{dU}{dt}$

$$C_v = \frac{d}{dT}\left(\frac{5}{2}RT\right) = \frac{5}{2}R$$

The molar specific heat capacity of a gas at constant volume is

$$C_v = \frac{7}{2}R.$$

As we know,

$$C_p - C_v = R$$

Therefore, the molar specific heat of a gas at constant pressure is

$$C_p = R + C_v$$
$$= R + \frac{5}{2}R$$
$$= \frac{7}{2}R$$

Hence, the correct option is (B).

45. The rms speed of any homogeneous gas sample is given by:

$$V_{rms} = \sqrt{\frac{3RT}{M}}$$

Here, M and R is constant,

Therefore,

$$V_{rms} \propto \sqrt{T}$$

If the temperature is increased to 3 times, then V_{rms} is increased by $\sqrt{3}$ times.

Hence, the correct option is (D).

46. We know that,

$$C_v = \frac{dU}{dt}$$
$$C_v = \frac{d}{dT}\left(\frac{5}{2}RT\right)$$
$$= \frac{5}{2}R$$

The molar specific heat capacity of a gas at constant volume is

$$C_v = \frac{7}{2}R.$$

As we know,

$$C_p - C_V = R$$

Therefore, the molar specific heat of a gas at constant pressure is

$$C_p = R + C_v$$
$$= R + \frac{5}{2}R$$
$$= \frac{7}{2}R$$

Hence, the correct option is (C).

47. Ferro Magnetic material is having the property of creating a B-H curve.

From the following options

Permalloy, Nickel and cobalt are having ferromagnetic properties.

Titanium will be having very paramagnetic properties.

Lead is having diamagnetic properties.

Therefore, titanium and lead will not show B-H characteristics.

Hence, the correct option is (D).

48. When the temperature exceeds the transition temperature, a ferromagnetic material becomes similar to paramagnetic material because randomness in the orientation of dipoles increases due to increased temperature and ferromagnetic material lose their magnetic property.

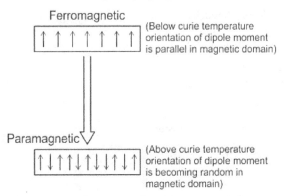

Hence, the correct option is (D).

49. Given,

$$V_i = V_{BE} + R_B i_B \ldots(1)$$
$$20 = 500 \times 10^3 \times i_B$$
$$i_B = 40\mu A$$
$$V_0 = V_{CE} - R_C i_C \ldots(2)$$
$$20 = 4 \times 10^3 i_C$$
$$i_C = 5\ mA$$
$$\beta = \frac{I_C}{I_B} = \frac{5\ mA}{40\mu A} = 125$$

Hence, the correct option is (C).

50. The dynamic resistance of the diode is directly proportional to the temperature.

The dynamic resistance can be defined from the I-V characteristic of a diode in forward bias. It is defined as the ratio of a small change to voltage to a small change in current, i.e.

$$r_d = \left(\frac{\Delta V}{\Delta I}\right) = \frac{\eta V_T}{I}$$

V_T = Thermal voltage

I = Bias current

$V_T = \dfrac{kT}{q}$

$V_T \propto T$

The dynamic resistance is given by the inverse of the slope of $i - v$ characteristics as shown:

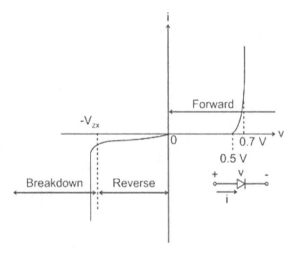

Hence, the correct option is (A).

51. We can see from the curve of both the compounds:

- Solubility increases as temperature increase with different rate.
- Therefore, statement in option (C) is incorrect as it says solubility decreases with increase in temperature.

Hence, the correct option is (C).

52. The expression for the buffer capacity is as follows:

Buffer capacity = $\dfrac{\text{Number of moles of acid or base added per litre}}{\text{Change in } pH}$

$10ml$ of $0.2M$ acid is added to $250ml$ of a buffer solution.

Number of moles of acid added $= \dfrac{0.2 \times 10}{1000}$

Therefore, the number of moles of acid added per litre,

$= \dfrac{0.2 \times 10}{1000} \times \dfrac{1000}{250}$

$= 0.008$

Change in $pH = 6.34 - 6.32 = 0.02$

Substituting values in the above expression, we get,

Buffer capacity $= \dfrac{0.008}{0.02} = 0.4$

Therefore, the buffer capacity is 0.4.

Hence, the correct option is (D).

53. Aryl amines react with nitrous acid to produce diazonium salts.

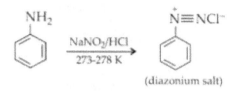

(diazonium salt)

Hence, the correct option is (B).

54. The electromeric effect is a temporary effect brought into play at the requirement of attacking reagent. Electromeric effect refers to a molecular polarizability effect occurring by an intra-molecular electron displacement. It is the temporary effect.

Hence, the correct option is (B).

55. In the structure of CrO_5, it has four O atoms as peroxide which have oxidation number $= -1$ and one O as oxide (double bonded O) atom with oxidation number $= -2$.

Let the oxidation number of Cr is x.

Then,

$x + 4 \times (-1) + 1 \times (-2) = 0$

or, $x = +6$

The oxidation number of Cr in CrO_5 is $+6$.

Hence, the correct option is (C).

56. For first order reaction,

$[A] = [A_0]e^{-kt}$

Where,

k = First order rate constant

$[A]_0$ = Initial concentration

$[A]$ = Concentration at time 't'

From the above equation we can draw:

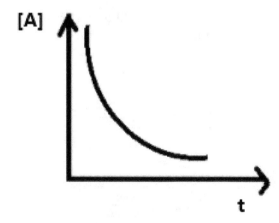

Thus we can say that the concentration of reactants will exponentially decrease with time.

Hence, the correct option is (B).

57. The rate of a zero order reaction is independent of the concentration of the reactants. The reaction proceeds at a constant rate throughout.

In some reactions, the rate is apparently independent of the reactant concentration. The rates of these zero order reactions do not vary with increasing nor decreasing reactants concentrations. This means that the rate of the reaction is equal to the rate constant.

Hence, the correct option is (B).

58. For an elementary reaction, the molecularity is equal to the order of the reaction. Thus, the rate law for the given reaction will be:

$r = k[A]^2[B]$

Now, the concentration here is basically moles per unit volume.

So, decreasing the volume by half will double the concentration of both the reactants.

Thus, the rates can be compared as:

$r_1 = k[A]^2[B]$

$r_2 = k[2A]^2[2B]$

$= 8k[A]^2[B]$

$= 8r_1$

Therefore, rate increases by eight times.

Hence, the correct option is (C).

59. During osmosis, the flow of water through a semi-permeable membrane is from a solution having lower concentration only.

Osmosis is a process by which molecules of a solvent tend to pass through a semipermeable membrane from a less concentrated solution into a more concentrated one. The flow of water through a semipermeable membrane is from both sides of semipermeable membrane with unequal flow rates.

Hence, the correct option is (D).

60. Assume the mass of benzene be $30\ g$ in the total mass of the solution of $100\ g$.

Mass of $CCl_4 = (100 - 30)g$

$= 70\ g$

Molar mass of benzene $(C_6H_6) = (6 \times 12 + 6 \times 1) g mol^{-1}$

$= 78\ g\ mol^{-1}$

Therefore,

Number of moles of $C_6H_6 = \dfrac{Mass}{Molar\ Mass}$

$= \dfrac{30}{78}\ mol$

$= 0.3846\ mol$

Molar mass of $(CCl_4) = (1 \times 12 + 4 \times 355)\ g\ mol^{-1}$

$= 154\ g\ mol^{-1}$

Therefore,

Number of moles of $CCl_4 = \dfrac{Mass}{Molar\ Mass}$

$= \dfrac{70}{154}\ mol$

$= 0.4545\ mol$

Therefore,

Mole fraction of benzene $= \dfrac{Number\ of\ moles\ of\ C_6H_6}{Number\ of\ moles\ of\ C_6H_6 + Number\ of\ moles\ of\ CCl_4}$

$= \dfrac{0.3846}{0.3846 + 0.4545}$

$= 0.458$

Hence, the correct option is (D).

61. Given that:

Vapour pressure of heptane, $p_1^\circ = 105.2 kPa$

Vapour pressure of octane, $p_2^\circ = 46.8 kPa$

We know that,

Number of moles $= \dfrac{Mass}{Molar\ Mass}$

Molar mass of heptane $(C_7H_{16}) = 7 \times 12 + 16 \times 1 = 100\ g\ mol^{-1}$

Therefore, number of moles of heptane $= \dfrac{26}{100} = 0.26\ mol$

Molar mass of octane $(C_8H_{18}) = 8 \times 12 + 18 \times 1 = 114\ g\ mol^{-1}$

Therefore, number of moles of octane $= \dfrac{35}{114} = 0.31\ mol$

Mole fraction of heptane, $x_1 = \dfrac{Number\ of\ moles\ of\ heptane}{Number\ of\ moles\ of\ heptane + Number\ of\ moles\ of\ octane}$

$= \dfrac{0.26}{0.26 + 0.31}$

$= 0.456$

Therefore, mole fraction of octane, $x_2 = 1 - 0.456 = 0.544$

Now, partial pressure of heptane,

$p_1 = x_1 p_1^\circ$

$= 0.456 \times 105.2$

$= 47.97 kPa$

Partial pressure of octane,

$p_2 = x_2 p_2^{\circ}$

$= 0.544 \times 46.8$

$= 25.46 kPa$

Therefore, vapour pressure of solution,

$p_{total} = p_1 + p_2$

$= 47.97 + 25.46$

$= 73.43 kPa$

Hence, the correct option is (B).

62. R is a constant and is not a thermodynamic coordinate.

Each thermodynamic process is distinguished from other process in energetic character according to which parameters as temperature, pressure or volume. While R is a gas constant which is not a thermodynamical coordinate.

Hence, the correct option is (A).

63. For the process to occur under adiabatic conditions, the correct condition is $q = 0$.

When a thermodynamic system undergoes a change in such a way that no exchange of heat takes place between Systems and surroundings, the process is known as an adiabatic process. During the adiabatic process, there is no exchange of heat that takes place between the system and the surroundings.

Hence, the correct option is (C).

64. Hess's law is applicable for the determination of heat of transition, formation and reaction.

Hess's Law of Constant Heat Summation:

The standard enthalpy of a reaction, which takes place in several steps, is the sum of the standard enthalpies of intermediate reactions into which the overall reactions may be divided at the sarme temperature.

$\Delta H = \Delta H_1 + \Delta H_2 + \Delta H_3$

It is applicable to determine heat of formation, transition, reaction, hydration, etc.

Hence, the correct option is (D).

65. Since the general formula is AX with coordination number 6, the crystal could be considered as $NaCl$. Thus, it is evident that the ratio lies between 0.414 and 0.732 because of its octahedral structure.

The value ranging between 0.414 and 0.732 is obtained by dividing the radius of positive ion by that of negative ion.

Hence, the correct option is (B).

66. The amorphous solids are the solids which have short range order and are isotropic in nature which means that the physical properties are same along the crystal length.

Thus the option (D) is incorrect as amorphous solids are isotropic nature.

Hence, the correct option is (D).

67. Correct match:

Column 1	Column 2
1. HCL	c. Polar solids
2. CCl4	d. Non polar solids
3. CaF2	b. Ionic solids
4. AlN	a. Covalent solids

HCl is an example of polar molecular solids which are bonded together by dipole-dipole interaction.

CCl4 is an example of non polar solids which are bonded together by dispersion or London forces.

CaF2 is an example of ionic solids which are bonded together by coulombic or electrostatic force of attraction.

Al-N is an example of covalent solids which are bonded together by covalent bonding.

Hence, the correct option is (C).

68. All gases except He and H_2 exhibit negative deviation at a lower temperature.

The ideal gas equation is not applicable to real gas. Hence, we use the real gas equation which involves the compressibility factor. The value of compressibility factor is as follow:

$Z = \dfrac{PV}{RT}$

Hydrogen and helium are very lighter gas. The attraction between these gases is very less. The value of van der waal coefficient is very less for hydrogen and helium. Hence the pressure exerted is high. So the value of Z that is compressibility factor is greater than 1 even at lower temperature. Hence it shows positive deviation. For other gases there is considerable attraction and hence the compressibility factor is less that 1 so they show the negative deviation. Due to lower temperature the kinetic energy lowers and hence the attraction in between gases increases.

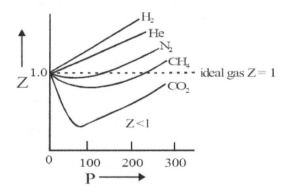

Hence, the correct option is (C).

69. When you heat a sample of gas, the particles move faster to the particles that make up the gas.

When heat is added to a substance, the molecules and atoms vibrate faster. As atoms vibrate faster, the space between atoms increases. The motion and spacing of the particles determines the state of matter of the substance. The end result of increased molecular motion is that the object expands and takes up more space.

Mass of the object remains the same, however solids, liquids and gases all expand when heat is added.

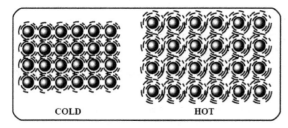

Hence, the correct option is (A).

70. Due to low ionization enthalpies, alkali metals are strongly electropositive or metallic in nature and electropositive nature increases from Lithium to caesium due to decrease in ionization enthalpy.

Hence, the correct option is (B).

71. We know that,

Molecular weight of $CaCl_2$ = 111g/mol

Ions in one calcium chloride molecule = $Ca^{+2} + 2Cl^- $ = 3 ions

Now no. of molecules in 111g of $CaCl_2$ = Avogadros number

= 6.02 × 1023 molecules

So number of ions in 111g of $CaCl_2$

= 3 × 6.02 × 10²³ ions

= 3 moles

Hence, the correct option is (C).

72. Each water molecule can form a maximum of four hydrogen bonds with neighboring water molecules. The two hydrogens of the water molecule can form hydrogen bonds with other oxygens in ice, and the two lone pairs of electrons on the oxygen of the water molecule can attract other hydrogens in ice. So, 4 hydrogen bonds are possible with a molecule of water.

Hence, the correct option is (D).

73. There is adsorption of common ion on the colloidal solution and an electrical double layer is formed. Thus, the dispersed phase in a lyophobic colloidal solution is stabilized.

$$\underbrace{Fe(OH)_3 FR^{3+}}_{\text{Fixed part}} : \underbrace{3Cl}_{\text{Mobile part}}$$

Hence, the correct option is (D).

74. Given,

Wavelength of violet light $= 400 \, nm = 400 \times 10^{-9} \, m$

Wavelength of red light $= 750 \, nm = 750 \times 10^{-9} \, m$

As we know,

The speed of light,

$c = 3 \times 10^8$ m/s

Frequency of violet light is given as,

$$\nu = \frac{c}{\lambda}$$

$$= \frac{3.00 \times 10^8}{400 \times 10^{-9}}$$

$$= 7.50 \times 10^{14} \text{ Hz}$$

Frequency of red light is given as,

$$\nu = \frac{c}{\lambda}$$

$$= \frac{3.00 \times 10^8}{750 \times 10^{-9}}$$

$$= 4 \times 10^{14} \text{ Hz}$$

Hence, the correct option is (A).

75. A bicycloalkene cannot have the formula of C_2H_6.

C_2H_6 has two degree of unsaturation (two H_2 less than saturated hydrocarbons), therefore it can be a diene, a cycloalkene or a bicycloalkane but it cannot be a bicycloalkene because it has three degrees of unsaturation.

Hence, the correct option is (D).

76. $\frac{E_{H^+}}{H_2} = \frac{E^\circ_{H^+}}{H_2} - \frac{0.059}{2} \log \frac{P_{H_2}}{[(H^+)]^2}$

$\frac{E_{H^+}}{H_2} = -\frac{059}{2}P_{H_2} + .059\log[H^+]$

If $[H^+]$ is increased by a factor of n then,

$\frac{E_{H^+}}{H_2} = \frac{0.059}{2}P_{H_2} + 0.059\log[(H^+)] + 0.059\log n$

Thus, $\Delta E = .059\log n$

Thus, $\log n = \frac{\Delta E}{.059} = \frac{.0282}{.059} = .4780 \approx \log 3$

So, $n = 3$

Hence, the correct option is (B).

77. At equilibrium, the relation between the free energy of the reaction and equilibrium constant is as follows,

$\Delta G° = -RT\ln K_p$

If $K_p = 1$ at equilibrium

$\Delta G' = -RT\ln 1$

or $\Delta G° = 0$

Hence, the correct option is (C).

78. $2Cl^- \rightarrow Cl_{2(g)} + 2e^-$

$W = \frac{E}{96500} \times it$

$0.1 \times 71 = \frac{35.5}{96500} \times 3 \times t$

$\therefore t = 6433.33 s$

Or $t = 107.22\ min \approx 110\ min$

Hence, the correct option is (B).

79. The complex $[Co(NH_3)_5(NO_2)]^{2+}$ and $[Co(NH_3)_5(ONO)]^{2+}$ are called linkage isomers due to presence of NO_2 ligand. It is an ambidentate ligands are capable of coordinating in more than one way i.e., NO_2^-/ONO^-.

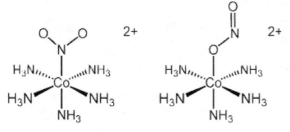

Hence, the correct option is (B).

80. Neutral ligand means ligand with no charge on it.

Example: H₂O, NH₃, CO, C₂H₄...

ONO⁻ has a charge on it, therefore it is not a neutral ligand.

Hence, the correct option is (C).

81. The name of the complex cation is written first followed by the name of the complex anion. The names of the ligands are written in alphabetical order. The roman numerals IV and II are written in parenthesis to indicate the oxidation state of platinum in complex cation and complex anion. The prefix tetra is used to indicate the number of amine and chloro ligands. So, the name of the complex $[Pt(NH_3)_4Cl_2][PtCl_4]$ is tetraamminedichloroplatinum(IV) tetrachloroplatinate(II).

Hence, the correct option is (A).

82. Boiling points of carbonyl compounds are higher than those of alkanes due to dipole-dipole interactions.

The boiling points of aldehydes and ketones (carbonyl compounds) are higher than boiling point of non-polar alkanes due to the presence of dipole-dipole interactions between molecules of carbonyl compounds which are much stronger than Van der Waals forces between molecules of alkanes.

So, energy required to break the interaction between carbonyl compound molecules is more than that of forces between molecules of alkane and therefore, boiling point is higher.

Hence, the correct option is (B).

83. $HOCl \rightarrow OH^- + Cl^+$

Cl^+ shall attack acetylene as an electrophile and OH^- will end the addition with a nucleophilic addition.

Therefore, the final reaction will be:

$CH \equiv CH + 2HOCl \longrightarrow$
$CH(OH)_2 - CHCl_2 \xrightarrow[\text{Unstable}]{-H_2O} CHCl_2 - CHO$

Hence, the correct option is (A).

84. Presence of one vinyl (or ethenyl) group gives formaldehyde as one of the product in ozonolysis.

CH₂=CH- on ozonolysis will give HCHO.

- Ozonolysis is an organic reaction where the unsaturated bonds of alkenes, alkynes, or azo compounds are cleaved with ozone.
- Alkenes and alkynes form organic compounds in which the multiple carbon–carbon bond has been replaced by a carbonyl group while azo compounds form nitrosamines.

$\underset{\text{2-methyl Prop-1-ene}}{\overset{H}{\underset{H}{>}}C=C\overset{CH_3}{\underset{CH_3}{<}}} + O_3 \longrightarrow \underset{\text{Formaldehyde}}{HCHO} + \underset{\text{Acetone}}{O=C\overset{CH_3}{\underset{CH_3}{<}}}$

Hence, the correct option is (B).

85. Under ultra-violet light, three chlorine molecules add to benzene to produce benzene hexachloride, C₆H₆Cl₆ which is also called gammaxane. Benzene hexachloride is an isomer of hexachlorocyclohexane with a chemical formula C₆H₆Cl₆. It is also known as Lindane or hexachloride.

Uses of Benzene hexachloride ($C_6H_6Cl_6$):

- Benzene hexachloride is used as an insecticide on crops, in forestry, for seed treatment.
- It is used in the treatment of head and body lice.
- It is used in pharmaceuticals.
- It is used to treat scabies.
- It is used in shampoo.

Hence, the correct option is (B).

86. Phenol is also known as Carbolic acid. In 1865, the British surgeon Joseph Lister used phenol as an antiseptic to sterilize his operating field.

Phenol is an aromatic organic compound characterized by a hydroxyl (—OH) group attached to a carbon atom that is part of an aromatic ring.

Besides serving as the generic name for the entire family, the term phenol is also the specific name of its simplest member, monohydroxybenzene (C_6H_5OH).

Hence, the correct option is (B).

87. Soaps are sodium or potassium salts of long-chain of carboxylic acids.

Sodium salts of fatty acids are called hard soaps and potassium salts of fatty acids are called soft soaps.

Soaps are sodium or potassium salts of long-chain fatty acids.

Alcohol carries one hydroxyl functional group (at least) which is bound to a saturated carbon atom. The molecular formula is $C_nH_{2n+1}OH$.

Aldehydes carry a functional group with the structure – CHO. In this, a carbon atom shares a double bond with an oxygen atom, a single bond with a hydrogen atom, and a single bond with another atom.

Esters are derived from carboxylic acids (-COOH group). The hydrogen is replaced by a hydrocarbon group in esters.

Hence, the correct option is (A).

88. An enzyme brings about reduction in activation energy. Enzymes are proteins which accelerate the rate of the reaction. The substrate and product have different energy state. The energy gap between the substrate and the product is known as activation energy which is the minimum energy required to initiate a reaction. The binding energy is the source of energy used by enzyme to lower the activation energy of reaction. Activation energy is the minimum energy required from outside to overcome the energy barrier of reactants. The enzymes lower the activation energy and lead to the faster conversion of substrate to the product.

Hence, the correct option is (D).

89. The enzymes hexokinase which catalyses glucose to glucose-6-phosphate in glycolysis is inhibited by glucose- 6-phosphate. This is an example of feedback allosteric inhibition. Hexokinase is a protein that phosphorylates a six-carbon sugar, a hexose, to a hexose phosphate. In many tissues and creatures, glucose is the most significant substrate of hexokinases, and glucose 6-phosphate the most significant item. Hexokinase has a high proclivity for glucose, the hexokinase is allosterically hindered by its item which is glucose-6-phosphate. At the point when the centralization of glucose-6-phosphate expands, it ties with the compound at its allosteric site and achieves the conformational change in the protein.

Hence, the correct option is (A).

90. Starch and Cellulose occur naturally.

Natural occurring polymers are protein, nucleic acid, cellulose, starch.

Starch is a polysaccharide comprising glucose monomers joined in a 1,4 linkages. The chemical formula of the starch molecule is $(C_6H_{10}O_5)_n$.

Cellulose is a structural component of plant cell walls, it comprises about 33 percent of all vegetable matter and is the most abundant of all naturally occurring organic compounds.

Hence, the correct option is (B).

91. Teflon: A synthetic material that gets used to cover the surface of some object and transmit nonstick properties to it is called Teflon.

It has a high melting point and it does not react with other substances easily. It has non-stick qualities that are the reason used in many pots, frying pans, and other culinary items.

The chemical formula of Teflon is given by $(C_2F_4)_n$.

Hence, the correct option is (A).

92. The Hofmann reaction is an organic reaction used to convert a primary amide to a primary amine. In the Hofmann reaction, an amide is treated with bromine and base (usually NaOH or KOH).

Upon heating, an intermediate isocyanate is formed, which is not isolated. In the presence of water, the isocyanate loses carbon dioxide to give an amine.

From the above explanation, we can see that Hofmann bromamide reaction is the one in which an amide is treated with bromine and a base to prepare amines from lower amines.

Hence, the correct option is (C).

93. Gabriel phthalimide synthesis is used for the preparation of primary amines, phthalimide on treatment with ethanolic potassium hydroxide formed salts of phthalimide which in heating with alkyl halide followed by alkyl hydrolysis produce corresponding primary amines. Aromatic primary amines cannot be prepared by this synthesis because aryl halides do not undergo nucleophilic substitution with the anion formed by phthalimide.

The Gabriel phthalimide reaction transforms primary alkyl halides into primary amines.

From the given options, n-butylamine is the only aliphatic primary amine compound.

Actually, Gabriel phthalimide synthesis is used for the preparation of aliphatic primary amines. It involves nucleophilic substitution

(SN2) of alkyl halides by the anion formed by the phthalimide. Hence, aromatic primary amines cannot be prepared by this process.

Hence, the correct option is (A).

94. The ability of the transition metals to exhibit variable valency is generally attributed to the availability of more electrons in the (n-1) d orbitals which are closer to the outermost ns orbital in energy levels.

Hence, the correct option is (C).

95. Mercurous chloride (Hg_2Cl_2) does not undergo Chromyl chloride test. This is bceause the mercurous chloride show more covalent character than the other compound.

Apart from mercurous chloride, the chloride of gold, silver, and platinum also does not give Chromyl chloride test.

Hence, the correct option is (D).

96. A solution of $(-)-1$-chloro-1-phenylethane in toluene racemises slowly in the presence of a small amount of $SbCl_5$, due to the formation of carbocation. Carbocation has planar geomety. Hence, the nucleophile can attack from either side.

Carbocation intermediate

Hence, the correct option is (B).

97. Neon, argon, krypton and xenon are obtained by fractional distillation of air. Fractional distillation of liquid air gives oxygen, nitrogen and a mixture of noble gases. The individual noble gases are then separated by adsorption over coconut charcoal which adsorbs different gases at different temperatures.

Hence, the correct option is (D).

98. 3-Bromopropene has 3 C atoms in the parent chain with a double bond at C-1 and Br at C-3. This means that Br is attached to the C which is next to the C-C double bond, hence it is an allylic halide.

Hence, the correct option is (C).

99. For the particles in the nano form, the melting point reduces significantly. Other chemical properties are also changed as the dimensions of the object comes in the nano range.

Hence, the correct option is (B).

100. The elements of group 17 have seven electrons in the valence shell and hence their general electronic configuration is ns^2np^5, i.e., $ns^2np_x^2np_y^2np_z^1$. Thus, they contain one electron less than the nearest inert gas configuration.

Hence, the correct option is (A).

Physics & Chemistry : Mock Test 05

Physics

Q.1 A particle of mass $m = 5g$ is executing simple harmonic motion with an amplitude $0.3m$ and time period $\frac{\pi}{5}$ sec. The maximum value of force acting on the particle is:

[BITSAT, 2013]

A. 5N B. 4N C. 0.5N D. 0.15N

Q.2 The pulse rate of a normal person is 75 per min. The time period of heart is:

[BITSAT, 2013]

A. 0.8 s B. 0.75 s C. 1.25 s D. 1.75 s

Q.3 Two particles execute SHM of the same amplitude and frequency along the same straight line. If they pass each other when going in opposite directions, each time their displacement being half their amplitude, the phase difference between them is

A. $\frac{\pi}{2}$ B. $\frac{\pi}{6}$ C. $\frac{2\pi}{3}$ D. $\frac{2\pi}{7}$

Q.4 A convex lens of refractive index 1.49 is immersed in a certain liquid. For the lens to act as a transparent plane sheet, what should be the refractive index of the liquid?

A. Less than 1.49 B. Greater than 1.49
C. Equal to 1.49 D. None of these

Q.5 When a beam of light passes through a prism, which of the following color(s) deviates more?

A. Red B. Yellow C. Green D. Violet

Q.6 If gravitational mass of a body on the moon be denoted by M_m and that on the earth be M_e, then:

A. $M_m = \frac{1}{6} M_e$ B. $M_m = M_e$
C. $M_m = 2M_e$ D. $M_m = 6M_e$

Q.7 The kinetic energy of the fastest moving photo electron from a metal of work function 2.8 eV is 2 eV. If the frequency of light is doubled, then find the maximum kinetic energy of photo electron.

A. 6.8eV B. 68eV C. -6.8eV D. -68eV

Q.8 The graph shows variation of stopping potential V_0 versus frequency of incident radiation v for two photosensitive metals A and B. Which of the two metals has higher threshold frequency?

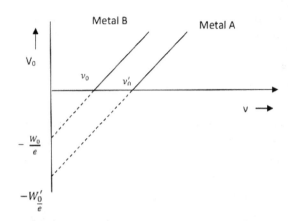

A. B
B. A
C. Both A anb B has same threshold frequency
D. None of the above

Q.9 The number of silicon atoms per m^3 is 5×10^{28}. This is doped simultaneously with 5×10^{22} atoms per m^3 of Arsenic and 5×10^{20} per m^3 atoms of Indium. Calculate the number of electrons and holes. Given that $n_i = 15 \times 10^{16} \ m^{-3}$.

A. $5.95 \times 10^{22} \ m^{-3}$ and $5.5 \times 10^9 \ m^{-3}$
B. $4.95 \times 10^{22} \ m^{-3}$ and $4.5 \times 10^9 \ m^{-3}$
C. $6.95 \times 10^{22} \ m^{-3}$ and $6.5 \times 10^9 \ m^{-3}$
D. $3.95 \times 10^{22} \ m^{-3}$ and $3.5 \times 10^9 \ m^{-3}$

Q.10 _____ affects the heat of reaction which is based on Kirchoff's equation.

A. Molecularity B. Temperature
C. Pressure D. Volume

Q.11 An ideal refrigerator has a freezer at a temperature of $-13°C$. The coefficient of performance of the engine is 5. The temperature at which heat is rejected will be:

A. $30.5°C$ B. $32.5°C$ C. $39°C$ D. $38°C$

Q.12 A refrigerator is to maintain eatables kept inside at $9°C$. If room temperature is $36°C$, calculate the coefficient of performance.

A. 10.44 B. 11.44 C. 9.04 D. 11.84

Q.13 Which series of hydrogen spectrum corresponds to ultraviolet region?

A. Balmer series B. Brackett series
C. Paschen series D. Lyman series

Q.14 A nucleus with $Z = 92$ emits the following in a sequence
$\alpha, \alpha, \beta^-, \beta^-, \alpha, \alpha, \alpha, \alpha, \beta^-, \beta^-, \alpha, \beta^+, \beta^+, \alpha$. The Z of the resulting nucleus is:

A. 76 **B.** 78 **C.** 82 **D.** 74

Q.15 An electron is moving in an orbit of a hydrogen atom at the 4th energy level. Find the number of spectral lines for a transition from here to the ground state.
A. 8 **B.** 3 **C.** 6 **D.** 10

Q.16 Arrange the α – rays, β – rays, and γ – gamma rays in decreasing order of penetrating powers.
A. α – rays > β – rays > γ – rays
B. γ – rays > β – rays > α -rays
C. α – rays = β – rays = γ – rays
D. α – rays < β – rays > γ – rays

Q.17 If the radius of the earth is 6400 km then angular velocity for a point on its equator will be:
[UPSESSB TGT Science, 2016]
A. 7.3×10^{-5} **B.** 7.3×10^{-6}
C. 10×10^{-5} **D.** 1.5×10^{-5}

Q.18 The angular momentum of a moving body remains constant if:
[UPSESSB TGT Science, 2016]
A. Net external force is applied
B. Net pressure is applied
C. Net external torque
D. Net external torque is not applied

Q.19 When one joule of energy is consumed in one second, then the power used is said to be?
A. One watt **B.** One coulomb
C. One volt **D.** One ampere

Q.20 The process of electroplating, using the phenomenon of electrolysis, is primarily based on:
A. Electromagnetic induction
B. Chemical effect of electric current
C. Heating effect of electric current
D. Magnetic effect of electric current

Q.21 Electromagnetic waves of frequencies higher than $9\sqrt{2}MHz$ are found to be reflected by the ionosphere on a particular day at a place. The maximum electron density in the ionosphere is:
A. $\sqrt{5} \times 10^{23} m^{-3}$ **B.** $\sqrt{2} \times 10^{12} m^{-3}$
C. $2 \times 10^{12} m^{-3}$ **D.** $5 \times 10^{12} m^{-3}$

Q.22 A metallic rod of mass per unit length $0.5\ kg\ m^{-1}$ is lying horizontally on a smooth inclined plane which makes an angle of $30°$ with the horizontal. The rod is not allowed to slide down by flowing a current through it when a magnetic field of induction $0.25\ T$ is acting on it in the vertical direction. The current flowing in the rod to keep it stationary is:
A. 14.76 A **B.** 5.98 A **C.** 7.14 A **D.** 11.32 A

Q.23 If a coil of 40 turns and area $4.0\ cm^2$ is suddenly removed from a magnetic field, it is observed that a charge of $2.0 \times 10^{-4}\ C$ flows into the coil. If the resistance of the coil is $80\ \Omega$, the magnetic flux density in Wb/m^2 is:
A. 0.5 **B.** 1 **C.** 1.5 **D.** 2

Q.24 When a bus starts suddenly, the passengers are pushed back. This is an example of which of the following?
A. Newton's first law
B. Newton's second law
C. Newton's third law
D. None of these

Q.25 On heating, solid is directly converted into a gaseous state. This process is called _____.
A. Sublimation **B.** Evaporation
C. Diffusion **D.** Condensation

Q.26 A soap bubble, having radius of $1\ mm$, is blown from a detergent solution having a surface tension of $2.5 \times 10^{-2}\ N/m$. The pressure inside the bubble equals at a point Z_0 below the free surface of water in a container. Taking $g = 10\ m/s^2$, density of water $= 10^3\ kg/m^3$, the value of Z_0 is :
[NEET UG, 2019]
A. $100\ cm$ **B.** $10\ cm$ **C.** $1\ cm$ **D.** $0.5\ cm$

Q.27 A small hole of area of cross-section 2 mm² is present near the bottom of a fully filled open tank of height 2 m. Taking g = 10 m/s², the rate of flow of water through the open hole would be nearly
[NEET UG, 2019]
A. 12.6 × 10⁻⁶ m³/s **B.** 8.9 × 10⁻⁶ m³/s
C. 2.23 × 10⁻⁶ m³/s **D.** 6.4 × 10⁻⁶ m³/s

Q.28 A copper sphere of mass $2g$ contains nearly 2×10^{22} atoms. The charge on the nucleus of each atom is $29e$. What fraction of the electrons must be removed from the sphere to give it a charge of $+2\mu C$?
A. 2.16×10^{-12} **B.** 3.15×10^{-11}
C. 3.15×10^{-12} **D.** 2.16×10^{-11}

Q.29 Calculate the Coulomb force between 2 alpha particles separated by $3.2 \times 10^{-15}m$.
A. 60N **B.** 50N **C.** 90N **D.** 70N

Q.30 The electric field at a point is:
A. Always continuous
B. Continuous if there is a charge at that point
C. Discontinuous only if there is a negative charge at that point
D. Discontinuous if there is a charge at that point

Q.31 What happens to the capacitance of a parallel plate capacitor when the area of the plates, as well as the distance between them, is halved?
A. It doubles **B.** It becomes 4 times
C. It remains the same **D.** It becomes one-half

Q.32 In a particular circuit, a coil having a self-inductance of $2H$ is required to carry a current of $4A$. A capacitor rated for $400V$ is used across the coil in order to prevent sparking during breaking of the circuit. The value of capacitor needed is:
A. $120\mu F$
B. $100\mu F$
C. $400\mu F$
D. $200\mu F$

Q.33 If the magnetic flux through each turn of the coil consisting of 200 turns is $(t^2 - 3t)$ m-wb, where t is in seconds, then the induced emf in the coil at $t = 4$ sec is:
A. -1 V
B. 1 V
C. -0.1 V
D. 0.1 V

Q.34 The direction of induced emf can be founded by _____.
A. Laplace's Law
B. Fleming's right hand rule
C. Kirchhoff's Voltage Law
D. Lenz's Law

Q.35 According to Faraday's law, the voltage v induced in the coil with N turns and magnetic flux ϕ is:
A. $v = \frac{1}{N}\frac{d\phi}{dt}$
B. $v = N^2 \frac{d\phi}{dt}$
C. $v = N\frac{d\phi}{dt}$
D. $v = N\frac{d^2\phi}{dt^2}$

Q.36 A source emitting wavelengths 480 nm and 600 nm is used in Young's Double Slit Experiment. The separation between the slits is 0.25 mm. The interference is observed 1.5 m away from the slits. The linear separation between first maxima of the two wavelengths is:
A. 0.72 mm
B. 0.62 mm
C. 0.76 mm
D. 0.27 mm

Q.37 Two waves having their intensities in the ratio of $9:1$ produce interference. In the interference pattern, the ratio of maximum to minimum intensity is equal to:
A. $\frac{4}{1}$
B. $\frac{8}{4}$
C. $\frac{2}{3}$
D. $\frac{1}{2}$

Q.38 What should be the angular speed with which the earth have to rotate on its axis so that a person on the equator would weight $\frac{3}{5}$th as much as present?
A. 7.8×10^{-4} rad/sec
B. 1106×10^{-3} rad/sec
C. 110.610^{-3} rad/sec
D. 1.10610^{-5} rad/sec

Q.39 Two moles of an ideal gas with $\frac{C_P}{C_V} = \frac{5}{3}$ are mixed with 3 moles of another ideal gas with $\frac{C_P}{C_V} = \frac{4}{3}$. The value of $\frac{C_P}{C_V}$ for the mixture is:
A. 1.45
B. 1.50
C. 1.47
D. 1.42

Q.40 Consider a mixture of n moles of helium gas and $2n$ moles of oxygen gas (molecules taken to be rigid) as an ideal gas. Its $\frac{C_P}{C_V}$ value will be:
A. $\frac{19}{13}$
B. $\frac{67}{45}$
C. $\frac{40}{27}$
D. $\frac{23}{15}$

Q.41 Average power loss in an induction coil is:
A. $\frac{1}{2}LI^2$
B. $2L^2$
C. $\frac{1}{4}LI^2$
D. 0

Q.42 The resistance of a wire of length l and area of cross-section a is $x\ ohm$. If the wire is stretched to double its length, its resistance would become:
A. $2x\ ohm$
B. $0.5x\ ohm$
C. $4x\ ohm$
D. $6x\ ohm$

Q.43 The resistance for a unit length of the potentiometer wire is $1.2\ \Omega m^{-1}$. If the potential gradient is $0.009\ Vcm^{-1}$, the value of the current in ampere in the primary circuit will be:-
A. 0.4
B. 0.75
C. 0.5
D. 0.25

Q.44 Among the following properties describing diamagnetism identify the property that is wrongly stated:
a) Diamagnetic material do not have permanent magnetic moment.
b) Diamagnetism is explained in terms of electromagnetic induction
c) Diamagnetic materials have a small positive susceptibility
d) The magnetic moment of individual electrons neutralise each other
A. a
B. b
C. c
D. d

Q.45 The susceptibility of a ferromagnetic material is found to be X at a temperature of 27°C. Its susceptibility at 627 °C will be _____.
A. $3X$
B. $\frac{X}{3}$
C. $2X$
D. $\frac{Xi}{2}$

Q.46 A wave is first reflected by a rigid boundary and then by a non-rigid boundary. If there is no energy loss in both the cases, then which of the following quantity will remain the same in both the cases:
A. Phase difference between the incident and the reflected wave
B. Frequency of the reflected wave
C. Both (A) and (B)
D. None of these

Q.47 The circular motion of a particle with constant speed is:
A. Periodic but not simple harmonic
B. Neither periodic nor simple harmonic
C. Periodic and simple harmonic
D. Simple harmonic but not periodic

Q.48 Two waves each of amplitude 'a_0' produce resultant wave of amplitude 'a_0' on superposition. The phase difference between the two waves is:
A. $\frac{\pi}{3}$
B. $\frac{2\pi}{3}$
C. $\frac{\pi}{2}$
D. $\frac{\pi}{4}$

Q.49 Which one of the following parameters is used for distinguishing between a small signal and a large signal amplifier?
A. Voltage gain
B. Frequency response
C. Harmonic distortion
D. Input/output impedances

Q.50 The majority charge carriers in n-type semiconductors are:

A. Holes B. Electrons
C. Neutrons D. Protons

Chemistry

Q.51 How many litres of water must be added to 1 litre of an aqueous solution of HCl with a pH of 1 to create an aqueous solution with pH of 2?
A. 0.9 L   B. 2.0 L   C. 9.0 L   D. 0.1 L

Q.52 Given that at $800k$ the concentrations are as follows: $N_2 = 3.0 \times 10^{-3}M, O_2 = 4.2 \times 10^{-3}M$ and $NO = 2.8 \times 10^{-3}M$, what is the equilibrium constant for the reaction $N_{2(g)} + O_{2(g)} \rightleftharpoons 2NO_{(g)}$?
A. 0.622   B. 0.7   C. 0.8   D. 0.94

Q.53 Arrange the following compounds in decreasing order of basicity:
I. Ethylamine
II. 2 - amino ethanol
III. 3 - amino - 1 - Propanol
A. I > II > III   B. III > I > II
C. I > III > II   D. I < II > III

Q.54 C_2H_6 compound has:
A. 8 covalent bonds
B. 6 covalent bonds and 1 ionic bond
C. 7 covalent bonds
D. 7 Ionic Relations

Q.55 Direction: The following questions consist of two statements, one labelled as Assertion and the other Reason. Examine both the statements carefully and mark the correct choice according to the instructions given below.
Assertion
O_2 is a stronger reducing agent than F_2.
Reason
F_2 is more electronegative.
A. Both Assertion and Reason are correct and Reason is the correct explanation for Assertion
B. Both Assertion and Reason are correct but Reason is not the correct explanation for Assertion
C. Assertion is correct but Reason is incorrect
D. Both Assertion and Reason are incorrect

Q.56 The higher the temperature _____.
A. Lower the energy   B. Higher the energy
C. Moderate energy   D. None of above

Q.57 Why do most chemical reaction rates increase rapidly as the temperature rises?
A. The fraction of molecular with kinetic energy grater than the activation energy increases rapidly with temperature
B. The average kinetic increases as temperature rises
C. The activation energy decreases as temperature rise
D. More collisions take place between particle so that the reaction can occur

Q.58 The rate of chemical reaction depends on the nature of reactants because:
A. The number of bonds broken in the reactant molecules and the number of bonds formed in product molecules changes
B. Some of the reactants are solids at the room temperature
C. Some of the reactants are coloured
D. Some of rectants are liquid at room temperature

Q.59 The vapour pressure of a solvent decreased by 10 mm of mercury when a non-volatile solute was added to the solvent. The mole fraction of the solute in the solution is 0.2. What should be the mole fraction of the solvent, if the decrease in the vapour pressure is to be 20 mm of mercury?
A. 0.8   B. 0.6   C. 0.4   D. 0.2

Q.60 An aqueous solution of 2% non-volatile solute exerts a pressure of 1.004 bar at the normal boiling point of the solvent. What is the molar mass of the solute?
A. $44.8 \; g \; mol^{-1}$ B. $42.5 \; g \; mol^{-1}$
C. $41.35 \; g \; mol^{-1}$ D. $50.35 \; g \; mol^{-1}$

Q.61 Calculate the amount of benzoic acid (C_6H_5COOH) required for preparing 250 mL of $0.15M$ solution in methanol.
A. 4.680 g   B. 4.790 g   C. 4.875 g   D. 4.575 g

Q.62 A reaction, $A + B \rightarrow C + D + q$ is found to have a positive entropy change. The reaction will be:
A. possible at high temperature
B. possible only at low temperature
C. not possible at any temperature
D. possible at any temperature

Q.63 In a process, $701 \; J$ of heat is absorbed by a system and $394 \; J$ of work is done by the system. What is the change in internal energy for the process?
A. 307 J   B. 207 J   C. 107 J   D. 407 J

Q.64 The reaction of cyanamide, $NH_2CN(s)$ with dioxygen was carried out in a bomb calorimeter and ΔU was found to be $-742.7 KJ mol^{-1}$ at $298 \; K$. Calculate the enthalpy change for the reaction at $298 \; K$.

$NH_4CN_{(g)} + \frac{3}{2}O_{2(g)} \rightarrow N_{2(g)} + CO_{2(g)} + H_2O_{(l)}$

A. $741.5 \; kJ \; mol^{-1}$ B. $-841.5 \; kJ \; mol^{-1}$
C. $841.5 \; kJ \; mol^{-1}$ D. $-741.5 \; kJ \; mol^{-1}$

Q.65 Graphite is one of the allotropes of carbon. Unlike diamond, it is an electrical conductor and a good lubricant. Graphite is a good conductor of electricity due to the presence of _____.
A. Lone pair of electrons
B. Anions
C. Cations
D. Free valence electrons

Q.66 In a CCP lattice of X and Y, X atoms are present at the corners while Y atoms are at face centres. Then, the formula of the compound would be if one of the X atoms from a corner is replaced by Z atoms (also monovalent)?
A. $X_7Y_{24}Z_2$ B. $X_7Y_{24}Z$ C. $X_{24}Y_7Z$ D. $ZY_{24}Z$

Q.67 What is the packing fraction of $^{56}_{26}Fe$?
(Isotopic mass $= 55.92066$)
A. -14.167 B. 173.90 C. -15.187 D. -73.90

Q.68 What happens to the electropositive character of elements on moving from left to right in a periodic table?
A. Increase
B. Decrease
C. First increase then decrease
D. First decrease then increase

Q.69 Which of the following is the correct order of the atomic radii of the elements oxygen, fluorine, and nitrogen?
A. O < F < N B. N < F < O
C. O < N < F D. F < O < N

Q.70 What is the other name for group 18th elements?
A. Noble gases B. Alkali metals
C. Alkali earth metals D. Halogens

Q.71 Alkaline earth metals show $+1$ Oxidation state and their atomic volume _____ down the group.
A. Irregularity B. Increase
C. Decrease D. None of these

Q.72 The hydrocarbon in which all the 4 valencies of carbon are fully occupied is called as _____.
A. Alkene B. Alkyne
C. Alkane D. Cycloalkane

Q.73 The rates of diffusion of gases are inversely proportional to square root of their densities. This statement refers to _____.
A. Daltons Law B. Grahams Law
C. Avogadros Law D. None of the Above

Q.74 Which of the following is not a type of van der Waal's forces?
A. Dipole – dipole forces
B. Dipole – induced dipole forces
C. Ion – dipole forces
D. London forces

Q.75 Among the following mixtures, dipole-dipole as the major interaction is present in:
A. Benzene and ethanol
B. Acetonitrile and acetone
C. KCl and water
D. Benzene and carbon tetrachloride

Q.76 Which method is used to prepare colloidal solution?
A. Mond Process
B. Ostwald Process
C. Van Arkel Method
D. Bredig's Arc Method

Q.77 Calculate (a) wavenumber and (b) frequency of yellow radiation having wavelength $5800 Å$.
A. $1.724 \times 10^2\ cm^{-1}$, 5.172×10^{10} Hz
B. $2.724 \times 10^4\ cm^{-1}$, 5.172×10^{14} Hz
C. $5.724 \times 10^4\ cm^{-1}$, 5.172×10^{14} Hz
D. $1.724 \times 10^4\ cm^{-1}$, 5.172×10^{14} Hz

Q.78 The result of the operation 2.5×1.25 should be which of the following on the basis of significant figures?
A. 3.125 B. 3.13 C. 3.1 D. 31.25

Q.79 The standard reduction potential for the half-cell reaction, $Cl_2 + 2e^- \rightarrow 2Cl^-$ will be:
$Pt^{2+} + 2Cl^- \rightarrow Pt + Cl_2, E^o_{cell} = -0.15\ V$;
$Pt^{2+} + 2e^- \rightarrow Pt, E^o = 1.20\ V$
A. $-1.35\ V$ B. $+1.35\ V$
C. $-1.05\ V$ D. $+1.05v$

Q.80 When lead storage battery is charged:
A. Lead dioxide dissolves
B. Sulphuric acid is regenerated
C. The lead electrode becomes coated with lead sulphate
D. The amount of sulphuric acid decreases

Q.81 A $0.05M\ NaOH$ solution offered a resistance of $31.6\ \Omega$ in a conductivity cell is $0.367\ cm^{-1}$, find out the specific conductance of the sodium hydroxide solution.
A. $0.0216\ ohm^{-1}cm^{-1}$
B. $0.0116\ ohm^{-1}cm^{-1}$
C. $0.156\ ohm^{-1}cm^{-1}$
D. $0.356\ ohm^{-1}cm^{-1}$

Q.82 Which of the following is the coordination entity in $K_2[Zn(OH)_4]$?
A. K^+ B. Zn^{2+}
C. OH^- D. $[Zn(OH)_4]^{2-}$

Q.83 Identify the Lewis acid in $K_3[Al(C_2O_4)_3]$.
A. K^+ B. Al
C. Al^{3+} D. $[Al(C_2O_4)_3]^{3-}$

Q.84 Which of the following is the central atom/ion in $[CoCl(NH_3)_5]^{2+}$?
A. Co B. Co^{2+} C. Co^{3+} D. Cl^-

Q.85 Which of the following gives benzoic acid on oxidation?
A. Chlorophenol B. Chlorotoluene
C. Chlorobenzene D. Benzyl chloride

Q.86 Ionic species are stabilised by the dispersal of charge, which of the following carboxylate ions is the most positive charge?
A. $CH_3 - \overset{\overset{O}{\|}}{C} - O^{\ominus}$

B. $Cl-CH_2-\overset{O}{\underset{|}{C}}-O^{\ominus}$

C. $F-CH_2-\overset{O}{\underset{|}{C}}-O^{\ominus}$

D. $F-\underset{|}{CH}-\overset{O}{\underset{|}{C}}-O^{\ominus}$ (with F below)

Q.87 Which of the following names is correct for $CH_2-\underset{CHO}{|}$

$\underset{CHO}{CH}-\underset{CHO}{CH_2}$?

A. 3- Formaldehyde-1,3-dial
B. 2, 3, 4- Triformylpropane
C. 2-Formylmethylbutane-1, 4-dial
D. Propane-1, 2, 3-tricarbaldehyde

Q.88 Ethyl alcohol is industrially prepared from ethylene by:
A. Permanganate oxidation
B. Catalytic reduction
C. Absorbing in H_2SO_4 followed by hydrolysis
D. All the three

Q.89 Phenol on hydrogenation with Ni at 433K gives:
A. Benzene
B. Cyclohexane
C. Cyclohexanol
D. n-hexanol

Q.90 From which of the following tertiary butyl alcohol is obtained by the action of methyl magnesium bromide?
A. HCHO
B. CH_3CHO
C. CH_3COCH_3
D. CO_2

Q.91 The enormous diversity of protein molecules is due mainly to the diversity of:
A. Amino acid sequences within the protein molecule
B. Peptide bonds
C. R groups on the amino acids
D. Amino groups on the amino acids

Q.92 Length of one turn of the helix in a B-form DNA is approximately _____.
A. $3.4\ nm$
B. $0.34\ nm$
C. Both (A) and (B)
D. None of these

Q.93 What is Teflon?
A. $(C_2F_4)_n$
B. $(C_4F_2)_n$
C. $(k_2Cr_2O_7)_n$
D. $(CF)_n$

Q.94 Which of these are examples of condensation polymers?
A. Terylene
B. Maltose
C. Nylon 6,6
D. All of these

Q.95 Which of the following is the functional group of Amine?
A. Oxygen   B. Nitrogen   C. Helium   D. Barium

Q.96 Why are the compounds of transition metal generally coloured?
A. Due to s being filled before d (Aufbau principle)
B. Due to presence of unpaired electron
C. Unfilled d orbital
D. d-d transition

Q.97 A reduction in atomic size with increase in atomic number is a characteristic of elements of:
A. d-block
B. d-block
C. Radioactive series
D. High atomic masses

Q.98 Acetone is mixed with bleaching powder to give:
A. Chloroform
B. Acetaldehyde
C. Ethanol
D. Phosgene

Q.99 The common name of Chloropicrin is _____.
A. Coal gas
B. Tear gas
C. Laughing gas
D. Water gas

Q.100 Name the product obtained when methylamine (CH_3NH_2) is treated with nitrous acid is:
A. CH_3OH
B. $CH_3-O-N=O$
C. CH_3OCH_3
D. None of these

Physics & Chemistry : Mock Test - 5

// Smart Answer Sheet //

Correct Indicates percentage of students who answered questions correctly.

Skipped Indicates percentage of students who skipped questions.

Q.	Ans.	Correct / Skipped	Q.	Ans.	Correct / Skipped	Q.	Ans.	Correct / Skipped	Q.	Ans.	Correct / Skipped	Q.	Ans.	Correct / Skipped
1	D	50.33 % / 1.25 %	17	A	49.14 % / 1.15 %	33	A	63.82 % / 1.41 %	49	D	44.65 % / 1.8 %	65	D	64.78 % / 1.21 %
2	A	57.24 % / 1.27 %	18	D	79.99 % / 0.0 %	34	D	68.91 % / 1.43 %	50	B	60.3 % / 1.46 %	66	B	12.87 % / 4.8 %
3	C	67.4 % / 1.84 %	19	A	76.39 % / 0.0 %	35	C	53.27 % / 1.14 %	51	C	89.89 % / 0.0 %	67	A	40.19 % / 1.88 %
4	C	47.46 % / 1.28 %	20	B	89.93 % / 0.0 %	36	A	63.9 % / 1.16 %	52	A	65.61 % / 1.01 %	68	B	27.19 % / 4.12 %
5	D	88.7 % / 0.0 %	21	C	68.33 % / 1.66 %	37	A	64.45 % / 1.35 %	53	C	23.03 % / 4.0 %	69	D	26.24 % / 4.61 %
6	B	47.67 % / 1.04 %	22	D	66.32 % / 1.54 %	38	A	45.51 % / 1.55 %	54	C	64.27 % / 1.22 %	70	A	43.91 % / 1.13 %
7	A	77.87 % / 0.0 %	23	B	60.77 % / 1.82 %	39	D	68.25 % / 2.0 %	55	A	45.15 % / 1.88 %	71	C	46.83 % / 1.59 %
8	B	44.33 % / 1.51 %	24	A	78.23 % / 0.0 %	40	A	46.85 % / 1.65 %	56	B	76.86 % / 0.0 %	72	C	81.77 % / 0.0 %
9	B	69.82 % / 1.09 %	25	A	60.16 % / 1.39 %	41	D	44.81 % / 1.39 %	57	D	86.29 % / 0.0 %	73	B	44.84 % / 1.03 %
10	B	53.81 % / 1.38 %	26	C	61.95 % / 1.26 %	42	C	47.74 % / 1.13 %	58	A	15.19 % / 4.9 %	74	C	53.51 % / 1.79 %
11	C	68.93 % / 1.54 %	27	A	68.68 % / 1.63 %	43	B	54.33 % / 1.23 %	59	B	29.89 % / 3.84 %	75	B	11.53 % / 4.49 %
12	A	88.26 % / 0.0 %	28	D	26.29 % / 4.82 %	44	C	45.12 % / 1.93 %	60	C	63.67 % / 1.73 %	76	D	41.58 % / 1.09 %
13	D	84.16 % / 0.0 %	29	C	87.11 % / 0.0 %	45	B	46.81 % / 1.81 %	61	D	89.49 % / 0.0 %	77	D	40.15 % / 1.72 %
14	B	23.25 % / 4.79 %	30	D	89.9 % / 0.0 %	46	B	68.11 % / 1.69 %	62	D	63.25 % / 1.01 %	78	C	57.03 % / 1.69 %
15	C	82.12 % / 0.0 %	31	C	61.95 % / 1.43 %	47	A	59.53 % / 1.6 %	63	A	21.73 % / 4.72 %	79	B	25.23 % / 3.39 %
16	B	66.24 % / 1.71 %	32	D	64.35 % / 1.52 %	48	B	47.95 % / 1.57 %	64	D	21.47 % / 3.32 %	80	B	86.12 % / 0.0 %

Physics & Chemistry : Mock Test - 5

Q.	Ans.	Correct / Skipped
81	B	62.01 % / 1.2 %
82	D	50.21 % / 1.74 %
83	C	42.82 % / 1.44 %
84	C	81.11 % / 0.0 %

Q.	Ans.	Correct / Skipped
85	D	83.02 % / 0.0 %
86	D	44.62 % / 1.72 %
87	D	45.62 % / 1.41 %
88	C	21.83 % / 4.33 %

Q.	Ans.	Correct / Skipped
89	C	57.24 % / 1.53 %
90	C	64.23 % / 1.44 %
91	A	84.81 % / 0.0 %
92	A	87.16 % / 0.0 %

Q.	Ans.	Correct / Skipped
93	A	83.01 % / 0.0 %
94	D	51.65 % / 1.35 %
95	B	23.76 % / 4.77 %
96	B	62.49 % / 1.87 %

Q.	Ans.	Correct / Skipped
97	B	53.42 % / 1.6 %
98	A	41.12 % / 1.17 %
99	B	51.81 % / 1.91 %
100	A	69.78 % / 1.97 %

Performance Analysis	
Avg. Score (%)	49.0%
Toppers Score (%)	60.0%
Your Score	

//Hints and Solutions//

1. We know,

Maximum acceleration $a_{max} = \omega^2 A = \frac{4\pi^2}{T^2} A$

$= \frac{4\pi^2}{\left(\frac{\pi}{5}\right)^2} \times 0.3 = 30 \, m/s^2$

Maximum force

$F_{max} = ma_{max} = \frac{5}{1000} \times 30 = 0.15 N$

Hence, the correct option is (D).

2. The beat frequency of heart is

$v = \frac{75}{(1min)} = \frac{75}{60s} = 1.25 \, s^{-1}$

= 1.25 Hz

The time period of heart is

$T = \frac{1}{v} = \frac{1}{1.25 s^{-1}} = 0.8s$

Hence, the correct option is (A).

3. Equation of simple harmonic wave is

$y = A \sin(\omega t + \phi)$

Here, $y = \frac{A}{2}$

$\therefore A\sin(\omega t + \phi) = \frac{A}{2}$

So, $\delta = \omega t + \phi = \frac{\pi}{6}$ or $\frac{5\pi}{6}$

So, the phase difference of the two particles when they are crossing each other at $y = \frac{A}{2}$ in opposite directions are

$\delta = (\delta_1 - \delta_2)$

$= \left(\frac{5\pi}{6} - \frac{\pi}{6}\right)$

$= \left(\frac{2\pi}{3}\right)$

Hence, the correct option is (C).

4. In a transparent plane sheet, the thickness of the sheet is negligibly small that it allows light to travel through it with negligible deviation.

- The speed of light varies in different media.
- For a lens to act as a transparent sheet when placed in liquid refraction should not take place. So, either its thickness must be negligibly small or the speed of light in the liquid and lens must be the same.
- The former is not possible, as the lens cannot be altered to a thin sheet.

- Thus, the speed of the light in the lens must match that in the liquid. This is possible only if the two media have the same optical density i.e., refractive index.

Thus, the refractive index of the liquid must be equal to that of the lens i.e., 1.49.

Hence, the correct option is (C).

5. As we know, the bending of light is inversely proportional to the wavelength of the light.

Bending $\propto \frac{1}{Wavelength}$

Different colors bend differently on passing through a prism and the bending of colour depends on wavelength.

Higher wavelengths bend less, whereas shorter wavelength bend more.

- Violet: $380 - 450$ nm
- Green: $495 - 570$ nm
- Yellow: $570 - 590$ nm
- Red: $620 - 750$ nm

Out of all colors violet has the least wavelength and therefore, it bends the most and red has the highest wavelength, so it bends the least.

Hence, the correct option is (D).

6. Mass is independent of the place where it is measured. Weight can be different at different places with different gravitational field.

Mass of a body is constant that neither depends on the location of the body nor on the gravitational force exerted on the body. So mass of the body will remain unchanged on moon i.e., $M_m = M_e$

Hence, the correct option is (B).

7. Given:

$\phi = 2.8 eV, E = 2 eV$

We know that Maximum kinetic energy $(E) = hv - \phi$

Put the given values in above formula.

$2 = hv - 2.8$

$\Rightarrow hv = 4.8 eV$

New frequency $v' = 2v$

So, $E' = hv' - \phi$

$\Rightarrow E' = 2\,hv - \phi$

Put the given values in above formula.

$= 2 \times 4.8 - 2.8$

$= 6.8 eV$

Hence, the correct option is (A).

8. Metal A has higher threshold frequency,

We know that for a given photosensitive material,

The stopping potential varies linearly with the frequency of the incident radiation.

Also,

Work function,

$$\phi_0 = h\nu_0$$

Also,

$\phi_0 = e \times$ magnitude of intercept on potential axis.

Here for metal A, y - intercept is more negative.

Hence, the correct option is (B).

9. Here $N_D = 5 \times 10^{22}\ m^{-3}$,

$N_A = 5 \times 10^{20}\ m^{-3}, n_i = 1.5 \times 10^{16}\ m^{-3}$

For the semiconductor to remain electrically neutral,

$N_D - N_A = n_e - n_h$ ......(1)

Also

$n_e n_h = n_i^2$

$(n_e + n_h)^2 = (n_e - n_h)^2 + 2n_e n_h$

$= (N_D - N_A)^2 + 4n_i^2$ ......(2)

$n_e + n_h = \sqrt{(N_D - N_A)^2 + 4n_i^2}$

Adding equations (1) and (2), we get

$n_e = \frac{1}{2}(N_D - N_A) + \sqrt{(N_D - N_A)^2 + 4n_i^2}$

$= \frac{1}{2}\left[(5 \times 10^{22} - 0.05 \times 10^{22}) + \sqrt{(4.95 \times 10^{22})^2 + 4 \times (1.5 \times 10^{16})^2}\right]$

$\approx \frac{1}{2}\left[4.95 \times 10^{22} + \sqrt{(4.95 \times 10^{22})^2}\right]$

$= 4.95 \times 10^{22}\ m^{-3}$

$n_h = \frac{n_i^2}{n_e}$

$= \frac{(1.5 \times 10^{16})^2}{4.95 \times 10^{22}} = \frac{2.25 \times 10^{32}}{4.95 \times 10^{22}}$

$= 4.5 \times 10^9\ m^{-3}$

Hence, the correct option is (B).

10. Kirchhoff's Law describes the enthalpy of a reaction's variation with temperature changes. In general, enthalpy of any substance increases with temperature, which means both the products and the reactants' enthalpies increase. The overall enthalpy of the reaction will change if the increase in the enthalpy of products and reactants is different.

At constant pressure, the heat capacity is equal to change in enthalpy divided by the change in temperature.

$$c_p = \frac{\Delta H}{\Delta T}$$

Therefore, if the heat capacities do not vary with temperature then the change in enthalpy is a function of the difference in temperature and heat capacities. The amount that the enthalpy changes by is proportional to the product of temperature change and change in heat capacities of products and reactants.

Hence, the correct option is (B).

11. Given that, the temperature of freezer,

$T_2 = -13°C$

$\Rightarrow\quad T_2 = -13 + 273 = 260K$

Coefficient of performance, $\beta = 5$

The coefficient of performance is defined as,

$\beta = \frac{T_2}{T_1 - T_2}$

$\Rightarrow 5 = \frac{260}{T_1 - 260}$

$\Rightarrow T_1 - 260 = \frac{260}{5}$

$\Rightarrow T_1 - 260 = 52$

$T_1 = (52 + 260)K = 312K$

$T_1 = (312 - 273)°C$

$T_1 = 39°C$

Hence, the correct option is (C).

12. Here, the temperature inside the refrigerator can be provided as,

$T_1 = 9°C = 282K$

Room temperature is given as,

$T_2 = 36°C = 309K$

Coefficient of performance can be given by the relation,

$COP = \frac{T_1}{(T_2 - T_1)}$

$\Rightarrow COP = \frac{282}{(309 - 282)}$

$\Rightarrow COP = 10.44$

Clearly, the coefficient of performance of the mentioned refrigerator is 10.44.

Hence, the correct option is (A).

13. Lyman series of hydrogen spectrum corresponds to ultraviolet region.

The Lyman series: It includes the lines emitted by transitions of the electron from an outer orbit of quantum number $n_2 > 1$ to the 1st orbit of quantum number $n_1 = 1$. All the energy wavelengths in the Lyman series lie in the ultraviolet band.

Hence, the correct option is (D).

14. Given:

A nucleons with $Z = 92$

Partical emission Sequence →
$2\alpha, 2\beta^{-1}, 4\alpha, 2\beta^{-1}, \alpha, 2\beta^+, \alpha$

Total $= 8\alpha$ particles, $4\beta^{-1}, 2\beta^+$ particles emitted.

we know that:

1α particle decreases Z by 2.

$1\beta^+$ decay decreases Z by 1.

$1\beta^-$ decay increases Z by 1.

$Z_{\text{final}} = 92 - 8\alpha_{\text{decay}} - 2\beta^+_{\text{decay}} + 4 \text{ beta } \overline{decay}$

$= 92 - 16 - 2 + 4$

$Z_{final} = 78$

Hence, the correct option is (B).

15. Given that transition is from n = 4 to n = 1 (ground state). So transition spectral lines

$N = \dfrac{n(n-1)}{2}$

$N = \dfrac{4(4-1)}{2} = 6$

n = 5 ──────────────────
n = 4 ──────────────────
n = 3 ──────────────────
n = 2 ──────────────────
n = 1 ──────────────────

Hence, the correct option is (C).

16. Nuclear Radiations:

According to Rutherford's experiment when a sample of a radioactive substance is put in a lead box and allows the emission of radiation through a small hole only.

When the radiation enters into the external electric field, they split into three parts (α – rays, β – rays, and γ – gamma rays).

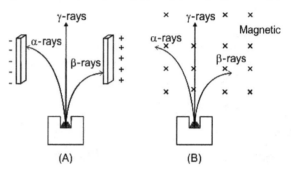

The penetration power of β – rays is 100 times that of α – rays. They are absorbed by the aluminum foil of 5 mm thickness.

The penetration power of γ – rays is 1000 times that of α – rays. They can penetrate a 30 cm thick iron block.

The decrsesing order of penetrating powers is γ – rays > β – rays > α – rays.

Hence, the correct option is (B).

17. Angular velocity: The time rate of change of angular displacement of a particle is called its angular velocity. It is denoted by ω.

It is measured in radian per second (rad/sec).

$\omega = \dfrac{d\theta}{dt}$

Where dθ = change in angular displacement and dt = change in time.

Given: Radius of earth = 6400 km.

$T = \dfrac{2\pi}{\omega}$

Where $\omega =$ angular velocity.

$\omega = \dfrac{2\pi}{T} = \dfrac{2 \times 3.14}{24 \times 60 \times 60} = 7.3 \times 10^{-5}$ radian /sec

So, $\omega = 7.3 \times 10^{-5}$ radian /sec

Hence, the correct option is (A).

18. When the net external torque acting on a system is zero, the total angular momentum of the system remains constant. Therefore the angular momentum of a moving body remains constant if net external torque is not applied.

Hence, the correct option is (D).

19. The rate at which electrical energy is dissipated into other forms of energy is called electrical power i.e.

$P = \dfrac{W}{t} = VI = I^2 R = \dfrac{V^2}{R}$

Where, V = Potential difference, R = Resistance and I = current.

If, $W = 1$ Joule and $t = 1$ second, then $P = 1$ watt

Thus, the power of an electric circuit is said to be one watt or 1 ampere volt if one joule of energy is consumed in one second.

Hence, the correct option is (A).

20. The process of electroplating, using the phenomenon of electrolysis, is primarily based on chemical effect of electric current.

- The phenomenon of producing heat by the electric current is called the heating effect of electric current.
- The amount of heat produced (H) in joules = I²Rt

Where, I is current, R is resistance and t is the time taken

- Due to the heating effect of the current, the filament of the bulb gets heated to a high temperature and it starts glowing.
- Similarly, the metals are melted and coated on another material to prevent corrosion. It is a chemical effect of electric current.

Hence, the correct option is (B).

21. The frequency of electromagnetic waves:

$v = 9\sqrt{\text{maximum electron density}}$

$v = 9\sqrt{d_{max}}$

$\Rightarrow 9\sqrt{2} \times 10^6 = 9\sqrt{d_{max}}$

$\Rightarrow \sqrt{2} \times 10^6 = \sqrt{d_{max}}$

$\Rightarrow d_{max} = 2 \times 10^{12} m^{-3}$

∴ The maximum electron density in the ionosphere is $2 \times 10^{12} m^{-3}$.

Hence, the correct option is (C).

22. Given,

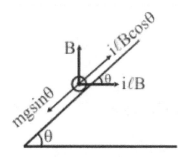

$B = 0.25\ T$

$\dfrac{m}{l} = 0.5 \dfrac{kg}{m}$

$\theta = 30°$

$F = Bil$

$F\cos 30$ balances $mg\sin 30$

∴ (Bil) $\cos 30° = mg\sin 30$

$i = \dfrac{m}{l}\dfrac{g}{B}\dfrac{\sin 30}{\cos 30}$

$= \dfrac{0.5 \times 9.8}{0.25 \times 866} \times \dfrac{1}{2}$

$= 11.32\ A$

Hence, the correct option is (D).

23. $\Delta Q = \dfrac{\Delta \varphi}{R}$

$= \dfrac{n \times BA}{R}$

$\Rightarrow B = \dfrac{\Delta Q . R}{nA}$

$= \dfrac{2 \times 10^{-4} \times 80}{40 \times 4 \times 10^{-4}}$

$= 1 Wb/m^2$

Hence, the correct option is (B).

24. When a bus starts suddenly, the passengers are pushed back. This is an example of Newton's first law.

According to Newton's first law of motion, an object will remain at rest or in uniform motion in a straight line unless acted upon by an external force. It is also called the law of inertia.

When a bus suddenly starts moving, the passengers fall backward due to the law of inertia of rest or first law of Newton. Because the body was in the state of rest and when the bus suddenly starts moving the lower body tends to be in motion, but the upper body still remains in a state of rest due to which it feels a jerk and falls backward.

Hence, the correct option is (A).

25. The conversion of a solid directly into vapors is called sublimation.

Sublimation: It is the conversion of a solid directly into vapors. Sublimation takes place when the boiling point is less than the melting point.

The heat required to change a unit mass of solid directly into vapors at a given temperature is called the heat of sublimation at that temperature.

Hence, the correct option is (A).

26. Given,

Excess pressure $= \dfrac{4T}{R'}$

Gauge pressure $= \rho g Z_0$

Now,

$P_0 + \dfrac{4T}{R} = P_0 + \rho g Z_0$

$Z_0 = \dfrac{4T}{R \times \rho g}$

$Z_0 = \dfrac{4 \times 2.5 \times 10^{-2}}{10^{-3} \times 1000 \times 10}$

$Z_0 = 1 \, cm$

Hence, the correct option is (C).

27. Rate of flow liquid:

$Q = au = a\sqrt{2gh}$

$= 2 \times 10^{-6} \, m^2 \times \sqrt{2 \times 10 \times 2} \, m/s$

$= 2 \times 2 \times 3.14 \times 10^{-6} \, m^3/s$

$= 12.56 \times 10^{-6} \, m^3/s$

$= 12.6 \times 10^{-6} \, m^3/s$

Hence, the correct option is (A).

28. Given a mass of copper slab $= 2g$ contains 2×10^{22} atoms.

We have to find the fraction of electrons that must be removed from sphere to give it $+2\mu C$ charge.

Charge on nucleus of each atom $= 29e$

$\therefore$ Net charge on $2g$ sphere

$= (29e) \times (2 \times 10^{22}) = 5.8 \times 10^{23} ec$

$\therefore$ Number of electrons on sphere $= 5.8 \times 10^{23}$

$\therefore$ Number of electrons removed to give $2\mu c$ charge $= \dfrac{q}{e}$

$= \dfrac{2 \times 10^{-6}}{1.6 \times 10^{-19}}$

$= 1.25 \times 10^{13}$

Fraction of electrons removed $= \dfrac{1.25 \times 10^{13}}{\text{Total number of electrons in sphere}}$

$= \dfrac{1.25 \times 10^{13}}{29 \times 2 \times 10^{22}}$

$= 2.16 \times 10^{-11}$

Hence, the correct option is (D).

29. Given,

Charge on an alpha particle, $q_1 = q_2 = +2e$

Distance between the particles, $r = 3.2 \times 10^{-15} m$

We know that:

Charge on an electron, $e = 1.6 \times 10^{-19}$

and, $\dfrac{1}{4\pi\epsilon\epsilon_0} = 9 \times 10^9$

Now, using coulomb's law, we get,

Force acting on the particles is given by,

$F = \dfrac{1}{4\pi\epsilon_0} \dfrac{q_1 q_2}{r^2}$

$F = \dfrac{9 \times 10^9 \times 2 \times 1.6 \times 10^{-19} \times 2 \times 1.6 \times 10^{-19}}{3.2 \times 10^{-15} \times 3.2 \times 10^{-15}} N$

$F = 90 N$

Hence, the correct option is (C).

30. The electric field at a point is discontinuous if there is a charge at that point.

The electric field due to any charge will be continuous, if there is no other charge in the medium. It will be discontinuous if there is a charge at the point under consideration.

Hence, the correct option is (D).

31. We know that:

A capacitor consists of two plates of a conductor and a dielectric insulator between them:

$C = \dfrac{\epsilon A}{d}$

Where

$C =$ capacitance in farad

$\epsilon =$ Permittivity of dielectric

$A =$ area of plate overlap in square meters

$d =$ distance between plates in meters

If the area of the plates is halved i.e., $\dfrac{A}{2}$ and the distance between them is halved i.e., $\dfrac{d}{2}$, then new capacitance is:

$C' = \dfrac{\epsilon \frac{A}{2}}{\frac{d}{2}}$

$\therefore C' = C$

Hence, the correct option is (C).

32. Given: $L = 2H, I = 4A, V_C = 400V$

Energy stored by the inductor (E_L) is given by,

$E_L = \dfrac{1}{2} L I^2$

Energy stored by a capacitor (E_C) is given by,

$E_C = \dfrac{1}{2} C V^2$

From the above concept,

$\frac{1}{2}LI^2 = \frac{1}{2}CV^2$

$LI^2 = CV^2$

$2 \times (4)^2 = C(400)^2$

$C = \frac{32}{160000}$

$C = 200\mu F$

Hence, the correct option is (D).

33. Concept:

According to Faraday's law, the induced emf in a coil (having N turns) is the rate of change of magnetic flux linked with coil,

$e = -N\frac{d\phi}{dt}$

N = number of turns in the coil

ϕ = magnetic flux link with the coil

Calculation:

Given that $\phi = (t^2 - 3t)$ m-wb and $N = 200$

Induced emf in coil $e = -N\frac{d\phi}{dt}$

$e = -200\frac{d}{dt}(t^2 - 3t) \times 10^{-3}$

$e = -200(2t - 3) \times 10^{-3}$

Then the induced emf in the coil at $t = 4$

$e = -200(2 \times 4 - 3) \times 10^{-3} = -1$ v

Hence, the correct option is (A).

34. The direction of induced emf can be founded by Lenz's Law.

According to Lenz's law, the direction of induced emf or current in a circuit is such as to oppose the cause that produces it.

Laplace's law indicates that the tension on the wall of a sphere is the product of the pressure times the radius of the chamber and the tension is inversely related to the thickness of the wall.

Fleming's right-hand rule shows the direction of induced current but it gives no relation between the direction of induced emf or current in a circuit is such as to oppose the cause that produces it.

Kirchoff's second law is also known as loop rule or voltage law (KVL) and according to it "the algebraic sum of the changes in potential in a complete traversal of a mesh (closed-loop) is zero", i.e. $\Sigma V = 0$.

Hence, the correct option is (D).

35. Faraday's first law of electromagnetic induction:

It states that whenever a conductor is placed in a varying magnetic field, emf is induced which is called induced emf. If the conductor circuit is closed, the current will also circulate through the circuit and this current is called induced current.

Faraday's second law of electromagnetic induction:

It states that the magnitude of the voltage induced in the coil is equal to the rate of change of flux that linkages with the coil. The flux linkage of the coil is the product of number of turns in the coil and flux associated with the coil.

$v = -N\frac{d\phi}{dt}$

Where N = number of turns, $d\phi$ = change in magnetic flux and v = induced voltage.

The negative sign says that it opposes the change in magnetic flux which is explained by Lenz law.

Hence, the correct option is (C).

36. First Maxima $= \frac{D\lambda}{d}$

$\beta_1 = \frac{1.5 \times 480 \times 10^{-9}}{0.25 \times 10^{-3}}$

$= 2.880 \times 10^{-3}$ m

$\beta_2 = \frac{1.5 \times 600 \times 10^{-9}}{0.25 \times 10^{-3}}$

$= 3.600 \times 10^{-3}$ m

So, $\beta_2 - \beta_1 = 0.72 \times 10^{-3}$ m

$= 0.72$ mm

Hence, the correct option is (A).

37. Let the intensities of the two waves be I_1 and I_2.

Given,

$I_1 : I_2 = 9 : 1$

Ratio of maximum and minimum intensities $\frac{I_{max}}{I_{min}} = \left(\frac{\sqrt{I_1} + \sqrt{I_2}}{\sqrt{I_1} - \sqrt{I_2}}\right)^2$

or,

$\frac{I_{max}}{I_{min}} = \left(\frac{\sqrt{\frac{I_1}{I_2}} + 1}{\sqrt{\frac{I_1}{I_2}} - 1}\right)^2$

or

$\frac{I_{max}}{I_{min}} = \left(\frac{\sqrt{9} + 1}{\sqrt{9} - 1}\right)^2$

$= \left(\frac{3+1}{3-1}\right)^2$

$\frac{I_{max}}{I_{min}} = \frac{16}{4}$

$= \frac{4}{1}$

Hence, the correct option is (A).

38. Given,

Actual weight on the equator $= W = mg$

Where $'m'$ is the mass and $'g'$ is the gravity.

According to the given condition,

Weight on the equator $= W' = mg'$

Weight on the equator $= W' = \frac{3}{5}mg$ .... (i)

We know that, $\lambda = 0$ at the equator.

Now,

$mg' = mg - mR\omega^2 \cos\lambda$

$\frac{3}{5}mg = mg - mR\omega^2 \cos 0 (\because \lambda = 0)$

$\frac{3}{5}mg = mg - mR\omega^2(1)(\because \cos 0 = 1)$

$\frac{3}{5}mg = mg - mR\omega^2$

$mR\omega^2 = mg - \frac{3}{5}mg$

$mR\omega^2 = \left(1 - \frac{3}{5}\right)mg$

$mR\omega^2 = \frac{2}{5}mg$

$R\omega^2 = \frac{2}{5}g$

$\omega^2 = \frac{2g}{5R}$

$\omega^2 = \frac{(2 \times 10)}{(5 \times 6.4 \times 10^5)}$

($\because R = $ Radius of Earth $= 6400 \, km = 6.4 \times 10^5 \, m$)

$\omega = \sqrt{(6.25 \times 10^{-7})}$

$\omega = 7.8 \times 10^{-4} \, rad/sec$

Hence, the correct option is (A).

39. Given that,

$n_1 = 2, \frac{C_{P_1}}{C_{V_1}} = \frac{5}{3}, n_2 = 3$ and $\frac{C_{P_2}}{C_{V_2}} = \frac{4}{3}$

We know that,

$\left(\frac{C_P}{C_V}\right)_{mix} = \frac{n_1 C_{P_1} + n_2 C_{P_2}}{n_1 C_{V_1} + n_2 C_{V_2}}$ ....(1)

And $C_P - C_V = nR$

$\Rightarrow \frac{C_P - 1}{C_V} = \frac{nR}{C_V}$

Rearranging the Eq.(1), we get,

$\frac{n_1}{\frac{C_{P_1}}{C_{V_1}} - 1} + \frac{n_2}{\frac{C_{P_2}}{C_{V_2}} - 1} = \frac{n_1 + n_2}{\left(\frac{C_P}{C_V}\right)_{mix} - 1}$

$\Rightarrow \frac{2}{\frac{5}{3} - 1} + \frac{3}{\frac{4}{3} - 1} = \frac{5}{\left(\frac{C_P}{C_V}\right)_{mix} - 1}$

$\Rightarrow \frac{2 \times 3}{2} + \frac{3 \times 3}{1} = \frac{5}{\left(\frac{C_P}{C_V}\right)_{mix} - 1}$

$\Rightarrow 12 = \frac{5}{\left(\frac{C_P}{C_V}\right)_{mix} - 1}$

$\Rightarrow \left(\frac{C_P}{C_V}\right)_{mix} - 1 = \frac{5}{12}$

$\Rightarrow \left(\frac{C_P}{C_V}\right)_{mix} = \frac{5}{12} + 1$

$= \frac{17}{12}$

$= 1.42$

Hence, the correct option is (D).

40. Given that:

$n_{He} = n, C_{V_{HE}} = \frac{3R}{2}$

$C_{P_{He}} = \frac{5R}{2}$

$n_{O_2} = 2n$

$C_{V_{O_2}} = \frac{5R}{2}$

$C_{P_{O_2}} = \frac{7R}{2}$

$\frac{C_{P_{mix}}}{C_{V_{mix}}} = \frac{n_{He}C_{P_{He}} + n_{O_2}C_{P_{O_2}}}{n_{He}C_{V_{He}} + n_{O_2}C_{V_{O_2}}}$

$= \frac{n \times \left(\frac{5R}{2}\right) + 2n \times \left(\frac{7R}{2}\right)}{n \times \left(\frac{3R}{2}\right) + 2n \times \left(\frac{5R}{2}\right)} = \frac{\frac{19n}{2}}{\frac{13n}{2}} = \frac{19}{13}$

Hence, the correct option is (A).

41. For a pure inductor circuit:

$\phi = 90°$ ($\because$ current lags the voltage by $90°$ in the purely inductive circuit)

$\cos\phi = \cos 90° = 0$

$P = V_{rms} I_{rms} \times 0$

$P = 0 \, W$

The average power supplied to an inductor over one complete alternating current cycle is 0.

Hence, the correct option is (D).

42. When we stretch the wire then length increases but cross-sectional are decreases. But the total volume of the wire will remain constant. So we will write the formula of resistance in terms of volume (V).

Volume $(V) = area(A) \times$ length (l)

So,

$A = \dfrac{V}{l}$

Resistance $(R) = \dfrac{\rho l}{A}$

$= \dfrac{\rho l}{\frac{V}{l}}$

$= \dfrac{\rho l^2}{V}$

$= x$

Now if length is doubled,

New length $(l') = 2l$

New Resistance $(R') = \dfrac{\rho (2l)^2}{V}$

$= \dfrac{4\rho l^2}{V}$

$= 4x \quad [\because R = \dfrac{4\rho l^2}{V} = x]$

Hence, the correct option is (C).

43. Given,

Resistance along the unit length, $\dfrac{R}{L} = 1.2 \; \Omega m^{-1}$

The potential gradient, $K = 0.009 \; Vcm^{-1} = 0.9 \; Vm^{-1}$

By using the formula (1), the potential difference along the circuit is calculated.

$V = \dfrac{K}{L}$

Substituting the values in the above equation,

$V = \dfrac{0.9}{L} \cdots - (1)$

Using the formula (2),

$V = IR$

Substituting the (1) and $R = 1.2 \; L$ in the above equation,

$\dfrac{0.9}{L} = I \times 1.2 \; L$

By grouping the similar terms,

$I = \dfrac{0.9}{1.2 L^2}$

Since the length of the wire is not given, it is taken as $1 \; m$

$I = \dfrac{0.9}{1.2}$

$I = 0.75 \; A$

So the current flows through the primary circuit is $0.75 \; A$.

Hence, the correct option is (B).

44. The motion of all the electrons in an atom of a diamagnetic is in random motion and thus they do not have a permanent magnetic moment. Therefore option (A) is correct.

The magnetic moment of the two being equal and opposite, cancel each (in the absence of an external magnetic field) so that net magnetic each atom is zero. Therefore option (D) is correct.

Magnetic susceptibility of diamagnetic materials is small and negative i.e. -1 ≤ x ≤ 0. Therefore option (C) is incorrect.

Hence, the correct option is (C).

45. Given,

$T_1 = 27 + 273 = 300 \; K$

$T_2 = 27 + 627 = 900 \; K$

Since we know that $i.e. X \propto \dfrac{1}{T}$

$\dfrac{X1}{X2} = \dfrac{T_2}{T_1}$

$\dfrac{X}{X2} = \dfrac{900}{300}$

$X_2 = \dfrac{X}{3}$

Hence, the correct option is (B).

46. If a pulse travelling along a stretched string and is reflected by the rigid boundary.

Assuming there is no absorption of energy by the boundary, the reflected wave has the same frequency and amplitude as the incident pulse but it suffers a phase change of π or $180°$ on reflection.

If the boundary point is not rigid but completely free to move (such as in the case of a string tied to a freely moving ring on a rod), the reflected pulse has the same phase, amplitude and frequency (assuming no energy dissipation) as the incident pulse.

Hence, the correct option is (B).

47. The circular motion of a particle with constant speed is uniform circular motion.

Due to constant speed, the object will cover equal distances in equal intervals of time. Hence, the circular motion will be repeated in equal intervals of time. So, it is a periodic motion.

In a circular motion, the object cannot oscillate about a fixed position as it travels circular distances. Thus, it is not a simple harmonic motion.

Hence, the correct option is (A).

48. Given,

$A_1 = A_2 = a_0$ and $A = a_0$

We know that

$A = \sqrt{A_1^2 + A_2^2 + 2A_1 A_2 \cos\phi}$

$a_0 = \sqrt{a_0^2 + a_0^2 + 2a_0 a_0 \cos\phi}$

$a_0^2 = 2a_0^2 + 2a_0^2 \cos\phi$

$\frac{-1}{2} = \cos\phi$

$\phi = \frac{2\pi}{3}$

Hence, the correct option is (B).

49. Input/output impedances used for distinguishing between a small signal and a large signal amplifier.

Amplifier has high input impedance and low output impedance. Small signal deals with very low amplitude signals and it is apply-input side of amplifier. Large signal deals with very high amplitude signal.

Hence, the correct option is (D).

50. The majority charge carriers in n-type semiconductors are electrons.

The n-type conductors have electrons as major charge carriers. This is because n-type conductors have pentavalent (5 valence electrons) impurities like phosphorous, etc.

Elements of Group 5 have five valence electrons, i.e. 1 extra from the Group 4 elements. 4 out of 5 electrons get bonded with the neighbouring Silicon atoms and 1 electron per atom remains extra with the Group 5 elements.

Thus, electrons are the major charge carriers in n-type semiconductors. p-type semiconductors have impurities of elements from Group 3 and holes are majority charge carriers in them.

Hence, the correct option is (B).

51. Initial $pH = 1$, i.e., $[H^+] = 0.1$ mole/litre

New $pH = 2$, i.e., $[H^+] = 0.01$ mole/litre

In case of dilution:

$M_1 V_1 = M_2 V_2$

Given here:

$V_1 = 1$ litre.

$0.1 \times 1 = 0.01 \times V_2$

$V_2 = 10$ litre.

Volume of water added $= 10 - 1 = 9$ litre.

Hence, the correct option is (C).

52. Given reaction,

$N_{2(g)} + O_{2(g)} \rightleftharpoons 2NO_{(g)}$,

We know that:

The equilibrium constant is given by:

$\frac{[NO]^2}{[N_2][O_2]}$

So, the equilibrium constant K is given by,

$\frac{(2.8 \times 10^{-3} M)(2.8 \times 10^{-3} M)}{(3.0 \times 10^{-3} M)(4.2 \times 10^{-3} M)} = 0.622$

There are no units as $\Delta n_g = 0$.

Hence, the correct option is (A).

53. The electron-withdrawing inductive effect of the -OH group decreases the electron density on nitrogen, thus lowering the basicity of amines. This effect diminishes with distance from the amino group.

Thus, ethylamine > 3 - amino - 1 - propanol > 2 - amino ethanol

Hence, the correct option is (C).

54. C_2H_6 compound has 7 covalent bonds.

The structure of the Ethane molecule is given below.

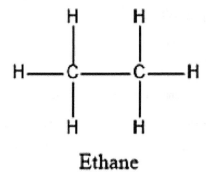

Ethane

From the above structure, we can see that the Ethane molecule has 6 C-H covalent bonds and one C-C covalent bond. Therefore, on adding the covalent bonds of C-C and C-H covalent bonds, we can say that the Ethane molecule has 7 covalent bonds.

Hence, the correct option is (C).

55. Fluorine acts as a stronger oxidizing agent than oxygen because it is more electronegative than oxygen. So, it can easily attract electrons and get reduced. Thus, oxygen is a strong reducing agent than fluorine.

Therefore, both the Assertion and Reason are correct and Reason is the correct, explanation for Assertion.

Hence, the correct option is (A).

56. The higher the temperature higher the energy.

Usually conducting a reaction at a higher temperature delivers more energy into the system and increases the reaction rate by

causing more collisions between particles, as explained by collision theory. However, the main reason that temperature increases the rate of reaction is that more of the colliding particles will have the necessary activation energy resulting in more successful collisions (when bonds are formed between reactants).

Hence, the correct option is (B).

57. As the temperature rises, more collisions start taking place which results in an increase in rate of the chemical reaction.

With rise in temperature, fraction of molecules possessing kinetic energy greater than the activation energy increases. Only such molecules are able to cause effective collisions and result in the formation of product. Thus, as the fraction of such molecules increases, rate of the reaction increases.

Hence, the correct option is (D).

58. The rate of a chemical reaction depends on the nature of reactants because the number of bonds broken in the reactant molecules and the number of bonds formed in product molecules changes.

In other words, the ease with which bonds are formed and the ease with which bonds are broken determines the rate of the chemical reaction.

Hence, the correct option is (A).

59. Given:

Mole fraction of solute in first solution $= 0.2$

According to Raoult's law, the relative lowering of vapour pressure is equal to the mole fraction of solute, i.e.,

$$\frac{p^\circ - p}{p^\circ} = \frac{n}{n+N}$$

or, $\frac{\Delta p}{p^\circ} = \frac{n}{n+N}$

The decrease in vapour pressure is 10 mm Hg:

$$\frac{10}{p^\circ} = 0.2$$

$\therefore p^\circ = 50$ mm ....(1)

For other solution of same solvent, the decrease in vapor pressure is 20 mm Hg:

$$\frac{20}{p^\circ} = \frac{n}{n+N}$$

or, $\frac{20}{50} = \frac{n}{n+N}$ (from (1))

$0.4 = \frac{n}{n+N}$ (mole fraction of solute)

$\because$ Mole fraction of solvent $+$ mole fraction of solute $= 1$

So, mole fraction of solvent $= 1 - 0.4 = 0.6$

Hence, the correct option is (B).

60. Given that:

Vapour pressure of the solution at normal boiling point, $p_1 = 1.004$ bar

Vapour pressure of pure water at normal boiling point, $p_1^\circ = 1.013$ bar

Mass of solute, $w_2 = 2\ g$

Mass of solvent (water), $w_1 = 100 - 2 = 98\ g$

Molar Mass of solvent (water),

$M_1(H_2O) = 2 \times 1 + 16 \times 1 = 18\ g\ mol^{-1}$

According to Raoult's law,

$$\frac{p_1^\circ - p_1}{p_1^\circ} = \frac{w_2 \times M_1}{M_2 \times w_1}$$

$$\Rightarrow \frac{1.013 - 1.004}{1.013} = \frac{2 \times 18}{M_2 \times 98}$$

$$\Rightarrow \frac{0.009}{1.013} = \frac{2 \times 18}{M_2 \times 98}$$

$$M_2 = \frac{1.013 \times 2 \times 18}{0.009 \times 98}$$

$$M_2 = 41.35\ g\ mol^{-1}$$

Hence, the correct option is (C).

61. 0.15 M solution of benzoic acid in methanol means,

1000 mL of solution contains 0.15 mol of benzoic acid.

Therefore, $250\ mL$ of solution contains $\frac{0.15 \times 250}{1000}$ mol of benzoic acid

$= 0.0375$ mol of benzoic acid

Molar mass of benzoic acid
$(C_6H_5COOH) = 7 \times 12 + 6 \times 1 + 2 \times 16 = 122\ g\ mol^{-1}$

Therefore, required benzoic acid $= 0.0375\ mol \times 122\ g\ mol^{-1} = 4.575\ g$

Hence, the correct option is (D).

62. A reaction, $A + B \rightarrow C + D + q$ is found to have a positive entropy change. The reaction will be possible at any temperature.

For a reaction to be spontaneous, ΔG should be negative
$\Delta G = \Delta H - T\Delta S$

According to the question, for the given reaction,

$\Delta S =$ positive

$\Delta H =$ negative (since heat is evolved)

That results in $\Delta G =$ negative

Therefore, the reaction is spontaneous at any temperature.

Hence, the correct option is (D).

63. According to the first law of thermodynamics,

$\Delta U = q + W$ .... (i)

Where,

ΔU = change in internal energy for a process

q = heat

W = work

Given,

$q = +701\ J$ (Since heat is absorbed)

$W = -394\ J$ (Since work is done by the system)

Substituting the values in expression (i), we get

$\Delta U = 701\ J + (-394\ J)$

$\Delta U = 307\ J$

Hence, the change in internal energy for the given process is $307\ J$.

Hence, the correct option is (A).

64. Enthalpy change for a reaction (ΔH) is given by the expression,

$\Delta H = \Delta U + \Delta n_g RT$

Where,

ΔU = change in internal energy

Δn_g = change in number of moles

For the given reaction,

$\Delta n_g = \sum n_g$ (products) - $\sum n_g$ (reactants)

$\Delta n_g = (2 - 1.5)$ moles

$\Delta n_g = +0.5$ moles

And, $\Delta U = -742.7\ kJ\ mol^{-1}$

$T = 298\ K$

$R = 8.314 \times 10^{-3}\ kJ\ mol^{-1}\ K^{-1}$

Substituting the values in the expression of ΔH

$\Delta H = (-742.7\ kJ\ mol^{-1}) + (+0.5\ mol)(298\ K)\ 8.314 \times 10^{-3} kJ mol^{-1}\ K^{-1}$

$\Delta H = -742.7 + 1.2$

$\Delta H = -741.5\ kJ\ mol^{-1}$

Hence, the correct option is (D).

65. Graphite is one of the allotropes of carbon. Unlike diamond, it is an electrical conductor and a good lubricant. Graphite is a good conductor of electricity due to the presence of free valence electrons.

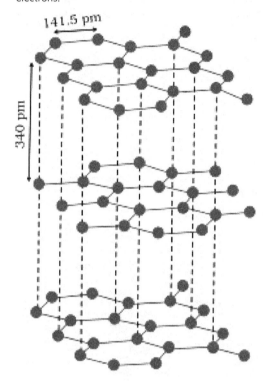

This property of graphite is due to the carbon atoms arranged in different layers and each atom is covalently bonded on three of its neighbouring atoms in the same layer. The fourth valence electrons of each atom are present between different layers and are free to move about. These free electrons in graphite make it a good conductor of electricity.

Hence, the correct option is (D).

66. Effective number of atoms of X, Y and Z are:

According to question:

For X:

Number of atoms $= \frac{1}{8} \times 7$ (out of 8 corners, X is occupying 7)

For Y:

Number of atoms $= \frac{1}{2} \times 6 = 3$ (Y is occupying all face centers)

For Z:

Number of atoms $= \frac{1}{8}$ (Z is occupying one corner out of 8)

Therefore, the formula of the compound will be:

$X_7 Y_3 Z_{\frac{1}{8}}$

$= X_7 Y_{24} Z$

Hence, the correct option is (B).

67. Given that:

Isotopic mass $= 55.92066$

Mass number $= 56$

We know that:

Packing fraction $= \dfrac{\text{Isotopic mass - Mass number}}{\text{Mass number}} \times 10^4$

$= \dfrac{55.92066-56}{56} \times 10^4$

$= -14.167$

Hence, the correct option is (A).

68. On moving from left to right in a periodic table the electropositive character of elements decrease.

Electropositive character of an element is its ability to lose electrons and form positive ions. Now, as on moving from left to right in a period of periodic table, the nuclear charge increases due to the gradual increase in number of protons, so the valence electrons are pulled more strongly by the nucleus. Thus, it becomes more and more difficult for the atoms to lose electrons causing a decrease in the electropositive character of elements on moving from left to right in a periodic table.

Hence, the correct option is (B).

69. F < O < N is the correct order of the atomic radii of the elements oxygen, fluorine, and nitrogen.

Oxygen (8), fluorine (9), and nitrogen (7) belong to the same period of the periodic table, in the order nitrogen, oxygen, and fluorine. Now in a period, on moving from left to right the atomic radius of the elements decreases. Therefore, the atomic radius of nitrogen is the largest.

Hence, the correct option is (D).

70. The other name for group 18th elements is noble gas.

Noble gas are very stable due to having the maximum number of valence electrons their outermost shell can hold, so they rarely react with other elements.

Hence, the correct option is (A).

71. Alkaline earth metals show $+1$ Oxidation state and their atomic volume decrease down the group.

The alkali metal atom show only $+1$ Oxidation State, because of their unipositive Ion at the time the stable noble gas configuration. The atomic volume of alkali metals is the highest in its period and goes on increasing down the group from top to bottom.

Hence, the correct option is (C).

72. The hydrocarbon in which all the 4 valencies of carbon are fully occupied is called as alkane.

Alkanes, the saturated hydrocarbons are those in which the carbon atoms are bonded covalently to each other (fully occupied). Each carbon atom is tetrahedrally surrounded by H-atoms.

Hence, the correct option is (C).

73. The rates of diffusion of gases are inversely proportional to square root of their densities. This statement refers to Grahams Law.

Graham's law states that the rate of diffusion of a gas is inversely proportional to the square root of its molecular weight and in the same conditions of temperature and pressure, the molar mass is proportional to the mass density. Therefore the rate of diffusion of different gases is inversely proportional to the square root of their mass densities.

$r \alpha \dfrac{1}{\sqrt{d}}$ and $r \alpha \dfrac{1}{\sqrt{M}}$

Hence, the correct option is (B).

74. Ion – dipole forces is not a type of van der Waal's forces.

Ion-dipole forces are generated between polar water molecules and a sodium ion. The oxygen atom in the water molecule has a slight negative charge and is attracted to the positive sodium ion. These intermolecular ion-dipole forces are much weaker than covalent or ionic bonds. It is not considered as van der waals force as van der waals force will come into concept when the molecules will be uncharged.

Hence, the correct option is (C).

75.

Molecules	Interactions
Benzene and ethanol	Dispersion forces
Acetonitrile and acetone	Dipole-dipole
KCl and water	Ion-dipole
Benzene and carbon tetrachloride	London forces

Dipole-dipole as the major interaction is present in Acetonitrile and acetone.

Dipole-dipole interactions occur among the polar molecules. Polar molecules have permanent dipoles. The positive pole of one molecule is thus attracted by the negative pole of the other molecule. The magnitude of dipole-dipole forces in different polar molecules is predicted on the basis of the polarity of the molecules, which in turn depends upon the electronegativities of the atoms present in the molecule and the geometry of the molecule (in the case of polyatomic molecules, containing more than two atoms in a molecule).

Both acetone and acetonitrile contain a polar bond. Both molecules have what is called a Hydrogen Bond Acceptor, but neither of them has a Hydrogen Bond Donor. So these two molecules will interact with each other through their polar regions (dipole regions - forming a Dipole-Dipole interaction).

Hence, the correct option is (B).

76. Bredig's arc method is a method of preparation of the colloidal solution of metals such as silver or gold. This method consists of both dispersion and condensation. An arc is struck in electrodes, under the surface of water containing stabilising agents. The heat of the arc vaporises some of the metal which then condenses into cold water.

Hence, the correct option is (D).

77. Given,

Wavelength $= 5800\text{Å} = 5800 \times 10^{-10}\ m$

As we know,

The speed of light,

$c = 3 \times 10^8\ m/s$

(a) Wavenumber is given as,

$\bar{v} = \dfrac{1}{\lambda}$

$= \dfrac{1}{5800 \times 10^{-10}}$

$= 1.724 \times 10^6\ m^{-1}$

$= 1.724 \times 10^4\ cm^{-1}$

(b) The frequency is given as,

$v = \dfrac{c}{\lambda}$

$= \dfrac{3 \times 10^8}{5800 \times 10^{-10}}$

$= 5.172 \times 10^{14}$ Hz

Hence, the correct option is (D).

78. Here,

$2.5 \times 1.25 = 3.125$

The rule says: Answer to a multiplication or division should be rounded off to a same number of significant figures as possessed by the least precise term in the calculation.

Since 2.5 has least numbers of significant figure i.e., two, thus, the result should have 2 significant figure i.e., 3.1.

Hence, the correct option is (C).

79. A galvanic cell or simple battery is made of two electrodes. Each of the electrodes of a galvanic cell is known as a half cell. In a battery, the two half cells form an oxidizing-reducing couple.

When two half cells are connected via an electric conductor and salt bridge, an electrochemical reaction is started.

The given reaction is,

$Pt^{2+} + 2Cl^{-} \rightarrow Pt + Cl_2, E^{0}_{cell} = -0.15\ V$

Anode:

$2Cl^{(-)} \rightarrow Cl_2 + 2e^{-}$

Cathode:

$Pt^{2+} + 2e^{-} \rightarrow Pt$

The EMF of a cell is given by the following expressions:

EMF of a cell $=$ Reduction potential of cathode $-$ Reduction potential of anode

$\therefore E_{cell} = E_R - E_L$

$-0.15 = E_{Pt^{2+}/Pt} - E_{Cl_2/Cl^{(-)}}$

$-0.15 = 1.20 - E$

$E = 1.20 + 0.15$

$E = 1.35V$

Hence, the correct option is (B).

80. During the charging of the lead storage battery, the sulphuric acid is regenerated.

- Sulphuric acid acts as an electrolyte in lead storage batteries.
- Thus, lead storage batteries can be used again and again by regenerating the sulphuric acid.

Hence, the correct option is (B).

81. Given that:

Resistance, $(R) = 3.16\Omega$

Cell constant $= 0.367\ cm^{-1}$

We know that:

Conductance, $(C) = \dfrac{1}{R}$

$= \dfrac{1}{3.16 ohm}$

$= 0.0316\ ohm^{-1}$

Specific conductance, $(\kappa) =$ Conductance $\times$ cell constant

$= 0.0316\ ohm^{-1} \times 0.367\ cm^{-1}$

$= 0.0116\ ohm^{-1} cm^{-1}$

Hence, the correct option is (B).

82. $[Zn(OH)_4]^{2-}$ is the coordination entity in $K_2[Zn(OH)_4]$.

A coordination entity consists of a central metal atom bonded to a fixed number of atoms/molecules. Here, K^{+} is the counter ion, OH is the molecule bonded to the central atom which is Zn.

Hence, the correct option is (D).

83. Al^{3+} is Lewis acid in $K_3[Al(C_2O_4)_3]$.

Aluminium ion is the Lewis acid as it can accept 3 electrons from the donor atom to form the complex $[Al(C_2O_4)_3]^{3-}$.

A Lewis acid is a species that can accept an electron pair. All cations are Lewis acids. Since the central atom of a coordination complex is metal and always accepts electrons, it is a Lewis acid.

Hence, the correct option is (C).

84. Co^{3+} is the central atom/ion in $[CoCl(NH_3)_5]^{2+}$.

The central ion in the given complex ion is cobalt as it accepts electrons to form a bond with Cl atom and ammonia molecules. Since the primary valence of Co in this compound is $+3$, the in in Co^{3+}.

Hence, the correct option is (C).

85. Benzyl chloride gives benzoic acid on oxidation.

The reaction takes place as follows:

$C_6H_5CH_2Cl + 2KOH + 2[O] \longrightarrow C_6H_5COOK + KCl + H_2O$

Hence, the correct option is (D).

86. Ionic species are stabilized by the dispersal of charge.

The carboxylate ion (F_2CHCOO^-) is the most stable.

The negative charge on O is dispersed through resonance in the carboxylate group.

The negative charge is further dispersed due to negative inductive effect (-I effect) of two F atoms present on alpha carbon atoms.

Hence, the correct option is (D).

87. Given compound:

$$\underset{CHO}{CH_2} - \underset{CHO}{CH} - \underset{CHO}{CH_2}$$

Numbering the carbon atoms, we get:

$$\overset{3}{\underset{CHO}{CH_2}} - \overset{2}{\underset{CHO}{CH}} - \overset{1}{\underset{CHO}{CH_2}}$$

- Since there are three carbon atoms in long chain and it contains 3 -CHO groups (one on each carbon atom).
- IUPAC suffix "aldehyde" will added due to presence of functional group -CHO.

Therefore, the correct IUPAC name will be propane-1, 2, 3-tricarbaldehyde.

Hence, the correct option is (D).

88. Ethyl alcohol is industrially prepared from ethylene by Absorbing in H₂SO₄ followed by hydrolysis.

Acid-catalyzed hydration of Alkene:

Alkenes react with water (hydrolysis) In the presence of acid as a catalyst to form alcohols.

$$>C=C< + H_2O \overset{H^+}{\rightleftharpoons} >\underset{H}{C}-\underset{OH}{C}<$$

In the case of unsymmetrical alkenes, the addition reaction occurs in accordance with Markovnikov's rule.

Mechanism:
Step 1: Protonation of an alkene to form carbocation by an electrophilic attack of hydronium ion (H₃O⁺).

$$>C=C< + H-\overset{H}{\underset{H}{O^+}}-H \rightleftharpoons -\overset{}{\underset{}{C}}-\overset{+}{\underset{}{C}}< + H_2\ddot{O}$$

Step 2: Nucleophilic attack of water on carbocation.

Step 3: Deprotonation to form an alcohol.

$$-\overset{H}{\underset{}{C}}-\overset{H}{\underset{}{C}}-\overset{H}{\underset{}{O^+}}-H + H_2\ddot{O} \longrightarrow -\overset{H}{\underset{}{C}}-\overset{:\ddot{O}H}{\underset{}{C}}- + H_3\overset{+}{O}$$

Industrial preparation of Ethyl alcohol:

- Ethanol reacts with sulphuric acid to form an intermediate product.
- This is followed by hydrolysis to give ethanol and H₂SO₄ as byproducts.
- Here, the H₂SO₄ formed as a byproduct is reused for further reaction with ethyl alcohol.

The reaction is as follows:

$$CH_2 = CH_2 \overset{H_2SO_4}{\longrightarrow} CH_3 - CH_2 - HSO_4 \overset{Hydrolysis}{\longrightarrow}$$
$$CH_3CH_2 - OH + H_2SO_4$$

Hence, the correct option is (C).

89. Phenol on hydrogenation with Ni at 433K gives cyclohexanol.

The hydrogenation reaction is the addition of hydrogen to compounds.

Raney Ni, which is a finely divided Nickel powder is used in the hydrogenation process because it adsorbs the hydrogen molecules and provides high catalytic efficiency.

When phenol is treated with Ni at 433K, it converts to Cyclohexanol.

It is a highly selective reaction.

The reaction of reduction of phenol is given as:

When phenol is reacted with zinc dust it forms benzene.

Zinc oxidized itself and become ZnO and reduces phenol to benzene.

Hence, the correct option is (C).

90. Tertiary butyl alcohol is obtained by the action of methyl magnesium bromide on acetone CH₃COCH₃.

Methyl magnesium bromide is CH₃MgX and falls in the category of Grignard Reagents. The methyl group bears a partial negative charge and the metal bears a partial positive charge. Ketones react with a Grignard reagent to give tertiary alcohols as addition products.

Aldehydes give secondary alcohol and formaldehyde gives primary alcohol. The reaction is a step-up reaction as the number of carbon atoms increases in the product.

The reaction of acetone with methyl magnesium halide is given as follows:

$$CH_3 - \underset{\underset{Acetone}{}}{\overset{CH_3}{\underset{}{C}}} = O + CH_3MgBr \longrightarrow$$

$$CH_3 - \underset{\underset{CH_3}{|}}{\overset{CH_3}{\underset{|}{C}}} - MgBr \xrightarrow{H^+/H_2O} CH_3 - \underset{\underset{CH_3}{|}}{\overset{CH_3}{\underset{|}{C}}} = O + Mg\underset{Br}{\overset{OH}{\diagup}}$$

Addition product   t-Butyl alcohol

The product of the reaction is tertiary butyl alcohol.

Hence, the correct option is (C).

91. The enormous diversity of protein molecules is due mainly to the diversity of amino acid sequences within the protein molecule. Proteins are building blocks of the body. The proteins are made up of amino acids. The amino acids are linked together by peptide bonds to form a protein. The amino acids consist of amine group made up of nitrogen and hydrogen and the carboxyl group at the end and a side chain of R group which is specific to a particular amino acid. This specific group brings a variability to the proteins. If R group is H it is glycine while if it is CH_2, it is alanine. The sequence of amino acids determines the protein.

Hence, the correct option is (A).

92. B-form DNA is the common form of DNA exists under normal physiological condition. The double strands of B-DNA run in opposite directions. In a DNA molecule, the two strands are not parallel but intertwined with each other. Each strand looks like a helix. This structure, also known as the B form, the helix makes a turn every $3.4 \, nm$.

Hence, the correct option is (A).

93. (C₂F₄)ₙ is Teflon.

A synthetic material that gets used to cover the surface of some object and transmit nonstick properties to it is called Teflon. Teflon is a fluorocarbon.

It has a high melting point and it does not react with other substances easily. It has non-stick qualities that are the reason used in many pots, frying pans, and other culinary items.

Hence, the correct option is (A).

94. Terylene, Nylon 6,6, Maltose are examples of condensation polymers.

Nylon 6,6 is condensation polymer of 1,6-diaminohexane and hexanedioic acid.

Maltose is condensation polymer of glucose.

Terylene is condensation polymer of ethylene glycol and terphthallic acid.

Hence, the correct option is (D).

95. Amines:

- An amine is a functional group with a nitrogen atom having a lone pair.
- Basically, Amines are derived from ammonia (NH3).
- Nitrogen has a valency of 5, that's why it makes a trivalent with a lone pair.

Uses:

Amines are used in water purification, medicine manufacturing, and insecticides, and pesticides.

These are also used in the production of Amino acids.

It is also used in pain-relieving medicines.

Types:

Amines are generally of four types:

- Primary Amines
- Secondary Amines
- Tertiary Amines
- Cyclic Amines

Amines can be obtained from Halogen alkanes.

Hence, the correct option is (B).

96. Coloured compound of transition elements is assosiated with partially filled (n-1)d orbitals. the transition metal ions containing unpaired d-electrons undergoes electronic transition from one d-orbital to another. during this d-d transition process the electrons absorb certain energy from the radiation and emit the remainder of energy as colored light. the color of ion is complementary of the color absorbed by it. hence, colored ion is formed due to d-d transition which falls in visible region for all transition elements.

Hence, the correct option is (B).

97. A reduction in atomic size with increase in atomic number is a characteristic of f-block elements.

This is due to poor shielding of f electrons. The extent of actinoid contraction is greater than lanthanoid contraction.

With increase in atomic number i.e. in moving down a group, the number of the principal shell increases and therefore, the size of the atom increases. But in case of f block elements there is a steady decrease in atomic size with increase in atomic number due to lanthanide contraction. As we move through the lanthanide series, 4f electrons are being added one at each step.

The mutual shielding effect of f electrons is very little. This is due to the shape of the f orbitals. The nuclear charge, however increases by one at each step. Hence, the inward pull experienced by the 4f electrons increases. This causes a reduction in the size of the entire 4fn shell.

Hence, the correct option is (B).

98. Acetone reacts with bleaching powder $CaOCl_2$ and undergoes a haloform reaction to give chloroform as the product.

The reaction is as follows:

$CH_3COCH_3 + 3CaOCl_2 \rightarrow CH_3COCl_3 + 3CaOH$

$CH_3COCl_3 + CaOH \rightarrow CH_3COOCa + CHCl_3$
(chloroform)

So, Acetone reacts with bleaching powder to give chloroform.

Hence, the correct option is (A).

99. The common name of hloropicrin is Tear gas.

Chloropicrin is used as an insecticide and also called tear gas. Its formula is CCl₃NO₂ Chemically it is called trichloronitromethane.

It is used as a warning agent when it is added at 2% or less by weight to methyl bromide. It is used in riots and war-like situations. It has an intensely irritating odour. It is nitromethane.

Hence, the correct option is (B).

100. CH_3NH_2 is primary alkyl amine and undergoes reaction with HNO_2 to give methanol in the following manner.

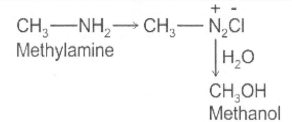

The reaction takes place at very low temperatures of about $0° - 5°C$. The intermediate is methyldiazonium, which upon hydrolysis gives methanol. Nitrogen is also produced as a side product.

Hence, the correct option is (A).

Physics & Chemistry : Mock Test 06

Physics

Q.1 Which of the following is not essential for the simple harmonic motion?

[UPSESSB TGT Science, 2019]

A. Inertia
B. Restoring force
C. Material medium
D. Gravity

Q.2 The ends of a rod of length l and mass m are attached to two identical springs as shown in the figure. The rod is free to rotate about its center O. The rod is depressed slightly at end A and released. The time period of the resulting oscillation is:

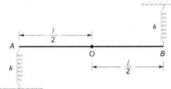

A. $2\pi\sqrt{\dfrac{m}{2k}}$ B. $2\pi\sqrt{\dfrac{2m}{k}}$ C. $\pi\sqrt{\dfrac{2m}{3k}}$ D. $\pi\sqrt{\dfrac{3m}{2k}}$

Q.3 When sounded together, a column of air and a tuning fork produce 4 beats per second. The tuning fork gives the lower note. The temperature of the air is 15°C. When the temperature falls to 10°C, the two produce 3 beats per second. Find the frequency of the fork.

A. 100 Hz   B. 110 Hz   C. 120 Hz   D. 130 Hz

Q.4 Which of the following figures represents the variation of particle momentum and associated de Broglie wavelength?

A.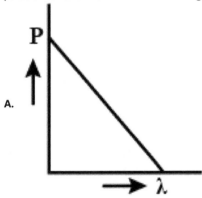

B.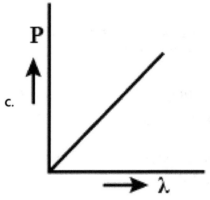

C.

D.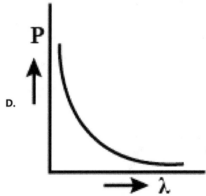

Q.5 A radio transmitter operates at a frequency $880 kHz$ and a power of $10 kW$. The number of photons emitted per second is:

A. 1.71×10^{31}
B. 1.327×10^{25}
C. 1.327×10^{37}
D. 1.327×10^{45}

Q.6 In an intrinsic semiconductor, the energy gap E_g is $12 eV$. Its hole mobility is very much smaller than electron mobility and is independent of temperature. What is the ratio between conductivity at $600\ K$ and that at $300\ K$? Assume that the temperature dependence of intrinsic carrier

concentration n_i is expressed as $n_i = n_0 \exp\left[\frac{-E_g}{2k_BT}\right]$ where n_0 is a constant and $k_B = 8.62 \times 10^{-5} eVK^{-1}$ is the Boltzmann constant.

A. $\exp(12.6) = 1 \times 10^5$
B. $\exp(13.6) = 1 \times 10^5$
C. $\exp(14.6) = 1 \times 10^5$
D. $\exp(11.6) = 1 \times 10^5$

Q.7 The heat given to a substance during the phase change is called _____.
A. Specific heat
B. Latent heat
C. Thermal capacity
D. None of these

Q.8 The spectrum of an oil flame is an example for _____.
A. line absorption spectrum
B. band emission specturm
C. line emission spectrum
D. continuous emission spectrum

Q.9 The relation between half-life $\left(t_{\frac{1}{2}}\right)$ of a radioactive sample and its mean life is:
A. $t_{\frac{1}{2}} = 0.693\tau$
B. $t_{\frac{1}{2}} = \tau$
C. $t_{\frac{1}{2}} = 2.303\tau$
D. $\frac{1}{t_{\frac{1}{2}}} = 0.693\tau$

Q.10 Half life of-a radio-active substance is 2 years. The amount of substance left after 6 years is:
A. $\frac{1}{16}$
B. $\frac{1}{8}$
C. $\frac{1}{4}$
D. $\frac{1}{6}$

Q.11 The focal lengths of objective and eyepiece of a telescope is 20 cm and 4 cm respectively. Find the magnification produced by the telescope.
A. 10
B. 6
C. 5
D. 80

Q.12 An object is placed at a distance of 10 cm in front of a double convex lens made of glass of refractive index 1.5. Both the radii of curvature of the lens are 20 cm in magnitude. What is the position of the image formed?
A. -35 cm
B. 10 cm
C. -20 cm
D. 20 cm

Q.13 For a sound wave, frequency is $8800\ Hz$ and speed is $352\ m/s$ in a given medium. The wavelength of the wave is:
A. 0.4 m
B. 0.03 m
C. 0.25 m
D. 0.04 m

Q.14 'VA' is the unit of which one?
A. Electric resistance
B. Electric energy
C. Electric power
D. Electric current

Q.15 The meter bridge is used to:
A. Measure the electric current in a circuit
B. Measure the potential difference across a resistance
C. Measure the resistance of a resistor
D. Measure the power supplied in the circuit

Q.16 A wire in the form of a circular loop of radius $10cm$ lies with its plane normal to a magnetic field $100T$. If the wire is pulled to take a square shape in the same plane in time $0.1s$, then the emf induced in the loop is given by:
A. 6.2V
B. 6.4V
C. 1.7V
D. 6.7V

Q.17 A wheel with 10 metallic spokes each $0.5\ m$ long is rotated with a speed of 120 rev/min in a plane normal to the horizontal component of earth's magnetic field H_E at a place. If $H_E = 0.4G$ at the place, what is the induced emf between the axle and the rim of the wheel? Note that $1G = 10^{-4}\ T$.
A. $6.28 \times 10^{-5}\ V$
B. $4.28 \times 10^{-5}\ V$
C. $4.48 \times 10^{-5}\ V$
D. $3.28 \times 10^{-5}\ V$

Q.18 A thin semicircular conducting ring of radius R is falling with its plane vertical in horizontal magnetic induction $\vec{B}$. At the position MNQ, the speed of the ring is V, and the potential difference developed across the ring is:
A. Zero
B. $\frac{1}{2}Bv\pi R^2$ and M is at a higher potential
C. πRBv and Q is at a higher potential
D. $2RBv$ and Q is at a higher potential

Q.19 The resistance of a wire at room temperature $30°C$ is found to be 10Ω. Now, to increase the resistance by 10% the temperature of the wire must be [The temperature coefficient of resistance of the material of wire is $0.002°C$].
A. $36°C$
B. $83°C$
C. $63°C$
D. $33°C$

Q.20 If a full-wave rectifier circuit is operating from 50 Hz mains, then the fundamental frequency in the ripple will be
A. 70.7 Hz
B. 100 Hz
C. 25 Hz
D. 59 Hz

Q.21 What is the relation between α and β in a transistor?
A. $\alpha = \frac{1-\beta}{\beta}$
B. $\alpha = \frac{\beta}{1-\beta}$
C. $\alpha = \frac{\beta}{1+\beta}$
D. $\alpha = \frac{1+\beta}{\beta}$

Q.22 A p-n junction acts as a _____.
A. Controlled switch
B. Bidirectional switch
C. Unidirectional switch
D. None of these

Q.23 The universal constant of gravitation _____.
A. Has no units and dimensions as it is a constant
B. Its value remains constant in all system of units
C. That's not depends upon the nature of the medium in which the bodies are placed
D. Its a force of repulsion

Q.24 A gas is compressed to half of its initial volume isothermally. The same gas is compressed again until the volume reduces to half through an adiabatic process. Then:
A. Work done during isothermal compression is more
B. Work done is independent of the processes used for compression
C. Work done is more during the adiabatic process
D. Work done is dependent on the atomicity of the gas

Q.25 A point on $P-V$ diagram shows:
A. A thermodynamic process
B. The state of the system
C. Work done on or by the system
D. None of the above

Q.26 A quantity of heat Q is supplied to a monoatomic ideal gas which expands at constant pressure. The fraction of heat that goes into work done by the gas is:
A. $\frac{2}{5}$ B. $\frac{3}{5}$ C. $\frac{2}{3}$ D. $\frac{4}{5}$

Q.27 A ball balanced on a vertical rod is an example of:
A. Stable equilibrium
B. Unstable equilibrium
C. Neutral equilibrium
D. Perfect equilibrium

Q.28 What did Archimedes determine after discovering the Archimedes principle?
A. Purity of milk
B. Purity of gold in the king's crown
C. Design concept of ship
D. Design concept of submarine

Q.29 Bernoulli's equation is applied to:
A. Venturimeter
B. Orifice meter
C. Pitot tube meter
D. All of the above

Q.30 Which of the following material has the highest relative permittivity?
A. Water
B. Transformer Oil
C. Epoxy Resin
D. Mica

Q.31 Figure shows tracks of three charged particles in a uniform electrostatic field, which particle has the highest charge to mass ratio?

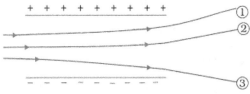

A. 1
B. 2
C. 3
D. None of the above

Q.32 Which of the following statements about electric field lines associated with electric charges is false?
A. Electric field lines can be either straight or curved
B. Electric field lines form closed loops
C. Electric field lines begin on positive charges and end on negative charges
D. Electric field lines do not intersect

Q.33 The electric field strength of a charge:
A. Increases with distance
B. Decreases with a cube of the distance
C. Decreases with distance
D. Decreases with the square of the distance

Q.34 What is the absolute permittivity of a substance?
A. The ratio of electric field intensity with magnetic field density, which produces that field density.
B. The ratio of electric field intensity with electric field density, which produces that field intensity.
C. The ratio of magnetic field density with electric field intensity, which produces that field density.
D. The ratio of electric field density with electric field intensity, which produces that field density.

Q.35 If the conductor is stationary and the field is changing (varying), then emf induced in it. Such an emf is known as:
A. Self-induced emf
B. Back emf
C. Static-induced emf
D. Dynamically-induced emf

Q.36 A hollow metallic sphere of radius r is kept at a potential of 1 volt. The total electric flux coming out of the concentric spherical surface of radius $R(>r)$ is:
A. $4\pi\varepsilon_0 r$
B. $4\pi\varepsilon_0 r^2$
C. $4\pi\varepsilon_0 R$
D. None of these

Q.37 Electric displacement density D at any point on the spherical surface of radius r with a charge Q at the center in a medium with dielectric constant ε is:
A. $\frac{Q}{(4\pi\varepsilon r^2)}$
B. $\frac{Q}{(4\pi r^2)}$
C. $\left(\frac{Q}{4\pi\varepsilon r^2}\right)$
D. $\frac{Q}{(4\pi r)^2}$

Q.38 Two-point masses of 0.3kg and 0.7kg are fixed at the ends of a rod which is of length 1.4m and of negligible mass. The rod is set rotating about an axis perpendicular to its length with a uniform angular speed. The point on the rod through which the axis should pass in order that the work required for rotation of the rod is minimum is located at a distance of:
A. 0.42 m from the mass of 0.3kg
B. 0.70 m from the mass of 0.7kg
C. 0.98m from the mass of 0.3kg
D. 0.98m from the mass of 0.7kg

Q.39 A bob of mass M is suspended by a massless string of length L. The horizontal velocity V at position A is just sufficient to make it reach point B. The angle at which the speed of the bob is half of that at A satisfies.

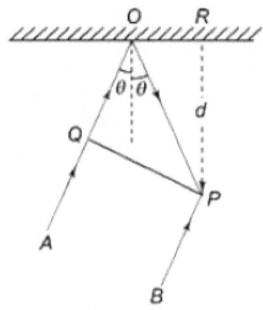

A. 2.1 mm   B. 1.9 mm   C. 1.8 mm   D. 1.7 mm

Q.44 In the figure given below, PQ represents a plane wavefront and AO and BP represent the corresponding extreme rays of monochromatic light of wavelength λ. The value of angle θ for which the ray BP and the reflected ray OP interfere constructively is given by

A. $\theta = \frac{\pi}{2}$
B. $\frac{\pi}{4} < \theta < \frac{\pi}{2}$
C. $\frac{\pi}{2} < \theta < 3\frac{\pi}{4}$
D. $\frac{3\pi}{2} < \theta < \pi$

Q.40 Light of wavelength 6900 Å is incident on a biprism of refracting angle 1° and refractive index 1.5. Interference fringes are observed on a screen 80 cm away from the biprism. If the distance between the source and the biprism is 20 cm, then the fringe width will be -

A. 0.098 mm   B. 0.197 mm
C. 0.395 mm   D. 0.049 mm

Q.41 4 g of a gas occupies 22.4 liters at NTP. The specific heat capacity of the gas at constant volume is 5.0 J/K-mol. If the speed of sound in this gas at NTP is 952 m/s, then the heat capacity at constant pressure is (Take gas constant R = 8.3 J/K-mol)

A. 7 J/K-mol   B. 7.5 J/K-mol
C. 8 J/K-mol   D. 8.5 J/K-mol

Q.42 Unpolarised light is incident from air on a plane surface of a material of refractive index $'\mu'$. At a particular angle of incidence $'i'$, it is found that the reflected and refracted rays are perpendicular to each other. Which of the following options is correct for this situation?

[NEET UG, 2018]

A. $i = \sin^{-1}\left(\frac{1}{\mu}\right)$
B. Reflected light is polarised with its electric vector perpendicular to the plane of incidence
C. Reflected light is polarised with its electric vector parallel to the plane of incidence
D. $i = \tan^{-1}\left(\frac{1}{\mu}\right)$

Q.43 In Young's double slit experiment the separation d between the slits is $2\ mm$, the wavelength λ of the light used is $5896Å$ and distance D between the screen and slits is $100\ cm$. It is found that the angular width of the fringes is $0.20°$. To increase the fringe angular width to $0.21°$ (with same λ and D) the separation between the slits needs to be changed to:

A. $\cos\theta = \frac{\lambda}{2d}$
B. $\cos\theta = \frac{\lambda}{4d}$
C. $\sec\theta = \frac{\lambda}{3d}$
D. $\sec\theta = \frac{2\lambda}{3d}$

Q.45 The displacement of a body from a reference point is given by $\sqrt{x} = 2t + 3$ where x is in metres and t in seconds. This shows that the body is:

A. At rest   B. Accelerated
C. Decelerated   D. In uniform motion

Q.46 Find the temperature at which root-mean-square speed of an oxygen molecule will be sufficient to take it away from the surface of the earth. Given: escape speed from the surface of the earth $= 11.2\ km\ s^{-1}$, mass of an oxygen molecule $= 2.76 \times 10^{-26}\ kg$, Boltzmann constant $= 1.38 \times 10^{-23}\ J\ K^{-1}$

A. $5.16 \times 10^4 K$ B. $8.36 \times 10^4 K$
C. $2.45 \times 10^4 K$ D. $9.12 \times 10^4 K$

Q.47 A given quantity of an ideal gas is at pressure P and absolute temperature T. The isothermal bulk modulus of the gas is

A. $\frac{2}{3}P$ B. P C. $\frac{3}{2}P$ D. $2P$

Q.48 A $100A$ current is flowing in an overhead power cable. Find the magnitude of the magnetic field at a distance $2\ m$ from the cable.

A. $10^{-5}\ T$ **B.** $10^{-6}\ T$ **C.** $10^{-7}\ T$ **D.** $10^{-4}\ T$

Q.49 The magnetic field due to a straight current-carrying wire is-
A. inversely proportional to the current in the wire
B. directly proportional to the current in the wire
C. inversely proportional to the square of the current in the wire
D. does not depend on the current in the wire

Q.50 Which of the following is not the characteristics of Planck's black body radiation distribution:
A. As temperature increases, the peak of the curve shift towards higher wavelength
B. Spectral emissive power varies continuously with the change in wavelength
C. At a given wavelength, as temperature increases, emissive power also increases
D. Total emissive power is proportional to T^4

Chemistry

Q.51 _____ is the most electropositive and _____ is the most electronegative element of the third period of the modern periodic table.
A. Sodium, Potassium
B. Magnesium, Aluminium
C. Sodium, Chlorine
D. Aluminium, Chlorine

A. B **B.** D **C.** A **D.** C

Q.52 The Electronic configuration of Magnesium is _____.
A. $1s^2, 2s^2, 2p^4, 3s^2$ **B.** $1s^2, 2s^2, 2p^6, 3s^1$
C. $1s^2, 2s^2, 2p^6, 3s^2$ **D.** $1s^2, 2s^2, 2p^7, 3s^2$

Q.53 $50ml$ of $0.6M NaOH$ is added to $100ml$ of $0.6M$ acetic acid. What is the additional volume of $1.2M NaOH$ required for making the solution of $pH 4.74$? The ionization constant of acetic acid is 1.8×10^{-5}

A. 0 **B.** 2 **C.** 4 **D.** 10

Q.54 At equilibrium, $500ml$ vessel contains $1.5M$ of each A, B, C, D if $0.5M$ of C and D expelled out then what would be the K_c?

A. 1 **B.** $\frac{1}{9}$ **C.** $\frac{4}{9}$ **D.** $\frac{5}{9}$

Q.55 Nitration of aniline in strong acidic medium also gives m-nitroaniline because

[NEET UG, 2018]

A. In absence of substituents nitro group always goes to m-position.
B. In electrophilic substitution reactions amino group is meta directive
C. Inspite of substituents nitro group always goes to only m-position.
D. In acidic (strong) medium aniline is present as anilinium ion.

Q.56 $2K(s) + F_2(g) \rightarrow 2K^+F^-(s)$ is a type of _____ reaction.
A. Disproportionation **B.** Combustion
C. Corrosion **D.** Redox

Q.57 The oxidative rusting of iron under Earth's atmosphere is _____.
A. Fast reaction
B. Slow reaction
C. Moderate rate reaction
D. Both (A) and (C)

Q.58 _____ is the unit for the rate of a chemical reaction.
A. Mole ^{-1}s **B.** Mole $^{-1}s^{-1}$
C. Mole $1s$ **D.** Mole $^{-1}$

Q.59 The most common molecular collisions are in between:
A. 2 molecules **B.** 3 molecules
C. 4 molecules **D.** 5 molecules

Q.60 The freezing point of equimolal aqueous solution will be highest for:
A. $C_6H_5NH_3^+Cl^-$ **B.** $Ca(NO_3)_2$
C. $La(NO_3)_2$ **D.** $C_6H_{12}O_6$

Q.61 A solution containing $1.8\ g$ of a compound (empirical formula CH_2O) in $40\ g$ of water is observed to freeze at $-0.465 C$. The molecular formula of the compound is (K_f of water $= 1.86\ kg\ kmol^{-1}$)
A. $C_2H_4O_2$ **B.** C_3H_6
C. $C_4H_8O_4$ **D.** $C_6H_{12}O_6$

Q.62 $1.00\ g$ of a non-electrolyte solute (molar mass $250\ g\ mol^{-1}$) was dissolved in $51.2\ g$ of benzene. If the freezing point depression constant, K_f of benzene is $5.12\ k\ kgmol^{-1}$, the freezing point of benzene will be lowered by:

A. $0.4\ K$ **B.** $0.3\ K$ **C.** $0.5\ K$ **D.** $0.2\ K$

Q.63 Calculate the number of kJ of heat necessary to raise the temperature of $60\ g$ of aluminium from $35°C$ to $55°C$. Molar heat capacity of Al is $24J\ mol^{-1}K^{-1}$.
A. 2.07 kJ **B.** 3.07 kJ **C.** 1.07 kJ **D.** 4.07 kJ

Q.64 A well-stoppered thermos flask contains some ice cubes. This is an example of:
A. Closed system
B. Open system
C. Isolated system
D. Non-thermodynamics system

Q.65 Hess's law of constant heat summation is based on:
A. $E = mc^2$
B. conservation of mass
C. first law of thermodynamics
D. $E = h\nu$

Q.66 In a cubic unit cell, seven of the eight corners are occupied by atom A and faces are occupied by B. The general formula of the substance having this type of structure would be:
A. A_7B_{14} B. $A_{14}B_7$ C. A_7B_{24} D. A_9B_{24}

Q.67 Crystalline solids are _____ in nature.
A. pseudo solids
B. anisotropic
C. isotropic
D. short range order

Q.68 Which of the following is the correct definition for crystal lattice?
A. An arrangement of atoms in space.
B. Three dimensional arrangement of points in space.
C. A regular arrangement of the points in space.
D. None of the above

Q.69 Who proposed the concept of dispersion force?
A. Heitler and London
B. Van der Waals
C. Gay Lussac
D. Fritz London

Q.70 What will be the minimum pressure required to compress $500 dm^3$ of air at 1 bar to $200 dm^3$ at $30°C$?
A. 12.5 bar B. 3.5 bar C. 1.5 bar D. 2.5 bar

Q.71 Which of the following is true regarding the reactivity order of alkali metals towards hydrogen?
A. $Li < Na < K > Rb$
B. $Li < Na < K < Rb < Cs$
C. $Li > Na < Cs$
D. $Li < Rb > Cs$

Q.72 Which of the following is not a heteroatom?
A. Oxygen B. Nitrogen C. Carbon D. Sulphur

Q.73 Which of the following represents the correct order of increasing first ionization enthalpy for Ca, Ba, S, Se and Ar.
A. $Ca < S < Ba < Se < A$
B. $S < Se < Ca < Ba < Ar$
C. $Ba < Ca < Se < S < Ar$
D. $Ca < Ba < S < Se < Ar$

Q.74 Starting from alumina would obtain:
A. Aluminium nitride
B. Aluminium
C. Aluminium oxide
D. Aluminium silicate

Q.75 The element with atomic number 35 belongs to:
A. s-block B. p-block C. d-block D. f-block

Q.76 The structure of IF_7 is:
A. Pentagonal bipyramidal
B. Square pyramidal
C. Trigonal bipyramidal
D. Octahedral

Q.77 Which of the following is a lyophobic colloidal solution?
A. Gold solution
B. Aqueous starch solution
C. Polymer solvent in some organic solvents
D. Aqueous protein solution

Q.78 Calculate energy of one mole of photons of radiation whose frequency is 5×10^{14} Hz.
A. $199.51\ kJ\ mol^{-1}$ B. $201.51\ kJ\ mol^{-1}$
C. $193.51\ kJ\ mol^{-1}$ D. $199.51\ J\ mol$

Q.79 A compound processes 8% sulphur by mass. The least molecular mass is:
A. 200 B. 400 C. 155 D. 355

Q.80 Three faradays of electricity are passed through molten Al_2O_3, aqueous solution of $CuSO_4$, and molten $NaCl$ taken in separate electrolytic cells. The amounts of Al, Cu and Na deposited at the cathodes will be in the molar ratio:
A. $1:2:3$ B. $3:2:1$
C. $1:1.5:3$ D. $1.5:2:3$

Q.81 For the cell reaction $2Fe^{3+}(aq) + 2I^-(aq) \rightarrow 2Fe^{2+}(aq) + I_2(aq)$
$E^\ominus_{cell} = 0.24V$ at $298K$. The standard Gibbs energy $(\Delta_r G^\ominus)$ of the cell reaction is: [Given that Faraday constant $F = 96500\ C\ mol^{-1}$]

[NEET UG, 2019]

A. $-46.32\ kJ\ mol^{-1}$ B. $-23.16\ kJ\ mol^{-1}$
C. $46.32\ kJ\ mol^{-1}$ D. $23.16\ kJ\ mol^{-1}$

Q.82 The conductivity of $0.05M$ solution of $MgCl_2$ is $194.5 \Omega - 1\ cm^2\ mol - 1$ at $25°C$. A cell with electrodes that are $1.50\ cm^2$ in surface area and $0.5\ cm$ apart is filled with the above solution. The resistance shown by the solution is
A. 25.2Ω B. 34.27Ω C. 42.52Ω D. 51.7Ω

Q.83 Which of the following ligands form a chelate?
A. Acetate B. Oxalate
C. Cyanide D. Ammonia

Q.84 The complex ion which has no d-electrons in the central metal atom is:
A. $[MnO_4]^-$ B. $[Co(NH_3)_6]^{3+}$
C. $[Fe(CN)_6]^{3-}$ D. $[Cr(H_2O)_6]^{3+}$

Q.85 Pick out the correct statement with respect to $[Mn(CN)_6]^{3-}$:
A. It is dsp^2 hybridised and square planar
B. It is sp^3d^2 hybridised and octahedral
C. It is sp^3d^2 hybridised and tetrahedral
D. It is d^2sp^3 hybridised and octahedral

Q.86
$R - CH = CRO^- + CH_2 - N^+R_2 \rightarrow NR_2 - CH_2 - CHR - CRO$

The given reaction in an example of:

[Graduate Pharmacy Aptitude Test, 2015]

A. Arndt-Eistert homologation
B. Mannich reaction
C. Michael addition

D. Chichibabin amination reaction

Q.87 The carbonyl stretching frequency for simple aldehydes, ketones, and carboxylic acids is about $1710\ cm^{-1}$, where the carbonyl stretching frequency for esters is about .... cm^{-1}:

[Graduate Pharmacy Aptitude Test, 2015]

A. 1650 B. 1700 C. 1750 D. 1850

Q.88 Arrange the following esters as per decreasing order of rate of saponification:
(I) Ethyl benzoate
(II) Ethyl p- methoxybenzoate
(III) Ethyl p- chlorobenzoate
(IV) Ethyl p-nitrobenzoate

[Graduate Pharmacy Aptitude Test, 2015]

A. $I > II > III > IV$ B. $IV > III > II > I$
C. $IV > III > I > II$ D. $II > IV > I > III$

Q.89 Which of the following combination doesn't evolve Cl_2 gas?
A. $HCl(aq) + KMnO_4$
B. $HCl + MnO_2$
C. $HCl + I_2$
D. $HCl + F_2$

Q.90 In the given reaction

$(A) + (B) \xrightarrow[5°C]{NaOH} CH_3 - \underset{\underset{CH_3}{|}}{\overset{\overset{OH}{|}}{CH}} - CH - CH$

A and B will respectively be:
A. $H_3C - CH_2 - CHO$ and $CH_3 - CH_2 - CHO$
B. $H_3C - CHO$ and $CH_3 - CH_2 - CHO$
C. $H_3C - CHO$ and $CH_3 - CHO$
D. $H_3C - CHO$ and $H_3C - \underset{\underset{CH_3}{|}}{\overset{\overset{OH}{|}}{C}} - CHO$

Q.91 In the reaction sequence

$CH_3 - CH_2 - COOH \xrightarrow{H_2O_2} [X] \xrightarrow{\Delta} [Y]$

$[Y]$ will be:
A. $CH_3 - \overset{\overset{OH}{|}}{CH} - COOH$
B. $CH_2 = CH - COOH$
C. $\overset{\overset{OH}{|}}{CH_2} - CH_2 - COOH$
D. Lactide

Q.92 Which of the following does not reduce Benedict's solution?
A. Sucrose B. Aldehyde
C. Glucose D. Fructose

Q.93 The most basic amino acid is:
A. Glutamine B. Glycine
C. Asparagine D. Histidine

Q.94 The term PVC used in plastic industry stands for:
A. Polyvinyl chloride
B. Polyvinyl carbonate
C. Phosphor vanadium chloride
D. Phospho vinyl chloride

Q.95 Which of the following polymer is thermosetting polymer?
A. Terylene B. Polystyrene
C. Bakelite D. Neoprene

Q.96 Biomass is used instead of extensive use of petroleum. This is an application of:
A. Green revolution
B. Waste management
C. Green chemistry
D. Revolution resource recovery

Q.97 _____ is an environment-friendly product and better than halons which are used to extinguish fire.
A. Ibuprofen B. Pyrocool
C. Carcinogen D. Carbon-dioxide

Q.98 Which compound is used in Ultra-violet calibration?
A. Hg_2Cl_2 B. $HgCl_2$
C. $K_2Cr_2O_7$ D. $KMnO_4$

Q.99 Which compound forms double salt with sulphates of alkali metals?
A. Ferric oxide B. Silver nitrate
C. Ferric chloride D. Ferrous sulphate

Q.100 Elimination reaction of 2-Bromo-pentane to form pent-2-ene is:
(a) β-Elimination reaction
(b) Follows Zaitsev rule
(c) Dehydrohalogenation reaction
(d) Dehydration reaction

[NEET UG, 2020], [MPPEB Sub Engineer (Mechanical), 2020]

A. (a), (c), (d) B. (b), (c), (d)
C. (a), (b), (d) D. (a), (b), (c)

Physics & Chemistry : Mock Test - 6

// Smart Answer Sheet //

Correct Indicates percentage of students who answered questions correctly.

Skipped Indicates percentage of students who skipped questions.

Q.	Ans.	Correct / Skipped	Q.	Ans.	Correct / Skipped	Q.	Ans.	Correct / Skipped	Q.	Ans.	Correct / Skipped	Q.	Ans.	Correct / Skipped
1	D	41.74 % / 1.88 %	17	A	60.99 % / 1.48 %	33	D	46.01 % / 1.23 %	49	B	40.43 % / 1.89 %	65	C	66.25 % / 1.99 %
2	C	23.04 % / 3.55 %	18	D	21.14 % / 4.88 %	34	D	89.63 % / 0.0 %	50	A	12.2 % / 3.36 %	66	C	59.88 % / 1.77 %
3	B	22.55 % / 4.53 %	19	B	48.72 % / 1.98 %	35	C	85.26 % / 0.0 %	51	D	57.66 % / 1.91 %	67	B	84.33 % / 0.0 %
4	D	82.51 % / 0.0 %	20	B	54.92 % / 1.17 %	36	A	52.65 % / 1.17 %	52	C	46.05 % / 1.06 %	68	C	40.95 % / 1.62 %
5	A	56.4 % / 1.89 %	21	C	65.96 % / 1.12 %	37	B	56.79 % / 1.52 %	53	A	68.49 % / 1.73 %	69	D	59.59 % / 1.7 %
6	D	22.13 % / 3.64 %	22	D	66.64 % / 1.99 %	38	C	56.27 % / 1.14 %	54	C	23.52 % / 4.87 %	70	D	68.51 % / 1.12 %
7	B	79.53 % / 0.0 %	23	C	69.0 % / 1.29 %	39	D	13.7 % / 3.84 %	55	D	59.54 % / 1.62 %	71	B	61.32 % / 1.22 %
8	D	55.42 % / 1.0 %	24	C	54.35 % / 2.0 %	40	B	58.37 % / 1.09 %	56	D	79.92 % / 0.0 %	72	C	77.71 % / 0.0 %
9	A	58.29 % / 1.64 %	25	B	78.18 % / 0.0 %	41	C	43.05 % / 1.24 %	57	B	78.93 % / 0.0 %	73	C	49.27 % / 1.24 %
10	B	88.43 % / 0.0 %	26	A	58.46 % / 1.98 %	42	B	80.5 % / 0.0 %	58	B	19.6 % / 3.87 %	74	A	19.65 % / 3.01 %
11	C	87.21 % / 0.0 %	27	B	85.54 % / 0.0 %	43	B	49.17 % / 1.62 %	59	A	11.48 % / 3.58 %	75	B	61.71 % / 1.97 %
12	C	41.76 % / 1.57 %	28	B	76.76 % / 0.0 %	44	B	67.36 % / 1.73 %	60	D	89.08 % / 0.0 %	76	A	42.27 % / 1.17 %
13	D	78.51 % / 0.0 %	29	D	41.45 % / 1.24 %	45	A	42.64 % / 1.44 %	61	D	44.72 % / 1.48 %	77	A	54.13 % / 1.39 %
14	C	87.07 % / 0.0 %	30	A	83.78 % / 0.0 %	46	B	68.49 % / 1.88 %	62	A	63.38 % / 1.76 %	78	A	62.84 % / 1.03 %
15	C	87.56 % / 0.0 %	31	C	60.29 % / 1.27 %	47	B	64.8 % / 1.74 %	63	C	45.49 % / 1.15 %	79	B	11.68 % / 3.12 %
16	D	52.14 % / 1.39 %	32	B	43.92 % / 1.54 %	48	A	58.09 % / 1.87 %	64	C	82.58 % / 0.0 %	80	C	63.78 % / 1.88 %

301

Physics & Chemistry : Mock Test - 6

Q.	Ans.	Correct / Skipped	Q.	Ans.	Correct / Skipped	Q.	Ans.	Correct / Skipped	Q.	Ans.	Correct / Skipped	Q.	Ans.	Correct / Skipped
81	A	14.04 % / 3.6 %	85	D	20.49 % / 4.25 %	89	C	51.83 % / 1.8 %	93	D	85.36 % / 0.0 %	97	B	47.34 % / 1.58 %
82	B	54.22 % / 1.71 %	86	B	78.33 % / 0.0 %	90	B	40.24 % / 1.82 %	94	A	86.88 % / 0.0 %	98	C	52.85 % / 1.24 %
83	B	62.28 % / 1.83 %	87	C	48.8 % / 1.37 %	91	B	41.52 % / 1.97 %	95	C	89.0 % / 0.0 %	99	D	59.7 % / 1.99 %
84	A	57.74 % / 1.13 %	88	C	49.38 % / 1.71 %	92	A	89.57 % / 0.0 %	96	C	59.78 % / 1.35 %	100	D	23.25 % / 4.19 %

Performance Analysis	
Avg. Score (%)	61.0%
Toppers Score (%)	71.0%
Your Score	

//Hints and Solutions//

1. The simple harmonic motion requires a restoring force, as that brings the objects back to the equilibrium position.

Restoring force requires inertia, as that keeps the object moving through equilibrium, resulting in harmonic motion.

Inertia requires elasticity, as that is the source of the restoring force, elasticity results in the spring constant (k).

Vibrations in spring are possible without gravity.

Gravity is not necessary for spring motion, it may be necessary for pendulum harmonic motion.

Also, the pendulum is not an example of perfect SHM.

So, gravity is not essential for simple harmonic motion.

Hence, the correct option is (D).

2. Let the rod be depressed by a small amount x Both the springs are compressed by x.

When the rod is released, the restoring torque is given by

$$\tau = (kx) \times \frac{l}{2} + (kx) \times \frac{l}{2}$$

$$= (kx)l$$

Now $\tan\theta = \frac{x}{\frac{l}{2}} = \frac{2x}{l}$. since θ is small, \(\tan \theta=\theta,\) where θ is expressed in radian.

Thus $\theta = \frac{2x}{l}$ or $x = \frac{\theta l}{2}$.

So, $\tau = k\left(\frac{\theta l}{2}\right) \times l = \frac{k\theta l^2}{2}$

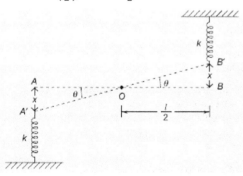

If I is the moment of inertia of the rod about O, then

or $I\frac{d^2\theta}{dt^2} = -\left(\frac{kl^2}{2}\right)\theta$

$\frac{d^2\theta}{dt^2} = -\left(\frac{kl^2}{2I}\right)\theta$

Since $\frac{d^2\theta}{dt^2} \propto (-\theta)$, the motion is simple harmonic whose angular frequency is given by

$\omega = \sqrt{\frac{kl^2}{2I}}$

Now $\omega = \frac{2\pi}{T}$ and $I = \frac{ml^2}{12}$.

Therefore, we have

$\frac{2\pi}{T} = \sqrt{\frac{kl^2}{2} \times \frac{12}{ml^2}} = \sqrt{\frac{6k}{m}}$

or $T = \pi\sqrt{\frac{2m}{3k}}$

Hence, the correct option is (C).

3. Let v = Frequency of the tuning fork, v_1 = Frequency of the air column At $15°C, v_1 = v + 4$

At $10°C, v_1 = v + 3$

We know, velocity u $= v\lambda$

$\therefore U_{15} = (V + 4)\lambda$

and $u_{10} = (v + 3)\lambda$

$\therefore \frac{u_{15}}{u_{10}} = \frac{v+4}{v+3}$ .....(1)

Also, $\frac{u_{15}}{u_{10}} = \sqrt{\frac{273+15}{273+10}} = \sqrt{\frac{288}{283}}$ ....(2)

From (1) and (2), we get

$\frac{v+4}{v+3} = \left(\frac{288}{283}\right)^{\frac{1}{2}} = \left(1 + \frac{5}{283}\right)^{\frac{1}{2}}$

Using binomial expansion and neglecting higher terms, we get

$\frac{v+4}{v+3} = \left(1 + \frac{1}{2} \times \frac{5}{283}\right) = 1 + \frac{5}{566}$

$\frac{(v+3)+1}{v+3} = 1 + \frac{5}{566}$

Or, $1 + \frac{1}{(v+3)} = 1 + \frac{5}{566}$

$\therefore \frac{1}{(v+3)} = 1 + \frac{5}{566}$

Or, $(v + 3) = 113.2$

$\therefore v = 110.2 Hz \simeq 110 Hz$

Hence, the correct option is (B).

4.

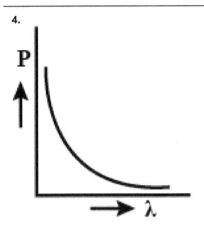

The de-Broglie wavelength is given by

$\lambda = \dfrac{n}{P}$

$\lambda \propto \dfrac{1}{P},$

$\lambda P =$ constant

Hence, the correct option is (D).

5. Power of transmitter,

$P = 10 kW$

$= 10 \times 10^3 W$

Frequency of the transmitter,

$v = 880 kHz$

$= 880 \times 10^3\ Hz$

Number of photons emitted per second

$N = \dfrac{P}{hv} = \dfrac{10 \times 10^3}{6.6 \times 10^{-34} \times 880 \times 10^3}$

$N = 1.71 \times 10^{31}$ photons emitted per second.

Hence, the correct option is (A).

6. As $\mu_e \gg \mu_{h'}$ and for an intrinsic semiconductor

$n_c = n_h = n_i$

∴ Conductivity is given by

$\sigma = e(n_e\mu_e + n_h\mu_h)$

$= en_i(\mu_e + \mu_h) = en_i\mu_e \quad [\because \mu_e \gg \mu_h]$

But $n_i = n_0 \exp\left[\dfrac{-E_g}{2k_BT}\right]$

∴ $\sigma = e\mu_e n_0 \exp\left[\dfrac{-E_g}{2k_BT}\right]$

Here all the pre-exponential terms are assumed independent of temperature. So we can put a constant

$\sigma_0 = e\mu_e n_0$

and express the conductivity as

$\sigma = \sigma_0 \exp\left[\dfrac{-E_g}{2k_BT}\right]$

Now $\dfrac{E_g}{2} = \dfrac{1.2}{2} = 0.6 eV, k_B = 8.62 \times 10^{-5} eVK^{-1}$

∴ $\sigma(600\ K) = \sigma_0 \exp\left[\dfrac{-0.6}{8.62 \times 10^{-5} \times 600}\right]$

$\sigma(300\ K) = \sigma_0 \exp\left[\dfrac{-0.6}{8.62 \times 10^{-5} \times 300}\right]$

Hence,

$\dfrac{\sigma(600\ K)}{\sigma(300\ K)} = \dfrac{\exp\left[\dfrac{-0.6}{8.62 \times 10^{-5} \times 600}\right]}{\exp\left[\dfrac{-0.6}{8.62 \times 10^{-5} \times 300}\right]}$

$= \exp\left[\dfrac{0.6}{8.62 \times 10^{-5}}\left(\dfrac{1}{300} - \dfrac{1}{600}\right)\right]$

$= \exp\left[\dfrac{0.6 \times 10^5}{8.62 \times 600}\right]$

$= \exp(11.6) = 1 \times 10^5$

This shows that the conductivity of a semiconductor increases rapidly with the rise in temperature.

Hence, the correct option is (D).

7. The heat given to the substance during the phase change is called latent heat. It can be either the latent heat of fusion or the latent heat of vaporization depending upon the phase change.

These are some important terms used related to latent heat:

- Liquid to solid: Latent heat of solidification
- Liquid to vapour: Latent heat of evaporation/vaporization (CD)
- Vapour to liquid: Latent heat of condensation

Hence, the correct option is (B).

8. The spectrum of an oil flame is an example for continuous emission spectrum.

Spectrum: When white light falls on a prism, different wavelengths' waves are deviated in different directions by the prism. The image obtained is coloured images of the slit and this image is called a spectrum. The spectra obtained are classified mainly into two types:

(i) emission spectra and (ii) absorption spectra.

(i) Continuous emission spectrum: It consists of unbroken luminous bands of all wavelengths containing all the colours from violet to red. These spectra depend on the temperature of the source only and are independent of the characteristic of the source.

For example: Incandescent solids, Carbon arc, liquids, electric filament lamps, etc.

(ii) Continuous absorption spectrum: When a pure green glass plate is placed in the path of white light, it absorbs everything except green and so it gives a continuous absorption spectrum.

Since the spectrum of an oil flame consists of continuously varying wavelengths in a definite wavelength range, it is an example of a continuous emission spectrum.

Hence, the correct option is (D).

9. As we know, the mean life (τ) of a radio-active delay is equal to the inverse of the wavelength (λ).

$$\tau = \frac{1}{\lambda} \quad ...(i)$$

Now as we know that wavelength (λ) is inversely proportional to half-life of radio-active sample.

$\lambda \propto \frac{1}{t_{\frac{1}{2}}} = \frac{k}{t_{\frac{1}{2}}}$, where k = proportionality constant, $t_{\frac{1}{2}}$ = half-life of radioactive sample.

And the value of $k = \ln 2 = 0.693$.

$$\lambda = \frac{0.693}{t_{\frac{1}{2}}} \quad ...(ii)$$

Now from equation (i) and (ii) we have,

$$\lambda = \frac{1}{\tau} = \frac{0.693}{t_{\frac{1}{2}}}$$

On simplifying it we get,

$$t_{\frac{1}{2}} = 0.693\tau$$

Hence, the correct option is (A).

10. Given:

Half-life = 2 years, total time = 6 years, and let the initial amount of radioactive substance (N_0)= 1

Since, half-life is 2 years so 6 years is equal to 3 half-lives.

We know that the fraction of substance remains after n half-lives,

$$N' = \frac{N_0}{2^n}$$

Where N' = amount remaining after n half-lives and N_0 = initial amount

So, $N' = \frac{N_0}{2^3}$

$\Rightarrow N' = \frac{N_0}{8} = \frac{1}{8}$

Hence, the correct option is (B).

11. Given that:

$f_0 = 20$ cm

$f_e = 4$ cm

The magnification of a telescope is given by:

$M = \frac{f_0}{f_e} \quad ... (1)$

Where, f_0 is the focal length of the objective and f_e is the focal length of the eyepiece.

Putting the value in equation (1),

Magnification, $M = \frac{f_0}{f_e} = \frac{20}{4} = 5$

Hence, the correct option is (C).

12. Given,

Distance of the object from the lens $= u = -10$ cm

Refractive index of the lens $= \mu = 1.5$

Radii of curvature of the lens are 20 cm in magnitude

$R_1 = 20$ cm and $R_2 = -20$ cm

(As per sign convention)

According to Len's Maker's formula

$$\frac{1}{f} = (\mu - 1)\left(\frac{1}{R_1} - \frac{1}{R_2}\right)$$

$$= (1.5 - 1)\left(\frac{1}{20} - \frac{1}{-20}\right)$$

$$= 0.5 \times \frac{2}{20} = \frac{1}{20} \text{ or,}$$

$$f = 20 \text{ cm}$$

From the Lens equation,

$$\frac{1}{v} - \frac{1}{u} = \frac{1}{f}$$

$$\frac{1}{v} = \frac{1}{f} + \frac{1}{u} \text{ or,}$$

$$v = \frac{fu}{u+f}$$

$$= \frac{20 \times (-10)}{-10 + 20}$$

$$= \frac{-200}{10}$$

$$= -20 \text{ cm}$$

The image is formed 20 cm on the same side as the object.

Hence, the correct option is (C).

13. Given,

Velocity $(v) = 352 \, m/s$

Frequency $(f) = 8800 \, Hz$

We know that,

Wavelength $(\lambda) = \frac{v}{f}$

$$\lambda = \frac{352}{8800}$$

= 0.04 m

Hence, the correct option is (D).

14. Volt-ampere (VA) is a measurement of electric power in a direct current (DC) electrical circuit. The VA specification is also used in alternating current (AC) circuits, but it is less precise in this application, because it represents apparent power, which often differs from true power .

In a DC circuit, 1 VA is the equivalent of one watt (1 W). The power, P (in watts) in a DC circuit is equal to the product of the voltage V (in volts) and the current I (in amperes):

P = VI

Hence, the correct option is (C).

15. Meter Bridge: It is an electrical instruments based on the principle of Wheatstone bridge and is used to measure the resistance of a resistor.

The metre bridge, also known as the slide wire bridge consists of a one metre long wire of uniform cross sectional area, fixed on a wooden block. A scale is attached to the block. Two gaps are formed on it by using thick metal strips in order to make the Wheat stones bridge.

The formula meter bridge is given below:

ρ = Lπr2X

Where, L be the length of the wire and r be its radius.

Hence, the correct option is (C).

16. Given:

Radius of wire $= 10cm$

Magnetic field $= 100T$

Time $= 0.1s$

Average induced emf in loop,

$2\pi R = 4L$

Therefore,

$L = \frac{\pi R}{2}$

$\Rightarrow \pi \times \frac{10}{2} = 5\pi cm$

$\Delta s = S_i - S_f$

$\Rightarrow \pi r^2 - L^2$

$= \pi(0.1)^2 - (5\pi)^2 \times 10°4$

$= 0.0067$

Now,

$e = \frac{\Delta \phi}{\Delta t}$

$\Rightarrow \frac{B.\Delta s}{\Delta t} = 100 \times \frac{0.0067}{0.1}$

= 6.7V

Hence, the correct option is (D).

17. Induced $emf = \left(\frac{1}{2}\right) \omega BR^2$

$= \left(\frac{1}{2}\right) \times 4\pi \times 0.4 \times 10^{-4} \times (0.5)^2$

$= 6.28 \times 10^{-5} V$

The number of spokes is immaterial because the emf's across the spokes are in parallel.

Hence, the correct option is (A).

18. We know that,

$E = \frac{d\phi}{dt} = \frac{BdA}{dt}$

When it is just about to move out:

$dA = 2R(vdt)$

$\frac{dA}{dt} = 2Rv$

So, $E = 2BRV$

Hence, the correct option is (D).

19. According to the question

Temperature coefficient of resistance of the wire,

$\alpha = \frac{0.002}{°C}$

Resistance at temperature,

$30°C = R_{30} = 10\Omega$

We know,

$R_T = R_0(1 + \alpha T)$

Putting the value of R_{30}, α and T in above equation we have

$10 = R_0(1 + 30\alpha)$ ... (i)

After 10% increase in resistance the new resistance becomes

$10 + 10 \times \frac{10}{100} = 11\Omega$

Again, for the new resistance we have

$11 = R_0(1 + \alpha T)$ ... (ii)

Dividing equation (ii) by (i), we get

$\frac{11}{10} = \frac{R_0(1+\alpha T)}{R_0(1+30\alpha)}$

R_0 gets cancelled out as it's the same material and same reference temperature.

Or, $\frac{11}{10} = \frac{(1+\alpha T)}{(1+30\alpha)}$

Or, $11(1 + 30\alpha) = 10(1 + \alpha T)$

Or, $11 + 330\alpha = 10 + 10\alpha T$

Or, $1 + 330\alpha = 10\alpha T$

Or, $\frac{1+330\alpha}{10\alpha} = T$

Putting the value of α, we get

$T = \frac{1+330\times 0.002}{10\times 0.002}$

Or, $T = 83°C$

Hence, the correct option is (B).

20. A full-wave rectifier consists of two junction diodes, so, its efficiency is twice that of a half-wave rectifier.

For full-wave rectifier, ripple frequency $= 2 \times$ input frequency

$= 2 \times 50$

$= 100$ Hz

Hence, the correct option is (B).

21. The common-emitter current gain (β) is the ratio of the transistor's collector current to the transistor's base current

i.e., $\beta = \frac{I_C}{I_B}$

And the common base DC current gain (α) is the ratio of the collector current of the transistor to the emitter current of the transistor i.e., $\beta = \frac{I_C}{I_B}$

Transistor currents are related by the following relation:

$I_E = I_B + I_C$

α can now be written as:

$\alpha = \frac{I_C}{I_B + I_C}$

On dividing both the numerator and the denominator by I_B, we get:

$\alpha = \frac{\frac{I_C}{I_B}}{\frac{1+I_C}{I_B}}$

Since $\beta = \frac{I_C}{I_B}$

$\alpha = \frac{\beta}{\beta + 1}$

Hence, the correct option is (C).

22. A p-n junction acts as a Unidirectional switch. A unilateral device is a device that conducts only in one direction. p-n junction diodes conduct only when the p region is connected to higher voltage and the n region is connected to lower voltage. When reverse biased, it acts as an open circuit.

The symbol for a diode is as shown:

Hence, the correct option is (D).

23. The universal constant of gravity is not one that depends on the nature of the medium in which the bodies are placed.

The gravitational constant can be defined as the constant relating the force exerted on the objects to the mass and distance between the objects. The value of the universal gravitation constant is found to be $G = 6.673 \times 10^{-11} Nm^2/kg^2$.

Hence, the correct option is (C).

24. A gas is compressed to half of its initial volume isothermally. The same gas is compressed again until the volume reduces to half through an adiabatic process. Then work done is more during the adiabatic process.

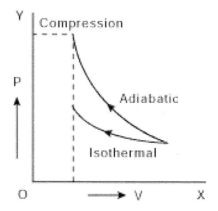

From the graph we can see that for compression of gas, area under the curve for adiabatic is more than isothermal process. Therefore, compressing the gas through adiabatic process will require more work to be done.

$W_{ext} =$ negative of area with volume-axis

W (adiabatic) $> W$ (isothermal)

Hence, the correct option is (C).

25. A point on $P - V$ diagram shows the state of the system. Each point on a $P - V$ diagram corresponds to a different state of the gas. The pressure is given on the vertical axis and the volume is given on the horizontal axis, as seen below.

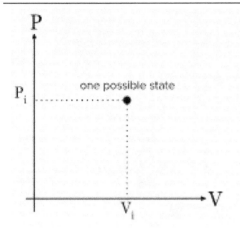

Every point on a $P-V$ diagram represents a different state for the gas (one for every possible volume and pressure).

Hence, the correct option is (B).

26. The heat Q is converted into the internal energy and work. According to the first law of thermodynamics,

$$Q = U + W$$
$$nC_p \Delta T = nC_v \Delta T + W$$

The defraction of heat converted to work is given as

$$\frac{W}{Q} = \frac{nC_p \Delta T - nC_v \Delta T}{nC_p \Delta T}$$
$$= \frac{C_p - C_v}{C_p}$$
$$= \frac{\frac{5}{2}R - \frac{3}{2}R}{\frac{5}{2}R}$$
$$= \frac{2}{5}$$

Hence, the correct option is (A).

27. A ball balanced on a vertical rod is an example of unstable equilibrium. A system is in unstable equilibrium if, when displaced from equilibrium, it experiences a net force or torque in the same direction as the displacement from equilibrium.

If a ball is placed on vertical rod, it is in unstable equilibrium because once it is displaced from its place, it will experience the net force in the direction of displacement and never come back to its original position. The potential energy of the ball is maximum at this point.

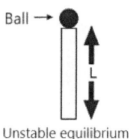

Unstable equilibrium

Hence, the correct option is (B).

28. Archimedes principle:

- It states that a body when wholly or partially immersed in liquid experiences an upward thrust which is equal to the volume of the liquid.
- Archimedes Principle is also known as the physical law of buoyancy.
- Purity of gold in the king's crown, Archimedes determine after discovering the Archimedes principle.
- Hydrometer, Ships, and Submarines work on the Archimedes Principle.
- A Ship/boat floats on the basis of the Archimedes Principle.

Hence, the correct option is (B).

29. Bernoulli's principle: For a streamlined flow of an ideal liquid in a varying cross-section tube the total energy per unit volume remains constant throughout the fluid.

- From above it is clear that Bernoulli's equation states that the summation of pressure head, kinetic head, and datum/potential head is constant for steady, incompressible, rotational, and non-viscous flow.
- In other words, an increase in the speed of the fluid occurs simultaneously with a decrease in pressure or a decrease in the fluid's potential energy i.e. the total energy of a flowing system remains constant until an external force is applied.
- So Bernoulli's equation refers to the conservation of energy.
- All of the above are the measuring devices like Venturimeter, Orifice meter, and Pitot tube meter works on the Bernoulli's theorem.

Hence, the correct option is (D).

30. The relative permittivity of the water is highest among the other materials given.

Permittivity describes the amount of charge needed to generate one unit of electric flux in a particular medium. Accordingly, a charge will yield more electric flux in a medium with low permittivity than in a medium with high permittivity. Thus, permittivity is the measure of a material's ability to resist an electric field.

Relative permittivity is the ratio of its absolute permittivity ' ϵ' to free space (empty of matter) permittivity ' ϵ_0' i.e.,

$\epsilon_r = \dfrac{\epsilon}{\epsilon_0}$

Hence, the correct option is (A).

31. Opposite charges attract each cither and same charges repel each other. Particles 1 and 2 both move towards the positively charged plate and repel away from the negatively charged plate. Hence, these two particles are negatively charged.

It can also be observed that particle 3 moves towards the negatively charged plate and repels away from the positively charged plate. Hence, particle 3 is positively charged.

The charge to mass ratio (emf) is directly proportional to the displacement or amount of deflection for a given velocity. Since the deflection of particle 3 is the maximum, it has the highest charge to mass ratio.

Hence, the correct option is (C).

32. Electric field lines form closed loops this statement about electric field lines associated with electric charges is false.

The imaginary lines which are used to represent the electric field are called electric field lines. The field lines emerge from a positive charge and terminate at a negative charge. They originate and end at right angles to the surface of the charge. Electric field lines do not make a loop. The magnitude of the electric field will be maximum where the number of field lines is maximum.

Hence, the correct option is (B).

33. The electric field strength of a charge decreases with the square of the distance.

We know that

$E = \dfrac{Q}{4\pi\epsilon l^2}$

E = electrical field

Q = charge

r = distance

One feature of this electric field strength formula is that it illustrates an inverse square relationship between electric field strength and distance. The strength of an electric field as created by source charge Q is inversely related to the square of the distance from the source.

Therefore, the electric field strength of a charge decreases with the square of the distance.

Hence, the correct option is (D).

34. The absolute permittivity of a substance is the ratio of electric field density with electric field intensity, which produces that field density.

Absolute permittivity is defined as the measure of permittivity in a vacuum. It is the resistance encountered when forming an electric field in a vacuum. It is the ratio of electric field density with electric field intensity, which produces that field density. The absolute permittivity is normally symbolized by ε_0. The permittivity of free space (vacuum) is equal to approximately 8.85×10^{-12} Farads/meter (F/m).

Hence, the correct option is (D).

35. Static-induced emf: When the conductor is stationary and the field is changing (varying) then the emf induced in the conductor is called static induced emf.

Example: Transformer

Dynamically-induced emf: When the conductor is rotating and the field is stationary, then the emf induced in the conductor is called dynamically induced emf.

Example: DC Generator, AC generator

Hence, the correct option is (C).

36. Concept:

By Gauss law, $\varepsilon\oint \vec{E}.\vec{ds} = Q_{encl}$

Thus, $\varepsilon\oint \vec{E}.\vec{ds} = \varepsilon_0 E(4\pi r^2)$

$\phi = \oint \vec{E}.\vec{ds}$

Where ϕ = flux coming out of the concentric sphere.

r = radius of the sphere

Calculation:

Since electric potential can be defined as:

$V = \dfrac{Q}{4\pi\varepsilon_0 r}$

$V = 1V$ (given)

$Q = 4\pi\varepsilon_0 r$

$\phi = \varepsilon\oint \vec{E}.\vec{ds} = 4\pi\varepsilon_0 r$

Hence, the correct option is (A).

37. The electric field intensity due to a point charge Q at any spherical surface of radius r is given by:

$E = \dfrac{Q}{4\pi\varepsilon r^2}$

ε = permittivity of the material / medium.

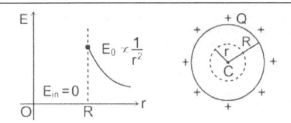

If we multiply the electric field intensity E by permittivity ε, we get a new vector D

$D = E \times \varepsilon$

$D = \dfrac{Q}{4\pi\varepsilon r^2} \times \varepsilon$

$D = \dfrac{Q}{(4\pi r^2)}$

Hence, the correct option is (B).

38. Here it is given that the angular velocity is constant so the kinetic energy will be dependent only on the inertia and work done to rotate the rod will be dependent on the kinetic energy so indirectly the work done is dependent on the moment of inertia of the body. So, for the work to be done to be minimum the moment of inertia for the rod must be minimum.

Let us assume that the required point is O. And from the given conditions we will draw a diagram which shows the exact condition which is given in the question. So, the diagram is as follows,

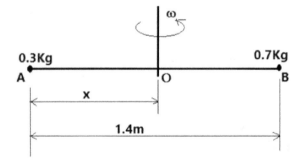

Given that the mass of the rod is negligible.

From the work energy theorem,

$W_{\text{all forces}} = \dfrac{1}{2}I\omega^2$, where ω is constant, so the $W_{\text{allforces}}$ will be minimum when I will be minimum.

So now we will write the expression for the moment of inertia.

Let the point O is at the distance of x from one end, then the moment of inertia,

$I = 0.3 \times (x)^2 + 0.7 \times (1.4 - x)^2$

Now I is to be minimum so the differentiation will be zero for I to be minimum.

So, $\dfrac{dI}{dx} = 0$

$\dfrac{d}{dx}[0.3 \times (x)^2 + 0.7 \times (1.4 - x)^2] = 0$

$\Rightarrow 0.3 \times 2x - 0.7 \times 2(1.4 - x) = 0$

$\Rightarrow 0.6x - (0.7 \times 2.8) + (0.7 \times 2x) = 0$

$\Rightarrow 0.6x - 1.96 + 1.4x = 0$

$\Rightarrow x = \dfrac{1.96}{2}$

$\Rightarrow x = 0.98 m$

So, the point on the rod through which the axis should pass in order that the work required for rotation of the rod is minimum is located at a distance of 0.98m from the mass of 0.3kg

Hence, the correct option is (C).

39. This is the case of vertical motion when the body just completes the circle.

Here,

$v = \sqrt{5gL}$

$v = \sqrt{5gL}$

Applying energy conservation,

$\dfrac{1}{2}mv_0^2 = \dfrac{1}{2}mv^2 + mgl(1 - \cos\theta) --- (1)$

where v_0 is the horizontal velocity at the bottom point, v is the velocity of bob where the bob inclined θ with vertical.
Also, we know the relation between the velocity at the topmost and velocity at the bottom point.

$mg(2 \text{ l}) = \dfrac{1}{2}mv_0^2 - \dfrac{1}{2}mv_{top}^2 ----(2)$

Since v_0 is just sufficient

$\dfrac{mv_{top}^2}{1} = T + mg$

$T = 0$

$v_{top} = \sqrt{gl}$

Then equation 2 becomes,

$v_0 = \sqrt{5gl}$

According to the question $v = \dfrac{v_0}{2}$

So from equation (1)

$\dfrac{1}{2}m(5\text{ }g) = \dfrac{1}{2}m\left(\dfrac{5gl}{4}\right) + mgl(1 - \cos\theta)$

$\dfrac{(20mgl - 5mgl)}{8} = mgl(1 - \cos\theta)$

$(1 - \cos\theta) = \dfrac{15}{8}$

$Cos\theta = \dfrac{7}{s}$

So, $\dfrac{3\pi}{2} < \theta < \pi$

Hence, the correct option is (D).

40. Fresnel's Biprims:

It is an instrument that can be used to obtain fringes due to interference and to calculate the wavelength of monochromatic light. Bi-prism produces interference pattern from a single source due to the creation of two virtual coherent sources as the light passes through the prism.

When a monochromatic light source is kept in front of biprism, two coherent virtual sources S_1 and S_2 are produced.

Fringes are of equal width (w).

$$w = \frac{\lambda D}{d}$$

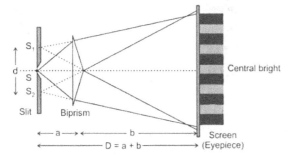

Let the separation between S_1 and S_2 be 'd' and the distance of slits and the screen from the biprism be a and b respectively i.e. D=(a+b).

If the angle of the prism is α and the refractive index is μ then

d = 2a(μ − 1)α

$$w = \frac{D\lambda}{2d} = \frac{D\lambda}{2a(\mu-1)\alpha}$$

Given λ = 6900 Å, μ = 1.5, α = 1° = $\left(\frac{\pi}{180}\right)$ = 0.0174 radians;

b = 80 cm, a = 20 cm, ⇒ D = a + b = 100 cm = 1 m;

Now the fringe width will be

$$w = \frac{1 \times 6900 \times 10^{-10}}{2 \times 20 \times 10^{-2} \times (1.5-1) \times 0.0174}$$

⇒ w = 0.197 mm

Hence, the correct option is (B).

41. At NTP, one mole of gas occupies 22.4 litres of volume.

The speed of the sound is given by

$$v = \sqrt{\frac{\gamma RT}{M}}$$

Where

$$\gamma = \frac{C_P}{C_V}$$

Given 4 g of a gas occupies 22.4 litres at NTP, CV = 5.0 J/K-mol, V = 952 m/s; R = 8.3 J/K-mol;

From the given 4 g of gas occupies 22.4 litres at NTP ⇒ M = 4 g/mol;

From the above equations, CP is given by

$$C_P = \frac{C_V M V^2}{RT}$$

$$\Rightarrow CP = \frac{5 \times 4 \times 10^{-3} \times 952^2}{8.3 \times 273}$$

⇒ C_V = 8 J/K-mol;

Hence, the correct option is (C).

42. The Reflected ray of light, when the angle of incidence is Brewster angle, would comprise of only the other component of light wave which is oscillating in a direction perpendicular to vibration of electric field vectors.

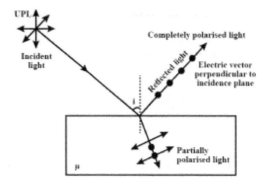

Hence, the correct option is (B).

43. Since in YDSE, angular width is given by :

Angular Width A.W. $= \frac{\beta}{D} = \frac{\lambda}{d}$

For a given wavelength,

$A.W._1 \, d_1 = A.W._2 \, d_2$

$\Rightarrow 0.20 \times 2 = 0.21 \times d_2$

$\Rightarrow d_2 = 1.9 \, mm$

Hence, the correct option is (B).

44. In this figure Q and P are at the same phase. Therefore, at P point the path difference between ray BP and reflected ray OP.

We can say, angles of QO and OP are the same.

In triangle POR, $OP = \frac{PR}{cos\theta} = \frac{d}{cos\theta}$

In triangle QOP, $QO = OP\sin(90° - 2\theta) = OP\cos 2\theta$

$\Delta = OP\cos 2\theta + OP$

$= OP(\cos 2\theta + 1)$

$= 2OP\cos^2\theta$

$= 2 \times \frac{d}{cos\theta} \times \cos^2\theta$

$= 2d\cos\theta$

Now, path difference is $\frac{\lambda}{2}$

Due to reflection at point P

$\Delta = \frac{\lambda}{2}, \frac{3\lambda}{2} \ldots\ldots\ldots$

$2d\cos\theta = \frac{\lambda}{2}, \frac{3\lambda}{2} \ldots\ldots$

$\cos\theta = \frac{\lambda}{4d}, \frac{3\lambda}{4d} \ldots\ldots\ldots$

Hence, the correct option is (B).

45. From the given equation we can find the time of the motion

$t = x^{\frac{1}{2}} + 3$

Since the displacement is the function of time and distance We can write it as

$f(t) = (t-3)^2$

On differentiating the above equation we get the velocity

$v(t) = 2(t-3)$

At origin, the velocity is zero so the time after the initiation of motion the velocity becomes zero at $3sec$

So the displacement is zero and the body is at rest.

Hence the correct option is (A).

46. As we know, Kinetic energy $= \frac{3}{2}k_B T$

$\frac{3}{2}k_B T = \frac{1}{2}mv_{es}^2$

Temperature, $T = \frac{mv_{cn}^2}{3k_B}$ ... (i)

Here, escape velocity, $v_{es} = 11.2\ km/s = 11.2 \times 10^3\ m/s$

$m = 2.76 \times 10^{-26}\ kg$ (mass)

$k_B = 1.38 \times 10^{-23} JK^{-1}$ (Boltzmann's constant)

Putting value in (i) so, we get,

$T = \frac{(11.2 \times 10^3)^2 \times 2.76 \times 10^{-26}}{3 \times 1.38 \times 10^{-23}}$

or, $T = \frac{346.2144 \times 10^{-20}}{4.14 \times 10^{-21}}$

$\therefore T = 8.36 \times 10^4 K$

Hence, the correct option is (B).

47. Given:

An ideal gas is at pressure P and absolute temperature T.

We have to find the isothermal bulk modulus of the gas.

The equation of state for an ideal gas in an isothermal process is

PV = constant ....(i)

where,

P: pressure of the gas

V: volume occupied by the gas

Differentiating eq. (i), we have

P dV + VdP = 0

$\Rightarrow \left(\frac{dP}{dV}\right) = -\left(\frac{P}{V}\right)$......(ii)

Now, the bulk modulus of an ideal gas is

$B = -\left[\frac{dP}{\left(\frac{dV}{V}\right)}\right]$ ......(iii)

$\Rightarrow B = -\left(\frac{dP}{dV}\right)V$

Using eq. (ii) and eq. (iii), we get

$\Rightarrow B = -\left(\frac{-P}{V}\right)V$

$\Rightarrow B = P$

Hence, the correct option is (B).

48. Given $l = 100\ A, r = 2\ m$, and $\mu_0 = 4\pi \times 10^{-7}\ N/A^2$

We know that an overhead power cable will be of infinite length, so,

$\Rightarrow \theta_1 = \theta_2 = 90°$

The magnetic field intensity at a distance r from a current-carrying wire is given as,

$\Rightarrow B = \frac{\mu_0 I}{4\pi r}(\sin\theta_1 + \sin\theta_2)$

$\Rightarrow B = \frac{4\pi \times 10^{-7} \times 100}{4\pi \times 2}(\sin 90 + \sin 90)$

$\Rightarrow B = \frac{4\pi \times 10^{-7} \times 100}{4\pi \times 2}(\sin 90 + \sin 90)$

$\Rightarrow B = 50 \times 2 \times 10^{-7}\ T$

$\Rightarrow B = 10^{-5}\ T$

Hence, the correct option is (A).

49. The magnetic field due to a straight current-carrying wire is directly proportional to the current in the wire.

Magnetic field intensity, $B = \frac{\mu_0 I}{2\pi r}$

$\Rightarrow B \propto I$

Hence, the correct option is (B).

50. Planck's law describes the spectral density of electromagnetic radiation emitted by a black body in thermal equilibrium at a given temperature T.

Planck's law for the energy E_λ radiated per unit volume by a cavity of a blackbody in the wavelength interval λ to $\lambda + \Delta\lambda$ can be written in terms of Planck's constant (h), the speed of light

$(c = \lambda \times v)$, the Boltzmann constant (k), and the absolute temperature (T):

Energy per unit volume per unit wavelength:

$$E_\lambda = \frac{8\pi hc}{\lambda^5} \times \frac{1}{e^{\frac{hc}{kT\lambda}}-1}$$

Energy per unit volume per unit frequency:

$$E_v = \frac{8\pi h}{c^3} \times \frac{v^3}{e^{\frac{hv}{kT}}-1}$$

So Planck's distribution function:

$$E(\omega, T) = \frac{1}{e^{\frac{h\omega}{\tau}}-1}$$

As temperature increases, the peak of the curve shift towards a lower wavelength.

Hence, the correct option is (A).

51. Sodium is the most electropositive and Chlorine is the most electronegative element of the third period of the modern periodic table.

Electronegativity is a measure of the tendency of an atom to attract a bonding pair of electrons.

Electropositivity is the measure of the ability of elements to donate electrons to form positive ions.

Electronegativity increases from left to right across a period of elements.

Hence, the correct option is (D).

52. The valency of a Magnesium (Mg) atom is +2. The number of electrons present in the outermost orbit of an atom is called Valency. We know the outer electronic configuration of Magnesium is $1s^2, 2s^2, 2p^6, 3s^2$.

Hence, the correct option is (C).

53. Given that:

$50ml$ of $0.6M NaOH$ would react with $50ml$ of $0.6M$ acetic acid.

Therefore,

[Acid] left = $50ml$ of $0.6M$ present in $150ml$ = $0.2M$

[Salt] present = $50ml$ of $0.6M$ present in $150ml$ = $0.2M$

$pKa = -\log 1.8 \times 10^{-5} = 4.74$

$pH = pKa + \frac{\log[salt]}{[Acid]}$

$= 4.74 + \frac{\log 0.2}{0.2}$

$= 4.74$

To make a solution of $pH = 4.74$,

[Acid] = [Salt]

Therefore, no extra amount of acid is required to be added at all.

Hence, the correct option is (A).

54. The given reaction is:

$A + B \rightarrow C + D$

Intially, $[A] = [B] = [C] = [D] = M$

Now change in $[C]$ = change in $[D] = M$

So, remaining $[C] = [D] = 1.5M - 0.5M = 1.0M$

$K = \frac{[C][D]}{[A][B]}$

$K = \frac{1 \times 1}{1.5 \times 1.5}$

$K = \frac{4}{9}$

Hence, the correct option is (C).

55. Nitration of aniline in strong acidic medium also gives m-nitroaniline because in acidic (strong) medium aniline is present as anilinium ion. Amino $-NH_2$ group is ortho-para directing but $-NH_3^+$ group is meta directing.

$C_6H_5 - NH_2 + H^+ \xrightarrow{\text{strong acid, nitrating mixture}} C_6H_5 - NH_3^+ \xrightarrow{NO_2^+} m-$ nitroaniline

Hence, the correct option is (D).

56. $2K(s) + F_2(g) \rightarrow 2K^+F^-(s)$ is a type of redox reaction.

- The oxidation number of K increases from 0 to $+1$ and the oxidation number of F_2 decreases from 0 to -1.
- Therefore, K is oxidized and F_2 is reduced.
- Thus, it is a redox reaction.

Hence, the correct option is (D).

57. The oxidative rusting of iron under Earth's atmosphere is slow reaction.

The reaction rate (rate of reaction) or speed of reaction for a reactant or product in a particular reaction is intuitively defined as how fast or slow a reaction takes place. For example, the oxidative rusting of iron under Earth's atmosphere is a slow reaction that can take many years.

Hence, the correct option is (B).

58. The rate of a chemical reaction is the change in concentration over the change in time and is a metric of the "speed" at which a chemical reactions occurs and can be defined in terms of two observables:

1. The Rate of Disappearance of Reactants: $\frac{[-\Delta \text{ Reactants}]}{\Delta \text{ time}}$

2. The Rate of Formation of Products: $\frac{[\Delta \text{Products}]}{\Delta \text{time}}$

Thus, the units for the rate is Molarity per Seconds $\left(\frac{M}{s}\right)$. or Moles per litre per second (moles $^{-1}s^{-1}$).

Hence, the correct option is (B).

59. The most molecular collision are in between 2 molecules.

The collision theory is based on the assumption that for a reaction to occur it is necessary for the reacting species to come together or collide with one another. Collision theory states that when suitable particles of the reactant hit each other, only a certain amount of collisions result in a perceptible or notable change, these successful changes are called successful collisions.

Hence, the correct option is (A).

60. Colligative properties are the properties of a solution which solely depends on the number of particles of the solute and not on the type or nature of the solute. Freezing point of a solution is one such colligative property. Whenever we add a solute to the solution, it lowers the original freezing point of the solution and this depression in freezing point can be calculated with the help pf below formula:

$$\Delta T_f = i \times K_f \times m$$

Where ΔT_f is the freezing point depression, i is the Van't Hoff factor, K_f is the freezing constant and m is the molality. Van't Hoff factor, it depends on the degree of association/dissociation of solute in the solution and the number of ions produced in the solution. so, we can write this as

$$\alpha = \frac{i-1}{n-1}$$

According to this, we get the information that for greater value of n, greater will be the Van't Hoff factor, where n is number of ions produced on dissolution in a solvent. Let us check it for all the four compounds given to us.

For $C_6H_5NH_3Cl, n = 3$

For $Ca(NO_3)_2, n = 3$

For $La(NO_3)_3, n = 4$

For $C_6H_{12}O_6, n = 1$

The lowest Van't Hoff factor will result in the lowest depression in freezing point and thus, the solution will have the highest freezing point. Since glucose has the lowest i, it will have the highest freezing point.

Hence, the correct option is (D).

61. Let compound be B.

Water be A.

$\Delta T_f = T_f^0 - T_{FS}$

Here, $T_f^0 = 0$

Therefore,

$\Delta T_f = 0° - (-0.465)$

$\Delta T_f = 0.465°C$

Given:

$K_f = 1.86 \ kg \ Kmol^{-1}$

Weight of compound, $w_B = 1.8 gm$

Let Molecular weight of compound, $M_B = x$

Weight of water, $w_A = 40 \ g$

We know that:

$\Delta T_f = K_f \cdot \frac{w_B}{M_B} \times \frac{1000}{w_A}$

$0.465 = \frac{1.86 \times 1.8 \times 1000}{x \times 40}$

$x = 180 \ g/mol$

So, empirical mass of $(CH_2O) = (12 \times 1) + (2 \times 1) + (16 \times 1)$

$= 30$

$n = \frac{\text{Molecular Mass}}{\text{Empirical formula mass}}$

$= \frac{180}{30}$

$n = 6$

So, molecular formula $=$ (Emperical formula $)_n$

$= (CH_2O)_6$

$= C_6H_{12}O_6$

Hence, the correct option is (D).

62. Given that:

Weight of solute $= 1.00 \ g$

Molar Mass of the solute $= 250 \ g \ mol^{-1}$

Weight of solvent $= 51.2 \ g = 0.0512 \ kg$

We know that:

Molality of non- electrolyte solute $= \frac{\frac{\text{weight of solute in gram}}{\text{molecular weight of solute}}}{\text{weight of solvent in } kg}$

$= \frac{\frac{1}{250}}{0.0512}$

$= \frac{1}{250 \times 0.0512}$

$= 0.0781 \ m$

As we know:

$\Delta T_f = K_f \times$ molality of solution

$= 5.12 \times 0.0781$

$= 0.4\ K$

Hence, the correct option is (A).

63. From the expression of heat (q),

$q = mc\Delta T$

Where,

$c =$ molar heat capacity

$m =$ mass of substance

$\Delta T =$ change in temperature

Given,

$m = 60\ g$

$c = 24\ J\text{mol}^{-1}K^{-1}$

$\Delta T = (55 - 35)°C$

$\Delta T = (328 - 308)K = 20\ K$

Substituting the values in the expression of heat:

$q = \left(\frac{60}{27}\ mol\right)(24 Jmol^{-1}\ K^{-1})(20\ K)$

$q = 1066.7\ J$

$q = 1.07\ kJ$

Hence, the correct option is (C).

64. A well-stoppered thermos flask contains some ice cubes. This is an example of an isolated system.

An isolated system is a thermodynamic system that can not exchange either energy or matter outside the boundaries of the system. In a thermos, ice can be kept for many hours because the walls of the thermos are insulated and it does not allow heat to flow out of the flask.

Hence, the correct option is (C).

65. Hess's law of constant heat summation is based on the first law of thermodynamics.

Hess's law of constant heat summation states that " Regardless of multiple stages, total enthalpy changes is the sum of all the changes."

Mathematically Hess law can be represented as;

$\Delta H_{net} = \Sigma \Delta H_Y$

Where, $\Delta H_{net} =$ Net enthalpy change

$\Delta H_r =$ Sum of enthalpy change of reactions

So, Enthalpy change is a state function as it depends on the final and initial stage and not on the path followed by the system. So, It resembles internal energy as internal energy is also a state function.

The first law of thermodynamics states that " Some part of internal energy of the system is used to heat the system while another part is used for work done."

So, Hess's law of constant heat summation is based on the first law of thermodynamics as both suggest the conversation of energy.

Hence, the correct option is (C).

66. Seven of the eight corners are occupied by atom $A = \frac{1}{8} \times 7 = \frac{7}{8}$

Faces are occupied by $B = \frac{1}{2} \times 6 = 3$

$A:B = \frac{7}{8} : 3 = 7:24$

Thus, the general formula will be A_7B_{24}.

Hence, the correct option is (C).

67. Crystalline solids are anisotropic in nature.

- It is because the arrangement of constituent particles is regular and ordered along all the directions.
- Therefore, the value of any physical property (electrical resistance or refractive index) would be different along each direction.
- That is, some of their physical index show different values when measured along different directions in the same crystal.

Hence, the correct option is (B).

68.

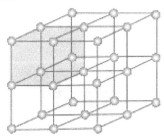

The three dimensional arrangement of constituent particles in a crystal is represented in such a way each particle is taken as a point, the arrangement is called as crystal lattice.

Thus, a regular arrangement of the points in space is the correct definition of crystal lattice.

Hence, the correct option is (C).

69. Fritz London the concept of dispersion force.

The London dispersion force is the weakest intermolecular force. The London dispersion force is a temporary attractive force that results when the electrons in two adjacent atoms occupy positions that make the atoms form temporary dipoles. This force is sometimes called an induced dipole-induced dipole attraction.

London forces are the attractive forces that cause nonpolar substances to condense to liquids and to freeze into solids when the temperature is lowered sufficiently.

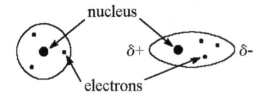

symmetrical distribution   unsymmetrical distribution

Hence, the correct option is (D).

70. Initial pressure $p_1 = 1$ bar

Initial volume, $V_1 = 500 dm^3$

Final volume, $V_2 = 200 dm^3$

Since the temperature remains constant, the final pressure (p_2) can be calculated using

Boyle's law.

According to Boyle's law,

$p_1V_1 = p_2V_2$

$\Rightarrow p_2 = \frac{p_1V_1}{V_2}$

$= \frac{1 \times 500}{200}$ bar

$= 2.5$ bar

Therefore, the minimum pressure required is 2.5 bar.

Hence, the correct option is (D).

71. Two moles of alkali metal reacts with one mole of hydrogen molecule in order to form 2 moles of alkali metal hydride. The correct order of reactivity of alkali metals towards hydrogen is $Li < Na < K < Rb < Cs$.

Hence, the correct option is (B).

72. A heteroatom is any atom other than carbon or hydrogen atom. All the others apart from carbon mentioned above are heteroatoms. In other words, a heteroatom is a non-carbon atom present in a carbon structure.

Carbon or hydrogen (termed a heteroatom) is bonded to carbon. All heteroatoms have a greater or lesser attraction for electrons than does carbon. Thus, each bond between a carbon and a heteroatom is polar, and the degree of polarity depends on the difference between the electron-attracting properties of the two.

Hence, the correct option is (C).

73. $Ba < Ca < Se < S < Ar$ represents the correct order of increasing first ionization enthalpy for Ca, Ba, S, Se and Ar.

Ionisation energy increases along a period from left to right and decreases down a group. The position of given elements in the periodic table is as:

	2	16	18
	Ca	S	Ar
	Ba	Se	

Thus, the order of increasing ΔH_{t_1} is $Ba < Ca < Se < S < Ar$.

Hence, the correct option is (C).

74. Starting from alumina would obtain 'Aluminium nitride'.

Aluminium nitride can be synthesized by the Carbothermal reduction of an Aluminium oxide in the presence of gaseous nitrogen at $1800°C$. The reaction is as follows:

$Al_2O_3 + 3C + N_2 \xrightarrow{1800°C} 2AlN + 3CO$

Aluminium nitride is a solid nitride of aluminium. It has a high thermal conductivity of up to $321\ W/(m \cdot K)$ and is an electrical insulator. Its wurtzite phase has a bandgap of $\sim 6eV$ at room temperature and has a potential application in optoelectronics operating at deep ultraviolet frequencies.

75. The element with atomic number 35 belongs to p-block.

The elements are classified into four blocks s, p, d, f block. The electronic configuration to the atomic number 35. The electronic configuration of the element with atomic number 35 is $1s^2 2s^2 2p^6 3s^2 3p^6 3d^{10} 4s^2 4p^5$ the last valence electrons enter into p orbital. The last valence electrons enter into the p-orbital so they are classified under p-block elements. From the periodic table, we know that Atomic number 35 belongs to Bromine.

The p-block comprise group 13 to 18 and these together with the s-block elements are called representative elements or main group elements. Its outermost electronic configuration varies from $ns^2 np^1 - ns^2 np^6$. the outermost electronic configuration for s block, d block and f block are $ns^1 - ns^2, (n-1)d^{1-10}ns^{0-2}, (n-2)f^{1-14}(n-1)d^{0-1}ns^2$ respectively.

Hence, the correct option is (B).

76. The structure of the IF_7 molecule is Pentagonal Bipyramidal. Iodine (I) is the central metal atom and Fluorine (F) is the monovalent atom. Also, it is a neutral molecule (i.e., the negative and positive charge is zero). In IF_7, the central atom I is attached to 7 fluorine atoms through 7 sigma bonds. So, the steric number is 7 here. Therefore, the hybridization of a central atom in IF_7 is sp^3d^3. IF_7 has seven bond pairs and zero lone pairs of electrons.

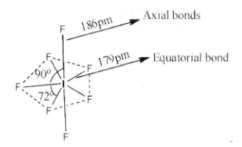

Hence, the correct option is (A).

77. Gold solution is lyophobic colloidal solution. Gold particles have very less affinity towards dispersion medium, therefore its solution can be easily coagulated.

When Lyophobic colloids are mixed with the suitable liquid, very weak force of attraction exists between colloidal particles and liquid and system does not pass into colloidal state readily.

Hence, the correct option is (A).

78. Given,

Frequency, $\nu = 5 \times 10^{14}\ Hz$

As we know, Planck constant is given as,

$h = 6.626 \times 10^{-34} Js$

Energy of one photon is given by the expression,

$E = h\nu$

$E = (6.626 \times 10^{-34}\ J\ s) \times (5 \times 10^{14}\ s^{-1})$

$= 3.313 \times 10^{-19}\ J$

As we know,

Avogadro's number $= 6.022 \times 10^{23}\ mol^{-1}$

Energy of one mole of photons,

$= (3.313 \times 10^{-19}\ J) \times (6.022 \times 10^{23}\ mol^{-1})$

$= 199.51\ kJ\ mol^{-1}$

Hence, the correct option is (A).

79. The compound having the least molecular mass should contain the minimum amount of sulphur or simply 1 atom of sulphur.

Let the molecular mass of the compound (in amu) be x.

Mass of sulphur in the compond $= 8\%$ of the total molecular mass of x

$= \dfrac{8x}{100}$

Since, the molecular mass of one mole of sulphur is 32, the compound must contain this amount of sulphur, i.e.,

$\dfrac{8x}{100} = 32$

$\Rightarrow x = 400$

Hence, the correct option is (B).

80. $Al^{+3} + 3e^- \rightarrow Al$

3 Faraday of electricity will produce 1 mol Al

$Cu^{+2} + 2e^- \rightarrow Cu$

2 Faraday electricity produces 1 mol Cu

3 Faraday electricity produces $\dfrac{3}{2}$ mol Cu

$Na^+ + e^- \rightarrow Na$

1 Faraday electricity produces 1 mol Na

3 Faraday electricity produces 3 mol Na

Ratio $= 1 : \dfrac{3}{2} : 3$

$\Rightarrow 1 : 1.5 : 3$

Hence, the correct option is (C).

81. Given:

The reaction is $2Fe^{3+}(aq) + 2I^-(aq) \rightarrow 2Fe^{2+}(aq) + I_2(aq)$

$E^0_{cell} = 0.24\ V$

Temperature = 298 K

faraday constant, $F = 96500 C mol^{-1}$

Standard Gibbs energy of the cell reaction

We know that change in Gibbs free energy can be given by -

$\Delta G^0 = -nFE^0_{cell}$

Where 'n' is the number of electrons transferred

F is faraday constant

From the above reaction, we see that Fe has accepted one electron and its oxidation state is changed by +1. For two atoms of Fe, there is transfer of two electrons which are donated by iodide.

So, n = 2

Thus,

$\Delta G^0 = -nFE^0_{cell}$

$\Delta G^0 = -2 \times 96500 \times 0.24$

$\Delta G^0 = -46320 J^{-1}_{mol}$

$\Delta G^0 = -46.32 kJ mol^{-1}$

The value of standard Gibbs energy of a cell reaction is positive or greater than 1 if the reaction is non spontaneous, negative or less than 1 in case the reaction is spontaneous and zero if the reaction is at equilibrium.

Hence, the correct option is (A).

82. Molar conductivity $= \dfrac{\text{Concentration of electrolyte(C)}}{\text{Specific conductance (K)}}$

$\Rightarrow K = Nm \times C = 194.5 O^{-1}\ cm^2\ mol^{-1} \times 0.05 mo l^{-1}$

$\Rightarrow K = 9.725 \Omega^{-1}\ cm^2\ L^{-1}$

$1\ L = 1000\ cm^3; 1\ L - 1 = 10^{-3}\ cm^{-3}$

as $\dfrac{1}{R} = \dfrac{KA}{1}$

$A \to$ Area of cross-section of cell;

$1 \to$ length of electrode cell;

$R \to$ Resistance

$\Rightarrow \dfrac{1}{R} = \dfrac{9.725 \Omega^{-1}\ cm^2 \times 10^{-3}\ cm^{-3} 1.50\ cm^2}{0.50\ cm} = 0.0290^{-1}$

$\Rightarrow R = 34.27 \Omega$

Hence, the correct option is (B).

83. In chelation, ring formation occurs because two atoms from the same ligand coordinate with the metal atom. This cannot happen if the ligand is monodentate.

Oxalate is a bidentate ligand so it forms a chelate. It can coordinate with both of its negatively charged O atoms.

Acetate, cyanide and ammonia are monodentate ligands. They do not form chelates.

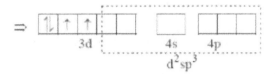

Hence, the correct option is (B).

84. The complex ion which has no d-electrons in the central metal atom is $[MnO_4]^-$.

The atomic number of $Mn = Z = 25$

So, the electronic configuration of $Mn = [Ar]3d^5 4s^2$

In $[MnO_4]^-$,

The oxidation state of $Mn = +7$

The electronic configuration of $Mn^{7+} = [Ar]3d^0 4s^0$

The electronic configuration of $Co^{+3} = [Ar]3d^6 4s^0$

The electronic configuration of $Fe^{+3} = [Ar]3d^5 4s^0$

The electronic configuration of $Cr^{+3} = [Ar]3d^3 4s^0$

As $[MnO_4]^-$ does not have any d-electron in central metal atom. But Co^{3+}, Fe^{3+} and Cr^{3+} have (6,5 and 3) d-electrons respectively.

Hence, the correct option is (A).

85. In the complex $[Mn(CN)_6]^{3-}$, the oxidation state of Mn is +3. Mn^{3+} ion has d^4 outer electronic configuration. It is an inner orbital complex. Inner d orbitals are used which results in d^2sp^3 hybridisation.

So, the molecular geometry is octahedral.

E.C. of $Mn^{+3} \to 3d^4$

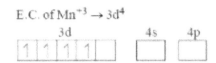

The presence of a strong field ligand CN⁻ causes pairing of electrons.

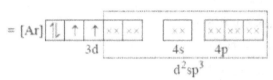

As, coordination number of Mn = 6, so it will form an octahedral complex.

∴ [Mn(CN)₆]³⁻

= [Ar] ...
  3d   4s   4p

d^2sp^3

Hence, the correct option is (D).

86. The given reaction in an example of Mannich reaction.

The reaction is named after chemist Carl Mannich. The Mannich reaction is an example of nucleophilic addition of an amine to a carbonyl group followed by dehydration to the Schiff base.

The Mannich reaction is an organic reaction which consists of an amino alkylation of an acidic proton placed next to a carbonyl functional group by formaldehyde and a primary or secondary amine or ammonia. The final product is a β-amino-carbonyl compound also known as a Mannich base. Reactions between aldimines and α-methylene carbonyls are also considered Mannich reactions because these imines form between amines and aldehydes. The reaction is named after chemist Carl Mannich.

Hence, the correct option is (B).

87. The carbonyl stretching frequency for esters is about 1750 cm^{-1}

Carbonyl stretching peaks generally fall between 1900 and 1600 cm-1 (assume all peak positions hereafter are in wavenumber units), a relatively unique part of the IR spectrum. This area is sometimes referred to as the carbonyl stretching region as a result. Esters have a memorable pattern of three intense peaks at ~1700, ~1200, and ~1100 from the C=O. The peak at 1742 is of course the carbonyl stretch, and for saturated esters in general this peak falls from 1755 to 1735.

Hence, the correct option is (C).

88. The following esters as per decreasing order of rate of saponification are:

Ethyl p-nitrobenzoate>Ethyl p- chlorobenzoate>Ethyl p-methoxybenzoate>Ethyl benzoate.

Ethyl benzoate is a benzoate ester obtained by condensation of benzoic acid and ethanol. It is a volatile oil component found in ripe kiwifruit, cranberry juice, and palm kernel oil. It has a role as a flavouring agent, a fragrance and a volatile oil component. It is a benzoate ester and an ethyl ester.

Hence, the correct option is (C).

89. Here $HCl + I_2$ combination doesn't evolve Cl_2 gas.

$HCl + I_2 \rightarrow$ No reaction

$8HCl + KMnO_4 \rightarrow MnCl_2 + \frac{5}{2}Cl_2 \uparrow +KCl + 4H_2O$

$4HCl + MnO_2 \rightarrow MnCl_2 + Cl_2 \uparrow +2H_2O$

$HCl + F_2 \rightarrow HF + Cl_2 \uparrow$

Hence, the correct option is (C).

90. Compound is β-hydroxy aldehyde hence the reaction is aldol addition. A and B can be known by retro aldol addition as follows:

$CH_3 - CH_2 - \overset{\overset{O-H}{|}}{CH} - CHO \Rightarrow CH_3 - CHO + CH_3 - CH_2 - CHO$
$\qquad\qquad\qquad |$
$\qquad\qquad\quad CH_3$

Hence, the correct option is (B).

91. Here Y is prop- 2-enoic-acid as shown by below given reaction:

$CH_3 - CH_2 - COOH \xrightarrow{H_2O_2} \overset{\overset{OH}{|}}{CH_2} - CH_2 - COOH$
$\xrightarrow{\Delta} CH_2 = CH - COOH$

$\qquad\qquad\qquad \beta - $ Hydroxy acid

Hence, the correct option is (B).

92. Sucrose does not reduce Benedict's solution. Sucrose contains two sugars (fructose and glucose) joined by their glycosidic bond in such a way as to prevent the glucose isomerizing to aldehyde, or the fructose to alpha-hydroxy-ketone form. Sucrose is thus a non-reducing sugar which does not react with Benedict's soution.

Hence, the correct option is (A).

93. The most basic amino acid is Histidine. Only Arginine and Histidine are basic amino acids even out of these two, histidine is weakly charged under physiological ph. Histidine is one of that type of amino acids that can be converted to intermediates of the tricarboxylic acid (TCA) cycle. Histidine, along with some other amino acids such as proline and arginine, takes part in deamination, which is a process in which its amino group is removed. The biosynthesis of the histidine has been majorly studied in prokaryotes like E. coli.

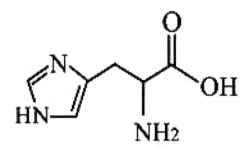

Hence, the correct option is (D).

94. Polymerization of vinyl chloride (monomer) results in the production of polyvinylchloride or PVC.

This is a plastic that has the chemical formula: $CH_2=CHCl$.

PVC is one of the most used plastic materials in the world. It is cost-effective and highly resistant to chemicals. By adding some additives, it can be made ductile and elastic. PVC is used in an enormous range of domestic and industrial products, from raincoats and shower curtains to window frames and indoor plumbing.

PVC's inherent flame retardant and excellent electrical insulation properties make it ideal for cabling applications.

Hence, the correct option is (A).

95. Bakelite is a thermosetting polymer.

The thermosetting polymer is a polymer that can be irreversibly hardened to the desired shape. It is hardened by the process of curing of a soft solid or viscous liquid prepolymer or resin. Curing is induced by heat or suitable radiation and may be promoted by high pressure, or mixing with a catalyst.

Once hardened, a thermoset cannot be melted for reshaping. Some examples of a thermosetting polymer are Polyurethanes, Polyurea, Bakelite, Urea-formaldehyde, etc.

Hence, the correct option is (C).

96. Biomass is used instead of extensive use of petroleum. This is an application of green chemistry. Use of petroleum creates lots of gases which are harmful to the environment.

In order to decrease human consumption of petroleum, chemists have investigated methods for producing polymers from renewable resources such as biomass.

Nature Works polylactic acid (PLA) is a polymer of naturally occurring lactic acid (LA), which on consumption creates no waste and hence, is an environment-friendly compound. It is an application of Green chemistry.

Hence, the correct option is (C).

97. Pyrocool is an environment-friendly product and better than halons which are used to extinguish fire.

Pyrocool is a product which is environmentally benign foam discovered using concept of Green chemistry. Large-scale fires such as oil tankers and jet airplane can be extinguished in a short time and in a better way than previous use of the halons.

Hence, the correct option is (B).

98. $K_2Cr_2O_7$ compound is used in Ultra-violet calibration.

Potassium dichromate $(K_2Cr_2O_7)$ is especially useful in the visible range but also useful in UV. Potassium dichromate itself is stable and available in high purity. In dilute perchloric acid solution, it has a linear response with good temperature stability and also stable as solution.

Hence, the correct option is (C).

99. Ferrous sulphate compound forms double salt with sulphates of alkali metals.

Ferrous sulphate forms double salts with sulphates of alkali metals with general formula $R_2SO_4 \cdot FeSO_4 \cdot 6H_2O$. With ammonium sulphate, it forms a double salt known as Mohr's salt. It ionises in solution to gives Fe^{2+}, NH_4^+ and SO_4^{2-} ions.

Hence, the correct option is (D).

100. This reaction is an example of β-elimination. Hydrogen is removed from β-carbon and halogen from α-carbon, so dehydrohalogenation reaction.

Pent-2-ene is major product known as Saytzeff's product and it is more stable alkene than Pent-1-ene.

Generally, in E_2 reaction Zaitsev alkene is formed as a major product (more stable alkene).

$$CH_3-\underset{\underset{Br}{|}}{\overset{\alpha}{CH}}-\underset{\beta}{\overset{H}{CH}}-CH_2-CH_3 \xrightarrow[E2]{Na^+\bar{O}Et} CH_3-CH=CH-CH_2-CH_3 + EtOH$$

sec.alkyl halide

Hence, the correct option is (D).

Physics & Chemistry : Mock Test 07

Physics

Q.1 A particle of mass m is located in a one dimensional field where potential energy is given by:
$V(x) = A(1 - \cos px)$ where A and p are constants. The period of small oscillations of the particle is:

A. $2\pi\sqrt{\frac{m}{(Ap)}}$
B. $2\pi\sqrt{\frac{m}{(Ap^2)}}$
C. $2\pi\sqrt{\frac{m}{A}}$
D. $\frac{1}{2\pi}\sqrt{\frac{Ap}{m}}$

Q.2 A horizontal platform with an object placed on it is executing SHM in the vertical direction. The amplitude of oscillation is $2.5\ cm$. What must be the least period of these oscillations so that the object is not detached from the platform.

A. π sec B. $\frac{\pi}{5}$ sec C. $\frac{\pi}{10}$ sec D. $\frac{\pi}{15}$ sec

Q.3 For a particle executing SHM, the displacement x is given by $x = A\cos\omega t$. Identify the graph which represents the variation of potential energy (PE) as a function of time t and displacement x.

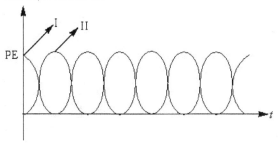

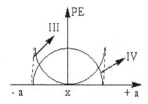

A. I, III B. II, IV C. II, III D. I, IV

Q.4 Two identical coherent waves of intensity I_0 are superimposed at a point. If the resultant intensity at this point is three times of I_0 then find the phase difference between the two waves at this point.

A. $\frac{\pi}{6}$ B. $\frac{\pi}{4}$ C. $\frac{\pi}{3}$ D. None of these

Q.5 The focal length and the diameter of the objective lens of a microscope are 15 cm and 6.1 cm respectively. Find the minimum separation of the microscope for the light of wavelength $4000\ \overset{\circ}{A}$.

A. 1.2×10^{-6} m B. 0.6×10^{-6} m
C. 1.4×10^{-6} m D. None of these

Q.6 All electrons ejected from a surface by incident light of wavelength $200\ nm$ can be stopped before traveling $1\ m$ in the direction of a uniform electric field of $4NC^{-1}$. The work function of the surface is:

A. $4eV$ B. $6.2eV$ C. $2eV$ D. $2.2eV$

Q.7 A radiation of energy 'E' falls normally on a perfectly reflecting surface. The momentum transferred to the surface is: (c = velocity of light)

A. $\frac{E}{c}$ B. $\frac{2E}{c}$ C. $\frac{2E}{c^2}$ D. $\frac{E}{c^2}$

Q.8 In a p-n junction diode, the current I can be expressed as $I = I_0 \exp\left(\frac{eV}{2k_BT} - 1\right)$, where I_0 is called the reverse saturation current, V is the voltage across the diode and is positive for forward bias and negative for reverse bias, and I is the current through the diode, k_B is the Boltzmann constant $(8.6 \times 10^{-5} eV/K)$ and T is the absolute temperature. If for a given diode $I_0 = 5 \times 10^{-12} A$ and $T = 300K$, forward current is flowing at forward volatge of $0.6V$ then, what will be the increase in current if the voltage across the diode is increased to $0.7V$?

A. 3.972 A B. 4.972 A C. 2.972 A D. 5.972 A

Q.9 What temperature are Fahrenheit and Celsius equal?

A. $-40°$ B. 574.59 C. 40 D. -574.59

Q.10 Successive emission of an α-particle and two β-particles by an atom of a radioactive element results in the formation of its:

A. isobar B. isotope
C. isomer D. None of these

Q.11 The electron in a hydrogen atom makes a transition of n_1 to n_2, where n_1 and n_2 are the principal quantum number of the two states. The time period of the electron in the initial state is eight times that in the final state. Then according to Bohr's atomic model, the possible value of n_1 and n_2 are:

A. $n_1 = 4$ and $n_2 = 2$ B. $n_1 = 8$ and $n_2 = 2$
C. $n_1 = 5$ and $n_2 = 2$ D. $n_1 = 6$ and $n_2 = 2$

Q.12 In a Rutherford's α-scattering experiment with thin gold foil, 8100 scintillations per minute are observed at an angle of 60°. What will be the number of scintillations per minute at an angle of 120°?

A. 90 B. 70 C. 80 D. 100

Q.13 What is the mass of an object that requires a force of $90\ N$ to accelerate at a rate of $2.6\ m/s^2$?
A. $44.6\ kg$ B. $34.6\ kg$ C. $54.6\ kg$ D. $48\ kg$

Q.14 In electromagnetic induction, the induced e.m.f. in a coil is independent of:
A. Magnetic field
B. Time
C. The resistance of the coil
D. Area of the coil

Q.15 On what application does speedometer works?
A. Lenz's law
B. Eddy current
C. Electromagnetic induction
D. Mutual inductance

Q.16 A long solenoid of diameter $0.1\ m$ has 2×10^4 turns per metre. At the centre of the solenoid, a coil of 100 turns and radius $0.01\ m$ is placed with its axis coinciding with the solenoid axis. The current in the solenoid reduces at a constant rate to $0A$ from $4A$ in $0.05s$. If the resistance of the coil is $10\pi^2 \Omega$, the total charge flowing through the coil during this time is.
A. π^2 B. $32\pi^2$ C. $4\pi^2$ D. $32\mu C$

Q.17 The relationship between the electric field E and the current density J in a conducting medium (where σ is the conductivity) is:
A. $J = \sigma^2 E$ B. $J = \frac{E}{\sigma}$ C. $J = \frac{\sigma}{E}$ D. $J = \sigma E$

Q.18 Current in an Intrinsic semiconductor is equal to:
A. Electron current
B. Hole Current
C. Electron current + Hole Current
D. Displacement current

Q.19 The weight of a body at the centre of the earth is _____.
A. Infinite
B. Zero
C. Same as that on the surface of the earth
D. Half of that on the surface of the earth

Q.20 The work done in an isothermal expansion of a gas depends upon:
A. Temperature only
B. Expansion ratio only
C. Both temperature and expansion ratio
D. Neither temperature nor expansion ratio

Q.21 Which of the following is a thermodynamics law?
A. Zeroth law of thermodynamics
B. Faraday's Law of thermodynamics
C. Ideal Gas Law of thermodynamics
D. Boyle's Law of thermodynamics

Q.22 Which of the following is an application of thermodynamics?

A. Refrigerators   B. Gas compressors
C. Power plants   D. All of the above

Q.23 A metal ball immersed in alcohol weighs W₁ at 0°C and W₂ at 59°C. The coefficient of cubical expansion of the metal is less than that of alcohol. If the density of the metal is large compared to that of alcohol, then
A. $W_1 > W_2$ B. $W_1 = W_2$
C. $W_1 < W_2$ D. None of them

Q.24 An open U-tube contains mercury. When $11.2\ cm$ of water is poured into one of the arms of the tube, how high does the mercury rise in the other arm from its initial level?
A. $0.56\ cm$ B. $1.35\ cm$ C. $0.41\ cm$ D. $2.32\ cm$

Q.25 Find the magnitude of the resultant force on a charge of $1\mu C$ held at P due to two charges of $+2 \times 10^{-8}C$ and $-10^{-8}C$ at A and B respectively.
Given: $AP = 10cm$
And, $BP = 5cm$
$\angle APB = 90°$

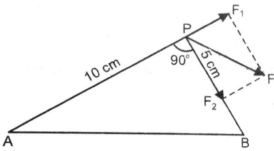

A. $6.024 \times 10^{-4} N$ B. $4.025 \times 10^{-3} N$
C. $4.024 \times 10^{-2} N$ D. $5.034 \times 10^{-2} N$

Q.26 A regular hexagon of side $10 cm$ has a charge $5 \mu C$ at each of its vertices. Calculate the potential at the center of the hexagon.
A. $1.7 \times 10^6 V$ B. $0.7 \times 10^6 V$
C. $2.7 \times 10^6 V$ D. $3..7 \times 10^6 V$

Q.27 In a parallel plate capacitor with air between the plates, each plate has an area of $6 \times 10^{-3} m^2$ and the distance between the plates is $3mm$. Calculate the capacitance of the capacitor. If this capacitor is connected to a $100V$ supply, what is the charge on each plate of the capacitor?
A. $1.771 \times 10^{-9} C$ B. $2.771 \times 10^{-9} C$
C. $3.771 \times 10^{-9} C$ D. $4.771 \times 10^{-9} C$

Q.28 Electric flux is a _____ field, and its density is a _____ field.
A. Vector, vector   B. Scalar, vector
C. Vector, scalar   D. Scalar, scalar

Q.29 The electric flux from a unit positive charge kept in a cuboidal box is:
A. ε_0^{-1} B. $4\pi\varepsilon_0$ C. ε_0 D. $4\pi\varepsilon_0^{-1}$

Q.30 Find the magnitude of the electric field intensity in a sample of silver having conductivity $\sigma = 6.17 \times 10^7$ mho/m, permittivity $\mu = 0.006$ m 2/Vs and drift velocity 1 mm/s.
A. $\frac{1}{10}$ V/m B. $\frac{1}{3}$ V/m C. $\frac{1}{2}$ V/m D. $\frac{1}{6}$ V/m

Q.31 Speed of sound is maximum in:
A. Vaccum B. Gases C. Liquids D. Solids

Q.32 Two waves of intensities I and $4I$ superpose. What will be the maximum and minimum intensities?
A. $5I, 3I$ B. $9I, I$ C. $9I, 3I$ D. $5I, I$

Q.33 In Young's double slit experiment the 10th maximum, of wavelength λ_1 is at a distance of y_1 from the central maximum. When the wavelength of the source is changed to λ_2, 5th maximum is at a distance of y_2 from its central maximum. The ratio of $\frac{y_1}{y_2}$ is:
A. $\frac{2\lambda_1}{\lambda_2}$ B. $\frac{2\lambda_2}{\lambda_1}$ C. $\frac{\lambda_1}{2\lambda_2}$ D. $\frac{\lambda_2}{2\lambda_1}$

Q.34 A beam of light of wavelength $600nm$ from a distant source falls on a single slit $1.0mm$ wide and the resulting diffraction pattern is observed on a screen $2m$ away. The distance between the first dark fringes on either side of the central bright fringe is;
A. $1.2cm$ B. $1.2mm$ C. $2.4cm$ D. $2.4mm$

Q.35 The displacement of a body from a reference point is given by $\sqrt{x} = 2t + 3$, where x is in metres and t is in seconds. The initial velocity of the body is:
A. Zero B. $11m/s$ C. $13m/s$ D. $12m/s$

Q.36 Cooking gas containers are kept in a lorry moving with uniform speed. The temperature of the gas molecules inside will _____.
A. Increase
B. Decrease
C. Remain the same
D. Decreases for some, while the increase for others

Q.37 A cylinder of fixed capacity 44.8 litres contains helium gas at standard temperature and pressure. What is the amount of heat needed to raise the temperature of the gas in the cylinder by $15.0°C$? ($R = 8.31\ J\ mol^{-1}\ K^{-1}$)
A. 265 J B. 310.10 J C. 373.95 J D. 387.97 J

Q.38 The heat generated while transferring 96000 coulomb of charge in one hour through a potential difference of 50 V is:
A. $4.8 \times 10^4 J$ B. $1.33 \times 10^3 J$
C. $4.8 \times 10^6 J$ D. $1.33 \times 10^4 J$

Q.39 Potential gradient is defined as:
A. Fall of potential per unit length of the wire
B. Fall of potential per unit area of the wire
C. Fall of potential between two ends of the wire
D. Potential at any one end of the wire

Q.40 Emission of light in an LED results due to:
A. Emission of electrons
B. Photovoltaic Effect
C. Generation of Electromagnetic Radiation
D. Conversion of Heat to Electrical Energy

Q.41 The rms speed of gas at $27°C$ is V. If the temperature of the gas is raised to $327°C$, then the rms speed of a gas is:
A. V B. $\frac{V}{\sqrt{2}}$ C. $\sqrt{2}$ D. $3V$

Q.42 On passing A.C. through an inductor:
A. Voltage leads the current
B. Voltage and current remain in phase
C. Voltage lags behinds the current
D. Voltage drop is equal to I × Z

Q.43 At very low frequencies a series R-C circuit behaves as almost purely:
A. Resistive B. Inductive
C. Capacitive D. None of the above

Q.44 Which one of the following material is a diamagnetic material?
A. Copper B. Nickel
C. Iron D. Aluminum

Q.45 When a ferromagnetic material is heated above the curie temperature, it becomes:
A. Paramagnetic material
B. Non-magnetic material
C. Diamagnetic material
D. Strongly charged

Q.46 The waves produced by a motor boat sailing in water are _____.
A. Transverse
B. Longitudinal
C. Longitudinal and transverse
D. Stationary

Q.47 The angular velocity of a planet revolving in an elliptical orbit around the sun increases, when it comes closer to the sun. This is due to _____.
A. Conservation of momentum
B. Newton's second law of motion
C. Conservation of angular momentum
D. Law of angular velocity

Q.48 In a hand driven grinding machine, the handle is put _____.
A. Perpendicular to the stone
B. Near the circumference of the stone
C. A few distances above the stone
D. As far away from the stone

Q.49 If two conducting spheres A and B of radius a and b respectively are at the same potential. Then the ratio of the charge of A and B is:

A. a : b B. b : a C. 2a : b D. 2b : a

Q.50 Two charges of $+4\mu C$ and $-16\mu C$ are separated from each other by a distance of $0.6\ m$. At what distance should a third charge of $+6\mu C$ be placed from $+4\mu C$ so that no force exerts on it will be zero?

A. $0.4\ m$ B. $0.6\ m$ C. $1.2\ m$ D. $0.3\ m$

Chemistry

Q.51 What is packing efficiency in simple cubic lattice?
A. 52.4% B. 55.4% C. 56.5% D. 53.6%

Q.52 Pick out the crystalline substance from the following.
A. Coal B. Wax C. Clay D. Sugar

Q.53 Which of the following is not a crystalline solid?
A. Common salt B. Sugar
C. Iron D. Rubber

Q.54 K_c for the reaction $A+B \underset{K_2}{\overset{K_1}{\rightleftharpoons}} C+D$, is equal to:

A. $\frac{K_1}{K_2}$ B. $K_1 K_2$
C. $K_1 - K_2$ D. $K_1 + K_2$

Q.55 The addition of NaCl to AgCl decreases the solubility of AgCl because _____.
A. Solubility product decreases
B. Solubility product remains constant
C. Solution becomes unsaturated
D. Solution becomes super saturated

Q.56 What is the common name of the simplest aromatic amine?
A. Aniline B. Benzylamine
C. Benzenamine D. Aminobenzene

Q.57 At same temperature and pressure, equal volumes of gases contain the same number of:
A. Molecules B. Electrons
C. Protons D. Particles

Q.58 Identify the compounds which are reduced and oxidised in the following reaction.
$3\ N_2H_4 + 2BrO_3^- \rightarrow 3\ N_2 + 2Br^- + 6H_2O$
A. N_2H_4 is oxidised and BrO_3^- is reduced.
B. BrO_3^- is oxidised and N_2H_4 is reduced.
C. BrO_3^- is both reduced and oxidised.
D. This is not a redox reaction.

Q.59 A rain in 50% completed om shown and 75% in 4 hours. Find the order of reaction:
A. First order B. Second order
C. Third order D. Fourth order

Q.60 Rate of the reaction depends on:
A. Temperature
B. Concentration of the reactants
C. Presence of catalyst

D. All of the above

Q.61 The study of chemical kinetics becomes highly complicate if there occurs:
A. Side reaction B. Surface reaction
C. Both (A) and (B) D. None of these

Q.62 A 5 molar solution of H_2SO_4 is diluted from 1 litre to a volume of 10 litres, the normality of the resulting solution will be:
A. 0.1 N B. 5 N C. 0.5 N D. 1 N

Q.63 If 6.84 solution of cane sugar (Molecular weight $= 342$) is isotonic with 1.52% solution of thiocarbonate, then the mol. wt. of thiocarbonate is:
A. 152 B. 60 C. 76 D. 180

Q.64 Volume of $0.1M\ K_2Cr_2O_7$ required to oxidize $35 ml$ of $0.5M\ FeSO_4$ solution is:
A. $29.2 ml$ B. $145 ml$ C. $175 ml$ D. $58.9 ml$

Q.65 The heat change associated with reactions at constant volume is due to the difference in which property of the reactants and the products?
A. internal energy B. enthalpy
C. heat capacity D. free energy

Q.66 Which type of molecular motion does contribute towards internal energy for an ideal mono-atomic gas?
A. Translational B. Rotational
C. Vibrational D. All of the above

Q.67 Actual flame temperature is always lower than the adiabatic flame temperature because there is _____.
A. no possibility of obtaining complete combustion at high temperature
B. always a loss of heat from the flame
C. both (A) and (B)
D. none of these

Q.68 At $0°C$, the density of certain oxide of a gas at 2 bar is the same as that of dinitrogen at 5 bar. What is the molecular mass of the oxide?
A. $50\ g/mol$ B. $60\ g/mol$
C. $70\ g/mol$ D. None of the above

Q.69 The theory which explains that gases consist of molecules, which are in rapid option is known as:
A. Daltons Atomic Theory
B. Bohr's Theory
C. Rutherfords Atomic Theory
D. Kinetic Molecular Theory

Q.70 Lithium fluoride is _____ in water.
A. completely soluble B. soluble
C. insoluble D. Cannot say

Q.71 By the presence of a halogen atom in the ring, what is the effect of this on basic properties of aniline?
A. Increased B. Decreased

Physics & Chemistry : Mock Test - 7

C. Unchanged D. Doubled

Q.72 Which of the following is a linear molecule?
A. ClO_2 B. CO_2 C. NO_2 D. SO_2

Q.73 The substance which increases the rate of a chemical reaction is called _____.
A. Inhibitor   B. Promoter
C. Catalyst   D. Moderator

Q.74 A 100 watt bulb emits monochromatic light of wavelength $400\ nm$. Calculate the number of photons emitted per second by the bulb.
A. $3 \times 10^{20}\ s^{-1}$ B. $2.012 \times 10^{20}\ s^{-1}$
C. $5 \times 10^{20}\ s^{-1}$ D. $2.012 \times 10^{19}\ s^{-1}$

Q.75 Choose the process by which liquid hydrocarbons can be converted to gaseous hydrocarbons.
A. Hydrolysis
B. Oxidation
C. Cracking
D. Distillation under reduced pressure

Q.76 In electrolytic conductors, the conductance is due to:
A. Flow of free mobile electrons
B. Movement of ions
C. Either movement of electrons or ions
D. Cannot be said

Q.77 Which of the following metals is not obtained by the electrolysis of aqueous solution of its salt?
A. Cu   B. Pb   C. Mg   D. Ag

Q.78 Given below are half-cell reactions:
$Mn^{2+} + 2e^- \to Mn$; $E° = -1.18$ V
$2(Mn^{3+} + e^- \to Mn^{2+})$; $E° = +1.51$ V
$E°$ for $3Mn^{2+} \Rightarrow Mn + 2Mn^{3+}$ will be
A. – 0.33 V; the reaction will not occur
B. – 0.33 V; the reaction will occur
C. – 2.69 V; the reaction will not occur
D. – 2.69 V; the reaction will occur

Q.79 Which of the following isomers will give a white precipitate with $BaCl_2$ solution?
A. $[Co(NH_3)_5SO_4]Br$
B. $[Co(NH_3)_5Br]SO_4$
C. $[Co(NH_3)_4(SO_4)_2]Br$
D. $[Co(NH_3)_4Br(SO_4)]$

Q.80 $[Pt(NH_3)_4][CuCl_4]$ and $[Cu(NH_3)_4][PtCl_4]$ are known as:
A. Ionisation isomers
B. Coordination isomers
C. Linkage isomers
D. Polymerisation isomers

Q.81 Meso tartaric acid does not show optical activity because:
A. It has two chiral centres.
B. It shows external compensation.
C. It has a plane of symmetry.
D. It has an erythro form.

Q.82 One mole of an organic compound (A) with the formula C₃H₈O reacts completely with two moles of HI to form X and Y. When Y is boiled with aqueous alkali it forms Z. Z answers the iodoform test. The compound (A) is-
A. Propan – 2 – ol   B. Propan- 1- ol
C. Ethoxy ethane   D. Methoxy ethane

Q.83 Partial reduction of phenyl cyanide with stannous chloride and passing dry HCl gas in ether solution followed by hydrolysis of the aldimine stannic chloride with water to form benzaldehyde is called as which of the following method of preparation of benzaldehyde?
A. Gattermann Koch synthesis
B. Etards reaction
C. Gattermann reaction
D. Stephen's reaction

Q.84 Which of the following reactions will not result in the formation of carbon-carbon bonds?
A. Reimer Tiemann reaction
B. Cannizzaro reaction
C. Wurtz reaction
D. Friedel Crafts acylation

Q.85 Which one of the following is the functional group in Propanone?
A. Ketone   B. Carboxylic acid
C. Alcohol   D. Aldehyde

Q.86 Stephen's reduction converts ethane nitrile into:
A. Acetic Anhydride   B. Ethanal
C. Propanone   D. Ethyl carbylamine

Q.87 Hydrogenation of benzoyl chloride in the presence of Pd on BaSO₄ gives:
A. Benzyl alcohol   B. Benzaldehyde
C. Benzoic acid   D. Phenol

Q.88 The helical structure of protein is stabilized by:
A. Hydrogen bonds   B. Disulphide bonds
C. Peptide bonds   D. None of these

Q.89 The K_m value of the enzyme is the value of the substrate concentration at which the reaction reaches to _____.
A. $\frac{1}{2}V_{max}$ B. Zero   C. $\frac{1}{4}V_{max}$ D. $2V_{max}$

Q.90 The monomer caprolactam is polymerised to obtain which polymer?
[UP Police Constable, 2019]
A. Teflon   B. Nylon 6   C. Bakelite   D. Kevlar

Q.91 Cellulose is a linear polymer of:
A. α-glucose   B. β-D glucose
C. α-fructose   D. None of these

Q.92 Identify the non-toxic and green solvent.
A. Liquified carbondioxide

B. Benzene
C. Carbon tetrachloride
D. Toluene

Q.93 Which of the following is a green solvent used for bleaching clothes?
A. Hydrogen peroxide   B. Tetrachloroethene
C. Benzene   D. Toluene

Q.94 CF_xCl_y [where x + y = 4], why these compounds are not used?
A. These are fluoro carbons
B. These are difficult to synthesise
C. They deplete ozone layer
D. These are very expensive

Q.95 In the common naming system, the prefix sym- is used for haloarenes with ____ halogen atoms.
A. 1   B. 2   C. 3   D. 4

Q.96 Which compound is used in Ultra-violet calibration?
A. Hg_2Cl_2 B. $HgCl_2$
C. $K_2Cr_2O_7$ D. $KMnO_4$

Q.97 Which block elements are known as inner transition elements?
A. s-block   B. p-block   C. d-block   D. f-block

Q.98 Which of the following is not poisonous?
A. H_2O B. H_2S C. H_2Se D. H_2Te

Q.99 Which of the following halogen exists as a solid at room temperature?
A. Chlorine   B. Fluorine   C. Iodine   D. Bromine

Q.100 Which among the following noble gases does not form clathrates?
A. Argon   B. Xenon   C. Krypton   D. Helium

Physics & Chemistry : Mock Test - 7

// Smart Answer Sheet //

Correct Indicates percentage of students who answered questions correctly.

Skipped Indicates percentage of students who skipped questions.

Q.	Ans.	Correct / Skipped	Q.	Ans.	Correct / Skipped	Q.	Ans.	Correct / Skipped	Q.	Ans.	Correct / Skipped	Q.	Ans.	Correct / Skipped
1	B	64.71 % / 1.63 %	17	D	69.51 % / 1.3 %	33	A	54.22 % / 1.54 %	49	A	63.65 % / 1.71 %	65	A	80.21 % / 0.0 %
2	C	46.96 % / 1.56 %	18	C	65.92 % / 1.68 %	34	D	25.02 % / 4.53 %	50	B	51.29 % / 1.52 %	66	A	41.94 % / 1.19 %
3	A	68.26 % / 1.71 %	19	B	85.93 % / 0.0 %	35	D	16.48 % / 3.69 %	51	A	49.98 % / 1.94 %	67	C	77.78 % / 0.0 %
4	C	58.65 % / 1.17 %	20	C	43.92 % / 1.73 %	36	C	78.83 % / 0.0 %	52	D	86.54 % / 0.0 %	68	C	16.77 % / 3.96 %
5	A	66.17 % / 1.68 %	21	C	77.49 % / 0.0 %	37	C	55.44 % / 1.25 %	53	D	44.8 % / 1.93 %	69	D	77.36 % / 0.0 %
6	D	12.9 % / 4.7 %	22	D	56.84 % / 1.27 %	38	C	59.46 % / 1.05 %	54	A	66.74 % / 1.19 %	70	C	78.01 % / 0.0 %
7	B	87.96 % / 0.0 %	23	C	66.27 % / 1.1 %	39	A	49.15 % / 1.58 %	55	D	82.03 % / 0.0 %	71	A	82.08 % / 0.0 %
8	C	21.07 % / 4.3 %	24	C	68.91 % / 1.09 %	40	C	45.21 % / 1.98 %	56	A	17.55 % / 4.11 %	72	B	55.06 % / 1.51 %
9	A	52.06 % / 1.65 %	25	C	69.4 % / 1.44 %	41	C	52.12 % / 1.37 %	57	A	85.81 % / 0.0 %	73	C	57.33 % / 1.41 %
10	B	54.56 % / 1.76 %	26	C	54.09 % / 1.97 %	42	A	68.75 % / 1.82 %	58	A	40.03 % / 1.82 %	74	B	19.7 % / 4.46 %
11	D	13.53 % / 3.22 %	27	A	19.92 % / 4.67 %	43	C	44.08 % / 1.48 %	59	A	55.15 % / 1.3 %	75	C	47.7 % / 1.95 %
12	D	25.9 % / 4.55 %	28	B	19.91 % / 4.41 %	44	A	63.42 % / 1.62 %	60	D	77.87 % / 0.0 %	76	B	86.34 % / 0.0 %
13	B	83.56 % / 0.0 %	29	A	52.31 % / 1.87 %	45	A	69.42 % / 1.86 %	61	C	16.46 % / 3.77 %	77	C	45.28 % / 1.41 %
14	C	62.24 % / 1.8 %	30	D	40.64 % / 1.69 %	46	C	81.01 % / 0.0 %	62	D	51.54 % / 1.35 %	78	C	55.8 % / 1.16 %
15	B	65.39 % / 1.1 %	31	D	80.49 % / 0.0 %	47	C	49.41 % / 1.04 %	63	C	63.2 % / 1.59 %	79	B	41.37 % / 1.33 %
16	D	50.55 % / 1.4 %	32	B	89.5 % / 0.0 %	48	B	47.2 % / 1.84 %	64	A	66.92 % / 1.34 %	80	B	52.53 % / 1.86 %

Physics & Chemistry : Mock Test - 7

Q.	Ans.	Correct / Skipped
81	C	89.74 % / 0.0 %
82	D	49.0 % / 1.54 %
83	D	58.0 % / 1.62 %
84	B	67.13 % / 1.19 %

Q.	Ans.	Correct / Skipped
85	A	81.87 % / 0.0 %
86	B	46.62 % / 1.84 %
87	B	60.33 % / 1.68 %
88	A	40.59 % / 1.42 %

Q.	Ans.	Correct / Skipped
89	A	15.56 % / 3.36 %
90	B	86.83 % / 0.0 %
91	B	59.37 % / 1.36 %
92	A	82.74 % / 0.0 %

Q.	Ans.	Correct / Skipped
93	A	51.82 % / 1.09 %
94	C	69.36 % / 1.64 %
95	C	62.33 % / 1.16 %
96	C	41.23 % / 1.78 %

Q.	Ans.	Correct / Skipped
97	D	50.84 % / 1.49 %
98	A	41.61 % / 1.44 %
99	B	53.41 % / 1.83 %
100	D	48.32 % / 1.43 %

Performance Analysis	
Avg. Score (%)	28.0%
Toppers Score (%)	55.0%
Your Score	

//Hints and Solutions//

1. We are given that a particle of mass m is located in a one dimensional potential field and the potential energy is given by:

$$V(x) = A(1 - \cos px)$$

So, we can find the force experienced by the particle as,

$$F = -\frac{dV}{dx} = -Ap\sin px$$

For small oscillations, we have,

$$F \approx -Ap^2 x$$

The acceleration would be given by,

$$a = \frac{F}{m} = -\frac{Ap^2}{m}x \quad ....(i)$$

Also we know that,

$$a = \frac{F}{m} = -\omega^2 x \quad ....(ii)$$

So from (i) and (ii),

$$\omega = \sqrt{\frac{Ap^2}{m}}$$

We know that,

Period, $T = \frac{2\pi}{\omega} = 2\pi\sqrt{\frac{m}{Ap^2}}$

Hence, the correct option is (B).

2. Equating the equation for forces, we get,

$m\omega^2 a = mg$, where m = mass, ω = angular frequency and a = amplitude.

$$\omega = \sqrt{\frac{g}{a}}$$

Now, formula for time period of simple pendulum is,

$$T = \frac{2\pi}{\omega} = 2\pi\sqrt{\frac{a}{g}} = 2\pi\sqrt{\frac{2.5}{1000}} = \frac{\pi}{10} \sec$$

Hence, the correct option is (C).

3. $x = A\cos\omega t$

$$PE = \frac{kx^2}{2}$$

$$PE = \frac{kA^2(\cos t)^2}{2} = \frac{kA^2(1+\cos 2t)}{2}$$

At $t = 0$, PE is maximum and at $t = \pi$ PE is minimum.

The Graph I is for PE and when $x = 0$ $PE = 0$

and when x = maximum or $x = A$, $PE = \frac{kA^2}{2}$

Therefore, Graph III is for PE.

Hence, the correct option is (A).

4. Given:

Intensity $= I_0$, and Resultant intensity $I = 3I_0$, the resultant intensity at that point is given as,

$$I = 4I_0 \cos^2\left(\frac{\phi}{2}\right)$$

$$\Rightarrow 3I_0 = 4I_0 \cos^2\left(\frac{\phi}{2}\right)$$

$$\Rightarrow \cos\left(\frac{\phi}{2}\right) = \frac{\sqrt{3}}{2}$$

$$\Rightarrow \frac{\phi}{2} = \frac{\pi}{6}$$

$$\Rightarrow \phi = \frac{\pi}{3}$$

Hence, the correct option is (C).

5. Given:

$f = 15 \times 10^{-2}$ m

$D = 6.1$ cm

$= 6.1 \times 10^{-2}$ m

And $\lambda = 4000 \, \overset{\circ}{A}$

$= 4000 \times 10^{-10}$ m

We know that the minimum separation of the microscope is given as,

$$d_{min} = \frac{1.22 f \lambda}{D}$$

Where,

λ = wavelength of light

f = focal length of the objective lens

D = diameter of the objective lens

$$= \frac{1.22 \times 15 \times 10^{-2} \times 4000 \times 10^{-10}}{6.1 \times 10^{-2}}$$

$= 1.2 \times 10^{-6}$ m

Hence, the correct option is (A).

6. The Einstein's equation for photoelectric effect is,

$$eV_0 = \frac{hc}{\lambda} - W$$

where,

V_0 = stopping potential

λ = wavelength of incident light

W = work function of metal.

$E = 4NC^{-1}$, $d = 1m$

$V_0 = \frac{E}{d} = \frac{4}{1} = 4$ volt

$\lambda = 200\ nm = 200 \times 10^{-9}\ m$

Thus, $W = \frac{hc}{\lambda} - eV_0$

$= \frac{(6.62 \times 10^{-34})(3 \times 10^8)}{200 \times 10^{-9}} - (1.6 \times 10^{-19})4$

$= 3.53 \times 10^{-19}\ J$

$= \frac{3.53 \times 10^{-19}}{1.6 \times 10^{-19}}$ (as $1eV = 1.6 \times 10^{-19}\ J$)

$= 2.2\ eV$

Hence, the correct option is (D).

7. We know that the energy carried by the photon is given by the following equation:-

$E = pc$ Which can also be written as follows:-

$p = \frac{E}{c}$ ....(i)

Where p denotes momentum, E is energy and c is speed of light.

One important fact is that the momentum incidence on the surface is equal to the momentum reflected from the surface. But reflected momentum is in the opposite direction.

Therefore, change in momentum, $\Delta p = p_i - p_r$

Where p_i and p_r are incident and reflected momentum respectively.

$p_i = \frac{E}{c}$ ....(ii)

Since, $p_i = p_r$ ....(iii)

So, $p_r = \frac{-E}{c}$

(p_r is in opposite direction of p_i)

But change in momentum is given as follows:-

$\Delta p = p_i - p_r$ ....(iv)

Putting value of (ii) and (iii) in (iv), we have

$\Rightarrow \Delta p = \frac{E}{c} - \frac{-E}{c}$

$\Rightarrow \Delta p = \frac{E}{c} + \frac{E}{c}$

$\Rightarrow \Delta p = \frac{2E}{c}$

Hence, the correct option is (B).

8. The current I through a junction diode is given as

$I = I_0 \left[\exp\left(\frac{eV}{k_BT}\right) - 1\right]$

$I_0 = 5 \times 10^{-12}\ A, T = 300\ K$

$k_B = 8.6 \times 10^{-5} eVK^{-1}$

$= 8.6 \times 10^{-5} \times 1.6 \times 10^{-19} JK^{-1}$

When $V = 0.6\ V$

$\frac{eV}{k_BT} = \frac{1.6 \times 10^{-19} \times 0.6}{8.6 \times 1.6 \times 10^{-24} \times 300}$

$= \frac{600}{8.6 \times 3} = 23.26$

$\therefore I = I_0 \left[\exp\left(\frac{eV}{k_BT}\right) - 1\right]$

$= 5 \times 10^{-12} [\exp(23.26) - 1] A$

$= 5 \times 10^{-12} [1.2586 \times 10^{10} - 1] A$

$= 5 \times 10^{-12} \times 1.2586 \times 10^{10}\ A$

$= 0.06293\ A$

When $V = 0.7\ V$,

$\frac{eV}{k_BT} = \frac{1.6 \times 10^{-19} \times 0.7}{8.6 \times 1.6 \times 10^{-24}} = 27.13$

$\therefore I = I_0 \left[\exp\left(\frac{eV}{k_BT}\right) - 1\right]$

$= 5 \times 10^{-12} [\exp(27.13) - 1] A$

$= 5 \times 10^{-12} [6.07 \times 10^{11} - 1] A$

$= 5 \times 10^{-12} \times 6.07 \times 10^{11}\ A = 3.035\ A$

Increase in current,

$\Delta I = 3.035 - 0.06293 = 2.972\ A$

Hence, the correct option is (C).

9. Concept:

Temperature: It is the measure of the degree of hotness and coldness of a body. The SI unit of temperature is Kelvin (K).

Fahrenheit and Celsius are measurements of temperature and are related to each other as follows:

$C = (F - 32) \times \frac{5}{9}$

Where C is the temperature in Celsius and F is the temperature in Fahrenheit.

Calculation:

Since we need temperature in fahrenheit and celsius to be equal:

Now, let $C = F = x$

So,

$x = (x - 32) \times \frac{5}{9}$

or, $9x = 5x - 160$

or, $4x = -160$

or, $x = -40$

Therefore, $-40°C = -40°F$

Hence, the correct option is (A).

10. Alpha decay: A nuclear decay process where an unstable nucleus changes to another element by shooting out a particle composed of two protons and two neutrons.

Beta decay: A type of radioactive decay in which a beta particle (fast energetic electron or positron) is emitted from an atomic nucleus, transforming the original nuclide to an isobar of that nuclide.

α-decay:

$$^A_ZX \rightarrow ^{A-4}_{Z-2}Y + \alpha$$

β-decay:

$$^A_ZX \rightarrow ^A_{Z+1}Y + \beta^-$$

Successive emission of 1α and 2β particles will eventually cause no change in the atomic number of the daughter nuclei.

So, the daughter nuclei is an isotope of the present nuclei.

Hence, the correct option is (B).

11. Given:

$T_1 = 8T_2$ and $Z = 1$ (for hydrogen)

We know that the time period for the electron moving in the nth orbit is given as,

$$T_n = \frac{4\epsilon_0^2 n^3 h^3}{mZ^2 e^4} \quad \ldots \ldots (i)$$

Where ϵ_o = permittivity, h = Planck's constant, m = mass of the electron, Z = atomic number and e = charge on the electron

By equation (i), the time period of the electron in the hydrogen atom is given as $(Z = 1)$,

$$T_n = \frac{4\epsilon_0^2 n^3 h^3}{m \times 1^2 \times e^4}$$

$\Rightarrow T_n \propto n^3 \quad \ldots(ii)$

By equation (ii),

$T_1 \propto n_1^3 \quad \ldots(iii)$

$T_2 \propto n_2^3 \quad \ldots(iv)$

Divide equation (iii) and equation (iv),

$$\frac{T_1}{T_2} = \frac{n_1^3}{n_2^3}$$

$\Rightarrow \frac{n_1^3}{n_2^3} = \frac{8T_2}{T_2}$

$\Rightarrow \frac{n_1}{n_2} = \frac{2}{1}$

$\Rightarrow n_1 = 2n_2 \quad \ldots(v)$

When $n_2 = 2$

$\Rightarrow n_1 = 2 \times 2$

$\Rightarrow n_1 = 4$

Hence, the correct option is (D).

12. Given:

Number of scintillations per minute at an angle 60°, n_1 = 8100 m

Number of scintillations per minute at an angle 120°, n_2 =?

The scattering in the Rutherford's experiment is proportional to $\cot^4 \frac{\phi}{2}$.

$$\Rightarrow \frac{n_2}{n_1} = \frac{\cot^4 \frac{\phi_2}{2}}{\cot^4 \frac{\phi_1}{2}}$$

Therefore,

$$\frac{n_2}{n_1} = \frac{\cot^4\left(\frac{120°}{2}\right)}{\cot^4\left(\frac{60°}{2}\right)}$$

$$= \frac{\cot^4 60°}{\cot^4 30°}$$

$$= \left(\frac{\frac{1}{\sqrt{3}}}{\sqrt{3}}\right)^4$$

$$= \frac{1}{81}$$

$$n_2 = \frac{1}{81} \times n_1$$

Put the value of n_1 in above equation,

$$= \frac{1}{81} \times 8100$$

$$= 100$$

Hence, the correct option is (D).

13. Given,

Force, $F = 90\ N$

Acceleration, $a = 2.6\ m/s^2$

The force required to accelerate a body of mass m with acceleration a is given by,

$$F = ma$$

$90 = m \times 2.6$

$m = \frac{90}{2.6}$

$m = 34.6 \, kg$

Hence, the correct option is (B).

14. As magnetic flux is equal to:

Φ = BA cosθ

Then, induced e.m.f is equal to:

$e = -N \frac{d(BA\cos\theta)}{dt}$

From the above equation, it is clear that the induced e.m.f. in a coil depends on the magnetic field (B), area of the coil (A), the number of turns (N), the angle between the area and magnetic field (θ), and the change in time (dt).

Therefore, induced e.m.f. in a coil is independent of resistance of the coil.

Hence, the correct option is (C).

15. Eddy Current:

- When a changing magnetic flux is applied to a bulk piece of conducting material then circulating currents is called eddy currents are induced in the material.
- Because the resistance of the bulk conductor is usually low, eddy currents often have large magnitudes and heat the conductor.

Speedometers: In a speedometer, a magnet rotates with the speed at the vehicle. The magnet is placed inside an aluminum drum which is carefully pivoted and held in position by a hairspring.

As the magnet rotates, eddy currents are set up in the drum which opposes the motion of the magnet. A torque is exerted on the drum in the opposite direction which deflects the drum through an angle depending on the speed of the vehicle.

Hence, the correct option is (B).

16. Given:

Number of turns, $n = 100$

Radius, $r = 0.01 \, m$

Resistance, $R = 10\pi^2 \, \Omega$

As we know,

$\epsilon = \frac{-Nd\phi}{dt}$

$= R\epsilon = \frac{-RNd\phi}{dt}, \quad \Delta I = \frac{-RNd\phi}{dt}$

$\frac{\Delta}{\Delta t} = \frac{-N}{R} \frac{\Delta \phi}{\Delta t}$

$\Delta q = -[\frac{N}{R}(\frac{\Delta \phi}{\Delta t})]\Delta t$

$-ve$ sign shows that induced emf opposes the change in flux

$\Delta q = \frac{\mu_0 ni\pi r^2}{R}$

$\Delta q = \frac{4\pi \times 10^{-7} \times 100 \times 4 \times \pi \times (0.01)^2}{10\pi^2}$

$= 32\mu C$

Hence, the correct option is (D).

17. Ohms' law states that at a constant temperature, the current through a resistance is directly proportional to the potential difference across the resistance, i.e.

V = R I   ---(1)

Where V is the potential difference, R is resistance and I is current flowing.

R = Resistance of the conductor, defined as:

$R = \frac{\rho l}{A}$ ···(2)

ρ = Resistivity of the conductor which is related to the conductivity as:

$\sigma = \frac{1}{\rho}$ ...(3)

The electric current per unit area (J) is called current density, i.e.,

$J = \frac{Current \, (I)}{Area \, (A)}$

Using Equation (1), (2), and (3), we get

$V = \frac{\rho l}{A} \times I$

$V = \left(\frac{1}{\sigma}\right) \times l \times \frac{I}{A}$

$V = \left(\frac{1}{\sigma}\right) \times l \times J$

Rearranging the above, we get

$J = \sigma \times \frac{V}{l} = \sigma E$

Hence, the correct option is (D).

18. Current in an Intrinsic semiconductor is equal to Electron current + Hole Current.

It is a crystal having all atoms of the same nature i.e. extremely pure semiconductor is called an intrinsic semiconductor.

Example: pure silicon, germanium.

At room temperature (300 Kelvin), the electrons in the valence band are moved to the conduction band. When an electron leaves the valence band it creates a vacancy known as a hole. A hole attracts electrons as it is positively charged.

In intrinsic semiconductors number of free electrons is equal to the number of holes. i.e., $n_e = n_h$

Since there is an equal number of both the electrons and holes in an intrinsic semiconductor, the current contribution will be equal from both the charge carriers.

The total current passing through intrinsic semiconductors is given by:

I = I$_e$ + I$_h$

I$_e$ = Electron Current

I$_h$ = Hole current

This is explained with the help of the following diagram:

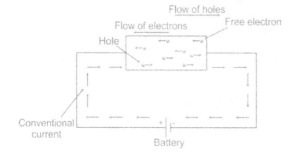

Hence, the correct option is (C).

19. The weight of a body at the centre of the earth is zero.

The weight of a body at the centre of earth is zero because value of g is zero. As we move a body closer to the centre of the earth, the mass of the earth between the centre of the earth and the body keeps decreasing. This causes the force acting from the centre of the earth on the body to decrease.

Hence, the correct option is (B).

20. The work done in an isothermal expansion of a gas depends upon both temperature and expansion ratio.

The work done in an isothermal process is given by:

$$W = nRT\ln\left(\frac{V_1}{V_0}\right) \Rightarrow W \propto T, \ln\left(\frac{V_1}{V_0}\right)$$

V_1 and V_0 are the final and initial volumes respectively, thus it represents the change in volume during expansion. Therefore, work done in an isothermal change of a gas depends on both the temperature and volume expansion ratio.

Hence, the correct option is (C).

21. Thermodynamics is primarily based on a set of four rules that are universally applicable when applied to systems that fall within their respective limitations. They are as follows:

- Zeroth law of thermodynamics
- First law of thermodynamics
- Second law of thermodynamics
- Third law of thermodynamics

Hence, the correct option is (C).

22. The second law of thermodynamics applies to all refrigerators, deep freezers, industrial refrigeration systems, all forms of air-conditioning systems, heat pumps, and so on.

Thermodynamic cycles govern the operation of all forms of air and gas compressors, blowers, and fans. The study of the feasibility of employing various forms of renewable energy sources for household and commercial purposes is an important topic area of thermodynamics.

Hence, the correct option is (D).

23. Since it is given that the coefficient of cubical expansion of alcohol is more than that of the metal.

Upthrust = (volume of the metal ball)× (density of liquid)×g

With the increase in temperature volume of the ball will increase and the density of the liquid will decrease. But the coefficient of cubical expansion of liquid is more. Hence the second effect is more dominating. Therefore upthrust, at higher temperatures will be less, or apparent weight will be more.

Hence, the correct option is (C).

24. At the same level in the two limbs of a U-tube, the pressure is the same. On pouring water on the left side, mercury rises $x\ cm$ (say) from its previous level in the right limb of the U-tube creating a difference of levels of mercury by $2x\ cm$.

Equating pressures at A and B, we get

$P_A = P_B$

$\therefore 11.2 \times 10^{-2} \times \rho_{\text{water}} \times g = 2x \times \rho_{\text{mercury}} \times g$

$\Rightarrow 11.2 \times 10^{-2} \times 1000\ kg/m^3$
$= 2x \times 13600 \times kg/m^3$

$\Rightarrow x = \frac{11.2 \times 10^{-2} \times 1000\ m}{2 \times 13600} = 0.41\ cm$

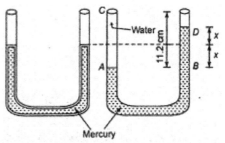

Hence, the correct option is (C).

25. Here, $F = ?$

Charge at P,

$q = 1\mu C = 10^{-6} C$

Charge at A,

$q_1 = +2 \times 10^{-8} C$

Charge at B,

$q_2 = -10^{-8} C$

$AP = 10 cm = 0.1 m$

$BP = 5 cm = 0.05 m$

$\angle APB = 90°$

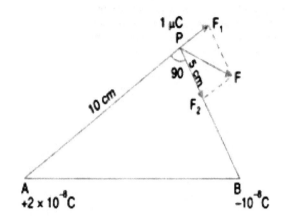

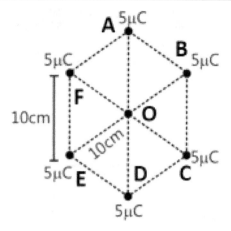

Force at P due to q_1 charge at A,

$F_1 = \dfrac{1}{4\pi\epsilon_0} \dfrac{q_1 q}{(AP)^2}$, along AP produced,

$= \dfrac{9\times 10^9 \times 2\times 10^{-8}\times 10^{-6}}{(0.1)^2}$

$= 18 \times 10^{-3} N$

Force at P due to q_2 charge at B,

$F_2 = \dfrac{1}{4\pi\epsilon_0} \dfrac{q_2 q}{(BP)^2}$, along BP

$= \dfrac{9\times 10^9 \times 10^{-8}\times 10^{-6}}{(0.05)^2}$

$= 36 \times 10^{-3} N$

As angle between $\vec{F_1}$ and $\vec{F_2}$ is $90°$,

∴ Resultant force $F = \sqrt{F_1^2 + F_2^2}$

$F = \sqrt{(18\times 10^{-3})^2 + (36\times 10^{-3})^2}$

$= 18 \times 10^{-3} \times 2.236$

$F = 4.024 \times 10^{-2} N$

Hence, the correct option is (C).

26. The given figure represents six equal charges, $q = 5 \times 10^{-6} C$, at hexagon's vertices.

Sides of the hexagon, $AB = BC = CD = DE = EF = FA = 10 cm$

The distance of O from each vertex, $d = 10 cm$

Electric potential at point O,

$V = \dfrac{6q}{4\pi\varepsilon_0 d}$

Where, ε_0 is the Permittivity of free space

Value of $\dfrac{1}{4\pi\varepsilon_0} = 9 \times 10^9 NC^{-2} m^{-2}$

$V = \dfrac{6\times 9\times 10^9 \times 5\times 10^{-6}}{0.1}$

$V = 2.7 \times 10^6 V$

Clearly, the potential at the hexagon's centre is $2.7 \times 10^6 V$.

Hence, the correct option is (C).

27. It is provided that,

Area of parallel plate capacitor's each plate, $A = 6 \times 10^{-3} m^2$

Distance separating the plates, $d = 3mm = 3\times 10^{-3} m$

Supply voltage, $V = 100 V$

The formula for parallel plate capacitor's Capacitance is given by,

$C = \dfrac{\varepsilon_0 A}{d}$

Where, ε_0 is the Permittivity of free space

$\varepsilon_0 = 8.854 \times 10^{-12} C^2 N^{-1} m^{-2}$

$C = \dfrac{8.854\times 10^{-12} \times 6 \times 10^{-3}}{3\times 10^{-3}}$

$C = 17.71 \times 10^{-12} F$

The formula for Potential V is related with charge q and capacitance C is given by,

$V = \frac{q}{C}$

$q = CV = 100 \times 17.71 \times 10^{-12}$

$q = 1.771 \times 10^{-9} C$

Hence, the correct option is (A).

28. Electric Flux:

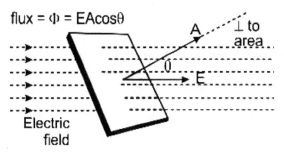

It is defined as the number of electric field lines associated with an area element.

Electric flux is a scalar quantity calculated as a dot product of Electric Field with area vector, i.e. $\phi = E.A = EA\cos\theta$

The SI unit of the electric flux is N-m ^{2}/C.

Electric flux density (D) is a vector quantity because it is simply the product of the vector quantity electric field and the scalar quantity permittivity of the medium, i.e.

$\vec{D} = \varepsilon \vec{E}$

Its unit is Coulomb per square meter.

Hence, the correct option is (B).

29. Concept:

Gauss's Law for electric field: It states that the total electric flux emerging out of a closed surface is directly proportional to the charge enclosed by this closed surface. It is expressed as:

$\phi = \frac{q}{\varepsilon_0}$

Where ϕ is the electric flux, q is the charge enclosed in the closed surface and ε_0 is the electric constant.

Calculation:

Since a unit positive charge is given, $q = +1$ unit

Therefore, electric flux from the surface $\phi = \frac{q}{\varepsilon_0} = \frac{1}{\varepsilon_0} = \varepsilon_0^{-1}$

Hence, the correct option is (A).

30. Concept:

The magnitude of the electric field intensity is the ratio of drift velocity and the permittivity i.e.

$E = \frac{V_d}{\mu}$

Calculation:

Given that,

$\sigma = 6.17 \times 10^7$ mho/m,

$\mu = 0.006$ m 2/Vs

$V_d = 1$ mm/sec $= 10^{-3}$ m/sec

$V_d = \mu E$

$V_d = 10^{-3}$ m/sec

$V_d = \mu E$

So,

$E = \frac{V_d}{\mu} = \frac{10^{-3}}{6 \times 10^{-3}}$

$= \frac{1}{6}$ V/m

Hence, the correct option is (D).

31. Speed of sound is maximum in solids and decreases from solids to liquids and liquids to gases.

Molecules in a solid medium are very close together and sound is a wave due to which the molecules of the solid collide rapidly, due to which the sound moves rapidly in the solid.

Hence, the correct option is (D).

32. Given,

Two waves of intensities $= I, 4I$

$I_{max} = \left(\sqrt{I_1} + \sqrt{I_2}\right)^2$

$= \left(\sqrt{I} + \sqrt{4I}\right)^2$

$I_{max} = \left(3\sqrt{I}\right)^2$

$I_{max} = 9I$

$I_{min} = \left(\sqrt{I_1} - \sqrt{I_2}\right)^2$

$I_{min} = \left(\sqrt{I} - \sqrt{4I}\right)^2$

$\Rightarrow \left(-\sqrt{I}\right)^2 = I$

Hence, the correct option is (B).

33. Position fringe from central maxima:

$y_1 = \frac{n\lambda_1 D}{d}$

Given: $n = 10$

$\therefore y_1 = \frac{10\lambda_1 D}{d}$ .....(i)

For second source:

$y_2 = \frac{5\lambda_2 D}{d}$ .....(ii)

Divide equation (i) by (ii)

$\therefore \frac{y_1}{y_2} = \frac{\frac{10\lambda_1 D}{d}}{\frac{5\lambda_2 D}{d}}$

$\Rightarrow \frac{y_1}{y_2} = \frac{2\lambda_1}{\lambda_2}$

Hence, the correct option is (A).

34. For a dark fringe to form,

$\frac{dy}{D} = \lambda$

$y = \frac{D\lambda}{d}$

$= \frac{2 \times 600 \times 10^{-9}}{10^{-3}} = 1.2mm$

Distance between the first dark fringes on either side of central bright fringe is-

$2 \times y = 2.4mm$

Hence, the correct option is (D).

35. Equation is given as

$\sqrt{x} = 2t + 3$

Taking square both side

$\left(\sqrt{x}\right)^2 = (2t+3)^2$

$x = (2t+3)^2$

$x = (2t)^2 + (3)^2 + 2(2t)(3)$

$x = 4t^2 + 12t + 9$

Taking derivative both side relative to $'t'$

$\frac{dx}{dt} = 2(4t) + 12$

$\frac{dx}{dt} = 8t + 12$

We know that,

$v = \frac{dx}{dt}$

Hence, $v = 8t + 12$

at $t = 0$

$v = 8(0) + 12$

$v = 12m/s$

Then, the initial velocity is $12m/s$.

Hence, the correct option is (D).

36. The centre of mass of the gas molecules moves with uniform speed along with the lorry. As there is no change in relative motion, the translational kinetic energy and hence the temperature of the gas molecules will remain the same.

Hence, the correct option is (C).

37. The volume of 1 mole of He at $STP = 22.4$ litres

Total volume of He at $STP = 44.8$ litres

$\therefore$ No. of moles of He, $n = \frac{\text{Total volume of He}}{\text{The volume of 1 mole of He}} = \frac{44.8}{22.4} = 2$

Molar specific heat of He (monoatomic gas) at constant volume,

$C_V = \frac{3}{2}R = \frac{3}{2} \times 8.31 \, J \, mol^{-1} \, K^{-1}$

$\Delta T = 15°C$

Heat required, $Q = nC_V \Delta T = 2 \times \frac{3}{2} \times 8.31 \times 15$

$Q = 373.95 \, J$

Hence, the correct option is (C).

38. Given:

$I = \frac{Q}{t} = \frac{96000}{3600} = \frac{80}{3} A$

$V = 50$ v

$t = 1$ hour $= 3600$ sec

Where, $I =$ current, $R =$ resistance, $t =$ the time taken, $V =$ electric potential and $Q =$ quantity of charge flowing

We know that:

The amount of heat produced (H) in joules is:

$H = VIt$

$\Rightarrow H = 50 \times \frac{80}{3} \times 3600$

$\Rightarrow H = 4.8 \times 10^6 J$

Hence, the correct option is (C).

39. Potential gradient (k): Potential difference (or fall in potential) per unit length of wire is called potential gradient i.e.,

$k = \frac{V}{l}$

Where, $V =$ Potential difference and $l =$ length of the wire

Potential gradient directly depends upon:

- The resistance per unit length (R/L) of potentiometer wire.
- The radius of potentiometer wire (i.e., Area of crosssection)
- The specific resistance of the material of potentiometer wire (i.e., ρ)
- The current flowing through potentiometer wire (I).

Hence, the correct option is (A).

40. Emission of light in an LED results due to Generation of Electromagnetic Radiation.

When an electron from n-type semiconductor of the diode moves to p-type semiconductor under the influence of an externally applied electric field, it emits a photon with energy equivalent to the energy bandgap of the p-n junction.

Light-Emitting Diode (LED): In an LED, this energy lies in the visible region of electromagnetic radiation, and the photon released is perceived as light.

An LED in this way converts electrical energy into light energy and light is an example of electromagnetic radiation.

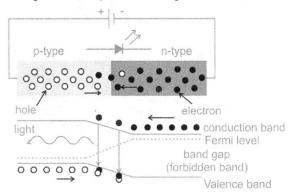

Hence, the correct option is (C).

41. Given: Initial rms velocity $(V_{rms1}) = V$, initial temperature $(T_1) = 27°C = 300\ K$ and final temperature $(T_2) = 327°C = 600\ K$

As the sample is the same, therefore the molecular mass will be the same. So,

$\Rightarrow V_{rms} \propto \sqrt{T}$

$\Rightarrow \dfrac{V_{rms1}}{V_{rms2}} = \sqrt{\dfrac{T_1}{T_2}}$

$\Rightarrow \dfrac{V}{V_{rms2}} = \sqrt{\dfrac{300}{600}} = \dfrac{1}{\sqrt{2}}$

$\Rightarrow V_{rms2} = V\sqrt{2}$

Hence, the correct option is (C).

42. On passing A.C. through an Inductor voltage leads the current.

$V_{L(t)} = L\dfrac{di_{L(t)}}{dt}$

If $i_{L(t)} = I_{max}\sin(\omega t)$ then:

$V_{L(t)} = L\dfrac{d}{dt}I_{max}\sin(\omega t + \theta)$

$= \omega L I_{max}\cos(\omega t + \theta)$

Then the voltage across an AC inductance will be defined as:

$V_L = \omega L I_{max}\sin(\omega t + 90°)$

Where: $V_L = I\omega L$ which is the voltage amplitude and $\theta = +90°$ which is the phase difference or phase angle between the voltage and current.

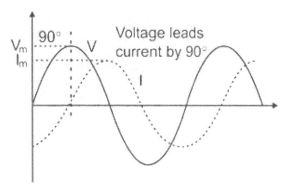

Hence, the correct option is (A).

43. Capacitive reactance is given by, $X_c = \dfrac{1}{2\pi f C}$

It is inversely proportional to frequency. So, at very low frequencies, the impedance is very high. At low frequencies, resistance is almost negligible compared to capacitive reactance. therefore series RC circuit acts as a capacitive circuit.

Hence, the correct option is (C).

44. Copper is a diamagnetic material.

Diamagnetic Substances: The substances which are weekly magnetized when placed in an external magnetic field, in a direction opposite to the applied field are called diamagnetic substances.

Example: Copper, lead, gold, silver, zinc, antimony, bismuth, etc.

Hence, the correct option is (A).

45. When ferromagnetic material heated beyond curie temperature, turns into paramagnetic material, as the ferromagnetic domains become random.

Ferromagnetism: Ferromagnetism is the presence of magnetic domains which are aligned in the same direction in magnetic materials. The most common examples of ferromagnetic materials are metals such as iron, nickel, cobalt, and metal alloys.

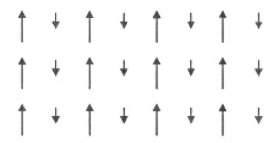

Antiferromagnetism:

- Antiferromagnetism is the presence of magnetic domains that are aligned in opposite directions in magnetic materials.
- These opposite magnetic domains have equal magnetic moments which are canceled out (since they are in opposite directions).
- This makes the net moment of material zero. This type of material is known as antiferromagnetic materials.

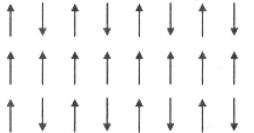

Order or Magnetic Domains in Antiferromagnetic Materials

Hence, the correct option is (A).

46. Transverse waves are generated on the water surface. Inside water longitudinal waves longitudinal waves are produced due to vibrations of the rudder.

Hence, the correct option is (C).

47. The angular velocity of a planet revolving in an elliptic orbit around the sun increases when it comes closer to the sun increases when it comes closer to the sun because its moment of inertia about the axis through the sun decreases. When it goes far away from the sun, its moment of inertia decreases so as to conserve angular momentum.

Hence, the correct option is (C).

48. For a given force, torque can be increased if the perpendicular distance of the point of application of the force from the axis of rotation is increased. Hence the handle put near the circumference produces maximum torque.

Hence, the correct option is (B).

49. Given: Radius of capacitor A = a, Radius of capacitor B = b, and Potential on both capacitors is the same i.e., $V_A = V_B = V$

As we know, the charge on the capacitor/conductor is given by:

$\Rightarrow Q = CV$

$\Rightarrow Q = (4\pi\epsilon_0 R)V$

For conducting spheres A, the charge on it is:

$\Rightarrow Q_A = (4\pi\epsilon_0 a)V$ .....(i)

For conducting spheres B. the charge on it is:

$\Rightarrow Q_B = (4\pi\epsilon_0 b)V$ .....(ii)

On dividing equations (i) and (ii), we get

$\Rightarrow \dfrac{Q_A}{Q_B} = \dfrac{4\pi\epsilon_0 a}{4\pi\epsilon_0 b} = \dfrac{a}{b}$

Hence, the correct option is (A).

50. Consider new charge $+4\mu C$ is placed dm apart from old $+4\mu C$ charge and $(x + 0.6)m$ apart from $-16\mu C$ charge.

Let,

$q_A = +4\mu C$ at point A

$q_B = -16\mu C$ at point B

$q_C = +6\mu C$ at point C

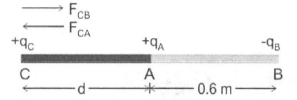

Since, net force on charge q_C will zero.

$\therefore |F_{CA}| = |F_{CB}|$

From above concept,

$\dfrac{Kq_A q_C}{d^2} = \dfrac{Kq_B q_C}{(0.6+d)^2}$

$\dfrac{24}{d^2} = \dfrac{96}{(0.6+d)^2}$

$4d^2 = (0.6 + d)^2$

$4d^2 = 0.36 + d^2 + 1.2d$

$3d^2 - 1.2d - 0.36 = 0$

$d_1 = -0.2m$

$d_2 = +0.6m$

So, according to option + 0.6 m distance should a third charge of + 6 µC be placed from + 4 µC so that no force exerts on it will be zero.

Hence, the correct option is (B).

51. Let the edge length or side of the cube be 'a', and the radius of each particle be 'r'.

Then, we know that:

For simple cubic lattice:

$a = 2r$

Volume of cube $= a^3$

$= 8r^3$

In simple cube, each unit cell has only one sphere,

Volume of sphere $= \dfrac{4}{3}\pi r^3$

Packing efficiency = $\frac{\text{Volume of a sphere}}{\text{Volume of the cube}} \times 100\%$

$= \frac{\frac{4}{3}\pi r^3}{8r^3} \times 100$

$= 52.4\%$

Hence, the correct option is (A).

52. In sugar, the constituent particles are arranged in a specific manner. Therefore, it is a crystalline solid.

The solids in which the constituent particles of matter are arranged and organized in a specific manner are called crystalline solids.

In coal, wax, and clay the constituent particles are arranged in a random manner. Therefore, these are an amorphous solid.

Hence, the correct option is (D).

53. Common salt, sugar and iron are crystalline solids whereas rubber is an amorphous solid as it does not have well developed perfectly ordered crystalline structure. Other amorphous solids include tar, glass, plastic, butter etc.

Hence, the correct option is (D).

54. K_c = Equilibrium constant

$A + B \underset{K_2}{\overset{K_1}{\rightleftharpoons}} C + D$

$K_c = \frac{K_1}{K_2} = \frac{[C][D]}{[A][B]}$

As at equilibrium,

Rate of forward reaction = rate of backward reaction,

$r_f = r_b$

$K_1[A][B] = K_2[C][D]$

$K_c = \frac{K_1}{K_2} = \frac{[A][B]}{[C][D]}$

Hence, the correct option is (A).

55. $NaCl$ is highly soluble and when it is added to $AgCl$, it decreases the solubility of $AgCl$ because of common ion Cl and solution become super saturated.

Hence, the correct option is (D).

56. The simplest amine is C₆H₅NH₂ and is known as aniline. This name is also accepted as the IUPAC name. Its actual IUPAC name is benzenamine, or it may also be written as aminobenzene.

Hence, the correct option is (A).

57. At same temperature and pressure, equal volumes of gases contain the same number of molecules.

Avogadro's hypothesis:

- All gases containing equal moles if substance occupy the same volume at the same temperature and pressure.
- Therefore, equal volumes of gases will have an equal number of particles that can be atoms or molecules.

Hence, the correct option is (A).

58. Separating the oxidation and reduction reaction from the redox reaction:

$3\,N_2H_4 + 2BrO_3^- \rightarrow 3\,N_2 + 2Br^- + 6H_2O$

Assigning the oxidation number on central atom (N and Br) in each molecules by considering oxidation number of $H = +1, O = -2$, we get oxidation state as:

$3\,\overset{-2}{N_2}H_4 + 2[\overset{+5}{Br}O_3]^- \rightarrow 3\,\overset{0}{N_2} + 2\overset{-1}{Br}^- + 6H_2O$

As the oxidation number of N changes from -2 to 0 as:

$N_2H_4 \rightarrow N_2$

Its a oxidation reaction where N_2H_4 gets oxidized.

Similarly, as the oxidation number of Br changes from $+5$ to -1 as:

$BrO_3^- \rightarrow Br^-$

Its a reduction reaction where BrO_3^- gets reduced.

Hence, the correct option is (A).

59. 50% reaction completes in 2 hours. That is, half life of reaction is 2 hours

$t_{(\frac{1}{2})} = 2$ hours. Also given that, $t_{(\frac{3}{4})} = 4$ hours

We can observe that,

$t_{(\frac{3}{4})} = 2 \times t_{(\frac{1}{2})}$

Thus, relation holds true only in first order

Hence, the correct option is (A).

60. Rate of reaction depends on temperature, concentration of the reactants and presence of catalyst.

Example:

1. At higher temperature, particles collide more frequently and with greater similarity.

2. $CH_4(g) + 2O_2(g) \rightarrow CO_2(g) + 2H_2O$ Faster rate

$C_{25}H_{52}(g) + 38O_2 \rightarrow 25CO_2(g) + 26H_2O$ Slow rate

So, reaction depends on nature of reactants.

3. A catalyst is a species that speeds up a chemical reaction with being chemically changed upon completion of reaction.

Hence, the correct option is (D).

61. The study of chemical kinetics becomes highly complicate if there occurs side reactions or surface reactions. These reactions bring changes in the value of rate constant and not help to proceeds the reaction in the right manner.

Hence, the correct option is (C).

62. Given,

$M_1 = 5$ molar

$V_1 = 1$ litre

$V_2 = 10$ litre

According to Dilation Formula,

$M_1 V_1 = M_2 V_2$

$\Rightarrow M_2 = 0.5$

Normality = Molarity $\times$ Equivalent number

Equivalent number refers to how many ions are acting in the solution, the number of those ions is called the gram equivalent number.

Here, the Equivalent number $= 2$

$N_2 = 0.5 \times 2 = 1.0$ N

Hence, the correct option is (D).

63. Isotonic solutions have some osmotic pressure hence, their molarities will be equal.

Molarity $= \dfrac{10 \times \left(\dfrac{w}{v}\%\right)}{M}$

Molarity of solution of cane sugar = Molarity of solution of thiocarbonate

$\dfrac{10 \times 6.84}{342} = \dfrac{10 \times 1.52}{x}$

$\Rightarrow x = \dfrac{10 \times 152 \times 342}{10 \times 684}$

$\Rightarrow x = \dfrac{152}{2}$

$\Rightarrow x = 76$

Hence, the correct option is (C).

64. $K_2Cr_2O_7 + 6FeSO_4 + 7H_2SO_4 \rightarrow K_2SO_4 + Cr_2(SO_4)_3 + 3Fe_2(SO_4)_3 + 7H_2O$

For $K_2Cr_2O_7, M = 0.1M, n_1 = 1, V_1 = ?$

For $FeSO_4, M = 0.5M, n_2 = 6, V_2 = 35ml$

According to Dilation Formula,

$\dfrac{M_1 V_1}{n_1} = \dfrac{M_2 V_2}{n_2}$

$\Rightarrow \dfrac{0.1 \times V_1}{1} = \dfrac{0.5 \times 35}{6}$

$\Rightarrow V_1 = 29.2 ml$

Hence, the correct option is (A).

65. The heat change associated with reactions at constant volume is due to the difference in the internal energy of the reactants and the products.

First Law of Thermodynamics dictates that $\Delta Q = \Delta U + \Delta W$

At constant $V, \Delta W = 0$

So, $\Delta Q = \Delta U$

So at constant volume, heat change takes place due to a change in the internal energy of the system.

Hence, the correct option is (A).

66. In an ideal mono-atomic gas, the internal energy is contributed only due to the translational kinetic energy.

For example, if we take He or Ne, the atoms are not bound to each other and hence they do not vibrate. Rotational energy is neglected since their atomic moment of inertia is minimal and higher energy excitation electronically also is not possible (except at very high temperatures). Thus, the internal energy changes in an ideal monoatomic gas are purely translational and there are 3 degrees of freedom. In other words, translation can take place in $3D$ space i.e. $x, y,$ and z directions.

Hence, the correct option is (A).

67. Actual flame temperature is always lower than the adiabatic flame temperature because there is no possibility of obtaining complete combustion at a high temperature and there is always a loss of heat from the flame.

The constant volume adiabatic flame temperature is the temperature that results from a complete combustion process that occurs without any work, heat transfer or changes in kinetic or potential energy. The constant pressure adiabatic flame temperature is the temperature that results from a complete combustion process that occurs without any heat transfer or changes in kinetic or potential energy. Its temperature is lower than the constant volume process because some of the energy is utilized to change the volume of the system (i.e., generate work).

Hence, the correct option is (C).

68. Density (d) of substance at temperature (T) can be given by the expression,

$d = \dfrac{Mp}{RT}$

Now, density of oxide (d_1) is given by,

$d_1 = \dfrac{M_1 p_1}{RT}$

Where, M_1 and p_1 are the mass and pressure of the oxide respectively.

Density of dinitrogen gas (d_2) is given by,

$d_2 = \frac{M_2 p_2}{RT}$

Where, M_2 and p_2 are the mass and pressure of the oxide respectively.

According to the given question,

$d_1 = d_2$

Therefore,

$M_1 p_1 = M_2 p_2$

Given,

$p_1 = 2 bar$

$p_2 = 5 bar$

Molecular mass of nitrogen, $M_2 = 28\ g/mol$

Now, $M_1 = \frac{M_2 p_2}{p_1}$

$= \frac{28 \times 5}{2}$

$= 70\ g/mol$

The molecular mass of the oxide is $70\ g/mol$.

Hence, the correct option is (C).

69. The theory which explains that gases consist of molecules, which are in rapid option is known as Kinetic Molecular Theory. Kinetic Molecular Theory states that gas particles are in constant motion and exhibit perfectly elastic collisions. Kinetic Molecular Theory can be used to explain both Charles' and Boyle's Laws. The average kinetic energy of a collection of gas particles is directly proportional to absolute temperature only.

Hence, the correct option is (D).

70. Lithium fluoride is insoluble in water.

All alkali halides except Lithium fluoride are soluble in water, this is because Lithium fluoride is soluble in nonpolar solvents as it has a strong covalent bond. Lithium fluoride is represented by the formula LiF.

Hence, the correct option is (C).

71. By the presence of a halogen atom in the ring, basic properties of aniline is increased because it is more electronegative so donation of electron will be easy, so basicity increases.

Hence, the correct option is (A).

72. CO_2 is a linear molecule because of sp-hybridization around the carbon atom.

The linear shape is the shape in which atoms are deployed in a straight line under $180°$ angle. Therefore, molecules with linear electron-pair geometries have sp hybridization at the center of the atom.

CO_2 has a linear shape so this is due to the VSEPR (valence shell electron repulsion) theory and the different number of electrons in each molecule.

In CO_2, the central C atom has 4 valence electrons. All are used up to form four bonds with O atoms. Thus, it has zero lone pair. As the carbon is in the center because it has lower electronegativity. If we only take a single bond from $C - O$, then carbon does not form a stable octet of electrons so that's why we need to form a double bond $C = O = C$. The bonding electrons around the carbon repel equally so the molecule is linear.

Hence, the correct option is (B).

73. A catalyst is a substance added to it to increase the rate of a chemical reaction.

Example:

1) Finely divided iron is used as a catalyst in the formation of ammonia(Haber process).

$N_2(g) + 3H_2(g) \Leftrightarrow 2NH_3(g)$

2) Vanadium pentoxide (V_2O_5) is used as a catalyst in the combination of sulphur dioxide and oxygen to form sulphur trioxide

$2SO_2(g) + O_2(g) \Leftrightarrow 2SO_3(g)$

Hence, the correct option is (C).

74. Given,

Power of the bulb $= 100 watt = 100\ J\ s^{-1}$

Wavelength, $\lambda = 400 \times 10^{-9} m$

Planck's constant, $h = 6.626 \times 10^{-34} Js$

The speed of light, $= 3 \times 10^8\ m\ s^{-1}$

Energy of one photon, $E = h\nu$

$= \frac{hc}{\lambda}$

$= \frac{6.626 \times 10^{-34} \times 3 \times 10^8}{400 \times 10^{-9}}$

$= 4.969 \times 10^{-19}\ J$

Number of photons emitted $= \frac{\text{Power of the bulb}}{\text{Energy of one photon}}$

$= \frac{100}{4.969 \times 10^{-19}}$

$= 2.012 \times 10^{20}\ s^{-1}$

Hence, the correct option is (B).

75. The process by which liquid hydrocarbons can be converted to gaseous hydrocarbons is cracking.

On cracking or pyrolysis, the hydrocarbon with higher molecular mass gives a mixture of hydrocarbons having lower molecular mass. Therefore, we can say that by cracking a liquid hydrocarbon can be converted into a mixture of gaseous hydrocarbons.

Hence, the correct option is (C).

76. In metallic conductors, the conductance is due to the flow of free mobile electrons and in electrolytic conductors, the conductance is due to the movement of ions in a solution of fused electrolyte.
Hence, the correct option is (B).

77. Highly reactive metals with lower reduction potentials than hydrogen are not obtained by electrolysis of aqueous solutions of their salts since their cations cannot be reduced at cathode in presence of water. Instead of reduction of these metal cations, water undergoes reduction. Mg are reactive metals with lower reduction potentials.

Usually d-block elements are less reactive and hence can be prepared by electrolysis of their aqueous solutions.
Hence, the correct option is (C).

78. Standard electrode potential of reaction will not change due to multiply the half-cell reactions with some numbers,

To get the main eq. we have to reverse 2nd equation given in question and add them

So, $E_3 = E_2 + E_1$

$E_3 = -1.18 + (-1.51)$

$E_3 = -2.69V$

The reaction is not possible as the ΔG will come +ve for this case and that indicates the reaction is non-spontaneous.

Hence, the correct option is (C).

79. SO_4^{2-} will give a precipitate with $BaCl_2$ only if the sulphate ion is not present in the coordination sphere. Only then it will be able to dissociate as an anion in aqueous solution.
The complex $[Co(NH_3)_5Br]SO_4$ dissociates to give $[Co(NH_3)_5Br]^{2+}$ and SO_4^{2-} ions. SO_4^{2-} ion reacts with barium chloride to give white precipitate of $BaSO_4$.
$[Co(NH_3)_5Br]SO_4 \rightleftharpoons [Co(NH_3)_5Br]^{2+} + SO_4^{2-}$
$SO_4^{2-} + BaCl_2 \rightarrow BaSO_4$ (white ppt.) $\downarrow +2Cl^-$
Hence, the correct option is (B).

80. Different complex ions have the same molecular formula. Ligands are interchanged between the complex cation and complex anion. These types of complexes are called coordination isomers.

In $[Pt(NH_3)_4][CuCl_4]$, ammonia ligands are attached to Pt metal and chloride ligands are attached to Cu metal.

In $[Cu(NH_3)_4][PtCl_4]$, ammonia ligands are attached to Cu metal and chloride ligands are attached to Pt metal.

Hence, the correct option is (B).

81. Meso tartaric acid is optically inactive because it has a plane of symmetry.

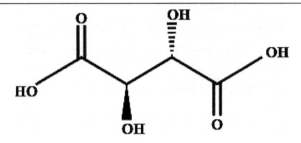

Hence, the correct option is (C).

82. The final product is Methoxy ethane which can be represented by the following reaction:

$C_2H_5O \xrightarrow{\text{Excess HI}} CH_3-I - CH_3-CH_2-I \xrightarrow[\text{NaOH}]{\text{aqueous}} [CH_3-CH]-H$
$(CH_3-CH_2-O-CH_3)$ (X) (Y) $\qquad\qquad\qquad$ OH
$\qquad\qquad\qquad\qquad\qquad\qquad\qquad\qquad\qquad\qquad$ (Z) (iodoform test)

The reaction finally is also used to prove the iodoform test valid.

Hence, the correct option is (D).

83. Partial reduction of phenyl cyanide with stannous chloride and passing dry HCl gas in ether solution followed by hydrolysis of the aldimine stannic chloride with water to form benzaldehyde is called Stephan's reaction. The reaction mechanism is given as follows:

R–C≡N $\xrightarrow{HCl}$ [RC=NH]$^+$Cl$^-$ $\xrightarrow{SnCl_2 + HCl}$ [RCH=NH_2]$_2$; SnCl$_6^{2-}$ $\xrightarrow{H_2O}$ RCHO + NH_3

Mechanism of stephens Reactions

R–C≡N $\xrightarrow{H^+}$ R–C≡N–H $\longrightarrow$ R–C=NH
$\qquad\qquad\qquad\qquad\qquad\qquad\qquad\qquad$ |Cl$^-$
$\qquad\qquad\qquad\qquad\qquad\qquad\qquad$ R–C=NH
$\qquad\qquad\qquad\qquad\qquad\qquad\qquad$ |Cl
$\qquad\qquad\qquad\qquad\qquad\qquad\qquad$ |SnCl$_2$/HCl
$\qquad\qquad\qquad\qquad\qquad\qquad\qquad$ 20°C
R–CHO $\xleftarrow{\text{Steam Distillation}}$ R–HC=NH

Following is the example of Stephen's reaction:

⬠–CN $\xrightarrow[\text{(ii) } H_2O/\Delta]{\text{(i) } SnCl_2/HCl}$ ⬠–CHO

Ph–CN $\xrightarrow[\text{(ii) } H_2O/\Delta]{\text{(i) } SnCl_2/HCl}$ Ph–CHO

Hence, the correct option is (D).

84. (B) Cannizaro reaction:

$\underset{\text{Formaldehyde}}{HCHO} \xrightarrow{50\% NaOH} \underset{\text{Sodium formate}}{HCOO^{\ominus}Na^{\oplus}} + \underset{\text{Methanol}}{CH_3OH}$

(A) Reimer Tiemann reaction:

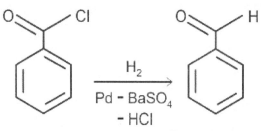

(C) Wurtz reaction:

$$H_3C-I + 2Na + I-CH_3 \rightarrow CH_3-CH_3 + 2NaI$$

Methyl iodide → Ethane

(D) Friedel Crafts reaction:

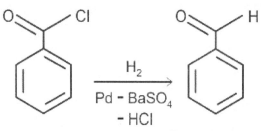

From the above images, it is clear that the Cannizaro reaction will not result in the formation of carbon-carbon bonds.

Hence, the correct option is (B).

85. In propanone($(CH_3)_2CO$), the functional group present is a ketone (- C=O) group.

Acetone also is known as Propanone is an organic compound with the formula $(CH_3)_2CO$.

In propanol (C_3H_7OH), the functional group present is an alcohol (- OH) group.

In propanoic acid (C_2H_5COOH), the functional group present is a carboxylic acid (- COOH) group.

In ethanal (CH_3CHO), the functional group present is an aldehyde(- CHO) group.

In propanal (C_2H_5CHO), the functional group present is an aldehyde(- CHO) group.

Hence, the correct option is (A).

86. Stephen's reduction converts ethane nitrile into ethanal or Acetaldehyde.

When ethane nitrile is treated with Sn/HCl, it undergoes Stephen's reaction to form Acetaldehyde.

The reaction is:

$R-CN + 2[H] \xrightarrow{SnCl_2/dil.HCl} R-CH=NHHCl \xrightarrow{H_3O^+} RCHO + NH_4Cl$
Alkyl cyanide → Imine hydrochloride → Aldehyde

a. $CH_3-C\equiv N + 2[H] \xrightarrow{SnCl_2/dil.HCl} CH_3-CH=NHHCl \xrightarrow{H_3O^+} CH_3-CHO + NH_4Cl$
Acetonitrile → Imine complex → Acetaldehyde

b. $C_6H_5-C\equiv N + 2[H] \xrightarrow{SnCl_2/dil.HCl} C_6H_5-C\equiv NHHCl \xrightarrow{H_3O^+} C_6H_5-CHO + NH_4Cl$
Benzonitrile → Imine complex → Benzaldehyde

The reaction is more efficient when aromatic nitriles are used rather than aliphatic nitriles. The reaction is a redox reaction and electron-withdrawing substituents can improve the rate of the reaction.

Hence, the correct option is (B).

87. When Benzoyl chloride reacts with hydrogen in presence of palladium catalyst and barium sulphate, benzaldehyde is formed. This is known as Rosenmund reaction.

It is a reduction reaction where hydrogen is added to benzoyl chloride in presence of a catalyst. The catalyst is poisoned with sulfur or quinoline to prevent over reduction of the compound to alcohol.

The alcohol formed then may react with the benzoyl chloride to form esters, thus the presence of catalyst poison is very important.

The reaction can be given as follows:

Example of Rosenmund Reduction

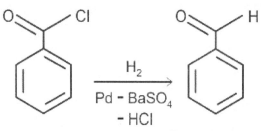

Benzoyl chloride → Benzaldehyde

Hence, the correct option is (B).

88. The helical structure of proteins or the alpha helix is the secondary structure of proteins and it is stabilized by hydrogen bonds. In helical structure, the carbonyl oxygen atoms in $C = O$ points in one direction, towards the amide hydrogen atoms in N- H groups, 4 residues away. These groups together form a hydrogen bond, one of the main forces of secondary structure stabilization in proteins.

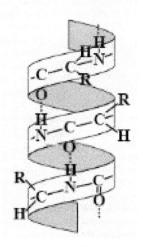

Hence, the correct option is (A).

89. The catalytic efficiency of an enzyme is described by the K_m value or Michaelis Menten constant. The Michaelis constant is the substrate concentration at which the reaction rate is one half the maximum. The K_m describes the affinity of enzyme for a substrate molecule. Greater the affinity lower is the K_m value and sooner the V_{max} can be attained.

According to Michaelis-Menten equation K_m is equal to substrate concentration at which the velocity is half the maximum. Michaelis and Menten proposed a hypothesis for enzyme for action according to which the enzyme molecule combines with a substrate complex which further dissociates to form product and enzyme back.

Hence, the correct option is (A).

90. Nylon 6 is only made from one kind of monomer, a monomer called caprolactam.

Nylon 6 is a polymer that is mainly used in the manufacturing sector. Having high tensile strength, fatigue resistance, and toughness, it is used in the manufacture of industrial yarn.

Structure of Nylon-6:

Caprolactum   Nylon-6

Hence, the correct option is (B).

91. Cellulose is a linear polymer of β-D-glucose units, which in contrast to starch, is oriented with $-CH_2OH$ groups alternating above and below the plane of the cellulose molecule thus producing long, unbranched chains. The absence of side chains allows cellulose molecules to lie close together and form rigid structures. Cellulose is the major structural material of plants. Wood is largely cellulose, and cotton is almost pure cellulose.

Hence, the correct option is (B).

92. When compared to conventional solvents, liquified CO_2 leaves a lower amount of residue. It is also a non-toxic and attractive solvent for temperature-sensitive materials.

Hence, the correct option is (A).

93. Hydrogen peroxide can easily breakdown into water and oxygen. It is a good oxidizing agent and a strong bleaching agent. Use of H_2O_2 gives better results and makes use of a lesser amount of water.

Hence, the correct option is (A).

94. CFC molecules are made up of chlorine, fluorine and carbon atoms and are extremely stable. This extreme stability allows CFC's to slowly make their way into the stratosphere (most molecules decompose before they can cross into the stratosphere from the troposphere).

Hence, the correct option is (C).

95. The prefix sym- is used for trihaloarenes with same halogen atom at alternate positions in the benzene ring (1, 3, 5). The prefixes o-, m- and p- are used for dihaloarenes depending on the relative positions of the two identical halogen atoms on the aromatic ring.

Hence, the correct option is (C).

96. Potassium dichromate ($K_2Cr_2O_7$) is especially useful in the visible range but also useful in UV. Potassium dichromate itself is stable and available in high purity. In dilute perchloric acid solution, it has a linear response with good temperature stability and also stable as solution.

Hence, the correct option is (C).

97. Inner transition elements are f-block i.e. 4f and 5f. They include elements from 57 to 71 and 89 to 103. The 4f elements are lanthanoids (57 – 71) and 5f are actinides (89 – 113). Most of the actinides are radioactive.

Hence, the correct option is (D).

98. The hydride of Oxygen, i.e., H_2O is a colourless, odourless liquid while the hydrides of all the other group 16 elements are unpleasant, foul smelling, poisonous gases. H_2O has the highest boiling point of 373 K amongst the hydrides of group 16 elements.

Hence, the correct option is (A).

99. The strength of the van der Waals between molecules forces increases as the size of the halogen increases from fluorine to iodine. As a result, F_2 and Cl_2 are gases at room temperature, Br_2 is a liquid whereas I_2 is a solid.

Hence, the correct option is (B).

100. Noble gases can form compounds in which the gases are entrapped in the cavities of crystal lattices. Such compounds are called clathrates. Only Argon, Krypton, Xenon and Radon are known to form clathrates among the noble gases.

Hence, the correct option is (D).

Physics & Chemistry : Mock Test 08

Physics

Q.1 A particle is executing linear simple harmonic motion of amplitude $'A'$. What fraction of the total energy is kinetic when the displacement is half the amplitude?
A. $\frac{1}{4}$
B. $\frac{1}{2\sqrt{2}}$
C. $\frac{1}{2}$
D. $\frac{3}{4}$

Q.2 A particle is performing linear Simple harmonic motion. What fraction of the total energy is potential, with the displacement is half the amplitude?
A. 0.33
B. 0.75
C. 0.5
D. 0.25

Q.3 A sonometer wire, with a suspended mass of $M = 1\ kg$, is in resonance with a given tuning fork. The apparatus is taken to the moon where the acceleration due to gravity is $\frac{1}{6}$ that on earth. To obtain resonance on moon, the value of M should be
A. $1\ kg$
B. $6\ kg$
C. $7\ kg$
D. $36\ kg$

Q.4 Which of the following is used in a magnifying glass?
A. Convex lens
B. Concave lens
C. Convex mirror
D. Concave mirror

Q.5 When light enters from rarer medium to denser medium then its:
A. Frequency increases speed decreases
B. Frequency is same but wavelength is smaller in denser medium then in rarer
C. Frequency is same but wavelength is greater in denser medium then in rarer
D. Frequency decrease and wavelength same

Q.6 The work function of tungsten is $4.50eV$. The wavelength of the fastest electron emitted when light whose photon energy is $5.50eV$ falls on a tungsten surface, is?
A. $1.29 \times 10^{-9}m$
B. $1.24 \times 10^{-19}m$
C. $1.24 \times 10^{-9}m$
D. $1.24 \times 10^{9}m$

Q.7 When the energy of the incident radiation is increased by 20%. The kinetic energy of the photoelectrons emitted from a metal surface increased from $0.5eV$ to $0.8eV$. The work function of the metal is:
A. $0.65eV$
B. $1.0eV$
C. $1.3eV$
D. $1.5eV$

Q.8 In an unbiased p-n junction, holes diffuse from the p-region to the n-region because:
A. Free electrons in the n-region attract them
B. They move across the junction by the potential difference
C. Hole concentration in p-region is more as compared to n-region
D. All the above

Q.9 The ice point of water in Kelvin scale is _____.

A. $273.15K$
B. $373.15K$
C. $0K$
D. $-273.15K$

Q.10 If the empirical formula for the observed wavelengths (λ) for hydrogen is $\frac{1}{\lambda} = R\left(\frac{1}{3^2} - \frac{1}{n^2}\right)$, where $'n'$ is integral values higher than 3, then it represents the _____ series.
A. Balmer
B. Lyman
C. Brackett
D. Paschen

Q.11 Which of the following statement(s) are correct for the Bohr model?
A. The Bohr model is applicable to hydrogenic atoms only
B. The Bohr's model correctly predicts the frequencies of the light emitted by hydrogenic atoms
C. Both (A) and (B)
D. None of these

Q.12 When an electron jumps from the orbit n = 2 to n = 4, then wavelength of the radiations absorbed will be _____ (R is Rydberg's constant)
A. $\frac{16}{3R}$
B. $\frac{16}{5R}$
C. $\frac{5R}{16}$
D. $\frac{3R}{16}$

Q.13 Which has highest penetrating power?
A. β-rays
B. γ-rays
C. α-rays
D. Cathode rays

Q.14 Due to an acceleration of $2\ m/s^2$, the velocity of a body increases from $20\ m/s$ to $30\ m/s$ in a certain period. Find the displacement (in m) of the body in that period.
A. 650
B. 125
C. 250
D. 325

Q.15 In electromagnetic induction, the induced e.m.f. in a coil is independent of:
A. Change in the flux
B. Time
C. The resistance of the circuit
D. None of the above

Q.16 Mutual inductance of two coils can be increased by:
A. Decreasing the number of turns in the coils
B. Increasing the number of turns in the coils
C. Winding the coils on wooden core
D. None of the above

Q.17 In a coil current changes from 4A to 2A in 0.05 sec, if induced e.m.f. is 8 volt then self-inductance of the coil is:
A. 0.5 H
B. 0.35 H
C. 0.2 H
D. 2mH

Q.18 In a transistor, if the base current changes from 40 mA to 50 mA then the collector current changes from 600 mA to 1000 mA then its β is:
A. 40
B. 800
C. 3
D. 400

Q.19 In the BJT symbol, the arrow in the emitter shows the direction of:

A. Holes
B. Electrons
C. Holes in PNP and electrons in NPN
D. Electrons in PNP and holes in NPN

Q.20 Where does a body has the maximum weight?
A. At the poles
B. In an orbiting satellite
C. At the equator
D. On the moon

Q.21 Two identical finite bodies of constant heat capacity at temperatures T_1 and T_2 are available to do work in a heat engine. The final temperature T_f reached by the bodies on delivery of maximum work is:
A. $T_F = \frac{T_1+T_2}{2}$
B. $T_f = \sqrt{T_1 T_2}$
C. $T_f = T_1 = T_2$
D. $T_f = \sqrt{T_1^2 + T_2^2}$

Q.22 Which of the following laws was expressed by Nernst?
A. The first law of thermodynamics
B. The second law of thermodynamics
C. Third law of thermodynamics
D. None of the above

Q.23 Two bodies at different temperatures T_1 and T_2 if brought in thermal contact:
A. Do not settle settle down at mean temperature
B. Settle down at mean temperature
C. Settle down at any temperature
D. None of the above

Q.24 The transverse displacement of a string fixed at both ends is given by

$$y = 0.06\sin\left(\frac{2\pi x}{3}\right)\cos(120\pi t)$$

x and y are in metres and t is in seconds. The length of the string is 1.5 m and its mass is 3.0×10^{-2} kg. What is the tension in the string?
A. $648N$ B. $724N$ C. $832N$ D. $980N$

Q.25 The radius of one arm of a hydraulic lift is four times the radius of the other arm. What force should be applied on the narrow arm to lift 100 kg?
A. $26.5N$ B. $62.5N$ C. $6.25N$ D. $8.3N$

Q.26 A $12pF$ capacitor is connected to a $50V$ battery. How much electrostatic energy is stored in the capacitor?
A. $2.5 \times 10^{-8} J$
B. $3.5 \times 10^{-8} J$
C. $4.5 \times 10^{-8} J$
D. $1.5 \times 10^{-8} J$

Q.27 A $600pF$ capacitor is charged by a $200V$ supply. It is then disconnected from the supply and is connected to another uncharged $600pF$ capacitor. How much electrostatic energy is lost in the process?
A. $5 \times 10^{-6} J$
B. $6 \times 10^{-6} J$
C. $7 \times 10^{-6} J$
D. $8 \times 10^{-6} J$

Q.28 In a hydrogen atom, the electron and proton are bound at a distance of about $d = 0.53 \mathring{A}$. Estimate the potential energy of the system in eV, taking the zero of the potential energy at an infinite separation of the electron from the proton.
A. $-27.2 eV$
B. $17.2 eV$
C. $27.2 eV$
D. $37.2 eV$

Q.29 What is the area of the plates of a $2F$ parallel plate capacitor, given that the separation between the plates is $0.5cm$?
A. $4130 km^2$
B. $3130 km^2$
C. $1130 km^2$
D. $2130 km^2$

Q.30 A cylindrical capacitor has two co-axial cylinders of length $15cm$ and radii $1.5cm$ and $1.4cm$. The outer cylinder is earthed and the inner cylinder is given a charge of $3.5\mu C$. Determine the capacitance of the system and the potential of the inner cylinder. Neglect end effects (i.e., bending of field lines at the ends).
A. $3.92 \times 10^4 V$
B. $4.92 \times 10^4 V$
C. $5.92 \times 10^4 V$
D. $2.92 \times 10^4 V$

Q.31 A piece of writing paper that is 10 cm wide, 15 cm long and 0.05 mm thick has a dielectric strength of 8 kV/mm. if it is placed between two copper plates and subjected to an increasing voltage, it will break down at:
A. 8 kV   B. 4 kV   C. 0.4 kV   D. 0.8 kV

Q.32 In a certain region, the electric potential distribution is as shown in the figure:

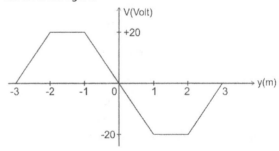

The corresponding plot of the electric field component will be:

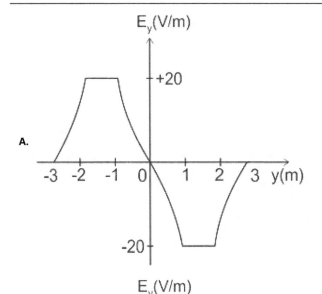

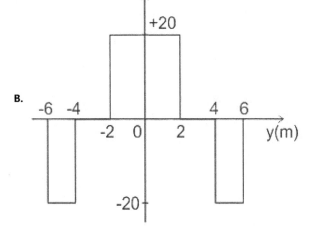

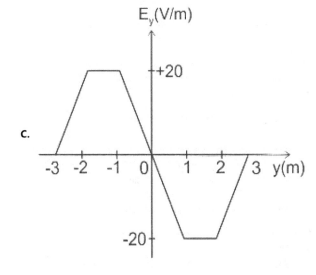

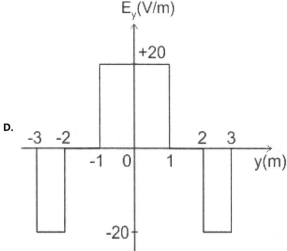

Q.33 Consider the expression $\tan\theta_\eta = \dfrac{\tau}{1+\sqrt{(1+\tau^2)}}$, where θ_η is the time phase between electric and magnetic field in a medium with conductivity σ_s permittivity ε and permeability μ. Then τ is given by which of the following expression:

A. $\dfrac{\omega\varepsilon}{\sigma}$ B. $\dfrac{\sigma}{\omega\varepsilon}$ C. $\dfrac{\sigma}{\omega\mu}$ D. $\dfrac{\omega\mu}{\sigma}$

Q.34 Which of the following statement is correct about longitudinal mechanical waves?

A. The longitudinal mechanical waves which lie in the frequency range $20 Hz$ to $20000\ Hz$ are called audible or sound waves
B. The longitudinal mechanical waves having frequencies less than $20 Hz$ are called infrasonic
C. The longitudinal mechanical waves having frequencies greater than $20,000 Hz$ are called ultrasonic waves
D. All of the above

Q.35 A swimmer can swim in still water with the speed of $5ms^{-1}$. While crossing a river his average speed is $3ms^{-1}$. If he crosses the river in the shortest possible time, what is the speed of the flow of water?

A. $2ms^{-1}$ B. $4ms^{-1}$ C. $6ms^{-1}$ D. $8ms^{-1}$

Q.36 An equilateral triangle is made of three wires of equal resistances 4 Ω. Find the equivalent resistance across any one side.

A. 4 Ω B. 8 Ω C. $\dfrac{4}{3}$ Ω D. $\dfrac{8}{3}$ Ω

Q.37 Two resistances of 10 Ω and 30 Ω are parallel connected in a circuit. The equivalent resistance of the circuit will be:

A. 20 Ω B. 40 Ω C. 15 Ω D. 7.5 Ω

Q.38 In which type of extrinsic semiconductor are electrons the major charge carriers?

A. n type B. p type
C. (A) and (B) both D. None of the above

Q.39 What is the average velocity of the molecules of an ideal gas?

A. Infinity   B. Constant   C. Unstable   D. Zero

Q.40 The ratio of mean kinetic energy per mole of hydrogen and oxygen at a given temperature is:
A. 1 : 16   B. 1 : 8   C. 1 : 4   D. 1 : 1

Q.41 Same gas is filled in two containers of same volume, same temperature and with pressure of ratio 1 : 2. The ratio of their rms speeds is:
A. 1 : 2   B. 2 : 1   C. 1 : 4   D. 1 : 1

Q.42 What is the cause of diffraction?
A. Interference of primary wavelets
B. Interference of secondary wavelets
C. Reflection of primary wavelets
D. Reflection of secondary wavelets

Q.43 A small circular disc is placed in the path of light from a distant source. Identify the nature of the fringe produced.
A. Dual   B. Narrow   C. Dark   D. Bright

Q.44 What should be the order of the size of an obstacle or aperture for diffraction light?
A. Order of wavelength of light
B. Order of wavelength of obstacle
C. Order in ranges of micrometer
D. Order in ranges of nanometer

Q.45 What is the power factor in a pure inductive or capacitive circuit?
A. -1   B. 0   C. 1   D. Infinity

Q.46 How many types of power can be defined in an AC circuit?
A. 3   B. 2   C. 1   D. 5

Q.47 The susceptibility is independent of temperature in which material?
A. Paramagnetic   B. Ferromagnetic
C. Diamagnetic   D. Ferromagnetic

Q.48 Piezoelectric effect is analogous to which phenomenon?
A. Electrostriction   B. Magnetostriction
C. Anisotropy   D. Magnetization

Q.49 A rigid body is rotating about an axis. One force F_1 acts on the body such that its vector passes through the axis of rotation. Another force F_2 acts on it such that it is perpendicular to the axis of rotation and at a point 5cm from the axis. This force F_2 is perpendicular to the radius vector at its point of application. Find the net torque on the body. Let F_1 = 10N & F_2 = 5N.
A. 0   B. 10.25 Nm
C. 0.25 Nm   D. 10 Nm

Q.50 A ring of radius 7cm is rotating about the central axis perpendicular to its plane. A force acts on it, tangentially, such that it does a work of 10J in a complete rotation. Find the value of that force.
A. $\frac{0.5}{7\pi} N$ B. $35\pi N$ C. $\frac{500}{7\pi} N$ D. $0.7 N$

Chemistry

Q.51 The pH of a solution obtained by mixing $100ml$ of $0.2M CH_3COOH$ with $100ml$ of $0.2M NaOH$ would be $(pK_{aCH_3COOH} = 4.74)$
A. 4.74   B. 8.87   C. 9.1   D. 8.57

Q.52 Which of the following salts is the most basic in aqueous solution?
[JEE Main Advanced, 2018]
A. $Pb(CH_3COO)_2$ B. $Al(CN)_3$
C. CH_3COOK D. $FeCl_3$

Q.53 Which of the following amines would undergo diazotization?
A. Primary aliphatic amines
B. Primary aromatic amines
C. Both (A) and (B)
D. None of these

Q.54 Classification means ___ of things.
A. Dividing   B. Grouping
C. Removal   D. None of these

Q.55 In which of the following conditions, the potential for the following half-cell reaction is maximum?
$2H^+ + 2e \rightarrow H_2$
A. $1.0M\ HCl$
B. A solution having $pH = 4$
C. Pure water
D. $1.0M\ NaOH$

Q.56 On increasing the temperature by $10°C$:
A. Number of collisions get doubled
B. Value of rate constant does not change
C. The energy of activation increases
D. The number of fruitful collisions gets doubled

Q.57 The rate of reaction becomes 2 times for every 10° rise in temperature. How much will the rate of reaction will increase, when the temperature is increased from 30°C to 80°C?
A. 31   B. 32   C. 36   D. 45

Q.58 The rate of reaction increase by the increase of temperature because:
A. Collision frequency is increased.
B. Energy of products decreases.
C. The fraction of molecules possessing energy $\geq E_T$ (threshold energy) increases.
D. Mechanism of a reaction is changed.

Q.59 A solution of acetone in ethanol:
A. Shows a negative deviation from Raoult's law
B. Shows a positive deviation from Raoult's law
C. Behave like a near ideal solution
D. Obeys Raoult's law

Q.60 Determine the molarity of $30\ g$ of $CO(NO)_3.6H_2O$ in $4.3\ L$ of solution.
A. 0.034 M B. 0.025 M C. 0.023 M D. 0.052 M

Q.61 If a solution prepared by dissolving 1.0 g of polymer of molar mass 185,000 in 450 mL of water at 37°C, calculate the osmotic pressure in Pascal exerted by it?
A. 31 Pa B. 30 Pa C. 32 Pa D. 33 Pa

Q.62 Two bodies at different temperatures are mixed in a calorimeter. Which of the following quantities remains conserved?
A. sum of the temperatures of the two bodies
B. total heat of the two bodies
C. total internal energy of the two bodies
D. internal energy of each body

Q.63 Thermodynamics is not concerned about:
A. the rate at which a reaction proceeds
B. the feasibility of a chemical reaction
C. the extent to which a chemical reaction proceeds
D. energy changes involved in a chemical reaction

Q.64 Which of the following statements is not true regarding the laws of thermodynamics?
A. It deals with energy changes of microscopic systems
B. It does not depend on the rate at which these energy transformations are carried out
C. It depends on the initial and final states of a system undergoing the change
D. None of these

Q.65 A solid has a 'BCC' structure. If the distance of nearest approach between two atoms is 1.73Å, the edge length of the cell is:
A. 314.20 pm B. 1.41 pm
C. 200 pm   D. 215 pm

Q.66 CsBr crystallises in a body centred cubic lattice. The unit cell length is $436.6 pm$. Given that the atomic mass of $Cs - 133$ and that of $Br = 80$ amu and Avogadro number being $6.02 \times 10^{23}\ mol^{-1}$, the density of CsBr is:
A. $42.5\ g/cm^3$ B. $0.425\ g/cm^3$
C. $8.25\ g/cm^3$ D. $4.25\ g/cm^3$

Q.67 Which of the following is not a crystalline solid?
A. Potassium Chloride   B. Caesium Chloride
C. Glass   D. Rhombic sulphur

Q.68 Alkali metals dissolving in Ammonia liquid give the blue solution, this is due to the formation of ammoniated _____.
A. Ions
B. Metal cations only
C. Metal cations and electrons
D. Electrons only

Q.69 The functional group present in organic, acid is –

A. $-COOH$ B. $-OH$
C. $-CHO$ D. $C=O$

Q.70 $34.05\ mL$ of phosphorus vapour weighs $0.0625\ g$ at $546°C$ and 0.1 bar pressure. What is the molar mass of phosphorus?
A. $1257.5 gmol^{-1}$ B. $1147.5 gmol^{-1}$
C. $1247.5 gmol^{-1}$ D. $1244.5 gmol^{-1}$

Q.71 A gas deviates from ideal behavior at a high pressure because its molecules:
A. Attract one another
B. Show the Tyndall Effect
C. Have kinetic energy
D. Are bound by covalent bonds

Q.72 The hybrid state of sulphur in SO_3 molecule is:
A. sp^3d B. sp^3 C. sp^3d^2 D. sp^2

Q.73 Which one of the following is a lyophilic colloidal solution?
A. Smoke
B. Gold sol
C. Starch aqueous solution
D. Cloud

Q.74 When electromagnetic radiation of wavelength $300\ nm$ falls on the surface of sodium, electrons are emitted with a kinetic energy of $1.68 \times 10^5\ J\ mol^{-1}$. What is the minimum energy needed to remove an electron from sodium?
A. $6.84 \times 10^{-19} J$ B. $6 \times 10^{-19} J$
C. $3.84 \times 10^{-19} J$ D. $5 \times 10^{-19} J$

Q.75 Hydrocarbons having single bonds are known as:
A. Saturated hydrocarbon
B. Unsaturated hydrocarbon
C. Alkyne
D. None of above

Q.76 A standard hydrogen electrode has a zero potential because:
A. Hydrogen can be most easily oxidised
B. Hydrogen has only one electron
C. The electrode potential is assumed to be zero
D. Hydrogen is the lightest element

Q.77 Following reactions are taking place in a Galvanic cell,
$Zn \to Zn^{2+} + 2e^-; Ag^+ + e^- \to Ag$
Which of the given representations is the correct method of depicting the cell?
A. $Zn_{(s)}|Zn^{2+}_{(aq)} \parallel Ag^+_{(aq)}|Ag_{(s)}$
B. $Zn^{2+}|Zn \parallel Ag|Ag^+$
C. $Zn_{(aq)}|Zn^{2+}_{(s)} \parallel Ag^+_{(s)}|Ag_{(aq)}$
D. $Zn_{(s)}|Ag^+_{(aq)} \parallel Zn^{2+}_{(aq)}|Ag_{(s)}$

Q.78 Given below are the half-cell reactions:
$Mn^{2+} + 2e^- \to Mn; E^o = -1.18V$
$2(Mn^{3+} + e^- \to Mn^{2+}); E^o = +1.51V$

The E^o for $3Mn^{2+} \rightarrow Mn + 2Mn^{3+}$ will be:
A. $-0.33V$; the reaction will not occur
B. $-0.33V$; the reaction will occur
C. $-2.69\ V$; the reaction will not occur
D. $-2.69\ V$; the reaction will occur

Q.79 The ligand $N(CH_2CH_2NH_2)_3$:
A. Bidentate
B. Tridentate
C. Tetradentate
D. Pentadentate

Q.80 The I.U.P.A.C name of the coordination compound $K_3[Fe(CN)_6]$ is:
A. Potassium hexacyanoferrate(II)
B. Potassium hexacyanoferrate(III)
C. Potassium hexacyanoiron(II)
D. Tripotassium hexacyanoiron(II)

Q.81 The name of the compound $[Co(NH_3)_5NO_2]Cl_2$ will be:
A. Pentaamminonitrocobalt(II) chloride
B. Pentaamminenitrochloridecobaltate(III)
C. Pentaamminenitrocobalt(III) chloride
D. Pentanitrosoamminechlorocobaltate(III)

Q.82 There is a large difference in the boiling points of butanal and butan-1-ol due to:
A. Intermolecular hydrogen bonding in butan-1-ol
B. Intramolecular hydrogen bonding in butanal
C. Higher molecular mass of butan-1-ol
D. Resonance shown by butanal

Q.83 Order of esterification strength of alcohols is?
A. $3° > 1° > 2°$
B. $2° > 3° > 1°$
C. $1° > 2° > 3°$
D. None of these

Q.84 Carboxylic acids dimerise due to:
A. High molecular weight
B. Coordinate bonding
C. Intermolecular hydrogen bonding
D. Covalent bonding

Q.85 Which substance is produced when alcohol is added with petrol and used as a fuel?
A. Only oxygen
B. Only carbon-dioxide
C. Only water
D. Carbon-dioxide and water both

Q.86 Which of the following alcohol is most reactive with Lucas Reagent?
A. Ethanol
B. Methanol
C. Isopropyl alcohol
D. Tertiary Butyl alcohol

Q.87 Ethyl alcohol is denatured by adding:
A. Glycerol
B. Methanol and pyridine
C. Aniline
D. Ether and ethanol

Q.88 Which one of the following group contains biocatalysts?
A. Glucose, amino acids, fatty acids
B. Peptidase, amylase, rennin
C. Rhodopsin, pepsin, steapsin
D. Myosin, oxytocin, adrenalin

Q.89 Enzymes that catalyse removal of groups from substrates by mechanisms other than hydrolysis, and addition of groups to double bonds, are called _____.
A. Lyases
B. Dehydrogenases
C. Hydrolases
D. None of these

Q.90 Semi-synthetic polymers among the following is:
A. Cellulose acetate
B. Nylon-6,6
C. BUNA-S
D. Polythene

Q.91 Natural rubber has:
A. All trans-configuration
B. Alternate cis - and trans-configuration
C. Random cis - and trans-configuration
D. All cis-configuration

Q.92 Which of the following is amphoteric?
A. CrO
B. Cr_2O_3
C. CrO_5
D. CrO_3

Q.93 Which of the following tests does AgCl not answer?
A. Chromyl chloride test
B. Baeyer's reagent test
C. Alkaline test
D. Acidic test

Q.94 Which of the following noble gases can diffuse through rubber?
A. Helium
B. Xenon
C. Argon
D. Krypton

Q.95 What is the correct order of enthalpy of dissociation of halogens?
A. $F_2 > Cl_2 > Br_2 > I_2$
B. $Cl_2 > Br_2 > F_2 > I_2$
C. $Cl_2 > F_2 > Br_2 > I_2$
D. $F_2 > Br_2 > Cl_2 > I_2$

Q.96 What is the correct order of reactivity of group 16 elements?
A. $O > Se > S > Te > Po$
B. $S > O > Te > Po > Se$
C. $S > O > Se > Te > Po$
D. $O > S > Se > Te > Po$

Q.97 What is the atomicity of halogens?
A. Monoatomic
B. Diatomic
C. Triatomic
D. Octatomic

Q.98 The Hinsberg's method is used for which of the following?
A. Preparation of primary amines
B. Preparation of secondary amines
C. Preparation of tertiary amines
D. Separation of amine mixtures

Q.99 Which of the following gas was traditionally used to bleach paper?

A. Sulfur
B. Carbon dioxide
C. Chlorine
D. Fluorine

Q.100 Name the conventional solvent that was used for dry cleaning purposes which later confirmed to be a suspected carcinogen.

A. Supercritical CO_2
B. Phenanthrene
C. Tetrachloroethene
D. Benzene aldehyde

Physics & Chemistry : Mock Test - 8

// Smart Answer Sheet //

Correct Indicates percentage of students who answered questions correctly.

Skipped Indicates percentage of students who skipped questions.

Q.	Ans.	Correct / Skipped	Q.	Ans.	Correct / Skipped	Q.	Ans.	Correct / Skipped	Q.	Ans.	Correct / Skipped	Q.	Ans.	Correct / Skipped
1	D	57.16 % / 1.04 %	17	C	65.64 % / 1.2 %	33	B	20.7 % / 3.54 %	49	C	67.57 % / 1.96 %	65	C	79.44 % / 0.0 %
2	D	47.42 % / 1.15 %	18	A	40.37 % / 1.25 %	34	D	53.39 % / 1.19 %	50	C	65.16 % / 1.84 %	66	D	19.4 % / 3.42 %
3	B	79.82 % / 0.0 %	19	A	40.1 % / 1.8 %	35	B	59.22 % / 1.08 %	51	B	30.93 % / 3.63 %	67	C	27.48 % / 3.07 %
4	A	85.98 % / 0.0 %	20	A	83.25 % / 0.0 %	36	D	63.6 % / 1.5 %	52	C	48.38 % / 1.13 %	68	C	64.53 % / 1.14 %
5	B	66.53 % / 1.94 %	21	B	21.92 % / 4.16 %	37	D	50.64 % / 1.42 %	53	B	69.09 % / 1.58 %	69	A	85.87 % / 0.0 %
6	C	45.82 % / 1.56 %	22	C	60.34 % / 1.27 %	38	A	68.87 % / 1.58 %	54	B	89.63 % / 0.0 %	70	C	59.6 % / 1.43 %
7	B	63.86 % / 1.94 %	23	A	53.03 % / 1.16 %	39	D	82.2 % / 0.0 %	55	A	45.15 % / 1.08 %	71	A	84.57 % / 0.0 %
8	C	83.06 % / 0.0 %	24	A	65.26 % / 1.48 %	40	D	64.33 % / 1.73 %	56	D	83.41 % / 0.0 %	72	D	53.11 % / 1.86 %
9	A	52.42 % / 1.21 %	25	B	49.93 % / 1.44 %	41	D	64.96 % / 1.15 %	57	B	25.76 % / 4.88 %	73	C	50.93 % / 1.31 %
10	D	86.88 % / 0.0 %	26	D	88.99 % / 0.0 %	42	B	44.58 % / 1.75 %	58	C	87.2 % / 0.0 %	74	C	31.2 % / 3.55 %
11	C	53.43 % / 1.05 %	27	B	20.81 % / 4.58 %	43	D	60.75 % / 1.04 %	59	B	40.05 % / 1.65 %	75	A	83.74 % / 0.0 %
12	A	56.43 % / 1.46 %	28	A	58.25 % / 1.77 %	44	A	56.43 % / 1.94 %	60	C	45.09 % / 1.27 %	76	C	78.76 % / 0.0 %
13	B	44.22 % / 1.67 %	29	C	57.23 % / 1.05 %	45	B	49.11 % / 1.97 %	61	A	24.78 % / 4.57 %	77	A	26.87 % / 3.92 %
14	B	76.74 % / 0.0 %	30	D	28.06 % / 3.46 %	46	A	65.33 % / 1.28 %	62	C	81.82 % / 0.0 %	78	C	28.29 % / 3.5 %
15	C	77.91 % / 0.0 %	31	C	77.12 % / 0.0 %	47	C	50.25 % / 1.61 %	63	A	68.85 % / 1.58 %	79	C	79.94 % / 0.0 %
16	B	83.23 % / 0.0 %	32	D	45.8 % / 1.94 %	48	B	62.0 % / 1.49 %	64	A	67.04 % / 1.05 %	80	B	53.53 % / 1.57 %

Physics & Chemistry : Mock Test - 8

Q.	Ans.	Correct / Skipped	Q.	Ans.	Correct / Skipped	Q.	Ans.	Correct / Skipped	Q.	Ans.	Correct / Skipped	Q.	Ans.	Correct / Skipped
81	C	57.36 % / 1.81 %	85	D	87.46 % / 0.0 %	89	A	61.64 % / 1.68 %	93	A	69.32 % / 1.05 %	97	B	64.37 % / 1.42 %
82	A	79.37 % / 0.0 %	86	D	59.35 % / 1.06 %	90	A	79.84 % / 0.0 %	94	A	56.76 % / 1.35 %	98	D	58.19 % / 1.14 %
83	C	69.42 % / 1.28 %	87	B	17.23 % / 4.0 %	91	D	69.79 % / 1.37 %	95	B	53.68 % / 1.32 %	99	C	46.93 % / 1.19 %
84	C	52.91 % / 1.33 %	88	B	48.11 % / 1.49 %	92	B	62.91 % / 1.25 %	96	D	69.78 % / 1.44 %	100	C	67.03 % / 1.13 %

Performance Analysis	
Avg. Score (%)	46.0%
Toppers Score (%)	73.0%
Your Score	

//Hints and Solutions//

1. $KE = \frac{1}{2}m\omega^2(A^2 - x^2)$
$= \frac{1}{2}m\omega^2\left(A^2 - \frac{A^2}{4}\right)$
$= \frac{3}{4} \times \frac{1}{2}m\omega^2 A^2$
$\therefore KE = \frac{3}{4}T.E$

Hence, the correct option is (D).

2. The total energy of particle executing simple harmonic motion is,

$E = \frac{1}{2}m\omega^2 A^2$

Therefore, kinetic energy at position is,

$K = \frac{1}{2}m\omega^2(A^2 - V^2)$

Kinetic energy at position half the amplitude of oscillation is,

$K = \frac{1}{2}m\omega^2\left[A^2 - \left(\frac{A}{2}\right)^2\right]$
$= \frac{1}{2}m\omega^2\left(\frac{3}{4}A^2\right)$
$K = \frac{3}{4}E$

Potential energy ($P.E.$)
$= E - K$
$= E - \frac{3}{4}E$
$= \frac{E}{4}$

Ratio $= \frac{P.E.}{E}$
$= \frac{\frac{E}{4}}{E}$
$= 0.25$

Now, Potential energy will be 0.25 of the total energy.

Hence, the correct option is (D).

3. The suspended mass M on the sonometer wire is $1\ kg$.

$M = 1\ kg$

The resonance tension T of the sonometer wire is balanced by the weight Mg of the suspended mass.

$T = Mg$

Substitute Mg for T in equation (1).

$f = \frac{1}{2l}\sqrt{\frac{Mg}{m}}$

Rewrite the above equation for the resonance frequency f' on the moon.

$f' = \frac{1}{2l}\sqrt{\frac{M'g'}{m}}$

Here, g' is the acceleration due to gravity on the moon.

The acceleration due to gravity g' on the moon is $\frac{1}{6}$ that on the earth.

$g' = \frac{1}{6}g$

We want to obtain the same resonance frequency on the earth and the moon.

$f = f'$

Substitute $\frac{1}{2l}\sqrt{\frac{Mg}{m}}$ for f and $\frac{1}{2l}\sqrt{\frac{M'g'}{m}}$ for f' in the above equation.

$\frac{1}{2l}\sqrt{\frac{Mg}{m}} = \frac{1}{2l}\sqrt{\frac{M'g'}{m}}$

$\Rightarrow \sqrt{Mg} = \sqrt{M'g'}$

$\Rightarrow Mg = M'g'$

Rearrange the above equation for M'.

$M' = \frac{Mg}{g'}$

Substitute $\frac{1}{6}g$ for g' and $1\ kg$ for M in the above equation.

$M' = \frac{(1\ kg)g}{\frac{1}{6}g}$

$\Rightarrow M' = 6\ kg$

Therefore, the mass M on the moon should be $6\ kg$.

Hence, the correct option is (C).

4. A magnifying glass uses a convex lens because these lenses cause light rays to converge, or come together. As the light rays enter the convex lens present in the magnifying glass, these rays become focused on a specific focal point in front of the center of the lens. Furthermore, if the magnifying glass is at an optimal distance, this generates the maximum magnification of the object.

Therefore, a magnifying glass comprises a simple convex lens.

Hence, the correct option is (A).

5. We know the relation between frequency (f) wavelength (λ) and speed (v):

$v = f\lambda$

When light passes from rarer medium to denser medium frequency remain the same but speed decrease $v=$ constant

$\therefore \lambda$ decreases

- Option (B) is correct because in refraction frequency is the same and the wavelength decreases as light travel from rarer to denser.
- Option (A) is incorrect because frequency doesn't change in refraction.
- Option (C) is incorrect because wavelength decreases as light travel from rarer to denser.
- Option (D) is incorrect because frequency doesn't change in refraction.

Hence, the correct option is (B).

6. Given:

$E = 5.5 eV$

$\phi = 4.5 eV$

Therefore, the kinetic energy will be equal to

$K.E = E - \phi$

On substituting the values in above formula, we get

$K.E = (5.5 - 4.5)eV$

$\Rightarrow K.E = 1 eV$

Wavelength $(\lambda) = \frac{h}{\sqrt{2M_e \times K \cdot E}}$

λ is the wavelength.

h is the Planck's constant 6.6×10^{-34}.

M_e is the mass of an electron 9.1×10^{-31}.

$K.E$, is the kinetic energy $= 1.16 \times 10^{-19}$.

So on substituting the values in the formula of wavelength, we get

$\lambda = \frac{6.6 \times 10^{-34}}{\sqrt{2 \times 9.1 \times 10^{-31} \times 1 \times 1.16 \times 10^{-19}}}$

$\Rightarrow \lambda = 1.24 \times 10^{-9} m$

Hence, the correct option is (C).

7. Given:

Incident Energy is increased by 20%.

$KE_1 = 0.5 eV =$ initial kinetic energy

$KE_2 = 0.8 eV =$ final kinetic energy

$E_1 = E =$ initial incident energy

According to the question.

$E_2 = E_1 + E_1 \times 20\%$

$= E_1 + 0.2 E_1$

$= 1.2 E_1 = 1.2 E$

Let ϕ is the work function of metal. According to Einstein equation:-

$E = \phi + KE$

$E_1 = \phi + KE_1 = E$

Put the value of KE_1 in above equation,

$E_1 = \phi + 0.5 = E$ .....(i)

$E_2 = \phi + KE_2 = 1.2 E$

Put the value of KE_2 in above equation,

$E_2 = \phi + 0.8 = 1.2 E$ .....(ii)

Divide equation (i) by equation (ii),

$\frac{E_1}{E_2} = \frac{\phi + 0.5}{\phi + 0.8} = \frac{E}{1.2 E} = \frac{1}{1.2}$

$\Rightarrow 1.2 \phi + 0.6 = \phi + 0.8$

$\Rightarrow 0.2 \phi = 0.2$

$\phi = \frac{0.2}{0.2} = 1 eV$

Work function of metal is $\phi = 1 ev$.

Hence, the correct option is (B).

8. In an unbiased p-n junction, holes diffuse from the p-region to n-region because hole concentration in p-region is more compared to n-junction. As the diffusion of charge carriers across the junction takes place from higher concentration to lower concentration.

Hence, the correct option is (C).

9. Concept:

Temperature: It is the measure of the degree of hotness and coldness of a body. The SI unit of temperature is Kelvin (K). The major temperature scales are:

Celsius scale: It is also known as the centigrade scale and the most commonly used scale. It is defined from assigning $0°C$ to $100°C$ of freezing and boiling point of water at 1 atmospheric pressure.

Kelvin scale: It is the base unit of temperature, denoted with K. There are no negative numbers on the Kelvin scale as the lowest is $0K$.

The relation between Celsius and Kelvin is given by:

$°C + 273.15 = K$

Given:

The ice point of water $= 0°C$

Temperature $(T) = 0°C$

$°C + 273.15 = K$

$\Rightarrow K = 273.15 K$

Hence, the correct option is (A).

10. It represents the **Paschen** series.

Hydrogen Spectrum and Spectral series: When a hydrogen atom is excited, it returns to its normal unexcited (or ground state) state by emitting the energy it had absorbed earlier.

This energy is given out by the atom in the form of radiations of different wavelengths as the electron jumps down from a higher to a lower orbit. The transition from different orbits causes different wavelengths, these constitute spectral series which are characteristic of the atom emitting them. When observed through a spectroscope, these radiations are imaged as sharp and straight vertical lines of a single colour.

Mainly there are five series and each series is named after it's discovered as Lyman series ($n_1 = 1$), Balmer series ($n_1 = 2$), Paschen series ($n_1 = 3$), Bracket series ($n_1 = 4$), and Pfund series ($n_1 = 5$).

Hence, the correct option is (D).

11. Both statements (A) and (B) are correct for the Bohr model.

The Bohr model is applicable to hydrogenic atoms. It cannot be extended even to mere two-electron atoms such as helium.

- The analysis of atoms with more than one electron was attempted on the lines of Bohr's model for hydrogenic atoms but did not meet with any success.
- The formulation of the Bohr model involves electrical force between the positively charged nucleus and electron. It does not include the electrical forces between electrons which necessarily appear in multi-electron atoms.

Bohr's model correctly predicts the frequencies of the light emitted by hydrogenic atoms, the model is unable to explain the relative intensities of the frequencies in the spectrum.

Hence, the correct option is (C).

12. Given:

$Z = 1, n_1 = 2, n_2 = 4$

We know that wavelength,

$\frac{1}{\lambda} = Z^2 R \left(\frac{1}{n_1^2} - \frac{1}{n_2^2}\right)$

$= R \left(\frac{1}{2^2} - \frac{1}{4^2}\right)$

$= R \left(\frac{1}{4} - \frac{1}{16}\right)$

$\Rightarrow \lambda = \frac{16}{3R}$

Hence, the correct option is (A).

13. Radioactivity: The phenomenon of spontaneous emission of radiations by heavy elements is called radioactivity. The elements which show this phenomenon is called radioactive elements.

Nuclear Radiations: According to Rutherford's experiment when a sample of a radioactive substance is put in a lead box and allows the emission of radiation through a small hole only.

- When the radiation enters the external electric field, they split into three parts (α – rays, β – rays, and γ – gamma rays).

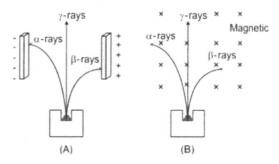

(A)   (B)

- The penetration power of β – rays is 100 times that of α – rays. They are absorbed by the aluminum foil of 5 mm thickness.
- The penetration power of γ – rays is 1000 times that of α – rays. They can penetrate a 30 cm thick iron block.
- The increasing order of penetrating powers is α – rays < β – rays < γ – rays.
- Thus, Gamma rays have the highest penetrating power.

Hence, the correct option is (B).

14. Given,

Acceleration, $a = 2 \, m/s^2$

$u = 20 \, m/s$

$v = 30 \, m/s$

From equation of motion,

$v^2 - u^2 = 2as$

$\Rightarrow s = \frac{(v^2 - u^2)}{(2 \times a)}$

$\Rightarrow s = \frac{(30^2 - 20^2)}{(2 \times 2)}$

$\Rightarrow s = \frac{500}{4}$

$\Rightarrow s = 125 \, m$

Hence, the correct option is (B).

15. Faraday's Laws of Electromagnetic Induction:

- First law: Whenever the number of magnetic lines of force (magnetic flux) passing through a circuit changes an emf is produced in the circuit called induced emf. The induced emf persists only as long as there is change or cutting of flux.
- Second law: The induced emf is given by the rate of change of magnetic flux linked with the circuit i.e.,

$$e = -\frac{d\phi}{dt}$$

Where $d\phi$ = change in magnetic flux, dt = change in time and e = induced emf.

The negative sign indicates that induced emf (e) opposes the change of flux.

From the above equation, it is clear that induced e.m.f. in a coil is depends on the change in the flux and time and independent of the resistance of the circuit.

Hence, the correct option is (C).

16. Mutual induction between the two coils of area A, number of turns N_1 and N_2 with the length of secondary or primary l is given by,

$$M = \frac{\mu_0 N_1 N_2 A}{l}$$

From the above formula, the mutual inductance of two coils can be increased by increasing the number of turns in the coils.

Hence, the correct option is (B).

17. As we know,

Self-inductance of a solenoid is given by,

$$L = \frac{\mu_0 N^2 A}{l}$$

Where μ_0 = Absolute permeability, N = Number of turns, l = length of the solenoid, the resistance of the coil $(R) = 4\Omega$, and A = Area of the solenoid

Induced e.m.f can be given as,

$$V_l = -L \frac{dI}{dt} \quad \text{...(1)}$$

Where

V_L = induced voltage in volts

N = self-inductance of the coil

$\frac{dI}{dt}$ = rate of change of current in ampere/second

Given,

$I_1 = 4A, I_2 = 2A, dt = 0.05 sec, V_L = 8$ volt

$\Rightarrow dI = I_2 - I_1 = (2 - 4) = -2A$

From equation (1), we get

$$8 = -L \frac{(-2)}{0.05}$$

$\Rightarrow L = 0.2H$

Hence, the correct option is (C).

18. In a transistor, small changes in the base current result in large changes in collector current.

The ratio of change in output current to the change in input current is called amplification or gain.

For a.c. input, the gain is denoted by β_{ac}.

Mathematically, we define the AC current gain as:

$$\beta_{ac} = \frac{(1000-600) \times 10^{-3}}{(50-40) \times 10^{-6}}$$

$$\beta_{ac} = 40$$

Hence, the correct option is (A).

19. BJT stands for Bipolar junction transistor.

- B = Bipolar (because conduction is due to two opposite types of carriers Holes and electrons)
- J = Junction refers to the two PN junctions between emitter and base, and collector and base.
- BJT's are current-driven devices.
- The current through the two terminals is controlled by a current at the third terminal (base).
- It is a bipolar device (current conduction by both types of carriers, i.e., majority and minority electrons and holes)
- It has a low input impedance.

The arrow on the symbol for bipolar transistors indicates the PN junction between base and emitter and points in the direction in which conventional current travels, i.e. the direction of holes.

NPN:

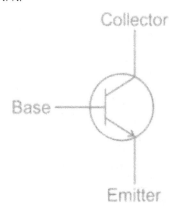

When the emitter-base is forward biased, holes from the base (p-type) start to flow to the emitter side (n-type) and electrons start to flow from the emitter to the base. The direction, however, represents the direction of the hole flow.

PNP:

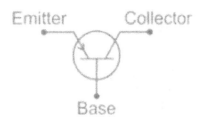

When the emitter-base junction is forward biased, holes from the emitter start to flow to the base. The direction of the arrow also indicates the same.

Hence, the correct option is (A).

20. The weight of an object is maximum at poles as the gravity is slightly higher at the poles and hence the weight there is more as compared to anywhere else.

Hence, the correct option is (A).

21.

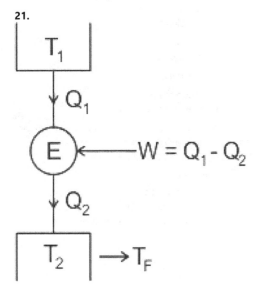

Assume $T_1 > T_2$

$Q_1 = C_p(T_1 - T_f)$

$Q_2 = C_p(T_f - T_2)$

$\therefore W = Q_1 - Q_2 = C_p(T_1 + T_2 - 2T_f)$

For 'W' to be maximum, T_f to be minimum

$\Delta S_1 = \int_{T_1}^{T_f} C_p \frac{dT}{T} = C_p \ln \frac{T_f}{T_1}$

$\Delta S_2 = \int_{T_1}^{T_f} C_p \frac{dT}{T} = C_p \ln \frac{T_f}{T_2}$

As,

$(\Delta S)_{univ} \geq 0$

$C_p \ln \frac{T_f}{T_1} + C_p \ln \frac{T_f}{T_2} \geq 0$

$\therefore C_p \ln \left[\frac{T_f^2}{T_1 T_2}\right] \geq 0$

Now,

For T_f to be minimum

$\ln \frac{T_f^2}{T_1 T_2} = 0 \quad \therefore \ln \frac{T_f^2}{T_1 T_2} = \ln 1$

$\therefore T_f = \sqrt{T_1 T_2}$

Hence, the correct option is (B).

22. The third law was developed by Walther Nernst during the years $1906-12$, and is therefore often referred to as Nernst's theorem or Nernst's postulate. The third law of thermodynamics states that the entropy of a system at absolute zero is a well-defined constant. This is because a system at zero temperature exists in its ground state, so that its entropy is determined only by the degeneracy of the ground state.

In 1912 Nernst stated the law thus: "It is impossible for any procedure to lead to the isotherm $T = 0$ in a finite number of steps."

Hence, the correct option is (C).

23. If two bodies at different temperatures T_1 and T_2 are brought in thermal contact, heat is said to flow from the body at higher temperature to the body at lower temperature until an equilibrium is obtained, i.e., until a point at which the temperatures of both the bodies becomes the same. The equilibrium temperature turns out to be the same as the mean temperature, which can be denoted as $\frac{(T_1+T_2)}{2}$ only when thermal capacities of the two bodies are the same.

Hence, the correct option is (A).

24. Wavelength, $\lambda = \frac{2\pi}{k} = \frac{2\pi}{\frac{2\pi}{3}} = 3\ m$

Frequency, $f = \frac{\omega}{2\pi} = \frac{120\pi}{2\pi} = 60\ Hz$

Speed, $v = f\lambda = 180\ m/s$

Speed of a wave in a string is given by

$v = \sqrt{\frac{T}{\mu}}$

$\Rightarrow T = \frac{v^2 m}{l}$

$\Rightarrow T = \frac{180^2 \times 3 \times 10^{-2}}{1.5}$

$\Rightarrow T = 648 N$

Hence, the correct option is (A).

25. By Pascal's law,

$\frac{F}{A} = \frac{f}{a}$

or $f = \frac{Fa}{A}$

$\Rightarrow f = \frac{100g \times \pi r^2}{\pi \times (4r)^2}$

$\Rightarrow f = 6.25g$

$\Rightarrow f = 62.5N$

Hence, the correct option is (B).

26. It is provided that,

Capacitance of the capacitor, $C = 12pF = 12 \times 10^{-12}F$

Potential difference, $V = 50V$

The formula for stored electrostatic energy in the capacitor is given by,

$E = \frac{1}{2}CV^2$

$E = \frac{1}{2} \times 12 \times 10^{-12} \times 50^2$

$E = 1.5 \times 10^{-8}J$

Therefore, the stored electrostatic energy in the capacitor is $1.5 \times 10^{-8}J$.

Hence, the correct option is (D).

27. It is provided that,

Capacitance of the capacitor, $C = 600pF$

Potential difference, $V = 200V$

The formula for stored electrostatic energy in the capacitor is given by,

$E = \frac{1}{2}CV^2$

$E = \frac{1}{2} \times 600 \times 10^{-12} \times 200^2$

$E = 1.2 \times 10^{-5}J$

If supply is removed from the capacitor and another capacitor of capacitance $C = 600pF$ is joined to it, then equivalent capacitance of the series combination is given by

$\frac{1}{C'} = \frac{1}{C} + \frac{1}{C}$

$\frac{1}{C'} = \frac{1}{600} + \frac{1}{600}$

$\frac{1}{C'} = \frac{2}{600}$

$C' = 300pF$

New electrostatic energy will be,

$E' = \frac{1}{2}C'V^2$

$E' = \frac{1}{2} \times 300 \times 10^{-12} \times 200^2$

$E' = 0.6 \times 10^{-5}J$

Loss in electrostatic energy $= E - E'$

$E - E' = 1.2 \times 10^{-5} - 0.6 \times 10^{-5} = 0.6 \times 10^{-5}J$

$E - E' = 6 \times 10^{-6}J$

Clearly, the lost electrostatic energy in the process is $6 \times 10^{-6}J$.

Hence, the correct option is (B).

28. Provided that,

The distance separating electron-proton of a hydrogen atom,

$d = 0.53 \overset{\circ}{A}$

Charge on an electron, $q_1 = -1.6 \times 10^{-19}C$

Charge on a proton, $q_2 = 1.6 \times 10^{-19}C$

The value of potential is zero at infinity.

Potential energy of the system is,

$U = 0 - \frac{q_1 q_2}{4\pi \varepsilon_o d}$

$U = 0 - \frac{9 \times 10^9 \times (1.6 \times 10^{-19})^2}{0.53 \times 10^{-10}}$

$U = -43.7 \times 10^{-19}J$

$V = -27.2eV$

Clearly, the potential energy of the system is $-27.2eV$.

Hence, the correct option is (A).

29. It is provided that,

The capacitance of a parallel capacitor, $C = 2F$

Distance separating the two plates, $d = 0.5cm = 0.5 \times 10^{-2}m$

The formula for parallel plate capacitor's capacitance is given by,

$C = \frac{\varepsilon_o A}{d}$

Where, ε_o is the Permittivity of free space

$\varepsilon_o = 8.854 \times 10^{-12}C^2N^{-1}m^{-2}$

We get,

$A = \frac{Cd}{\varepsilon_o}$

$A = \frac{2 \times 0.5 \times 10^{-2}}{8.854 \times 10^{-12}} = 1130km^2$

Hence, the correct option is (C).

30. It is provided that,

Co-axial cylinder's length, $1 = 15cm = 0.15m$

Outer cylinder's radius, $r_1 = 1.5cm = 0.015m$

Radius of inner cylinder, $r_2 = 1.4cm = 0.014m$

Charge on the inner cylinder, $q = 3.5\mu C = 3.5 \times 10^{-6} C$

The formula for co-axial cylinder's capacitance of radii r_1 and r_2 is given by,

$$C = \frac{2\pi \varepsilon_0 l}{\log_e\left(\frac{r_1}{r_2}\right)}$$

Where, ε_0 is the Permittivity of free space

$\varepsilon_0 = 8.854 \times 10^{-12} C^2 N^{-1} m^{-2}$

$$C = \frac{2\pi \times 8.854 \times 10^{-12} \times 0.15}{2.303 \log_{10}\left(\frac{0.015}{0.014}\right)}$$

$C = 1.2 \times 10^{-10} F$

The difference in potential of the inner cylinder is given by,

$V = \frac{q}{C}$

$V = \frac{3.5 \times 10^{-6}}{1.2 \times 10^{-10}} = 2.92 \times 10^4 V$

The difference in potential will be $2.92 \times 10^4 V$.

Hence, the correct option is (D).

31. Concept:

Electric field intensity between two parallel conducting plates can be calculated as:

$E = \frac{V}{I}$

Where $E = $ Electric field intensity

$V = $ supply voltage supplied by the source.

$I = $ distance by which parallel conducting plates are separated.

Calculation:

Given:

$I = 0.05$ mm

$E = 8$ kV/mm

The maximum voltage that can be applied before breakdown is:

$V = E \times I$

$8 \times 0.05 = 0.4$ kV

Hence, the correct option is (C).

32. Concept:

Electric field intensity at any point is equal to the negative gradient of electric potential at the point, i.e.

$E = -\nabla V$

$V = $ Electric potential

Application:

So, the y-component of the field is:

$E_y = -\frac{\partial V}{\partial y}$

For the interval $-3 \leq y \leq -2$:

$V = 20(y+3)$

$E_y = -\frac{\partial V}{\partial y} = -20 \; V/m$

For the interval $-1 \leq y \leq +1$:

$V = -20y$

$E_y = -\frac{\partial V}{\partial y} = 20 V/m$

For the interval $1 \leq y \leq 2$:

$V = -20$

$\therefore E_y = -\frac{\partial V}{\partial y} = 0$

For the interval $2 \leq y \leq 3$:

$V = 20(y-3)$

$E_y = -\frac{\partial V}{\partial y} = -20 \; V/m$

Therefore, the plot field component Ey with respect to y for the defined intervals will be the same as in option (D).

Hence, the correct option is (D).

33. For perfect conductor $\theta_\eta = 45°$

$\tan\theta_\eta = 1$

Now, if $\tau = \frac{\omega\varepsilon}{\sigma} = 0$ ($\because \sigma \approx \infty$ for conductors)

Using $\tau = 0$ we obtain $\tan\theta_\eta = 0$ which is not consistent.

However, if we take $\tau = \frac{\sigma}{\omega\varepsilon}$ we get

$\tau = \frac{\sigma}{\omega\varepsilon} = \infty$ ($\because \sigma = \infty$ for conductor)

And $\lim_{\tau \to \infty} \frac{\tau}{1+\sqrt{1+\tau^2}} = 1$

Thus, $\tau = \frac{\sigma}{\omega\varepsilon}$.

Hence, the correct option is (B).

34. The longitudinal mechanical waves which lie in the frequency range $20Hz$ to $20000Hz$ are called audible or sound waves and having frequencies less than $20Hz$ are called infrasonic and having frequencies greater than $20,000Hz$ are called ultrasonic waves.

Sound or Audible waves are sensitive to human ear and are generated by the vibrating bodies like tuning fork, vocal cords etc. Infrasonic waves are produced by sources of bigger size such as earth quakes, volcanic eruptions, ocean waves etc. Human ear cannot detect Ultrasonic waves.

Hence, the correct option is (D).

35.

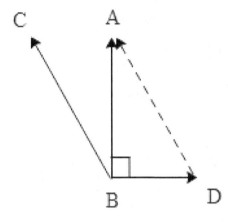

Considering the above figure let us say a swimmer at point B wishes to cross the river such that the time taken is the minimum. Therefore he has to make sure he is moving in a perpendicular path i.e. in the above figure is AB. The direction of the flow of water is BD with speed (V_W). Hence the swimmer actually has to swim with his speed (V_S) that is still water in direction CB such that he actually moves perpendicular. It is given to us that the average speed of the swimmer in the river is V_A i.e. along with path AB. Applying the Pythagoras theorem to the triangle ABD

we get,

$V_S^2 = V_A^2 + V_W^2$

$\Rightarrow 5^2 = 3^3 + V_W^2$

$\Rightarrow V_W^2 = 25 - 9$

$= 16$

$\Rightarrow V_W = 4$

Hence, the correct option is (B)

36.

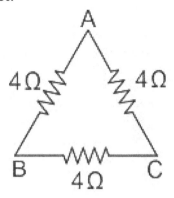

Here, 4 Ω across AB and AC are in a series combination, the equivalent resistance is:

$S = R_1 + R_2 = 4\Omega + 4\Omega = 8\Omega$

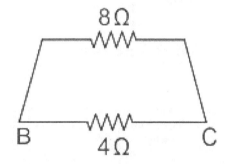

Now 4 Ω and 8 Ω are connected in parallel combination, the equivalent resistance is:

$\frac{1}{R_{eq}} = \frac{1}{8} + \frac{1}{4} = \frac{3}{8}$

$\Rightarrow R_{eq} = \frac{8}{3}\Omega$

Hence, the correct option is (D).

37. When the terminals of two or more resistances are connected at the same two points and the potential difference across them is equal is called resistances in parallel.

The net resistanceIequivalent resistance(R) of resistances in parallel is given by:

$\frac{1}{R_{eff}} = \frac{1}{R_1} + \frac{1}{R_2}$

Given:

$R_1 = 10\Omega$ and $R_2 = 30\Omega$

Since, they are parallel connected $\frac{1}{R_{eff}} = \frac{1}{10} + \frac{1}{30}$

$R_{eff} = \frac{10 \times 30}{10+30} = \frac{300}{40} = 7.5\Omega$

Hence, the correct option is (D).

38. Electrons are the major charge carriers in n-type semiconductors.

Semiconductor: The material which is not a good conductor or a good insulator is called a semiconductor.

- For example: Silicon, Germanium, etc.

Intrinsic semiconductor: The pure form of semiconductor is called an intrinsic semiconductor.

Extrinsic semiconductor: The impurity atoms added are called dopants and semiconductors doped with the impurity atoms are called extrinsic or doped semiconductors.

- P-type semiconductor: The semiconductor having holes as majority charge carriers and electrons as a minority charge carrier is called as p-type semiconductor.
- N-type semiconductor: The semiconductor having electrons as majority charge carriers and holes as a minority charge carrier is called as n-type semiconductor.

Hence, the correct option is (A).

39. The average velocity of the molecules of an ideal gas is zero because the molecules possess all sorts of velocities in all possible directions so their vector sum and hence the average is zero.

Hence, the correct option is (D).

40. According to kinetic energy theory, if we increase the temperature of a gas, it will increase the average kinetic energy of the molecule, which will increase the motion of the molecules.

This increased motion increases the outward pressure of the gas. The average kinetic energy of translation per molecules of the gas is related to temperature by the relationship:

$$\Rightarrow KE = \frac{3}{2} k_B T$$

Where E = kinetic energy, k_B = Boltzmann constant and T = temperature

From the above equation, it is clear that the average kinetic energy of the gas molecule is directly proportional to the absolute temperature of the gas.

As the temperature of both gases is the same. Therefore, the average kinetic energy of O_2 and H_2 is the same.

Hence, the correct option is (D).

41. Root mean square velocity of the gas: Root mean square velocity (RMS value) is the square root of the mean of squares of the velocity of individual gas molecules.

It is given as:

$$\Rightarrow v_{rms} = \sqrt{\frac{3RT}{M}}$$

Since the same gas is filled in two containers of the same volume, same temperature, and with the pressure of ratio 1 : 2.

Given: $M_1 = M_2 = M, V_1 = V_2 = V, T_1 = T_2 = T$ and $\frac{P_1}{P_2} = \frac{1}{2}$

The rms speed of the gas is given as,

$$\Rightarrow v_{rms} = \sqrt{\frac{3RT}{M}} \quad \ldots(1)$$

The rms speed for container 1 is given as,

$$\Rightarrow v_{rms1} = \sqrt{\frac{3RT}{M}} \quad \ldots(2)$$

The rms speed for container 2 is given as,

$$\Rightarrow v_{rms2} = \sqrt{\frac{3RT}{M}}$$

By equation (2) and equation (3),

$$\Rightarrow \frac{v_{rms1}}{v_{rms2}} = \frac{1}{1}$$

Hence, the correct option is (D).

42. Diffraction occurs due to interference of secondary wavelets between different portions of a wavefront allowed to pass across a small aperture or obstacle. Interference can be either constructive or destructive. When interference is constructive, the intensity of the wave will increase.

Hence, the correct option is (B).

43. Waves from the distant source are diffracted by the edge of the disc. These diffracted waves interfere constructively at the center of the shadow and produce a bright fringe. Therefore, the nature of the fringe produced is bright.

Hence, the correct option is (D).

44. The size of the obstacle or aperture should be of the order of the wavelength of light used. Therefore, the size of an obstacle is not of the order of obstacle, or micrometer or nanometer.

Hence, the correct option is (A).

45. A circuit which contains only inductance is called a pure inductive circuit and a circuit containing only a pure capacitor is known as a pure capacitive circuit. In a pure inductive circuit or a pure capacitive circuit, the current is lagging or ahead by 90 degrees from the voltage. The power factor is the cosine of the angle between the voltage and the current. Therefore:

$$\phi = \frac{\pi}{2} \rightarrow \text{Power factor} \left(\cos\frac{\pi}{2}\right) = 0$$

Hence, the correct option is (B).

46. In an AC circuit, we can define three types of power, namely, Instantaneous power, Average power, and Apparent power. A circuit element produces or dissipates power according to the equation → P = IV, where I is the current through the element and V is the voltage across it.

Hence, the correct option is (A).

47. In the diamagnetic materials, the susceptibility is very small and negative. Thus the susceptibility will be independent of the temperature. The atoms of solids having closed shells and metals like gold have this property.

Hence, the correct option is (C).

48. The piezoelectric effect is the mechanical strain caused on a material like quartz when subjected to an electric field. The same is observed in a ferromagnetic material called magnetostriction.

Hence, the correct option is (B).

49. The force F_1 passes through the axis of rotation, so it will not produce a torque.

The force F_2 is perpendicular to axis and radius, so it will provide a torque = r×F_2 about the axis of rotation, where 'r' is the distance of point of application of force F_2 from the axis of rotation.

Therefore, torque = r × F_2 = 0.05 × 5 Nm

= 0.25 Nm

Hence, the correct option is (C).

50. Let the force be 'F'. Work done will be = Tθ,

where T is the torque & is the angular displacement = 2π rad.

Work = Tθ = 10

∴ T(2π) = 10

∴ $T = \frac{5}{\pi} Nm$

Also, $T = r \times F$

∴ $\frac{5}{\pi} = 0.07 \times F$

∴ $F = \frac{500}{7\pi} N$

Hence, the correct option is (C).

51. CH_3COONa is salt of strong base and weak acid.

$NaOH + CH_3COOH \rightarrow CH_3COONa + H_2O$

$100\ mL$ of $0.2M CH_3COOH = 0.2 \times 100 = 20\ m\ mol$ of CH_3COOH

$100\ mL$ of $0.2M NaOH = 0.2 \times 100 = 20\ m$ mol of $NaOH$

$20\ m$ mol of $NaOH$ reacts with $20\ m$ mol of CH_3COOH to form $20\ m$ mol of CH_3COONa.

Concentration of $CH_3COONa = 20 mmoles/200ml = 0.1M$

$pH = \frac{pKw}{2} + \frac{pKa}{2} + \frac{\log C}{2}$

$pH = 7 + 2.37 + \frac{1}{2}[\log(0.1)]$

$pH = 9.37 + \frac{1}{2}[-1]$

$= 9.37 - 0.5$

$= 8.87$

Hence, the correct option is (B).

52. The nature of the solution depends on the strength of its cationic and anionic part. A salt solution will contain anionic and cationic part. Cation will come from the base and anion will come from the acid.

The overall nature of the solution will depend on how strong/weak the acid/base is.

All options are discussed below:

- $Pb(CH_3COO)_2$ is a salt of weak base $Pb(OH)_2$ and a weak acid CH_3COOH, thus, the solution will be nearly neutral.
- $Al(CN)_3$ is a salt of a weak base $Al(OH)_3$ and weak acid (HCN), thus, the solution will be nearly neutral.
- CH_3COOK is a salt of a strong base (KOH) and weak acid CH_3COOH, thus, the solution will be basic in nature.
- $FeCl_3$ is a salt of the strong acid (HCl) and weak base $Fe(OH)_3$, thus, it is an acidic salt. On hydrolysis, it gives $3H^+$ in the solution.

Hence, the correct option is (C).

53. The chemical process used in converting a primary aromatic amine into the corresponding diazonium salt of the amine is commonly referred to as diazotization.
Hence, the correct option is (B).

54. Classification means grouping of things.

The sorting of objects into groups with each group having its own characteristic properties, is called classification of objects.

All the objects having similar characteristics properties are placed in one group different groups and the objects having different properties are placed in different groups.

Hence, the correct option is (B).

55. In the given options,

(A) Concentration of H^+ in $1.0M\ HCl = 1M$

(B) Since, pH of solution is 4.

So, concentration of $H^+ = 10^{-4}M$

(C) pH of pure water $= 7$

So, concetration of $H^+ = 10^{-7}M$

(D) Concentration of H^+ in $1.0M\ NaOH$ is much less than the all the above options.

Since, concentration of H^+ is highest in option (A). So, potential of option (A) is maximum.

Hence, the correct option is (A).

56. Increasing the temperature of the substance, increases the fraction of molecules which collide with energies greater than Ea.

For every $10°C$ rise in temperature, the fraction of molecules having energy equal to or greater than Ea gets doubled leading to doubling the rate of reaction.

So, the number of fruitful collisions gets doubled.

Hence, the correct option is (D).

57. Given,

The rate of reaction becomes 2 times for every 10° rise in temperature.

The temperature is increased from 30°C to 80°C, thus the temperature is raised by 50°C.

Thus, the temperature coefficient of the reaction = 2 when the temperature is increased by 50°C.

As we know,

$\frac{r_2}{r_1} = 2^n$ .....(1)

Where,

r_2 = Rate at 80°C

r_1 = Rate at 30°C

And n $= \frac{\Delta T}{10}$

When temperature increases from 30°C to 80°C, change in temperature,

n $= \frac{80-30}{10} = 5$

From equation (1), we get

$\frac{r_2}{r_1} = 2^5$

= 32 times

Hence, the correct option is (B).

58. Every chemical reaction whether exothermic or endothermic has an energy barrier that has to be overcome before reactants can be transformed into products. If the reactant molecules have sufficient energy, they can reach the peak of the energy barrier after the collision and then they can go to the right side of the slope and consequently, change into products.

If the activation energy for a reaction is low, the fraction of effective collisions will be large and the reaction will be fast. On the other hand, if the activation energy is high, then the fraction of effective collisions will be small and the reaction will be slow.

When the temperature is increased, the number of active molecules increases, i.e., the number of effective collisions will increase and the rate of reaction will increase.

Hence, the correct option is (C).

59. A solution of acetone in ethanol shows a positive deviation from Raoult's law.

- It is due to miscibility of these two liquids with a difference of polarity and length of the hydrocarbon chain.
- Positive derivation occurs when vapour pressure of the component is greater than expected value.
- Acetone and ethanol both the components escape easily showing higher vapour pressure than the expected value.

Hence, the correct option is (B).

60. Given that:

Mass of $CO(NO)_3 \cdot 6H_2O = 30\ g$

Volume of solution $= 4.3\ L$

We know that,

$\text{Molarity} = \frac{\text{Moles of Solute}}{\text{Volume of solution in litre}}$

Molar mass of
$CO(NO)_3 \cdot 6H_2O = 59 + 2(14 + 3 \times 16) + 6 \times 18$
$= 291\ g\ mol^{-1}$

Therefore,

Moles of Moles of $CO(NO)_3 \cdot 6H_2O = \frac{\text{Mass}}{\text{Molar Mass}}$

$= \frac{30}{291}\ mol$

$= 0.103\ mol$

Therefore,

$\text{Molarity} = \frac{0.103\ mol}{4.3L}$

$= 0.023 M$

Hence, the correct option is (C).

61. It is given that:

Volume of water $(V) = 450\ mL = 0.45\ L$

Temperature $(T) = 37 + 273 = 310\ K$

Number of moles of the polymer, $n = \frac{\text{Mass of polymer}}{\text{Molar Mass of polymer}}$

$= \frac{1}{185000}\ mol$

We know that:

Osmotic pressure, $\pi = \frac{n}{V}RT$

where, $R = 8.314 \times 10^3\ PaLK^{-1}\ mol^{-1}$

$= \frac{1}{185000}\ mol \times \frac{1}{0.45L} \times 8.314 \times 10^3\ PaLK^{-1}\ mol^{-1} \times 310\ K$

$= 30.98\ Pa$

$= 31\ Pa$

Hence, the correct option is (A).

62. Two bodies at different temperatures are mixed in a calorimeter. The total internal energy of the two bodies remains conserved.

There is no heat lost since the calorimeter is insulated. If we consider both the liquids together as one system, then the work done by the system is zero.

From first law of thermodynamics,

$\Delta U = Q - W$

$\Delta U = 0$

Since there is no change in internal energy, the internal energy of the system remains constant.

Hence, the correct option is (C).

63. Thermodynamics is not concerned about the rate at which a reaction proceeds.

Thermodynamics tells us about the feasibility, energy changes, and extent of a chemical reaction. It does not tell us about the rate of the reaction. The kinetics of the reaction are concerned about the rate at which the reaction proceeds.

Hence, the correct option is (A).

64. It deals with energy changes of microscopic systems this statement is not true regarding the laws of thermodynamics.

The laws of thermodynamics deal with energy changes of macroscopic systems involving a large number of molecules rather than microscopic systems containing a few molecules. Laws of thermodynamics apply only when a system is in equilibrium or moves from one equilibrium state to another equilibrium state.

Hence, the correct option is (A).

65. If a is the edge length of the cube and r is the radius of each atom.

Distance of nearest approach between two atoms $= 2r = 1.73$ Å.

Therefore,

$r = \dfrac{1.73}{2} = 0.865$ Å

For BCC lattice, the relation of edge length and radius of the atom is,

$\sqrt{3}a = 4r$

$a = \dfrac{4r}{\sqrt{3}}$

$a = \dfrac{4 \times 0.865}{\sqrt{3}}$

$a = 1.99 = 2$Å $= 200 pm$

The edge length of the BCC lattice is $200 pm$.

Hence, the correct option is (C).

66. We know that:

Density, $\rho = \dfrac{Z \times M}{a^3 \times N_0}$

where,

Z: no. of atoms in the bcc unit cell $= 2$

M: molar mass of $CsBr = 133 + 80 = 213$

a: edge length of unit cell $= 436.6 pm$

$= 436.6 \times 10^{-10}$ cm

Therefore,

Density, $\rho = \dfrac{2 \times 213}{(436.6 \times 10^{-10})^3 \times 6.02 \times 10^{23}}$

$= 8.50\ g/cm^3$

For a unit cell $= \dfrac{8.50}{2} = 4.25\ g/cm^3$

Hence, the correct option is (D).

67. Crystalline solids are solids that have their atoms, molecules, and ions highly repetitive in nature and arranged in a specific pattern.

Potassium Chloride, Caesium Chloride, and rhombic sulphur are crystalline solids whereas glass is an amorphous solid.

Hence, the correct option is (C).

68. Alkali metals give deep blue solution due to the formation of ammonia the metal cations and electrons, the blue colour is due to the oxidation of ammonia electron to higher energy levels and the absorption of photons occurs in the red region of the spectrum.

Hence, the correct option is (C).

69. The functional group present every organic acid is $-COOH$ as it dissociate in water as $-COO^-$ and H^+.

Organic acids, such as acetic acid, all contain a functional group called a carboxyl group.

Hence, the correct option is (A).

70. Given:

$p = 0.1$ bar

V $= 34.05$ mL $= 34.05 \times 10^{-3}$ L $= 34.05 \times 10^{-3}$ dm^{-3}

$R = 0.083$ bar $dm^3 K^{-1} mol^{-1}$

$T = 546°C = (546 + 273)K = 819\ K$

The number of moles (n) can be calculated using the ideal gas equation as:

$pV = nRT$

$\Rightarrow n = \dfrac{pV}{RT}$

$= \dfrac{0.1 \times 34.05 \times 10^{-3}}{0.083 \times 819}$

$= 5.01 \times 10^{-5}\ mol$

Therefore, molar mass of phosphorus $= \dfrac{0.0625}{5.01 \times 10^{-5}} = 1247.5 g mol^{-1}$

Hence, the correct option is (C).

71. A gas deviates from ideal behavior at a high pressure because its molecules attract one another.

At high pressure, the volume is decreased appreciably, so the attractive forces become large and the molecules are crowded together. Thus, pressure correction is necessary and the gas deviates more from ideal behaviour.

Hence, the correct option is (A).

72. The sulphur is the central atom in the molecule SO_3 and has six valence electrons. The oxygen atom given is the divalent therefore, the number of monovalent electrons is zero. There is no cationic charge or anionic charge present on the molecule so the value is taken as zero. So, the hybridization of the SO_3 molecule is three which shows the hybridization as sp^2 hybridization which means there is no sigma bond present in the structure and there is a double bond present.

In SO_3 molecule, S atom remains sp^2 hybrid, so, it is trigonal planar structure.

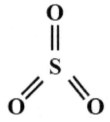

Hence, the correct option is (D).

73. Starch aqueous solution is a lyophilic colloidal solution.

Lyophilic colloids are liquid loving colloids. When these colloids are mixed with suitable liquid high force of attraction exists between colloidal particles and liquid.

Hence, the correct option is (C).

74. Given,

Wavelength, $\lambda = 300\ nm = 300 \times 10^{-9}\ m$

Planck's constant, $h = 6.626 \times 10^{-34} Js$

The speed of light, $= 3 \times 10^8\ m\ s^{-1}$

Energy of one photon, $E = h\nu$

$= \dfrac{hc}{\lambda}$

$= \dfrac{6.626 \times 10^{-34}\ J\ s \times 3.0 \times 10^8\ m\ s}{300 \times 10^{-1}\ m}$

$= 6.626 \times 10^{-19}\ J$

As we know,

Avogadro's number $= 6.022 \times 10\ mol^{-1}$

The energy of one mole of photons,

$= 6.626 \times 10^{-19}\ J \times 6.022 \times 10^{23}\ mol^{-1}$

$= 3.99 \times 10^5\ J\ mol$

The minimum energy needed to remove one mole of electrons from sodium $= (3.99 - 1.68) \times 10^5\ J\ mol^{-1}$

$= 2.31 \times 10^5\ J\ mol^{-1}$

The minimum energy for one electron $= \dfrac{2.31 \times 10^5\ J\ mol^{-1}}{6.022 \times 10^{23}\ electrons\ mol^{-1}}$

$= 3.84 \times 10^{-19}\ J$

Hence, the correct option is (C).

75. Hydrocarbons having single bonds are known as saturated hydrocarbon.

Saturated hydrocarbons are known as an alkane. These are also known as paraffin. Unsaturated hydrocarbons are having double or triple bonds i.e., alkenes and alkynes. A Saturated hydrocarbon is a hydrocarbon in which all the carbon-carbon bonds are single bonds.

Hence, the correct option is (A).

76. A standard hydrogen electrode has a zero potential because the electrode potential is assumed to be zero.

Potential is a relative term i.e., it is always measured with respect to a reference. In electrochemistry, hydrogen is taken to be the reference to measure the potential and therefore, to form a basis for comparison with all other electrode reactions, hydrogen's standard electrode potential is declared to be zero volts at all temperatures.

Hence, the correct option is (C).

77. The representation of the Galvanic cell is done as below:

Oxidation (left part) || Reduction (right part).

Aqueous elements have to be near the salt bridge in the representation. One has to remember that, in an electrochemical cell, reduction occurs at cathode and oxidation occurs at the anode.

Here in this question, option (A) satisfies the representation rules and thus, is the correct answer.

$Zn + 2Ag^+ \rightarrow Zn^{2+} + 2Ag$ can be represented as:

$Zn_{(s)} | Zn^{2+}_{(aq)} \parallel Ag^+_{(aq)} | Ag_{(s)}$

Hence, the correct option is (A).

78. Standard electrode potential of reaction will not change due to multiply the half-cell reactions with some numbers.

$Mn^{2+} + 2e^- \rightarrow Mn, E° = -1.18\ V$ .... (i)

$2(Mn^{3+} + e^- \rightarrow Mn^{2+}), E° = +1.51\ V$ ...... (ii)

Subtracting equation (ii) from equation (i), we get

$3Mn^{2+} \rightarrow Mn + 2Mn^{3+}$

$E° = -1.18 - (+1.51) = -2.69\ V$

Since, the value of $E°$ is negative, therefore, the reaction is non-spontaneous.

Hence, the correct option is (C).

79. Number of donor atoms in $N(CH_2CH_2NH_2)_3$ is four so it is a tetradentate ligand. Each nitrogen atom is a donor atom.

$H_2\ddot{N} - CH_2 - CH_2 - \underset{\underset{\underset{\overset{|}{:}NH_2}{\overset{|}{CH_2}}}{\overset{|}{CH_2}}}{\ddot{N}} - CH_2 - CH_2 - \ddot{N}H_2$

Hence, the correct option is (C).

80. The I.U.P.A.C name of the coordination compound $K_3[Fe(CN)_6]$ is Potassium hexacyanoferrate(III).

In this complex, there are six CN so they are named hexacyano and the cyanide ligand has -1 charge. So the iron overall has -3 charge, so the name of the central metal atom ends with -ate followed by the charge in roman letters.

Thus, the name of the complex is Potassium hexacyanoferrate(III).

Hence, the correct option is (B).

81. The name of the compound $[Co(NH_3)_5NO_2]Cl_2$ will be Pentaamminenitrocobalt(III) chloride.

Ligands are named in alphabetical order. The oxidation number of cobalt is $+3$ as the oxidation numbers of the nitro group and chlorine are -1 each. Option (A) is ruled out as cobalt has $+2$ oxidation state. Option (B) and (D) are ruled out as Co is written as cobaltate which indicates that Co is part of a complex anion. Also, in option (D), nitroso should be replaced with nitro.

Hence, the correct option is (C).

82. There is a large difference in the boiling points of butanal and butan-1-ol due to intermolecular hydrogen bonding in butan-1-ol.

Butan-1-ol has polar O–H bond due to which it shows intermolecular H-bonding which is not possible in case of butanal due to absence of polar bond.

Hence, the correct option is (A).

83. Order of reactivity of different alcohols towards esterification is $1° > 2° > 3°$.

Thus, as the steric hinderance (or bulkiness) increases from primary to secondary to tertiary alcohol, the order of esterification decreases.

Hence, the correct option is (C).

84. Carboxylic acids form dimers by hydrogen bonding of the acidic hydrogen and the carbonyl oxygen when anhydrous.

Due to the small size and strong hydrogen bonding between the molecule (intermolecular), they overlap and form a dimer in aqueous condition.

For example, acetic acid forms a dimer in the gas phase, where the monomer units are held together by hydrogen bonds.

Dimerization of acetic acid

Hence, the correct option is (C).

85. Carbon-dioxide and water both are produced when alcohol is added to petrol and used as a fuel.

For example, Ethanol is used as an additive in gasoline (Petrol) by some countries as its impact on the environment is much lower than gasoline or diesel. When ethanol combusts, it releases, mainly carbon dioxide and water.

$C_2H_5OH + 3\ O_2 \rightarrow 2\ CO_2 + 3\ H_2O + heat$

Hence, the correct option is (D).

86. Tertiary butyl alcohol is most reactive with Lucas Reagent.

Ethanol is a primary alcohol and does not give instant turbidity with Lucas Reagent. Methanol is also primary alcohol that does not give turbidity with Lucas Reagent. Isopropyl alcohol is secondary alcohol that gives turbidity with Lucas Reagent after 5 to 10 minutes.

Tertiary butyl alcohol is tertiary alcohol that gives turbidity instantaneously on reaction with Lucas Reagent. The reaction can be given as follows:

$\underset{\text{2-methylpropan-2-ol (3°)}}{CH_3-\underset{\underset{CH_3}{|}}{\overset{\overset{CH_3}{|}}{C}}-OH} + HCl \xrightarrow{\text{anhydrous } ZnCl_2} \underset{\text{2-chloro-2-methylpropane (immediate appearance of turbidity)}}{CH_3-\underset{\underset{CH_3}{|}}{\overset{\overset{CH_3}{|}}{C}}-Cl} + H_2O$

$\underset{\text{propan-2-ol (2°)}}{CH_3-\underset{\underset{CH_3}{|}}{CH}-OH} + HCl \xrightarrow{\text{anhydrous } ZnCl_2} \underset{\text{2-chloropropane (slow appearance of turbidity)}}{CH_3-\underset{\underset{CH_3}{|}}{CH}-Cl} + H_2O$

$\underset{\text{ethanol (1°)}}{CH_3-CH_2-OH} + HCl \xrightarrow{\text{anhydrous } ZnCl_2}$ No reaction at room temperature (Turbidity appears only on heating)

Hence, the correct option is (D).

87. Ethyl alcohol is denatured by adding methanol and pyridine.

Denatured alcohol, also called methylated spirits or wood spirit or denatured rectified spirit, is ethanol that has additives to make it poisonous, bad-tasting, foul-smelling, to discourage recreational consumption. It is sometimes dyed so that it can be identified visually. Pyridine, Methanol or both can be added to make denatured alcohol poisonous, and denatonium can be added to make it bitter.

Hence, the correct option is (B).

88. The group of peptidase, amylase, rennin contains biocatalysts. In humans salivary amylase enzyme breaks down starch. Renin is a proteolytic enzyme related to pepsin that synthesized by chief cells in the stomach of some animals. Peptidases are enzymes that cleave peptide bonds, yielding proteins and peptides. Biocatalyst is the substance which is used in the biochemical reaction and this increases the speed of the biochemical reaction. The enzyme accelerates the chemical reaction and that enzyme will not change the state of the equilibrium. This type of enzyme is known as biocatalyst.

Hence, the correct option is (B).

89. Enzymes that catalyse removal of groups from substrates by mechanisms other than hydrolysis, and addition of groups to double bonds, are called lyases. A lyase is an enzyme that catalyzes the breaking (an elimination reaction) of various chemical bonds by means other than hydrolysis (a substitution reaction) and oxidation. Lyase-catalyzed reactions break the bond between a carbon atom and another atom such as oxygen, sulfur, or another carbon atom.

Hence, the correct option is (A).

90. Semi-synthetic polymers among the following is Cellulose acetate.

Semi-synthetic polymers are the polymers made by modification of the properties of the natural polymers. Cellulose derivatives as cellulose acetate (rayon) and cellulose nitrate, are usually semi-synthetic as they involve natural substances too. Nylon-6,6 , BUNA-S, polythene are synthetic polymers.

Hence, the correct option is (A).

91. Natural rubber has all cis-configuration.

The repeating unit has the cis-configuration in natural rubber with chain extensions on the same side of the ethylene double bond. This is essential for elasticity. If the configuration is trans, the polymer is either a hard plastic or like gutta-percha.

Natural rubber
All *cis*-configuration

Hence, the correct option is (D).

92. Chromium(atomic no.24, symbol-Cr) forms many oxides. Some of its common oxidation states are +2, +3 and +6. Chromium (III) oxide (green in colour) is amphoteric, i.e., it can react as both acid and base. Its formula is Cr_2O_3.

Hence, the correct option is (B).

93. Chromyl chloride test is done for detecting the presence of Cl^- ions. The chlorides of silver, lead, mercury and antimony are covalent in nature and thus do not generate Cl^- ions and so they do not give the chromyl chloride test also. So, heavy metal chlorides don't give this test because they are not ionic.

Hence, the correct option is (A).

94. Hydrogen is the lightest and the smallest noble gas, having an atomic number of 2. Owing to its small size and inert nature, it has the unusual property of diffusing through most commonly used laboratory materials such as rubber, glass or plastic.

Hence, the correct option is (A).

95. Enthalpy of dissociation decreases as the bond distance increases from F_2 to I_2 due to a corresponding increase in the size of the atom as we move down the group from F to I. The F-F bond dissociation enthalpy is, however, smaller than that of Cl-Cl and even smaller than that of Br-Br. This is due to the reason that F atom is very small and hence the electron-electron repulsions between the lone pairs of electrons are very large.

Hence, the correct option is (B).

96. Oxygen is the most reactive group 16 element. Its reactivity is only slightly less than the most reactive elements, halogens. Sulphur is also very reactive particularly at high temperatures which helps in the cleavage of S-S bonds present in S_8 molecules. However, as we move down the group, the reactivity decreases, i.e., O > S > Se > Te > Po.

Hence, the correct option is (D).

97. Each halogen has one electron less than the nearest inert gas. As a result, halogens are very reactive elements. They readily share their single unpaired electron with other atoms to form covalent bonds. Thus, all halogens exist as diatomic molecules.

Hence, the correct option is (B).

98. The Hinsberg reaction is a test for the detection of primary, secondary and tertiary amines. In this test, the amine is shaken well with Hinsberg reagent in the presence of aqueous alkali (either KOH or NaOH). A reagent containing an aqueous sodium hydroxide solution and benzenesulfonyl chloride is added to a substrate.

Hence, the correct option is (D).

99. Chlorine gas was used to bleach paper. It has good oxidizing properties. Nowadays H_2O_2 with a suitable catalyst is used for bleaching purposes as it does not contaminate groundwater.

Hence, the correct option is (C).

100. Tetrachloroethene was used as a solvent for dry cleaning purposes. It is a suspected carcinogen and groundwater contaminant. It is replaced by greener solvent like supercritical CO_2.

Hence, the correct option is (C).

Physics & Chemistry : Mock Test 09

Physics

Q.1 Diagram shows a bar magnet and two infinite long wires W_1 and W_2 carrying equal currents in opposite directions. The magnet is free to move and rotate. P is the mid-point of magnet. For this situation mark out the correct statement(s).

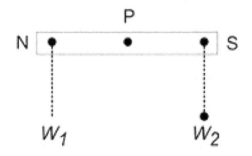

A. Magnet experiences a net torque in clockwise direction and zero net force.
B. Magnet experiences a net force towards left and a net torque in anti-clockwise direction.
C. Magnet experiences a net force towards right and a net torque in anti-clockwise direction.
D. Magnet experiences zero net force and a net torque in anti-clockwise direction.

Q.2 A toroidal solenoid has 3000 turns and a mean radius of $10\ cm$. It has a soft iron core of relative permeability 2000. What is the magnitude of the magnetic field in the core, when a current of $1\ A$ is passed through the solenoid?
A. $0.012\ T$ B. $0.12\ T$ C. $1.2\ T$ D. $12\ T$

Q.3 When $100V$ DC is applied across a solenoid, a current of $1A$ flows in it. When $100V\ AC$ is applied across the same coil, the current drops to $0.5\ A$. If the frequency of the AC source is $50\ Hz$, the resistance and inductance of the solenoid respectively are:
A. 100Ω and $0.55H$ B. 200Ω and $0.8H$
C. 200Ω and $1.0H$ D. 200Ω and $0.89H$

Q.4 A full-wave rectifier is fed with ac mains of frequency 50 Hz. What is the fundamental frequency of the ripple in the output current?
A. 25 Hz B. 50 Hz C. 75 Hz D. 100 Hz

Q.5 In the figure, given that V_{BB} supply can vary from 0 to $5.0V, V_{CC} = 5V, \beta_{dc} = 200, R_B = 100k\Omega, R_C = 1k\Omega$ and $V_{BE} = 1.0V$. The minimum base current and the input voltage at which the transistor will go to saturation, will be respectively:

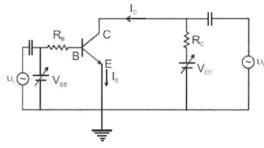

A. $20\mu A$ and $3.5\ V$ B. $25\mu A$ and $3.5\ V$
C. $25\mu A$ and $2.5\ V$ D. $20\mu A$ and $2.8\ V$

Q.6 A source emitting wavelengths 480 nm and 600 nm is used in Young's Double Slit Experiment. The separation between the slits is 0.25 mm. The interference is observed 1.5 m away from the slits. The linear separation between the first maxima of the two wavelengths is:
A. 0.72 mm B. 0.62 mm C. 0.76 mm D. 0.27 mm

Q.7 A spring of force constant K is cut into two pieces such that one piece is double the length of the other. The force constant of the longer piece will be:
A. $\frac{2K}{3}$ B. $\frac{3K}{2}$ C. $3K$ D. $6K$

Q.8 A simple pendulum is executing simple harmonic motion with a time period T. If the length of the pendulum is increased by 21%, the increase in the time period of the pendulum of increased length is:
A. 10% B. 21% C. 30% D. 50%

Q.9 When unpolarized light beam is incident from air onto glass $(n = 1.5)$ at the polarizing angle then:
A. Reflected beam is 100 percent polarized
B. Reflected and refracted beams are partially polarized
C. The refracted beam is 100 percent polarized
D. All of the above

Q.10 Mirage is an example of _____.
A. Reflection of light
B. Refraction of light
C. Total internal reflection of light
D. Scattering of light

Q.11 Outdoors on the winter, why does a piece of metal feel colder than piece of wood?
A. Metal is a good conductor of heat than wood
B. Wood is a good conductor of heat than metal
C. Wood conducts heat faster than metal
D. Both the metals and wood are bad conductors of heat

Q.12 The coolant in a chemical or a nuclear plant (i.e., the liquid used to prevent the different parts of a plant from getting too hot) should have:

A. Low specific heat
B. High specific heat
C. High Latent heat
D. None of the above

Q.13 In changing the state of a gas adiabatically from an equilibrium state A to another equilibrium state B, an amount of work equal to $22.3J$ is done on the system. If the gas is taken from state A to B via a process in which the net heat absorbed by the system is $9.35cal$, how much is the net work done by the system in the latter case? (Take $1cal = 4.19J$)

A. 12.39J B. 12.08J C. 15.88J D. 16.88J

Q.14 A steam engine delivers $5.4 \times 10^8 J$ of work per minute and services $3.6 \times 10^9 J$ of heat per minute from its boiler. What is the efficiency of the engine? How much heat is wasted per minute?

A. $5.06 \times 10^{-9}J$
B. $3.06 \times 10^9 J$
C. $8.06 \times 10^{19}J$
D. $1.05 \times 10^8 J$

Q.15 A spring balance is attached to the ceiling of a lift. A man hangs his bag on the spring and the spring reads $49\ N$, when the lift is stationary. If the lift moves downward with an acceleration of $5\ m/s^2$, the reading of the spring balance will be:

A. 24 N B. 74 N C. 15 N D. 49 N

Q.16 When photons of energy hv fall on an aluminium plate (of work function E₀), photoelectrons of maximum kinetic energy K are ejected. If the frequency of the radiation is doubled, the maximum kinetic energy of the ejected photoelectrons will be:

A. $K + E_0$ B. $2K$ C. K D. $K + hv$

Q.17 Light of wavelength 4000Å is incident on a metal surface. The maximum kinetic energy of emitted photoelectron is 2eV. What is the work function of the metal surface?

A. 4eV B. 1eV C. 2eV D. 6eV

Q.18 A piece of metal floats on mercury. The coefficients of volume expansion of the metal and mercury are λ_1 and λ_2, respectively. If their temperature is increased by ΔT, the fraction of the volume of metal submerged in mercury changes by a factor of:

A. $\left(\frac{1+\gamma_2 \Delta T}{1+\gamma_1 \Delta T}\right)$
B. $\left(\frac{1+\gamma_2 \Delta T}{1-\gamma_1 \Delta T}\right)$
C. $\left(\frac{1-\gamma_2 \Delta T}{1+\gamma_1 \Delta T}\right)$
D. $\frac{\gamma_2}{\gamma_1}$

Q.19 A metal plate of area $10^3\ cm^2$ rests on a layer of oil 6 mm thick. A tangential force of $10^2\ N$ is applied on it to move it with a constant velocity of $6\ cm\ s^{-1}$. The coefficient of viscosity of the liquid is

A. 0.1 poise B. 0.5 poise
C. 0.7 poise D. 0.9 poise

Q.20 In a Van de Graaff type generator, a spherical metal shell is to be a $15 \times 10^6 V$ electrode. The dielectric strength of the gas surrounding the electrode is $5 \times 10^7 Vm^{-1}$. What is the minimum radius of the spherical shell required?

A. 30cm B. 3m C. 90cm D. 150cm

Q.21 A $4\mu F$ capacitor is charged by a $200V$ supply. It is then disconnected from the supply and is connected to another uncharged $2\mu F$ capacitor. How much electrostatic energy of the first capacitor is lost in the form of heat and electromagnetic radiation?

A. 1.0267J B. 0.0267J C. 2.0267J D. 3.0267J

Q.22 The plates of a parallel plate capacitor have an area of $90cm^2$ each and are separated by $2.5mm$. The capacitor is charged by connecting it to a $400V$ supply. How much electrostatic energy is stored by the capacitor?

A. $2.55 \times 10^6 J$
B. $3.55 \times 10^6 J$
C. $4.55 \times 10^6 J$
D. $5.55 \times 10^6 J$

Q.23 The direction of the electric field due to the positive charge is:

A. Away from the charge
B. Towards the charge
C. Both (A) and (B)
D. None of the above

Q.24 The ability of charged bodies to exert force on one another is attributed to the existence of:

A. Electrons B. Protons
C. Neutrons D. Electric field

Q.25 A charge 'Q' is divided between two point charges. What should be the values of these charges on the objects so that the force between them is maximum?

A. $\frac{Q}{3}$ B. $\frac{Q}{2}$ C. $(Q-2)$ D. $2Q$

Q.26 The electric field strength of a charge _____.

A. Increases with distance
B. Decreases with cube of distance
C. Decreases with distance
D. Decreases with square of distance

Q.27 The force between two charges Q_1 and Q_2 is given by _____.

A. Newton's law B. Coulomb's law
C. Faraday's law D. Ampere's law

Q.28 An aeroplane execute a horizontal loop at a speed of $720\ kmph$ with its wings banked at $45°$. What is the radius of the loop? Take $g = 10\ ms^{-2}$

A. $4\ km$ B. $4.5\ km$ C. $7.2\ km$ D. $2\ km$

Q.29 The speed of the particle is increasing at the rate of a m/s^2 when it is rotating in the circular path of radius R. Find the acceleration of the particle when its speed is v.

A. a
B. $\frac{v^2}{R}$
C. $\sqrt{a^2 + \frac{v^2}{R}}$
D. $\sqrt{a^2 + \frac{v^4}{R^2}}$

Q.30 Two vibrating strings of the same material, but lengths L and $2L$ have radii $2r$ and r, respectively. They are stretched under the same tension. Both the strings vibrate in their fundamental modes, the one of length L with frequency v_1 and the other with frequency v_2. The ratio $\frac{v_1}{v_2}$ is

A. 2 B. 4 C. 8 D. 1

Q.31 A sound absorber attenuates the sound level by $20dB$. The intensity decreases by a factor of:

A. 1000 B. 10000 C. 10 D. 100

Q.32 Two amplifiers are connected one after the other in series (cascaded). The first amplifier has a voltage gain of 10 and the second has a voltage gain of 20. If the input signal is 0.01 volt, calculate the output AC signal.

A. 1 V B. 3 V C. 4 V D. 2 V

Q.33 The moment of the force, $\vec{F} = 4\hat{i} + 5\hat{j} - 6\hat{k}$ at $(2,0,-3)$, about the point $(2,-2,-2)$, is given by
[NEET UG, 2018]

A. $-7\hat{i} - 8\hat{j} - 4\hat{k}$ B. $-4\hat{i} - \hat{j} - 8\hat{k}$
C. $-8\hat{i} - 4\hat{j} - 7\hat{k}$ D. $-7\hat{i} - 4\hat{j} - 8\hat{k}$

Q.34 A gaseous mixture consists of $16\ g$ of helium and $16\ g$ of oxygen. The ratio C_P/C_V of the mixture is:

A. 1.59 B. 1.62 C. 1.4 D. 1.54

Q.35 The respectively speeds of five molecules are 2,1,5,1.6,1.6 and 1.2 km/sec. The most probable speed in km/sec will be:

A. 2 B. 1.58 C. 1.6 D. 1.31

Q.36 The amount of energy released when one microgram of matter is annihilated is:

A. $25kWh$ B. $9 \times 10^{10} kWh$
C. $3 \times 10^{10} kWh$ D. $0.5 \times 10^5 kWh$

Q.37 β-decay means emission of electron from:

A. innermost electron orbit
B. a stable nucleus
C. outermost electron orbit
D. radioactive nucleus

Q.38 Atomic mass unit (u) is equivalent to _____ the mass of carbon isotope C-12.

A. 12 times B. $\frac{1}{12}$th C. $\frac{1}{6}$th D. 6 times

Q.39 The capacitance of a reverse biased PN junction:

A. Increases as reverse bias is increased
B. Decreases as reverse bias is increased
C. Decreases as reverse bias is decreased
D. Is insignificantly low

Q.40 Find the reverse saturation current at $35°C$ for a junction which has $I_0 = 30nA$ at $25°C$.

A. 25 nA B. 40 nA C. 60 nA D. 20 nA

Q.41 The value of universal gravitational constant G is _____.

A. $6.67 \times 10^{-11} \frac{Nm^2}{kg}$ B. $6.67 \times 10^{-11} \frac{Nm^2}{kg^2}$

C. $66.7 \times 10^{-11} \frac{Nm^2}{kg^2}$ D. $66.7 \times 10^{-11} \frac{Nm^2}{kg}$

Q.42 An open pipe is suddenly closed at one end with the result that the frequency of third harmonic of the closed pipe is found to be higher by $100Hz$ than the fundamental frequency of the open pipe. The fundamental frequency of the open pipe is:

A. $200Hz$ B. $300Hz$ C. $240Hz$ D. $480Hz$

Q.43 In the circuit given, the correct relation to a balanced Wheatstone bridge is:

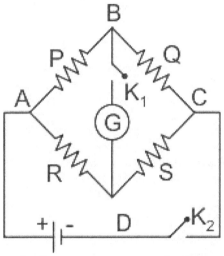

A. $\frac{P}{S} = \frac{R}{Q}$ B. $\frac{P}{Q} = \frac{S}{R}$
C. $\frac{P}{R} = \frac{Q}{S}$ D. None of these

Q.44 Keeping voltage constant, if more lamps are put into a series circuit, the overall current in the circuit:

A. Increases B. Decreases
C. Remains the same D. Becomes infinite

Q.45 If $f(t) = A\sin\omega t + B\cos\omega t$ is written as $f(t) = D\sin(\omega t + \varphi)$ then ' φ ' is equal to?

A. $\tan^{-1}\left(\frac{A}{B}\right)$ B. $\sqrt{(A^2 + B^2)}$
C. $\tan^{-1}\left(\frac{B}{A}\right)$ D. $A + B$

Q.46 The displacement equation for two waves undergoing superposition are $y_1 = 4\sin\omega t$, $y_2 = 3\sin\left(\omega t + \frac{\pi}{2}\right)$, then resultant amplitude will be:

A. 5 cm B. 7 cm C. 1 cm D. 0 cm

Q.47 In a ferromagnetic material, the losses due to hysteresis are:

A. Directly proportional to the supply frequency.
B. Inversely proportional to the supply frequency
C. Inversely proportional to square of the supply frequency
D. Directly proportional to square of the supply frequency

Q.48 The reluctance offered by a magnetic material is highest when it is:

A. Diamagnetic B. Paramagnetic
C. Ferromagnetic D. None of these

Q.49 The _____ is the curve characteristic of a material or element or alloy's magnetic properties.
A. Eddy current loss
B. B-H curve
C. Hysteresis
D. Iron loss

Q.50 "Whenever two (or more) waves travel through the same medium at the same time, the net displacement of the medium at any point in space or time, is simply the sum of the individual wave displacements." This statement is the principle _____.
A. Doppler effect
B. Resonance
C. Superposition
D. Harmonics

Chemistry

Q.51 The phenomenon in which polar crystals on heating produce electricity is called:
A. Pyro-electricity
B. Piezo-electricity
C. Ferro-electricity
D. Ferri-electricity

Q.52 In stoichiometric defect, the ratio of positive and negative ions as indicated by a chemical formula of the compound:
A. Decreases
B. Increases
C. Changes by a factor of 2
D. Remains the same

Q.53 The arrangement of X^- ions around A^+ ion in solid AX is given in the figure (not drawn to scale). If the radius of X^- is $250 pm$, what is the radius of A^+?

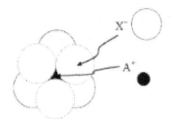

A. $104 pm$
B. $125 pm$
C. $183 pm$
D. $57 pm$

Q.54 $\log \dfrac{K_p}{K_c} + \log RT = 0$ is true relationship for which of the following reaction(s)?
A. $PCl_5 \rightleftharpoons PCl_3 + Cl_2$
B. $2SO_2 + O_2 \rightleftharpoons 2SO_3$
C. $N_2 + 3H_2 \rightleftharpoons 2NH_3$
D. Both (B) and (C)

Q.55 If the concentrations of two weak acids are different and degrees of ionisation (α) are very less, then their relative strengths can be compared by:
A. $\dfrac{[H^+]_1}{[H^+]_2}$
B. $\dfrac{\alpha_1}{\alpha_2}$
C. $\dfrac{C_1 \alpha_1^2}{C_2 \alpha_2^2}$
D. Both (A) and (C)

Q.56 Match List - I with List - II and select the correct answer by using the codes given below the list:

List – I (Petroleum fraction)		List – II (Composition)	
(a)	Gasoline	(i)	C_8 to C_{16}
(b)	Kerosine	(ii)	C_4 to C_9
(c)	Heavy oil	(iii)	C_{10} to C_{18}
(d)	Diesel	(iv)	C_{16} to C_{30}

A. (a) - (i), (b) - (ii), (c) - (iv), (d) - (iii)
B. (a) - (ii), (b) - (i), (c) - (iii), (d) - (iv)
C. (a) - (ii), (b) - (i), (c) - (iv), (d) - (iii)
D. (a) - (i), (b) - (ii), (c) - (iii), (d) - (iv)

Q.57 Identify disproportionation reaction.
A. $CH_4 + 2O_2 \rightarrow CO_2 + 2H_2O$
B. $CH_4 + 4Cl_2 \rightarrow CCl_4 + 4HCl$
C. $2F_2 + 2OH^- \rightarrow 2F^- + OF_2 + H_2O$
D. $2NO_2 + 2OH^- \rightarrow NO_2^- + NO_3^- + H_2O$

Q.58 Chemical kinetics a branch of physical chemistry deals with:
A. Structure of molecules
B. Heat changes in a reaction
C. Physical changes in a reaction
D. Rate of reactions

Q.59 In the reaction $2A + B \rightarrow A_2B$, if the concentration of A is doubled and that of B is halved, then the rate of the reaction will:
A. Increase 2 times
B. Increase 4 times
C. Decrease 2 times
D. Remain the same

Q.60 For producing the effective collisions, the colliding molecules must posses:
A. First order reactions
B. Second order reactions
C. Bimolecular reactions
D. Zeroth order reactions

Q.61 A solution containing $10\ g$ per dm^3 of urea (molecular mass $= 60\ g\ mol^{-1}$) is isotonic with a 5% solution of a non-volatile solute. The molecular mass of this non-volatile solute is:
A. $300\ g\ mol^{-1}$
B. $350\ g\ mol^{-1}$
C. $200\ g\ mol^{-1}$
D. $250\ g\ mol^{-1}$

Q.62 If $22\ g$ of benzene is dissolved in $122\ g$ of carbon tetrachloride, determine the mass percentage of carbon tetrachloride (CCl_4) and benzene (C_6H_6).
A. 80.72%
B. 84.72%
C. 85.70%
D. 80.20%

Q.63 At 300 K, 36 g of glucose present in a litre of its solution has an osmotic pressure of 4.98 bar. If the osmotic pressure of the solution is 1.52 bars at the same temperature, what would be its concentration?
A. 0.061 mol
B. 0.063 mol
C. 0.065 mol
D. 0.070 mol

Q.64 Which of the following is a closed system?
A. Pressure cooker
B. Rocket engine during propulsion
C. Tea placed in a steel kettle

D. Jet engine

Q.65 The state of a thermodynamic system is described by its measurable or macroscopic (bulk) properties. These are:
A. Pressure, volume, temperature and amount
B. Volume, temperature and amount
C. Pressure and temperature
D. Pressure and volume

Q.66 Among the following the state function(s) is (are):
(i) Internal energy
(ii) Irreversible expansion work
(iii) Reversible expansion work
(iv) Molar enthalpy
A. (i) and (iv)
B. (ii) and (iii)
C. (i), (ii) and (iii)
D. (i) only

Q.67 Which isotope is used in the nuclear power plants to generate electricity?
A. Uranium 235
B. Iodine 131
C. Cobalt 60
D. Uranium 238

Q.68 Which of the following elements is found at room temperature in the same physical state as water?
A. Iodine   B. Bromine   C. Chlorine   D. Florine

Q.69 An element with electronic configuration 2,8,2 belongs to which period and group?
A. 2, 3   B. 4, 3   C. 2, 1   D. 3, 2

Q.70 In Mendeleev table, the triad of VIII group is :
A. Ru, Rh, Pd
B. Cu, Ag, Au
C. N, O, F
D. Tl, Pb, Bi

Q.71 The eighth group of Mendeleev's periodic table is divided into how many subgroups?
A. 2   B. 0   C. 4   D. 1

Q.72 Why are aluminum items such as pressure cookers, saucepans, etc. anodized?
A. To increase their conductivity.
B. To increase their tensile strength.
C. To prevent them from rusting.
D. To make them lighter and shinier.

Q.73 What is the valency of carbon?
A. Pentavalent
B. Divalent
C. Trivalent
D. Tetravalent

Q.74 At the same temperature, the average molar kinetic energy of N_2 and CO is:
A. $KE_1 > KE_2$
B. $KE_1 < KE_2$
C. $KE_1 = KE_2$
D. None of the given

Q.75 Calculate the total pressure in a mixture of $8\ g$ of dioxygen and $4\ g$ of dihydrogen confined in a vessel of $1 dm^3$ at $27°C$. $(R = 0.083\ bar\ dm^3\ K^{-1}\ mol^{-1})$.
A. $55.025\ bar$
B. $56.025\ bar$
C. $50.035\ bar$
D. $51.025\ bar$

Q.76 What is the main factor responsible for weak acidic nature of $B - F$ bonds in BF_3?
A. Large electronegativity of F
B. Three centered two electron bonds in BF_3
C. $p\pi - d\pi$ back bonding
D. $p\pi - p\pi$ back bonding

Q.77 Substances that decrease the activity of a catalyst are known as:
A. Controllers
B. Promoters
C. Poisons
D. Initiators

Q.78 Which of the following properties are similar for isotopes?
A. Physical properties
B. Chemical properties
C. Both physical and chemical properties
D. Neither physical nor chemical properties

Q.79 Which one of the following element forms interstitial compounds?
A. Fe   B. Co   C. Ni   D. Sc

Q.80 Calculate the heat of formation of diborane $[B_2H_6(g)]$ at $298\ K$ if the heat of combustion of it is $-1941\ kJ/mol$ and heats of formation of $B_2O_3(s)$ and $H_2O(g)$ are $-2368\ kJ/mol$ and $-241.8\ kJ/mol$ respectively.
A. $-11.992\ kJ/mol$
B. $-1152.4\ kJ/mol$
C. $10.992\ kJ/mol$
D. $-10.992\ kJ/mol$

Q.81 A current of $0.75\ A$ is passed through an acidic solution of $CuSO_4$ for 10 minutes. The volume of oxygen liberated at anode (at STP) will be:
A. $26.11\ mL$
B. $26.1\ mL$
C. $39.15\ mL$
D. $52.2\ mL$

Q.82 One Faraday of electricity is passed through molten Al_2O_3 aqueous solution of $CuSO_4$ and molten $NaCl$ taken in three different electrolytic cells connected in series. The mole ratio of Al, Cu and Na deposited at the respective cathode is:
A. $2:3:6$ B. $6:2:3$ C. $6:3:2$ D. $1:2:3$

Q.83 Which of the following cannot be a ligand?
A. Ni^{2+} B. Cl^- C. H_2O D. NH_3

Q.84 Which is the donor atom in the coordinate bond shown below?

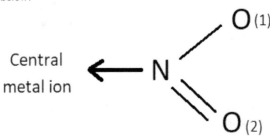

A. N
B. O(1)
C. O(2)
D. Both N and O

Q.85 What is the coordination number of chromium in $K_3[Cr(C_2O_4)_3]$?
A. 1 B. 2 C. 3 D. 6

Q.86 Arrange the following in increasing order of acidic character:
i. Phenol
ii. 2,4-Dinitrophenol
iii. 3,5-Dinitrophenol
iv. 2,4,6-Trinitrophenol
A. i < ii < iii < iv
B. i < iii < ii < iv
C. ii < i < iv < iii
D. ii < iii < i < iv

Q.87 The end product $'C'$ in the following sequence of chemical reactions is:

$$CH_3COOH \xrightarrow{CaCO_3} A \xrightarrow{Heat} B \xrightarrow{NH_2OH} C$$

A. Acetaldehyde oxime
B. Formaldehyde oxime
C. Methyl nitrate
D. Acetoxime

Q.88 In the mechanism of Hoffmann reaction, which intermediate rearranges to alkyl isocyanate?
A. Bromamide B. Nitrene
C. Nitroso D. Amide

Q.89 Order of reactivity of alcohols towards sodium metal is:
A. Primary > secondary > tertiary
B. Primary > secondary < tertiary
C. Primary < secondary > tertiary
D. Primary < secondary < tertiary

Q.90 The compound A on treatment with Na gives B, and with PCl_5 gives C. B and C react together to give diethyl ether. A, B and C are in the order.

[NEET UG, 2018]

A. $C_2H_5Cl, C_2H_6, C_2H_5OH$
B. $C_2H_5OH, C_2H_5Cl, C_2H_5ONa$
C. $C_2H_5OH, C_2H_6, C_2H_5Cl$
D. $C_2H_5OH, C_2H_5ONa, C_2H_5Cl$

Q.91 An oxygen containing organic compound upon oxidation forms a carboxylic acid as the only organic product with its molecular mass higher by 14 units. The organic compound is:
A. A ketone B. An aldehyde
C. A primary alcohol D. A secondary alcohol

Q.92 Oils are rich in:
A. Glycerol that possesses three hydroxyl groups
B. Esters of fatty acids
C. Fats that are generally liquid at room temperature
D. None of the above

Q.93 Bonds that do not exist in tertiary structure of proteins:
A. Phosphodiester bonds
B. Hydrophobic bonds
C. Ionic bonds
D. Covalent bonds

Q.94 Which of the following is fully fluorinated polymer?
A. Neoprene B. Teflon
C. Thiokol D. PVC

Q.95 The formation of amide linkage and ester linkage occurs through the condensation mechanism. Both reaction loses same substance during polymerisation. Identify the substance:
A. Alcohol B. Water
C. Aldehyde D. Ester

Q.96 Green chemistry is the design of chemical products and processes that reduce or eliminate the use and generation of hazardous substances. Identify the technique used in this area.
A. Bioamplification
B. Polymer manufacturing
C. Pesticide synthesis
D. Use of sunlight and Microwave-assisted reaction

Q.97 According to the green chemistry, the chemical involved in the production must be _____
A. Non toxic
B. Toxic
C. Highly toxic
D. Produces the toxic by products

Q.98 In the rate equation, when the concentration of reactants is unity then the rate is equal to:
A. Specific rate constant
B. Average rate constant
C. Instantaneous rate constant
D. None of the above

Q.99 The aqueous solution of which of the following compounds is the best conductor of electric current?
A. Acetic acid B. Hydrochloric acid
C. Ammonia D. Fructose

Q.100 Which of the following compounds is formed on the electrolytic reduction of nitrobenzene in presence of strong acid?
A. Azoxybenzene B. Aniline
C. Azobenzene D. p-aminophenol

Physics & Chemistry : Mock Test - 9

// Smart Answer Sheet //

Correct — Indicates percentage of students who answered questions correctly.

Skipped — Indicates percentage of students who skipped questions.

Q.	Ans.	Correct / Skipped	Q.	Ans.	Correct / Skipped	Q.	Ans.	Correct / Skipped	Q.	Ans.	Correct / Skipped	Q.	Ans.	Correct / Skipped
1	B	10.83 % / 3.21 %	17	B	50.09 % / 1.32 %	33	D	15.63 % / 3.8 %	49	A	64.6 % / 1.3 %	65	A	45.19 % / 1.63 %
2	D	54.82 % / 1.92 %	18	A	56.51 % / 1.99 %	34	B	27.68 % / 4.1 %	50	C	69.16 % / 1.73 %	66	A	45.88 % / 1.95 %
3	A	22.41 % / 3.41 %	19	A	45.78 % / 1.01 %	35	D	62.74 % / 1.8 %	51	A	42.27 % / 1.28 %	67	A	53.02 % / 1.9 %
4	D	58.99 % / 1.45 %	20	A	19.79 % / 3.7 %	36	A	41.74 % / 1.49 %	52	D	77.28 % / 0.0 %	68	B	63.02 % / 1.3 %
5	B	64.54 % / 1.15 %	21	B	61.06 % / 1.96 %	37	D	57.66 % / 1.38 %	53	A	56.41 % / 1.55 %	69	D	18.24 % / 4.1 %
6	A	51.87 % / 1.67 %	22	A	56.04 % / 1.76 %	38	B	58.13 % / 1.21 %	54	B	56.85 % / 1.56 %	70	A	54.02 % / 1.63 %
7	B	47.67 % / 1.99 %	23	A	79.96 % / 0.0 %	39	B	50.12 % / 1.26 %	55	D	76.19 % / 0.0 %	71	B	64.98 % / 1.14 %
8	A	24.93 % / 4.33 %	24	D	76.99 % / 0.0 %	40	C	15.9 % / 4.51 %	56	C	22.21 % / 4.37 %	72	C	43.1 % / 1.07 %
9	A	47.82 % / 1.89 %	25	B	88.6 % / 0.0 %	41	B	84.68 % / 0.0 %	57	D	43.69 % / 1.44 %	73	D	83.15 % / 0.0 %
10	C	79.7 % / 0.0 %	26	D	85.48 % / 0.0 %	42	A	20.69 % / 3.88 %	58	D	85.96 % / 0.0 %	74	C	43.37 % / 1.51 %
11	A	40.25 % / 1.21 %	27	B	53.59 % / 1.69 %	43	C	57.5 % / 1.91 %	59	A	21.85 % / 3.48 %	75	B	29.49 % / 4.23 %
12	B	43.42 % / 1.29 %	28	A	40.39 % / 1.38 %	44	B	60.59 % / 1.46 %	60	C	43.46 % / 1.07 %	76	D	17.55 % / 3.17 %
13	D	50.02 % / 1.03 %	29	D	53.06 % / 1.56 %	45	C	55.67 % / 1.53 %	61	A	67.41 % / 1.14 %	77	C	21.97 % / 4.39 %
14	B	57.63 % / 1.67 %	30	D	26.89 % / 4.97 %	46	A	40.54 % / 1.46 %	62	B	32.97 % / 4.73 %	78	B	80.01 % / 0.0 %
15	A	60.99 % / 1.87 %	31	D	47.2 % / 1.31 %	47	A	81.92 % / 0.0 %	63	A	54.44 % / 1.45 %	79	C	32.71 % / 4.48 %
16	D	24.21 % / 3.23 %	32	D	66.33 % / 1.57 %	48	A	79.56 % / 0.0 %	64	A	86.08 % / 0.0 %	80	B	51.54 % / 1.84 %

Physics & Chemistry : Mock Test - 9

Q.	Ans.	Correct / Skipped
81	A	54.5 % / 1.34 %
82	A	46.71 % / 1.58 %
83	A	47.03 % / 1.94 %
84	A	32.41 % / 4.13 %

Q.	Ans.	Correct / Skipped
85	D	69.47 % / 1.23 %
86	B	57.64 % / 1.51 %
87	D	54.88 % / 1.8 %
88	B	48.53 % / 1.27 %

Q.	Ans.	Correct / Skipped
89	A	31.39 % / 4.17 %
90	D	25.81 % / 3.87 %
91	C	11.19 % / 4.47 %
92	A	81.23 % / 0.0 %

Q.	Ans.	Correct / Skipped
93	A	43.91 % / 1.2 %
94	B	85.71 % / 0.0 %
95	B	59.35 % / 1.41 %
96	D	58.67 % / 1.36 %

Q.	Ans.	Correct / Skipped
97	A	89.14 % / 0.0 %
98	A	47.27 % / 1.45 %
99	B	59.9 % / 1.21 %
100	D	55.07 % / 1.44 %

Performance Analysis	
Avg. Score (%)	44.0%
Toppers Score (%)	65.0%
Your Score	

//Hints and Solutions//

1. Both the poles of the magnet experience a force due to magnetic field produced by wires W_1 and W_2

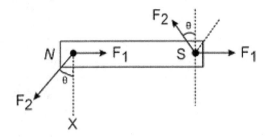

North pole experiences a force F_1 due to W_1, and F_2 due to W_2 shown in diagram. Similarly, south pole experience a force F_1 due to W_2 and F_2 due to W_1.

From free body diagram of magnet, it is clear that magnet experiences a net force towards right and a torque in anti-clockwise direction.

Hence, the correct option is (B).

2. Given,

$N = 3000$

$r = 10\,cm = 0.1\,m$

$n = \dfrac{N}{2\pi r}$

$\mu_r = 2000$

$I = 1A$

For a solenoid magnetic field, $B = \mu n I = \mu_r n_0 n I$

$B = 2000 \times 4\pi \times 10^{-7} \times \dfrac{N}{2\pi r} \times 1$

$= 2000 \times 4 \times 10^{-7} \times \dfrac{3000}{2\pi \times 0.1} \times 1 = 12T$

Hence, the correct option is (D).

3. Impedance $= \dfrac{V_{xc}}{I_{x:}} = \dfrac{100\,V}{0.5\,A} = 200\Omega$

$R = \dfrac{V_{cc}}{I_{dz}} = \dfrac{100}{1} = 100\Omega$

$L\omega = \sqrt{\text{impedance}^2 - R^2}$

$= \sqrt{200^2 - 100^2} = 173.2$

$L = \dfrac{173.2}{\omega}$

$= \dfrac{173.2}{2\pi 50} = 0.55H$

Hence, the correct option is (A).

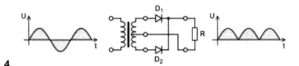

4.

If we consider this, the output frequency is certainly twice that of the input frequency.

So, if the input frequency is 50 Hz, the output frequency will be 100 Hz.

It is visible from the signal waveform shown in the image using color.

What happens is, the negative side of the signal appears at the positive side after the rectification. Since the signal to be rectified is usually symmetric in nature, the frequency of the signal at output is doubled.

Also, rectification is a process of converting alternating current into the unidirectional current. It is a part of the DC power generation unit. In a direct current, we ideally require a zero frequency signal. Thus, circuits like filter circuit and voltage regulation circuit further reduce this variable voltage to a fixed voltage by stabilizing it and removing all frequency components.

Hence, the correct option is (D).

5. At saturation,

$V_{CE} = 0$

$V_{CE} = V_{CC} - I_C R_C$

$I_C = \dfrac{V_{CC}}{R_C}$

$= 5 \times 10^{-3}\,A$

Given,

$\beta_{dc} = \dfrac{I_C}{I_B}$

$I_B = \dfrac{5 \times 10^{-3}}{200}$

$I_B = 25\mu A$

At input side $V_{BB} = I_B R_B + V_{BE}$

$= (25\,mA)(100k\Omega) + 1\,V$

$V_{BB} = 3.5\,V$

Hence, the correct option is (B).

6. First Maxima $= \dfrac{D\lambda}{d}$

$\beta_1 = \dfrac{1.5 \times 480 \times 10^{-9}}{0.25 \times 10^{-3}}$

$= 2.880 \times 10^{-3}\,m$

$\beta_2 = \dfrac{1.5 \times 600 \times 10^{-9}}{0.25 \times 10^{-3}}$

$= 3.600 \times 10^{-3}$ m

So, $\beta_2 - \beta_1 = 0.72 \times 10^{-3}$ m

$= 0.72$ mm

Hence, the correct option is (A).

7. Given,

$K =$ Force constant of the spring

$C =$ Proportionality constant

$l =$ Length of the spring

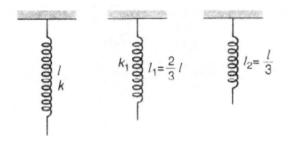

According to the question,

The force constant of a spring is inversely proportional to be the length of the spring. Let the original length of the spring be l and spring constant be K

Therefore,

$K \times l = \dfrac{2l}{3} \times K'$

$\Rightarrow K' = \dfrac{3}{2} K$

Hence, the correct option is (B).

8. Given, initial time period of the simple pendulum, $T_1 = T$

Initial length of the pendulum, L_1

Let final length of the pendulum, L_2

$L_2 = 1.21 \, L_1$

Time period of Simple pendulum,

$T = 2\pi \sqrt{\dfrac{L_1}{g}} \Rightarrow T \propto \sqrt{L}$

$\Rightarrow \dfrac{T_2}{T_1} = \sqrt{\dfrac{L_2}{L_1}} = \sqrt{\dfrac{1.21 \, L_1}{L_1}} = \sqrt{1.21}$

$\Rightarrow T_2 = 1.1 \, T_1$

$\Rightarrow T_2$ has increased by 10%.

Hence, the correct option is (A).

9. The unpolarized light has two electric field components, one perpendicular to the plane of incidence (represented by dots) and the other in the plane of incidence (represented by arrows).

When an unpolarized light beam is an incident from the air onto glass $(n = 1.5)$ at the polarizing angle (ip), most of these vibrations of electric vector get transmitted and are not reflected. Therefore, light refracted is a mixture of polarized light and unpolarized light. i.e., it is partially polarized.

The reflected light, therefore, contains vibrations of an electric vector perpendicular to the plane of incidence.

Thus, the reflected light is completely plane-polarized in a direction perpendicular to the plane of incidence and thus, reflected beam is polarized 100 percent.

Hence, the correct option is (A).

10. Mirage is an example of total internal reflection of light.

On hot summer days, the air near the ground becomes hotter than the air at higher levels.

The refractive index of air increases with its density. Hotter air is less dense and has a smaller refractive index than cooler air. If the air currents are small, that is, the air is still, the optical density at different layers of air increases with height.

As a result, light from a tall object such as a tree passes through a medium whose refractive index decreases towards the ground.

Thus, a ray of light from such an object successively bends away from the normal and undergoes total internal reflection, if the angle of incidence for the air near the ground exceeds the critical angle.

Hence, the correct option is (C).

11. Concept:

There are three methods of heat transfer between the two systems. They are conduction, convection, and radiation.

- **Conduction** is a method of heat transfer in solids and heat transfer takes place without the movement of particles.
- **Convection** is a method of heat transfer in fluids (gases and liquids) and heat transfer takes place due to the movement of particles.
- **Radiation** is a method of heat transfer where heat is transferred from one place to another without affecting the medium of heat transfer.

Both are at the same temperature, the metal will feel colder than the wood because of the thermal conductivity of the metal, compared to the wood is more.

Metal extract more heat from your hand than wood in a given time. Therefore, you perceive the metal as being colder than the wood.

Hence, the correct option is (A).

12. The coolant in a chemical or nuclear plant must have a high specific heat as it is known that higher the specific heat of the coolant, higher is its heat-absorbing capacity and vice-versa.

Thus, a liquid which has a high specific heat is the best coolant to be utilized in a nuclear or chemical plant. This prevents different parts of the plant from becoming too hot.

Hence, the correct option is (B).

13. It is provided that the work done (W) on the system when the gas transforms from state A to state B is $22.3J$.

This is an adiabatic process. Thus, the change in heat is zero.

$\Rightarrow \Delta Q = 0$

(As the work is done on the system)

Using the first law of thermodynamics,

$\Delta Q = \Delta U + \Delta W$

where,

$\Rightarrow \Delta W = -22.3J$

on putting the above value we get,

$\Rightarrow \Delta U = 22.3J$

ΔU = change in the internal energy of the gas

When the gas transforms from state A to state B via a process, the net heat absorbed by the system is given by

$\Delta Q = 9.35 cal = 9.35 \times 4.19J = 39.1765J$

Heat absorbed can be given by the equation,

$\Delta Q = \Delta U + \Delta W$

$\Rightarrow \Delta W = \Delta Q - \Delta U = 39.1765 - 22.3 = 16.8765J$

Clearly, $16.88J$ of work is done by the system.

Hence, the correct option is (D).

14. Work done by the steam engine per minute, $W = 5.4 \times 10^8 J$

Heat supplied from the boiler, $H = 3.6 \times 10^9 J$

Efficiency of the engine $= \dfrac{\text{Output Energy}}{\text{Input Energy}}$

$\Rightarrow \eta = \dfrac{W}{H}$

$\Rightarrow \eta = \dfrac{5.4 \times 10^8}{3.6 \times 10^9}$

$\Rightarrow \eta = 0.15$

Thus, the percentage efficiency of the engine is 15.

Amount of heat wasted $= 3.6 \times 10^9 - 5.4 \times 10^8$

$= 30.6 \times 10^8$

$= 3.06 \times 10^9 J$

Clearly, the amount of heat wasted per minute is $3.06 \times 10^9 J$.

Hence, the correct option is (B).

15. When the lift is stationary spring force balances weight:

$kx = mg = 49\ N \ldots (1)$

Where,

k = force constant of spring

x = elongation

True weight $= 49\ N$

From equation (1), we get

$k = \dfrac{49}{x}$

$m = \dfrac{49}{9.8} = 5\ kg$

when lift moves with acceleration $5\ m/s^2$ downward we have:

$kx_2 = mg - 5 \times m$

Where,

Pseudo force in lift frame $= 5m$ upward

x_2 = new elongation

$\Rightarrow kx_2 = 49 - 5 \times 5 = 24\ N$

So new reading in spring balance $= 24\ N$

Hence, the correct option is (A).

16. Given:

Energy of photons $= h\nu$

Work function of surface $= E_0$

Maximum kinetic energy $= K$

Now, frequency is doubled

The energy of photon is used in liberating the electron from metal surface and in imparting the kinetic energy to emitted photoelectron.

According to Einstein's photoelectric effect energy of photon = KE photoelectron + Work function of metal i.e.,

$h\nu = \dfrac{1}{2}mv^2 + E_0$

$h\nu = K_{max} + E_0$

$K_{max} = h\nu - E_0 \ldots\ldots$ (i)

Now, we have given,

$\nu' = 2\nu$

Therefore, $K_{max} = h(2\nu) - E_0$

$K'_{max} = 2h\nu - E_0$

From Equation (i) and (ii), we have

$K'_{max} = 2(K_{max} + E_0) - E_0$

$= 2K_{max} + E_0$

$= K_{max} + (K_{max} + E_0)$

$= K_{max} + h\nu$ [From Equation (i)]

$K_{max} = K$

$\therefore K'_{max} = K + h\nu$

The photoelectric emission is an instantaneous process. The time lag between the incidence of radiations and emission of photoelectrons is very small, less than even 10^{-8} second.

Hence, the correct option is (D).

17. Given:

The wavelength of the incident light $= 4000 Å$

$KE = 2eV$

The relation for kinetic energy of a photoelectron is given by $KE = h\nu$ - work function or $KE = h\nu - W$

$KE = \frac{hc}{\lambda} - W$ or $W = \frac{hc}{\lambda} - KE$

$W = \frac{6.6 \times 10^{-34} \times 3 \times 10^8}{4000 \times 10^{-10}} - 2eV$

$= 4.95 \times 10^{-19} J - 2eV$

$= \frac{4.95 \times 10^{-19}}{1.6 \times 10^{-19}} - 2eV$

$= 3eV - 2eV$

$= 1eV$

Hence, the correct option is (B).

18. Using the relation for floating, $vd_{Hg} = Vd_m$

Fraction of volume of metal submerged in mercury $\frac{\mu}{v} = \frac{d_m}{d_{Hy}} = K_{1(say)}$

When temperature is increased by ΔT

$\frac{v}{V} = \frac{d_m}{d_{itg}} = K_{2(say)}$

Now,

$\frac{K_2}{K_1} = \frac{dm \times d_{Hg}}{dm \times d^+_{Hg}} = \frac{d_m^2 \times d^+_{Hg}(1+\gamma_2 \Delta T)}{dm(1+\gamma_1 \Delta T) \times d_{Hg}}$

$\frac{K_2}{K_1} = (1 + \gamma_2 \Delta T)(1 + \gamma_1 \Delta T)^{-1}$

$\frac{K_2}{K_1} = (1 + \gamma_2 \Delta T)(1 - \gamma_1 \Delta T)$ $\frac{K_2}{K_1} = 1 + (\gamma_2 - \gamma_1) \Delta T$

$Y_2 - Y_1 = K_2 > K_1$
$Y_2 > Y_1 = K_2 > K_1$

Hence, the correct option is (A).

19. $\eta = \frac{F}{A\left(\frac{dv}{dy}\right)}$

$\therefore \eta = \frac{10^{-2}}{(10^3 \times 10^{-4})\left(\frac{6 \times 10^{-2}}{6 \times 10^{-3}}\right)}$

$= \frac{10^{-2} \times 6 \times 10^{-3}}{10^{-1} \times 6 \times 10^{-2}}$

$\eta = 10^{-2} Nsm^{-2} = 0.1$ poise

Hence, the correct option is (A).

20. It is provided that,

Potential difference, $V = 15 \times 10^6 V$

Surroundings gas's dielectric strength $= 5 \times 10^7 Vm^{-1}$

Electric field intensity is equal to the dielectric strength, $E = 5 \times 10^7 Vm^{-1}$

The formula for spherical shell's minimum radius required for the purpose is given by,

$r = \frac{V}{E}$

$r = \frac{15 \times 10^6}{5 \times 10^7} = 0.3 m = 30 cm$

Clearly, the required minimum radius of the spherical shell is $30 cm$.

Hence, the correct option is (A).

21. It is provided that,

A charged capacitor has capacitance, $C_1 = 4\mu F = 4 \times 10^{-6} F$

Supply voltage, $V_1 = 200V$

Electrostatic energy stored in C_1 capacitor is given by,

$E_1 = \frac{1}{2} C_1 V_1^2$

$E_1 = \frac{1}{2} \times 4 \times 10^{-6} \times 200^2$

$E_1 = 8 \times 10^{-2} J$

An uncharged capacitor's capacitance, $C_2 = 2\mu F = 2 \times 10^{-6} F$

When C_2 is joined to the circuit, the potential attained by it is V_2.

According to the conservation of charge,

$V_2(C_1 + C_2) = V_1 C_1$

$V_2(4 + 2) \times 10^{-6} = 200 \times 4 \times 10^{-6}$

$V_2 = \frac{400}{3} V$

The formula for electrostatic energy for the two capacitors combination is given by,

$E_2 = \frac{1}{2}V_2^2(C_1 + C_2)$

$E_2 = \frac{1}{2}\left(\frac{400}{3}\right)^2 (4+2) \times 10^{-6}$

$E_2 = 5.33 \times 10^{-2} J$

The amount of lost electrostatic energy by the capacitor is, =
$E_1 - E_2 = 0.08 - 0.0533 = 0.0267 J$

Therefore, the lost electrostatic energy is $0.0267 J$.

Hence, the correct option is (B).

22. It is provided that,

Area of the parallel capacitor's plates, $A = 90 cm^2 = 90 \times 10^{-4} m^2$

Distance separating the plates, $d = 2.5 mm = 2.5 \times 10^{-3} m$

Potential difference across the pates, $V = 400V$

The formula for capacitance will be,

$C = \frac{\varepsilon_0 A}{d}$

Electrostatic energy stored in capacitor is given by,

$E_1 = \frac{1}{2}CV^2$

$E_1 = \frac{1}{2}\frac{\varepsilon_0 A}{d}V^2$

Where, ε_o is the Permittivity of free space

$\varepsilon_0 = 8.854 \times 10^{-12} C^2 N^{-1} m^{-2}$

$E_1 = \frac{1}{2}\frac{8.854 \times 10^{-12} \times 90 \times 10^{-4}}{2.5 \times 10^{-3}} 400^2$

$E_1 = 2.55 \times 10^6 J$

The stored electrostatic energy inside the capacitor is, $2.55 \times 10^6 J$.

Hence, the correct option is (A).

23. The direction of the electric field due to the positive charge is away from the charge.

Conventionally the direction of the electric field due to a charge is defined as the direction along which a positive test charge experiences a force due to the given charge at that point in space. Since like charges repel and unlike charges attract, the electric field of a positive charge would point away from it and the other way around for a negative charge.

Hence, the correct option is (A).

24. The ability of charged bodies to exert force on one another is attributed to the existence of an electric field.

The electric field is the space around a charge in which another charged particle experiences a force that is said to have an electric field in it.

wherein

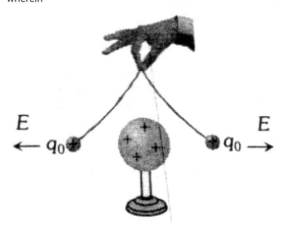

One charge exert force on another charge due to the electric field produced by one charge and this field will exert force on another charge.

Hence, the correct option is (D).

25. The force between two charges separated by a distance r is given by:

$\vec{F} = \frac{q_1 q_2}{4\pi \varepsilon_0 r^2} \hat{a_r}$

Let the two objects be A and B.

Let the total Charge $= Q$

Let the charge on $A = q$

$\therefore$ The charge on B will be:

$Q_B = Q - q$

The force between the two objects will be:

$F_{AB} = \frac{Q_A Q_B}{4\pi r^2} = \frac{q(Q-q)}{4\pi r^2}$

For the force to be maximum, we differentiate the above with respect to q and equate to 0, i.e.

$\frac{dF_{AB}}{dq} = 0$

$\Rightarrow \frac{1}{4\pi r^2} = \frac{dq}{dq}(Q - q) = 0$

$\Rightarrow \frac{d}{dq}(Qq - q^2) = 0$

$\Rightarrow Q - 2q = 0$

$\Rightarrow Q = 2q$

$\Rightarrow q = \frac{Q}{2}$

∴ The charges must be $\frac{Q}{2}$ for the force between the two objects to be maximum.

Hence, the correct option is (B).

26. We know that:

$E = \frac{Q}{4\pi\varepsilon r^2}$

E = electrical field

Q = charge

r = distance

∴ The electric field strength of a charge decreases with square of distance.

Hence, the correct option is (D).

27. Coulomb's Law: It states that the force between two charged particles will be directly proportional to the product of the quantity of the two charges.

$F \propto Q_1 Q_2$

Secondly, it is also inversely proportional to the square of the distance between them, i.e.

$F \propto \frac{1}{r^2}$

∴ The force between two charges Q_1 and Q_2 is given by:

$F = k \frac{Q_1 Q_2}{r^2}$

Where k is the proportionality constant and is equal to 9×10^9 Nm 2/C 2.

Hence, the correct option is (B).

28. Given that $v = 720 \; kmph$

$= 720 \times \frac{5}{18} \; m/s$

$= 200 \; m/s$

$\theta = 45°$

$g = 10 \; m/s^2$

Bank angle,

$\tan\theta = \frac{v^2}{rg}$

$r = \frac{200^2}{10 \times \tan 45°} = 4000 \; m$

$r = 4 \; km$

Hence, the correct option is (A).

29. Given:

R = radius of the path
The tangential acceleration is given as,

$\Rightarrow a_t = a$

The centripetal acceleration is given as,

$\Rightarrow a_c = \frac{v^2}{R}$

When two vectors act perpendicular to each other, the resultant vector is given as,

$\Rightarrow R = \sqrt{P^2 + Q^2}$

Where P and Q are the two vectors

Since acceleration is a vector quantity so the resultant acceleration of the rotating particle is given as,

$\Rightarrow a_R = \sqrt{a^2 + \left(\frac{v^2}{R}\right)^2}$

$\Rightarrow a_R = \sqrt{a^2 + \frac{v^4}{R^2}}$

Hence, the correct option is (D).

30. Fundamental frequency is given by

$v = \frac{1}{2l}\sqrt{\frac{T}{\mu}}$ (with both the ends fixed)

∴ Fundamental frequency

$v \propto \frac{1}{l\sqrt{\mu}}$ (for same tension in both strings)

Where, μ = mass per unit length of wire

$= \rho.A (\rho = $ density $)$

$= \rho(\pi r^2)$ or $\sqrt{\mu} \propto r$

∴ $v \propto \frac{1}{rl}$

∴ $\frac{v_1}{v_2} = \left(\frac{r_2}{r_1}\right)\left(\frac{l_2}{l_1}\right) = \left(\frac{r}{2r}\right)\left(\frac{2L}{L}\right) = 1$

Hence, the correct option is (D).

31. From the formula: $\Delta L = 10 \log 10 \frac{l_1}{l_2}$

We are given: $\Delta L = 20 \; dB$

Substitute this value in the formula:

$20 = 10 \log 10 \frac{l_1}{l_2}$

$\log 10 \frac{l_1}{l_2} = 2$

$\frac{l_1}{l_2} = 10^2 = 100$

Hence, the correct option is (D).

32. Given:

The voltage gain of the first amplifier, $V_1 = 10$

The voltage gain of the second amplifier, $V_2 = 20$

The voltage of the input signal, $V_i = 0.01 \; V$

The voltage of output AC signal $= V_o$

The total voltage gain of a two-stage amplifier is given by the product of voltage gains of both the stages,

i.e., $V = V_1 \times V_2 = 10 \times 20 = 200$

It can be calculated by the relation: $V = \frac{V_o}{V_i}$

$V_o = V \times V_i = 200 \times 0.01 = 2 \; V$

33. The force given as $\vec{F} = 4\vec{j} + 5\vec{j} - 6\vec{k}$

The force acting the point $(2, 0, -3)$

The point under construction $(2, -2, -2)$

Position vector $(2, 0, -3)$ w.r.to $(2, -2, -2)$

$\vec{r} = (2-2)i + (0-(-2j+(-3-2)\vec{k} = 0\vec{i} + 2\vec{j} - \vec{k}$

Moment of force is $\vec{M} = \vec{r} \times \vec{f}$

$M = \left(0i + 2\vec{j} - \vec{k}\right) \times \left(4i + 4j - 6\vec{k}\right)$

$M = \begin{vmatrix} i & j & k \\ 0 & 2 & -1 \\ 4 & 5 & -6 \end{vmatrix}$

$= -7\vec{i} - 4\vec{j} - 8\vec{k}$

Hence, the correct option is (D).

34. Given,

$M_{He} = 4$, $m_{He} = 16\,g$

$M_{ox} = 32$, $m_{ox} = 16\,g$

Specific heat of mixture at constant volume is given by,

$C_V = \dfrac{n_1 C_{V_1} + n_2 C_{V_2}}{n_1 + n_2}$ ......(1)

For Helium gas,

Number of moles, $n_1 = \dfrac{m_{He}}{M_{He}}$

$n_1 = \dfrac{16}{4} = 4$

$\gamma_1 = \dfrac{5}{3}$

Foe Oxygen Gas,

Number of moles, $n_2 = \dfrac{m_{Ox}}{M_{Ox}}$

$n_2 = \dfrac{16}{32} = \dfrac{1}{2}$

$\gamma_2 = \dfrac{7}{5}$

And specific heat constant volume of helium gas,

$C_{V_1} = \dfrac{R}{\gamma_1 - 1} = \dfrac{R}{\frac{5}{3}-1} = \dfrac{3}{2}R$

The specific heat of oxygen at constant volume,

$C_{V_2} = \dfrac{R}{\gamma_2 - 1} = \dfrac{R}{\frac{7}{5}-1} = \dfrac{5}{2}R$

From equation (1),

$C_V = \dfrac{4 \times \frac{3}{2}R + \frac{1}{2} \times \frac{5}{2}R}{4 + \frac{1}{2}}$

$= \dfrac{6R + \frac{5}{4}R}{\frac{9}{2}}$

$= \dfrac{29R \times 2}{9 \times 4} = \dfrac{29R}{18}$

Now, $C_V = \dfrac{R}{\gamma - 1}$

$\Rightarrow \gamma - 1 = \dfrac{R}{C_V}$

or $\gamma = \dfrac{R}{C_V} + 1 = \dfrac{R}{\frac{29}{18}R} + 1$

$\dfrac{C_p}{C_V} = \dfrac{18}{29} + 1$

$= \dfrac{18 + 29}{29} = 1.62$

Hence, the correct option is (B).

35. Given:

v_1, v_2, v_3, v_4, v_5 are $2, 1.5, 1.6, 1.6, 1.2$ respectivily.
RMS velocity of gas molecules is,

$v_{rms} = \sqrt{\dfrac{(v_1^2 + v_2^2 + v_3^2 + v_4^2 + v_5^2)}{5}}$

$v_{rms} = \sqrt{\dfrac{(2^2 + 1.5^2 + 1.6^2 + 1.6^2 + 1.2^2)}{5}}$

$v_{rms} = \sqrt{\dfrac{12.8}{5}}$

$v_{rms} = 1.6\,m/s$

Most probable speed is,

$v_{mp} = \sqrt{\dfrac{2}{3}} \times v_{rms}$

$v_{mp} = 0.816 \times 1.6$

$v_{mp} = 1.306 \approx 1.31\,km/s$

Therefore, the most probable speed of the gas is 1.31 km/s.
Hence, the correct option is (D).

36. According to Einstein's mass energy equivalence:

$E = mc^2$

$= 10^{-6} \times 10^{-3} \times (3 \times 10^8)^2 J$

$= 9 \times 10^7 J$

As we know, 1 kilowatt hour $(1kWh) = 3.6 \times 10^6\,J$

$\therefore E = 9 \times 10^7 J \times \dfrac{1kWh}{3.6 \times 10^6 J}$

$= \dfrac{900}{36} kWh$

$= 25\,kWh$

Hence, the correct option is (A).

37. β-emission takes place from a radioactive nucleus as:

$$^{32}_{15}P \xrightarrow{-\beta} {}^{32}_{16}S + {}_{-1}e^0 + \overline{v}$$

where $\overline{v}$ is the anti-neutrino.

In β^+ decay a positron is emitted as:

$$^{22}_{11}Na \rightarrow {}^{22}_{10}Ne + {}_{+1}e^0 + v$$

where v is the neutrino.

Hence, the correct option is (D).

38. Following are the important points of atomic mass unit:

- An atomic mass unit (symbolized as "amu") is defined as basically $\frac{1}{12}^{th}$ of the mass of an atom of carbon-12(C-12).
- The carbon-12 (C-12) atom has a total of six neutrons and six protons in the nucleus.
- In simple terms, 1 AMU is the average of the neutron rest mass and the proton rest mass within a nucleus.
- Another term of the Atomic Mass unit is Dalton.
- 1 Atomic Mass unit or 1 Dalton $= 1.66 \times 10^{-27} \, kg$.

From above it is clear that the atomic mass unit (u) is equivalent to $\frac{1}{12}^{th}$ the mass of carbon isotope C-12.

Hence, the correct option is (B).

39. The capacitance is given by,

$$C = \frac{\epsilon A}{d}$$

When reverse bias increases, the depletion region width "d" increases.

As "d" increases, the capacitance decreases.

Hence, the correct option is (B).

40. Reverse saturation current of the diode doubles for every $10°$ rise in temperature.

Mathematically, if reverse saturation current is I_0 at a temperature T_1 and I_0 at temperature T_2 then:

$$I_0 = I_0 2^{(T_2 - T_1)/10}$$

Given

$I_0 = 30nA$ at $T_1 = 25°$

At $T_2 = 35°$, the reverse saturation current will be:

$I_0 = 3 \times 2^{(35-25)/10} nA$

$I_0 = 30 \times 2^1 nA$

$I_0 = 60nA$

Hence, the correct option is (C).

41. Gravitational force between two objects of mass m_1 and m_2 separated by a distance r, $F = \frac{Gm_1 m_2}{r^2}$

$$\Rightarrow G = \frac{Fr^2}{m_1 m_2}$$

Value of universal gravitational constant G is $6.67 \times 10^{-11} \frac{Nm^2}{kg^2}$.

Hence, the correct option is (B).

42. Fundamental frequency of open pipe $f_0 = \frac{v}{2l}$

Fundamental frequency of closed pipe $f'_0 = \frac{v}{4l}$

Where, $v =$ velocity of sound in air, $l =$ length of pipe.

Now,

$\frac{f_0}{f'_0} = 2 \Rightarrow f_0 = 2f'_0$

According to the question,

$3f'_0 = f_0 + 100$

$\Rightarrow 3 \times \frac{f_0}{2} = f_0 + 100$

$\Rightarrow 3f_0 = 2f_0 + 200$

$\Rightarrow f_0 = 200Hz$

Hence, correct option is (A).

43. The bridge is said to be balanced when deflection in the galvanometer is zero i.e., no current flows through the galvanometer or in other words $V_B = V_D$

In the balanced condition $\frac{P}{Q} = \frac{R}{S}$, on mutually changing the position of cell and galvanometer, this condition will not change.

Therefore, in the circuit given, the correct relation to a balanced Wheatstone bridge is $\frac{P}{R} = \frac{Q}{S}$.

Hence, the correct option is (C).

44. In a series circuit, the total resistance in the circuit is equal to the sum of all the resistances in the circuit.

- A lamp is nothing but resistance, hence with the addition of a lamp the total resistance of the circuit will increase.
- Now when the voltage is kept constant the current in the circuit will decrease with the increase of resistance in accordance with ohm's Law (I = V/R) (with an increase in denominator value of fraction decreases).

- Thus, on adding more lamps into a series circuit, the overall current in the circuit will decrease if the voltage is kept constant.
- The opposite will happen in a circuit where lamps/resistors will be connected parallel.

Hence, the correct option is (B).

45.

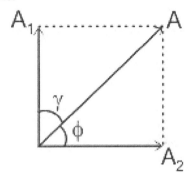

Two waves

$y_1 = A_1 \sin(\omega t - \gamma_1), y_2 = A_2 \sin(\omega t - \gamma_2)$

Then by the principle of superposition,

$y = y_1 + y_2$

$y = A_1 \sin(\omega t - \gamma_1) + A_2 \sin(\omega t - \gamma_2)$

∴ The phase difference between the two waves is

$\phi = (\omega t - \gamma_2) - (\omega t - \gamma_1)$

$\phi = \gamma_1 - \gamma_2$

$y = A \sin(\omega t - \phi)$

Resultant wave is

$A = \sqrt{A_1^2 + A_2^2 + 2A_1 A_2 \cos(\gamma_1 - \gamma_2)}$

Given that:

$f(t) = A \sin\omega t + B\cos\omega t$

$f(t) = \sqrt{A^2 + B^2} \sin(\omega t + \varphi)$

$\tan\varphi = \dfrac{B}{A}$

$\varphi = \tan^{-1}\left(\dfrac{B}{A}\right)$

Hence, the correct option is (C).

46. Given:

$y_1 = 4\sin(\omega t)$ and $y_2 = 3\sin\left(\omega t + \dfrac{\pi}{2}\right)$

The resultant amplitude of the wave after superposition of two waves:

$\Rightarrow A = \sqrt{a^2 + b^2 + 2a \times b \times \cos\phi}$

Where, a = amplitude of wave 1, b = amplitude of wave 2, and ϕ = phase difference

Here, $a = 4\,cm$, $b = 3\,cm$ and $\phi = \dfrac{\pi}{2}$

$\Rightarrow A = \sqrt{4^2 + 3^2 + 2 \times 4 \times 3 \times \cos\dfrac{\pi}{2}}$

$\Rightarrow A = \sqrt{25}$

$\Rightarrow A = 5\,cm$

Hence, the correct option is (A).

47. In a ferromagnetic material, the losses due to hysteresis are directly proportional to the supply frequency.

It is due to the reversal of magnetization of the transformer core whenever it is subjected to the alternating nature of the magnetizing force.

The power consumed by the magnitude domains to change their orientation after every half cycle whenever core is subjected to alternating nature of magnetizing force is called as hysteresis loss.

Hysteresis loss can be determined by using the Steinmetz formula given by

$W_h = \eta B_{max}^2 fV$

Where

x is the Steinmetz constant, B_m = maximum flux density

f = frequency of magnetization or supply frequency, V = volume of the core

So, from the above expression we can observe that hysteresis loss is directly proportional to frequency.

Hence, the correct option is (A).

48. The reluctance offered by a magnetic material is highest when it is diamagnetic.

Order of reluctance offered by a magnetic material is

Ferromagnetic < Paramagnetic < Diamagnetic

Actually, diamagnetic substances placed in the magnetic field, acquire feeble magnetism opposite to the direction of the magnetic field.

Hence, the correct option is (A).

49. The Eddy current loss is the curve characteristic of a material or element or alloy's magnetic properties.

It will be subjected to the increasing value of magnetic field strength (H) and the corresponding flux density (B) measured the result is shown in the below figure by the curve O-a-b.

At point b, if the field intensity (H) is increased further the flux density (B') will not increase any more, this is called saturation b-y is called solution flux density. Now if the H increased in the opposite direction the flux density decreases until the point d here the flux density (B) is zero.

The magnetic field strength (points between O and d) require to remove the residual magnetism i.e. reduce B to zero called a coercive force.

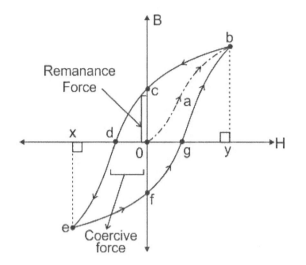

Now if H is increased further in the reverse direction causes the flux density to increase in the reverse direction all the saturation point e. If H is varied backwards OX to O-Y, the flux Density (B) follows the curve b-c-d-d.

Hence, the correct option is (A).

50. "Whenever two (or more) waves travel through the same medium at the same time, the net displacement of the medium at any point in space or time, is simply the sum of the individual wave displacements." This statement is the principle superposition.

Principle of Superposition of waves:

- According to the Principle of Superposition of waves, when two or more waves are traveling in a medium and superimpose on each other, the resultant displacement (y) at any given instant is given by the vector sum of the displacements of individual waves.
- An antinode is a point on the wave where the amplitude is maximum and hence it is the wave crest.
- Node is a point where the amplitude of oscillation is zero, i.e. displacement is minimum from the mean.

Hence, the correct option is (C).

51. Some of the polar crystals when heated produce an electric current. This phenomenon is called Pyro-electricity or pyroelectric effect.

Pyroelectric sensors are most commonly used sensor type, for measuring the Power and Energy of Lasers. They have a fast response in measurement compared to other sensor types. But, the pyroelectric sensor can measure only pulsed lasers that have a repetitively pulsed energy up to 25 kHz.

Hence, the correct option is (A).

52. The defects in which the stoichiometry of a crystal is not affected, are called stoichiometric defects. Thus, in such defects, the ratio of positive and negative ions are the same as indicated by a chemical formula of the compound. The compounds in which the number of positive and negative ions are exactly in the ratios indicated by their chemical formulae are called stoichiometric compounds. The defects that do not disturb the stoichiometry (the ratio of numbers of positive and negative ions) are called stoichiometric defects.

Hence, the correct option is (D).

53. According to the given figure, A^+ is present in the octahedral void of X^-.

The limiting radius in octahedral void is related to the radius of sphere as

$r_{void} = 0.414 r_{sphere}$

$r_{A^+} = 0.414 r_X$

$= 0.414 \times 250 = 103.5$

$\approx 104 pm$

Hence, the correct option is (A).

54. We have:

$K_p = K_c (RT)^{\Delta n}$

$\Rightarrow \log K_p = \log K_c + \Delta n \log RT$

$\Rightarrow \log K_p - \log K_c = \Delta n \log RT$

$\Rightarrow \log \left(\frac{K_p}{K_c}\right) - \Delta n \log RT = 0$

If $\Delta n = -1$,

$\Rightarrow \log \frac{K_p}{K_c} + \log RT = 0$ ....(i)

For the reaction,

$2SO_3 + O_2 \rightleftharpoons 2SO_2$

$\Delta n = -1$, so, the reaction (i) is valid.

Hence, the correct option is (B).

55. As we know, for acids, higher the dissociation, the higher is the hydrogen ion concentrations and acid will be stronger.

So, their strength can be compare by $\frac{[H^+]_1}{[H^+]_2}$

Also, we can compare their strength by their dissociation constants. Higher is the constant value, stronger is the acid for a weak acid.

$K_a = C\alpha^2$

So, we can compare their strength by:

$\frac{K_{a1}}{K_{a2}} = \frac{C_1 \alpha_1^2}{C_2 \alpha_2^2}$

Hence, the correct option is (D).

56.

Fraction	Carbon Atoms	Uses
Gas	C_1 to C_4	Bottled Gas
Gasoline	C_4 to C_{12}	Petrol
Naphtha	C_7 to C_{14}	Petrochemicals
Kerosene	C_{11} to C_{15}	Aviation fuels
Gas Oil	C_{15} to C_{19}	Diesel
Lubricant	C_{20} to C_{30}	Lubricating Oils
Fuel Oil	C_{30} to C_{40}	Ships/Power station fuel
Wax	C_{21} to C_{50}	Candles
Bitumen	C_{50} +	Road surfaces

So, correct match

List – I (Petroleum fraction)		List – II (Composition)	
(a)	Gasoline	(ii)	C_4 to C_9
(b)	Kerosine	(i)	C_8 to C_{16}
(c)	Heavy oil	(iv)	C_{16} to C_{30}
(d)	Diesel	(iii)	C_{10} to C_{18}

Hence, the correct option is (C).

57. Disproportionation reaction is a redox reaction in which a compound of intermediate oxidation state converts to two different compounds, one of higher and one of lower oxidation states.

(A) $\overset{+4}{C}H_4 + 2\overset{0}{O}_2 \rightarrow \overset{+4}{C}\overset{-2}{O}_2 + 2H_2O$: Not a disproportionate reaction.

(B) $\overset{4+}{C}H_4 + 4\overset{0}{C}l_2 \rightarrow \overset{+4}{C}\overset{-1}{C}l_4 + 4HCl$: Not a disproportionate reaction.

(C) $2\overset{0}{F}_2 + 2\overset{-2}{O}H^- \rightarrow 2\overset{-1}{F}^- + \overset{+2}{O}\overset{-1}{F}_2 + H_2O$: Redox reaction but not disproportionate reaction.

(D) $2\overset{+4}{N}O_2 + 2OH^- \rightarrow \overset{+3}{N}O_2^- + \overset{+5}{N}O_3^- + H_2O$: N changes from $+4$ to $+3$ and $+5$. Thus its a disproportionate reaction.

Hence, the correct option is (D).

58. Chemical kinetics is branch of physical chemistry that is concerned with understanding the rates of chemical reactions.

Structures and physical changes are deal in solid state and while studying liquids. Thermochemistry deals with energy changes in chemical reactions.

Hence, the correct option is (D).

59. Equation of reaction: $2A + B \leftrightarrow A_2B$

The concentration of A is doubled

The concentration of B is halved

To find: no. of times the rate of reaction will change

We know that the expression for the rate of reaction is given by

$R = K[A]^2[B]$ ..... (i)

where, K is the equilibrium constant

Now, we have

New $[A] = [2 \times A]$ .... (ii)

New $[B] = [\frac{1}{2} \times B]$ .... (iii)

Therefore,

New $R = K \times$ New $[A]^2 \times$ New $[B]$

substituting the values from (i) & (ii), we get

New R

$= K[2 \times A]^2[\frac{1}{2} \times B]$

$= K \times 4 \times [A]^2 \times \frac{1}{2} \times [B]$

$= 2 \times K[A]^2[B]$ ...... (iv)

Therefore, from equation (i) \& (iv) we can conclude that, after the concentration of A is doubled and B is halved the rate of reaction increases by 2 times.

Hence, the correct option is (A).

60. For producing the effective collisions, the colliding molecules must posses bimolecular reactions.

Bimolecular reaction originates from a collision between two reactants. Whether or not a collision results in a chemical reaction is determined by the energy of the reactants and their orientation.

The total energy of the two reactants must be in excess of the activation energy (Ea), and the reactants must be in a favorable orientation for the chemical reaction to occur. While there are many different orientations possible for the collisions, usually not all of them will result in a chemical reaction. For most reactions, if the orientation is not correct, the reactants will bounce off of each other without a chemical reaction.

Hence, the correct option is (C).

61. It is given that:

The solution contains $10\ g$ per dm^3 urea.

And, we know that:

The chemical formula of urea is CH_4N_2O.

So, molecular mass of urea $= 12 + 4 \times (1) + 2 \times (14) + 16$

$= 60\ gmol^{-1}$

So, the molarity of urea $= \dfrac{\text{mass concentration}}{\text{molar mass}}$

$= \left(\dfrac{10 g/dm^3}{60}\right)$

$= \dfrac{1}{6} mol/dm^3$

Let's assume the molar mass of the non-volatile solution is 'm'.

Physics & Chemistry : Mock Test - 9

So, the molarity of non- volatile solute = $\dfrac{\text{mass concentration}}{\text{molar mass}}$

$= \dfrac{50 g/dm^3}{m}$

Both solutions are isotonic with each other means concentration of both solutions are same:

Molarity of urea = Molarity of non-volatile solution

$\dfrac{1}{6} mol/dm^3 = \dfrac{50\ g/dm^3}{m}$

By solving the above equation we get the value of 'm' as:

$m = 50 \times 6\ gmol^{-1}$

$= 300\ gmol^{-1}$

So, the molecular mass of non-volatile solute is $300\ gmol^{-1}$.

Hence, the correct option is (A).

62. Given that:

Mass of benzene, $(C_6H_6) = 22$

Mass of Carbon tetra chloride, $(CCl_4) = 122$

We know that:

Mass percentage of Benzene $(C_6H_6) =$
$\dfrac{\text{Mass of } C_6H_6}{\text{Total mass of the solution}} \times 100$

$= \dfrac{\text{Mass of } C_6H_6}{\text{Mass of } C_6H_6 + \text{Mass of } CCl_4} \times 100$

$= \dfrac{22}{22+122} \times 100$

$= 15.28\%$

Mass percentage of Carbon Tetrachloride $(CCl_4) =$
$\dfrac{\text{Mass of } CCl_4}{\text{Total mass of the solution}} \times 100$

$= \dfrac{\text{Mass of } CCl_4}{\text{Mass of } C_6H_6 + \text{Mass of } CCl_4} \times 100$

$= \dfrac{122}{22+122} \times 100$

$= 84.72\%$

Hence, the correct option is (B).

63. Given that:

Mass of glucose $= 36\ g$

Molar mass of Glucose $(C_6H_{12}O_6) = 12 \times 6 + 1 \times 12 + 16 \times 6 = 180$

$\pi_1 = 4.98$ bar

$\pi_2 = 1.52$ bar

Mole fraction of glucose, $C_1 = \dfrac{\text{Mass}}{\text{Molar Mass}}$

$= \dfrac{36}{180}$

$C_2 = ?$

Now, according to van't hoff equation:

$\pi = CRT$

Putting the values in above equation, we get:

$4.98 = \left(\dfrac{36}{180}\right) RT \quad \cdots (1)$

$1.52 = C_2 RT \quad \cdots (2)$

Now dividing equation (2) by (1), we get:

$\dfrac{(C_2 \times 180)}{36} = \dfrac{1.52}{4.98}$

or, $C_2 = 0.061$

Therefore concentration of second solution is $0.061 M$.

Hence, the correct option is (A).

64. A pressure cooker is a closed system.

There will be no interactions with the surroundings. For example, the contents of a pressure cooker on a stove with its lid tightly closed and the whistle in position is a closed system as no mass can enter or leave the pressure cooker, but heat can be transferred to it.

Hence, the correct option is (A).

65. The state of a thermodynamic system is described by its measurable or macroscopic (bulk) properties. These are pressure, volume, temperature, and amount.

State of the System: The state of a thermodynamic system is described by its measurable (or macroscopic) or bulk properties. Thus, the state of a gas can be described by quoting its pressure (p), volume (v), temperature (T), and amount (n). These variables are called state variables or state functions because their values depend only on the state of the system and not on how it is reached.

Hence, the correct option is (A).

66. Among the following, the state functions are Internal energy and Molar enthalpy.

The sum of all energies of a chemical system is called the internal energy (U) of the system. The internal energy may change under the following conditions:

- Heat passes into or out of the system
- Work done on or by the system
- Matter enters or leaves the system

Molar enthalpy is also a state function. Enthalpy is the sum of internal energy and pressure-volume or work. It is defined in terms of state functions. Enthalpy is a state function because it only depends on the initial and final conditions, and not on the path taken to establish these conditions. Therefore, the integral of state functions can be taken using only two values, the final and initial values.

Hence, the correct option is (A).

67. Uranium 235 is used in nuclear power plants to generate electricity. It is the fuel most widely used by nuclear plants for nuclear fission.

Uranium is the most widely used fuel by nuclear power plants for nuclear fission. Nuclear power plants use a certain type of uranium U-235—as fuel because its atoms are easily split apart. Although uranium is about 100 times more common than silver, U-235 is relatively rare at just over 0.7% of natural uranium.

Hence, the correct option is (A).

68. Bromine (Br) is a chemical element with atomic number 35 of a halogen group or group 17. It is a faint reddish-brown material at room temperature.

Bromine is a chemical element with the symbol Br and atomic number 35. It is the third-lightest halogen and is a volatile red-brown liquid at room temperature that evaporates readily to form a similarly coloured vapour. Its properties are intermediate between those of chlorine and iodine.

Hence, the correct option is (B).

69. Element with electronic configuration 2,8,2 belongs to the 3rd period and 2nd group. The valence electrons give us the idea of group numbers. As the electrons are divided into 3 different shells therefore the period number is 3. The element with electronic configuration 2, 8 has a complete octet. Therefore, it is a noble gas. It will be found in group 18 with all the other noble gases.

Hence, the correct option is (D).

70. Group VIII of Mendeleev's table consists of three triads known as transition triads and they are:

i) Iron, Cobalt, and Nickel

ii) Ruthenium, Rhodium, and Palladium (Ru, Rh, Pd)

iii) Osmium, Iridium, and Platinium

Hence, the correct option is (A).

71. In Mendeleev's, periodic table groups were divided into two subgroups. Groups from I to VII are meant for normal elements, and group VIII is for transition elements. Groups I to VII have been divided into two subgroups while group VIII is meant for three elements.

So, the eighth group in Mendeleev's periodic table was not divided into any group.

Hence, the correct option is (B).

72. Anodized aluminium is sealed so that the metal cannot leach into food or react with acidic foods.

- Unlike ordinary, lightweight aluminium pots and pans, which are highly reactive with acidic foods (like tomatoes), anodized aluminium cookware is safe.
- It can be present in the food we eat and the water we drink.

Anodized aluminium is still very conductive, but the surface is much harder than regular aluminium.

- It is much more durable than, say, a nonstick pan.
- On the other hand, like a nonstick pan, you should never wash it in the dishwasher, as it will ruin the surfaces in both cases.

Hence, the correct option is (C).

73. The atomic number of carbon is 6 and thus it has 4 valence electrons. So, it can either accept 4 electrons or donate 4 electrons in order to become stable. But it is difficult for carbon to neither lose 4 electrons due to its strong force of attraction with the nucleus nor gain 4 electrons since the protons in the nucleus are not sufficient to hold 8 electrons in them. Therefore, carbon forms 4 covalent bonds with other atoms, thereby, exhibiting tetravalency.

Hence, the correct option is (D).

74. At the same temperature, the average molar kinetic energy of N_2 and CO is $KE_1 = KE_2$.

For same temp. kinetic energies would be equal for all molecules, what ever their molecular weights will be, it doesn't matter. Average kinetic energy does not depend on the nature of the gas and their weight. It only depends on temperature. These same temperature condition is given. So, kinetic energies are same.

Hence, the correct option is (C).

75. Given,

Mass of dioxygen $(O_2) = 8\ g$

Thus, number of moles of $O_2 = \frac{8}{32} = 0.25\ mol$

Mass of dihydrogen $(H_2) = 4\ g$

$H_2 = \frac{4}{2} = 2\ mol$

Therefore, total number of moles in the mixture $= 0.25 + 2 = 2.25\ mol$

Given,

$V = 1 dm^3$

$n = 2.25\ mol$

$R = 0.083\ bar\ dm^3\ K^{-1}\ mol^{-1}$

$T = 27°C = 300\ K$

Total pressure (p) can be calculated as:

$pV = nRT$

$\Rightarrow p = \frac{nRT}{V}$

$$= \frac{2.25 \times 0.083 \times 300}{1}$$

$$= 56.025 \ bar$$

Hence, the correct option is (B).

76. $p\pi - p\pi$ back-bonding is the main factor responsible for the weak acidic nature of $B - F$ bonds in BF_3.

BF_3 is the formula of the inorganic compound boron trifluoride. It is a boron trihalide. In general, the boron trihalides can act as Lewis acids because they can very easily form adducts with electron-pair donors (which are termed as Lewis bases).

Since according to Lewis's concept, a substance which accepts electron pairs are acids and substances which donate electron pairs are bases, thus the boron trihalides which possess a sextet of electrons accept an electron pair to complete its octet and thus behaves as Lewis acids. Thus, all the three boron trihalides which are boron trifluoride, boron trichloride and boron tribromide are capable of forming stable adducts with Lewis bases.

Among the boron trihalides, boron trifluoride is the weakest Lewis acid. Each of the three boron trihalides has a planar trigonal geometry which arises because of the sp^2 hybridization of the boron atom in an excited state. Now, one of the $2p$ orbitals remains vacant and unhybridized in sp^2 hybridization and a halogen atom has a partially filled p orbital. Thus the partially filled halogen p orbital and the unhybridized orbital of boron will overlap and form a B-F sigma bond, whereas the rest of the three halogen orbitals will have one lone pair of electrons each. Now, the filled p_z orbital of the halogen atom will overlap laterally with the vacant boron p_z orbital and will form an $F \to B\pi$ - bond which is called $p\pi - p\pi$ back bonding.

backbonding

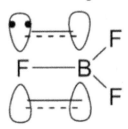

filled p-orbital of F   empty p-orbital of B

Hence, the correct option is (D).

77. Catalysts are chemical compounds that increase a reaction without getting consumed. Certain chemical molecules affect the working of catalysts. One of them are poisons which actually inhibit the functioning of catalysts. They decrease the activity of a catalyst which altogether slower down the chemical process or inhibits in occurring so.

Hence, the correct option is (C).

78. Isotopes have same atomic numbers but different mass numbers. This also means that the isotopes have the same number of electrons.

Chemical properties are determined by electronic configuration. So, with the same electronic configuration, they have similar chemical properties.

Hence, the correct option is (B).

79. Nickel (Ni) element forms interstitial compounds.

- It is known that a compound which is formed from a small atom whose radius is small enough that it sits in an interstitial "hole" in a metal lattice is known as an interstitial.

- When we move from left to right in a period then there occurs a decrease in size of the atoms. And, atoms with smaller size are able to sit in an interstitial hole.

- Out of the given options nickel is smaller in size. As a result it will be able to form an interstitial compound, whereas, Sc, Fe and Co are all larger in size than nickel. Therefore, they will not form interstitial compounds.

Hence, the correct option is (C).

80. The combustion of diborane includes following reaction:
$B_2H_{6(g)} + 3O_{2(g)} \to B_2O_{3(s)} + 3H_2O_{(g)}$
According to Hess Law of heat summation :
$\Delta H_{combustion} = [\Delta H_{form B_2O_3}(s) + 3\Delta H_{form H_2O}(g)] - \Delta H_{form B_2H_6}$
$\Delta H_{combustion} =$ Heat of combustion of diborane
$= -1941 \ kJ$
$\Delta H_{form B_2O_3(g)} =$
Heat of formation of borane oxide $= -2368 \ kJ$
$\Delta H_{form H_2O(g)} =$ Heat of formation of water $= -241.8 \ kJ$
$\Delta H_{form B_2H_6}(g) =$ Heat of formation fo diborane Putting the values in the equation above,
We get :
$-1941 = [-2368 + 3(-241.8)] - \Delta H_{form B_2H_6}$
$\Delta H_{form B_2H_6} = [-2368 - 725.4] + 1941$
$= -3093.4 + 1941$
$= -1152.4 \ kJ/mol.$
The heat of the formation of diborane is $= -1152.4 \ kJ/mol$.

Hence, the correct option is (B).

81. Given:-

Time $(t) = 10 min$

$= 10 \times 60$

$= 600 \ s$

Current passed $(i) = 0.75 \ A$

From Faraday's law of electrolysis, $Q = nF$

Whereas, n is the no. of moles of electrons used

$\Rightarrow i \times t = nF (\because q = I \times t)$

$\Rightarrow n = \frac{i \times t}{F}$

$\Rightarrow n = \frac{0.75 \times 600}{96500} = \frac{4.5}{965} \, mol$

Now, $H_2O \rightarrow 4H^+ + O_2 + 4e^-$

Amount of O_2 released at STP when 4 mole of electrons are used $= 22400 \, mL$

Amount of O_2 released at STP when $\frac{4.5}{965}$ mole of electrons are used $= \frac{22400}{4} \times \left(\frac{4.5}{965}\right)$

$= 26.11 \, mL$

Hence the volume of oxygen liberated at the anode (at STP) will be $26.11 mL$.

Hence, the correct option is (A).

82. $Al^{3+} + 3e^- \rightarrow Al$

$Cu^{2+} + 2e^- \rightarrow Cu$

$Na^+ + e^- \rightarrow Na$

Thus, $1F$ will deposit $\frac{1}{3}$ mole of Al, $\frac{1}{2}$ mole of Cu and 1 mole of Na

$\therefore$ Molar ratio $= \frac{1}{3} : \frac{1}{2} : 1$

$= 2 : 3 : 6$

Hence, the correct option is (A).

83. Ni^{2+} cannot be a ligand.

The ions/molecules bound to the central atom/ion is called a ligand. Ni^{2+} is a metal ion, and according to Werner, the secondary valences can be satisfied only by neutral molecules or negative ions. Cl^-, H_2O and NH_3 are all possible ligands.

Hence, the correct option is (A).

84. N is the donor atom in the coordinate bond shown below.

[Diagram: Central metal ion ← N with O(1) single bond and O(2) double bond]

This is nitrite-N, formed by ambidentate ligand NO^{2-} ion when it bonds through its N atom to the central metal ion. The other form is nitrite-O, which is formed when NO^{2-} coordinates through the O(1) atom.

Hence, the correct option is (A).

85. 6 is the coordination number of chromium in $K_3[Cr(C_2O_4)_3]$.

There are three oxalate groups attached to the central ion in the given compound, but since oxalate is a didentate ligand, there are a total of 6 donor atoms to which the metal is directly bonded. Thus, the CN of Cr in $K_3[Cr(C_2O_4)_3]$ is 6.

Coordination number is also known as the secondary valence of a central metal ion in a complex and is defined as the number of donor atoms it is directly bonded to. Hence, the coordination number is a quantity associated with the metal ion.

Hence, the correct option is (D).

86. The increasing order of acidic strength is phenol < 3, 5-dinitrophenol < 2,4-Dinitrophenol < 2, 4, 6-trinitrophenol group being electron-withdrawing in nature, increases the acidic strength of phenol.

Hence, the correct option is (B).

87.
$2CH_3COOH \xrightarrow{CaCO_3} \underset{A}{(CH_3COO)_2Ca} \xrightarrow[-CaCO_3]{\Delta}$

$\underset{B}{CH_3COCH_3} \xrightarrow[-H_2O]{NH_2OH} \underset{(acetoxime)}{(CH_3)_2C=N-OH}$

The acetic acid in presence of $CaCO_3$ gives calcium acetate, which on heating gives ketone.

Final product is acetone oxime (acetoxime).

Hence, the correct option is (D).

88. The Hofmann rearrangement is the organic reaction of a primary amide to a primary amine with one fewer carbon atom. The reaction involves oxidation of the nitrogen followed by rearrangement of the carbonyl and nitrogen to give an isocyanate intermediate.

Hence, the correct option is (B).

89. In the reaction of alcohols with sodium metal, bond cleavage of the $O\,H$ bond takes place.

The ease of breakage of the $O-H$ bond in alcohols is an indication of the acidity of alcohols.

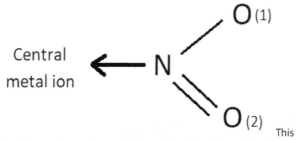

We know that the ease of this bond breakage follows the order primary > secondary > tertiary.

So, the ease of reactivity of sodium follow the order.

RCH_2OH > R₂CHOH > R₃C—OH

1° alcohol   2° alcohol   3° alcohol

Hence, the correct option is (A).

90. The compound A is ethanol C_2H_5OH. The compound A on treatment with Na gives sodium ethoxide (C_2H_5ONa) which is compound B.

$$C_2H_5OH \xrightarrow[-H_2]{Na} C_2H_5ONa$$

The compound A on treatment with PCl_5 gives ethyl chloride $(C_2H_5 - Cl)$ which is compound C.

$$C_2H_5OH \xrightarrow{PCl_5} C_2H_5 - Cl + HCl + POCl_3$$

B and C react together to give diethyl ether.

$$C_2H_5ONa + C_2H_5Cl \rightarrow C_2H_5OC_2H_5 + NaCl$$

A, B and C are in the order $C_2H_5OH, C_2H_5ONa, C_2H_5Cl$.

Hence, the correct option is (D).

91. An oxygen containing organic compound upon oxidation forms a carboxylic as the only organic product with its molecular mass higher by 14 units. The organic compound is a primary alcohol.

Primary alcohol is easily oxidized to carboxylic acid. $-CH_2 - OH \rightarrow -COOH$. The net process is addition of one O atom and removal of two H atoms. In the net process, the molecular mass increases by 14 units. The atomic masses of O and H are $16 \ g/mol$ and $1 \ g/mol$ respectively. $16 - 2(1) = 14$.

A secondary alcohol on oxidation gives ketone. When drastic conditions are used for the oxidation of ketone, the carbon skeleton breaks.

Hence, the correct option is (C).

92. Oils are rich in glycerol that possesses three hydroxyl groups. Glycerol can be found in the triglyceride structure of oils/fats, and the content ranges from approximately 9 to 13.5%. Glycerol residue, a by-product of glycerol refining from a palm kernel oil methyl ester plant, is found to be good source of glycerol and medium chain fatty acids.

Hence, the correct option is (A).

93. The tertiary structure of a protein consists of the way a polypeptide is formed of a complex molecular shape. This is caused by R-group interactions such as ionic and hydrogen bonds, disulphide bridges, and hydrophobic & hydrophilic interactions. Bonds that do not exist in tertiary structure of proteins are Phosphodiester bonds. A phosphodiester bond occurs when exactly two of the hydroxyl groups in phosphoric acid react with hydroxyl groups on other molecules to form two ester bonds.

Hence, the correct option is (A).

94. ($CF_2 - CF_2$) is Teflon, which is fully fluorinated polymer.

Teflon is actually made of a chemical compound named polytetrafluoroethylene (PTFE) which is a synthetic fluoropolymer which has been under use for various purposes. The discoverer of PTFE named Roy Plunkett found the same while working for DuPont in New Jersey in 1938 by accident.

Hence, the correct option is (B).

95. Both the formation of amide and ester linkage occurs due to the loss of water. For amide linkage, Amine and carboxylic acid reacts and releases water, but in the case of ester linkage, alcohol and carboxylic acid reacts and loses water.

Hence, the correct option is (B).

96. Photochemical reaction occurs when light energy gets absorbed by a substances' molecule. It is a green route as no byproduct will be formed. Vitamin D3 synthesis is assisted by a photochemical reaction.

Waste Management is all the activities and actions required to manage waste from its inception to its final disposal.

Environmental Chemistry is the scientific study of the chemical and biochemical phenomena that occur in natural places. It should not be confused with Green Chemistry, which seeks to reduce potential pollution at its source.

Hence, the correct option is (D).

97. According to the green chemistry, the chemical involved in the production must be nontoxic.

It reduces pollution and protects the environment. By green synthesis, the products that are non-hazards to the nature are produced. So, no pollution takes place. Explanation: According to the green chemistry, the chemical involved in the production must be nontoxic.

Hence, the correct option is (A).

98. In the rate equation, when the concentration of reactants is unity then the rate is equal to specific rate constant.

We can say that at a given temperature, rate is equal to the rate constant of reaction when concentration of the reactant in unity. Thus rate constant is also known as specific reaction rate. Where all the terms have usual meaning. If CA=CB= I then r = k. Increasing the concentration of one or more reactants will often increase the rate of reaction. This occurs because a higher concentration of a reactant will lead to more collisions of that reactant in a specific time period.

Hence, the correct option is (A).

99. The aqueous solution of Hydrochloric acid is the best conductor of electric current because it is a strong acid as it dissociates completely into ions.

The aqueous solution of Hydrochloric acid, HCl is the best conductor of electric current as it is a strong electrolyte and is completely dissociated into ions. On the other hand, ammonia and acetic acid are weak electrolytes which undergo partial dissociation and fructose is a non-electrolyte. Hence, they are poor conductors of electricity.

Hence, the correct option is (B).

100. In a weakly acidic medium, nitrobenzene on electrolytic reduction gives aniline but under strongly acidic medium it gives p-aminophenol.

The electrolytic reduction of nitrobenzene in strongly acidic medium produces phenylhydroxylamine which rearranges to p-Aminophenol.

In weakly acidic medium, aniline is obtained whereas in alkaline medium, various mono and di-nuclear reduction products (such as nitrosobenzene, phenylhydroxylamine, azoxybenzene, azobenzene and hydrazobenzene) are obtained.

Hence, the correct option is (D).

Physics & Chemistry : Mock Test 10

Physics

Q.1 Two long straight conductors AOB and COD are perpendicular to each other and carry currents i_1 and i_2. The magnitude of the magnetic induction at a point P at a distance a from the point O in a direction perpendicular to the plane $ABCD$ is :

A. $\frac{\mu_0}{2\pi a}(i_1 + i_2)$
B. $\frac{\mu_0}{2\pi a}(i_1 - i_2)$
C. $\frac{\mu_0}{2\pi a}\sqrt{(i_1^2 + i_2^2)}$
D. $\frac{\mu_0}{2\pi a}\frac{i_1 i_2}{(i_1+i_2)}$

Q.2 A conducting circular loop is placed in a uniform magnetic field, $B = 0.025\,T$ with its plane perpendicular to the direction of the magnetic field. The radius of the loop is made to shrink at a constant rate of $1\,mm\,s^{-1}$. Find the induced emf in the loop when its radius is $2\,cm$, is:

A. $2\pi\mu V$ **B.** $\pi\mu V$ **C.** $\frac{\pi}{2}\mu V$ **D.** $2\mu V$

Q.3 A long solenoid of cross-sectional radius R has a thin insulated wire ring tightly put on its winding. One half of the ring has the resistance 10 times that of the other half. The magnetic induction produced by the solenoid varies with time as $B = bt$, whose b is a constant. Find the magnitude of the electric field strength in the ring.

A. $\left(\frac{9}{11}\right)Rb$ **B.** $\left(\frac{9}{22}\right)Rb$ **C.** $9Rb$ **D.** Rb

Q.4 For a p-type semiconductor, which of the following statements is true?

[NEET UG, 2019]

A. Electrons are the majority carriers and trivalent atoms are the dopants.
B. Holes are the majority carriers and trivalent atoms are the dopants.
C. Holes are the majority carriers and pentavalent atoms are the dopants.
D. Electrons are the majority carriers and pentavalent atoms are the dopants.

Q.5

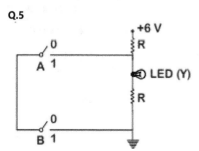

The correct Boolean operation represented by the circuit diagram drawn is :

[NEET UG, 2019]

A. AND **B.** OR **C.** NAND **D.** NOR

Q.6 A rod of mass 'M' and length '2L' is suspended at its middle by a wire. It exhibits torsional oscillations; If two masses each of 'm' are attached at distance '$\frac{L}{2}$' from its centre on both sides, it reduces the oscillation frequency by 20%. The value of ratio m/M is close to:

A. 0.77 **B.** 0.57 **C.** 0.37 **D.** 0.17

Q.7 A pendulum is hung from the roof of a sufficiently high building and is moving freely to and fro like a simple harmonic oscillator. The acceleration of the bob of the pendulum is $20\,m/s^2$ at a distance of $5\,m$ from the mean position. The time period of oscillation is

A. 2 second **B.** π second
C. 2π second **D.** 1 second

Q.8 The radius of circle, the period of revolution, initial position and sense of revolution are indicated in the fig.

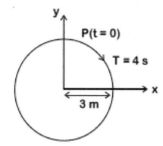

y - projection of the radius vector of rotating particle P is :

A. $y(t) = -3\cos 2\pi t$, where y in m
B. $y(t) = 4\sin\left(\frac{\pi t}{2}\right)$, where y in m
C. $y(t) = 3\cos\left(\frac{3\pi t}{2}\right)$, where y in m
D. $y(t) = 3\cos\left(\frac{\pi t}{2}\right)$, where y in m

Q.9 The displacement of the two coherent waves at any point is $y_1 = a\cos(\omega t)$ and $y_2 = a\cos(\omega t + \phi)$. The intensity of both waves is I_0. When they are superimposed the resultant intensity is equal to:

A. $4I_0\cos^2\left(\frac{\phi}{2}\right)$
B. $4I_0\sin^2\left(\frac{\phi}{2}\right)$
C. $4I_0$
D. None of these

Q.10 Unpolarized light of intensity I passes through polaroid P_1 and then through polaroid P_2 kept at an angle θ with P_1. The intensity of final wave is:

A. I
B. $I_0\cos\theta$
C. $I_0\cos^2\theta$
D. None of these

Q.11 The maximum velocity of the photoelectrons emitted from the surface is v when light of frequency n falls on a metal surface. If the incidence frequency is increased in $3n$. The maximum velocity of the ejected photoelectron will be:

A. $v > v\sqrt{3}$
B. $= v$
C. $\leq \sqrt{3}v$
D. None of these

Q.12 Calculate the velocity of the electron ejected from platinum surface when radiation of 2000A talks omit. The work function of the metal is $5eV$.
A. 6.54×10^2 m/s
B. 0.54×10^2 m/s
C. 6.5×10^2 m/s
D. 6.4×10^2 m/s

Q.13 If the earth suddenly stops rotating, then the value g at the equator, will ____.
A. Decrease
B. Increase
C. Remain the same
D. Be zero

Q.14 A machine gun is mounted on a $2000\ kg$ car on a horizontal frictionless surface. At some instant the gun fires bullets of mass $10gm$ with a velocity of $500\ m/sec$ with respect to the car. The number of bullets fired per second is ten. The average thrust on the system is:
A. 550 N
B. 50 N
C. 250 N
D. 250 dyne

Q.15 A body of density ρ is dropped from rest from a height h into a lake of density $\sigma(\sigma > \rho)$. The maximum depth the body sinks inside the liquid is (neglect viscous effect of liquid):
A. $\dfrac{h\sigma}{\sigma-\rho}$
B. $\dfrac{h\rho}{\sigma}$
C. $\dfrac{h\rho}{\sigma-\rho}$
D. $\dfrac{h\sigma}{\rho}$

Q.16 Viscosity is the property of liquids by virtue of which a:
A. Liquid opposes the relative motion of its layers
B. Liquid pushes neighboring molecules
C. Liquid attracts other molecules
D. Liquid becomes conducting

Q.17 An infinite line charge produces a field of $9 \times 10^4\ N/C$ at distance of $2\ cm$. Calculate the linear charge density.
A. $12\mu C/m$
B. $10\mu C/m$
C. $11\mu C/m$
D. $9\mu C/m$

Q.18 A dielectric slab of thickness $1.0\ cm$ and dielectric constant 5 is placed between the plates of a parallel plate capacitor of plate area $0.01\ m^2$ and separation $2.0\ cm$. Calculate the change in capacity on introduction of dielectric.
A. 4.425×10^{-13} Farad
B. 5.436×10^{-12} Farad
C. 2.95×10^{-12} Farad
D. 5.436×10^{-13} Farad

Q.19 Two long parallel conductors are placed $10\ mm$ apart from each other carrying a current of 150 Amperes. What will be force per meter length of each one?
A. $0.45\ N/m$
B. $0.1\ N/m$
C. $4.5\ N/m$
D. $9\ N/m$

Q.20 Two charges, one of $+5\mu C$ and another of $-5\mu C$ are kept $1\ mm$ apart. Calculate the dipole moment.
A. $10^8\ cm$
B. $10^{-8}\ cm$
C. $10^9\ cm$
D. $10^{-9}\ cm$

Q.21 By what factor, the electric force between two electrons greater than the gravitational force between them?
A. 5×10^{40}
B. 4×10^{42}
C. 5×10^{32}
D. 6×10^{45}

Q.22 False statement among the following statements regarding Coulombs law is ____.
A. Gives the force between two charges q_1 and q_2
B. The magnitude of the force of attraction (or repulsion) between two-point charges is directly proportional to the product of the quantity of the two charges
C. The magnitude of the force of attraction (or repulsion) between two-point charges is inversely proportional to the square of the distance between them
D. None of these

Q.23 An air-filled parallel plate capacitor is arranged such that the lower side of the upper plate carries a surface charge density of $2\ C/m\ 2$ and the upper side of the lower plate carries a surface charge density of $-2\ C/m\ 2$ as shown in the figure. The electric field intensity between the plates will be:

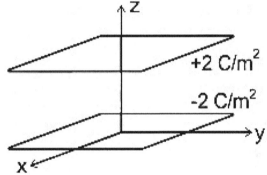

A. $-\dfrac{2}{\varepsilon_0}a_z$
B. $\dfrac{2}{\varepsilon_0}a_z$
C. $-\dfrac{4}{\varepsilon_0}a_z$
D. $\dfrac{4}{\varepsilon_0}a_z$

Q.24 Determine the energy density in free space created by a magnetic field with intensity $H = 10^3$ A/m.
A. 314 mJ/m 3
B. 314 µJ/m 3
C. 628 mJ/m 3
D. 628 µJ/m 3

Q.25 The speed of a swimmer in still water is 20 m/s. The speed of river water is 10 m/s and is flowing due east. If he is standing on the south bank and wishes to cross the river along the shortest path the angle at which he should make his strokes w.r.t. north is given by :

[NEET UG, 2019]

A. 30° west
B. 0°
C. 60° west
D. 45° west

Q.26 A harmonic transverse wave travelling on a string has an amplitude of $2\ cm$, wavelength of $1.25\ m$ and velocity of $5\ m/s$ in $+x$-direction. At $t = 0$, this wave has a crest at $x = 0$. Find the wave equation $y = f(x, t)$.

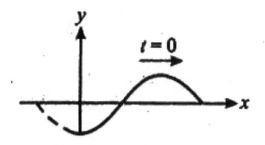

A. $y = 0.02\cos(8\pi t - 1.6\pi x)$
B. $y = 0.002\cos(4\pi t - 1.6\pi x)$.
C. $y = 0.008\cos(4\pi t - 2.6\pi x)$.
D. None of the above

Q.27 A sonometer wire, with a suspended mass of M = 1 kg, is in resonance with a given tuning fork. The apparatus is taken to the moon where the acceleration due to gravity is $\frac{1}{6}$ that on the earth. To obtain resonance on the moon, the value of M should be:

A. 1 kg   B. $\sqrt{6}$ kg   C. 6 kg   D. 36 kg

Q.28 An observer moves towards a stationary source of sound with a velocity of one-tenth of the velocity of sound. The apparent increase in frequency is:

A. Zero   B. 5%   C. 10%   D. 0.1%

Q.29 A p-n photodiode is fabricated from a semiconductor with a band gap of $2.8eV$. At what energy of photon it can detect a wavelength of $6000\ nm$?

A. $0.207eV$ B. $1.207eV$ C. $0.507eV$ D. $0.907eV$

Q.30 $200°$ Celsius = _____Fahrenheit.

A. $-73°F$ B. $-328°F$ C. $392°F$ D. $73°F$

Q.31 Consider a gas of triatomic molecules. The molecules are assumed to the triangular and made of massless rigid rods whose vertices are occupied by atoms. The internal energy of a mole of the gas at temperature T is:

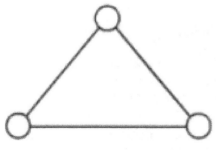

A. $\frac{9}{2}RT$ B. $\frac{3}{2}RT$ C. $\frac{5}{2}RT$ D. $3RT$

Q.32 The molar specific heat of oxygen at constant pressure $C_p = 7.03\ cal/mol°C$ and $R = 8.32\ J/mol°C$. The amount of heat taken by 5 moles of oxygen when heated at constant volume from $10°C$ to $20°C$ will be approximately.

A. 25 cal   B. 50 cal   C. 253 cal   D. 500 cal

Q.33 An electric heater supplies heat to a system at a rate of $100W$. If the system performs work at a rate of 75 Joules per second. At what rate is the internal energy increasing?

A. $25W$ B. $20W$ C. $15W$ D. $35W$

Q.34 A thermodynamic system is taken from an original state to an intermediate state by the linear process shown in figure below

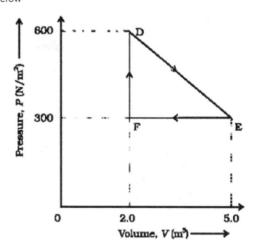

Its volume is then reduced to the original value from E to F by an isobaric process. Calculate the total work done by the gas from D to E to F.

A. $250J$ B. $450J$ C. $350J$ D. $550J$

Q.35 In the total work done by the system along the path ADC is $85J$ find the volume at point C.

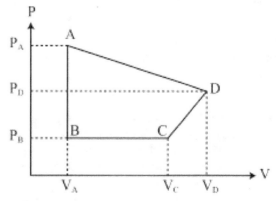

A. 4.033 lltres   B. 1.003 litres
C. 2.233 litres   D. 1.233 litres

Q.36 If λ is the wavelength of a hydrogen atom from the transition $n = 3$ to $n = 1$, then what is the wavelength for doubly ionized lithium-ion for the same transition?

A. $\frac{\lambda}{3}$ B. 3λ C. $\frac{\lambda}{9}$ D. 9λ

Q.37 When radiation is incident on a photoelectron emitter, the stopping potential is found to be $9\ V$. If $\frac{e}{m}$ for the

electron is $1.8 \times 10^{11} CKg^{-1}$, the maximum velocity the ejected electron is:
A. $6 \times 10^5 \, m \, s^{-1}$
B. $8 \times 10^5 \, m \, s^{-1}$
C. $1.8 \times 10^6 \, m \, s^{-1}$
D. $1.8 \times 10^5 \, m \, s^{-1}$

Q.38 If the ratio of the radius of a nucleus with 61 neutrons to that of helium nucleus is 3, then the atomic number of this nucleus is:
A. 27   B. 47   C. 51   D. 61

Q.39 Which of the following are the characteristics of a Junction Field Effect Transistor?
1. High input resistance
2. Good thermal stability
3. High current gain
4. Noisier than bipolar junction transistor
A. 1 and 3   B. 1 and 2   C. 2 and 3   D. 3 and 4

Q.40 If for a silicon NPN transistor, the base-to-emitter voltage (V_{BE}) is 0.7 V and the collector-to-base voltage (V_{CB}) is 0.2 V, then the transistor is operating in the:
A. Normal active mode   B. Saturation mode
C. Inverse active mode   D. Cut-off mode

Q.41 A solid sphere & a hollow sphere of radius R are rolling down in inclined lane of height h. The ratio of velocities of solid sphere to Hollow sphere on reaching the bottom is:
A. $\sqrt{\frac{21}{25}}$ B. $\sqrt{\frac{25}{21}}$ C. $\sqrt{\frac{3}{5}}$ D. $\sqrt{\frac{5}{3}}$

Q.42 A thin ring of mass $5 \, kg$ and diameter $20 \, cm$ is rotating about its axis at $4200 rpm$. Find its angular momentum (in kgm^2/s)?
A. 44   B. 11   C. 22   D. 33

Q.43 Which of the following options is correctly depicting the formula of power?
A. $P = VI$
B. $P = \frac{V^2}{R}$
C. $P = I^2 R$
D. All of the above

Q.44 If two unequal resistors connected in parallel then:
A. The voltage is different in both resistor.
B. The current is same in both resistor.
C. The voltage is large in one of the smaller resistor.
D. The current is large in smaller resistor.

Q.45 Two waves represented by $y_1 = a\sin\left(\omega t + \frac{\pi}{6}\right), y_2 = a\cos\omega t$, the resultant amplitude will be:
A. a B. $a\sqrt{2}$ C. $a\sqrt{3}$ D. $2a$

Q.46 A wave is first reflected by a boundary P and then by a boundary Q without dissipating energy. If the boundary P is rigid and the boundary Q is non-rigid, then find the fraction of the amplitude of the reflected wave by boundary P to the reflected wave by boundary Q.
A. 0
B. ∞

C. $1 : 1$ D. None of above

Q.47 The superposition of two waves of slightly different frequencies moving in the same direction leads to:
A. Interference   B. Beats
C. Stationary waves   D. None of these

Q.48 The relative permeability of ferromagnetic material is _____.
A. Less than unity   B. Equal to unity
C. Larger than unity   D. Not equal to unity

Q.49 Which of the following materials has permanent magnetic dipoles?
A. Ferromagnetic material
B. Anti-ferromagnetic material
C. Diamagnetic material
D. Paramagnetic material

Q.50 Which magnetic material obeys Curie's law in which the magnetic moment is localized at the atomic or the ionic sites where there is no interaction between neighboring magnetic moments?
A. Diamagnetic Materials
B. Paramagnetic Materials
C. Ferromagnetic Materials
D. Anti-ferromagnetic Materials

Chemistry

Q.51 Which of the following formulae represents limestone?
A. $CaSO_4$ B. $CaCO_3$ C. CaO D. $MgSO_4$

Q.52 Which of the following metals does not form amalgams?
A. Zinc   B. Copper
C. Magnesium   D. Iron

Q.53 The value of K_c for the reaction: $A + 3B \rightleftharpoons 2C$ at $400°C$ is 0.5. Calculate the value of K_p.
A. 1.64×10^{-4} B. 1.64×10^{-6}
C. 1.64×10^{-5} D. 1.64×10^{-3}

Q.54 Which of the following is an example of solid-liquid equilibrium?
A. Water and steam at hundred degrees centigrade
B. Water and ice at 0-degree centigrade
C. The point where Ammonia is sublimized
D. Boiling point of water

Q.55 Techniques like titration, precipitation, spectroscopy, chromatography, etc. commonly used in _____.
A. Organic chemistry
B. Inorganic chemistry
C. Analytical chemistry
D. Physical chemistry

Q.56 In the reaction, $Cl_2 + OH^- \rightarrow Cl^- + ClO_3 + H_2O$, chlorine is:
A. Oxidised

B. Reduced
C. Oxidised as well as reduced
D. Neither oxidised nor reduced

Q.57 Which statements are correct in terms of chemical kinetic stuides?
A. The quenching of a reaction can be made by cooling the reaction mixture.
B. The quenching of a reaction can be made by diluting the reaction mixture.
C. The reaction is supposed to be completed if it is kept for long time or strongly heated.
D. All of the above

Q.58 For a reaction 2A + B → C + D, the active mass of B is kept constant but that of A is tripled. The rate of reaction will:
A. Decrease by 3 times
B. Increased by 9 times
C. Increase by 3 times
D. Unpredictable

Q.59 _____ increases effective collisions without increasing average energy.
A. An increase in the reactant concentration
B. An increase in the temperature
C. A decrease in pressure
D. Catalysts

Q.60 According to Fajan's rule, which of the following ions shows the greatest polarising power?
A. Li⁺   B. Cs⁺   C. K⁺   D. Na⁺

Q.61 Which condition is not satisfied by an ideal solution?
A. $\Delta_{mix}V = 0$
B. $\Delta_{mix}S = 0$
C. Obeyance to Raoult's Law
D. $\Delta_{mix}H = 0$

Q.62 p_A and p_B are the vapour pressure of pure liquid components, A and B, respectively of an ideal binary solution. If x_A represents the mole fraction of component A, the total pressure of the solution will be
A. $p_A + x_A(p_B - p_A)$
B. $p_A + x_A(p_A - p_B)$
C. $p_B + x_A(p_B - p_A)$
D. $p_B + x_A(p_A - p_B)$

Q.63 _____ is a quantity that represents the total energy of the system.
A. Chemical energy
B. Electrical energy
C. Internal energy
D. Mechanical energy

Q.64 The enthalpy change of a reaction does not depend on:
A. Different intermediate reactions
B. Initial and final enthalpy change of a reaction
C. Nature of reactants and products
D. The state of reactants and products

Q.65 The q is ___ when heat is transferred from the surroundings to the system and q is _____ when heat is transferred from system to the surroundings.

A. positive, negative
B. high, low
C. negative, positive
D. low, high

Q.66 Alkali halids do not show Frenkel defect because:
A. Cations and anions have almost equal size
B. There is a large difference in size of cations and anions
C. Cations and anions have a low coordination number
D. Anions cannot be accommodated in voids

Q.67 An elemental crystal has a density of $8570 \ kg/m^3$. The packing efficiency is 0.68. The closest distance of approach between neighbouring atom is $2.86 A$. What is the mass of one atom approximately?
A. $29 \ amu$ B. $39 \ amu$ C. $63 \ amu$ D. $93 \ amu$

Q.68 Which of the following exists as covalent crystals in the solid-state?
[JEE Main Advanced, 2013]
A. Sulphur
B. Phosphorous
C. Iodine
D. Silicon

Q.69 The element Californium belongs to the family of:
[UPSESSB TGT Science, 2016]
A. Actinide series
B. Alkali series
C. Lanthanide series
D. Alkaline earth series

Q.70 Pd has exceptional configuration $4d^{10}5s^2$, it belongs to:
[UPSESSB TGT Science, 2016]
A. 4th Period
B. 6th Period
C. 7th Period
D. 5th Period

Q.71 Which of the following pairs of atomic numbers represent elements belonging to the same group:
[UPSESSB TGT Science, 2016]
A. 11, 20   B. 12, 30   C. 13, 31   D. 14, 33

Q.72 Which of the following mixture is known as fusion mixture?
A. Sodium carbonate and potassium chloride
B. Sodium carbonate and potassium carbonate
C. Sodium bicarbonate and sodium carbonate
D. Potassium bicarbonate and sodium carbonate

Q.73 Butanone is a four-carbon compound with the functional group –
A. Carboxylic acid
B. Ketone
C. Aldehyde
D. Alcohol

Q.74 The relation between RMS velocity, average velocity and most probable velocity is:
A. $1:\sqrt{2}:\sqrt{3}$
B. $1:2:3$
C. $\sqrt{2}:\sqrt{\frac{8}{\pi}}:\sqrt{3}$
D. $\sqrt{2}:\sqrt{3}:\sqrt{\frac{8}{\pi}}$

Q.75 Name the liquid with higher vapour pressure in the following pairs:
A. Alcohol, Water, Petrol
B. Petrol, Water, Alcohol
C. Alcohol, Petrol, Water
D. None of the above

Q.76 Trigonal bipyramidal geometry is shown by:
A. $[XeF_8]^{2-}$
B. XeO_3F_2
C. $FXeOSO_2F$
D. None of these

Q.77 Fog is a colloidal solution of:
A. Solid particles dispersed in a gas
B. Gaseous particles dispersed in a liquid
C. Liquid particles dispersed in a gas
D. Solid particles dispersed in a liquid

Q.78 Which of the following energy state is filled by an electron after the completion of $4p$ orbital?
A. $5s$
B. $3d$
C. $4d$
D. $4f$

Q.79 Which of the following is/are saturated hydrocarbon?
A. C_2H_6
B. C_2H_4
C. C_2H_5
D. All of these

Q.80 A cell converts:
[Sainik School Entrance Class IX, 2022]
A. Electrical energy into chemical energy.
B. Chemical energy into electrical energy.
C. Magnetic energy into electrical energy.
D. Electrical energy into mechanical energy.

Q.81 During discharging of a lead storage battery, which of the following is/are true?
A. $PbSO_4$ is formed at both electrodes
B. Density of electrolytic solution decreases
C. (A) and (B) both
D. H_2SO_4 is produced

Q.82 E^o_{cell} for the reaction, $2H_2O \to H_3O^+ + OH^-$ at $25°C$ is $-0.8277\ V$. The equilibrium constant for the reaction is:
A. 10^{-14}
B. 10^{-23}
C. 10^{-7}
D. 10^{-21}

Q.83 In the complex $K_2Fe[Fe(CN)_6]$:
A. Both Fe atoms are in the same oxidation state.
B. Both Fe atoms are in different oxidation states.
C. The coordination number of ion is 4.
D. The complex is a high spin complex.

Q.84 Which of the following complex species is not expected to exhibit optical isomerism?
[JEE Main Advanced, 2013]
A. $[Co(en)_2Cl_2]^+$
B. $[Co(NH_3)_3Cl_3]$
C. $[Co\ (en)\ (NH_3)_2Cl_2]^+$
D. $[Co(en)_3]^{3+}$

Q.85 Which one of the following compounds will exhibit linkage isomerism?
A. $[Pt(NH_3)_2Cl_2]$
B. $[Co(NH_3)_2NO_2]Cl_2$
C. $[Co(NH_3)_4Cl_2]Cl$
D. $[Co(en)_2Cl_2]Cl$

Q.86 To detect the reducing and non reducing sugars, which of the following test is used?
A. Molisch's test
B. Biuret test
C. Fehling's test
D. Million's test

Q.87 Formic acid can be distinguished from acetic acid by reaction with:
A. $NaHCO_3$
B. dil, acidified $KMnO_4$
C. 2,4-dinitrophenylhydrazine
D. Na metal

Q.88 The compound which forms acetaldehyde when heated with dilute $NaOH$, is:
A. 1,1-dichloroethane
B. 1,1,1-trichlorethane
C. 1-chlorethane
D. 1,2-dichlorethane

Q.89 Starch is converted to ethanol by fermentation. What is the sequence of enzymes used?
A. Amylase, maltase, zymase
B. Diastase, maltase, zymase
C. Amylase, invertase, zymase
D. Amylase, zymase, maltase

Q.90 Identify the product A in the following reaction:

C. [structure: 1,3-diphenylpropane-1,3-dione]

D. [structure: 1,3-diphenylpropane-1,3-diol]

Q.91 The product formed in the reaction of dihydroquinone with potassium dichromate and conc. sulphuric acid is
A. 1,4 - benzoquinone
B. 1,2 - benzoquinone
C. Benzene
D. Cyclohexane-3,5-dienone

Q.92 Cleavage of specific covalent bonds and removal of groups without hydrolysis is the property of:
A. Lyases
B. Transferases
C. Isomerases
D. Hydrolases

Q.93 Which one of the following is included in essential amino acids?
A. Valine
B. Tryptophan
C. Leucine
D. All of the above

Q.94 Natural rubber is a polymer of isoprene. It is made to market quality through a process called vulcunisation. Name the new bonds introduced that stiffens rubber.
A. Sulphur cross links
B. Hydrogen bonds
C. Ionic link
D. Glycsidic link

Q.95 Which polymer among the following polymers does not soften on heating?
A. Bakelite
B. Polythene
C. Polystyrene
D. PVC

Q.96 Which of the following is a greener route to produce ethanal commercially?
A. Catalytic cracking of ethanol
B. Oxidation of ethene with an ionic catalyst
C. Steam reforming of methanol
D. Dehydrogenation of ethylene

Q.97 Which of the following is not a principle of Green Chemistry?
A. Green solvents and auxiliaries
B. Use of renewable feedstock
C. Hazardous chemical synthesis
D. Design for energy efficiency

Q.98 Which of the following natural amino acid is optically inactive?
A. Alanine
B. Glycine
C. Valine
D. Aspartic acid

Q.99 Nitrobenzene is subjected to reduction with Zn dust and ammonium chloride. The main product formed will be:
A. Benzenamine
B. Aniline
C. N-phenylhydroxylamine
D. None of the above

Q.100 In industrial processes, transition elements and their oxides are used as:
A. Surfactants
B. Insecticides
C. Catalyst
D. All of them

Physics & Chemistry : Mock Test - 10

// Smart Answer Sheet //

Correct — Indicates percentage of students who answered questions correctly.

Skipped — Indicates percentage of students who skipped questions.

Q.	Ans.	Correct / Skipped	Q.	Ans.	Correct / Skipped	Q.	Ans.	Correct / Skipped	Q.	Ans.	Correct / Skipped	Q.	Ans.	Correct / Skipped
1	C	57.08 % / 1.85 %	17	B	76.89 % / 0.0 %	33	A	89.52 % / 0.0 %	49	A	47.1 % / 1.07 %	65	A	51.39 % / 1.52 %
2	B	79.7 % / 0.0 %	18	C	12.52 % / 4.05 %	34	B	59.2 % / 1.32 %	50	B	52.64 % / 1.14 %	66	A	64.15 % / 1.16 %
3	B	69.77 % / 1.45 %	19	A	58.54 % / 1.36 %	35	D	19.92 % / 4.28 %	51	B	77.9 % / 0.0 %	67	D	21.96 % / 3.31 %
4	B	51.22 % / 1.4 %	20	D	80.71 % / 0.0 %	36	C	62.05 % / 1.99 %	52	D	24.4 % / 3.01 %	68	D	65.96 % / 1.59 %
5	C	55.38 % / 1.57 %	21	B	89.33 % / 0.0 %	37	C	58.86 % / 1.06 %	53	A	24.47 % / 4.16 %	69	A	69.46 % / 1.13 %
6	C	50.09 % / 1.52 %	22	D	41.5 % / 1.23 %	38	B	60.44 % / 1.08 %	54	B	88.58 % / 0.0 %	70	D	28.72 % / 4.78 %
7	B	80.46 % / 0.0 %	23	A	42.66 % / 1.81 %	39	B	60.03 % / 1.23 %	55	C	84.68 % / 0.0 %	71	C	48.87 % / 1.83 %
8	D	45.36 % / 1.51 %	24	C	40.69 % / 1.27 %	40	A	40.73 % / 1.12 %	56	C	69.09 % / 1.77 %	72	B	78.14 % / 0.0 %
9	A	11.63 % / 4.47 %	25	A	59.04 % / 1.62 %	41	B	42.51 % / 1.37 %	57	D	66.4 % / 1.88 %	73	B	77.07 % / 0.0 %
10	C	66.47 % / 1.16 %	26	A	50.7 % / 1.22 %	42	C	69.37 % / 1.69 %	58	B	14.01 % / 4.07 %	74	C	21.04 % / 3.38 %
11	A	31.42 % / 3.58 %	27	C	40.03 % / 1.62 %	43	D	83.41 % / 0.0 %	59	A	17.61 % / 4.2 %	75	C	84.67 % / 0.0 %
12	A	40.49 % / 1.62 %	28	C	64.61 % / 1.83 %	44	D	85.72 % / 0.0 %	60	A	68.55 % / 1.57 %	76	B	54.06 % / 1.8 %
13	B	89.11 % / 0.0 %	29	A	69.07 % / 1.26 %	45	C	49.12 % / 1.72 %	61	B	57.18 % / 1.25 %	77	C	59.85 % / 1.26 %
14	B	58.59 % / 1.16 %	30	C	54.64 % / 1.58 %	46	C	46.87 % / 1.2 %	62	D	46.41 % / 1.38 %	78	A	48.46 % / 1.69 %
15	C	64.55 % / 1.19 %	31	D	79.0 % / 0.0 %	47	B	78.52 % / 0.0 %	63	C	68.94 % / 1.74 %	79	A	76.28 % / 0.0 %
16	A	61.26 % / 2.0 %	32	C	11.14 % / 4.96 %	48	C	88.86 % / 0.0 %	64	A	44.12 % / 1.44 %	80	B	64.27 % / 1.3 %

Q.	Ans.	Correct / Skipped
81	C	24.38 % / 3.13 %
82	A	47.3 % / 1.49 %
83	A	57.02 % / 1.91 %
84	B	43.47 % / 1.65 %
85	B	54.38 % / 1.16 %
86	C	21.32 % / 4.81 %
87	C	65.59 % / 1.07 %
88	A	61.94 % / 1.51 %
89	B	51.75 % / 1.99 %
90	C	69.99 % / 1.35 %
91	A	42.26 % / 1.53 %
92	A	76.07 % / 0.0 %
93	D	64.58 % / 1.37 %
94	A	66.86 % / 1.46 %
95	A	83.76 % / 0.0 %
96	B	53.11 % / 1.75 %
97	C	77.98 % / 0.0 %
98	B	89.5 % / 0.0 %
99	B	43.71 % / 1.56 %
100	C	66.57 % / 1.54 %

Performance Analysis

Avg. Score (%)	51.0%
Toppers Score (%)	57.0%
Your Score	

//Hints and Solutions//

1. Conductors AOB and COD are perpendicular to each other shown in figure.

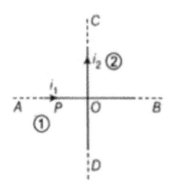

At distance a above O,

$B_1 = \dfrac{\mu_0 i_1}{2\pi a}$

And $B_2 = \dfrac{\mu_0 i_2}{2\pi a}$

B_1 is perpendicular to B_2.

Resultant of B_1 and B_2,

$B = \sqrt{B_1^2 + B_2^2}$

$= \dfrac{\mu_0}{2\pi a}\sqrt{i_1^2 + i_2^2}$

Hence, the correct option is (C).

2. Here,

Magnetic field, $B = 0.025\ T$

Radius of the loop, $r = 2\ cm = 2 \times 10^{-2}\ m$

Constant rate at which radius of the loop shrinks,

$\dfrac{dr}{dt} = 1 \times 10^{-3} ms^{-1}$

Magnetic flux linked with the loop is

$\phi = BA\cos\theta = B(\pi r^2)\cos 0° = B\pi r^2$

The magnitude of the induced emf is

$|\varepsilon| = \dfrac{d\phi}{dt} = \dfrac{d}{dt}(B\pi r^2) = B\pi 2r\dfrac{dr}{dt}$

$= 0.025 \times \pi \times 2 \times 2 \times 10^{-2} \times 1 \times 10^{-3}$

$= \pi \times 10^{-6} V = \pi\mu V$

Hence, the correct option is (B).

3. Both upper half and lower half will have the same effective area $\dfrac{\pi R^2}{2}$ so a change in flux will be same and induced emf will have the same value. But since the resistance is different due to which current must be different but the ring is as a whole is closed circuit so the electric field will be generated to make the current flow in both parts to be same.

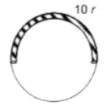

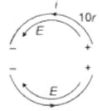

$e = \dfrac{-Nd\Phi}{dt}$

$= \dfrac{-NAdB}{dt}$

$= -b\pi a^2$ (since number of turns $N = 1$)

But $e = IR$

So, $IR - \ln R = b\pi a^2$

Therefore $IR(1-n) = b\pi a^2$

or $IR = \dfrac{b\pi a^2}{(1-n)}$

$d\Phi = \Phi_1 - \Phi_2$

$= \dfrac{-b\pi a^2}{(1-n)} - \dfrac{(b\pi a^2)}{2} = -b\pi a^2[\dfrac{1}{(1-n)} - \dfrac{1}{2}] = -b\pi a^2\dfrac{(1-n)}{2(1+n)}$

Electric field $(E) = \dfrac{e}{L}$ (Length), $E\pi a = -b\pi a^2 \dfrac{(1n)}{2(1+n)}$

or $E = \dfrac{-ba(1-n)}{2(1+n)}$

Since cross sectional radius $a = R$ and Resistance is one-half is 10 times another half, $n = 10$

$E = \dfrac{9}{22}Rb$

Hence, the correct option is (B).

4. Holes are the majority carriers and trivalent atoms are the dopants is the statement are true.

In a p-type semiconductor, the holes are the majority carriers, while the electrons are the minority carriers. A p-type semiconductor is obtained when trivalent atoms, such as aluminium, are doped in silicon atoms.

Semiconductors like germanium or silicon doped with any of the trivalent atoms like boron, indium or gallium are called p-type semiconductors. The impurity atom is surrounded by four silicon atoms. It provides the atoms to fill only three covalent bonds as it has only three valence electrons.

Hence, the correct option is (B).

5. From the given logic circuit LED will glow, when voltage across LED is high. This is out put of NAND gate.

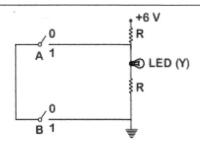

Truth Table

A	B	Y
0	0	1
0	1	1
1	0	1
1	1	0

A two-input NAND gate is a digital combination logic circuit that performs the logical inverse of an AND gate. While an AND gate outputs a logical "1" only if both inputs are logical "1," a NAND gate outputs a logical "0" for this same combination of inputs.

Hence, the correct option is (C).

6. It causes a twisting of such elements due to an external applied torque. Specifically, torsional vibrations (or torsional oscillations) can be defined as the periodical movement of a shaft. Therefore, such shaft twists ups around itself, alternating its turning direction.

We know that, the torsional oscillation frequency is given by the formula:

$$\omega = \frac{k}{\sqrt{I}}$$

Where,

k = Torsion constant

I = Moment of Inertia

Rod without mass:

The moment of inertia of rod is:

$$I = \frac{ML^2}{12}$$

Where,

M = Mass of rod = M (given)

L = Length of rod = $2L$ (given)

Now,

$$\Rightarrow I = \frac{M(2L)^2}{12}$$

$$\Rightarrow I = \frac{M(4L^2)}{12}$$

$$\therefore I = \frac{ML^2}{3}$$

Now, the torsional oscillation frequency of rod is:

$$\therefore \omega_1 = \frac{k}{\sqrt{\frac{ML^2}{3}}}$$

Rod with mass:

The moment of inertia of rod and two masses is:

$$I = \frac{ML^2}{12} + 2m(l)^2$$

Where,

m = Attached mass = m (given)

l = Length from which the mass is attached = $L/2$ (given)

M = Mass of rod = M (given)

L = Length of rod = $2L$ (given)

Now,

$$\Rightarrow I = \frac{M(2L)^2}{12} + 2m\left(\frac{L}{2}\right)^2$$

$$\Rightarrow I = \frac{ML^2}{3} + \frac{2mL^2}{4}$$

$$\therefore I = \frac{ML^2}{3} + \frac{mL^2}{2}$$

Now, the torsional oscillation frequency of rod with mass is:

$$\therefore \omega_2 = \frac{k}{\sqrt{\frac{ML^2}{3} + \frac{mL^2}{2}}}$$

From question, after the mass is attached its frequency which is reduced by $20\% (100\% - 20\% = 80\%)$

$\omega_2 = 80\%$ of ω_1

$$\omega_2 = \frac{80}{100}\omega_1$$

$$\Rightarrow \omega_2 = 0.8\omega_1$$

Now, substituting the torsional oscillation frequencies,

$$\Rightarrow \frac{k}{\sqrt{\frac{ML^2}{3} + \frac{mL^2}{2}}} = (0.8)\frac{k}{\sqrt{\frac{ML^2}{3}}}$$

$$\Rightarrow \frac{1}{\sqrt{\frac{ML^2}{3} + \frac{mL^2}{2}}} = \frac{0.8}{\sqrt{\frac{ML^2}{3}}}$$

Squaring on both sides,

$$\Rightarrow \frac{1}{\frac{ML^2}{3} + \frac{mL^2}{2}} = \frac{0.64}{\frac{ML^2}{3}}$$

$\Rightarrow \frac{ML^2}{3} = 0.64\left(\frac{ML^2}{3} + \frac{mL^2}{2}\right)$

$\Rightarrow \frac{ML^2}{3} = \left((0.64)\frac{ML^2}{3}\right) + \left((0.64)\frac{mL^2}{2}\right)$

$\Rightarrow \frac{ML^2}{3} - (0.64)\frac{ML^2}{3} = (0.64)\frac{mL^2}{2}$

$\Rightarrow (0.36)\frac{ML^2}{3} = (0.64)\frac{mL^2}{2}$

$\Rightarrow \frac{m}{M} = \frac{2}{3} \times \frac{0.36}{0.64}$

$\therefore \frac{m}{M} = 0.375$

Hence, the correct option is (C).

7. Since in SHM, magnitude of acceleration is given as

$a = \omega^2 x$

$20 = \omega^2 \times 5$

$\omega = 2$

Now, Time Period (T),

$T = \frac{2\pi}{\omega}$

$T = \pi second$

Hence, the correct option is (B).

8. At $t = 0, y$ displacement is maximum, so equation will be cosine function.

$T = 4\ s$

$\Rightarrow \omega = \frac{2\pi}{T}$

$= \frac{2\pi}{4} = \frac{\pi}{2} rad/s$

So,

$y = acos\omega t$

$y = 3\cos\frac{\pi}{2}t$, where y in m

Hence, the correct option is (D).

9. Given:

$y_1 = acos(\omega t), y_2 = acos(\omega t + \phi)$, and $I_0 =$ intensity of both the waves

If at any point the waves emerging from the source S_1 and S_2 are in opposite phase then we will have destructive interference and the resultant intensity will be zero.

Path difference $= \left(n + \frac{1}{2}\right)\lambda$ and $n = 0,1,2,3, ...$

Where, $\lambda =$ wavelength

Let at any point the phase difference between the displacements of the two waves is ϕ.

So, the displacement of the two waves is given as,

$y_1 = acos(\omega t)$

$\Rightarrow y_2 = acos(\omega t + \phi)$

When the waves are superimposed at this point the resultant displacement is given as,

$y = 2acos\left(\frac{\phi}{2}\right)\cos\left(\omega t + \frac{\phi}{2}\right)$

The amplitude of the resultant displacement is given as,

$A = 2acos\left(\frac{\phi}{2}\right)$

The intensity at that point is given as,

$I = 4I_0\cos^2\left(\frac{\phi}{2}\right)$

Hence, the correct option is (A).

10. Malus law states that the intensity of the polarized light transmitted through the analyzer varies as the square of the cosine of the angle between the plane of transmission of the analyzer and the plane of the polarizer.

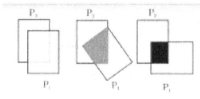

If unpolarized light is passed through two polaroids are placed at an angle θ to each other, the intensity of the polarized wave is:

$I = I_0\cos^2\theta$

Where, I is the intensity of the polarized wave, I_0 is the intensity of the unpolarized wave.

Hence, the correct option is (C).

11. Let the work function for the given metal be ϕ. When the light of the frequency n falls on the surface of the metal, the maximum kinetic energy of the ejected photoelectron is given by,

$K.E_{max} = nh - \phi$

$\frac{1}{2}mv^2 = nh - \phi$ ... (i)

When the light of the frequency 3n falls on the surface of the metal, the maximum kinetic energy of the ejected photoelectron is given by,

$K.E_{max} = 3nh - \phi$

Let the maximum velocity of the electron be v.

$\frac{1}{2}mv^2 = 3nh - \phi$ ... (ii)

Substituting $nh = \frac{1}{2}mv^2 + \phi$ from equation (i) to equation (ii)

$\frac{1}{2}mv^2 = 3\left(\frac{1}{2}mv^2 + \phi\right) - \phi$

$\frac{1}{2}mv^2 = \frac{3}{2}mv^2$

$\frac{1}{2}mv^2 - \frac{3}{2}mv^2 = 0$

The work function cannot be negative or zero.

Thus,

$\frac{1}{2}mv^2 - \frac{3}{2}mv^2 > 0$

$\Rightarrow v > v\sqrt{3}$

Hence, the correct option is (A).

12. Given:

$W = 5eV = 5 \times (1.6 \times 10^{-19})J = 8.0 \times 10^{-19} J$

Using Einstein's photoelectric equation, $E_1 = KE + W$

$E_1 = \frac{hc}{\lambda}$ .....(i)

$h = 6.63 \times 10^{-34}$, $c = 3 \times 10^8 m/s$, $\lambda = 200 \times 10^{-9} m$

Put the given values in (i).

$= \frac{(6.63 \times 10^{-34}) \times (3 \times 10^8)}{(200 \times 10^{-9})}$

$= 9.945 \times 10^{-19}$

$KE = E_1 - W$ .....(ii)

Put the given values in (ii).

$= 9.945 \times 10^{-19} - 8.0 \times 10^{-19}$

$= 1.945 \times 10^{-19} J$

Kinetic energy of the electron $(KE) = \frac{1}{2mv^2}$

$\Rightarrow v = \left[\frac{2KE}{m}\right]^{\frac{1}{2}}$ .....(iii)

Put the given values in (iii).

$v = \left[\frac{2(1.195 \times 10^{-19})}{9.1 \times 10^{-31}}\right]^{\frac{1}{2}}$

$= 6.54 \times 10^2 \ m/s$

Hence, the correct option is (A).

13. If the earth suddenly stops rotating, then the value g at the equator, will increase.

The effect of rotation of the earth on acceleration due to gravity is to decrease its value. Therefore if the earth stops rotating, the value of g will increase.

$g = g_e - R\omega^2 \cos^2 \alpha$

$R \rightarrow$ Radius of earth, $\omega \rightarrow$ Angular velocity of earth.

$\alpha \rightarrow$ lattitude angale.

Where, At equator, $\alpha = 0$

g, increases by a factor of $R\omega^2 \cos^2 \alpha$.

Hence, the correct option is (B).

14. Given,

Mass of car, $M = 2000 \ kg$

Mass of bullet, $m = 10 \times 10^{-3} \ kg$

Velocity of bullet, $u = 500 \ m/sec$

The number of bullets fired per second is ten. Then,

$\frac{N}{t} = 10$

$F_{avg} = \frac{\Delta P}{\Delta t}$

$= \frac{Nm(v_2 - v_1)}{t}$

$= 10 \times 10 \times 10^{-3} \times 5 \times 10^2$

$= 50 \ N$

Hence, the correct option is (B).

15. The velocity of body just before touching the lake surface is,

$v = \sqrt{2gh}$

Retardation in the lake,

$a = \frac{\text{upthrust-weight}}{a}$

$\Rightarrow \frac{V\rho g - V\rho g}{V\rho} = \left(\frac{\sigma - \rho}{\rho}\right)g$

Maximum depth $d_{max} = \frac{v^2}{2a}$

$\Rightarrow \frac{h\rho}{\sigma - \rho}$

Hence, the correct option is (C).

16. The property of viscosity of liquids arises when there is a relative motion between its layers. The viscous force acts in a direction opposite to the direction of motion, i.e. it opposes the motion.

Hence, the correct option is (A).

17. Given,

Electric field, $E = 9 \times 10^4 \ N/C$

Distance, $r = 2 \times 10^{-2} \ m$

Using the formula of electric field for uniformly charged wire,

$$E = \frac{\lambda}{2\pi r \varepsilon_0}$$

$$\therefore \lambda = E \cdot 2\pi r \cdot \varepsilon_0$$

where, λ is a linear charge density,

and, $\epsilon_0 = 8.854 \times 10^{-12}$

Then,

$$\lambda = 9 \times 10^4 \times 2\pi \times 2 \times 10^{-2} \times 8.854 \times 10^{-12}$$

$$\lambda = 10 \times 10^{-6}$$

Therefore,

Linear charge density, $\lambda = 10 \mu C/m$

Hence, the correct option is (B).

18. Given,

Thickness of the dielectric slab, $t = 1\, cm = 10^{-2}\, m$

Dielectric constant, $\varepsilon_r = K = 5$

Area of the plates of the capacitor, $A = 0.01\, m^2 = 10^{-2}\, m^2$

Distance between parallel plates of the capacitor, $d = 2\, cm = 2 \times 10^{-2}\, m$

We know that:

Capacity with air in between the plates,

$$C_0 = \frac{\epsilon_0 A}{d}$$

where, $\epsilon_0 = 8.854 \times 10^{-12}$

$$= \frac{8.85 \times 10^{-12} \times 10^{-2}}{2 \times 10^{-2}}$$

$$C_0 = 4.425 \times 10^{-12}\, \text{Farad}$$

Capacity with dielectric slab in between the plates,

$$C = \frac{\epsilon_0 A}{d - t\left(1 - \frac{1}{K}\right)}$$

$$= \frac{8.85 \times 10^{-12} \times 10^{-2}}{(2 \times 10^{-2}) - 10^{-2}\left(1 - \frac{1}{5}\right)}$$

$$C = 7.375 \times 10^{-12}\, \text{Farad}$$

Increase in capacity on introduction of dielectric:

$$C - C_0 = (7.375 \times 10^{-12}) - (4.425 \times 10^{-12})$$

$$= 2.95 \times 10^{-12}\, \text{Farad}$$

Hence, the correct option is (C).

19. We know the force per unit length between the two conductors is

$$\frac{F}{l} = \frac{\mu_0 I_1 I_2}{2\pi d}$$

Here d = distance = 10×10^{-3} meter

$$\mu_0 = 4\pi \times 10^{-7}\, F/m$$

And currents $I_1 = I_2 = 150$ Ampere

$$\therefore \frac{F}{l} = \frac{4\pi \times 10^{-7} \times 150 \times 150}{2\pi \times 10 \times 10^{-3}}$$

$$= 0.45\, N/m$$

Hence, the correct option is (A).

20. Given:

Charge on dipole is $\pm 5\mu C = \pm 5 \times 10^{-6} C$

Distance between the charges $= 1\, mm = 10^{-3}\, m$

We know that:

Dipole moment is given by:

$$P = q(2a)$$

$$= 5 \times 10^{-6} \times 1 \times 10^{-3}$$

$$= 10^{-9} cm$$

Hence, the correct option is (B).

21. We know that:

Electrostatic force $= \frac{KQ_1 Q_2}{r^2}$ ......(1)

Gravitational force $= \frac{Gm_1 m_2}{r^2}$ ......(2)

On dividing the two we get,

$$\frac{\text{Electrostatic Force}}{\text{Gravitational Force}} = \frac{\frac{KQ_1 Q_2}{r^2}}{\frac{Gm_1 m_2}{r^2}}$$

$$\frac{\text{Electrostatic Force}}{\text{Gravitational Force}} = \frac{9.0 \times 10^9 \times (1.6 \times 10^{-19})^2}{6.67 \times 10^{-11} \times (9.1 \times 10^{-31})^2}$$

Electrostatic Force $= 4 \times 10^{42}$ Gravitational Force

Therefore, electrostatic force between two electrons is greater than gravitational force by a factor of 10^{42}.

Hence, the correct option is (B).

22. Coulomb's Law: It states that the force between two charged particles will be directly proportional to the product of the quantity of the two charges.

$$F \propto q_1 q_2$$

Secondly, it is also inversely proportional to the square of the distance between them, i.e.

$$F \propto \frac{1}{r^2}$$

$\therefore$ The force between two charges q_1 and q_2 is given by:

$F = k\frac{q_1 q_2}{r^2}$

Where k is the proportionality constant and is equal to 9×10^9 Nm 2/C 2.

Hence, the correct option is (D).

23. Concept:

Electric field intensity at any point due to uniform surface charge distribution is defined as:

$E = \frac{\rho_s}{2\varepsilon_o} a_n$

Where ρ_s = surface charge density

a_n = unit vector normal to the sheet directed toward the point where the field is to be determined.

Application:

For the upper plate, $a_n = -a_z$.

∴ The electric field intensity due to the upper plate will be:

$E_U = \frac{2}{2\varepsilon_o}(-a_z)$

For the lower plate, $a_n = a_z$.

∴ The field intensity due to the lower plate will be:

$E_l = -\frac{2}{2\varepsilon_o}(a_z)$

So the net field between the plates will be:

$E = E_U + E_l$

$E = \frac{2}{2\varepsilon_o}(-a_z) + \left[-\frac{2}{2\varepsilon_o}(a_z)\right]$

$E = -\frac{4}{2\varepsilon_o} a_z = -\frac{2}{\varepsilon_o} a_z$

∴ The electric field intensity between the plates will be $-\frac{2}{\varepsilon_o} a_z$.

Hence, the correct option is (A).

24. Given:

Free space created by a magnetic field with intensity $H = 10^3$ A/m

Concept:

Energy density in free space created by a magnetic field with intensity is given by

$E = \frac{1}{2}\mu \left(\vec{H}\right)^2$ J/m 3

Where μ is the permeability

For free space, $\mu = \mu_0 = 4\pi \times 10^{-7}$

Calculation:

In free space, magnetic field intensity, $H = 10^3$ A/m.

In free space, $\mu = \mu_0 = 4\pi \times 10^{-7}$

$\Rightarrow E = \frac{1}{2} \times 4\pi \times 10^{-7} \times (10^3)^2 = 0.628$ J/m 2

$\Rightarrow E = 628$ mJ/m 3

∴ The energy density is 628 mJ/m 3

Hence, the correct option is (C).

25. $V_{SR} = 20\ m/s$

$V_{RG} = 10\ m/s$

$\overline{V}_{SG} = \overline{V}_{SR} + \overline{V}_{RG}$

So,

$\sin\theta = \frac{|\overline{V}_{RG}|}{|\overline{V}_{SR}|}$

$\sin\theta = \frac{10}{20}$

$\Rightarrow \sin\theta = \frac{1}{2}$

$\Rightarrow \theta = 30°$ west

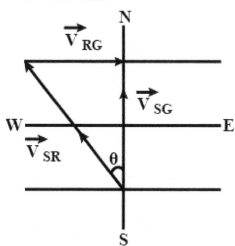

Hence, the correct option is (A).

26. The equation of the harmonic wave is

$y = A\sin(\omega t - kx + \phi)$

Where $t = 0, x = 0$ and $y = -A$

Since from the figure it is clear that the amplitude shows negative deviation i.e., $y = -A$

$\sin\phi = -1$ or $\phi = -\frac{\pi}{2}$

Then,

Physics & Chemistry : Mock Test - 10

$y = -A\cos(\omega t - kx)$,

Where,

$A = 0.02 m, \omega = v \times k$

$= v \times \dfrac{(2\pi)}{\lambda}$

$= 5 \times \dfrac{2\pi}{1.25} = 8\pi$, and $k = \dfrac{2\pi}{\lambda} = \dfrac{2\pi}{1.25} = 1.6\pi$

So,

$y = 0.02 \cos(8\pi t - 1.6\pi x)$.

Hence, the correct option is (A).

27. On earth: $v = \dfrac{1}{2l}\sqrt{\dfrac{Mg}{m}} = \dfrac{1}{2l}\sqrt{\dfrac{g}{m'}}$, since $M = 1$ kg

On moon $v' = \dfrac{1}{2l}\sqrt{\dfrac{Mg/6}{m}} = \dfrac{1}{2l}\sqrt{\dfrac{Mg}{6m}}$

For resonance $v = v'$ or $\dfrac{1}{2l}\sqrt{\dfrac{g}{m}} = \dfrac{1}{2l}\sqrt{\dfrac{Mg}{6m}}$

which gives $M = 6$ kg.

Hence, the correct option is (C).

28. $v' = v\left(1 + \dfrac{u_0}{v}\right)$

Given, $\dfrac{u_0}{v} = \dfrac{1}{10}$

Therefore, $v' = \dfrac{11}{10}v$

or $v' - v = \dfrac{11}{10}v - v = \dfrac{v}{10}$

The percentage increase in v is

$\dfrac{v'-v}{v} \times 100 = 10\%$

Hence, the correct option is (C).

29. Given:

The energy band gap of the given photodiode, $E_g = 2.8 eV$

The wavelength, $\lambda = 6000\, nm = 6000 \times 10^{-9}\, m$

The energy of a photon is given by the relation $E = \dfrac{hc}{\lambda}$

Where, $h =$ Planck's constant $= 6.626 \times 10^{-34}\, J\, s$

$c =$ Speed of light $= 3 \times 10^8\, m/s$

$E = \dfrac{6.626 \times 10^{-34} \times 3 \times 10^8}{6000 \times 10^{-9}} = 3.313 \times 10^{-20}\, J$

But $1.6 \times 10^{-19}\, J = 1 eV$

$E = 3.313 \times 10^{-20}\, J$

$\therefore E = 3.313 \times 10^{-20}\, J = \dfrac{3.313 \times 10^{-20}}{1.6 \times 10^{-19}} = 0.207 eV$

The energy of wavelength $6000\, nm$ is $0.207 eV$.

Hence, the correct option is (A).

30. The various temperature scales commonly used are Celsius (C), Kelvin (K), Fahrenheit (F) and Rankine (Ra).

$°F = \dfrac{9}{5}°C + 32$

$°F = \dfrac{9}{5} \times 200 + 32$

$= 360 + 32$

$= 392°F$

Hence, the correct option is (C).

31. A triatomic (non-linear) gas molecule has 6 degrees of freedom (3 translational, 3 rotational and no vibrational) at room temperature. According to the law of equipartition of energy, the average energy per molecule of a triatomic gas at room temperature T is

$\overline{E} = \dfrac{1}{2}fRT$

$= \dfrac{1}{2}6RT = 3RT$

Hence, the correct option is (D).

32. Molar heat is that amount of capacity in which heat is needed to raise the temperature of 1 mole of a substance by 1 kelvin or $1°C$ at constant volume. It is the amount of heat energy required per unit temperature. $C_p - C_v = R$.

Here R is the universal gas constant.

Now from the question:

Given $C_p = 7.03\, cal/mol°C$

$R = 8.32\, J/mol°C = \dfrac{8.32}{4.2}\, cal/mol°C$ (since 1 calorie=4.2 joule approx)

$T_1 = 10°C$ and $T_2 = 20°C$

Change in a temperature $\Delta T = T_2 - T_1 = 20 - 10 = 10°C$

Molar heat capacity at constant volume,

$C_p - C_v = R$

$C_v = C_p - R$

$C_v = 7.03\, cal/mol°C - \dfrac{8.32}{4.2}\, cal/mol°C$

$C_v = 5.05\, cal/mol°C$ approx

Amount of heat absorbed $\Delta Q = nC_v\Delta T$

$= (5 \times 5.05)10 \; cal$

$= 252.5 = 253 \; cal$ approx

Hence, the correct option is (C).

33. Heat is supplied to the system by an electric heater at a rate of $100W$.

Thus, heat supplied, $Q = 100J/s$

The system operates at a rate of $75J/s$.

Clearly, work done, $W = 75J/s$

Using the first law of thermodynamics,

$Q = U + W$

where,

U = internal energy

$\Rightarrow U = Q - W$

$\Rightarrow U = 100 - 75$

$\Rightarrow U = 25J/s$

$\Rightarrow U = 25W$

Hence, the correct option is (A).

34. Considering the given linear process in a thermodynamic system, it can be understood that,

Total work done by the gas from D to E to F is equal to the area of $\triangle DEF$.

Area of $\triangle DEF = \frac{1}{2} \times DF \times EF$

where,

DF = Change in pressure

$\Rightarrow DF = 600N/m^2 - 300N/m^2$

$\Rightarrow DF = 300N/m^2$

FE = Change in volume $= 5 - 2 = 3m^3$

Thus,

Area of $\triangle DEF = \frac{1}{2} \times 300 \times 3 = 450J$

Clearly, the total work done by the gas from D to E to F is $450J$.

Hence, the correct option is (B).

35. Work done along ADC = Work done along AD (expanding) - Work done along DC (contracting). Work done along AD can be easily calculated by calculating area under line AD which comes out to be $88J$

$85 = 88$ - Area under CD

Area under $CD = 3$

Let E be the intersection of lines from C and D and F and G be the x-intercepts from C and D respectively.

Area under $CD = \frac{1}{2} \times DE \times EC + CG \times EC$

$CD = \frac{1}{2}(P_D - P_B) \times (V_D - V_C) + P_B \times (V_D - V_C)3$

$= \frac{1}{2} \times 0.3 \times 10^5 \times (1.3 - V_C) + 0.3 \times 10^5 \times (1.3 - V_C)$

We know $10^{-3}m^3 = 1l$

Therefore, volume at point C is $V_C = 1.3 - \frac{3}{45 \times 10^4}$

$= 1.3 - 0.66 \times 10^3$

$= 1.233$ litres

Hence, the correct option is (D).

36. As given, λ is the wavelength of a hydrogen atom from the transition $n = 3$ to $n = 1$.

For wavelength,

$\frac{1}{\lambda} = RZ^2 \left(\frac{1}{n_1^2} - \frac{1}{n_2^2}\right)$

Here, transition is same.

So, $\lambda \propto \frac{1}{Z^2}$

$\frac{\lambda_H}{\lambda_{Li}} = \frac{(Z_{Li})^2}{(Z_H)^2}$

$\frac{\lambda_H}{\lambda_{Li}} = \frac{(3)^2}{(1)^2} = 9$

$\lambda_{Li} = \frac{\lambda_H}{9} = \frac{\lambda}{9}$

Hence, the correct option is (C).

37. Given,

The stopping potential $= 9 \; V$

$\frac{e}{m} = 1.8 \times 10^{11} CKg^{-1}$

By the law of conservation of energy,

$\frac{1}{2}mv^2_{max} = eV_0$

$\Rightarrow v_{max} = \sqrt{2\left(\frac{e}{m}\right)V_0}$

$\Rightarrow \sqrt{2 \times 1.8 \times 10^{11} \times 9}$

$\Rightarrow 18 \times 10^5 \; m \; s^{-1}$

$\Rightarrow 1.8 \times 10^6 \; m \; s^{-1}$

Hence, the correct option is (C).

38. As given, the ratio of the radius of a nucleus with 61 neutrons to that of helium nucleus is 3.

As we know, the radius is directly proportional to $\frac{1}{3}$ power of mass number,

i.e., $R \propto A^{\frac{1}{3}}$

or, $\frac{A_1}{A_2} = \left(\frac{R_1}{R_2}\right)^3$

$\Rightarrow \frac{A_2}{A_1} = \left(\frac{1}{3}\right)^3$

$\Rightarrow \frac{A_2}{A_1} = \frac{1}{27}$

$\Rightarrow \frac{A_2}{A_1} = 27$

$\Rightarrow A_2 = A_1 \times 27$

$A_2 = 4 \times 27 = 108$

$\Rightarrow Z_2 = A_2 - 61$

$Z_2 = 108 - 61 = 47$

Hence, the correct option is (B).

39.

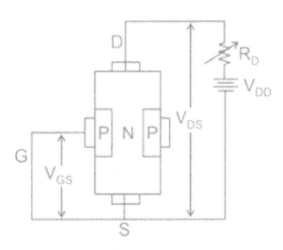

Here, Gate is reversed biased, so the current flow through the Gate is approximately zero. So, Input-impedance is very high in JFET Typically in megaohms.

Now, when the temperature increases mobility decreases according to the equation μ α T⁻ᵐ. So, the increase in current due to thermal generation is compensated by the decrement of mobility, So, FET has high thermal Stability.

Hence, the correct option is (B).

40. The modes of operation of an NPN BJT are as follow:

Emitter base junction	Collector Base junction	Mode
Reverse bias	Reverse bias	Cutoff
Reverse bias	Forward bias	Reverse active
Forward bias	Reverse bias	Active
Forward bias	Forward bias	Saturation

Given V_{BE} = 0.7 V which indicates a forward-biased Emitter-Base junction,
V_{CB} = 0.2 V which indicates a Reverse biased Collector-Base junction.
So, the mode of operation of the given transistor will be Normal active mode.

Hence, the correct option is (A).

41. In rolling without slipping through the distance L down the incline, the height of the rolling object changes by "h".

So, the gravitational potential energy changes by mgh.

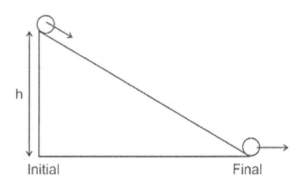

$\Rightarrow P.E = K.E_{\text{translation}} + KE_{\text{rotational}}$

$\Rightarrow mgh = \frac{1}{2}mv^2 + \frac{1}{2}I\omega^2 = \frac{1}{2}mv^2 + \frac{1}{2}I\left(\frac{v}{r}\right)^2$

$\Rightarrow 2mgh = mv^2\left(1 + \frac{I}{mr^2}\right)$

$\Rightarrow v = \sqrt{\frac{2gh}{\left(1 + \frac{I}{mr^2}\right)}}$

As we know that moment of inertia of solid sphere is

$\Rightarrow I = \frac{2}{5}mr^2$

∴ The velocity of the solid sphere is

$\Rightarrow v_{\text{solidsphere}} = \sqrt{\frac{10}{7}gh} \dots \dots (1)$

The moment of inertia of the hollow sphere is

$\Rightarrow I = \frac{2}{3}mr^2$

∴ The velocity of the hollow sphere is

$\Rightarrow v_{\text{hollowsphere}} = \sqrt{\frac{6}{5}gh} \dots \dots (2)$

On dividing equation 1 and 2, we get

$$\Rightarrow \frac{v_{\text{solid}}}{v_{\text{hollow}}} = \sqrt{\frac{25}{21}}$$

Hence, the correct option is (B).

42. Given:

Mass of the ring $(M) = 5\ kg$, diameter of the ring $(d) = 20\ cm$, radius of the ring $(r) = 10\ cm = 10^{-1}\ m$

$$v = 4200 rpm = \frac{4200}{60} rps = 70 rps$$

The moment of inertia of a uniform circular ring is

$$\Rightarrow I = MR^2$$

$$\Rightarrow I = 5 \times 10^{-2}$$

The relation between the angular momentum and moment of inertia is given by

$$\Rightarrow L = I\omega = mr^2 \times 2\pi V$$

$$\Rightarrow L = 5 \times 10^{-2} \times \frac{2 \times 22 \times 70}{7}$$

$$= 2200 \times 10^{-2} = 22 kg m^2/s$$

Hence, the correct option is (C).

43. The rate at which electrical energy is dissipated into other forms of energy is called electrical power i.e.,

$$P = \frac{W}{t} = VI = I^2 R = \frac{V^2}{R}$$

Where, $V = $ Potential diffrence, $R = $ Resistance and $I = $ current

From above equation it is clear that all options are correct.

Hence, the correct option is (D).

44. When the terminals of two or more resistances are connected at the same two points and the potential difference across them is equal is called resistances in parallel.

The net resistance/equivalent resistance(R) of resistances in parallel is given by:

$$\frac{1}{R} = \frac{1}{R_1} + \frac{1}{R_2}$$

Suppose two resistors R_1 and R_2 are connected in parallel $(R_1 > R_2)$

As we know that the voltage across both resistors is the same in parallel combination. Therefore, the current through R_1 is:

$$I_1 = \frac{V}{R_1}$$

Current through R_2:

$$I_2 = \frac{V}{R_2}$$

Since, $R_1 > R_2$,

Therefore, $I_1 < I_2$

Hence, the correct option is (D).

45. Given:

$$y_1 = a\sin\left(\omega t + \frac{\pi}{6}\right) \text{ and } y_2 = a\cos(\omega t)$$

$$\Rightarrow y_2 = a\cos(\omega t) = a\sin\left(\omega t + \frac{\pi}{2}\right)$$

The resultant amplitude of the wave after superposition of two waves:

$$\Rightarrow A = \sqrt{a^2 + b^2 + 2a \times b \times \cos\phi}$$

Where, $a = $ amplitude of wave $1, b = $ amplitude of wave 2, and $\phi = $ phase difference

Here, $a = a, b = a$ and $\phi = \frac{\pi}{2} - \frac{\pi}{6} = \frac{\pi}{3}$

$$\Rightarrow A = \sqrt{a^2 + a^2 + 2a \times a \times \cos\frac{\pi}{3}}$$

$$\Rightarrow A = \sqrt{3a^2}$$

$$\Rightarrow A = \sqrt{3}a$$

Hence, the correct option is (C).

46. We know that if a pulse travelling along a stretched string and is reflected by the rigid boundary.

- If there is no absorption of energy by the boundary, the reflected wave has the same frequency and amplitude as the incident pulse but it suffers a phase change of π or 180° on reflection.
- We know that if a pulse is reflected by a non-rigid boundary the reflected pulse has the same phase, amplitude, and frequency (assuming no energy dissipation) as the incident pulse.
- From the above explanation, it is clear that the amplitude of the reflected wave is always equal to the incident wave.

Hence, the correct option is (C).

47. The superposition of the waves may result in the following cases,

(i) The superposition of two waves of same frequencies moving in the same direction leads to Interference

(ii) The superposition of two waves of slightly different frequencies moving in the same direction leads to beats

(iii) The superposition of two waves of same frequencies moving in the opposite direction leads to stationary waves.

Hence, the correct option is (B).

48. The relative permeability of ferromagnetic material is larger than unity.

Ferromagnetic Substances: The substances which are strongly magnetized when placed in an external magnetic field in the same direction to the applied field are called ferromagnetic substances.

Properties:

- These are characterized by parallel alignment of magnetic dipoles
- These substances are strongly attracted by a magnet
- It develops strong magnetization in the direction of the applied magnetic field
- By removing the magnetizing filed, it does not lose its magnetization.

Hence, the correct option is (C).

49. Ferromagnetic materials has permanent magnetic dipoles. The ferromagnetic materials are those substances that exhibit strong magnetism in the same direction of the field when a magnetic field is applied to it.

when we consider some unpaired electrons, they will interact with each other between two atoms and they line up themselves in a tiny region with the direction of the magnetic field.

This mechanism of the ferromagnetic material is ferromagnetism. It can be defined as some materials (cobalt, gadolinium, iron etc) that will become permanent magnets with the use of a magnetic field.

Hence, the correct option is (A).

50. Paramagnetic Materials that obey this law are materials in which the magnetic moments are localized at the atomic or ionic sites and where there is no interaction between neighboring magnetic moments.

There are several theories of paramagnetism, which are valid for specific types of material. Langevin's model, which is true for materials with non-interacting localized electrons, states that each atom has a magnetic moment that is randomly oriented as a result of thermal agitation.

The application of a magnetic field creates a slight alignment of these moments and hence a low magnetization in the same direction as the applied field.

As the temperature increases, then the thermal agitation will increase and it will become harder to align the atomic magnetic moments and hence the susceptibility will decrease.

Hence, the correct option is (B).

51. $CaCO_3$ is the chemical formula of Calcium carbonate (Limestone).

- Limestone is a carbonate sedimentary rock composed primarily of calcium carbonate ($CaCO_3$).
- Limestone is the raw material used in the process of manufacturing cement.

Hence, the correct option is (B).

52. Alloys are substances that possess metallic character and are obtained by mixing metal with another metal or another element.

Either the mixture/alloy of mercury (Hg) with any other metal is called an amalgam whereas Tungsten, Platinum, Iron, and Tantalum are exceptions that do not form an amalgam.

The alloys of mercury with any other metal are termed amalgams and depending upon the proportion of mercury, they can be liquid, paste, or solid in nature.

One of the best examples of Amalgam is a mixture of mercury and silver which is used by the dentist for a dental filling.

From the above explanation, we can see that amalgams are an alloy of mercury and other metal like zinc copper magnesium except for iron.

i.e., Iron or Fe is the metal that can not be used to form an amalgam alloy.

Hence, the correct option is (D).

53. Given that:

$T = 673\ K,\ K_c = 0.5,$

We know that:

$R = 0.082$ litre bar $K^{-1}\ mol^{-1}$

$K_p = K_c[RT]^n$

Where,

$n =$ Concentration of products - concentration of reactants

$= 2 - 4$

$n = -2$

Then,

$K_p = 0.5 \times (0.082 \times 673)^{-2}$

$= 1.64 \times 10^{-4}\ atm$

Hence, the correct option is (A).

54. At zero degree centigrade, when water and ice are together the opposing process occurs simultaneously at the same rate, so the amount of ice and water remains constant. It is an example of a solid-liquid equilibrium.

Solid–liquid equilibrium is utilized to describe the phase formation and the compositions in many industrial processes. For example, a commonly used unit operation to separate substances in pure solid form from a liquid mixture is crystallization.

Hence, the correct option is (B).

55. Techniques like titration, precipitation, spectroscopy, chromatography, etc. commonly used in analytical chemistry.

A branch of chemistry that deals with the identification of compounds and mixtures (qualitative analysis) or the determination of the proportions of the constituents (quantitative analysis): techniques commonly used are titration, precipitation, spectroscopy, chromatography, etc.

Hence, the correct option is (C).

56. Given reaction is:

$Cl_2 + OH^- \rightarrow Cl^- + ClO_3 + H_2O$

The balanced reaction will be:

$3Cl_2 + 6OH^- \rightarrow 5Cl^- + ClO_3 + 3H_2O$

Oxidation number of $Cl_2 = 0$

Oxidation number Cl in $Cl^- = -1$

Oxidation number of Cl in ClO_3:

$\Rightarrow x + 3 \times (-2) = -1$

$\Rightarrow x = +5$

So, Cl_2 is oxidised as well as reduced.

Hence, the correct option is (C).

57. The quenching of a reaction can be made by cooling as well as diluting the reaction mixture. The reaction is supposed to be completed if it is kept for a long time or strongly heated. Quenching a reaction is used to deactivate any unreacted reagents. It is also done by adding an antisolvent to induce precipitation, and collecting or removing the solids.

Hence, the correct option is (D).

58. According to the given reaction, Rate = k [A]² [B]¹

When A becomes 3A i.e., triples, the rate will become: Rate = k [3A]² [B]¹ = 9k [A]² [B]

Thus, rate of reaction is increased by 9 times.

Hence, the correct option is (B).

59. An increase in the reactant concentration increase effective collisions without increasing average energy. This is due to the fact that molecules comes more and more closer, hence, they tends to collide more easily.

Hence, the correct option is (A).

60. According to Fajan's rules of polarization, the more the size of anion, the more easily will it be polarized, and hence compound will be more non-polar. Less the size of the cation, more will be its polarizing power and hence compound will be more non-polar. Now, among all the ions given to us, the Li⁺ ion is the smallest in size because it has lost 3 electrons so it becomes very small as compared to other ions (the effective nuclear charge increases to a maximum amount). So, It will have maximum polarizing power. Smaller cations that have higher positive charges will have better polarizing power because the positive charge is distributed in a relatively small area. Li⁺ ion has the highest polarising power among the alkali metal ions.

Hence, the correct option is (A).

61. An ideal solution is as followed:

Volume change (ΔV) of mixing should be zero.

Heat change (ΔH) on mixing should be zero.

Obey Raoult's law at every range of concentration.

$\Delta_{mix} S = 0$ is not satisfied.

Hence, the correct option is (B).

62. According to Raoult's law,

$P = x_A p_A + x_B p_B$ ....(i)

For binary solutions,

$x_A + x_B = 1, x_B = 1 - x_A$ ....(ii)

Putting value of x_B from equation (ii) to equation (i)

$P = x_A p_A + (1 - x_A) p_B = x_A p_A + p_B - x_A p_B$

$P = p_B + x_A (p_A - p_B)$

Hence, the correct option is (D).

63. Internal energy is a quantity that represents the total energy of the system.

Internal energy U of a system or a body with well-defined boundaries is the total of the kinetic energy due to the motion of molecules and the potential energy associated with the vibrational motion and electric energy of atoms within molecules. Internal energy also includes the energy in all the chemical bonds. From a microscopic point of view, internal energy may be found in many different forms. For any material or repulsion between the individual molecules.

Hence, the correct option is (C).

64. The enthalpy change of a reaction does not depend on different intermediate reactions.

The enthalpy change of a reaction is the value of the energy required or released during a reaction. Since, the value depends only on the energy of the reactants and products and is given by,

ΔH = (energy of products) - (energy of reactants)

So, it is a function of only initial reactants and final products and thus it does not depend on any intermediate products energy.

Hence, the correct option is (A).

65. The q is positive when heat is transferred from the surroundings to the system and q is negative when heat is transferred from the system to the surroundings.

The sign of q in this equation tells us whether the difference of energy in the initial system and the final system is endothermic or exothermic. If q is negative, then energy has been released from the system to its surroundings, if q is positive, then energy has been drawn in from the surroundings to the system.

Hence, the correct option is (A).

66. Frenkel defect is possible in the compounds in which the size of cations and anions are different. In this defect, the smaller ion comes to an interstitial place. In Alkali halides the size of cations and anions is almost equal. So the ion size is large and they cannot get into the interstitial site. So, these kinds of compounds do not show Frenkel defect.

Hence, the correct option is (A).

67. The packing efficiency $= 0.68$, means the given lattice is BCC

The closest distance of approach $= 2r$

$2r - 2.86A = a\sqrt{3}$

or $a = \dfrac{2 \times 2.86}{\sqrt{3}} = 3.30 A$

Let atomic weight of the element $= a$

$\therefore \dfrac{2 \times a}{36 \times 10^{23} \times (3.3)^3 \times 10^{-24}} = 8.57$

$a = 8.57 \times 3 \times (3.3)^3 \times 0.1$

$= 92.39 \simeq 93 \; amu$

Hence, the correct option is (D).

68. Covalent crystals are formed by sharing valence electrons between two atoms resulting in the formation of a covalent bond.

The covalent bonds extend in two or three dimensions forming a giant interlocking structure called a network.

Diamond and graphite are good examples of this type.

Silicon (Si): Covalent solid

Sulphur (S_8): Molecular solid

Phosphorus (P_4): Molecular solid

Iodine (I_2): Molecular solid

Hence, the correct option is (D).

69. In the periodic table, the Actinoid element or the actinide element, any of a series of 15 consecutive chemical elements from actinium to lawrencium (atomic numbers 89–103).

As a group, Actinoid elements are significant largely because of their property of being radioactive.

Curium (Cm), a synthetic chemical element having atomic number 96 comes under the Actinoid series of the periodic table.

Actinoid elements are actinium, thorium, protactinium, uranium, neptunium, plutonium, americium, curium, berkelium, californium, einsteinium, fermium, mendelevium, nobelium and lawrencium.

Hence, the correct option is (A).

70. Palladium (Pd) does not belong to 3d series of transition elements (Atomic number of Pd is 42).

Palladium (Pd) belongs to the 4d series which contain elements from Yttrium (Y) to Cadmium (Cd).

The d-block elements are called transition elements.

They are called d-block as their valency electrons enter the d-orbital.

$4d^{10}5s^2$ is the exceptional configuration of Pd. Its electronic configuration should be $[36Kr]4d^8 5s^2$

Thus, its Period $= 5$th (Highest orbit) Group $= ns + (n-1)d$ electrons

$= 2 + 8 = 10$

Hence, the correct option is (D).

71. Mosley gave the modern Long form of Periodic table where the base of classification was the atomic number.

According to Mosley's periodic law, the physical and chemical properties of elements are periodic functions of their Atomic number.

In the long-form periodic table, horizontal rows are called Periods and vertical rows are called groups.

Group 13 contains Aluminium (13) and Gallium (31).

Element with atomic number 12 is magnesium which belongs to group 2 and element with atomic number 30 is zinc which belongs to group 12.

Element with atomic number 11 is sodium which belongs to group 1 and element with atomic number 20 is calcium which belongs to group 2.

Element with atomic number 14 is silicon belonging to group 14 and 31 is Gallium from group 13.

So, 13, 31 pairs of atomic numbers represent elements belonging to the same group (Group 13).

Hence, the correct option is (C).

72. The mixture of sodium carbonate and potassium carbonate together is known as a fusion mixture. It is used for the qualitative test for organic compounds.

The fusion mixture is the mixture containing the salts of sodium (Na) and the potassium (K) salts. Generally used fusion mixture is the potassium carbonate and sodium carbonate mixture.

The mixture is called a fusion mixture, since they are fused with the organic compounds and various tests for the group analysis are done using this mixture.

Hence, the correct option is (B).

73. Butanone is a four-carbon compound with the functional group.

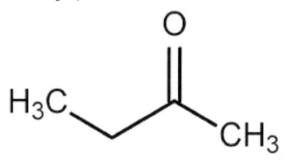

In ketones, the carbonyl group has 2 hydrocarbon groups attached to it. These can be either the ones containing benzene rings or alkyl groups. Ketone does not have a hydrogen atom attached to the carbonyl group. Butanone has a functional group ketonic group $(C = O)$.

Hence, the correct option is (B).

74. Root mean square velocity: The root-mean square (RMS) velocity is the value of the square root of the sum of the squares of the stacking velocity values divided by the number of values.

$$V_{rms} = \sqrt{\frac{3RT}{M}}$$

Most probable velocity: The velocity which is possessed by the maximum fraction of gaseous molecules at a particular time is known as most probable velocity.

$$V_{mp} = \sqrt{\frac{2RT}{M}}$$

Average velocity: Average velocity is the rate of change of position of an object. It can also be explained as total displacement in total time.

$$V_{avg} = \sqrt{\frac{8RT}{\pi m}}$$

If we compare these velocities, their ratio would be:

$V_{rms} : V_{avg} : V_{mp}$

$\sqrt{\frac{3RT}{M}} : \sqrt{\frac{8RT}{\pi m}} : \sqrt{\frac{2RT}{M}}$

R, T and M are present in all the three so they will cancel out.

$\sqrt{3} : \sqrt{\frac{8}{\pi}} : \sqrt{2}$

Hence, the correct option is (C).

75. The vapour pressure of the liquid is inversely proportional to the magnitude of the intermolecular forces of attraction present. Based on this, the liquid with higher vapour pressure in the different pairs is: (a) Alcohol, (b) Petrol, (c) Water.

Hence, the correct option is (C).

76. Trigonal bipyramidal geometry is shown by XeO_3F_2.

Trigonal bipyramidal geometry is seen in complexes that have hybridization of sp^3d and their coordination number is 5.

In the molecule XeO_3F_2, the steric number of Xe is 5 as there are 5 sigma bonds and 0 lone pairs. Therefore 5 steric number implies that the hybridization is sp^3d and therefore the geometry is trigonal bipyramidal.

Valence electrons in Xenon $= 8$

Contribution of each F atom $= 2$

∴ Coordination number $= (8 + 2) \div 2 = 5$

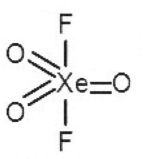

XeO₃F₂

Hence, the correct option is (B).

77. Fog is a colloidal solution of liquid particles dispersed in gas.

When a large mass of air consisting of the dust particles is cooled below its dew point, the moisture present in the air condenses on the surface of these particles forming fine droplets. These droplets float in the air due to their colloidal nature. This process forms fog. An example of aerosol in which dispersed phase is liquid and dispersion medium is gas is fog.

Hence, the correct option is (C).

78. When $4p$ orbital in any atom are filled completely, the next electron goes in $5s(n + 1 = 5 + 0 = 5)$ not in $4d(n + 1 = 4 + 2 = 6)$, electron first enters into the subshell which is having less $(n + 1)$ value (energy). So, the $5s$ is filled first than $4d$.

Hence, the correct option is (A).

79. The general formula for saturated hydrocarbons is C_nH_{2n+2}.

Alkane - C_nH_{2n+2}

Alkene - C_nH_{2n}

Alkyene - C_nH_{2n-2}

So, C_2H_6 is saturated hydrocarbon.

Hence, the correct option is (A).

80. A cell converts chemical energy into electrical energy.

- It consists of two solid electrodes and this solid electrodes are placed in an electrolyte and connected together by an electrical conductor such as wire.

- The two electrodes should be made up of two different metals and the electrolyte solution can be an alkaline, acidic or salt solution depending on the situation.

- These electrodes can be depicted as two half cells set up in different containers and are connected through a porous or salt solution.

Hence, the correct option is (B).

81. Oxidation at anode is represented by the half cell reaction:

$$Pb(s) + SO_4^{2-}(aq) \rightarrow PbSO_4(s) + 2e^-$$

Reduction at cathode is represented by the half cell reaction:

$PbO_2(s) + 4H^+(aq) + SO_4^{2-}(aq) + 2e^- \rightarrow PbSO_4(s) + 2H_2O(l)$

The overall cell reaction is:

$Pb(s) + PbO_2(s) + 2H_2SO_4(aq) \rightarrow 2PbSO_4(s) + 2H_2O(l)$

During discharging of a lead storage battery, sulfuric acid is consumed and water is produced.

Lead sulphate is formed at both electrodes.

Since sulfuric acid is consumed, the density of the electrolytic solution decreases.

Hence, the correct option is (C).

82. Given reaction,

$2H_2O \rightarrow H_3O^+ + OH^-$

And, $E^0_{cell} = -0.8277\ V$

It is evident from the cell reaction that it involves the transfer of one electron so that $n = 1$

We know a relation:

$\log K = \dfrac{E^0_{cell} \times n}{0.0591}$

$\log K = \dfrac{-0.8277 \times 1}{0.0591} = -14$

$\therefore K = 10^{-14}$

Hence, the correct option is (A).

83. In the complex $K_2Fe[Fe(CN)_6]$, both Fe atoms are in the same oxidation state.

Oxidation state of Fe in $K_2Fe[Fe(CN)_6]$,

$0 = 2 + 2x - 6$

$x = 2$

In the complex $K_2Fe[Fe(CN)_6]$, both the iron atoms have $+2$ oxidation state. Since six cyanide ions surround the iron atom, its coordination number is 6.

The Fe^{2+} ion in $[Fe(CN)_6]^{4-}$ has outer electronic configuration of $3d^6$. The complex is a low spin complex. It contains 0 unpaired electrons with a magnetic moment of 0 BM and is colourless.

Hence, the correct option is (A).

84. Optical isomerism is exhibited by only those complexes which lack elements of symmetry.

$[Co(NH_3)_3Cl_3]$ shows facial as well as meridional isomerism. But both the forms contain plane of symmetry.

Thus, this complex does not exhibit optical isomerism.

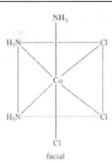
facial

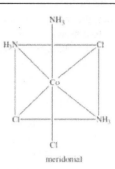
meridional

Hence, the correct option is (B).

85. $[Co(NH_3)_2NO_2]Cl_2$ will exhibit linkage isomerism.

The coordination complexes that show linkage isomerism have ambidentate ligands. Ambidentate ligands are those which have two donor atoms, but only one of the donor atoms can bind to the central metal atom at a time.

NO_2 is the ambidentate ligand in this coordination complex. This ligand is the reason the coordination complex shows linkage isomerism. When the central metal atom is bonded with nitrogen, the ligand is NO_2. When the metal atom is bonded with oxygen, the ligand is ONO.

$[Co(NH_3)_2NO_2]Cl_2$ will exhibit linkage isomerism as it contains nitrite ligand which has the same composition differing with the connectivity of the metal to a ligand. It can bind from N as well as from O side.

Hence, the correct option is (B).

86. (A) Molisch's test is a chemical test which is used to check for the presence of carbohydrates in a given analyte.

(B) The biuret test, also known as Piotrowski's test, is a chemical test used for detecting the presence of peptide bonds. In the presence of peptides, a copper (II) ion forms mauve-colored coordination complexes in an alkaline solution.

(C) Fehling's test is used for reducing sugars and non-reducing sugars, supplementary to the Tollens' reagent test. The test was developed by German chemist Hermann von Fehling in 1849.

(D) Millon's reagent is an analytical reagent used to detect the presence of soluble proteins.

Hence, the correct option is (C).

87. Formic acid and acetic acid can be distinguished using $2,4$-dinitrophenylhydrazine.

Formic acid is having aldehyde group, so it answers the above test. Forming yellow colour precipitate of $2,4$-dinirto phenyl hydrazone. Whereas acetic acid does not.

Hence, the correct option is (C).

88. When $CH_3CH(Cl)_2$ under go reaction with dilute sodium hydroxide dilute $NaOH$, it gives

$CH_3CH(Cl)_2 \rightarrow CH_3CH(OH)_2$ (unstable)

$CH_3CH(OH)_2 \rightarrow CH_3CHO + H_2O$

Thus acetaldehyde is formed from $1,1$-dichloroethane

When $CH_3C(Cl)_3$ under go reaction with dilute sodium hydroxide dilute $NaOH$, it gives

$CH_3C(Cl)_3 \rightarrow CH_3C(OH)_3$ (unstable)

$CH_3C(OH)_3 \rightarrow CH_3COOH + H_2O$

Thus acetic acid is formed from $1,1,1$-trichloroethane

Hence, the correct option is (A).

89. Starch is converted to ethanol by fermentation. The sequence of enzymes used is Diastase, maltase, zymase.

Hence, the correct option is (B).

90.

Hence, the correct option is (C).

91. The product formed in the reaction of dihydroquinone with potassium dichromate and concentration sulphuric acid is 1,4 - benzoquinone.

Hence, the correct option is (A).

92. Lyases are the'enzymes which cause cleavage, removal of groups without hydrolysis, addition of groups to double bonds or removal of a group producing double bond, e.g histidine decarboxylase break histidine to histamine and CO_2.

Hence, the correct option is (A).

93. Essential amino acids are those which cannot be synthesized by organisms in the body and are obtained from plants. The 9 essential amino acids are: histidine, isoleucine, leucine, lysine, methionine, phenylalanine, threonine, tryptophan, and valine.

Non-essential amino adds can be synthesized by the organism and may not be the requisite components of the diet, e.g., serine, cysteine, proline, glycine, alanine, asparagine, glutamine and tyrosine.

Hence, the correct option is (D).

94. Sulphur cross links stiffens rubber.

To improve upon the physical properties of rubber, a process of vulcanisation is carried out. This process consists of heating a mixture of raw rubber with sulphur and an appropriate additive at a temperature range between 373 K to 415 K. On vulcanisation, sulphur forms cross links at the reactive sites of double bonds and thus, the rubber gets stiffened.

Hence, the correct option is (A).

95. Bakelite does not soften on heating.

A plastic material, which cannot be repeatedly melted-molded again, is called a thermosetting plastic. Thermosetting plastics do not become soft on heating and they do not change their shape on heating. Bakelite is one example of a thermosetting plastic.

Hence, the correct option is (A).

96. Ethanal can be prepared by oxidation of ethene, in the presence of an ionic catalyst in an aqueous medium. This is a greener method and gives 90% of yield.

Micro waves are greener than the conventional methods in organic synthesis without solvents. The wide range of micro wave chemistry is extended recently too many aspects of organic synthesis.

Hence, the correct option is (B).

97. Synthetic methods should avoid using or generating substances toxic to humans and/or the environment. Hence less hazardous chemical synthesis is an important principle.

Principles of Green Chemistry. Green chemistry is the approach in chemical sciences that efficiently uses renewable raw materials, eliminating waste and avoiding the use of toxic and hazardous reagents and solvents in the manufacture and application of chemical products.

Hence, the correct option is (C).

98. An optically inactive substance is a substance which does not have optical activity, i.e. a substance which does not rotate the plane of plane-polarized light.

Almost all the natural amino acids except glycine are optically active. (i.e. glycine is optically inactive). This is because glycine does not have a chiral carbon in its structure. Optical activity is the ability of a substance to rotate the plane of polarization of a beam of light that is passed through it.

Hence, the correct option is (B).

99. Nitrobenzenes can be reduced in the presence of a strongly acidic and as well as neutral medium.

When reduced in presence of a strongly acidic medium such as tin HCl, nitrobenzene forms aniline.

When a neutral reducing agent such as zinc dust and aqueous ammonium chloride, forms nitrosobenzene which gets immediately converted to phenylhydroxylamine.

So, when Nitrobenzene is subjected to reduction with Zn dust and ammonium chloride, the main product is Aniline.

Hence, the correct option is (B).

100. In industrial processes, transition elements and their oxides are used as catalyst.

Iron one of the transition metal is used in construction and manufacturing industries. Titanium is used in construction of aircrafts, in artificial hip replacements and piping for nuclear power plants. Nickel is in the production of stainless steel. Copper is used in electrical wiring.

Hence, the correct option is (C).

// Notes //

// Notes //

CPSIA information can be obtained
at www.ICGtesting.com
Printed in the USA
BVHW021452130623
665881BV00012B/391